Preparing to Teach Texas Content Areas

Preparing to Teach Texas Content Areas

The TExES EC-4 Generalist and the ESL Supplement

EDITED BY

Janice L. Nath
University of Houston–Downtown

John M. Ramsey
University of Houston

Boston   New York   San Francisco
Mexico City   Montreal   Toronto   London   Madrid   Munich   Paris
Hong Kong   Singapore   Tokyo   Cape Town   Sydney

Executive Editor and Publisher: Stephen D. Dragin
Editorial Assistant: Katie Heimsoth
Marketing Manager: Weslie Sellinger
Production Editor: Gregory Erb
Editorial Production Service: Nesbitt Graphics, Inc.
Composition Buyer: Linda Cox
Manufacturing Buyer: Linda Morris
Electronic Composition: Nesbitt Graphics, Inc.
Interior Design: Tara Fisher, Nesbitt Graphics, Inc.
Cover Designer: Joel Gendron

For related titles and support materials, visit our online catalog at www. ablongman. com.

Between the time Web site information is gathered and then published, it is not unusual for some sites to have closed. Also, the transcription of URLs can result in typographical errors. The publisher would appreciate notification where these errors occur so that they may be corrected in subsequent editions.

ISBN 10: 0-205-50302-0
ISBN 13: 978-0-205-50302-5

Library of Congress Cataloging-in-Publication Data was not available at press time.

Printed in the United States of America

10 9 8 7 6 5 4 3 2 1 EDW 11 10 09 08 07

Special thanks to . . .

Esther Huff, an excellent mother, teacher, and editor,

Lisa Hill, University of Houston–Downtown,

Susan Paige, University of Houston–Downtown, and

Dr. K.K. Jenkins, University of Houston–Downtown, who is also an author.

Contents

Preface   xvii

About the Editors   xx

About the Authors   xxi

Chapter 1 Understanding How to Prepare for the TexES Generalist   1

Janice L. Nath

Cynthia G. Henry

Let's Talk About the Test   2
Standards, Domains, and Competencies   2
Item Formats   3

Several Months Before the Generalist   4
What Should I Do First?   4
How Should I Begin to Prepare for the Generalist?   5
How Should I Manage My Time?   5
What Material Management Skills Will I Need
   and How Do I Develop Them?   6

Keeping Up Momentum   7
How Should I Spend My Study Time; What Should I Concentrate
   on When I Only Have a Few Weeks Before Taking the Generalist?   7

Two Weeks Before the Generalist 9
How Can I Best Spend My Time Two Weeks Before the Generalist?   9
What Strategies Should I Use to Prepare for Multiple-Choice Exams?   9

One Week Before the Generalist   12
With Only One Week to Go, What Can I Do to Best Prepare
   for the Generalist?   12

The Night Before the Generalist   14
What Should I Do the Night Before the Generalist?   14

The Day of the Generalist   15
What Should I Do on the Day of the Generalist?   15

Summary   17

Chapter 2 Preparing to Teach Language Arts and Reading in Texas   18

Laveria F. Hutchison

Eleanore S. Tyson

Standard I Oral Language   20

Standard II Phonological and Phonemic Awareness   28

Standard III Alphabetic Principle   32

Standard IV Literacy Development and Practice 36

Standard V Word Analysis and Decoding 41

Standard VI Reading Fluency 44

Standard VII Reading Comprehension 48
>   Note Taking 52
>   Questioning 52
>   Listening—Thinking Strategy 54
>   SQ3R (Survey, Question, Read, Recite, and Review) 54

Standard VIII Development of Written Communication 61
>   Phase 1: Prewriting 63
>   Phase 2: Drafting 63
>   Phase 3: Revising 63
>   Phase 4: Editing 63
>   Phase 5: Publishing 63

Standard IX Writing Conventions 65

Standard X Assessment and Instruction of Developing Literacy 69

Summary 73

Glossary 73

References 76

A READING LESSON PLAN 78

DRAFT YOUR OWN LANGUAGE ARTS OR READING LESSON PLAN 81

OBSERVING LANGUAGE ARTS AND READING EXPERIENCES/ACTIVITIES 83

TEST YOURSELF ON READING AND LANGUAGE ARTS 88

Chapter 3 Preparing to Teach Mathematics in Texas 88

Rena M. Shull
Norene Vail Lowery
Charles E. Lamb

An Overview of Mathematics Today 89

An Introduction to the Mathematics Standards 90
>   Pre-Kindergarten Curriculum Guidelines 90
>   Mathematics Manipulatives 92
>   TEKS for Pre-K 93
>   Mathematics Standards and Sample Questions with Discussions 94

Standards I Number Concepts, VII Mathematical Learning and Instruction, and VIII Assessment 95

Standards I Number Concepts and II Patterns and Algebra 103

Standards III Geometry and Measurement and IV Probability and Statistics 109

Standards V Mathematical Processes and VI Mathematical Perspectives 117

Discussion 121

Summary 123

A Snapshot of Teaching Mathematics in the Elementary Classroom   **125**

Practice Questions   **128**

Content Practice Test   **131**

Glossary   **135**

References   **139**

Resources   **140**

A MATHEMATICS LESSON PLAN   141

DRAFT YOUR OWN MATHEMATICS LESSON PLAN   144

OBSERVING MATHEMATICS EXPERIENCES/ACTIVITIES   146

TEST YOURSELF ON MATHEMATICS   148

Chapter 4   Preparing to Teach Social Studies in Texas   **152**

Trenia L. Walker
Janice L. Nath

Elementary Social Studies Scope and Sequence in Texas   **155**

Standards I, II, and III Social Science Instruction   **156**

Implication of Child Development in Social Studies   **157**

Technology as a Teaching Tool   **158**

Intradisciplinary and Interdisciplinary Issues   **160**

Engaging *All* Students   **162**

Building Thinking Skills   **163**

Assessment and Evaluation   **163**

Reflective Teaching   **164**

Standards IV History and X Science, Technology, and Society   **165**

Teaching History   **167**

United States History and International Relations   **175**

Standards V and IX Geography and Culture   **212**

Teaching Geography   **213**

Materials for the Social Studies Classroom   **214**

Geography Content   **215**

Culture   **223**

Standards VI, VII, VIII Economics, Government, and Citizenship   **226**

Government Content   **228**

Citizenship   **236**

Economics   **238**

Summary   **246**

References   **246**

A SOCIAL STUDIES LESSON PLAN   248

DRAFT YOUR OWN SOCIAL STUDIES LESSON PLAN   250

OBSERVING SOCIAL STUDIES EXPERIENCES/ACTIVITIES   252

TEST YOURSELF FOR SOCIAL STUDIES   254

Chapter 5   Preparing to Teach Science in Texas   259

Mary E. Wingfield

Lynn S. Freeman

Standard I Science Instruction   260

Standard II Using Science Tools, Materials, Equipment, and Technologies   262

Standard III Science Inquiry   269

Standard IV Teaching Science   273

Standard V Assessment   275

Standard VI History and Nature of Science   276

Standard VII Personal and Social Decision Making   278

Standard VIII Physical Science   279

Standard IX Life Science   282

Standard X Earth and Space Science   285

Standard XI Unifying Themes   288

A TExES Science Lesson   289
    Lesson Evaluation Using the Standards   289

References   290

Resources   290

A SCIENCE LESSON PLAN   291

DRAFT YOUR OWN SCIENCE LESSON PLAN   293

OBSERVING SCIENCE EXPERIENCES/ACTIVITIES   295

TEST YOURSELF ON SCIENCE   297

Chapter 6   Preparing to Teach Art in Texas   299

Sara Wilson McKay

Janice L. Nath

TEKS-Related Correlations   300

Standard I Perception in Art   301
    The Elements of Art   303
    The Principles of Design   303

Standard II Creative Expression in Art   304

Standard III Appreciation of Art Histories and Diverse Cultures   307

Standard IV Analysis, Interpretation, and Evaluation of Art   312

Standard V Cognitive and Artistic Development   316

Discipline-Based Art Education (DBAE)   317
    Art-Making   319
    Art Criticism   319
    Art History   319
    Aesthetics   319
    Relating Language and Art   320
    Relating Science and Art   321
    Relating Mathematics and Art   321
    Relating Social Studies and Art   321

Summary   322

References   323

AN ART LESSON PLAN   324

DRAFT YOUR OWN ART LESSON PLAN   327

OBSERVING ART EXPERIENCES/ACTIVITIES   329

TEST YOURSELF ON ART   331

Chapter 7 **Preparing to Teach Music in Texas   334**

Janice L. Nath

Standard I Visual and Aural Knowledge   335

Duration   335

Rhythm   337

Pitch and Melody   340

Form   344

Dynamics   346

Tempo   347

Instrument Families   348

Timbre and Tone   348

Standard II Singing and Playing   351

Standard III Music Notation   352

Standard V Texas and American Music History   353

Texas Music   354

American Music   357

Musical Careers   361

Standard VI Evaluating Musical Performance   362

Teaching Children to Sing   362

Teaching Children to Move   365

Standard VII Planning and Implementing Effective Music Lessons   365

Music in the Domains   367

Remember Your Pedagogy   368

Music Connections   369

Technology and Music   374

Resources   375

The Home, Community, and Music   376

Health and Safety in Music   377

Special Needs Children at Music Time   377

Standard IX Assessment   380

Assessment and Evaluation   381

Standard X Professional Responsibilities   383

Copyright Laws and Music   384

Summary   385

A MUSIC LESSON PLAN   386

DRAFT YOUR OWN MUSIC LESSON PLAN   389

OBSERVING MUSIC EXPERIENCES/ACTIVITIES   391

TEST YOURSELF ON MUSIC   394

Chapter 8 Preparing to Teach Health and Physical Education in Texas   397

Mel E. Finkenberg
Janice L. Nath
John M. Ramsey

Standards I and II Health   399

Choosing a Healthy Life   400

School Health Facilities   402

Nutrition   402

Healthy Relationships   403

Teaching About Illness and Disease   404

Substance Abuse   405

Healthy Communication   406

Refusal Skills   407

Teaching About Violence   408

Stress   409

Technology and Health   410

Safety   411

Standards I–VI Physical Education   414

Movement   418

Growth and Development   421

Assessment and Evaluation   422

Positive Interactions and Personal Exploration in Physical Education   423

Designing and Implementing Activities   424

Summary   426

References   426

Suggested Readings   427

A HEALTH LESSON PLAN   428

DRAFT YOUR OWN HEALTH OR PHYSICAL EDUCATION LESSON PLAN   431

OBSERVING HEALTH AND/OR PHYSICAL EDUCATION EXPERIENCES/ACTIVITIES   433

TEST YOURSELF ON HEALTH AND PHYSICAL EDUCATION   435

Chapter 9 Preparing to Teach Theatre Arts in Texas   437

Kathryn L. Jenkins

Janice L. Nath

Joyce M. Dutcher

What Are Theatre Arts Experiences?   438
Dramatic Play   438
Drama Activities   439

What Are The TEKS in Theatre Arts for Students in EC-4 Classrooms?   440
Perception   440
Creative Expression/Performance   441
Historic and Cultural Heritage   442
Critical Evaluation   442

Why Include Theatre Arts in Daily Activities?   444

What Is the Teacher's Role in Theatre Arts in Early Childhood Education?   446
Instructional Roles   446
Noninstructional Roles   447

What Are the Main Aspects of Theatre Arts That Teachers Should Consider?   448

Bringing It All Together: How Do Teachers Plan for Activities That Address the Four Strands of the Theatre Arts TEKS?   453

How Can Theatre Arts Be Integrated into Other Content Areas?   453

Summary   456

Glossary   456

References   459

A THEATRE ARTS LESSON PLAN   460

DRAFT YOUR OWN THEATRE ARTS LESSON PLAN   464

OBSERVING THEATRE ARTS EXPERIENCES/ACTIVITIES   466

TEST YOURSELF ON THEATRE ARTS   469

Chapter 10 Teaching English as a Second Language in Texas   473

William J. Kortz, Jr.
Janice L. Nath

About Texas ESL Certification   474

Domain I Language Concepts and Language Acquisition/Preparation Before Teaching ESL or Before the Classroom   477

Standard I Concepts, Structure, and Conventions of English and Standard III L1 and L2 Language Acquisition   477

The Acquisition-Learning Hypothesis (Meaning to Structure with Two Theories Combined)   483

The Natural Order Hypothesis   484

The Affective Filter Hypothesis   484

The Input Hypothesis   485

The Monitor Hypothesis   486

Domain II ESL Instruction and Assessment/In the Classroom During Teaching   487

Standards I Concepts, Structure, and Conventions of English, III L1 and L2 Language Acquisition, IV ESL Methods and Instruction in the Classroom, V ESL Academic Content, Language, and Culture, and VI Formal and Informal Assessment   487

ESL Methods   488
Other Methodologies Recommended for the ESL Classroom   489
Teacher Strategies for ESL Learners   490
Technological Tools and Resources   491

Management and Teaching Strategies   491
Students Acquire Language in a Low-Anxiety Environment with Comprehensible Input: This Supports Listening and Speaking Skills 493

Speaking Supports Language Acquisition   494
Speech Emergence Is Distinguished by Grammatical Errors   494
Speech Emerges Step-by-Step   495
The Goal of the Natural Approach Is Communicative Competence   496
Comprehension Comes Before Production   497
Group Work Encourages Interaction and Creates Community   497
Interrelatedness   499

English Is an Alphabetic Language   499

Reading Comprehension   500
Transfer of Literacy   500
Individual Differences and Personal Factors   500

Applies Knowledge of Effective Practices, Resources, and Materials   **502**
Instructional Delivery   502

Test Design, Development, and Interpretation   **504**
Formal, Informal, and Authentic Assessments   504

Standardized Tests   **505**

State-Mandated LEP Policies   **506**
Instructional Relationships   507

Domain III Foundations, Culture, Family and Community/Outside the
Classroom/Continuous Professional Development and Community/
Resource Outreach   508

**Standards II Foundations of ESL, V ESL Academic Content, Language,
and Culture, and VII Family and Community Involvement**   **508**

Historical, Theoretical, and Policy Foundations   **508**
Types of ESL Programs   509
Make Appropriate Instructional and Management Decisions   509
Convergent Research Applied   510
Cultural and Linguistic Diversity   511
Diversity: Multicultural and Multilingual   512
Cultural Bias   512
Sensitivity and Respect   512

Strategies for Awareness   **513**

Teacher as an Advocate   **514**

Family Involvement   **515**

Family Collaboration   **515**

Community Members and Resources   **516**

Glossary   **518**

References   **524**

AN ESL LESSON PLAN   526

DRAFT YOUR OWN ESL LESSON PLAN   528

EVALUATION OF EC-4 EXPERIENCES/ACTIVITIES   530

TEST YOURSELF ON ESL   534

TEST YOURSELF ANSWERS AND RATIONALES FOR ESL   537

Name Index   **541**
Subject Index   **543**

Preface

The History

In 2002, the Texas State Board for Educator Certification (SBEC) implemented a new teacher examination testing program that supplanted the ExCETs (Examination for the Certification of Educators in Texas)—the testing program that had been in place for Texas educators since 1986. These new tests were named the Texas Examinations for Educator Standards (TExES). The main purpose for change was a more seamless, cohesive alignment between educator certification and the mandated student curriculum (the Texas Essential Knowledge and Skills [TEKS]). A special P-16 Initiative brought together SBEC, the Texas Education Agency (which regulates elementary and secondary public education), and the Texas Higher Education Coordinating Board (which oversees higher education) to initiate these new tests for many content areas and for the Pedagogy and Professional Responsibilities (PPR).

National Evaluation Systems (a private educational testing corporation) developed the TExES under contract from SBEC, but the state awarded its testing contract to Educational Testing Service (ETS) in 2006 with the understanding that, for the time, the testing framework would not change. ETS has agreed to continue to provide testing sites (both for paper-and-pencil and computer exams) and scoring of these examinations.

The redesigned testing program was based on educator standards that defined the rigorous content and professional knowledge and skills that an entry-level educator should possess. This book is focused on preparing prospective teachers for *one* of the certification examinations, the EC-4 Generalist examination for content areas in language arts/reading, mathematics, science, social studies, and fine arts with health and physical education.

The Audience: The Prospective Teacher for Younger Children

This book is intended for those who are seeking certification to teach younger children (EC-4) in Texas. These prospective teachers must meet an array of quality and preparation criteria, including at least two state-administered examinations (the PPR and the Generalist). This book addresses the standards, competencies, and associated content of the Generalist examination. The Generalist standards and competencies require knowledge and skills associated with early childhood and elementary curricular content developed directly from the TEKS (for children) and appropriate learning and assessment practices. The second examination required for EC-4 certification is the Pedagogy and Professional Responsibilities (PPR) examination. The PPR specifically focuses on the knowledge and skills associated with classroom pedagogy and professional ethics. If you are also studying for this test, we recommend *Becoming an EC-4 Teacher in Texas* by editors J. Nath and M. Cohen.

The Content: Generalist Subject Areas

This book is a preparation resource that can be used as either a primary source text or a supplemental review guide for this examination. Note that this book is not an SBEC publication; rather it is an effort by experienced and dedicated educators to contribute to the certification process for the benefit of the state's prospective teachers and their students. These educators are fully aware that passing this examination is not *all* that makes a good teacher. Each one of these authors has seen a number of wonderful teacher candidates who may not have easily passed the state examinations but who teach excellent lessons with children. However, we do submit that this is excellent information for *any* teacher of younger children to know.

There are seven areas of discipline knowledge solidly aligned with the TEKS (the basic mandated student curriculum of the State of Texas). These seven content areas are reading/language arts, mathematics, science, social studies, art, music, and health/physical education. There are three additional chapters, one on teaching theatre arts, one on preparing for the English as a Second Language (ESL) exam (which is now being required by many school districts), and a study skills chapter to assist examination-takers in the preparation process.

Each chapter is organized around the standards for that subject area. The chapter presents the standards, a list or summary of the competencies with discussion, an overview of the related knowledge base (i.e., the facts, concepts, skills, and appropriate practices), practice examination questions and discussion, an example lesson plan, a blank form for writing your own lesson plan, and an observation form for the classroom. However, due to the nature of each content area's standards and competencies, each chapter also has its own unique organization. For example, some subject areas have more standards than competencies while others have more competencies than standards. Thus, the length and organization of each chapter will vary.

Standards refer to broad, general goal statements related to each content area. They serve as an inclusive "umbrella" for that particular subject. **Competencies** are akin to objectives, operationalizing each standard into a number of more specific subcomponents of knowledge, skills, and appropriate practices. In some chapters, these competencies are paraphrased from the official text published by SBEC due to their length or redundancy.

The examination questions that are included both within chapters and at the end of each chapter use a multiple-choice format and are written at the comprehension, application, and analysis levels of Bloom's taxonomy. The content areas are not necessarily treated equally in terms of the number of questions for each. For example, the reading/language arts component of the examination represents about 40 percent of all examination questions. The mathematics, social studies, science, and combined fine arts, physical education and health components, on the other hand, represent 15 percent each of all examination questions. Because there is no separate section for theatre arts on this examination, these questions are integrated with other content areas. The ESL questions are exclusively for the ESL examination rather than for the Generalist examination.

The Rationale for This Book

Prospective Texas teachers currently come from all over the United States and the world. Their educational experiences and cultural backgrounds vary to a significant extent in terms of quantity and quality. Their prior knowledge about the U.S. public school curricula will also vary. However, Texas has mandated its own statewide curricula and requirements for teachers. Texas history under the subject area of social studies, for example, is a mandated curricular requirement, and Texas requires its teachers to have appropriate knowledge of that subject, regardless of other educational preparation and background. This book provides a resource tool for prospective Texas teachers to identify, review, and/or remediate the knowledge, skills, and appropriate practice required for the Generalist in all content areas covered by this examination. In addition, many districts are requiring their teachers to have completed an ESL certification prior to being hired or to obtain this supplemental certification as soon as they are able to do so. The ESL chapter will provide a basic review for passing the ESL TExES—an area crucial for teachers who will increasingly find children in their classrooms from many countries and who speak languages other than English.

The Organization of the Book

This book is divided into ten chapters. Chapter 1 presents both generic study skills and study skills specific to this exam, along with examination preparation guidelines. Chapter 2 begins the content areas with language arts and reading, perhaps the most important chapter in this book due to its emphasis of 40 percent on the Generalist. Chapter 3 offers information on mathematics; Chapter 4 covers social studies; Chapter 5 presents science; art is found in Chapter 6 and music in Chapter 7; Chapter 8 provides information on health and physical education; Chapter 9 imparts guidelines on theatre arts; and Chapter 10 discusses the ESL supplemental certification. Authors were tasked with offering as much content and other teaching information as possible, but all were restricted by length limitations. We hope that you will continue to seek more content information, theory, and ideas for good teaching. Each chapter concludes with a lesson plan (demonstrating how to implement the content area in the classroom), a blank form to complete for your own lesson plan, a classroom observation instrument to help focus on best practices for that subject, and a number of questions to retest your knowledge and test-taking skills.

SBEC: Additional Background

If you've ever wondered who makes up the rules under which one becomes certified as a teacher, counselor, principal, superintendent, or any of the other professional roles in public schools, the answer is the State Board for Educator Certification in Texas, currently a part of The Texas Education Agency. Since education is one of the powers reserved to the states under the Tenth Amendment to the U.S. Constitution, each state is really responsible for its own system of public education—including decisions about who is licensed to teach in that state.

The State Board for Educator Certification (SBEC) is the result of a 1995 action by the Texas Legislature. Its purpose is "to recognize public school educators as professionals and grant educators the authority to govern the standards of their profession." This Board is responsible to TEA and further to the Texas Legislature for overseeing all aspects of the preparation, assessment, certification, and standards of professional conduct of educators in the state's public schools and, in addition, for accountability of teacher preparation entities. Recently, SBEC has been in the process of reorganization under TEA, and many changes may take place in the next few years regarding this restructuring.

In the past several years, SBEC has brought about great change in Texas teacher certification. It has implemented an accountability system for entities that prepare educators (both institutions of higher learning and numerous alternative certification programs). It has also phased out the historic practice of issuing lifetime certificates in favor of certificates that are renewable every five years. A renewal currently requires documentation of professional development during the five-year life of the certificate to assure that educators stay current in their professional knowledge. SBEC has also changed (and will continue to change) the certification levels to better meet the emerging needs of schools in the state.

Structure

SBEC is currently composed of eleven voting members appointed by the Governor to six-year terms. These members are:

- four classroom teachers,
- one counselor,
- two school administrators, and
- four citizens of the state not employed in public schools.

There are also currently three <u>non</u>-voting members:

- one dean of a Texas college of education, appointed by the Governor,
- one staff member of Texas Education Agency, appointed by the Commissioner of Education, and
- one staff member of the Texas Higher Education Coordinating Board, appointed by the Commissioner of Higher Education.

Members

While members are appointed for six-year terms, as is usual with a group this size, individuals sometimes move or change positions so that they can no longer hold a certain seat (e.g., a classroom teacher becomes an assistant principal). To get the most up-to-date information on the current membership of the State Board for Educator Certification, the best source is their web site (www.sbec.state.tx.us). This web site contains a wealth of information on the SBEC Board, its current membership, scheduled meetings, agendas, minutes, and information on requirements and standards that apply to various types of certificates. It also provides press releases and reports generated by the Board and its staff and information on investigations and enforcement of certification standards and the Code of Ethics. You may download the standards and a practice booklet (with all of the competencies listed) for your tests from this site or from http://texes.ets.org. Go to the "Preparation Manuals" and then to the EC-4 Generalist site. Besides helping Texas educators become more familiar with many areas of education in Texas, it is also an excellent source of information for individuals who are certified in another state and who wish to become certified in Texas.

A Note From the Editors

We thank Lin Moore, Texas Women's University, for her comments on the manuscript.

Good luck to all prospective teachers on this test and in your classrooms! We hope that this book will help you pass the examination and will also help you become an excellent and knowledgeable teacher. May you give your best to children each and everyday!

About the Editors

Dr. Janice L. Nath is an associate professor in the Department of Urban Education and, currently, Associate Dean at the University of Houston—Downtown in the College of Public Service. She is the co-editor of a number of books on teacher preparation and certification, including: *Becoming a Teacher in Texas: A Course of Study for the Elementary* *and Secondary Professional Development ExCET, Becoming an EC-4 Teacher in Texas: A Course of Study for the Pedagogy and Professional Responsibilities (PPR) TExES; Becoming a Middle or High School Teacher in Texas: A Course of Study for the Pedagogy and Professional Responsibilities (PPR) TExES;* and *Preparing for the Texas PreK-4 Teacher Certification: A Guide to the Comprehensive TExES Content Areas Exam.* Teacher education is her main area of interest, along with technology in teacher education, action research, and others. She has been actively involved in field-based teacher education for many years and has served as the chair of AERA's (American Educational Research Association) Professional Development School Research SIG, chair of the Texas Coordinators for Teacher Certification Testing (formerly, the ExCET Coordinators Association), and chair and treasurer of CSOTTE (Consortium for State Organizations for Texas Teacher Education). In 2004, she was awarded her university's Scholarship/Creativity Award for research. Her other co-edited books investigate Professional Development School research and include: *Forging Alliances in Community and Thought: Research in Professional Development Schools* and *Professional Development Schools: Advances in Community Thought and Research.*

John M. Ramsey, Ph.D., is associate professor of science education at the University of Houston. He has served as department chair, director of teacher education, doctoral and masters advisor, and principal investigator for numerous funded projects. His professional experience includes more than thirty years in middle, secondary, and higher education. He has co-authored or co-edited nine books and published twenty-five refereed research articles. He has received the highest university teaching award granted at the University of Houston and was honored with the 2001 Research Excellence Award from the North American Association of Environmental Education. He has conducted more than 300 international and national professional development workshops and presentations and has served as a consultant for the United Nations, national and state agencies, international governments, non-government organizations, and businesses.

About the Authors

Dr. Joyce M. Dutcher, Ed.D., is currently an assistant professor in the Department of Urban Education at the University of Houston—Downtown. Dr. Dutcher's passion is to make a difference in the lives of young children. This can be seen in the early childhood courses that she teachers at the University or through community outreach initiatives like that at the House of Tiny Treasures, a preschool for Houston's homeless children. Prior to coming to UHD, Dr. Dutcher was an early childhood teacher, curriculum coordinator, and administrator in two of Texas' largest school districts. She regularly presents at conferences on topics related to early childhood, science education, and systemic educational reform.

Dr. Mel E. Finkenberg, Ed.D., is Regents Professor and Chair of the Department of Kinesiology and Health Science at Stephen F. Austin State University in Nacogdoches, Texas. Prior to his appointment at SFA, he served as Professor and Chair of the Department of Physical Education and Recreation/Leisure Studies at California State University, Los Angeles. Dr. Finkenberg has also been an exercise physiologist at NASA's Johnson Space Center and has taught elementary physical education. Dr. Finkenberg has been President of the Texas Association of Health, Physical Education, Recreation and Dance and was selected as the Association Scholar for 1999. He was awarded the Honor Award by this group as well. He served as Vice President for Physical Education of the Southern District American Alliance for Health, Physical Education Recreation and Dance. He recently received this association's Honor Award. At SFA, he was named Distinguished Professor and selected as the Phi Delta Kappa Educator of the Year. Dr.

Finkenberg has served as Vice President of the National Association for Physical Education in Higher Education. In 2001, he received that Association's Distinguished Administrator Award.

Dr. Lynn S. Freeman, an assistant professor at the University of Houston—Victoria, serves as coordinator for the post baccalaureate teacher certification program at the University of Houston-Cinco Ranch. Prior to joining UHV, Dr. Freeman was a clinical associate professor at University of Houston-Main Campus, where she taught elementary science methods and served as a Field Coordinator at many professional development sites. A science teacher prior to teaching in higher education, her research interests include teaching at-risk students and distance learning. In 2003, she was named Teacher of the Year by the West Houston Chamber of Commerce.

Dr. Cynthia Henry was formerly a clinical associate professor in the Department of Curriculum and Instruction at the University of Houston and served as the Coordinator for the Teacher Internship Program. She was also actively involved in field-based teacher education there. Dr. Henry currently works with gifted and talented students and ESL students near Atlanta, Georgia. She is co-editor of *Becoming a Teacher in Texas: A Course of Study for the Elementary and Secondary Professional Development ExCET*. Her research interests include teacher education, gifted and talented education, and parent involvement.

Dr. Laveria F. Hutchison is an associate professor at the University of Houston—Central Campus in Houston, Texas and is director of the middle and secondary certification program. She is the co-director of a recruitment project for mathematics and science teachers that is funded by the U.S. Department of Education. She received her doctoral degree from Ball State University in Muncie, Indiana.

Dr. Kathryn L. Jenkins, Ed.D., is currently assistant professor of Early Childhood Education in the Department of Urban Education at the University of Houston—Downtown. Outside of the collegiate level classroom, her current research is being conducted at the House of Tiny Treasures, a preschool for homeless children, ages 12 months–5 years. There, she is exploring the developmental levels of play and oral language as well as a professional development model that focuses on developmentally appropriate integration of multiple content areas. Additionally, Dr. Jenkins is investigating (in partnership with Dr. Joyce Dutcher) the enhancement of observation skills of preservice teachers using art through a collaborative with the Museum of Fine Arts in Houston. Prior to coming to the University of Houston—Downtown, Dr. Jenkins was a visiting and clinical professor at the University of Houston and an early childhood classroom teacher of Pre-K and kindergarten children.

Dr. William J. Kortz, Jr. currently serves as a University of Houston—Downtown faculty member in the Department of Urban Education teaching bilingual, ESL, and technology curriculum. He is a recipient of the Manchester Who's Who of Professionals and Business Executives (2005), the TExES Teacher Award at Sam Houston State University (2004), and the Positively Pasadena Award (1995) for teaching innovation. In addition, he is an active member of the National Association of Bilingual Education (NABE), the Texas Association of Bilingual Education (TABE), the Texas Alternative Certification Association (TACA), the Association for the Advancement of Computers in Education (AACE), Toastmasters International, and the National American Council for Online Learning (NACOL). He was previously a technology director for a distance learning initiative, The Texas Center for Academic Excellence (TXCAE) at Sam Houston State University. He has designed online programs for upper level courses in educational leadership and ESL certification at Texas A&M and Sam Houston State University. He has served as a public school bilingual teacher in grades 3–5 and an ESL teacher/coordinator in grades K–12. He has published eight Texas teacher certification guides which include

Pass the TExES Bilingual EC-4 and *Pass the TExES ESL EC-12*. Dr. Kortz has also taught over 150 TExES teacher certification seminars in districts, state educational region centers, and universities across Texas.

Charles E. Lamb, Ed.D., was a faculty member at the University of Texas at Austin from 1979–1994. He served as a faculty member at Texas A&M University from 1994–2001. As Professor Emeritus, he continues to teach part-time as well as serve on graduate committees. He frequently speaks at conference and does educational consulting.

Norene Vail Lowery, Ph.D., a former assistant professor of Mathematics Education at the University of Houston, recently returned to the public school venue and is now serving as the District Curriculum Specialist for Elementary Mathematics for the Katy Independent School District, Katy, Texas. Norene's research interests include assessment, curriculum, pedagogical content knowledge, and the integration of literature and mathematics.

Sara Wilson McKay, Ph.D., was assistant professor and program area coordinator of Art Education at the University of Houston. Her research interests include theories of vision and perception, cultural reproduction, and art and democracy. She advocates critical thinking in education through art experiences that emphasize the value of diverse points of view and multiple interpretations. She developed the Houston Area Visual Resource Center and has published about contemporary issues in elementary art education. Her work continued at North Texas University as a part of the North Texas Institute for Educators on the Visual Arts.

Dr. Rena M. Shull, Ph.D., is currently an assistant professor in the Department of Education at Rockhurst University in Kansas City, Missouri. Dr. Shull had previously taught mathematics methods as a visiting and clinical professor at the University of Houston, where she also served as a field coordinator for Professional Development School sites. From 1979 to 1993, she taught high school mathematics. Dr. Shull maintains an interest in number sense, research on lesson plan design, and the use of technology in the mathematics classroom.

Eleanore S. Tyson, Ed.D., is a clinical professor at the University of Houston—Central Campus. She teaches undergraduate and graduate literacy courses in the UH teacher preparation program. Among her favorite courses to teach are those in children's literature. She has also worked with Web-based lessons related to children's trade books. She currently serves on the board of the Greater Houston Area Reading Council and was recently appointed to a committee for the UH Library. Dr. Tyson received her doctoral degree from the University of Houston.

Dr. Trenia L. Walker is an assistant professor at Washington State University—Vancouver, Department of Teaching and Learning. Dr. Walker taught social studies methods at the University of Houston for several years, in addition to being a classroom history teacher in Houston ISD. Her current research explores transformative learning theories and the implications for technology, popular culture, and globalization in social studies teaching and learning.

Mary E. Wingfield, Ed.D., has been a science methods professor for preservice elementary teachers in the teacher preparation program at the University of Houston for many years. She has served on State Board of Educator Certification Oversight Teams to assist in review of certification performance at entities throughout the state. As a former science teacher, she is interested in helping to enhance the efficacy of new science teachers and in promoting scientific literacy in Texas elementary school children.

1 Understanding How to Prepare for the TExES Generalist

Janice L. Nath
University of Houston—Downtown

Cynthia G. Henry

Intuitively, we know that studying early and studying smart for the Generalist will pay off with a higher test score, but research also concludes that good things happen for those who work to improve their *study* and *test-taking skills* (in addition to simply knowing the content). Students with strong study skills find it easier to study, consistently earn better grades and higher test scores, and become more successful in life. Therefore, we begin with this chapter by giving you some strategies and hints to help you study for and complete this examination with success. This chapter is designed along a timeline and written in a question-and-answer format to facilitate your learning.

Let's Talk About the Test

Standards, Domains, and Competencies

The state provides guidelines that tell us exactly what knowledge and skills Texas children need to possess, how Texas teachers should go about their professional lives, and what knowledge teachers need for Texas classrooms. This information is found in three places: (1) the *Texas Essential Knowledge and Skills* (TEKS) established for students, (2) the TExES (Texas Examinations of Educator Standards) *Standard,* and (3) the TExES *Competencies* developed for teachers in both pedagogy and content. All three of these areas are important for teachers to learn, understand, and use. Because much of our knowledge about children, teaching, and content is in a constant state of change, it is important information for teachers to learn now but also to update continuously throughout their careers.

The process of development for this test is systematic. The TEKS for children are developed first (and are periodically updated), followed by the standards for teachers (which are *solidly* based on the TEKS). Committees for teacher standards, made up of Texas educators, parents, and business and community members, also consider current educational research as well as national standards that are set by content-area specialists within their specialized organizations (for example, the National Council of Teachers of Mathematics [NCTM]). Standards are established to cover all of the major content areas that are taught to children in Texas, and for the Generalist, these content areas have been divided into five *domains.* Each of these domains is an "umbrella" for one of the five tested areas. The following shows these five domains with the percentage each currently counts on the test.

Domain I	English Language Arts and Reading	40%
Domain II	Mathematics	15%
Domain III	Social Studies	15%
Domain IV	Science	15%
Domain V	Fine Arts, Health, and Physical Education	15%

After development of the teaching standards, committees turn to establishing a framework for testing. This framework provides the *competencies,* which are specific knowledge and skills for testing each domain. As you read these *competencies* under each domain, you will see two parts. The first is a *competency statement,* which is a general beginning statement about an area of knowledge under one of the domains. For example, in language arts, one such *competency statement* about *oral language* reads, "The teacher understands the importance of oral language, knows the developmental processes of oral language, and provides children with varied opportunities to develop listening and speaking skills." Directly following each of these broad statements, there is a list of *descriptive statements* that delineates or defines what Texas specifically wants teachers to know and be able to do. You can be expected to be directly tested on the competency statements and the specific details and vocabulary of these descriptive statements. For example, one of the many *descriptive statements* under the oral language competency statement above reads: "The beginning teacher knows basic linguistic concepts (e.g., phonemes, semantics, syntax, pragmatics)." Therefore, before testing you should ensure that you not only know the general statements but also the specific definition of terms inside the parentheses. By reading the TEKS, the standards, the competency statements, and the descriptive statements, you will know exactly what will appear on the test. The sequence of development is shown below:

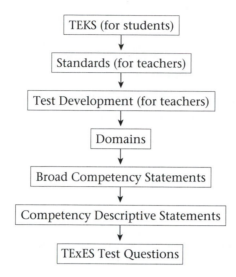

TEKS (for students)

↓

Standards (for teachers)

↓

Test Development (for teachers)

↓

Domains

↓

Broad Competency Statements

↓

Competency Descriptive Statements

↓

TExES Test Questions

The final process involves committees that design test questions in a multiple-choice format to assess knowledge of the teaching skills and content knowledge stated in these standards and competencies. These questions come in several formats.

Item Formats

All items are in multiple-choice format. However, they are arranged as single items, stimulus material items, and clustered items. Each of these formats is described below:

- ***Single item format:*** A single problem or question is presented with four answer choices. You are required to choose the correct response or ending statement and mark this on your answer sheet.
- ***Stimulus material item format:*** Following some type of stimulus material, a question is asked that may require you to analyze a given chart, graph, map, table, or so forth. The stimulus could also be a "real-world" classroom situation, a dialogue between a teacher and student, or an example(s) of a student's or students' work. When answering this type of question, be sure to read the stimulus *very* carefully.
- ***Clustered item format:*** A group of questions or problems is related in some way. There may be only two or three related questions—or there can be many questions, as with a *Teacher Decision Set* (which requires you to follow a long scenario, answering questions as the scene unfolds over several pages).

Here are a few helpful hints.

- When answering any of the questions, always make sure that you are answering from the point of view of the Texas standards and competencies (both for the Generalist and the PPR [Professional Pedagogy and Responsibilities]). No answer on the test will ever contradict the philosophies of these standards and competencies. It pays to learn these well.

- The test will have the same biases that the PPR TExES contains: student choice and responsibility, authentic assessment, self-assessment and reflection, relevant instruction, age-appropriate instruction, use of technology and the community as resources, use of cooperative groups, higher-level thinking, and so forth.
- If you have a choice of which of the two required tests you take first, it may be worth your taking the PPR initially so that you have a clear understanding of these issues and can better apply the desired Texas pedagogy and philosophies to the content-area questions.

We will discuss more testing strategies later in the chapter.

 ## Several Months Before the Generalist

What Should I Do First?

You should begin by thinking about the registration process for this exam well in advance so that you will be well prepared and can select the time and method that is best for you. It can be difficult to obtain a place at a particular location if you do not register early, so think about getting this underway as soon as you are ready to take the test.

There are currently two options for taking this test—a paper-and-pencil version or a computer-administered test (CAT). Think about which of these options might be best for you. For example, as a testing strategy, it may help you to be able to underline or otherwise mark in your test booklet, so the paper-and-pencil route may be optimal. If you do a great deal of work on the computer and feel more comfortable in that format, you may want to choose the electronic version (CAT). Use the Web site listed at the end of this chapter to find the yearly schedule for paper-and-pencil testing and/or when and where the CAT is offered. Most locations that offer the CAT are at Texas universities or colleges. The CAT is offered quite often, so this method can be more versatile. If you want to take the examination on the computer, you are currently allowed to retake it after 90 days if you do not do well.

If you are in a certification program, you may be required to take the Generalist during a particular phase of your program. If so, determine exactly when that is, but also be sure to check with your program about what *your* part of the registration process might be. Most programs have a certification officer or TExES coordinator. Find out who this is and check in with them often. If you are not required to adhere to a particular time for the Generalist, you should think carefully about your test date and take the proper steps to register for the date and time that is most beneficial to your situation. This is important because testing sites can fill up early, forcing you to drive further or to be assigned to a test at a time other than what may be your best. For instance, if you are a morning person, you will definitely want the morning session, or if you do not "get going" until later in the day, you would probably want to start your test after lunch. If your prime choice of sites is already closed, search for other sites in proximity on your own. The ETS site currently does not automatically show you options but may soon.

Make sure that you have decided on the best time and method to take the Generalist and have begun the registration process properly (either through the state or through your teacher preparation entity). Registration is available online, but you may still need approval if you are being recommended for certification through a university or alternative certification program (ACP). Your university or teacher preparation program may also have its own dead-

Helpful Hint:

To become a certified teacher you will also have to take the PPR (Pedagogy and Professional Roles) TExES. We highly suggest, however, that you do not plan to take more than one of these tests per testing day. Many people do not do well taking more than one test because they become tired and lose concentration as the day passes. Some teacher preparation entities do not allow you to take more than one test per day because of this concern. Plan your testing schedule carefully so you will have plenty of time to get a passing score on both examinations prior to obtaining a teaching position or, if you already have a teaching position, keeping your job.

lines or other requirements *prior* to the state deadline to obtain approval, so pay close attention to these dates as well. As a note, you also must go through the fingerprinting process to become certified in Texas, so be sure to allow time for that as well (instructions are on the SBEC Web site given at the end of the chapter).

Be very careful to sign up for the correct test. The test that you request is the *only* one that will be brought to the site for you. If you request the wrong test, you will be out of luck that day.

Be aware of the state's registration cutoff dates. Late registration and changes in registration cost you more money and can cost you a delayed test day. Early registration and close attention to filling out the *correct* information will help ensure that you are assigned your preference. If you have name changes or other changes in information previously given to the Texas educational data bank, be sure to take care of those changes earlier to avoid confusion and possibly losing a test date. Web site addresses and phone numbers for registration and information can be found at the end of this chapter.

How Should I Begin to Prepare for the Generalist?

Begin as soon as possible. Studying for this important exam can seem to be overwhelming when you first begin to look at all that you should know. There are *so* many questions that could be asked! The good news is that much of it will probably be a review of what you already know.

For the most benefit, break your task into smaller, more manageable steps. The key is to get organized by developing time management skills and material management skills. Start early to review and learn new information!

How Should I Manage My Time?

You must set both manageable time goals and workload goals for each study session. For example, if you begin studying for the exam four months before your test date, plan to study about three days a week for approximately 30 to 60 minutes per session. This is a manageable and reasonable study schedule for most. However, if you begin preparing for the Generalist one or two months before the test date, you will need to study more days during the week and spend more time in each study session to ensure that you sufficiently cover the materials on the test.

You may be taking classes, student teaching, or holding a teaching position or another job at the same time you are studying for this exam. If so, you will be juggling many dates and assignments. This is the time to purchase and use a daily planner (if you haven't already) that will allow you to write down all the dates that you need to

Helpful Hint:

Download the Preparation Manual at www.ets.org for some practice questions and other information

Helpful Hint:

Schedule your study sessions when you feel the most energetic and motivated. Understanding your patterns of mental energy and fatigue will help you get the most out of your study time.

remember. A good idea is to "back up deadlines" on your calendar by a day (if something is due on Nov. 3, back it up to Nov. 2) so that you are sure to meet the deadline. Scheduling your study sessions by writing them on your calendar (as you would an appointment with your doctor or dentist) will emphasize the importance of this time for you. Also, try to schedule your study sessions for the same time of the day or evening. This will help you develop and stick to a study routine.

Did you know that our brains more easily remember the first and last items we read as compared to items in the middle of a passage or list? This is important if you want to maximize the amount of material you can remember. Don't study continuously during your study sessions. It is better to take frequent study breaks to create as many beginnings and endings as possible without forfeiting any of those minutes you have set aside for your entire session. For example (as noted earlier), each chapter of this book is divided into sections to deal with separate domains, then further into smaller sections of separate standards. Several concepts are often covered in each of these subdivisions. Try to concentrate on one of these smaller sections for a bit, and then go on to another. When you take your breaks, however, they should not be too long. A brief two-to-five minute "mental vacation" is all that it takes to give your mind a rest (as it absorbs material you have just read). Some suggestions for brief study breaks include: listening to a favorite song, stretching your muscles by doing a few exercises, getting a quick drink or snack, or simply closing your eyes for a few moments. With that said, try not to let others interrupt your study sessions. Thirty minutes of "good time" can be more effective than two hours of study time that is constantly interrupted by others. Close the door and use your time to focus.

Helpful Hint:

If you are taking the PPR or another test, try to schedule some time in between exams to mentally rest before gearing up to study for the next one. This will allow you to better focus for the next exam.

For each of your study sessions, you must also set a workload goal that can be accomplished within the time allotted for your study session. For example, a reasonable workload goal would be to read five to ten pages of content material from a textbook or study guide or to work through several practice questions and their correct answers. Setting small time goals and workload goals is a powerful and effective way to overcome most study blocks that can often make a longer study session seem overwhelming. As Henry Ford once said, "Nothing is particularly hard if you divide it into small jobs" (www.brainyquote.com/quotes/quotes/h/henryford125392.html).

What Material Management Skills Will I Need and How Do I Develop Them?

You may have many materials that help you study for this test besides this book. The material management skills you will need include keeping your study materials organized and accessible. If your study materials are scattered throughout your house, apartment, dorm room, or other locations you will waste valuable time locating and organizing them before you can begin your study session. A procrastinator often subconsciously uses this excuse to put off studying. Find an easily accessible place, such as a desk, bookcase, or filing cabinet, and return all of your study materials to this location when you have finished using them. Using different colored file folders, manila file folders with colored labels for each content area, or a binder with tabs for each area is an effective method of organizing a large body of study material. For example, if you place all of your mathematics materials in a red file folder or binder section, you will quickly be able to locate them when you are ready to study that content area. Further organization of your materials may have to be done if the content contains multiple areas that you need to study and review separately. Because some domains contain many subsections, several file folders of the same color should be labeled separately with each content title—but stored together in a box, desk drawer, or binder for easy access.

As well as material management skills, there are other methods for creating an optimal study environment. These methods include:

- keeping your study environment at approximately 68 degrees, as cooler temperatures normally help improve concentration and memory,
- studying while facing a blank or neutral wall; looking at a wall of eye-catching posters or pictures can be distracting,
- ensuring your study environment is well-lit with high-watt, soft-light bulbs, because fluorescent or insufficient lighting can increase mental fatigue.

Keeping Up the Momentum

How Should I Spend My Study Time What Should I Concentrate on When I Only Have a Few Weeks Before Taking the Generalist?

ORGANIZE A STUDY GROUP. If you have been preparing on your own for a while, now is the time, if possible, to organize a study group for review sessions. However, make sure that it is a group that is serious about studying and providing positive support. Many times, other students or teachers who are also preparing for this examination can offer fresh insight into the content and can help maintain motivation for your study sessions. Discussing terms and concepts with others requires you to become actively involved with the material, and one of the best ways to learn something new is to explain and teach it to someone else. Learning theory tells us that retention is greatest when we teach others—use that to your advantage. Generating your own practice questions and answers and reviewing content material with a partner or a small group of other test takers is one of the most effective means of preparing for an important examination.

Helpful Hint:

Plan to do something fun after a study session. Studying for this examination requires hard work, commitment, and dedication on your part. Therefore, it is important to schedule an enjoyable activity with which to reward yourself after a study session.

At this point you should feel confident that you are covering new material and reviewing old material in an effective manner. Select those main subject areas in which you feel you are still struggling, and concentrate on those areas first. The Language Arts/Reading Domain is weighted more heavily (followed by mathematics, science, social studies, etc.), so focus on where you need it most with your group or individually, if you do not have much time.

USE YOUR SENSES. Successfully completing the Generalist requires you to know and remember a large amount of information. Using numerous sensory channels to store information is a powerful way to remember and recall what you have learned. Try to use your senses of sight, hearing, and touch during each study session. We know that learning theory tells us to use all modalities with children in teaching lessons. Try to make that work for *you* as well. Make it a habit to visualize, discuss, draw, diagram, and/or create flashcards for what you are reading and hearing. These strategies will help you make connections with the content material and, in turn, will help you recall the information you need when you take the examination. Specific memory models help as well. For example, you may have heard sayings, such as "Please Excuse My Dear Aunt Sally," in mathematics to help you remember the order of operations, but you can create your own models to help you remember some of the information needed for this test, too. For example, "**K**now **C**hildren **A**nd **A**lways **S**hare **E**verything" may help you remember the order of Bloom's taxonomy (**k**nowledge, **c**omprehension, **a**pplication, **a**nalysis, **s**ynthesis, and **e**valuation). Finding or creating little songs, rhymes, or funny pictures will help you retain the wealth of material required for this exam.

Helpful Hint:

In addition to studying with this guide, attend a university, district, regional, school-sponsored, or commercial review seminar. A specially prepared review can be a worthwhile investment and can offer additional insights and guidance in your preparation process. Take advantage of these opportunities, particularly if you have previously not done well on this examination.

USE YOUR TIME WISELY. Using your time wisely is a critical component in getting the most out of each study session. If you focus your attention and concentration powers on the materials you are studying, you will be more likely to stay motivated to accomplish your goals. To help, try the following suggestions:

- **Alternate your activities.** Use each study session to review two or more content areas. For example, do not spend an entire study session focusing only on basic science concepts. Switch over to history after a time. Changing topics within a content area or studying two completely different content areas during one session will help keep your mind fresh.
- **Take notes and selectively underline and/or highlight as you read.** Using this strategy will help you focus on the most critical ideas and concepts in the material. You may also want to use Post-it® notes on pages that are critical or write information that you feel you might forget easily on index cards. You will be forced to think about the information being presented and what it means to you, and you can take the cards with you to study when you are standing in line, grabbing a bite to eat, or have a few free minutes. Most importantly, this will stop you from getting to the end of a page or section and wondering what you have just read.
- **Begin and end on a positive note.** Incorporating this strategy is a simple way to maintain your focus and motivation for studying. If you are not a person who enjoys studying for long and difficult examinations, end your study session at a point where it is easy and logical for you to pick up and begin again. Beginning and ending on a positive note will go a long way towards keeping you motivated and helping you concentrate and focus.
- **Buy in!** If you are going to teach young children in Texas, you really must know all of this content information! It will be good for students and good

for you as a professional. This is expected as a part of your professional knowledge. Buying into this idea will help keep you motivated to learn it all and will help you to be a more knowledgeable teacher!

As a reminder, the number of indicators within each domain or content area reflects the coverage of the content area on the Generalist. Therefore, those domains or content areas with more indicators will have more questions on the exam. You will need to spend a greater percentage of your study time reviewing the material in those areas—for example, as shown earlier, language arts has (in the past) taken up to 40 percent of the test questions. Do not forget to look at current information on these percentages by going to the Web site listed at the end of the chapter.

 ## Two Weeks Before the Generalist

How Can I Best Spend My Time Two Weeks Before the Generalist?

PLAYING GAMES. Continue to review your study materials both individually and with your study partner or study group, if possible. You should have a good review schedule in place by now that meets your study needs. Now is also the time to test yourself before you are tested. One way to test yourself is to construct a final set of flashcards. These should include important terms, concepts, definitions, and key concepts for the standards and competencies that still seem hard to rmember. Carry these cards with you at all times so that you can review a few minutes here and there. Use them as traditional flashcards, or use them in a matching game.

Another idea is to use the content material and practice questions in this book to help you make up additional questions. Creating your own questions will help you begin thinking like the test developers. You may be surprised how closely your questions actually match the real test questions!

What Strategies Should I Use to Prepare for Multiple-Choice Exams?

TEST HINTS FOR MULTIPLE-CHOICE ITEMS. The Generalist, as you may remember, is written in a multiple-choice format. The Preparation Manual for this exam, which can be downloaded from www. sbec. state. tx. us or from www. ets. org, should be read carefully. This test is designed to make you think by recalling factual information, analyzing information, comparing it with other knowledge you have, or making decisions about information. You will be asked to answer each question by choosing one of several answers. Then you will mark your answer choice on a separate answer sheet (a scantron) or click on your choice on the computer. One of the best ways to answer multiple-choice questions is to narrow your answer options by using a process of elimination. Here are several helpful suggestions for narrowing your answer.

- **Focus on exactly what is being asked.** Examine the question or question stem and try to determine what the question is *really* asking. After selecting an answer, go back to check if your choice really is a match for the question. For example, if the question is asking you about the most effective *focus activity* for a science lesson, you will need to select an answer that talks about a *focus activity* rather than another part of the lesson plan. Many test takers miss answers because they fail to give this step proper attention. The test writers have deliberately designed many of these questions to be sure you have the ability to analyze carefully—so be very sure that you do!

- **Test your answer.** By *filling in the blank* with your choice and reading it back you can see if the answer you selected makes sense.
- **Watch grammar.** If the question demands a noun, look for an answer that is a noun, or if a verb is required to complete a question stem, be sure to select an answer that is a verb.
- **Analyze verbs.** Related to the hint above, you should *look closely at the verbs* to analyze what the question requires. This can also be a good indicator of the correct answer. For example, if a question contains the word *prepare,* the answer should indicate something to do with preparation; that is, something the teacher would do *prior* to teaching, or if the question deals with managing, the answer must have some aspect of classroom management. Some of these can be tricky, so analyze, analyze, analyze!
- **Read *all* answer choices before choosing an answer.**
- **Eliminate incorrect answers first.** Place an *X* next to the answer choices you know are incorrect (if you are taking the paper-and-pencil version). You will probably be able to eliminate one or two choices immediately after using this strategy. Be sure to *eliminate an answer that has any hint of negativity toward children or their parents.*
- **Read the question and the related paragraphs and other material carefully.** As you read, underline key information and circle key words or phrases—or note them carefully if you are taking the computer version. These definitely should include words that would change the answer (*first, last, next, best, least, not,* etc.). If you feel that three of the answers are similar, go back to the paragraph to make sure you did not miss one of these words that can change the meaning.
- **Remember that when two choices are similar to each other, one of them is usually the correct answer.**
- **Look for an "umbrella" situation.** If an answer can "cover" another answer, the "umbrella" is probably the correct answer. For example, if Choice *A* reads, "A teacher should establish time allotments ahead for each student's PowerPoints," and Choice *B* reads, "A teacher should give students a rubric, time to plan, and time to practice their PowerPoints," Choice *B* is a better umbrella answer because Choice *B* would cover time allotments in the rubric and in the planning stage, and it is more detailed.
- **Go with your first hunch.** Our first choice will be correct more often than not. Mark this first choice on every question. If you have a concern about it, place a small question mark beside the number and come back *if* there is time. If not, at least you have given it your best shot. *Unanswered questions are counted as wrong.* This is a long examination with considerable reading. If you have to come back to many unanswered questions, you may run out of time. Go ahead and mark something on every first pass.

STRATEGIES THAT ARE PARTICULAR TO THIS EXAMINATION.

- **Remember your pedagogy.** *Do not answer in ways that go against* good educational theory or *your PPR* (Pedagogy and Professional Responsibilities TExES test) competencies. Never, ever answer "against" any of these competencies or standards, even if you have seen practices in your school experiences that do not match them.

- **Know the standards.** Knowing the TEKS, standards, and competencies well for this exam will give you an edge. Pay close attention to the *vocabulary* in the competencies; know what every word means.

- **Think TEXASLAND!** Like at Disneyland, *assume that everything good for children is available* and select that answer. If you discard a choice because you think that it offers something not available or not seen in your experiences or in "real live" schools, you will get it wrong. *Put yourself in the place of children in the scenario.* Ask yourself what would be best or most exciting for me (*as a child*), and choose that answer. Think roses and rainbows, field trips and technology, parents who are eager to participate, and so forth. If an answer indicates that something would be less work or easier for the teacher—that is usually *not* the right answer. Texas wants you to work hard to offer the ultimate experiences for children.

- **Answer shorter items first.** Go through the exam and *answer the shorter items first* (*unless* they are part of a cluster group of questions or fall into a Teacher Decision Set; then do not do those during the first pass). This strategy may be particularly useful if you are a slower reader. After answering these single items, go back to others that have longer paragraphs or other more complicated stimulus data to analyze, along with the cluster items and the Teacher Decision Sets. (*Note: This strategy is not suggested for the PPR exam because there is so much that you would have to reread in that test.*)

- **Remember the Texas biases.** These include encouraging student choice and responsibility, higher-level thinking, authentic assessment, self-assessment, providing relevant instruction, age-appropriate instruction, use of technology and using the community as resources, using cooperative groups, and so forth.

- *Isolate the grade level* **on which the question is centered.** It can make a big difference in your answer. Your answer about instruction will be different for each grade level, so be sure to look for this information, in pedagogy questions.

- **Watch for trial times.** Remember that a number of the questions on this exam are *trial items* and are not graded as a part of your score. If a question seems "not quite right," go on rather than fixating on finding an answer for it. The test makers may simply be trying out a question for validity.

- *Mark all your answers first in the test booklet* **as well as on your scantron** (if you are taking the paper-and-pencil version). That way, should you discover that you are not on the correct number on your scantron, you can come back to your booklet where you have clearly marked the answers without wasting time rereading to find out where you went wrong.

Helpful Hint:

If the question is a scenario-based question, try to visualize the classroom and what is happening. Try to see the teacher acting in ways that reflect the Generalist and the PPR competencies and standards. "Cut to the chase" of what it is you believe the question is asking by ignoring superfluous information. Select your answer, and again, go back to the question to double-check if your selection answers that particular question.

Helpful Hint:

Remember that a blank answer is wrong on the Generalist. Even if you do not know the answer to a question, it is to your advantage to guess rather than to not answer at all. If you run out of time, quickly mark something for all items you did not have a chance to answer before you turn in your test.

One Week Before the Generalist

With Only One Week to Go, What Can I Do to Best Prepare for the Generalist?

There are several important issues to consider in the week before you take the Generalist. First, continue to review your study materials both individually and with a study partner or group (if possible). If you have been following a well-designed study schedule, this last week before the exam should be a review week. This is not the time to begin learning new content. At this point, you should feel confident with your knowledge base in almost all of the competencies, so spend your study time on the few competencies that you need to further practice and review. Remember to study the most heavily weighted (reading/language arts) items very well.

HOUSEKEEPING. You also have a few housekeeping chores to complete this week. First, read your test admission ticket carefully. Your admission ticket provides you with important information, such as the exam date, the exam administration site, the time of the exam, the exam for which you are registered, and what to bring to the exam. Remember that the testing company and the state do not guarantee either the time or the site that you originally requested. If your request for a site is already filled, they will have assigned you to the next closest site and/or another time. If you arrive at a different site or a different time from what is on your ticket, you will not be allowed to test. Mistakes are sometimes made for the actual test, so check carefully to make sure they have you down for the exact test you requested. There are no extra tests brought to a site, so if your requested test was incorrectly recorded and you did not catch it in time, again, you will not be allowed to test. If you are taking more than one exam on the same day (and we hope you are not), you will receive a separate admission ticket for each. Remember to take your admission ticket(s) with you to the exam site. You will not be allowed to enter a testing session without your ticket.

Make sure you know how to get to the test administration site. Although the address will be printed on your test admission ticket, you may want to consult a road map or MapQuest and/or make a dry run to the site a few days before your exam. This will help you figure out how long it will take you to drive to the site on your exam day and what traffic, road construction, and/or parking problems you may encounter along the way. Arriving in a rush of anxiety over getting there on time can cause you to begin the exam flustered and not at your best. Remember that if you arrive late to the site for registration, you may be refused admission to the test that day and refused a refund for missing your exam. If you are driving to a testing site from out of town, you may want to request an afternoon testing time or make a hotel reservation to avoid driving in the early morning hours. Be sure to book early—others may have the same idea.

Additional information about testing requirements, registration, test results, and obtaining a teaching certificate can be found in the Registration Bulletin on the Web site. It is always suggested to check this site several times prior to your test to find out the very latest information and possible changes. ETS is working to ensure that cancelled testing due to weather or other problems are posted as soon as they know on their Web site. This type of information could appear as late as the morning of a test, so check before you go.

TEST ANXIETY. This week you may be feeling some test anxiety about taking the Generalist. Test anxiety is a psychological response to a perceived threatening situation. Most of your fellow test takers will also be feeling a little anxious and nervous. In fact, feeling this way before an important exam is perfectly normal and can be beneficial, as it helps increase your alertness and improves your attention to the task at hand. However, many test takers who are "too calm" are not motivated to do their best work. Having "an edge" can be good, but feeling a great deal of anxiety and nervousness can interfere with your performance on the Generalist. Test takers who experience a high level of test anxiety can lose their concentration, feel their hearts pounding, experience lightheadedness, break out in a cold sweat, or be unable to recall simple information when completing the exam. Highly anxious test takers tend to score lower on tests than less anxious test takers. Try the following strategies to help you control test anxiety on this examination:

- **Register for only one test at a time.** We have said this several times because it is so important. Some people put these tests off and then reach their time limit when they *must* pass on a particular testing date or be ineligible to apply in time for the new school year, or they may even lose their jobs if they do not pass. This anxiety can be extremely detrimental to test taking. Research continues to show that some who attempt to take more than one test do not do well on one or both tests. Because these tests are such long reading tests, at a certain points anxiety and/or a loss of concentration can cause you to not be at your best.

- **Ensure that you are thoroughly prepared for the exam.** Many times test takers use test anxiety as an excuse for lack of studying for the exam. Overpreparation may be the best way to prevent test anxiety; the better you know the material, the more confident you will be about taking the test. However, remember that you do not have to make an "A" on this test to pass, so you do not have to answer every single question correctly. If you come across information you don't know, just go on and try to answer those items that you *do know* correctly.

- **Simulate the testing situation multiple times so that it is as close as possible to the real experience.** This includes taking timed practice tests, working with other test takers (as mentioned earlier), and completing chapter exercises that will help you visualize and experience what the Generalist is like. After completing the practice questions and exercises in this book, use them as a guide to help you generate additional questions for each competency. Remember that the test can ask questions selected from thousands of bits of information from all of the content areas. Practice tests can only hit a limited number of these items. Study for many details, even though you may not see them on the practice tests.

- **Reserve this day for this examination alone.** Trying to catch a plane, be a member of a wedding party, or even having a "big date" later that day or evening can cause you to lose concentration during the test. This is an expensive test and is not offered that often, so reserve this day for testing and focus on the test alone.

- **Arrive early.** Many test takers who must drive a considerable distance can begin to panic if they think they may not arrive in time for registration. Some sites have parking a considerable distance away, so those who arrive late may be rushing to get seated in time to begin. Both of these situations set up a negative beginning for the hours of testing to come.

Helpful Hint:

Do not answer questions based on your own personal classroom observations and teaching experiences *unless* these experiences match the same actions and philosophies found in the materials for this examination and other tests involving professional development philosophies (the PPR).

- **Do relaxation exercises and practice positive self-talk before and during the exam.** Take several slow, deep breaths before beginning the exam and visualize yourself successfully completing the test. Throughout the exam, say to yourself, "I have studied hard," "I know this material," and/or "I am confident that I am doing well."
- **Eliminate distractions.** If another test taker causes you to begin to lose your concentration or creates anxiety for any reason (tapping or making other noises, causing the table to move, etc.), ask the proctor to move you. Do not address the other person directly, as the proctor could view it as cheating (which could cause you to lose your test score for that day).

The Night Before the Generalist

What Should I Do the Night Before the Generalist?

Spend the night before the Generalist organizing for the exam the next day and doing a relaxing activity to take your mind off the task ahead. Read your admission ticket again to confirm you know where you are going and exactly what time you are expected to be there and in your seat. Also, collect all of the supplies you will need for the following day. These supplies include your valid admission ticket, two pieces of identification, sharpened no. 2 pencils with erasers, an accurate watch that does not beep, a snack, and a lunch if you are taking more than one exam on the same day (and, again, we hope you are not). Although you cannot eat or drink (other than water) inside the actual room, you may step outside for a break. Therefore, you may want to put an energy bar and/or a drink in your pocket or purse to give you a midtest boost, as there may be no snack machines available at the test site. At the time of publication, only water bottles with screw-on tops are being allowed inside the actual room where people are testing, but check the current registration information to insure that no changes in this requirement have been made.

You are required to bring identification with you to get into the site. The two pieces of identification you must bring (always check for changes) are:

- One government issued photo ID, in the name in which you are registered
- One secondary ID with a signature

In the Registration Bulletin you will find examples of acceptable forms of identification, what to do if you forget your required forms of identification, or what to do if you do not have photo identification with your current name, and so forth. Also, you will find a complete list of prohibited items. Many personal items are prohibited at the exam site, and you will be asked to store them at your own risk in a designated area if you should bring any of these with you. Here is current list of prohibited items.

briefcases	electronic pagers	watches that beep	calculators
backpacks	audiotapes	highlighters	calculator watches
packages	dictionaries	notebooks	any written or
textbooks	photographic or	scratch paper	unauthorized
spell checkers	recording devices	slide rules	materials
cellular phones			

Talking on a cell phone or using a cell photo phone may be interpreted as cheating and could cost you a test score. Leave your phone and other communication devices at home or in your car so you do not have to worry about them during the test. Visitors, including friends and relatives, must remain outside the test site. Remember to carefully read the most current Registration Bulletin to ensure you understand the most recent requirements for this examination.

After organizing your supplies for the following day, you should plan to do a relaxing and enjoyable activity to help take your mind off the task ahead of you. If you do plan to review this evening, spend only about an hour going over your notes or flipping through your flashcards. Do not use this time as a long study session to cram for tomorrow's exam.

Most importantly, you should go to bed early and get a good night's sleep. Waking up feeling refreshed will go a long way in helping you to feel confident about the task ahead. Sleeping is not a waste of time with a huge day in front of you.

The Day of the Generalist

What Should I Do on the Day of the Generalist?

BEFORE THE EXAM. When the big day is finally here, there are several things you can do to help yourself be as successful as possible. First, eat a nutritious breakfast if you are scheduled to take the exam in the morning, or eat a healthy lunch if you are scheduled to take the exam in the afternoon. Nutritionists suggest that foods high in protein and low in carbohydrates can produce mental alertness. Based on this suggestion, you will want to eat brain foods, such as lean meats and fish, leafy green vegetables, and peanuts, while avoiding cereals, pastas, potatoes, and breads. Also, don't overload on caffeine before taking the examination; this can impair your ability to concentrate and focus. You want to be as calm and relaxed as possible, and this is very difficult to do if you have infused your body with too much coffee or cola. An added distraction is that you may find your concentration broken by having to leave the test for too many restroom breaks.

Dress in loose, comfortable clothing, and don't forget any lucky charms if they are a psychological boost to you. It is a good idea to dress in layers so that you can take off or put on a jacket or sweater if the room temperature feels too hot or cold during the test. Feeling comfortable and relaxed will go a long way in helping you focus on the exam during the many hours of testing.

A third rule of thumb to follow on test day is to arrive early at the test site and sit by yourself in the testing room. By arriving early (as discussed earlier), you will not feel rushed and will have time to relax and become comfortable with the testing environment. If you can

Helpful Hint

For the paper-and-pencil version:
To avoid errors that have to do with being on a specific number in your test booklet and another number on your scantron, circle the answer you selected right in your examination booklet as you answer each question. That way, if you do see a mismatch with your scantron, you will not be forced to go back through the test and reread a number of questions to find out where your first mismatch occurred—you already have a record of the answers you selected in your booklet.

separate yourself from your fellow test takers, you will be able to tune out their chatter about how difficult they think this test is going to be and how worried they are about failing. If you cannot choose your seat and other test takers are talking around you, use this time to focus on all of the hard work you have put into studying for this exam and how that effort will pay off for you. Practice your positive self-talk and deep breathing exercises, if needed. When testing begins, however, be sure to be in your assigned seat, if applicable. You may not receive credit if you are not seated where you were assigned.

Sometimes the test may not begin on time, and there may be long lines. Do not let this delay bother you, as the monitors must give you the correct amount of time as soon as the test begins. If you have a major complaint about the site or the monitors, you may put this into writing and send it to ETS within seven days at their Web site (www.ets.org). They may set up a retest with no charge if the conditions at your testing site made it difficult to deliver a fair test.

ETS Paper-Based TExES Tests
Test Administration Services
Mail Stop 34-Q
Princeton, NJ 08541-6051
Fax: 1-609-771-7710
E-mail: TexasTas@ets.org

ETS Computer-Administered
TExES Tests
CAT Complaints
P.O. Box 6051
Princeton, NJ 08541-6051
Fax: 1-609-530-0551

DURING THE EXAM. After the examination has been distributed, read the test directions very carefully. This is especially important when taking a multiple-choice test like the Generalist because of the various types of item formats described earlier in this chapter. Test takers can also make serious mistakes when answers are required to be recorded on a separate scantron and scored by a test-scoring machine. Be sure to stop and check about every ten questions to make sure your scantron number matches the question number you are answering. If you do mismatch your answer sheet, it is much better to catch this early and correct it rather than realizing what you have done at the end of the test—or not catching it at all.

Time management is a big factor in the successful completion of this examination. Remember that if you do not control your time, it will control you. Because the room in which you are testing may not have a clock, you may not be able to see a clock from where you are sitting, or the clock may not be accurate, make sure you have an accurate watch that does not beep with you. Since the Generalist is a timed test, keeping track of the time you have left will help you budget your remaining time during the test session. Use all of the time allotted for the testing session by pacing yourself through the exam. There are difficult questions on this test, so do not spend too much time on any one question. Mark your first inclination and put a question mark beside it if you are uncertain, and then go on—with the aim to come back *if* you have time.

When you are first given your test booklet or see your computer test, note how many questions your particular exam has and divide your time by the number of questions. Also, factor in the number of minutes that you think that you will need to schedule for breaks. This

Helpful Hint:

Since the Generalist is very long and demanding, you may find it easier to take several short breaks during the testing session rather than working continuously through the exam. Try closing your eyes or putting your head on your desk or table for fifteen seconds (being sure not to nod off). If you feel yourself becoming tense, take a few deep breaths and practice positive self-talk, reminding yourself that you do know this material. Step outside for a moment and walk around briskly or have that energy bar in your purse or pocket.

will give you an idea of how many questions you have to answer per hour to finish—including brief breaks. Move at a consistent pace through the exam and monitor yourself to keep track of how much time you have left. Allow at least five minutes at the end of the test to thoroughly check your answer sheet, making sure that you have marked an answer for each question—even if you have to quickly just guess. If you guess correctly, you are ahead. If you leave the item blank, it is wrong. If you run out of time, mark all the remaining items with the same letter answer. Also, it would be a shame to lose a point for an incomplete erasure or a mark made outside the guidelines. Clean up your scantron very thoroughly. If you believe that you may have some stray marks *and* if you are within a point or two of passing, you can request a scantron recheck. Having your test rechecked is probably not worth it unless you have a very close-to-passing score. If your circumstances are such that you are out of time for keeping your job, and you do feel that your scantron was a bit messy, directions for rechecking your score are found in the Registration Bulletin.

SUMMARY

In conclusion, studying for and passing the Generalist is an important component in your becoming an effective Texas teacher. By following this schedule, organizing your time and materials, and using good study skills, you will have an excellent chance of being successful on this examination and entering the classroom as a competent and confident educator. Teachers who know their content well are miles ahead when it comes time to planning good lessons for children. This advantage is compounded by those who also understand how to teach the content well. We hope that you will find information about both of these areas in the chapters that follow and that you will take the time and effort to thoroughly learn about both—for yourself (in passing the exam) but, even more than that, for our children.

If you have questions about the Registration Bulletin, completing forms, test dates and registration deadlines, test cancellation, score reports, or other information regarding the Generalist, please write, call, or e-mail the following company (remembering that this information is current at the time of publication and can change):

ETS Web site: http://texes.ets.org/

Email: texes-excet_inquires@ets.org

TExES/ExCET Program
Oak Hill Technology, Inc.
Suite 710
4544 South Lamar Boulevard
Austin, TX 78745

Telephone: 866-902-5922
 (General Information and Registration)

For disability information: www.ets.org/disability or e-mail stassd@ets.org or 866-387-8602

If you have certification questions or questions about which tests you need, you may want to call or write the State Board of Educator Certification (SBEC) Information and Support Center currently located at TEA:

Texas Education Agency
Educator Certification & Standards
1701 North Congress Ave.
WBT 5-100
Austin, TX 78701-1494

Telephone: (888) 936-8400 (toll free)
 Local Number: 512-936-8400

E-mail address:sbec@tea.state.tx.us

Web site: http://www.sbec.state.tx.us
 (certification information)

Check for new Web sites and phone numbers if those listed above are no longer current. The information listed was current at the time of publication. However, the state changes its organizational structure, its testing structure, and so forth more often than you think. If you are in a teacher preparation program, stay in touch with a university advisor or certification officer to regularly review your program of study and any changes made in the state's testing requirements.

We wish you the best of luck on your examination.

2 Preparing to Teach Language Arts and Reading in Texas

Laveria F. Hutchison
University of Houston—Central Campus

Eleanore S. Tyson
University of Houston—Central Campus

This chapter discusses the English Language Arts and Reading (Early Childhood–Grade 4) section of the *EC-4 Generalist*. It includes standards for knowledge and classroom applications in literacy instruction and related areas, such as oral language, phonemic awareness, comprehension, developmental writing, and assessment. In addition to a basic discussion of language arts and reading, other areas that support literacy have been added to provide a more complete overview of this section for a new teacher. This is, perhaps, one of he most important chapters to learn. No matter what subject you are teaching, you will always be working with children on reading skills.

The authors of this chapter would like first to stress the importance of understanding the components of each of these standards as a test taker. As an example, let's consider *Standard VIII: Development of Written Communication.* First, the test taker needs to know each stage of the writing process and its meaning and relationship to the other English Language Arts and Reading standards and assessment procedures. Next, the test taker needs to understand the purpose and meaning of each test item that addresses this standard, and connections should be made with key terms given in the standard, the question, and response choices. In this way, a test taker determines the *best* answer that relates back to the standard. It is a circular process that goes from the standard to the purpose of the question and to the connection of response choices. As you study this chapter, you should also connect this information to your preparation for the Professional Roles and Responsibilities (PRR) TExES. There are questions in the Generalist that not only test content knowledge but also your knowledge of best teaching practices. It takes practice in order to become a successful TExES question analyzer, but you can acquire this skill.

You are encouraged to read each standard, the definition of each standard, and each practice question. In addition, you should read the information related to the standard and critically analyze the application question(s) that follow(s). The English Language Arts and Reading section of the Generalist consists of ten standards and provides test items for approximately 40 percent of the TExES test items. Additionally, these standards correlate with the Texas Essential Knowledge and Skills (TEKS) for English Language Arts and Reading. The TEKS tell teachers what knowledge and skills children should gain at each grade level. Of course, that means that teachers must know this information in order to teach these skills, and they must also know the best ways to teach this information. Table 2.1 summarizes the instructional components of the TEKS for language arts and reading for Pre-K through fourth grade.

Table 2.1   Summary of Pre-K–Grade 4 TEKS for Language Arts and Reading

Pre-K	Students interact with responsive adults and peers in a language- and print-rich instructional environment that provides opportunities for development in the following areas: **1.** Listening comprehension **3.** Functions of print **2.** Phonological awareness **4.** Letter knowledge
Kindergarten	Students engage in instructional activities that promote development of oral language usage, conceptual knowledge, narrative and expository print forms, alphabet usage, and letter formation.
Grade 1	Students engage in instructional activities that promote development of independent readers and writers by using various print forms, by providing reading materials that promote fluency and understanding, and by demonstrating the conventions of writing and spelling.
Grade 2	Students engage in instructional activities that promote development of independent readers by providing instruction that promotes sight vocabulary development, teaching and demonstrating a variety of word identification strategies, teaching comprehension skills, demonstrating graphic presentations, teaching note-taking procedures, and teaching conventions of writing and spelling.
Grade 3	Students engage in instructional activities that promote structural analysis skills, glossary skills, elements of the writing process, independent reading activities, and activities that provide a transition from manuscript writing to cursive writing.
Grade 4	Students engage in instructional activities that demonstrate story structure analysis, produce narrative and expository writing products, practice the parts of speech in a variety of written forms, emphasize awareness of correct spelling and grammar, and demonstrate application of the elements of writing.

As you read the information about each standard, you should try to capture the relationship between the TEKS and TExES. Additionally, you can find a listing of the TEKS on the following Web site: http://www.tea.state.tx.us/teks.

Standard I Oral Language

Competency 001: Teachers of young children understand the importance of oral language, know the developmental processes of oral language, and provide a variety of instructional opportunities for young children to develop listening and speaking skills.

The teacher knows basic linguistic concepts, knows developmental stages in acquiring oral language, plans oral language instruction based on assessment procedures, designs instructional practices that promote purposeful listening activities, provides various instructional activities that allow children to have opportunities to engage in oral language activities that involve adult and peer participation, and provides opportunities for children to evaluate the effectiveness of their own spoken language. The teacher needs to have an instructional environment that promotes discussions about books, objects, experiences, pictures, and other print and nonprint sources. Remember that the TEKS promote oral language development and instruction.

Try this practice question:

Mr. Jones teaches a kindergarten class comprised of a diverse population of students with varying language proficiency levels. Which activity from those listed below would be the *least* effective in encouraging language development for all his students?

A. Mr. Jones can facilitate a story writing activity in which all students contribute to the story as he writes the class story on chart paper. Class members can then act out the story they created.

B. Students can memorize and chorally present a poem selected by the teacher to be shared with parents in a class presentation.

C. Mr. Jones can create language centers where students can work during different times of the day that includes a listening center, a puppet center, and a grocery story center.

D. Mr. Jones arranges children in "Think, Pair, Share" cooperature groups to discuss the experiment as it progresses.

Choice A incorporates and includes the language and voice of all students in the classroom. Because students also see the teacher writing down what they say, children can understand how reading and writing are associated. Additional language use and oral expression are reinforced through the retelling and acting out of the story at the end. Choice B will not promote language proficiency unless students understand the words in the poem. There is an indication that, because it is a teacher-selected poem, the message of the poem may have more meaning for the teacher and parents than for the students. Choice C is also well rounded in the teacher's attempt to meet the language needs of all students, whether they can or cannot recognize rhyming words or whether their language proficiency level is highly communicative or weak. The activities described in the centers would promote the language development of all students at any level of proficiency. Choice D encourages communication through one of many types of cooperative grouping. Children have time to think about an answer, share it with a partner and, finally, with the group, so that children have reflection on what they will say, and opportunity to use it, with a partner then to test with a page group. Therefore, Choice B is correct as the *least* effective activity.

Children come to school with a myriad of backgrounds and with varying degrees of language proficiency. Children's differences in language development are strongly shaped and influenced by language used in the home. Children fortunate enough to have had a rich literacy background at home are often confident and articulate. Their oral language is frequently quite advanced for their age. On the other hand, there are those children who, for a variety of reasons, are shy or reluctant to speak or have not had the advantages of language development offered by some homes (including some where English is not spoken as a *first* language). Teachers must be aware of individual experiences with language to best meet the learning needs of their students. These children must feel comfortable speaking with another person at a personal and informal level before they will contribute to class discussions, speak out in a cooperative group, volunteer to take part in a skit, or give an oral report. When responding to questions about this standard, be aware that questions about students' language development will most likely focus on teacher awareness of individual students' background experiences with language and current language proficiency. The teacher's ability to meet students' learning needs with an appropriate instructional strategy (by considering individual students' learning and instructional levels, learning styles, personal backgrounds, and so forth) builds from students' present ability levels.

As the novice teacher begins to investigate the conceptual development of oral language, it is a good idea for him or her to review the features and stages of language development. A developed language base in young readers is important in learning to read. Although *learning theories* that explain the processes children follow in learning language are sometimes controversial, educators usually accept the following sequence (Jewell & Zintz, 1986):

1. Vocalizing sounds (crying or babbling) to obtain a response from a parent or caregiver.
2. Recognizing a stimulus-producing sound (hears a barking sound and looks at the family's dog).
3. Generalizing a word to identify an object (parent asks for the ball, and child responds by identifying the ball in a variety of ways such as looking at or touching the ball).
4. Speaking by age 3 years in phrases and sentences containing approximately four words; understanding the concept of "yes" and "no," asking and answering simple questions, and following directions such as "pick up the ball and give it to Mommy."
5. Developing language skills in preschoolers through focusing on using four to five words in a sentence, using a limited number of grammar rules, creating and orally presenting personal stories (about going to the zoo or to McDonald's), asking and answering questions, and describing objects and personal events.

6. Acquiring a speaking vocabulary of 2,000 to 3,000 words by kindergarten age and continuing to develop oral language competencies.
7. Developing a continuous ability to produce words that includes the use of social talk, correct grammar, and construction of oral and written complex sentences.

Basic related instructional components are generally apparent for the development of age-appropriate oral language skills. Early childhood teachers should foster a language-rich environment by displaying charts showing pictures of objects or actually displaying concrete objects that are being discussed in voice-recognition class, using picture books to enhance oral language development, providing technology, using word walls that display high-frequency sight words, displaying items that identify colors, introducing symbols that explain directions, and so forth. Instructional practices that integrate language development should provide expanded time-chunks for incorporating many or all of the entire language development components, hopefully engaging children in literacy as a whole. An intradisciplinary approach allows children to use a variety of cognitive resources, such as predictable books, literature-based basal readers, trade books, computers, newsprint, visual media, peers, libraries, teachers, and other adults. The discussion of this standard highlights several components of linguistic concepts, then proceeds to discuss those that beginning teachers should recognize as part of the decoding process.

One concept that EC-4 teachers should understand well is **decoding**, or unlocking the meaning of a word. Numerous studies by educational researchers have provided information on the processes young children use in decoding words. As children attempt to pronounce a word, they gain information from the way a word is spelled (**orthography**), the way a word is pronounced (**phonology**), the way a word is defined (**semantics**), the recognition of the sounds heard in a word (**segmentation**), the sentence structure (**syntax**), and the meaning of a word in its **contextual** setting. This is a challenging process for teachers to convey to children and for children to apply to the many text forms (or printed materials) encountered in classrooms.

Another element for beginning teachers to consider is that classroom instruction needs to relate to students from culturally and linguistically diverse backgrounds. Diverse backgrounds include those students who speak Standard English, who speak nonstandard English, who are bilingual, who are emerging English speakers, and who speak no English at all. Linguistic considerations include the various dialects and languages present in classrooms. Let us investigate some strategies and terms that connect with these young learners.

The **language experience approach (LEA)** is an instructional method that incorporates the various components of language arts by using children's experiences and backgrounds as a structure for developing stories—individually or in a heterogeneous group. These group or individually generated stories can discuss ideas about school activities, field trips, a trade book, observations, structured words, personal experiences, creative stories, or a variety of other topics. LEA is connected to *schema theory* by using students' experiences and backgrounds as a starting point for developing stories as the teacher writes down children's stories and responses. LEA allows them to observe the organization and mechanical functions of written language by observing the teacher print directionally from left to right and from top to bottom. Children also see printed word organization and spacing, punctuation, letter formation, and sentence structure. Additionally, children with limited

English proficiency (LEP) and with limited background experiences can bene-fit from LEA because they are better able to comprehend reading material that they themselves have dictated to the teacher.

Because the connection between LEA and children with limited English proficiency is mentioned, there is the need to discuss **nonstandard dialects**. These are dialects used by children who are bilingual, multilingual, and who speak only English. It is important to note that Standard English is a dialect that is effectively used by many members of society (we might say "business" English). *Nonstandard English* is often connected to the usage of grammatical variations in language production. A dialect may belong to a cultural group, and usage in that group requires certain language rules just as with Standard English. In relationship to LEA and how to most effectively deal with nonstan-dard English in classroom situations, consider the following conversational example between a student and a teacher:

Teacher: Have you decided on a title for your story?

Student: Yup. Me go write bout my cat are going to have kittens.

Teacher: Oh! I think that is a great idea. *You are going to write about how your cat* is going to have kittens. Let's get started.

The teacher accepts the child's idea that is stated in nonstandard English and models another way to restate the child's sentence using Standard English. Note that the teacher focuses on the ideas the child offers. The teacher is ac-cepting of the statement and not critical of the child's language used to give the idea in this conversation. It is important to note that a child's personal usage of oral and written language has an important multicultural aspect, be-cause not being accepting of a child's language production (especially when the language includes nonstandard English) could deter learning risks and lan-guage growth. However, teachers should: (1) always model many examples of correct and effective speech structures and writing examples in classroom situ-ations; (2) ask children to clarify their responses, and; (3) provide positive feedback that encourages Standard English. Many teachers feel that a goal for children is *bidialectism*. This means that children can feel less pressure using their home dialect as they learn to be successful in using Standard English in school and later in the business world.

It is important to state again that children enter school with oral and lis-tening vocabularies that have been developing since they were born. These vocabularies have been shaped by children's cognitive, linguistic, cultural, and experiential backgrounds. A teacher's goal should be to promote children's de-velopment of reading and writing vocabularies that closely parallel these oral and listening vocabularies. Piaget's word *schema* reminds us that it is easier to learn if we can attach new knowledge to something already known.

Language interference is the use of sounds, syntax, and vocabulary of two languages simultaneously as a child participates in literacy activities. **Bilingual education** involves presenting reading and other subject area mate-rials in the child's native language, while gradually introducing English. **English-as-a-Second Language** (ESL) teachers may work with children from a variety of countries and who speak a number of languages who are placed to-gether in one class. As the beginning teacher instructs children who are in the process of learning English (English Language Learners), it is important to ex-plain the common meanings of English words before beginning instruction and to use strategies such as LEA. Many ESL techniques are listed in the last chapter of this book.

In a language arts classroom, *listening* is another significant part of oral language learning. Students who become *active* listeners can remember important parts of a story, follow directions, respond to purpose-setting questions set by the teacher, participate in cooperative groups, and improve their vocabulary development. As students learn to listen critically, the teacher should provide students with practice in building on prior knowledge, in learning to synthesize information from more than one source, and in solving problems. As students learn to listen for appreciation, the teacher should emphasize the understanding of mood and of the use of figurative language. Although there are a variety of instructional components that can be used, note taking and questioning are two that are important in this area.

Note taking is a selective listening activity that allows children to organize ideas, identify main ideas, and provide study points. Teachers can model *developmentally appropriate* note taking for students by presenting a graphic organizer such as a graphic mapping activity or an outline of the content (which may be partially filled in), narrative stories, picture books, and oral presentations. As children learn the process of identifying and recording important information, they can engage in cooperative groups to compare ideas. You will find additional information about note taking in the discussion of Standard VII.

Questioning is another area that promotes effective listening and higher level thinking. Teacher questioning should promote responses from children that help them comprehend literal, inferential, and evaluative areas of ideas and meanings. You will find additional information about comprehension in the discussion of Standard VII.

Learning a language involves understanding how to analyze words. **Word analysis** is a strategy that includes three cueing systems that good readers develop and learn to use: **graphophonic** (sound/symbol relationships), **syntactic** (patterns of phrases, clauses, and sentences), and **semantics** (meaning of words and combinations of words). To become proficient in word analysis, children need to develop an effective sight vocabulary and know how to use contextual and structural analysis as well as phonics skills. All these are considered **facilitative** skills and are *not* considered reading. The actual understanding or comprehension of what has been read is the **functional** part of reading.

There are many strategies for developing and expanding vocabulary. Aside from using glossaries that are located in the back of textbooks, dictionaries, and thesauruses, students can use *word walls*, examine *homophones* and *homographs*, study *idioms*, *metaphors*, and *similes*, explore riddles and other word plays, engage in *word sorts*, and create semantic maps (word clusters) and semantic feature analysis grids. Below you will find descriptions of the highlighted words in this paragraph:

1. **Homographs.** Words spelled the same but have different pronunciations and meanings: for example, "She is wearing a red *bow*." "She will *bow* to the queen."
2. **Homophones.** Words that sound the same but have different spellings and meanings: for example, "He is wearing a *red* shirt," "He *read* the book."
3. **Idioms.** Figurative sayings that have special meanings: as an example, "*Keep your shirt on!*" basically means "Don't get angry."
4. **Metaphors.** Comparison of two unlike things without using *as* or *like;* an example is "*The moon was a silver dollar against the night sky.*"
5. **Semantic map** *(word cluster).* Writing a word or concept in the center circle (or bubble) of a cluster, drawing rays, writing information about the

word or concept, and making connections between the word or concept and the related unit of study.

6. **Similes.** Comparisons between two things of a different kind or quality using *like* or *as*. An example is "*The rain came down like transparent sheets.*"

7. **Word sorts.** Sorting a collection of words taken from a word wall or other source into two or more categories.

8. **Word wall.** A list of words children are learning or know posted on a poster (or an actual wall in a classroom) in a highly visible location.

A discussion of integrated language arts should include thematic learning units. **Thematic units** are used to connect the various components of language arts (speaking, reading, spelling, writing, and listening, etc.) with other content areas. Thematic units may have a focus in any content area (science, health, mathematics, etc.). Children enjoy units on, for example, butterflies, apples, shapes, cultures of other lands, and so forth. A first-grade thematic learning unit in social studies, for instance, could focus on "The Pilgrims Celebrating Thanksgiving at Plymouth." In this unit children might read (or their teacher can read to them) textbook information and **trade books**. Trade books are children's literature that teachers can sometimes use in instructional settings instead of basal readers or textbooks about the topic. Additionally in this example of a thematic unit, children could research this period of history by investigating lifestyles, tasting foods the Pilgrims found in America, and focusing on significant people, types of transportation used, and so forth. Children could examine a variety of sources, including computer-generated information, to collect information about the topic. It is important for teachers to consider instructional activities that address children's interests. As an example, the teacher might encourage children to participate in writing and/or performing a short play that highlights this significant period. The unit might focus on games that children played during those times (both Pilgrim and Native American) compared to games children play now. Mathematics elements might compare the difference between how much things cost during that period with the present, or they may measure to determine how large the houses were in Plymouth colony. Counting songs (with lyrics on a Thanksgiving theme) combine mathematics, reading, and music. Thematic units should contain a number of subject areas under the umbrella of one topic.

Another important language arts concept is *oral expression*. It takes practice and feedback to become adept in expressing oneself orally. Having a **conversation** with even one other person who is not a member of their own family may be a new experience for some children. A teacher's asking a child specific questions about his or her interests can help a child organize his or her thoughts and encourage the communication of information and ideas. Other informal speaking activities (such as role-playing using a telephone) encourage a child to adjust voice volume and wait for the other person's response. In this way, a child learns telephone etiquette as well as gains confidence. **Textless**, or **wordless**, **picture books** provide an opportunity for a young child to tell a story to the teacher. Because there is no text in these books, there is no correct way to relate the story, and the child has the freedom to interpret it any way he or she chooses. From this "reading," the teacher can assess a child's *sense of story* (a term used to describe a child's understanding of how a story begins, unfolds, and concludes) as well as vocabulary development and communication skills. **Show-and-tell** builds the speaker's confidence and stimulates conversation. It also provides an important link between home and school because the child brings something from home that is special to him or her. Children are more articulate when they are talking about something that is well known and important to them. **Discussions** about special events or favorite books can also afford opportunities for oral language development. **Puppets** are confidence builders with many children, as noted earlier. Children who refrain from speaking in class will frequently feel comfortable talking to (or through) a puppet. The puppet becomes the center of attention, so the child feels less self-conscious and can therefore be more articulate. Other strategies for encouraging oral language development include *interviews, oral reports, debates,* and *dramatic presentations*. In a language arts classroom, *active speaking* is recognized as a critical component of learning. Noise levels vary because students are encouraged to work in pairs or in larger cooperative groups. These groups encourage discussions, reactions, and negotiations. Teachers can promote active speaking in classroom situations by implementing activities such as:

1. **Rereading stories.** Asking children to talk about their favorite parts of the story and their favorite characters in the story.
2. **Retelling stories.** Teachers may have children use props, puppets, dolls, etc., in the retelling process to encourage comprehension and fluency. (See discussion of story retelling under Standard VII.)
3. **Choral reading** and speaking that allows children to orally share written words. Choral delivery can also be used in a thematic unit as children orally deliver a poem or in a science class to read a section of print.
4. **Readers' theater,** which involves children's reading from a prepared script or from a script that children have written. Children learn to project the voice of characters, bring characters to life, and have eye contact with their audience. This activity incorporates reading and oral fluency skills by student performances and listening skills by the audience.
5. Social classroom talk, or conversation, that encourages informal discussions about characters in books or formal discussions about the procedure to solve a problem.

In a language arts classroom, students should have the opportunity to *actively read* from a variety of sources such as books, poems, magazines, computer screens, and other types of print. Students are encouraged to *actively write* and read aloud such products as poems, creative stories, journal entries, drafts and edited works, records of science experiments, and many other types of writing products. Very young children may begin to develop products (such as shape books, picture books that show familiar objects, and letter books) and be encouraged to read or explain them to others.

Effective assessment practices are important as teachers collect information for the purpose of making decisions about instructional practices. Teachers of young children usually collect instructional information by the use of observations, from parents during conferences, from informal conversations, and from formal and informal tests. Observational data can be recorded on checklists, in field notes, in notebooks, or in any form that will allow the teacher to organize and summarize collected data. Parental input is important because parents can provide information about the child's home environment. Additionally, parents can be encouraged to promote literacy activities in the home by (1) placing labels on objects/things that are in the home such as *light, door, window,* or *bed;* (2) asking a variety of questions about favorite topics such as pets and toys; (3) rereading books or other materials that children seem to love and enjoy; (4) helping children place cut-out magazine pictures into categories such as "animals that bark," "things that people eat," "things that are green," etc.; (5) playing developmentally and age appropriate games; (6) providing many opportunities for conversation; (7) reading predictable books; (8) going to the community library to select books to read and reread at home; and (9) encouraging and showcasing schoolwork and other beginning attempts of literacy activities in the home. Formal assessments used in early literacy settings usually measure knowledge of letters, oral vocabulary development, recognition of words, and visual and auditory discrimination ability (Barrett, 1965). The informal and formal assessment procedures that highlight different instructional practices will be discussed again in Standard X.

Try these practice questions:

Mrs. Parlez has several Pre-K students in her class who are reluctant to speak in class. What activity might be *least* effective in stimulating the development of their oral language?

A. Have students use puppets to tell a familiar story.
B. Have students role-play telephone conversations.
C. Have students "read" aloud textless, or wordless, books.
D. Have each child bring a show-and-tell item to class and allow each child the option of describing it or not.

Consider what activity might encourage a shy or reluctant child to speak in a class setting. With regard to Choice *A*, young children will often speak using a puppet while they are too shy to speak face-to-face to an adult. Choice *B*, role-play conversations using a play telephone, offers a familiar and comfortable way for a young child to express himself or herself. Choice *C*, "read" aloud textless, or wordless, picture books affords a framework for oral storytelling. Since each of the above choices could be effectively used to promote oral language development, we can assume the correct answer is *D*. Show-and-tell is often used with young children because it permits them to talk about a topic or item that is important to them in a relaxed, accepting atmosphere. However, if they choose *not* to describe their item, it will not stimulate their oral language development. The answer is *D*.

Mr. Cate, a fourth-grade teacher, has invited a guest speaker to discuss the important events related to the upcoming rodeo. Realizing that the speaker's main objective is to present a wide range of information over a 30-minute time period, which of the following would be the *best* listening practice for Mr. Cate to implement for the children to use as they listen to the speaker?

A. Provide a list of purpose-setting questions.
B. Arrange the children into cooperative groups.
C. Provide a summary of the speaker's discussion.
D. Provide the children with an open note-taking sheet.

Remember that Mr. Cate wants to provide activities to support effective *listening* practices that would allow his children to identify purposes for listening to the speaker. The use of cooperative grouping, recommended in Choice *B*, could be an effective practice for peer engagement to discuss aspects of the speaker's ideas *after* the speaker has finished. Providing the children with either a written or an oral summary of the speaker's ideas, recommended in Choice *C*, could provide ideas about the speaker's presentation *afterwards*. The note-taking sheet, recommended in Choice *D*, does not provide a purpose for listening to the speaker. Having a purpose to listen to the speaker assists children in focusing on the content of the speaker's ideas, and this knowledge allows them to have the information necessary to engage in other activities. Response *A* is the *best* response because good questions give children an effective method for gaining information by providing a rationale for collecting information during the speech. The answer is *A*.

Students in Miss Lucio's urban kindergarten class dictated a story about their field trip to the fire station. What should she *not* expect in the content of their oral delivery?

   A. Standard English
   B. Inconsistent grammar structure
   C. Details about the field trip
   D. Events highlighting the field trip

Actually, *B, C,* and *D* are components of the Language Experience Approach (LEA) that are frequently found in dictated stories and that were discussed in Standard I; therefore, response *A* is what the teacher should *not* expect in a dictated story at this time in the young child's development. However, Standard English, or "business" English, is the target teachers try to reach with students.

Miss Chavez, a Pre-K teacher, plans to provide a list of at-home activities for parents to use. Which parental activities should she *not* suggest?

   A. Allow your child to assist in planning family activities.
   B. Read books to your child and allow your child to discuss the pictures.
   C. Use a scripted conversation developed by professional reading teachers to help reinforce vocabulary.
   D. Clip pictures from magazines that represent the color of the week.

In this situation, Miss Chavez could appropriately recommend Choices *A, B* and *D* to parents as activities that could foster literacy concepts.

The teacher could provide suggestions for vocabulary to be used at home but should not ask for scripted parent/child conversations. The answer is *C*.

Standard II Phonological and Phonemic Awareness

Competency 002: Teachers of young children understand the components of phonological and phonemic awareness and utilize a variety of approaches to help young children develop this awareness and its relationship to written language.

The teacher understands the significance of phonological and phonemic awareness instruction to the reading process, adjusts instruction to meet the developmental needs of children, uses assessment practices to plan instruction, and designs a variety of age-appropriate instructional activities. Remember that beginning in pre-kindergarten and continuing through grade 4, TEKS objectives require using of a variety of print and nonprint language activities that expose children to phonemic awareness instruction.

Use this kindergarten teacher's instructional activity to answer the practice question that follows the activity:

Miss Fuentes, a kindergarten teacher, asks Alex, Mario, Mac, Armando, and Trenia to come to the literacy table. Miss Fuentes plans to use an oral activity to practice rhyming words. Below is the activity she uses with the children.

I am going to say two words together. After I say the words, I will call on one of you to tell me if the words rhyme. If the words rhyme, say "yes." If the words do not rhyme, say "no."

She uses the following list:

1. top/pop
2. rag/big
3. sack/bat
4. look/book
5. sun/man
6. make/take
7. pig/peg
8. could/should

Identify the prereading skill the kindergarten teacher is using.

A. Segmenting of rhyming sounds
B. Auditory discrimination of rhyming pairs of words
C. Visual discrimination of rhyming pairs of words
D. Blending

Choice *B* is the correct response because the teacher is presenting pairs of words to the group of students for the purpose of having them orally identify rhyming pairs. A description of segmenting and blending will be presented later in this section. The answer is *B*.

This standard highlights the concept of **phonological awareness** (the ability to use letter-sound knowledge to identify an unknown word) and **phonemic awareness** (the ability to recognize that spoken words are made up of a sequence of individual sounds that contributes to the young reader's ability to recognize and pronounce unknown words) (Rubin, 2000). As a teacher starts to develop instructional activities that demonstrate to the young reader that words are made up of a series of sounds, it is important to realize that several reading researchers have found that *phonemic awareness* abilities are strong indicators and predictors of successful reading development (Cunningham, Cunningham, Hoffman, & Yopp, 1998; Juel, 1988; Stanovich, 1994). Phonemic awareness is a necessary skill for the young reader to acquire in learning to read and spell. According to Adams (1990), young readers should be able to perform the following *phonemic* awareness tasks that relate to learning to read and spell.

1. **Rhyming and Alliteration. Rhyming** requires the young reader to recognize rhymes or to produce patterns of rhyming words. Rhyming is believed to be the *least* difficult phonemic awareness task to develop because young children have usually been exposed to oral productions of rhyming word patterns from books that were read to them, singing songs, adults' oral play language, and other auditory media sources. Initially, rhyming, is developed through listening. Later, the young reader learns to identify rhyming patterns in various types of printed materials. The following sentence is an example of rhyming: The girl saw a *hat* when she was sitting next to a *cat*. **Alliteration** requires the young reader to recognize words in a sentence or

phrase that mostly begin with the same letter sound. The following sentence is an example of alliteration: T̲all T̲ella t̲ook t̲iny t̲ots t̲o t̲own.

2. **Blending.** This task requires the young reader to blend a series of orally produced sounds to form a word. As an example, the teacher would produce the separate sounds of /t/, /o/, /p/ to the reader and expect the reader to say *top*.

3. **Segmenting beginning and ending sounds in words.** The young reader who has the ability to hear sounds in words should be able to hear and identify sounds at the beginning or end of a word. The teacher could ask the reader to identify the sound heard at the beginning of the word top (the /t/) and also the sound heard at the end (the /p/).

As the young child develops *phonemic* awareness, he or she can recognize that words rhyme, that words can begin and end with either the same sound or a different sound, and that words are made of **phonemes** (the smallest unit of sound in a language that distinguishes one word from another word), which can be blended to form words.

It is important to mention that parents play a significant role in the development of children's *phonemic* awareness development by reading, saying, or singing rhymes together, playing oral language games, and encouraging early written expression by using scribbles and forms of invented spelling. **Invented spelling** is a written approximation based on how a child determines the spelling of a word. As an example, a kindergarten student might write the following sentence to describe his new puppy: M PUE ES QT AN VE TNE (My puppy is cute and very tiny). The discussion of Standard VIII (Development of Written Communication) will provide additional information related to invented spelling. Early childhood teachers and early elementary school teachers should provide examples of reading materials and language activities that parents can use in the home to promote *phonemic* awareness. The home reinforces the work that teachers do at school. Young children need to be able to: (1) associate sounds with letters in words; (2) learn the function of consonant sounds and letters in the initial, medial, and final position; and (3) see print in a variety of situations (big books, peer writing, word walls, trade books, basal readers, worksheets, charts, etc.).

Teachers of young children are encouraged to use *oral interaction* and *direct instruction* in demonstrating phonemic awareness patterns that show how sounds in words are manipulated. The following list provides an instructional structure for developing *phonemic* awareness.

1. *Promote language through different types of oral delivery.* Teachers of young children can use nursery rhymes, riddles, songs, read-aloud books, poems, and other creative ideas that provide sound production. Teachers can demonstrate the same types of activities to parents during the annual Open House/Back to School Night, at parent–teacher conferences, through newsletters, on a Web site, and at various types of parent educational meetings. Children should be asked to respond to questions and statements related to reading selections in both narrative and expository print sources. The teacher and/or parent can ask questions such as "Which two words rhyme?" "Which two words begin with the same sound?" and "Identify the sounds that you hear at the end of the first two words in the following sentence." Rhyming words are used frequently as an instructional activity for young children, and the teacher should spend time demonstrating that rhyming words sound the same at the *end* of each word used in the rhyming pattern. Additionally, teachers should encourage children to make up their own rhyming word patterns.

2. *Create games and activities that develop an awareness of sounds in words.* As children begin to develop an understanding of the concept of *phonemic* awareness, the teacher can purchase or develop games and activities that practice sound patterns in words. As an example, teachers can say a word (or children's names, for example) and ask children to clap the number of syllables heard as the teacher repeats the word. The Elkonin box (1963) is frequently used to practice phonemic awareness by placing a picture on an overhead projector or worksheet and drawing the appropriate number of boxes needed to represent the sounds heard in the word. The teacher might have a picture of the word *hat* and three boxes under the picture (each box represents a sound heard in the word *hat*). Children then place some type of marker (paper clips, plastic counters, pennies, beans, etc.) in each box as the teacher pronounces a word with that sound. As children advance in their understanding of phonemic awareness, the teacher should ask children to write the letter of each sound in the appropriate box. The teacher should have several examples of Elkonin boxes for the children to use. Another activity to help students delete or add phonemes to words is having an ending sound on tagboard (such as "at") with beginning sounds (c, f, m, etc.) that can be flipped in front or taken away. These flip charts can be teacher constructed on tagboard with the beginning phonemes on a binder ring. Technology programs abound for emerging readers, but a teacher must be sure that he or she uses a variety rather than *only* programs that are "worksheets" on the computer. One type of technology that helps students with difficulties in spelling in this area is voice recognition programs, where a computer "reports" in writing what a child says. The teacher must also make sure that *all* children are given appropriate grade-level reading activities and assignments.

3. *Design writing activities.* As children begin to develop an understanding of *phonemic* awareness, the teacher should provide classroom activities that allow children to experiment with language through writing words, phrases, sentences, paragraphs, and longer written segments. The more opportunities children are given to write, the better they will become at understanding and hearing the sounds in words they can use to invent the spelling patterns used to produce a word. As children become capable of segmenting sounds used to spell words, the teacher should encourage children to approximate, or invent, the spelling of words based on the sounds heard in words. Teachers should then provide instruction in classroom settings that will enhance spelling patterns. Additionally, teachers can use classroom word walls to display spelling patterns used in words, sight words, and so forth. Teachers should remember to encourage children to use words from the word wall in both oral and written language formats.

In classroom settings, teachers can assess a child's ability to use *phonemic* awareness through informal or formal means. Informal assessments that evaluate phonemic awareness include: (1) teacher *observations* of students' completing phonemic awareness tasks that require students to complete written tasks and produce oral responses, (2) teacher use of *rubrics* and *checklists* that identify the level of performance students have acquired using phonemic awareness tasks, and (3) other teacher-generated products that provide evidence of students' growth using phonemic awareness tasks.

One formal assessment instrument, the *Texas Primary Reading Inventory* (TPRI), is currently being used by teachers in Texas to determine children's ability to manipulate sounds in words and to determine how they understand these words. It is used in kindergarten through second grade and has been designed as an early reading assessment to determine young readers' early literacy and comprehension development (Carlson, Fletcher, Foorman, Francis, & Schatschneider, 2001). Table 2.2 shows the components of the TPRI's screening section and inventory section.

The *Yopp-Singer Test of Phonemic Segmentation* is another formal assessment used to measure children's ability to pronounce sounds in spoken words and to spell words. This is a 22-item assessment that requires children to respond to teacher-pronounced words by segmenting each pronounced word into separate sounds. This test allows teachers to identify students who need instruction and practice in *phonemic* awareness (Yopp, 1995).

Read this activity and respond to the question that follows:

Ms. Nguyen, a kindergarten teacher, asks students to "clap the number of syllables" heard in this list of words:

1. schoolhouse
2. building
3. pony
4. blue
5. Monday
6. hamburger
7. wagon
8. book

What is the purpose of this activity?

A. To determine the development of sight words.
B. To determine the ability to hear syllables.
C. To determine the readiness for teaching reading.
D. To determine the use of capital letters.

This activity allows Ms. Nguyen to determine how effectively her kindergarten children are hearing syllables in orally pronounced words. Therefore, Choice *B* is correct.

Standard III Alphabetic Principle

Competency 003: Teachers of young children understand the importance of the alphabetic principle to reading English—know the elements of the alphabetic principle, and provide instruction that helps children understand that printed words consists of graphic representation that relates to the sounds of spoken language in conventional and unintentional ways.

The teacher knows the elements of the alphabetic principle, understands individual differences as related to the alphabetic principle, provides instructional activities that assist children in gaining competence in determining sound/letter relationships, and uses assessment practices that determine skill development. Remember that the TEKS promote instruction that uses a variety of practices for developing print awareness, letter knowledge, word analysis strategies, and fluency development.

Table 2.2   Components of the *Texas Primary Reading Inventory*

Grade	Screening Section	Inventory Section
Kindergarten	Graphophonemic knowledge	Book and print awareness
	Phonemic awareness	Phonemic awareness
		Graphophonemic knowledge
		Listening comprehension
Grade 1	Graphophonemic knowledge	Phonemic awareness
	Word reading	Graphophonemic knowledge
	Phonemic awareness	Reading accuracy and fluency
		Listening comprehension
Grade 2	Word reading	Graphophonemic knowledge
		Reading accuracy and fluency
		Reading comprehension

Read the following activity and respond to the practice question:

What is the purpose of this activity? Have first-grade students name the letters of the alphabet. Have one sheet that lists the alphabet in sequence and one sheet that lists the alphabet in random order. Remember to present lowercase letters first in at least a 14-point print size. *You may repeat the same activity using uppercase letters.*

  A. To determine alphabet letter recognition.
  B. To determine the use of uppercase and lowercase letter formation.
  C. To determine readiness for formal reading instruction.
  D. To determine alphabetizing.

The purpose of this instructional activity is to determine letter recognition of both upper and lower case letters in sequential and random order. Choice *A* is correct.

This standard focuses on elements of the **alphabetic principle**, which states that there is a one-to-one correspondence between alphabet letters (*graphemes*) and sounds (*phonemes*). The English language does not have a systematic alphabet system that has only one sound for each of the twenty-six letters of the alphabet because these twenty-six letters have approximately forty-four different sounds (phonemes). As an example, Tompkins (2001) states that "long *e*, for instance, is spelled fourteen different ways in common words. Consider, for example, *me, meat, feet, people, yield, baby,* and *cookie*" (p. 164). In addition to the alphabetic principle, it is important to state that **graphophonemic knowledge** is the understanding that written words are made up of systematic letter patterns that represent sounds in pronounced words. This discussion will highlight instruction related to **letter recognition** (the relationship of letters in printed words to spoken language) and instructional activities used to enhance the development of letter recognition.

Letter naming, or *alphabetic recognition,* is an important skill to develop because children use this skill to acquire reading, spelling, and writing ability. It is important to mention that the *alphabet* is a series of abstract marks that are assigned identities and sounds for use in written contexts. As young children develop the skill of naming letters of the alphabet, they must learn to recognize the shapes of the uppercase manuscript letters, lowercase manuscript letters, uppercase cursive letters, and lowercase cursive letters. Additionally, young children need to identify letters based on formation, position on a line, length, and size. Children frequently have difficulty recognizing the difference between letters that look similar. As an example, the uppercase letters *E* and *F* and the lowercase letters *b* and *d* often confuse the young reader. Until recently, children who reversed or confused similarly formed letters (or words that contained similar letters) were considered to have learning deficits. However, today educators believe that constant exposure in a variety of instructional settings will assist children in developing the skills needed to overcome many of these somewhat common difficulties.

Many children enter school naming the letters of the alphabet by rote memory. However, teachers should realize that young children may not understand that these letter names connect to sound and writing. Children will need instruction in using the letters of the alphabet in random sequence and to learn, practice, and apply the basic sounds that each letter represents. According to Adams (1990) and Cramer (2004) automatic and instant recognition of letters, presented in sequence and randomly, allow children to focus on learning and applying sound-symbol relationships.

Most educators agree that beginning teachers should come to their classrooms with a variety of instructional methods and activities to teach the young child to recognize and apply letter-name knowledge. As an example, Mr. Robinson may plan a lesson using sandpaper letters and other manipulatives, tactile activities, alphabet songs, and books that teach and practice the "letter of the day." Mrs. Jordon may use a multisensory (seeing, hearing, touching, and movement) approach to teach and practice forming the "letter of the day" by using paints, shaving cream, body-letter formation, different colored markers, paper and pencil, clay, and sand. Both of these teachers understand that children should be encouraged to learn alphabet naming by direct instruction and through many types of exposure including visual, auditory, tactile, and kinesthetic. Additionally, teachers should use the consonant-vowel-consonant word pattern (C-V-C, for example in *bat*) to model blending (see discussion of *blending* under Standard II). The teacher should use pictures to enhance the idea that *letter naming* connects to the reading of words. For instance, as the teacher introduces the letter *h*, the teacher should show and pronounce the word *hat* and show a picture of a hat. Picture files of many things that relate to these sounds are valuable to show children (house, horse, hand, etc.) to increase understanding.

It is also an effective practice for the teacher to adjust instructional pacing to meet the needs of children. As the beginning teacher considers ways to teach concepts that relate to the alphabetic principle, he or she may want to consider the following instructional sequence: (1) teach letter names in random sequence, (2) teach the formation and sounds of letters in random sequence, (3) teach lessons that highlight one letter at a time, (4) teach the likenesses and differences in letters based on formation and sound, (5) reteach difficult letters, and (6) provide skill lessons for students experiencing difficulty in learning letters.

As teachers consider ways to assess children's usage of the alphabetic principle, it is important to realize that assessment should be frequent so that teachers can address the immediate instructional needs of learners. Teachers should initially assess children to determine their knowledge of the alphabet by asking them to name the written uppercase and lowercase letters of the alphabet presented in random order. This type of assessment allows the teacher to determine individual children's knowledge of letter names and to plan further instruction. Then the teacher should develop a variety of assessments to use to determine children's growth and development in identifying letters of the alphabet. These assessments can also include activities such as asking a child to identify specific uppercase or lowercase manuscript letters of the alphabet by naming letters as the teacher points to specific letters, by having the child point to specific letters as the teacher names a letter, or having the child match uppercase and lowercase manuscript letters presented in columns.

Most educators agree that the beginning teacher should ask parents to become involved in the development of young children's emergent literacy. Teachers, with the permission of the school's administrative staff, could develop several of the following activities for the purpose of involving parents:

1. Design grade-level workshops to demonstrate ways to assist with decoding words, reading and asking questions, and homework assignments.
2. Develop take-home kits that include books for the child to read, practice worksheets that highlight a specific skill, fun activities, and additional suggestions for things to do in the home. Parents should be encouraged to play many sound games with their children, relating the sound to the letter, and to words the child knows ("Brother is on his bike. What sound do you hear twice? That sound is a B.").
3. Produce a newsletter and a Web site that informs parents about classroom events, new skills that are being introduced, and other academic information. (Remember that English may not always be the language spoken at home.) Teacher-made VCR tapes can also be an effective way to reach parents.

Examine the following as an assessment activity. Then consider the question that follows:

Mr. Dwyer, a kindergarten teacher, places a teacher-made folder game in the literacy center. The directions ask students to match lowercase letters with the corresponding uppercase letters by pulling a length of yarn from one letter in the uppercase column to its corresponding letter in the lowercase column. What is the purpose of this activity?

   A. To practice letter association.
   B. To play a game.
   C. To practice writing the alphabet.
   D. To practice writing conventions.

In this instructional situation, Mr. Dwyer could use this activity to allow students to practice upper- and lowercase letter association. Then, following repeated instruction and practice (using games; computer activities; a variety of tactile products employing sandpaper letters, plastic letters, and other raised surfaces; books; and/or other literacy tools), he would use this as an assessment to determine students' growth in identifying upper-and lowercase letters. The correct answer is *A*.

Standard IV Literacy Development and Practice

Competency 004: Teachers of young children understand that literacy develops over time and progresses from emergent to proficient stages. Teachers use a variety of contexts to support the development of children's literacy.

The teacher understands literacy development from pre-kindergarten through conventional literacy acquisition, has an awareness of the different types of printed materials children use in instructional settings, and uses assessment practices in making decisions about instruction. Remember that the TEKS promotes knowing different types of print sources that teachers can use in instruction.

Try this practice question:

Which strategies should a teacher implement to foster students' enjoyment and appreciation of poetry?

    A. Reading poems, clapping out the rhyme in familiar rhymes, and recording a "top ten" set of poems for use in a listening center.
    B. Making personal collections of students' favorite poems, requiring memorization of poems, and dramatizing narrative poems.
    C. Illustrating Native American poetry, analyzing sections of poems, and sharing haiku with poetry pals in another classroom.
    D. Choral reading and peer editing.

First, consider which activity would lead to an *enjoyment* and *appreciation* of poetry. Since each item contains more than one activity, you must decide if *each* of those activities leads to true appreciation and enjoyment. Let us use the strategy of elimination on this item, so that if one choice does not promote enjoyment or appreciation, mark the entire item incorrect. For each suggested answer, underline or check those activities that would promote enjoyment and appreciation in poetry. In items *B, C,* and *D,* would *all* activities listed in each choice promote enjoyment? The activities in *A* would promote appreciation of poetry for younger children; therefore, Choice *A* is correct.

This standard emphasizes instruction related to literacy development skills, or emergent literacy, and the use of a variety of text structures such as children's literature and expository text in instructional settings. Teachers should understand the developmental steps that children encounter in learning to become proficient readers in order to identify, diagnose, and prepare for effective instruction. **Emergent literacy** refers to reading and writing experiences that a child encounters before formal literacy instruction begins. These experiences occur in the home, social environments, and preschool settings. During the development of *print association,* children become aware of different types of print found in their environment. They begin to recognize that print is meaningful, develop the ability to rhyme, engage in reading environmental print (for example, reading McDonald's or other favorite places when passing these locations in a car), and engage in story discussion during the reading of a favorite book. Children engaging in emergent literacy activities should receive meaningful direct guidance from an adult figure. Children should be allowed to develop language skills naturally; however, an adult can provide scaffolding to assist in gaining higher levels of understanding. **Scaffolding** refers to support for a learner as he or she enters a phase of readiness for a new skill. This is especially important the moment a child is ready to read. Educators believe that emergent literacy activities include pre-reading and prewriting activities that develop in a meaningful way. As an example, a young child may imitate an adult by "writing" a letter to an aunt or grandparent, even though that letter may contain scribbles that are only meaningful to the child. Also, the young child may learn to memorize a favorite book because a parent or teacher has read the same book to the child many times. As a reminder, *oral* language develops in the young child from the early developmental stages of babbling to developmental and mature speech so even Pre-K children will come to a teacher with a variety of experiences with language.

Teachers use a variety of strategies for building initial literacy skills. These include the use of children's text, using a pointer to demonstrate the left-to-right sequence for reading and showing the parts of a book. Teachers can demonstrate these concepts by using "big books" and other types of narrative reading sources in children's literature. As teachers assist children in developing literacy skills, it is important to realize that children are learning the alphabet in nonsequential order, acquiring phonemic awareness skills, developing a sight vocabulary, and learning to decode words that are encountered in isolated lists and in contextual settings. As elementary students develop into more proficient readers, they use a variety of decoding skills (e.g., phonics, context clues, and structural analysis), read with varied pitch and intonation, read with increased fluency and rate, develop *orthographic awareness* (correct spelling), recognize a greater number of sight words in both isolated lists and contextual text, and show an interest in a variety of text types. It is important to understand the stages that students experience in trying to become capable of reading various text types. Table 2.3 highlights literacy developmental stages in children from Pre-K to grade four.

Table 2.3   Literacy Developmental Stages

Pre-K children begin to do the following:

- Become aware of environmental print
- Recognize signs (as an example, a STOP sign) seen frequently
- Recognize a limited number of letters and numbers
- Interpret forms of their writing that represent their written messages
  (a child could interpret a series of lines he or she made to mean "I have a new bike.")
- Actively participate in reading and writing activities
- Orally make rhyming word patterns
- Listen to short stories and retell their favorite parts
- Recognize the orientation of print (left-to-right, top-to-bottom, and print usage)

Kindergarten children begin to do the following:

- Retell information from narrative and expository text sources
- Write letters of the alphabet (in uppercase form) and numbers
- Recognize the sound that letters make in the initial position
- Make an association with onsets and rimes in one-syllable words
- Write a limited number of sight words
- Engage in invented spelling to communicate in printed form
- Use more descriptive words in oral expression

(continued)

Table 2.3 Continued

First-grade children begin to do the following:

- Read stories and discuss stories
- Write stories
- Develop comprehension strategies for getting the main idea, predicting outcomes, understanding sequence, using contextual clues, etc.
- Develop reading fluency
- Use word identification strategies to determine an unknown word
- Use limited punctuation marks
- Use appropriate capitalization in words such as their first names and the first word in a sentence
- Develop spelling techniques for writing words
- Develop sight words

Second-grade children begin to do the following:

- Increase sight word recognition
- Read a variety of text sources such as expository, poems, notes from peers, invitations, etc.
- Read for different purposes such as for information, fun, etc.
- Read with fluency
- Use effective comprehension strategies
- Use word identification strategies to determine the pronunciation of an unknown word
- Use an increasing number of punctuation marks in written products
- Use the elements of the writing process
- Make the transition from invented spelling to correct spelling
- Use capitalization more extensively
- Engage in self-selected independent reading

Third-grade children begin to do the following:

- Increase sight word recognition
- Read with increased fluency, rate, and expression
- Use word identification strategies to determine the pronunciation and meaning of unknown words
- Use comprehension strategies to gain understanding of text sources
- Use reference sources to gain information
- Recognize the difference between narrative and expository text forms
- Write descriptively in different text forms such as expository paragraphs, stories, research reports, poems, letters, etc.
- Use effectively the elements of the writing process
- Proofread written products
- Develop and use an increased vocabulary
- Increase their ability to use correct spelling

Fourth-grade children begin to do the following:

- Increase sight word recognition that includes content area subjects
- Read a variety of text sources with increased understanding, fluency, rate, and expression
- Spell correctly in a variety of written forms such as paragraphs, poems, etc.
- Read longer text sources such as informational articles and trade books
- Produce effective written summaries
- Expand vocabulary usage
- Continue to use reference sources
- Use effective comprehension strategies to understand a variety of text sources
- Increase usage of punctuation

As you study Table 2.3, remember that the teacher should engage children in oral and written discussions of books, reread favorite stories to children, provide books on tape, provide games and activities that promote language development, model and instruct on strategies for determining the pronunciation of an unknown word, model comprehension strategies, provide opportunities for students to engage in higher-level thinking activities, teach and model the writing process, and produce other effective ways to promote classroom literacy.

Teachers should use many different types of children's literature. **Genres** (types) of children's literature include picture books, folk literature, realistic fiction, historical fiction, fantasy, science fiction, informational books, poetry, mysteries, and biographies. *Picture books* are those books in which the text and illustrations combine to form a meaningful whole. A special type of picture book is the *textless,* or *wordless,* picture book that relies solely on the illustrations to tell the story. Also included in the genre are alphabet books, counting books, picture books, and *concept books* (those that teach children about concepts or ideas, such as shapes, colors, and feelings). Although we often consider picture books appropriate only for our youngest readers, there are many quality picture books that can be successfully used with upper elementary students. *Folk literature* (folklore) encompasses those tales that were originally told orally. Such styles as fairy tales, tall tales, fables, myths, legends, epics, ballads, and folk songs all are part of folk literature and often engage students in moral lessons about human nature. *Realistic fiction* stories are those that occur in contemporary times and are quite popular with children because they present characters and situations with which they can identify. *Historical fiction* presents stories about characters and events of the past and can afford an effective way to introduce children to important periods in Texas, U.S., and world history. *Fantasy* and *science fiction,* stories in which anything can happen, can develop children's imagination as well as their creativity and sense of humor. *Expository texts* (informational books), or nonfiction literature, can pique children's interest about specific topics and help answer many of their questions. *Biographies,* books about real people both past and present, introduce children to persons with interesting and often inspiring life stories.

Poetry is another major genre, or type, of children's literature. Teachers often do not include poetry in classroom instruction, either because they have negative poetry memories from their own school days or because they lack knowledge on how to select poetry for their children. Those memories might include being required to memorize poems and then listen to each classmate recite the same selection in front of the class. This reduces the enjoyment of poetry for many young readers, as does having to overanalyze and determine the "real" meaning of poems in the upper elementary grades.

Poetry preference studies done over the past fifty years, in particular by Terry (1974) and Kutiper (1985), show that children have certain likes and dislikes regarding poetry. Children like poems to which they can relate—in other words, poems that deal with familiar experiences. They also like narrative poems, limericks, poems about animals, and poems with lots of sounds in them. When given the choice, children overwhelmingly prefer poems by contemporary writers to those by traditional writers. Sometimes young children do not like to read or hear haiku, though by fourth grade many begin to write, understand, and enjoy age-appropriate haiku.

Poetry is a genre that is meant to be heard. Children benefit from activities that promote listening to poetry or orally expressing poetry. Enjoyment comes from hearing favorite poems read or sung and by sharing them with others. This pleasure can then foster students' desire to create their own poems. Poem patterns such as couplets, triplets, biopoems, cinquains, and diamantes are both simple and fun for students to write. They can also feel a great sense of accomplishment when their poems are "published" or shared with others.

Teachers may use many of the genres discussed above to explore *seven literary elements*. These elements include: (1) setting, (2) character, (3) plot, (4) style, (5) point of view, (6) mood or emotional tone, and (7) theme, or the "abstract statement about life or humanity reflected in a story or poem" (McGee & Richgels, 2000, p. 116). Older elementary children should be encouraged to include these elements in their writing.

The **basal reader** is another text source used to develop children's literacy skills. Basal readers are designed to provide a sequence of skills that are introduced, practiced, and applied by having students read narrative and expository text sources. After reading basal reader stories, teachers often have children use corresponding workbooks, skills sheets, and other types of supplementary instructional materials to reinforce skills introduced in each lesson. Most often basal readers and their accompanying materials, including a teacher's edition, are those "reading books" provided by schools.

Try this practice question:

Mr. Chaparral is about to introduce a unit on the westward movement to his fourth-grade students. Which of the following strategies would be most effective in immersing his students in this subject?

A. Have students read the related chapter in their social studies textbook and answer the questions at the end of the chapter.
B. Organize the class into groups and let each group choose a novel on the topic.
C. Have students read diaries, biographies, and nonfiction books about the westward movement and collaboratively create an illustrated timeline for the bulletin board.
D. Assign everyone to read, with the teacher's assistance, Laura Ingalls Wilder's *Little House on the Prairie.* Then have students write a response to the story.

Consider which of the suggested activities would give students the most understanding of the westward movement. Choice A, reading the chapter in the textbook, gives the students only one perspective on this historical period (the textbook author's perspective), and answering the questions at the end of the chapter is tedious, boring, and solitary. Choice B, allowing groups of students to select a novel, does not provide a focus for a broader view of this lesson. Choice D, assigning everyone to read the same book, does not take into consideration that fourth-grade boys and girls prefer to read about characters that are the same gender they are. Boys would probably prefer to read a book in which there was a male character. Choice C, having students get into groups and choose their own book for reading and discussion, gives students responsibility by allowing them to schedule their reading, conduct their discussion, and plan their final presentations to the class. Reading diaries, biographies, and other nonfiction literature pertaining to the historical period gives students a truer perspective of what life was like then. Allowing them to collaborate on a timeline lets children take responsibility for organizing and executing their work. Since this response involves a broad range of related literature, collaborative learning, and student decision making, the correct answer is C. The teacher must remember that books should be at the appropriate reading level for elementary children.

Standard V Word Analysis and Decoding

Competency 005: Teachers understand the importance of word analysis and decoding to reading and provide many opportunities for children to improve their word analysis and decoding abilities.

The teacher knows that children develop word analysis and decoding skills in a predictable sequence, provides various instructional practices that allow children to develop skill in using word analysis and decoding strategies, uses a variety of assessment practices to determine children's word analysis and decoding development, exposes children to high-frequency sight words, and provides instruction in the relationship of word analysis to comprehension. Remember that the TEKS promotes instruction that emphasizes the introduction and independent usage of word analysis skills.

Try this practice question:

Mitch, a second grader, reads a word incorrectly in a sentence as he is reading orally to his teacher. After reading two more sentences, he goes back and corrects the error. What strategy did Mitch's teacher observe him using in determining his error?

- **A.** Application of onsets and rimes
- **B.** Context clues
- **C.** Structural analysis
- **D.** Sight words

Consider the approach Mitch used in determining the need to go back and reread the sentence. What clued him to the need to go back? Because Mitch is a second grader, he should have the ability to apply onsets (identification of the consonant at the beginning of a word) and rimes (identification of the consonants and vowels at the end of a syllable). However, it cannot be determined if he used this strategy because his self-correction was delayed until after reading two additional sentences. Therefore, Choice *A* is not correct. We know that he made a miscue in reading, and we know that his teacher did not stop his reading. He pronounced a word incorrectly but continued to read two more sentences. It appears that the *contextual setting* gave him a clue that assisted in determining that a word had been pronounced incorrectly in a previous sentence. Therefore, it is seeen that Mitch used *context clues* in determining the need to go back to reread the sentence that contained the error rather than structural analysis and sight words. Therefore, Choice *B* would be correct.

Teachers and administrative educators frequently discuss the sequence in which word analysis and decoding skills should be introduced to the reader. According to Blevins (1998), the following sequence should be considered when teaching young children to read using **word analysis skills.**

1. Teachers should introduce consonants and short vowels in combination. The purpose of this combination is to develop decodable words that children will encounter in print and can transfer to spelling words (examples: *bat, pet, sip, hot,* and *cup*).
2. Teachers should introduce single consonants before introducing consonant blends or clusters.

3. Teachers should introduce consonants that have high utility. As an example, the letter t has a higher utility—that is, it is found in more words than the letter z.

4. Teachers should begin to introduce more complex letter combinations, such as consonant blends (example: *fl* in the word *flag*) and diagraphs (example: *oa* in the word *float*).

Teachers should know the definition of **word recognition skills** and how to apply these skills in instructional situations. The following list provides significant terms, definitions, and some examples.

1. **Affix.** A structural element added to the beginning or ending of a root or base word in order to alter the meaning, pronunciation, or function. Example: prefixes and suffixes such as *un-* (uncontrollable) or *-ness* (happiness).

2. **Alphabetic principle.** The idea that individual letters represent individual speech sounds; therefore, words may be read by saying the sounds represented by the letters, and words may be spelled by writing the letters that represent the sounds.

3. **Consonant blend or cluster.** Two or three letters in the same syllable that are blended or heard when pronounced. Example: *tr* in *tree.*

4. **Consonant digraph.** A combination of two or more letters that represent a sound that is different from the speech sound that the letters represent individually. Examples: *ch* in *chop, sh* in *shop, th* in *thank, wh* in *whether,* and *ph* in *phone.*

5. **Decode.** Associating printed letters with the speech sounds the letters make to comprehend a word.

6. **Diphthong.** Two adjacent vowels in which each vowel is heard in the pronunciation. Examples: *ou* in *house, oi* in *oil, oy* in *boy,* and *ow* in *brown.*

7. **Explicit phonics instruction.** Providing children with direct phonics instruction that allows them to use decodable text sources that are made up of words and sounds that have been previously taught.

8. **Grapheme.** A written or printed letter symbol used to represent a speech sound (phoneme).

9. **Grapheme–phoneme relationship.** The relationship between printed letters and the sounds they represent.

10. **Logographic awareness.** The first stage children experience when learning about words. Words are learned as whole units that are sometimes embedded in a logo such as a stop sign or the arches in the McDonald's sign.

11. **Morpheme.** The smallest meaningful unit of language. Example: *cat* is a morpheme whose pronunciation consists of three phonemes (c/a/t).

12. **Onsets and rimes.** *Onsets* are the consonants that come at the beginning of syllables in words. Example: the *bl* in the word *blend* is an onset. *Rimes* are vowels and consonants at the end of a syllable. Example: *end* in the word *blend* is a rime.

13. **Orthography.** Correct spelling.

14. **Phoneme.** The smallest unit of sound in a language that distinguishes one word from another word. Example: *cat* and *hat* are distinguished as sounding different by considering their beginning consonant phonemes /c/ and /h/.

15. **Phonemic awareness.** The knowledge or understanding that speech consists of a series of sounds and that individual words can be divided into phonemes.

16. **Phonic analysis.** The process of applying knowledge of letter-sound relationships to words. Teachers ask for this when they instruct children to "sound out" a word.

17. **Schwa sound.** In many words that are multisyllabic, one of the syllables receives less or diminished stress. The sound of the vowel in the syllable that receives the diminished stress has a softening of the vowel sound that is identified as a *schwa* sound and often pronounced as the "uh" sound. The word *about* contains the schwa sound.

18. **Sight vocabulary.** Any words a reader can instantly recognize without having to use any type of word recognition strategy. When a word cannot be taught with any other word recognition strategies, such as onsets and rimes, it is usually taught as a sight word.

19. **Syllable.** Divisions of speech sounds within words. Each **syllable** has one vowel sound. An open syllable ends in a vowel, and a closed syllable ends in a consonant. Teachers should teach the following rules:

    a. When there are two consonants between two vowels, teach students that the syllable is divided between the two consonants, unless the two consonants are a blend or a digraph. Example: *traf/fic* represents the V-C-C-V pattern where both consonants are the same and *pen/cil* represents the V- C-C-V pattern where the consonants are different.

    b. When vowel digraphs or diphthongs appear in a word, teach students not to divide between these vowel combinations. Example: *ea/ger* (*ea* represents a digraph) and *pow/der* (*ow* represents a diphthong).

    c. When there is a vowel-consonant-vowel pattern noticed in the middle of a word, divide either before the consonant or after the consonant. If teachers instruct students to divide the word into a syllable before the consonant, students should notice that the first vowel sound is long. Example: *mo/ment* represents the V-C-V pattern that shows a long sound pronunciation of the vowel. If teachers instruct students to divide the word into a syllable after the consonant, students should notice that the first vowel sound is short. Example: *sev/en* represents the V-C-V pattern that shows a short sound pronunciation of the vowel.

    d. When there is a compound word, teach students to divide into syllables between the two words. Example: *seahorse* should be divided as *sea/horse*.

    e. When a word has an affix (prefix or suffix), teach students to divide into syllables between the base word and the affix. Example: *remove* should be divided as *re/move*.

20. **Vowel digraph.** Two adjacent vowels that represent one speech sound. Examples: *ee* in *feet, oo* in *foot, ea* in *meat,* and *ai* in *sail*.

21. **Word analysis.** An inclusive term that refers to *all methods* of word recognition. Phonics is one such method. Other methods include *picture clues* (using pictures and graphic aids to assist in word pronunciation and meaning), *context clues* (using surrounding text to aid in word pronunciation and meaning), *sight words,* and *structural analysis* (which focuses on root words, base words, affixes, compound words, syllable division, and contractions).

In addition to becoming acquainted with these terms, beginning teachers should teach these skills directly and assist students in applying word recognition skills in a variety of literacy settings. For example, as students read various selections of print orally, they will frequently encounter words that they mispronounce in context. Encouraging students to reread the section of print where the mistake (or **miscue**) occurred will often produce the correct pronunciation (by using **context clues** that connect the word to background). As students advance, they should be able to use individual fix-up strategies to help with their comprehension. Although teachers should provide students with a wide variety of print sources, they should remember to suggest books that can be read independently and have words that are consistently pronounceable in approximately 95 percent of the text. Putting students in a position where they obtain overall success with a bit of a challenge is optimal (according to motivational theory). Always remember to apply the concept of the **zone of proximal development** in reading, which means discovering the place where children can be successful with some assistance from an adult or a capable peer. Teachers should allow time for students to discuss the main ideas presented by the author, other concepts, and the students' own purposes for reading. To further enhance fluency, teachers should encourage students to reread favorite sections of print. Word recognition skills are important; however, teachers should provide significant exposure to new words so that these words will become automatically pronounced as sight words.

Now, consider the worksheet in Figure 2.1 to answer the following question:

Considering Maria's written responses on this worksheet, what assessment would be incorrect on the part of the teacher about her reading achievement?

A. She can read words that contain consonant blends.
B. She can read words that contain vowel digraphs.
C. She can use structural analysis skills.
D. She can understand the use of metaphor.

As you think about the correct answer, you should consider that one function of this standard is to provide information connecting the reader, the text, and the context. So, does Maria seem to do this? Yes, because she basically answers the questions correctly. Nicole could have extended her response to Question 4 by indicating that she quickly began to feel happy because she thought of a way to come back to the amusement park; however, not including this extension does not make her response incorrect because the text states that Maria felt sad. The correct response is *D* because the story contains no figurative language (like metaphors) and because she reads several words that contain the following decoding elements:

Consonant blends or clusters: *spend, blop, stuffed, train, bring, plays*
Vowel digraphs: *train, feels, leave*
Structural analysis: example of a word from the story: compound word, *doorbell*

You should notice that Maria reads other words that are examples of several of the decoding terms included in the list of terms defined under this standard. The answer is *D.*

Standard VI Reading Fluency

Competency 006: Teachers understand the importance of fluency to reading comprehension and provide many opportunities for children to improve their reading fluency.

The teacher understands the relationship of reading fluency to comprehension, provides instructional practices that develop reading fluency, assesses reading fluency, and realizes that fluency involves rate, accuracy, and intonation. Remember that the TEKS promotes the usage of instructional strategies that enhance reading fluency.

Read the worksheet below and answer the four questions. (A third-grade student completed this worksheet.)

Name: ___*Maria Jones*___   Date: ___*April 5, 200?*___

Read the following passage and answer the questions.

Nicole is in a hurry this morning because Whitney's mother is picking her up at 10:00. The girls are going to the amusement park to spend the day. Since Nicole just moved to Simons two weeks ago, she has not been to this park. She hears the doorbell, runs to open the door, and sees Whitney. "Are you ready?" Whitney asks. "I am," replies Nicole.

　　As Nicole enters the amusement park, she sees people who look as excited as she feels. She rides on the Big Blop, plays toss the ring and wins a stuffed rabbit, eats a hot dog, rides on the Turning Train, and goes to a puppet show. She tells Whitney's mother that this is the most fun she has had since coming to the new town. Whitney's mom tells the girls that it is time to go to the car for the ride home. As they leave the park, Nicole is sad because she is not ready to leave. Then she thinks, "My mom can bring us the next time."

1. Describe the way Nicole feels when she woke up. Why did she feel this way?

    Happy. She is going to the park.

2. How long has Nicole lived in her new town?

    Two weeks.

3. List the things the girls do at the amusement park.

    rides, plays toss the ring, eats seesashow

4. How does Nicole probably feel as she leaves the amusement park?

    she is sad.

FIGURE 2.1

Try this practice question:

Ms. Routt, a first-grade teacher, has noticed that two students have limited knowledge and use of sight words. Which activity would *not* provide further word recognition development?

A. Provide students with a variety of books at their independent reading levels.
B. Ask the students to select something different rather than to reread their favorite part of a book.
C. Allow the students to look at the print as the teacher reads the book.
D. Have the students read along taped versions of the books.

Each choice but one actually promotes literacy development. These children have had limited knowledge and use of sight words that could promote reading fluency. Therefore, they need to see and use print in a variety of ways and use stories of various types and in many different ways. This can be accomplished if Ms. Routt allows the children to actually see words in print and hear words that make up stories. Therefore, choice *B* correctly answers this question because the children are asked *not* to reread their favorite part of a book but to select something different. Rereading a motivating selection is an excellent way for students to gain word recognition. Additionally, big books, large print, colorful illustrations, and adequate spacing would be features that the teacher could use to assist the students in acquiring literacy development. The correct answer is *B.*

Reading fluency relates to a student's being able to: (1) orally read a text source by using accuracy in pronouncing words, (2) comprehend effectively because attention is given to textual meaning, (3) provide expression that includes attention to punctuation, and (4) read with a rate that is appropriate for the purpose identified for reading the text source. Table 2.4 provides an explanation of reading fluency components.

Children often experience reading difficulties that affect fluency as it relates to comprehension. A list of the *most common reading difficulties* that influence reading fluency and instructional practices that address these difficulties follows.

1. *Word-by-word reading* is described as a student's pausing after each word in printed text. This type of reading is often caused by limited sight word knowledge and overdependence on the usage of phonics. As remediation practices, the teacher could:
   a. assign reading materials at a lower level.
   b. use familiar reading materials that contain known sight words.
   c. have children dictate language experience stories that could be read aloud (review Standard I—LEA).

Table 2.4   The Components of Reading Fluency

Read orally a text source by using accuracy in pronouncing words.

The student can recognize most of the words in the text with automatic and immediate recognition. Students may read text sources at the independent level, which means that approximately 95 percent to 100 percent of the words are recognized and pronounced correctly. However, many students need opportunities to engage in repeated readings of the same text sources before they reach this level of automatic and immediate word recognition.

Comprehend effectively because attention is given to textual meaning and not just to word identification.

The student can comprehend text if he or she does not need to spend a significant amount of time decoding words. The frequent pausing to figure out a word alters the flow of reading, thus causing comprehension to receive less attention on the part of the reader. Basically, fluency (continuous flow of word recognition) results in comprehension. *It is important to note that some students engage in effective word naming without effectively comprehending the text source.* Teachers should remember to evaluate comprehension by asking questions/statements at various levels, to allow students to retell sections of print, and to use other strategies as well.

Provide expression that includes attention to punctuation.

The student reads with attention to phrasing, appropriate breathing, voice intonation, tone, and attention to all punctuation marks. *Prosody* is the term frequently used to identify these reading considerations (Dowhower, 1991). Think about how you would expect a student to read this sentence: *I have a new puppy!*

Read with a rate that is appropriate for the purpose identified for reading the text source.

   d. have children read along with taped text sources until fluency is reached.
   e. provide opportunities for children to read at their independent level daily.
   f. suggest reading materials for parents to have in the home that will allow children to practice using sight words and new exposure words.

2. *Insufficient knowledge of word recognition skills* refers to limited use of sight word knowledge, context clues, structural analysis, and other skills used to help in pronouncing an unknown word. As remediation practices, the teacher could:

   a. have children use sight words in isolation, phrases, and complete sentences.
   b. have children read a variety of print sources at the students' independent reading levels.
   c. have charts in the classroom that include onsets and rimes that appear in words that could be used in sentences (a word wall could be used).
   d. have available for children common affixes and words that contain the affixes written in complete sentences (a word wall could be used).
   e. have children continue to read text involving an unknown word. Have children consider the word's onset and the print following the unknown word.

3. *Ineffective comprehension* by a student is recognized when he or she is not able to tell about what has been read or is not able to respond to statements and questions posed about text that has been read. As remediation practices, the teacher could:

   a. develop questions and statements that encourage responses at different levels (recall, comprehension, etc.).
   b. encourage note taking and active listening.
   c. enhance word recognition knowledge.
   d. assign reading at appropriate levels.
   e. develop visual aids, such as pictures or felt-board figures, to show the sequence of a story that children are reading.
   f. explain the use of signal words and phrases (such as *first, also, on the other hand, in contrast, in comparison, next, then,* and *finally.*)
   g. demonstrate the steps of the Question-Answer Relationships strategy (QARs) that are outlined in the discussion of Standard VII.

Many schools promote reading fluency in programs such as DEAR (Drop Everything and Read) or SSR (Sustained Silent Reading). Programs such as these often ask everyone in the school (including the teacher-as-a-model) to select something from a large variety of reading material and read silently for a period of time—just for the enjoyment of it. Teachers have a part in guiding children to materials that will be interesting, exciting, and within their abilities.

Consider this practice question:

A second-grade teacher has noticed that Jamie is developing the reading behavior of a word-by-word reader; that is, she reads each word with a pause between it ("The . . . cat . . . ran . . . up . . . the . . . tree!"). Which strategy would be best for the teacher to use with this student?

   A. Providing the student with books of interest.
   B. Asking literal level questions.
   C. Assigning reading material at a lower level of difficulty.
   D. Encouraging the student to read orally in a small group.

Allowing a student to read books based on his or her interest (*A*) is an effective practice; however, these books may not promote fluency in reading orally because the books may not be written at the student's independent level. Asking literal questions (*B*) does allow the teacher to know if the student understands the stated concepts in a story, but this does not promote fluency. Assigning reading material at a lower level of difficulty allows the student to encounter known words. This practice and the practice of allowing the student to reread favorite books at the independent level would promote fluency. Encouraging students to read orally in a small group (*D*) often promotes anxiety. Therefore, Choice *C* is the most effective practice for the teacher to use with Jamie.

Standard VII Reading Comprehension

Competencies 007 and 008: Teachers understand the importance of reading for understanding, know the components of comprehension, and teach young children strategies for improving their comprehension.

The teacher knows the importance of reading for meaning, knows the levels of comprehension, provides effective strategies that enhance comprehension, uses a variety of assessment procedures, and instructs children on appropriate ways to gain information from expository text-sources. Remember that the TEKS promote comprehension developmental instruction that allows children to engage in a variety of strategies. The teacher also understands the importance of research and comprehension skills to children's academic success and provides children with instruction that promotes their acquisition and effective use of these skills in the content areas.

Try this practice question:

Ms. Jones has decided to assign a series of expository paragraphs about "Early Days in San Antonio" to her fourth-grade social studies students to read during class. Which of the following would be *most* effective to use before having the students read this information?

A. Summarize the paragraphs for students.
B. Determine what students already know about the topic.
C. Read a section to students to foster interest.
D. Give students a series of questions to answer as they read.

Actually, each of these activities could be considered appropriate for Ms. Jones to use with her students. However, we are looking for the *most* effective method. It is always an effective practice to determine students' *background knowledge* about a new topic because it would be difficult for students to gain contextual meaning or, in this case, have an adequate background or understanding of this time in Texas history. By determining students' background knowledge, the teacher could then decide the amount of preparation necessary before the students could begin this learning activity. If the teacher determines that the students have either little or no background knowledge, she will realize that they are not yet ready for this activity. Instead, she would need to provide background knowledge so that they would be able to make connections and to comprehend this new information. Therefore, the answer is Choice *B*.

As a discussion of comprehension strategies is presented, it is important to identify and briefly explain literal, inferential, and evaluative comprehension. **Literal comprehension** has readers respond correctly to questions and statements from stated text. A student, for example, could read, "The boy ran home from school." The teacher could ask this student to identify the specific details of where the boy had been and where the boy is going. This type of response does not require the student to incorporate any background experience or to consider thinking beyond the print. Other *literal comprehension* categories that the elementary teacher should implement are: (1) *identification of stated main ideas* in expository text structures (main ideas in narrative text structures are not usually stated directly for readers; instead, a sequential string of details are provided about characters, their problems, their solutions to the problems, and so on, that require the reader to identify a central theme or the general significance of the total narrative selection), (2) *identification of sequence of details,* (3) *identification of comparisons,* and (4) *identification of cause and effect relationships.*

Inferential comprehension has readers use ideas and information that are directly stated in the text along with their intuition, background, and experiences to reach a conclusion or a hypothesis. As students make inferences, the teacher should assist them in examining their schema-based information to identify additional ideas needed to make responses. It should be expected and accepted that, as students make inferences, their responses may differ from other students' responses. Student responses should be accepted as long as they are connected to the literal meaning of the text. One category of inferential comprehension that teachers use in instruction is *predicting outcomes* or *ideas.* Teachers of young children can ask students to "predict what they think a story or textbook chapter is about by looking at pictures or reading the title of the chapter," or, as a story develops, "predict what will happen next."

Evaluative comprehension requires that children compare information and ideas presented in the text with their own experiences, background, and values. These responses, given in their own words, might be about *reality versus fantasy, fact versus opinion,* and the *accuracy of information* that compares various written sources about the same topic. Comprehension can sometimes be a little tricky to teach, but teachers need to implement appropriate procedures for classroom usage that would assist students in effectively using text sources. It is also important for the teacher to develop and monitor comprehension before, during, and after the reading of a text source.

The *Directed Reading-Thinking Activity (DR-TA)* is a technique used to increase understanding of text structures. The DR-TA employs the following steps:

1. Assisting students in acquiring the skills needed during the reading of a text source. The teacher and students *survey* the material and *make predictions* from illustrations and other graphics. The teacher provides instruction by *introducing new technical terms* in isolation and in contextual settings, and the teacher assists students by providing teacher-directed and student-generated *questions* and statements to *provide purposes* for reading the selection.
2. Encouraging students to write *responses* to questions and statements as they read silently. Students should write their responses so that a discussion can be generated in the next step.
3. Continuing to develop comprehension by *discussing, clarifying responses,* and *redefining purposes* as students read orally and discuss sections of text that refer to the identified purpose-setting questions and statements.
4. *Rereading* the sections of the text silently and/or orally for continued instruction related to critical thinking (making inferences, drawing

conclusions, identifying the main idea, making judgments, etc.). The teacher assists students in *applying* the textual information to *real-life situations* and in identifying additional instructional needs noticed during the discussion and reading of the text.

5. *Expanding instruction* to include the use of research skills, technology-based activities, related supplementary recreational reading from trade books and other sources, and group projects to develop additional cross-curricular cognitive ideas. (Stauffer 1969, pp. 14–15).

K-W-L is a strategy often used to promote comprehension and active learning of expository and narrative text sources. This strategy allows students to use their prior knowledge to identify what they already *know*, to initiate curiosity by generating questions to show what they *want to know* about the topic, and to provide responses about what they *learned* after the lesson is concluded. Ogle (1992), the developer of K-W-L, recommends using the following diagram to record information (though there are a number of variations):

K—What I Know	W—What I Want to Know	L—What I Learned

Repeated story reading is a strategy that young children enjoy because they become so familiar with a text source that they can often read (or engage in pretend reading) on their own. Teachers should repeatedly read the story to children, encourage children to repeatedly read it, provide situations for them to discuss it, provide props (costumes, dolls, puppets, sticks on characters, etc.) to retell or dramatize it, and provide opportunities for children to engage in other literacy activities such as drawing and writing about the story.

Story retelling allows children to read or listen to a story that they will then retell. This activity allows children to participate in language development, comprehension skill enhancement, and story structure awareness. Children have an opportunity to use their background and experiences in retelling and explaining the main ideas and supporting details of the story; to practice listening skills (because the teacher should give children purposes to promote active listening); to practice the sequencing of what happened *first, second,* and *last* in the story; and to practice self-expression. Morrow (1989) recommends that when children experience difficulty in retelling a story, the teacher should ask about the story by using prompts such as:

1. What was the story about?
2. Who was the main character?
3. What was the main character's problem?
4. How did the character solve the problem?
5. How did the story end?
6. What was your favorite part?

It is important for teachers to remember that children can do story retellings in written form.

Summarizing is another skill area that needs to be considered as a significant comprehension strategy. In order to assist students in using summarizing effectively, teachers should: (1) demonstrate to students how and why to omit noncontributing information from the text, (2) explain what repeated details are and show why those details could be omitted in summarizing, and (3) continue to assist students in determining the author's main ideas or the overall general significance of a selection that could be used in a written summary. As teachers recognize that children are becoming proficient in developing effective summaries over smaller chunks of materials (paragraphs, subchapters, etc.), they usually begin to expose children to the skill of developing summaries over longer sections of print (summarizing a chapter, story, or novel). This process of combining extended sections to produce connected meanings can enhance understanding of the text.

The beginning teacher recognizes the importance of modeling and emphasizing strategies that are used to assist students in identifying concepts and information that they may and may not understand in their reading, writing, listening, and speaking activities. The teacher also recognizes that the cognitive concept of metacognition (metacognitive awareness, or self-regulation) is related to self-monitoring and provides instruction and activities that allow children to learn to self-monitor. This encourages children to assess their own cognitive growth, to identify inconsistent "missing areas," and to learn to use strategies that work best for themselves. As an example, Jody, a third grader, encounters an unknown geographical area that appears in the chapter of a social studies textbook, Jody realizes that ignoring the fact that she does not know anything about this area would alter her comprehension; therefore, she could decide to seek the pronunciation of the geographic area and to determine the location of this area by looking at a map. The correct pronunciation and an understanding of the area's location provide additional background that can enhance comprehension. Additionally, the teacher frequently self-monitors him- or herself. This means he or she reflects on instructional delivery by asking children specific questions to determine if they are comprehending. This allows the teacher to make adjustments, if needed, by using different words to teach the same concept, substituting words in oral delivery, and making directions clearer. In other words, the teacher is trying to make instruction more effective and meaningful for students (not simply repeating or saying it louder).

In classrooms today, *listening* has become an important part of the daily routine. **Oracy** is the concept that identifies and describes the differences between the skills of listening and speaking from the skills of reading and writing. Oracy should be considered in classrooms in order to assist students in functioning in an active discussion-based environment (Wilkinson, 1974). Active listening is essential in classroom settings because speaking and reading are connected to purposeful listening.

Several factors that influence listening instruction should be considered as students become active listeners in school settings: (1) the student's background as related to his or her experiences and to a cognitive knowledge base; (2) the level of language development; (3) the instructional level of the material being presented; (4) the speed, pitch, and intonation of the person providing the oral delivery of information; (5) the attention span of the listener; and (6) the instructional preparation of the listener, including having been given a purpose for listening, activities to organize the information, and activities that enhance memory for retaining the information that has been presented (Lundsteen, 1979).

This standard considers the use of listening activities as one way of assisting students in monitoring cognitive structures in classroom settings. It should be noted that effective listening needs instructional attention through various types of activities such as note taking, questioning, and listening-think-alouds.

Note Taking

Note taking, as mentioned earlier, is one of the most direct listening skills used in classrooms when seen as a teacher-produced method of delivering information to children in an oral form. Students must listen to succeed in this task. Note taking is also used when children use multiple sources such as encyclopedias, textbooks, interviews, charts, and narratives to collect information and record this information by making lists, answering questions, filling in note taking forms, and so forth. However, note taking is not stressed often enough in classroom situations. Let us examine a procedure that could be used to connect note taking, reading, and listening for elementary children. The teacher could begin the initial stage of note taking by providing a worksheet that outlines important points that will be expanded upon by the teacher later in oral delivery. Let us consider the components of a teacher-delivered talk or mini-lecture in an elementary science class about "How Plants Grow." The teacher has developed a note taking worksheet to be used by children to serve as purpose-setting points for effective listening. The following chart shows this type of example.

Topic: **How Plants Grow**	
Teacher provides questions for students.	*Each student provides answers to questions.*
1. How do plants start to grow?	Student provides a response.
2. What are the parts of a plant?	Student provides a response.
3. What does a plant need to grow?	Student provides a response.
4. Why are plants important to people?	Student provides a response.
Student summarizes information from the answer section.	
Student summary statements are based on information from the student's answers to the questions.	

Note taking allows children to learn how to determine significant details and main ideas from information. This type of filtering of significant information helps children to determine the major points provided by the teacher. Allowing children to use sample notes developed by the teacher, to compare notes taken in class by peers, and to make adjustments to individual notes provides children with a self-evaluation method. This type of self-assessment of the notes can often assist children in becoming more critical listeners (and readers).

Other graphic organizers also help children organize information and read for a purpose. Concept mapping shows a major focus (dogs) in a center circle and "radiates" related information (types, care, etc.) or details in connecting "bubbles." This helps students see main and subsidiary ideas very clearly. Other types of graphic organizers help students more easily comprehend visually areas such as cause-and-effect, storylines, timelines, and so forth.

Questioning

Questioning is one of the most used teaching strategies found in today's classrooms. Research, however, indicates that many teachers ask questions only at the literal or knowledge level. This is *lower-level* thinking, according to

Bloom's taxonomy (lower levels include knowledge, comprehension, and application; higher levels include analysis, synthesis, and evaluation). The first three levels provide basic thinking, but teachers' aims should always be to have children think at higher levels. In language arts, teachers often pose questions and statements as advanced organizers as a way of providing students with purposes for listening to orally delivered information and information found in text sources. These questions and statements should require responses that allow children to identify the main idea of a selection, determine details that discuss the main idea, and identify supporting details that further describe the initial details. The following are specific strategies that can be used by teachers to enhance questions and responses.

QUESTION-ANSWER RELATIONSHIPS (QARs). This is a directed-teaching strategy that develops students' awareness of the process used in answering questions. Steps should include:

1. Identifying *"right there"* questions that are literal and can be answered from information stated in the book and sometimes found in one sentence.
   a. An example question might be: What is Carmen's job?
   b. Answer that is stated in the text source: "Carmen has worked for the last ten years as a bus driver for elementary school students. She lives in Pasadena, but she works nearby in South Houston."
2. Identifying *"think and search"* questions, requiring students to draw a conclusion. They are told that the information needed to determine the answer to the question can be found in the text source, but it will be in more than one sentence. Students are instructed on how to link this information by putting several ideas together to determine a response.
   a. An example question might be: How would you describe Emily?
   b. The answer would come from several sections of text that described Emily. Students would need to put the description together from the entire text source that describes her.
3. Identifying *"author and you"* questions, requiring students to use text details plus their own background knowledge to make an inference. Children are instructed to determine answers by using text information and information they already know from their background; they must relate what they know to what is in their text source. Answers thus become more individualized rather than a single correct answer. As an example, children read a paragraph about "Going to the Zoo" on a very hot summer day. In the story a lady smiles and allows a little boy to go ahead of her on a ride. The children were asked to answer the following question: What type of person is the lady? The reader has to determine that the lady is probably a kind person because of her actions.
4. Identifying *"on your own"* questions connected to evaluative responses, background consideration, and creative thoughts to determine an answer. Children, for example, having read about the life of Abraham Lincoln, could then be asked to identify the characteristics of a leader.

Another way to view questioning is to look at the difference between *convergent questions* and *divergent questions*. **Convergent question** responses allow students to use their text source to answer questions because there is one correct answer to a question. On the other hand, **divergent question** responses would require students to use the text source, their background knowledge, and their understanding of the information in the text to answer a question. In other words, the teacher could expect to hear a variety of individualized answers that are connected to the text sources, all of which are correct.

RECIPROCAL QUESTIONING (REQUEST). Using ReQuest, students learn to pose their own questions and statements about content material being studied. Manzo (1969) recommends the following steps:

1. Teacher and students read the same passage silently.
2. Teacher closes the book and is questioned by students.
3. Roles change and the teacher begins to ask students questions.
4. Teacher assists students in developing logical responses to questions. When the teacher determines that children have an adequate knowledge of question-answer responses, the teacher then allows them to independently read to determine the answers to questions.
5. Teacher conducts a follow-up discussion. (pp. 124–125)

Listening–Thinking Strategy

The purpose of the listening–thinking strategy is to provide a format for teaching students how to develop predictive listening and comprehension. This strategy encourages students to make predictions as the teacher reads the title of a chapter or reads to an exciting point in a story. The teacher continues to read the selection and allows children to change or make new predictions. As the teacher reads to students, he or she uses pitch/intonation variations and storyline discussions to assist students in effectively listening to classroom discussions (Walker, 2000).

Many content areas utilize students' reading and writing skills in acquiring knowledge of concepts. It is important for students to understand that informational textbooks, or *expository texts*, contain such features as a preface, a table of contents, appendices, a glossary, and an index. In addition, each chapter within expository textbooks includes an introduction, headings, subheadings, graphics, purpose-setting questions, and a summary. Most expository texts are organized with the most important ideas stated first, with supporting ideas and descriptive details following in paragraph form. Students who understand this textbook structure can often distinguish the important/significant details from the less important details in reading material (Meyer, 1975). Additionally, authors of textbooks usually provide connective terms (such as *most important, however, because, after,* etc.) to help students connect one idea to another idea as they read information (Halliday & Hasan, 1976). Teaching this can help students locate information more quickly.

Content area teachers should identify specific strategies that can be embedded throughout lessons in social studies, science, health, and so forth. Every teacher is a reading teacher. During prereading activities, the teacher introduces activities that activate a child's schema and establish purposes for reading. As students read silently, teachers provide them with activities that continuously monitor comprehension. After children finish reading, teachers should assist them in determining relevant applications of the new information, in building schema and in extending comprehension skills by rereading portions of the textbook or other sources that supplement the chapter.

SQ3R (Survey, Question, Read, Recite, and Review)

In order to discuss Standard VII, which incorporates the structure of assisting young readers in learning to use expository text structures independently, an overview of *SQ3R* and its cognitive connections to other study strategies is needed. Also, it is necessary to indicate that this strategy is usually most effective with expository (informational-based) text-sources. In *SQ3R, S* means *survey,*

Q means *question,* and *3R* means *read, recite,* and *review.* Let us discuss each separately and make connections with other study strategies such as previewing, note taking, study guides, and test taking.

The *survey* step suggests that the reader with instructional guidance from the teacher: (1) previews the reading selection and notices the title of the chapter and the titles of the subchapter headings; (2) notices new vocabulary; (3) reads the introduction and summary of the entire chapter; (4) reads the first sentence in each paragraph as each subheading is considered and reads both the questions at the end of each subsection and at the end of the chapter; (5) reads sections in bold or other types of selected print; (6) studies graphic and visual information such as maps, illustrations, graphs, etc., and becomes familiar with the purpose of this information; and (7) notices other relevant information. In using this step, readers will notice the structure of a chapter, thus allowing them to determine a framework for reading and comprehending the information. Additionally, Vacca and Vacca (1986) recommend that, as children preview (by examining the introduction, illustrations, new vocabulary terms, subchapters, the summary, etc.), they can often determine the amount of time it will take to complete the task and determine what they already know about the topic.

The *question* step recommends that the teacher aid readers in determining what questions about the reading material can be answered from the text. These questions provide purposes for reading the selection and are designed to assist readers in paying close attention to the information that is being read. Questions can be formulated in several ways; however, the most common way to formulate questions in this step is to change the stated subchapter headings into questions. As an example, a chapter in a third-grade social studies textbook might be titled "Living in China." In this chapter, students could probably expect to find a subchapter heading titled "The People of China" that could be changed by the student into a question that is "Who are the people living in China?" This can result in factual information about China but also in a discussion about the differences among many Asian people (Japanese, Korean, Indian, Thai, etc.). Also, the teacher could prepare a study guide (study guides will be discussed later in this section), or a list of questions and statements that could be given to the students before beginning to read the text source.

The *read* step requires the student to answer the questions, or in some cases, the statements formulated in the question step. Opening the door to engage children in active reading through the use of questions and statements leads to connections of main idea information, details, and descriptive ideas. Imagine being given a reading assignment and being told that a test would follow on the next class day. You and some children already have metacognitive strategies in place that would allow comprehension, but others would get very little from this assignment and would probably not earn a passing grade. One of the reasons that some children might have difficulty passing such a test is that there was not a specific "road map" to follow to determine the understanding of the text material. As teachers, we do not want to always tell students exactly what they should learn as they read, but we do want to scaffold until they have acquired the metacognitive strategies that would allow independence in determining comprehension. For some students, this can be accomplished quickly, but for others it takes time to scaffold them on their way to becoming independent learners.

The *recite* step asks students to make either oral or written responses to the questions formulated in the *question* step. As students respond orally to answer these questions, teachers can additionally request readers to identify locations in the text that were used in making these responses, or children can provide written responses to the questions.

The *review* step allows pupils to evaluate the text information by rereading selected segments of the text so that they can verify their responses given during the recite step. Children can either read out loud or read silently the text sections that verify their answers. Remember, readers have had private time with the text source to answer the questions. After they have had an opportunity to read the text silently, it is instructionally appropriate to allow children to volunteer to read sections of the text orally that provide responses to questions generated in the question step. In reviewing the components' of DR-TA, we can remember that this strategy encourages reading out loud to answer questions and to verify responses to answers. However, in SQ3R oral reading comes *after* students have been given an opportunity to read the text source silently.

As we continue to discuss strategies that respond to this standard, the use of adjunct study materials such as study guides and graphic aids will be discussed in more detail. First, let us see exactly why adjunct study materials are important. According to Vacca and Vacca (1986), adjunct study materials add a way for children to interact and make connections with text material that is unfamiliar or difficult, to analyze and discuss ideas and concepts found in texts, and to scaffold students in comprehending the text being read.

Study guides prepared by the teacher or commercially by the textbook authors benefit students during active silent and oral reading. Study guides usually provide a set of questions or statements for children to use as they study text materials. Although there are several types of study guides, three types will be discussed. The *interlocking study guide* is a type of guide that frames a group of literal questions, a group of interpretive questions, and a group of evaluative questions to be answered by readers. The *noninterlocking guide* arranges questions and statements in a nonordered fashion that does not group questions according to literal, interpretive, and evaluative levels, but intermingles questions between the three levels. As an example, the first question could be an evaluative question, the second question could be literal, the third question could be interpretive, and so forth. The last type of study guide to be discussed is the *Guide-O-Rama*. Teachers using this type of guide determine the purpose for reading the selection needed to answer specific questions. Teachers would not require students to read the sections of text that did not address the purpose for reading. However, the teacher determines and shows, by signaling, what parts of the text need to be used to complete the task. As an example, Mrs. Bell asks her children to read page 127, paragraph 4 to answer a question about a famous woman scientist. This type of signaling is done throughout the chapter to gain specific information that relates to content-specific information.

Yet another study skill that needs discussion is the ability to *locate information*. The elementary teacher should assist students in learning to use an index. To assist children with index usage, the teacher could, for example, design an activity in a fourth-grade social studies class that asks readers to identify headings that contain information about the production of oil. Students identify headings, such as oil, production of oil, types of oil products, procedure used in processing oil, and sources of oil. After the list is formulated, children use the textbook's index to determine if the headings are listed. Note that the skill of alphabetical sequencing is necessary for this activity to be effectively completed. Readers identify page references and use them to actually find the information in the textbook. When the concept of locating information using a book index has been mastered, the teacher should encourage readers to use index entries of other reference sources such as encyclopedias, almanacs, and atlases. Additionally, children should be taught to use the table of contents of text sources to locate library sources and to use computer technology to locate various types of information. Older elementary students can be taught to bookmark information and the rudimentary concepts of copyrighting and plagarism with technology.

Interpreting graphic information is important in increasing comprehension, but children may need special instruction in this area. Readers encounter maps, cartoons, charts, and other types of diagrams in textbooks. Usually there is text association that connects the graphics to the text, but children often do not include graphics in reading of the text information. A map of the "Regions of Texas," for example, might be included in a fourth-grade social studies book and, to encourage children to interpret the information, the teacher could ask them to do the following on their own maps:

1. Outline the regions of Texas with yellow.
2. Color the water areas blue.
3. Trace the mountain range areas in brown.

This teacher-generated activity promotes graphic interpretation that allows students to make cognitive connections with print.

It is also important for the elementary teacher to include test-taking strategies for elementary students. Teachers want to encourage readers to become effective test takers by encouraging them to consider doing the following:

1. Scan the entire test before answering test items to determine the test format, the type of test questions, and the number of points for each item to determine the approximate amount of time to spend on most test items.
2. Answer the questions that you know first.
3. Look for giveaway answers on objective tests and words that indicate extremes in the answer (*best, least, none, never, always*, etc.).
4. Make an outline, list, or graphic organizer to begin answering essay-type questions. Students should be encouraged to identify and answer each part of an essay question.

Additionally, Carmen and Adams (1972) designed *SCORER* as a test-taking strategy. SCORER stands for and recommends the following: *S* stands for *schedule* and recommends that the test taker learns to predetermine the time they believe they will need to complete a test efficiently; *C* stands for *clue* and recommends that the test taker identify words that could assist in answering the question; *O* stands for *omit* and recommends that the test taker omit the hardest questions first and return to these difficult questions after known ones are answered; *R* stands for *read* and recommends that the test taker read each question carefully to determine if each part is fully understood (if taking an informal teacher-generated test, the test taker could seek clarification from the teacher); *E* stands for *estimate* and recommends that the test taker determine what should be included in a response (e.g., if taking an essay test, the test taker could make an outline of the information needed to complete the response); and *R* stands for *review* and recommends that the test taker read over the test before finally submitting it to the teacher. This strategy allows the teacher to expect a degree of responsibility from students during test-taking situations. One instructional part of teaching in Texas involves preparing children for the TAKS test. Even if you do not teach at a TAKS grade level, you still have the responsibility of assisting teachers who do teach at TAKS grade levels by preparing children with test-taking skills. This is a serious undertaking in Texas because of the amount of recognition and funding attached to test scores.

Consider the following practice questions that are related to comprehension:

Mr. Guntur, a third-grade teacher, reads a page of print from the science textbook to his students. Which of the following activities would be *most* effective in helping students gain the information?

- **A.** Have students take notes or fill in a graphic organizer.
- **B.** Give students a set of questions to consider.
- **C.** Have students determine the main idea.
- **D.** Give students study guide questions for homework.

The part that states "Mr. Guntur reads," cues us to consider that this should relate to listening skills. We can then decide which activity promotes active listening. Having children take notes or fill in a graphic organizer as they listen to Mr. Guntur read (Choice *A*) involves effective listening. Giving a set of questions to consider (*B*) is a good practice if questions are provided before reading or during reading. Giving students a study guide for homework (*D*) is also an effective practice, as is determining the main idea (*C*), but they are not *most* effective for *active* listening. Therefore, Choice *A* is the *best* answer because it recommends that the children take notes or fill in a graphic organizer as they listen to their teacher read a page of print. Remember one test-taking strategy that is effective on the TExES is to watch for cue words such as *most*, as in this question.

Mrs. Jones's students have completed reading paragraphs on the "Battle of the Alamo." Now she wants to help her children extend their understanding of this topic. Which of the following would be the *most* effective practice that she could use?

- **A.** Have students reread the paragraphs for determining a different purpose.
- **B.** Have students read information from different sources such as trade books, computer-generated information, and magazines.
- **C.** Have students develop a dramatic play that identifies fictional and/or nonfictional characters who lived during the "Battle of the Alamo."
- **D.** Have students write a paragraph that identifies the major events of the "Battle of the Alamo."

Mrs. Jones has effective instructional choices, but which choice would promote an understanding of the topic that would allow children to read, develop purposes, and analyze the information? Each choice has fragments of knowledge extension; however, Choice *C* promotes inferential comprehension. Having children develop a play would allow them to create characters based on their factual knowledge, and this activity would also promote an integrated usage of the levels of comprehension. The answer is *C.*

Miquel is a good reader who enjoys books on many topics. His teacher, Mrs. Canteo, knows that he demonstates self-monitoring skills in his social studies class books in order to learn a concept. Which of the following statements does *not* demonstrate self-monitoring?

- **A.** Asks himself self-structured questions as he reads text silently.
- **B.** Slows down his reading rate.
- **C.** Asks his teacher a question.
- **D.** Does not reread a difficult sentence.

Self-monitoring includes any technique that allows the learner to identify ways to completely understand a concept. Choices *A, B,* and *C* could be considered self-monitoring skills because they could be used by the student to determine a way to more effectively learn the concept. The question asks, "What is not . . .?" Therefore, *D* is the correct answer.

Tran, a third-grade student, is having difficulty understanding the main idea of sections of a text. Which of the following activities would be *most* appropriate for the teacher to suggest that Tran use to become more effective in determining the main idea?

   A. Show an example of a summarized paragraph.
   B. Have the student paraphrase major facts and ideas after each paragraph in a section.
   C. Teach the student underlining and note-taking strategies.
   D. Provide an outline prepared by the teacher.

The best choice is *B* because the student needs to develop a system for learning to determine the main idea of a selection. Although paraphrasing after each paragraph is time-consuming, this strategy allows the reader to use statements or purpose-setting questions to help determine main idea choices. The answer is *B*.

A first-grade teacher, Mrs. Beck, read a story to her students. Which of the following activities would help the teacher best determine if her students comprehended the story?

   A. Have students tell their favorite part of the story.
   B. Have students write about their favorite character.
   C. Have students illustrate the main parts of the story.
   D. Have students identify the setting of the story.

Consider which activity would give Mrs. Beck the *best* assessment of how well her students comprehended the story. Since each choice contains an activity, you must decide which is *best* for understanding the elements of the *entire* story. In Choice *A*, children are being asked to consider *only* their favorite part of the story. Response *B* asks pupils to write about a part of the story; whereas in *C*, they are required to illustrate the main parts of the story. This illustration would allow the teacher to assess students' understanding of the whole story rather than just one segment of the story. Choice *D*, again, only asks students for one specific element of the story. Therefore, Choice *C* is correct.

What would be a first-grade social studies teacher's most effective practice in getting students prepared to either read a chapter or to listen to the teacher read (with a purpose) a chapter on "Community Helpers in the United States?"

   A. Have students brainstorm and write (or draw) things they know about "Community Helpers in the United States."
   B. Have students define community helpers by using their textbook's picture and word glossary.
   C. Distribute a mapping activity and have students attempt to fill in information about community helpers.
   D. Have students view a film on community helpers.

This teacher is showing evidence that he or she knows ways to incorporate reading skills in other content areas. Decades ago, a social studies teacher probably would have assigned the reading without any initial preparation. However, today teachers use a variety of strategies to enhance decoding and comprehension. Let's look at the choices. Choice *A* is an effective practice because it investigates students' background knowledge and encourages them to write or draw about what they know. Choice *B* is not an effective practice because students have not discussed this topic; therefore, they may not select the best definition for the term as it relates to their social studies textbook. Choice *C* is not effective because students have not yet been given the type of instruction that would prepare them to fill in a mapping activity. Choice *D* *could be* effective, *if* the teacher had given students a purpose for viewing a film or if a film had been used as an extension to the lesson. Therefore, *A* is the most effective practice.

Mrs. Torres has found that her second-grade students experience difficulty comprehending their science textbook. Much of the difficulty appears related to new vocabulary and terminology presented in chapter discussions. Which of the following language arts strategies could she use to increase understanding of concepts presented in the science textbook?

  A. Students chorally read the text aloud and stop on each page to discuss words that they cannot pronounce.
  B. Students, individually or in pairs, are assigned a vocabulary word from the textbook. They are to paraphrase, or write in their own words, a definition of the vocabulary word.
  C. The teacher writes a synopsis, or summary, of each chapter in the textbook at a lower reading level to increase student comprehension of the text material.
  D. All of the above.

Choice *A* does not present a language arts skill that improves *comprehension* and learning of science *concepts;* this only promotes phonics knowledge (and possibly not very effectively). Choice *C* does not teach a language arts skill because students are not involved in lowering the reading level of the text source. Choice *B* empowers students to use their own language to create meaning of new vocabulary terms and concept knowledge in the science content area. *B* is the correct answer.

Mr. Campo, a fourth-grade teacher, has assigned students to read a science chapter for homework. Identify the *most* effective procedure Mr. Campo could recommend that students use to begin the assignment.

  A. Take thirty minutes to read the chapter.
  B. Preview the chapter before beginning to read.
  C. Identify a Web site that might have additional information about the chapter that they could access at home.
  D. Read the introduction to the chapter.

Remember that children are preparing to read the chapter as a homework assignment, and this means that Mr. Campo is recommending startups to assist in independently reading the assigned text. In this case, he would not suggest a time frame for completing the reading assignment (*A*) because students read at different rates. A Web site (*C*) would provide additional background information for the students. However, the Web site would probably be most effective in the *extension section* of the lesson because this question does not indicate that the teacher has established the level of students' background knowledge. Also, remember the possible technology bias from your Pedagogy and Professional Responsibilities TExES; that is, many lower socioeconomic status families may not have easy access to technology at home. An effective practice the teacher could recommend would be for the students to preview the chapter before beginning to read (*B*). The preview would allow students to notice new vocabulary terms, graphic aids, questions, and other features related to the chapter. Choice (*D*) may not be as inclusive. Another consideration would be for Mr. Campo to preview the chapter with children before assigning it as homework. Mr. Campo might find that students need assistance with skills such as the pronunciation of several words encountered during the preview. Therefore, *B* would be the *best* answer.

Mr. Baco, a second-grade teacher, has his students gather information about Native Americans from a social studies textbook, a trade book, a Web site, and field trip to a museum. Mr. Baco assigns students to work in cooperative groups to synthesize information found in each source. What is a purpose of this assignment?

  A. To illustrate how people dressed during this time.
  B. To notice how different sources describe a topic.
  C. To develop a paragraph.
  D. To practice reading from a variety of sources.

Mr. Baco obviously intends for the students to gain insight into the topic by using a variety of sources, and it is important to understand that he wants students to synthesize information found in different sources. Therefore, *B* is the correct response because students can see how different sources discuss and describe Native Americans.

Standard VIII Development of Written Communication

Competency 010: Teachers understand that writing to communicate is a developmental process and provide instruction that helps young children develop competence in written communication.

The teacher understands the emergent and developing stages of literacy that include writing styles, provides instruction that incorporates the elements of the writing process, uses instructional practices that provide opportunities for children to write in a variety of forms, and monitors children's writing development. Remember that the TEKS promotes using strategies that emphasize developmental writing and elements of the writing process. Additionally, the TEKS recommends that beginning teachers provide examples of the different types of writing selections.

Answer the practice question that relates to a classroom situation:

Ms. Keith, a fourth-grade social studies teacher, assigned the following task.

You are to interview a relative or friend who has fought in a war. Use the following as discussion areas during your interview: which country started the conflict, location of the war, time of the war, the causes of the conflict, when and where the major battles were located, the results of the peace agreement, and the role that the relative played. Ms. Keith asks the students to bring their notes to class in one week.

Sidney is excited about this assignment, understands the purpose of the assignment, interviews his aunt who served in the Gulf War, and brings his notes to Ms. Keith early. Ms. Keith notices the following about Sidney's notes: The notes are incomplete in content, words are spelled correctly, and punctuation and other mechanics are basically correct.

How can Ms. Keith best assist Sidney in producing notes that are more complete in content?

A. Have Sidney read examples of interview notes from his language arts textbook.
B. Encourage Sidney to prepare a draft of the notes.
C. Have Sidney reread his notes.
D. Have Sidney explain the purpose of the assignment.

Test taker 1 selected Choice *A*, believing that looking at examples from a commercial textbook and allowing Sidney to compare his notes would be adequate. Test taker 2 selected Choice *C* because Sidney seemed to skip the initial phases of the writing process, and test taker 3 selected *D* because the teacher engaged Sidney in an oral activity. To answer this question effectively, however, knowledge of the phases of the writing process would be helpful. However, the logic of the other test takers includes the usage of examples from textbooks and teacher connection with a student's product. But do these ideas address the writing process? The test taker should consider each choice, but the most effective response is *B*.

This standard addresses the developmental process that young children use to learn to communicate in written form. Baghban (1984) suggests that children learn to write in stages that are scaffolded, or supported, by teachers. The **emergent stage**, which usually begins before kindergarten, allows the child to produce print in a variety of forms such as scribbling, drawing, and a combination of letter formations and drawings. Teachers of young children should encourage the practice of these beginning efforts in forming letters, as it strengthens the connections of letter recognition in beginning to read, too. Children in the emergent stage should have a number of activities that help them recognize and form letter shapes. As mentioned earlier, these might include having students touch sandpaper letters, make letters out of clay, draw letters in sand trays or on their desks with shaving cream, as well as more traditional methods. Teachers will know if students are able to distinguish shapes through letter matching activities. Children will "read" their drawings in a story format as if they constructed a written source, often reading from left to right and top to bottom because they have observed adults reading to them. In this stage, the child may write his or her first name and may try to produce other popular words often using **invented spelling** forms (an example of invented spelling would be "*gone*" spelled as "*gon*" because of the way the child perceives how the word sounds). They may also write using the name of the letter to communicate (I LVV U or U C ME). The beginning writing stage, which usually starts in first grade, allows the child to continue to use invented spelling to label pictures and to write sentences and short stories. The teacher will notice that children begin to write sentences that describe personal items, show a developing awareness of correct spelling patterns (word walls are often used to show spelling pattern examples that could be used in both spelling and word pronunciation), and use a story form that shows a description of a beginning and an ending of a story. The **developing writing stage** begins to show a process for writing that is explained in the following section. Teachers need to assess students' writing by using writing products to look for development in **mechanics** (correct formation and use of lower- and uppercase letters, directionality from left to right, use of punctuation, etc.) and for development in spelling (review Standard IX for information about spelling development). It is useful to remember that children's fine motor skills may not match their knowledge. Teachers who provide a number of materials with which to write (crayons, markers, chalk, dry-erase boards, paints, etc.) may be able to help children much better. Children who feel frustrated with a traditional pencil and paper may be much more comfortable and skillful with other writing instruments.

This standard addresses the writing process that is used in the integrated language arts classroom. It should be noted that more than ten years ago teachers approached the process of writing in a much different way. At that time, teachers basically focused on having students produce papers that contained no spelling or grammar errors and that could easily be assigned a letter grade. Currently, teachers are focusing on the components of the writing process by using models that scaffold and encourage students to use different genres, such as creative stories, poetry, content-specific expository products, and other types of narrative products (Ziegler, 1981). They basically want children to enjoy producing ideas on paper first without being punished for mechanics. (As an aside, in management, teachers should avoid associating writing with punishment in assigning the writing of "lines" when children misbehave. We want children to enjoy writing rather than link it to negativity.) Teachers understand that students basically follow a process that is sequential. Most teachers assist children in understanding the phases of the writing process. Therefore, it is important to identify and discuss the following phases of the writing process.

Phase 1: Prewriting

This phase allows students to explore topics for consideration, identify ways to gather information about the topic, determine (with their teacher's help) the purpose for the writing assignment, determine the intended audience, and select the format of the product (that is, if the product will be a poem, a creative story, an expository response, etc.). Many teachers find that this is often the most difficult phase because students often cannot begin to get their ideas into written form.

Phase 2: Drafting

The students have gathered information about the topic. Therefore, during this phase they begin to write about the things they have learned. Students are encouraged to write and not be too concerned about mechanics such as spelling, grammar, and punctuation until revisions are made.

Phase 3: Revising

The teacher encourages children to be concerned with revising the content of their writing assignment but not yet consider correcting mechanics such as spelling and punctuation. Students are encouraged to consider their audience by selecting the most effective wording to convey clear meaning, provide supporting details, and present descriptive meaning. During the revision phase, teachers often encourage children to discuss their products with peers and to conference with the teacher. This exchange with peers and the teacher will often suggest more effective ways for revising their writing. This phase also fosters repeated exchanges because students continue to redevelop their content by considering comments from peers and from the teacher.

Phase 4: Editing

During the editing phase, the teacher encourages students to proofread their content by looking for mechanical errors such as misspelled words and incorrect punctuation. Teachers encourage children to collaborate with their peers for the purpose of assisting in proofreading to identify errors. Additionally, the teacher will often act as a proofreader.

Phase 5: Publishing

As noted in Phase 1, an important consideration for a writer is the audience who will read the content of the product. The writing products can be shared through books, verbal sharing, collections of stories and poems bound by the teacher in book form, reports, or other of types of oral and written forms. Children should also be encouraged to self-assess their progress by looking back at their work over time. This is possible by keeping portfolios.

The previous steps are often part of a **writing workshop** that lasts over several days. The teacher may use a routine format that includes: (1) a mini-lesson on a strategy that supports the writing experience (i.e., sequencing, techniques for getting ideas, etc.) for about 10 minutes; (2) a statement of purpose [for three or four minutes] in which students give their goals for the day; (3) a twenty-to-thirty-minute sustained writing block where the teacher pulls out students for conferences; and (4) a five-to ten-minute sharing time (Duthie, 1996).

Table 2.5   Content for Writing Selections

A summary paragraph should include:

- an accurate restatement, written in your own words, of the main ideas of the text;
- a restatement of supporting details; and
- omission of unimportant details.

A narrative paragraph should include:

- descriptive details to develop the characters, setting, and plot;
- a clear beginning, middle, and ending;
- a logical organization, with clues and transitions, to help the reader understand the order of events (examples of transitions would be *first, but, last, also,* and *next*);
- a consistent tone and point of view;
- language that is appropriate for the audience; and
- an explanation of the importance of the events and ideas.

A compare-and-contrast paragraph should include:

- the subject being compared and contrasted (a Venn diagram is an appropriate graphic aid to use);
- specific and relevant details;
- transitional words and phrases that signal similarities and differences; and
- a conclusion.

A conclusion paragraph should include:

- a summary of the main points;
- a description of personal feelings about the topic;
- a brief restatement of the thesis; and
- a provocative question or call for some type of action.

A cause-and-effect paragraph should include:

- a statement that includes the cause-and-effect relationship being examined;
- a connection between causes and effects; and
- facts, examples, and other details to illustrate each cause and effect.

A problem-solving paragraph should include:

- a concise explanation of the problem and its significance;
- a workable solution and details that explain and support the solution; and
- a conclusion that restates the problem.

As teachers help young children develop writing skills, the teacher should allow children to connect reading and writing (by either narrative or expository selections that students read themselves or that the teacher reads to the children). Teachers can accomplish this skill by asking children to reflect on ideas from various types of texts. As an example, children may be asked "What if" questions to promote children's thinking about text sources. The "What if" responses can be used as a writing activity. Teachers should encourage written text to include words from word walls and from phonemic awareness instruction (review Standards II, III, and IV to connect the usage of word recognition discussions).

Children must have a variety of situations that encourage writing. They should be encouraged to electronically mail (e-mail) pen pals who live in various parts of their state, the United States, and the world. Journal writing provides a way for children to express their literary experiences. They can participate by writing in various types of journals, such as those that center on describing a character from a story and those that have a short "story starter." It is important for the teacher of young children to model effective writing forms by responding to children's writing activities and by assisting them in using the phrases discussed above in the writing process. Many examples of the types of writing selections that students are encouraged to use should be provided. Table 2.5 provides a list, with suggested content, of these writing selections.

Children should also be encouraged to write for meaningfulness. When children see a direct link with the real world and writing communication, they are more motivated to learn (rather than filling out a worksheet). Letters that are really sent to friends, relatives, or guest speakers requesting or explaining something, communicating with technology, creating, entertainment, and so forth, make writing more valuable.

Try this practice question:

Students in Ms. Mitza's second-grade science class have been writing descriptive expository paragraphs about "Ocean Life," and the students are using the computer lab to do the assignment. As Ms. Mitza observes her students, she notices that they are composing their paragraphs, frequently doing a word count, and checking their spelling. She wants her students to use a variety of text sources to locate information and organize their paragraphs around main ideas as they revise.

Which of the following instructional strategies would be *most* effective in achieving this goal?

A. Providing a variety of text sources.
B. Modeling paragraph construction.
C. Asking children if they have described main points.
D. Encouraging students to graphically organize their paragraphs before beginning to write information.

Choice *C* is correct because the teacher wants her students to construct paragraphs that contain information related to their main topic. It is an effective practice to have a variety of text sources available and to encourage children to develop their own graphics as they construct their paragraphs. However, it is also important to remember that, in the revision phase, children are constructing text without being concerned about editing yet. The answer is *C.*

Standard IX Writing Conventions

Competency 009: Teachers understand how young children use writing conventions and how to help children develop proficiency in using writing conventions.

The teacher understands the stages children use in acquiring writing conventions, knows the stages of spelling development, uses systemic spelling instruction to teach letter patterns in words, and applies assessment practices to enhance instruction. Remember that the TEKS promote developmental application of the writing conventions.

	Sample 1 Pre-kindergarten (I have a kite.)
	Sample 2 Kindergarten (I am four.)
	Sample 3 Grade 1 (I have a puppy.)
	Sample 4 Grade 2 (I like my dog and cat. My dog is big.)

FIGURE 2.2 Devin's Portfolio Samples

Use the chart in Figure 2.2 to answer the practice question:

A third-grade teacher has just opened Devin's portfolio. The teacher notices four writing samples (pre-kindergarten, kindergarten, grade 1, and grade 2) that are a part of Devin's portfolio. What can the teacher determine about Devin's writing products?

A. His writing in Samples 1 through 3 shows little use of writing conventions.
B. His writing in Samples 1 through 4 shows development in spelling.
C. His writing in Sample 4 shows development in letter formation and punctuation but also shows errors in spelling.
D. His writing in Sample 3 shows that he understands the formation of only uppercase letters.

Think about all you know about children and their developmental stages for writing, spelling, punctuation, etc. Actually, Devin shows literacy development and progress with each of his portfolio products. So, let's think about each of the answer choices. Choice A does not give Devin credit for many things he does effectively. For example, in Sample 1, Devin uses spacing of scribbles to communicate his thoughts. In Sample 2, he is beginning to use uppercase letter formation and number formation, and he continues to demonstrate usage of spacing. In Sample 3, he is beginning to show usage of letter-sound association and punctuation. Choice *B* gives Devin credit for showing developmental spelling patterns. Choice *C* does give Devin credit for development in letter formation and punctuation, but sufficient credit regarding spelling is not given. Actually, he misspells two words (he writes *an* instead of *and*, and he writes *kat* instead of *cat*). But credit should be given for letter-sound association. Choice *D* indicates that Devin knows the formation of only uppercase letters. However, he is showing development in spelling and punctuation. Therefore, Choice *B* is the best answer.

It is important for the teacher of young children to understand that writing is an exciting activity that comes in a variety of forms (scribbles, drawings, and letter or number formations) that often will produce reversals, words, and sentences. Parents and teachers who encourage very young children "to write" strengthen the process of understanding that writing is an important activity and the ability to recognize the shape of writing will be required later on. Young children often write from the bottom up (not from the top down), write from right to left (not from left to right), and mix a variety of written forms to spell or invent the spelling of a word. Most young children have some exposure to print and have had the opportunity to observe the conventions of print (parents have read books to them, preschool and kindergarten teachers have used a variety of "big books," and they have had access to books for examination or reading). In order for the teacher to explain the importance of becoming aware of conventions used in writing, it is important to identify the types of conventions that could be used with young children. Spandel and Stiggins (1997) have identified several *conventions* that teachers should model and include in instruction. They recommend that teachers demonstrate: (1) left-to-right direction of print normally by pointing as they read orally; (2) the idea that people read/write from the top to the bottom of a page; (3) that space should be left on both sides of a word to show division; (4) that culmination pronunciation marks should be used; (5) an awareness of the proper usage of lowercase and capital letters; (6) an awareness and growth of correct spelling; (7) usage of left and right margins, neatness, developmental grammar usage; and (8) the awareness of a storyline. Teachers are encouraged to observe growth patterns and to collect samples of writing that document this growth over time.

As you recall from the discussion of Standard VIII (Development of Written Communication), children go through a developmental process in learning to construct meaning by using print. Students who are learning to spell go through a developmental process by using scribbles to indicate spelling approximations. Table 2.6 summarizes the stages of spelling development.

Table 2.6   Stages of Spelling Development

Prephonetic (pre-K to beginning/middle of kindergarten)

Students use scribbles that show a sense of directionality, symbols, and other forms to present written language. Students often understand the purpose of written forms of language because they see print in books, on signs, and on different items in their environment. However, students do not understand yet the concept of using letters to produce words.

Prephonetic/Semiphonetic (end of kindergarten to middle of grade 1)

Students are aware of some of the sounds of the alphabet. They begin to realize that letters of the alphabet stand for sounds they hear in a word.

(continued)

Table 2.6 Continued

Phonetic (middle of Grade 1)

Students understand the regular sounds of the alphabet and begin to use invented spelling. In most cases, words they spell can be interpreted (or read) by others because they spell by using the sounds in a word (for example, a student could spell *BOOKS* as *BOCZ*).

Transitional (end of Grade 1 to beginning of Grade 2)

Students begin to spell words based on how words sound. They are beginning to spell words based on how words look because they are experiencing more words in printed form. Usually students place a vowel in each syllable they write, and they are beginning to use limited structural analysis (prefixes, suffixes, and inflectional endings). They continue to use invented spelling, but it is used with some correct spelling. The student might spell *BOOKS* as *BOKS*.

Conventional (Grade 2 through Grade 4)

Students begin to spell more words consistently correctly and seem to understand the meaning of more words. They spell correctly one-syllable words that have a short vowel sound, and they understand and correctly use verb past tense. They have difficulty with dividing words into syllables and spelling words that have double consonants. At this point, the student should be able to spell *BOOKS* correctly.

Source: Adapted from Gentry, 1981.

Try this practice question:

The teacher wrote "excellent" on this first-grade student's story.

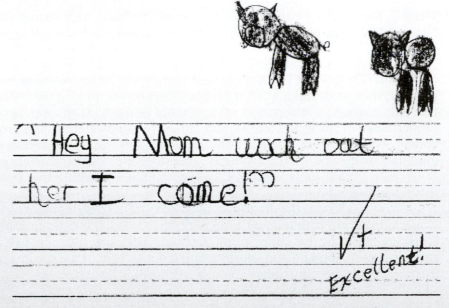

FIGURE 2.3 Why do you think the teacher wrote "excellent" on this first-grade student's story?

    A. The student used more than one type of punctuation mark.
    B. The student used left-to-right orientation.
    C. The student illustrated the story.
    D. The student demonstrated correct spelling.

This student correctly used several writing conventions (punctuation marks, left-to-right orientation, spacing, directionality, and capital letters). He did not spell correctly (D), but the child would still be in the inventive spelling stage. If these words had not yet been taught during spelling time, the teacher would want to concentrate more on *A*, *B*, and *C*. The child also included an illustration which clearly matches "the story." It is important to remember to provide a variety of writing examples to use in classroom settings. As an example, use word walls to display descriptive and other types of words, provide topics for students to use during writing sessions, have a variety of writing products available for students to access, and provide feedback to students for the purpose of developmental growth. The answer is *D*.

Standard X Assessment and Instruction of Developing Literacy

Competency 011 (Assessment of Developing Literacy): Teachers understand the basic principles of literacy assessment and use a variety of assessments to plan and implement literacy instruction.

The teacher uses a variety of formal and informal assessment techniques, analyzes children's reading and writing performance for instructional purposes, knows the procedure for determining children's reading levels, uses assessment practices for the purpose of preparing lessons, and communicates children's progress in literacy development to parents and other professionals. Remember that the TEKS promotes systematic assessment for the purpose of effective on-grade-level instruction.

Try this practice question:

During an informal assessment, Ms. Enzo recorded the way a first-grade student, Corbin, read the following sentence:

The boy likes to play baseball.

"She ba base."

Based on this sample, where should Mrs. Enzo focus *initial* reading instruction?

A. Automatic sight word recognition.
B. Picture clues.
C. Compound words.
D. Syllable division.

Ms. Enzo should provide instruction on sight word recognition so that textual meaning *can* be emphasized. Picture or illustration clues could be helpful, but the test item does not provide a picture for Corbin to use. Although baseball is a compound word and can be applied to syllable division, she would help Corbin *initially* by using instruction that focuses on sight word recognition. Therefore, Choice *A* is correct.

In today's classroom settings, assessment can usually be viewed as either formal or informal. Formal assessment often centers on norm-referenced standardized tests. Formal tests are published tests "for which norms based on the performances of large numbers of students have been developed" (McCormick, 1999, p. 80). Norms provide information for educators to compare the test performance of students with other students in a sample group. For example, in many Texas elementary schools, the Iowa Test of Basic Skills is administered to students. Their scores are then compared to what seems "normal" for a great number of test-takers at that level (e.g., students in your school in Texas would be compared to students in the same grade in Georgia). Additionally, *criterion-referenced* tests should be discussed. These are published tests, less formal than standardized tests, that provide information about the types of skills students have either mastered or not mastered. Criterion-referenced tests can be standardized, but the results are not used for comparison, so this type of test is usually not "normed." Scores are not compared to other students but to how well a student knows particular concepts. The TExES test is an example of a criterion-referenced test because scores will reflect a percentage of how many questions were answered correctly by a test taker. A criterion is the level of performance used to determine if a student has or has not mastered a task level, and criterion-referenced tests are based on specific objectives. As an example, a social studies objective might be stated: The student will demonstrate mastery by correctly identifying and describing five (5) rivers found in Texas.

The *Reading Miscue Inventory* helps teachers determine if students' reading **miscues** (words read differently from what is actually written) prevent them from obtaining correct information from the passage. This assessment assists in determining if children are using background and context clues to assist in reading. The Reading Miscue Inventory stresses that (1) reading is the ability to obtain meaning, (2) reading is not an absolute process because effective readers often substitute words, and (3) teachers should not treat all miscues the same way. Let's look at an example of a miscue that does not basically change the meaning of a sentence: <u>The boy saw a red *automobile*.</u> is read aloud by a child as <u>The boy saw a red *car*</u>. The teacher decides if the student has altered a word in a sentence significantly enough to change the meaning of the sentence, and, in this case, he has not. However, if the child had substituted *hat* for *automobile*, then the teacher would have realized that this miscue changed the entire meaning of the sentence and would signal serious difficulties in analyzing words.

Informal assessment (see additional information in Standard II) is a nonstandardized measure that could be an observation, a checklist, a teacher-generated test, an interest inventory, an interview, a portfolio, an informal reading inventory, a reading miscue inventory, or another type of measure that would give a teacher insight into student performance. Most informal assessments and the implementation processes have been a part of your schooling for years and are clearly understood. However, several need additional discussion.

Teachers use a **running record** to identify the number of correct words a student pronounced in lines of print. To conduct a running record, the teacher would use a blank sheet of paper to place check marks, or ticks, that represent each correctly pronounced word. The teacher would mark, or record, miscues and errors by using the same criteria used in marking informal reading inventory responses and miscues (Clay, 1985).

Portfolio assessment has become a much discussed concept in education. A **portfolio** is a collection of student-generated products that show growth, progress, or improvement over a period of time. Calfee and Perfumo (1993) suggest that the portfolio could include the following student-generated products identified by the teacher and/or by the student for their importance and use in a particular area of reading/writing: (1) rough, final, and published drafts; (2) content-entry journals; (3) tests and quizzes; (4) illustrations; (5) independent and group-generated projects; and (6) other types of literacy products. Each item should be carefully selected by the teacher and/or the student. The length of portfolios can vary from long and involved to rather brief.

Additionally, teachers' written comments should be maintained over time to document children's academic achievement history. Portfolio collections provide a meaningful picture for parents during conferences and for students to self-assess their own progress.

Another type of assessment is an **Informal Reading Inventory (IRI)**, which contains a series of graded paragraphs followed by a comprehension analysis. Teachers have many types of commercially prepared IRIs from which to select. Most contain the following components: (1) a graded word list to determine the starting paragraph level and basic information about a child's sight word vocabulary, (2) two sets of paragraphs with one to be read orally and the other to be read silently, and (3) a series of comprehension checks at different levels. The basic purpose of the IRI is to determine a child's (1) independent reading level [students can read at school or at home without assistance], (2) instructional reading level [students are challenged and require instruction from the teacher], (3) frustration level [students are experiencing material that is too difficult to read], and (4) listening capacity level [students can benefit from hearing the teacher read text aloud that will be followed by questions]. It is important to remember the criteria for determining reading levels as structured by an informal reading inventory (see Table 2.7).

Capacity level (also called hearing or listening level) is tested by the examiner reading to a child at the next level beyond his or her determined frustration level. The comprehension checks are administered until the child scores below 70 percent on questions related to the paragraphs that are read aloud to the child. The purpose of the capacity level, which measures listening comprehension, is to determine the level of reading material children could understand if they could read the material themselves (Spring & French, 1990).

Most educators agree that instruction is a cycle that should lead from lesson objectives to effective instructional activities to assessment and back to new objectives that target what the teacher noted during assessment. Let's look at how a first-grade teacher could assess the following written product and use the results to plan instructional activities and additional authentic assessment activities (see Figure 2.4 on page 72).

Let's assume that Mrs. Kumar has read *The Three Little Bears* to her class and has asked Emily to do a written retelling of the story (see Standard VII to review the components of story retelling). The teacher should note that Emily understood the following: (1) the family structure of the bears, (2) the name of the food they were going to eat, (3) what they did, and (4) what had happened to their food when they returned. Mrs. Kumar should assess the written retelling to determine instructional strategies that could be used to help Emily orally retell omitted details about the story. For example, Mrs. Kumar could ask Emily to tell about other characters in the story, other things that happened in the story, where the story took place, the main problem and how it was solved, and so forth. Additionally, Mrs. Kumar

Table 2.7   Reading Levels of an Informal Reading Inventory

Level	Word Recognition Accuracy Percentage	Comprehension Percentage
Independent	95 to 100% correct	90 to 100% correct
Instructional	90 to 94% correct	70 to 89% correct
Frustration	Below 90% correct	Below 70% correct

The Three Littl bear porrige and went for a Littl wake and wen They came bake Thre porrige wose gon

FIGURE 2.4

should assess Emily's writing conventions (see Standard IX to review writing conventions) and determine further activities that could be used in instruction. A teacher might plan an additional lesson on using punctuation at the end of a sentence, in which several activities would be given to provide the child practice in using an appropriate punctuation mark at the end of several different types of sentences. This brief discussion highlights that assessment and instructional practices should be used daily to make instructional decisions.

Try these practice questions:

Mr. Orion provides the following information about Patrick's reading performance during a parental conference:

"Patrick reads slightly above grade level. He enjoys reading orally in class and has a positive attitude about learning. There is some concern about the usage of miscues during oral reading. This is causing Patrick to make some comprehension mistakes. This is not necessarily a habit yet, but strategies that will assist Patrick in being more accurate in oral reading should be provided."

Which instructional practices would *not* be recommended?

A. Establishing strategies that would allow Patrick to use his own background knowledge to determine word selection during oral and silent reading.
B. Encouraging him to stop and seek assistance each time he encounters a word he cannot pronounce.
C. Instructing him to use context clues to determine unknown words.
D. Instructing Patrick on how to use metacognitive strategies to ask questions about the readings.

Actually, Patrick should have grade-appropriate sight word recognition. However, it would also be an appropriate practice to encourage him to use his own background in determining word choices, to use self-determined questions (using a metacognitive strategy) to assist in meaning, and to use context clues to determine unknown words. Therefore, Choice *B* would be correct and would *not* be recommended so as not to continuously break the flow of his reading, especially during independent reading.

Students in Mr. Canto's third-grade mathematics class have been writing journal entries to describe the process used in solving math problems. Mr. Canto has just requested that his students give him journal entries submitted over the last five Mondays. Which type of assessment is closest to Mr. Canto's request?

A. Portfolio assessment
B. Informal reading inventory
C. Criterion-referenced testing
D. Norm-referenced testing

Mr. Canto is using portfolio assessment considerations in his request to see a rather specific collection of student-generated products that could indicate a pattern of academic or nonacademic growth. For a complete portfolio, he would want to include many different products and have student input. Therefore, *A* is the correct response.

SUMMARY

This chapter discussed the instructional importance of acquiring knowledge about the concepts to be tested in the ten standards of the English Language Arts and Reading Early Childhood-Grade 4 TExES Generalist examination. This chapter should serve as a review of information that you have studied in coursework and applied in different types of instructional settings. As you connect this information to your current knowledge base, you will notice an increase in basic information that will assist you in preparing for this examination. In addition to acquiring a cognitive knowledge base needed to be successful when taking this examination, it is necessary to properly apply this information to successfully teach children in classroom settings. The importance of designing effective language arts and reading lessons cannot be overstated. Planning this type of instruction requires the development and use of activities that are meaningful and interesting—so that all children can participate in an effective learner-centered classroom environment. Therefore, educators who understand the process and reasons for designing and conducting effective instruction for reading and language arts will be able to identify and meet the needs of *all* children.

GLOSSARY

You should become familiar with the following terms so that you can establish an effective knowledge base. This knowledge base will provide you with more information when considering the most effective response to questions on the TExES.

Affix. A structural element added to the beginning or ending of a word in order to alter the meaning, pronunciation, or function (e.g., prefixes and suffixes).

Alliteration. Words in a sentence or phrase that begin mostly with the same letter sound.

Alphabetic principle. The idea that individual letters represent individual speech sounds; therefore, words may be read by saying the sounds represented by the letters, and words may be spelled by writing the letters that represent the sounds.

Alphabetic recognition. The ability to name letters of the alphabet.

Balanced approach to reading. The use of different strategies and approaches to teach reading.

Basal reader. A collection of stories that matches the instructional level of children.

Bilingual education. Instruction that involves presenting reading and other subject area materials in the child's native language while gradually introducing English.

Blending. The skill of combining separate sounds to create a word (/t/ /o/ /p/ = top)

Choral reading. Oral reading, often of poetry, involving more than one reader.

Consonant blend or cluster. Two or three letters in the same syllable that are blended or heard when pronounced (e.g., *"tr"* in *tree*).

Consonant digraph. A combination of two or more letters that represent a sound that is different from the speech sound that the letters represent individually (e.g., *ch* in *chop*).

Context clues. Words or phrases within a reading passage that give hints to vocabulary meaning.

Convergent question. A question with one correct answer (ex., what is the capital of Texas?)

Conversation. An activity involving two or more persons taking turns talking about a subject.

Debate. A discussion involving varying viewpoints on a central topic, where sides are supported.

Decode. Associating printed letters with the speech sounds the letters make; deciphering word meaning.

Dialect. A linguistic change or variation in speech pronounciation that is different from the standard, or original, pronunciation.

Diphthong. Two adjacent vowels in which each vowel is heard in the pronunciation (e.g., *ou* in *house*).

Discussion. Focused conversations about a specific topic.

Divergent question. A question that could have many correct answers (ex., what is the best way to limit polution?).

Emergent literacy. Children's reading and writing development before formal instruction in classroom settings.

Emergent writing stage. Beginning efforts in letter formation (scribbling, drawing, and a combination of these), usually starting before kindergarten age.

English as a Second Language (ESL). An instructional program that teaches English to students whose native language is not English.

Evaluative comprehension. Level of comprehension that requires children to compare information and ideas presented in a text with their own experiences, background, and values.

Facilitative. Skills such as word analysis that enable a reader to identify words.

Functional. The actual understanding or comprehension of what has been read.

Genre. A description of the type of text being read (e.g., poetry, biography, mystery, fantasy).

Grapheme. A printed letter symbol used to represent a speech sound (phoneme).

Graphophonemic knowledge. Written words are made up of systematic letter patterns that represent sounds in pronounced words.

Graphophonic. Sound/symbol relationship.

Homographs. Words spelled the same but having different pronunciations and meanings; for example: "She is wearing a red *bow*," and "She will *bow* to the queen."

Homophones. Words that sound the same but have different spellings and meanings; for example: "He is wearing a *red* shirt." "He *read* the book."

Idioms. Figurative sayings that have special meanings; for example, *"Keep your shirt on!"* basically means *"Don't get angry."*

Inferential comprehension. Level of comprehension that requires children to respond to questions and statements based on ideas and information that are directly stated in the text along with the use of their intuition, background, and experiences to reach a conclusion or a hypothesis.

Informal reading inventory (IRI). A series of graded paragraphs followed by a comprehension analysis used to determine a child's independent, instructional, and frustration level for reading.

Interview. One person asking another questions and recording their responses.

Invented spelling. Temporary spelling patterns young children use to approximate the spelling of words (e.g., a young child might write *"It wus a preti da"* instead of *"It was a pretty day."*

Language experience approach (LEA). An instructional method that incorporates children's experiences and backgrounds as a means of developing instructional reading stories.

Language interference. For ESL children, the use of sounds, syntax, and vocabulary of two languages simultaneously as a child participates in literacy activities.

Letter recognition. The relationship of letters in printed words to spoken language.

Literal comprehension. Level of comprehension that requires children to respond to questions and statements that directly relate to stated text.

Logographic awareness. The first stage children experience when learning about words. Words that are learned as whole units are sometimes embedded in a logo such as a stop sign or the arches in the McDonald's sign.

Metaphor. Comparison of two unlike things without using *as* or *like* (e.g., "The *moon* was an *orange* floating on the silver platter of the sea.").

Miscues. Words read differently than how they are written.

Morpheme. The smallest meaningful unit of language (e.g., *cat* is a *morpheme* whose pronunciation consists of three phonemes, c/a/t).

Nonstandard dialect. Grammatical variations in a language most often associated with a cultural group.

Onsets and **rimes.** *Onsets* are the consonants that come at the beginning of syllables in words—for example, the *bl* in the word *blend* is the onset. *Rimes* are vowels and consonants at the end of a syllable—for example, the *end* in the word *blend* is the rime.

Oracy. The concept that identifies and describes the differences between the *skills of listening and speaking* from the skills of reading and writing.

Oral reports. Individual or group reports delivered orally to an audience.

Orthography. Correct spelling.

Phoneme. The smallest unit of sound in a language that distinguishes one word from another word. Example: *cat* and *hat* are distinguished as sounding different by considering their beginning consonant phonemes /c/ and /h/.

Phonic analysis. The process of applying knowledge of letter-sound relationships to words. Teachers ask for this when they instruct children to "sound out" a word.

Phonemic awareness. The knowledge or understanding that speech consists of a series of sounds and that individual words can be divided into phonemes.

Phonics. Using letters and the sounds of letters to determine the pronunciation of a word.

Phonological awareness. The ability to use letter-sound knowledge to identify an unknown word.

Phonology. The study of speech sounds.

Portfolio. A collection of student-generated products that shows growth, progress, or improvement over a period of time.

Prosody. The rhythm of speech including phrasing, appropriate breathing, voice intonation, tone, and attention to all punctuation marks.

Puppets. Animal or human characters made from a variety of materials to be held or slipped over the hand and used in dramatic play.

Readers' theater. The oral presentation of drama by two or more readers using a printed script; normally used to create motivation and oral fluency.

Rhyming. Produce patterns of rhyming words.

Running record. An informal assessment that provides a record of a child's oral reading development and behavior.

Scaffolding. Support for a learner as he or she enters a phase of readiness for a new skill.

Schwa sound. In many words that have more than one syllable, one of the syllables receives less or diminished stress. The sound of the vowel in the syllable that receives the diminished stress has a softening of the vowel sound that is identified as a schwa sound and often pronounced as the "uh" sound. The word *about* contains the schwa sound.

Segmentation. The ability to identify and separate sounds in words (for purposes of blending).

Semantic feature analysis. Constructing a grid for a concept (example: mammals) where examples of the concept are listed vertically (example: cow, bat, squirrel) and features are listed horizontally (example: has fur, swims, flies). Students then decide which feature matches each word.

Semantic or concept map (word cluster). Writing a word or concept in the center circle of a cluster, drawing rays, writing information about the word or concept, in the "outer bubbles" and making connections between the word or concept and the related unit of study or details from readings.

Semantics. The way a word is defined.

Show-and-tell. A traditional informal speaking activity in which a child brings something from home that is special to him or her and tells the class about it.

Sight vocabulary. Any words a reader can recognize instantly without having to use a word recognition strategy. Many teachers have children personalize a word bank of the sight words they can read.

Similes. Comparison between two things of a different kind or quality using *like* or *as.* An example: *"The rain came down like transparent sheets."*

Syllable. Divisions of speech sounds within words.

Syntactic. Patterns of phrases, clauses, and sentences.

Syntax. Sentence structure.

Textless books (also known as **wordless books**). A picture book with few or no words in which the illustrations convey the story.

Thematic units. Instructionally generated learning activities that center on a topic of interest (such as a variety of content areas discussing "Butterflie").

Trade books. Children's literature sources that teachers sometimes use in instructional settings instead of textbooks.

Vowel digraph. Two adjacent vowels that represent one speech sound (e.g., *ee* in *feet*).

Word analysis. An inclusive term that refers to *all methods* of word recognition. Phonics is one such method. Other methods include *picture clues* (using pictures and graphic aids to assist in word pronunciation and meaning), *context clues* (using surrounding text to aid in word pronunciation and meaning), *sight words,* and *structural analysis* (which focuses on root words, base words, affixes, compound words, syllable division, and contractions).

Word sorts. Sorting a collection of words taken from a word wall or other sources into two or more categories.

Word wall. A list of words children are learning (or know) posted on a poster (or an actual wall in a classroom) in a highly visible location.

Writing or **Writer's Workshop.** An extended project that can involve narration of a story to the teacher or, in the case of older children, a writing assignment prompt, instruction on a small area of writing or punctuation, revision/editing, "publishing," and peer sharing. This is normally an interdisciplinary activity and occurs three to five times a week.

Zone of proximal development. Children learn within their instructional level or just beyond their instructional level with scaffolding from an adult or from a capable peer.

REFERENCES

Adams, M.J. (1990). *Beginning to read: Thinking and learning about print.* Cambridge, MA: Massachusetts Institute of Technology.

Baghban, M. (1984). *Our daughter learns to read and write: A case study from birth to three.* Newark, DE: International Reading Association.

Barrett, T.C. (1965). The relationship between measures of prereading visual discrimination and first grade reading achievement: A review of the literature. *Reading Research Quarterly, 1,* 51–76.

Blevins, W. (1998). *Phonics from a to z: A practical guide.* New York: Scholastic Professional Books.

Calfee, R.C., & Perfumo, P. (1993). Student portfolios: Opportunities for a revolution in assessment. *The Reading Teacher, 46,* 532–537.

Carlson, C., Fletcher, J., Foorman, B., Francis, D., & Schatschneider, C. (2001). *Texas primary reading inventory (TPRI) teacher's guide.* Austin: Texas Education Agency.

Carmen, R., & Adams, W. (1972). *Study skills: A student's guide to survival.* New York: Wiley.

Clay, M.M. (1985). *The early detection of reading difficulties: A diagnostic survey with recovery procedures.* Portsmouth, NH: Heinemann.

Cramer, R.L. (2004). *The language arts: A balanced approach to teaching reading, writing, listening, and thinking.* Boston: Pearson Education, Inc.

Cunningham, J.W., Cunningham, P. M., Hoffman, J. V., & Yopp, H. R. (1998). *Phonemic awareness and the teaching of reading: A position statement from the board of directors of the International Reading Association.* Newark, DE: International Reading Association.

Dowhower, S.L. (1991). Speaking of prosody: Fluency's unattended bedfellow. *Theory into Practice, 30,* 165–175.

Duthie, C. (1996). *True stories: Nonfiction literacy in the primary classroom.* York, ME: Stenhouse.

Elkonin, D.B. (1963). The psychology of mastering elements of reading. In B. Simon & J. Simon (Eds.), *Educational psychology in the U.S.S.R.* (pp. 165–179). London: Routledge and Kegan Paul.

Gentry, J.R. (1981). Learning to spell developmentally. *The Reading Teacher, 34,* 378–381.

Halliday, M., & Hasan, R. (1976). *Cohesion in English.* London: Longman.

Jewell, M., & Zintz, M.F. (1986). *Learning to read and write naturally.* Dubuque, IA: Kendall-Hunt.

Juel, C. (1988). Learning to read and write: A longitudinal study of fifty-four children from first through fourth grade. *Journal of Educational Psychology, 80,* 437–447.

Kutiper, K. (1985). *A survey of the adolescent poetry preferences of seventh, eighth, and ninth graders.* Unpublished doctoral dissertation, University of Houston, Houston, Texas.

Lundsteen, S. W. (1979). *Listening: Its impact at all levels on reading and the other language arts.* Urbana, IL: ERIC Clearinghouse on Reading and Communication Skills and the National Council of Teachers of English.

Manzo, A. V. (1969). The request procedure. *Journal of Reading, 13,* 123–126.

McCormick, S. (1999). *Instructing students who have literacy problems* (3rd ed.). Upper Saddle River, NJ: Prentice-Hall.

McGee, L., & Richgels, D. (2000). *Literacy's beginnings: Supporting young readers and writers.* Boston: Allyn and Bacon.

Meyer, B. (1975). *The organization of prose and its effect on memory.* Amsterdam: North-Holland.

Morrow, L. M. (1989). Using story retelling to develop comprehension. In K. D. Muth (Ed.), *Children's comprehension of text: Research into practice* (pp. 37–58). Newark, DE: International Reading Association.

National Reading Panel (2000). *Teaching children to read: An evidence-based assessment of the scientific research literature on reading and its implications for reading instruction.* Washington, DC: National Institute of Child Health and Human Development.

Ogle, D. M. (1992). KWL in action: Secondary teachers find applications that work. In E. K. Dishner. T. W. Bean, J. E. Readence, & D. W. Moore (Eds.), *Reading in the content areas: Improving classroom instruction* (3rd ed.), (pp. 270–281). Dubuque, IA: Kendall-Hunt.

Rey, H.A. (1957). *Curious George gets a medal.* Boston: Houghton Mifflin Company.

Rubin, D. (2000). *Teaching elementary language arts.* Boston: Allyn and Bacon.

Spandel, V., & Stiggins, R. (1997). *Creating writers: Linking writing assessment and instruction.* New York: Addison Wesley Longman.

Spring, C., & French, L. (1990). Identifying children with specific reading disabilities from listening and reading discrepancy scores. *Journal of Learning Disabilities, 23,* 53–58.

Stanovich, K.E. (1994). Romance and reality. *The Reading Teacher, 47,* 280–291.

Stauffer, R.G. (1969). *Teaching reading as a teaching process.* New York: Harper and Row.

Terry, C.A. (1974). *Children's poetry preferences: A national survey of upper elementary grades.* Urbana, IL: National Council of Teachers of English.

Tompkins, G.E. (2001). *Literacy for the 21st century: A balanced approach* (2nd ed.). Upper Saddle River, NJ: Prentice-Hall.

Vacca, R., & Vacca, J. A. (1986). *Content area reading.* Boston: Little, Brown and Company.

Walker, B.J. (2000). *Diagnostic teaching of reading.* New Jersey: Merrill.

Wilkinson, A. (1974). Oracy in English teaching. In H. DeStefana & S. Fox (Eds.), *Language and the language arts* (pp. 64–71). Boston: Little, Brown and Company.

Yopp, H.K. (1995). A test for assessing phonemic awareness in young children. *The Reading Teacher, 49,* 20–29.

Ziegler, A. (1981). *The writing workshop, Vol. 1.* New York: Teachers and Writers Collaborate.

A READING LESSON PLAN

The Letter B

Grade Level: Kindergarten/First

Main Subject Area: Reading

Integrated Subjects: Art/music

Time Frame/Constraints: 1 to 2 hours

Overall Goal(s): To have children associate /b/ sound with the upper- and lowercase letter *B*.

TAKS/TEKS OBJECTIVES:

§ 110.2/3. **English Language Arts** and **Reading, Kindergarten** (b) knowledge and skills (C) participate in rhymes, songs, conversations, and discussions (K-3); (E) listen responsively to stories and other texts read aloud, including selections from classic and contemporary works (K–3); and (D) know the difference between individual letters and printed words (K–1); (E) know the difference between capital and lowercase letters (K–1); (7) Reading/letter-sound relationships. The student uses letter-sound knowledge to decode written language. The student is expected to: (A) name and identify each letter of the alphabet (K–1); (B) understand that written words are composed of letters that represent sounds (K–1); and (C) learn and apply letter-sound correspondences of a set of consonants and vowels to begin to read (K–1); (10) Reading/literary response. The student responds to various texts. The student is expected to: (A) listen to stories being read aloud (K–1);

§ 117.2. **Art** Creative expression/performance. The student expresses ideas through original artworks, using a variety of media with appropriate skill. The student is expected to: (A) create artworks, using a variety of colors, forms, and lines; (B) arrange forms intuitively to create artworks; and (C) develop manipulative skills when drawing, painting, printmaking, and constructing artworks, using a variety of materials;

§ 117.3. **Music** (1) Perception. The student describes and analyzes musical sound and demonstrates musical artistry. The student is expected to: (C) identify repetition and contrast in music examples.

OBJECTIVES:

(To be given *after* the Concept Attainment Game).

- Students will draw a picture of something that starts with the letter "Aa."
- Students participate in the Concept Attainment Game on things that start with the letter "Bb."
- Students will listen to a Batman cartoon book or to *Brown Bear, Brown Bear*.
- Students will sing Bingo, clap the "beat" of the song, and "bark" to the song.
- Students, in groups, will construct a "B-Bag."
- Students will each make an upper- and lowercase "B" with brown beans.
- Students will complete a worksheet in which each correctly circles 8 out of 10 answers of words beginning with the /b/ sound.
- Students will orally identify pictures of animals whose names start with /b/.

Sponge Activity: Students will be asked to draw a picture showing yesterday's letter/sound ("A") on a piece of paper.

Environmental Concerns: Remember to go over "glue rules" during bean activity. Students should be in their core groups for the "B-Bag" activity; if not, be sure groups are heterogeneous.

Rationale(s): (To be given *after* the Concept Attainment Game). There are many words that start with the letter "B". If we want to be able to read and write those words, we must be able to recognize and pronounce that letter. How could we write Bobby, Bailey, or Brianna (or "B" names of classmates) if we didn't know about "B"—because all of their names begin with the letter "B"? How could we see if a restaurant had the foods we wanted to eat (burgers, barbeque on a bun, beans, bananas, etc.) could not recognize the letter "B"?

Focus or Set Induction: Concept Attainment Game. The teacher has two sets of large cards: (1) with 4–5 pictures of fruits and 4–5 pictures of vegetables [or any thing other than fruit] and (2) with at least 10 large pictures of things that begin with the letter "B" (boat, baby, bear, bag, bathtub, books, brown color, backpack, bacon, ball, balloon, banana, bell, buttons, etc.) and 10 cards with things that do not begin with "b" (camera, cat, umbrella, truck, dog, elephant, apples, eggplant, etc.). The teacher introduces the game by saying, "Today, boys and girls, we are going to play 'Guess What I'm Thinking.' I am going to show you some pictures that have some examples of what I'm thinking and some pictures that are not of what I am thinking. There are some rules for this game. You must raise your hand and be called on, and you can never say what "it" is that you believe is in my mind until the end of the game, but you can guess another example of what I am thinking or you can guess a nonexample (or "not it"—something you believe that I'm not thinking about) Let's play a sample game, so that you will see how to play." The teacher shows two cards with two different fruits (for example, apples and grapes and one card with a vegetable and tells students, "I'm going to put the cards that are examples of what I'm thinking of on this side of the board (marked "Yes" or "It"), and the ones that are not of what I'm thinking about on the other side (marked "No" or "Not It"). Now, who can give me another example of what I'm thinking?" When students say a particular fruit, the teacher adds the picture to the "Yes" side (or prints the word on the board if it is not on one of the cards). If it is a nonexample, it is placed on the "No" or "Not It" side. If students say "fruit" right away (the concept) you must say, "Well, maybe, but can you give me an example or a nonexample to test your guess?" When the cards are finished and it is fairly obvious that most students do know that the concept is fruit, the teacher asks one child to tell out loud what the concept is. If it is not correct, play a little longer. As a practice game, this should not last very long. Move on to the real game. The teacher begins by showing two examples of the /b/ cards and one nonexample, placing them under the correct label on the board and asks the class to say the name of each object in the picture out loud. Then the teacher asks students to give an example ("Yes" or "It") or a nonexample ("No" or "Not It"). Place answers in the correct area (either a picture or the printed word). Children should have a few guesses between adding pictures, but if they are off-track, always add a new card to the example side. When the teacher begins to see that children have an idea of the concept, he or she should switch modes to showing children a picture and asking on which side it belongs. Finally, children will be asked to give the concept— "words that begin with the letter 'B.'" If they do not get it, the teacher can have them go through all of the cards again and pronounce all of the words and/or give other hints. Finally, she or he should ask if students know other words that start with the letter "b" that were not mentioned.

MAKING CONNECTIONS:

1. Connections to Past or Future Learning: (Do not give until after the Concept Attainment Game). We learned how to make a letter "A" and learned about some of the sounds that "A" makes. Today, we will learn more about the sound that the letter "B" makes and how to make a lower- and uppercase letter "B."

2. Connections to the Community: Does anyone know a person whose name starts with the letter "B"? Do you know any businesses that start with the letter "B" (Burger King; Halfprice Books, bank, bakery, etc.; having pictures is a good idea).

3. Cultural Connections: Look at a list of names in the class or grade level that begins with the letter "B," research the cultural origin and share with students. Ask them if all languages have a "B." They do not—the Hawaiian language has no words with "B."

4. Connection to Student Interests and Experiences: What toys start with the letter "B"? (Barbie, baseball, baseball bat, baton, beachball, bears, baby doll, balloon).

Materials: 2 sets of cards for Concept Attainment Game (one for the practice game and one for the real game); Batman cartoon book or *Brown Bear, Brown Bear;* brown paper bags; stickers with "B" words; blue balloons and blue ribbons; beans and light brown construction paper; worksheet; PowerPoint slides with "B" words; animal cards.

Activities: Guided Practice: Teacher reads a Batman cartoon (or can make one up) with many "Bat words" or reads *Brown Bear, Brown Bear.* The class sings *Bingo*, and the teacher has children "bounce" when they hear the letter "B." Children then clap the "beat" as they sing again, and finally children substitute the word *bark* for all of the words as they sing the last time.

Children are grouped to construct a "B-bag." Each group has a brown paper lunch bag. The group is given a number of stickers. They are to pick out the stickers that have words beginning with the letter "B" and glue or stick them on their bags. When they are finished, all members of the group should raise their hands, and the teacher will come and tie a blue balloon onto their bags with a blue ribbon.

Independent Practice: Each child will make an upper- and a lowercase "B" by pasting brown beans on a sheet of light brown construction paper; children will correctly circle 8 out 10 items on a worksheet that begin with the letter "B."

Assessment: Individuals must complete their "B" sheet with brown beans. Children must circle 8 out of 10 items that begin with the letter "B" on a worksheet.

What will students do who finish early?

Children will view a teacher-constructed Power-Point Presentation with many pictures of items beginning with the letter "B."

Closure: The teacher will tell children that science cannot do without the letter "B" to identify animals. The teacher will hold up animal cards that start with the letter "B" (bat, butterfly, baboon, badger, beetle, bear, bee, bluebird, blackbird, bunny, etc.) or not (cat, dog, fish, monkey, elephant, giraffe, etc.) and have children identify orally those animals whose names begin with "B."

Modification for Students with Special Needs: Toby will need to sit next to the teacher during the closure to ensure that his attention is directly on the cards. The teacher may need to go back and have Toby identify the cards one-on-one. Travis will need extra help manipulating the beans. The teacher may ask him to put the beans in the sandbox rather than glue them.

Reflection: To be completed after teaching the lesson.

Center Connections: This lesson can be tied to centers in the following ways:

1. In the Art Center, children create their own *Brown Bear, Brown Bear* page with their choice of an animal whose name begins with "B" to be bound later for a class book.

2. In the Home Center, materials (clay, etc.) are available for "preparing" a number of bakery goods with a play oven to "bake" the item (encourage bread, biscuits, bagels, breakfast items, brownies, blueberry muffins, breadsticks, etc.). A "cookbook" should have pictures of "B" bakery products for children to see. Students are required to "bake" something with a "B" and show it to the teacher.

3. In the Gym Center, children balance a beanbag on their heads and try to keep their balance along a line of tape on the floor (simulating a balance beam). Children bounce a basketball and toss a beach ball. Children toss the beanbag into a Bozo the Clown's mouth.

4. In the Science Center, children use a balance to test many items for balanced weights. Children blow bubbles.

5. In the Math Center, children sort buttons by attributes (brown and blue; big and bigger, etc.).

DRAFT YOUR OWN LANGUAGE ARTS OR READING LESSON PLAN

Title of Lesson: _____

Grade Level: _____

Main Subject Area: _____

Subjects Integrated: _____

Time Frame/Constraints: _____

Overall Goal(s): _____

TEKS/TAKS Objectives: _____

_____

_____

Objectives: _____

_____

_____

Sponge Activity: _____

_____

_____

Environmental Concerns: _____

_____

_____

Rationale(s): _____

_____

_____

Focus or Set Induction: _____

_____

_____

Making Connections:

1. Connections to Past or Future Learning: _____

_____

2. Connections to the Community: _____

_____

3. Cultural Connections: _____

_____

4. Connections to Student Interests & Experiences: _____

_____

Materials: _____

_____

_____

Activities: Guided practice: _____

_____

_____

_____

_____

_____

_____

_____

_____

_____

_____

Independent practice: _____

_____

_____

_____

_____

_____

_____

_____

_____

_____

Assessment: _____

_____

_____

What will students do who finish early? _____

_____

_____

Closure: _____

_____

_____

Modification for Students with Special Needs: _____

_____

_____

Reflection: _____

_____

_____

OBSERVING LANGUAGE ARTS AND READING EXPERIENCES/ACTIVITIES

During your visit to an early childhood classroom, use the following form to provide feedback as well as to reflectively analyze the room, the materials, and the teacher.

The Classroom Environment	Observed	Not Observed	Response
1. There is ample space for movement by children and adults.			If not, how could the classroom be rearranged?
2. There is evidence that diversity is valued.			If so, describe. If not, what language arts elements could be included to address this issue?
3. The teacher uses activities that promote oral skills.			If so, explain the types of activities observed. If not, what types of activities could be added?
4. The teacher uses approaches that provide instruction in the development of phonological awareness.			If so, describe. If not, which approaches could be implemented?
5. The teacher uses approaches and materials that provide instruction in the alphabetic principle.			If so, describe. If not, what could be added?
6. There is evidence of exposure to print awareness.			If so, describe. If not, what could be added?
7. The teacher uses games, activities, and a variety of other instructional materials to teach and practice word analysis and decoding skills.			If so, list and describe their effectiveness. If not, what could be added?
8. The teacher uses a variety of text sources to promote comprehension skills, higher-level questioning, and critical thinking.			If so, list types. If not, what are some logical additions?
9. The teacher uses instructional practices to promote reading fluency.			If so, describe. If not, what practices could be added?
10. The teacher uses motivating instructional materials to teach the development of the writing process.			11. If so, describe. If not, what materials could be added?
1.1 There is evidence of instruction in the conventions of writing.			If so, describe. If not, what opportunities were missed?
12. The teacher uses a variety of informal, formal, and authentic assessment practices.			List and explain the assessment practices and their effectiveness. If not effective, what are some logical additions?
13. There is evidence that parental involvement in reading and language arts is encouraged.			If so, describe. If not, how could this be encouraged?

The Classroom Environment	Observed	Not Observed	Response
14. There is evidence that students have choices to some degree.			If so, describe. If not, how could this be accomplished?
15. There is evidence that state standards are used in lesson planning and implementation.			If so, describe. If not, how could they be incorporated into instructional planning?
16. Student work samples are displayed.			If so, describe. Is this effective? If not, list ideas on how this could become more effective.
17. There is evidence of the integration of technology usage in aspects of language arts/reading instruction.			If so, describe. If not, in what ways could this be accomplished?
18. The teacher engages students in both individual and group work.			If so, describe. If not, how could this be changed?
19. The teacher employs student reading and writing across the curriculum.			If so, describe. If not, describe some methods to accomplish this.
20. There is a language arts/reading center in the classroom.			If so, describe. If not, describe a center that could be added.
21. The teacher integrates movement into language arts/reading.			If so, describe. If not, how could it be added?
22. The teacher integrates music into language arts/reading.			If so, describe. If not, how could it be added?
23. The lesson begins with a motivating focus.			If so, describe. If not, what could be added
24. Language Arts/Reading displays are attractively presented in the classroom.			If so, describe. If not, what could be changed.
25. The teacher checks for understanding for *all* children			If so, describe. If not, what children are left out?
26. The lesson is presented in a logical manner.			If so, describe. If not, what should be rearranged and why?
27. The teacher uses an effective closure to end the lesson.			If so, describe. If not, what could be added.

TEST YOURSELF ON LANGUAGE ARTS AND READING

1. Mr. Binca, a second-grade teacher, noticed that Marsha had finished reading her library book. He asked her to select a couple of sentences to read out loud to him, and she read the following to him:

   The boy and his dad took a trip. They had fun because they went fishing in a pond. Mr. Binca noticed that Marsha hesitated as she began to read the word *fish* and read the word very slowly to sound like *f/i/sh*. Which phonemic awareness skill is Marsha using to read the word *fish*?
   A. Rhyming
   B. Segmenting
   C. Blending
   D. Visual discrimination

2. Mrs. Brown, a first-grade teacher, is providing individual practice for Milake. The teacher slowly pronounces *cup* as *c/u/p* and immediately asks Milake to pronounce the word. Which phonemic awareness skill is being used in this situation?
   A. Rhyming
   B. Segmenting
   C. Blending
   D. Auditory discrimination

3. A fourth-grade teacher assigned two writing prompt topics each week for students to use to construct written compositions. The teacher recently noticed that the students were not developing compositions that effectively used the writing conventions. Which of the following ideas might *best* improve the students' use of the writing conventions?
   A. Correct each composition and have the students re-write the compositions using the teacher's edits.
   B. Have students play "conventions detective" and look for their incorrect conventions.
   C. Design a series of PowerPoint presentations that provide instruction and practice games with the uses of capitalization and punctuation.
   D. Have the students learn to spell a new set of words each week.

4. Miss Binica teaches a Pre-K class and has noticed that two of her students do not participate in whole class oral language discussions. What could the teacher do to encourage the participation of these two students?
   A. Determine several things that these students enjoy doing and incorporate these ideas into her questioning so that she can discretely build the children's answers from short ones into longer ones.
   B. Read a story to the class. After reading and discussing the story, she could ask the two students to draw the sequence of the story and tell their favorite parts to other children in the class.
   C. Ask the students to re-tell their favorite story to another child in the class.
   D. Instruct these two children to individually stand in front of the class to tell about the story that they most liked during the week.

5. A fourth-grade student can instantly recognize, or read, most of the words in the newly adopted science textbook. The student only needs to use word analysis or decoding skills for two or three words. Which word analysis skill is this student mostly employing?
   A. Context clues
   B. Structural analysis
   C. Sight words
   D. Syllable division

6. A third-grade teacher wants her students to identify summary paragraphs in reading selections and to write summary paragraphs as a part of written compositions. How can this teacher best describe to students the components of a summary paragraph?
   A. There is a consistent tone and point of view.
   B. Descriptive words are used.
   C. The main ideas are restated, and essential supporting details of the text or composition are noted.
   D. The main problem is discussed.

7. Mrs. Mendosa, a first-grade teacher, reads *Curious George Gets a Medal* (Rey, 1957) to her students. She wants to develop sequencing skills with her students because she knows this skill can be used in other instructional areas such as mathematics, science, and social studies. Which of the following instructional activities would allow her to teach this skill?
   A. As she reads the story to her students, she would allow the students to re-tell each part of the story.

B. In small collaborative groups, the students would discuss the characteristics of the main character.

C. As the students write in their composition logs, they would write a summary of the story.

D. As Mrs. Mendosa reads various sections of *Curious George Gets a Medal,* the students would complete a chart that is arranged for them to record the various events that happen in the story.

8. Ms. Jackson frequently reads books to her pre-kindergarten class with rhyming texts. Often she will omit the final word and encourage the children to supply it. On what reading skill is Ms. Jackson focusing?
   A. Auditory discrimination of onsets in words
   B. Auditory discrimination of rimes in words
   C. Use of context clues
   D. Structural analysis

9. Miss Newton works with a small group of kindergarteners using a set of picture cards. She shows a card to the children, pronounces the name of the object, and asks them to say the letter that matches the sound they hear at the beginning of the word. Miss Newton is assessing:
   A. understanding of the alphabetic principle.
   B. ability to decode words.
   C. discrimination between onsets and rimes.
   D. sight vocabulary.

10. When Mrs. Rose shares big books with her pre-kindergarten students, she points to the words as she reads the story. Mrs. Rose is primarily teaching her students:
   A. sound–symbol relationships.
   B. the directionality of print.
   C. word boundaries.
   D. orthography.

TEST YOURSELF ANSWERS AND RATIONALES FOR LANGUAGE ARTS/READING

Answer 1: *Phonemic awareness* is the ability to recognize that spoken words are made up of a sequence of individual sounds that contributes to the young reader's ability to recognize and pronounce unknown words (Rubin, 2000). The National Reading Panel (2000) has indicated that phonemic awareness instruction is an essential instructional tool in helping the young reader to learn to independently pronounce words. Choice

B is correct because the reader was able to pronounce the individual sounds, or phonemes, in segments in the word *fish.* The answer is *B.*

Answer 2: The young child was able to say the word after her teacher slowly pronounced (or blended) the individual sounds, or phonemes, in the word. The correct answer is *C.*

Answer 3: Choice *A* does not necessarily provide a reason for why certain edits were made. Choice *B* could be fun but does not provide instruction. Choice *D* does not indicate how these words would be used in the instructional sequence of the writing process. Choice *C* is correct because it would provide information and structured application/structured practice for the students to see various ways of using the conventions. The correct answer is *C.*

Answer 4: We should immediately rule out Choice *D*. Even though giving students something to talk about that they enjoy encourages talking, standing in front of the class would be ineffective and stressful for these children. Choices *B* and *C* would encourage the students to talk to other classmates but not necessarily to speak out in a whole class format. Choice *A* considers using instructional topics that are of interest to the students and builds small successes that can grow into greater ones. Eventually, the students may become comfortable enough to participate in a whole-class setting. The correct answer is *A.*

Answer 5: The question stem indicates that the student can read "most of the words" in the textbook. This would indicate that the student is using sight words because most of the words are recognized without additional analysis. Choice *C* is the correct answer because the student is recognizing almost all of the words instantly. The answer is *C.*

Answer 6: A summary paragraph is an accurate restatement of the main ideas and supporting details. The summary paragraph omits unimportant details. If the summary paragraph is a part of a student's composition, the main idea should be written in the student's *own words.* The correct answer is *C.*

Answer 7: Choices *A, B,* and *C* are effective instructional activities. However, the question stem addresses the development of sequencing skills. The teacher could *best* achieve the development of sequencing skills by using an advanced organizer, such as a sequencing chart or story board, to be sure that they visually see the sequence of each main event. The answer is *D.*

Answer 8: Rhyming words share the same ending sound. By inviting students to provide the missing word in a phrase or sentence, Ms. Jackson is focusing on the ending part or rime of the word. Words with the same rime (or ending sound), rhyme. The correct answer is *B*.

Answer 9: The ability to *decode words* (*B*) and being able to discriminate between *onsets* and *rimes* (*C*) are skills that depend on knowledge of the alphabetic principle. *Sight vocabulary* (*D*) consists of words that children must learn to recognize without decoding strategies because they are irregular. The students in this scenario are learning that the printed symbol (grapheme) represents a sound (phoneme) (*A*). This is a very basic understanding in learning to read. The correct answer is *A*.

Answer 10: *Orthography* refers to correct spelling, so *D* would not be the best answer. *Sound-symbol relationships* (*A*) and *word boundaries* (*B*) may be taught using big books, but by tracking the print as she reads, Mrs. Rose is demonstrating the *direction* in which a text is read. Shared reading (using big books) enables the teacher to demonstrate one of the *conventions of print*—directionality. The correct answer is *B*.

3 Preparing to Teach Mathematics in Texas

Rena M. Shull
Rockhurst University

Norene Vail Lowery
University of Houston

Charles E. Lamb
Texas A&M University

This chapter presents three sections for test takers who will teach mathematics in EC-4 classrooms. The first section highlights the current emphases on the teaching and learning of mathematics. This overview describes the move from traditional mathematics teaching to elementary mathematics classrooms of today. The second section presents standards and competencies for the TExES with a brief elaboration. Sample question items that correspond to each area are given along with information for successful completion of the mathematics portion of the TExES Generalist exam. A snapshot teaching scenario follows this section with more practice questions and information addressing mathematics such as manipulatives, formulas, and other vital information for EC-4 mathematics. A glossary is found at the conclusion of the chapter with other helpful information and forms.

An Overview of Mathematics Today

The current vision of the EC-4 mathematics learning environment is probably not the same as most adults have experienced. Traditional classrooms normally adhered to curricular activities that were presented part-to-whole with emphasis on basic skills, memorization, textbook problems, and drill sheets, as students worked individually at their seats. Learning was teacher centered and teacher directed, and mathematical concepts were presented in a didactic manner. Having a correct answer was the single most way to have one's work evaluated, and assessment was separate from ongoing instruction. This description of a traditional classroom contradicts much of what cognitive research findings are discovering concerning human learning (Brooks & Brooks, 1993).

Reform efforts in mathematics education call for new ways of teaching and learning mathematics. The advances in cognitive psychology and the emergence of the constructivist approach to teaching and learning promote new methods of addressing mathematics in the classroom (Davis, Maher, & Noddings, 1990). Goals for mathematics education that affect curricular content, instructional strategies, the classroom learning environment, and the assessment of knowledge have been established by the National Council of Teachers of Mathematics (NCTM). Mathematics education should reflect these goals by helping students: (a) learn to value mathematics, (b) become confident in their own abilities, (c) become mathematical problem solvers, (d) learn to communicate mathematically, and (e) learn to reason mathematically (NCTM, 1989). The overall goal is to have students become mathematically literate.

National Standards (NCTM, 1989, 1991, 1995, 1998, 2000) for mathematics, the Texas Essential Knowledge and Skills (TEKS), and the Texas Assessment of Knowledge and Skills (TAKS) all promote *active* learning environments that are *learner centered*. Within this type of classroom, teachers seek to understand students' prior knowledge and connect it to current concepts. (Questioning strategies aim to develop higher-order thinking skills in children, and cognitive terminology such as classify, analyze, predict, create, and justify is used in learning interactions). While manipulatives are used to assist children in "seeing," "reflecting," and "thinking" to provide a concrete basis for those concepts that are abstract, learning centers are used to provide relevant, exploratory, and interactive contexts for learning mathematics both for individual students and small groups. Opportunities are created that address diversities in learning styles, gender, culture, multiple intelligences, and ability. Learners in these classrooms are not passive but *active* learners in all aspects.

Other strategies have changed as well. The incorporation of mathematical representations (models, tables, graphs, etc.) is promoted for children to develop better conceptual understanding of mathematical concepts. Elementary mathematics learning has moved beyond basic facts and procedures. The NCTM *Principles and Standards for School Mathematics* (2000) and the organization's Web site (www. nctm. org) provide teachers with developmentally appropriate, grade-level visions of teaching and learning mathematical content and process skills. Mathematics in today's classrooms should come alive through experiences that inform children of the value and utility of mathematics through historical aspects, present-day professions, and everyday living. The mathematical content and processes emphasize reasoning and authentic problem solving. Lessons connect mathematical ideas to other subject areas in *interdisciplinary* instruction and join together other mathematical concepts in *intradisciplinary* ways. Real-world contexts and applications also help children to value mathematics and see its relevance. Instruction should involve the use of a textbook as one of *many* resources, and children should utilize primary sources of data with manipulatives and physical materials. As technology advances, its uses in mathematics classes are also evolving. The use of calculators and computers support instruction. Assessment is not simply the end of the chapter test but is ongoing (formative) and interwoven with teaching by placing a focus on learning *processes*. Alternative forms of assessment (e.g., observations, checklists, interviews, performance tasks, journals, and portfolios) are incorporated in the assessment process.

The picture of a perfect twenty-first century mathematics classroom continues. A traditional teaching approach with rows of desks and individual seatwork gives way to an active mathematical learning environment with small groups of students problem-solving collaboratively. Children are encouraged to talk about mathematics as they work cooperatively to solve problems. Children become motivated to learn and discuss mathematics (both the content and processes) in an interactive, hands-on, minds-on approach. Reasoning and communicating are highly valued components in this classroom, and the classroom is a safe learning environment that is an active community of problem solvers (including the teacher as a co-learner and investigator). This creates a new role for the teacher as facilitator to children who are also in the process of constructing their own knowledge.

Introduction to the Mathematics Standards

There are eight elementary mathematics standards and four competencies. Within each of these is embedded the vision for improving teaching and learning mathematics. Each standard is designed and correlated with the TEKS (Texas Essential Knowledge and Skills) and the TAKS (Texas Assessment of Knowledge and Skills) that tests students on the TEKS. The first part of this section presents the Texas Education Commissioner's guidelines for pre-kindergarten curriculum; the second part presents the introductory information from the TEKS for the early childhood grades. At the time of this publication there were no state-*required* pre-kindergarten curriculum. None the less, EC-4 teachers are responsible for Pre-K children. The third part of this section presents the mathematics standards and competencies with sample questions and discussion.

Pre-Kindergarten Curriculum Guidelines

Mathematics learning builds on children's curiosity and enthusiasm and challenges children to explore ideas about patterns and relationships, order and predictability, and logic and meaning. Consequently, quality instruction occurs in environments that are rich in language, encourage children's thinking, and nurture children's explorations and ideas. These ideas include the concepts of number pattern, measurement, shape, space, and classification.

1. **Number and Operations:** Understanding the concept of "number" is fundamental to mathematics. Children come to school with rich and varied informal knowledge of number. A major goal is to build on this informal

base toward more thorough understanding and skills. Children move from beginning to develop basic counting techniques in pre-kindergarten to later understanding number size, relationships, and operations.

The child:

- arranges sets of concrete objects in one-to-one correspondence;
- counts by ones to ten or higher;
- counts concrete objects to five or higher;
- begins to compare the numbers of concrete objects using language (e.g., *same* or *equal, one more, more than,* or *less than*);
- begins to name *how many* are in a group of up to three (or more) objects without counting (e.g., recognizing two or three crayons in a box);
- recognizes and describes the concept of zero (meaning there are none);
- begins to demonstrate part of and whole with real objects (e.g., an orange, chocolate bar, etc.);
- begins to identify first and last in a series; and
- combines, separates, and names "how many" concrete objects.

2. **Patterns:** Recognizing patterns and relationships among objects is an important component in children's intellectual development. Children learn to organize their world by recognizing patterns and gradually begin to use patterns as a strategy for problem solving, forming generalizations, and developing the concepts of number, operation, shape, and space. *Pattern recognition is the first step in the development of algebraic thinking.*

The child:

- imitates pattern sounds and physical movements (e.g., clap, stomp, clap, stomp, . . .);
- recognizes and reproduces simple patterns of concrete objects (e.g., a string of beads that are yellow, blue, blue, yellow,);
- begins to recognize patterns in their environment (e.g., day follows night, repeated phrases in storybooks, patterns in carpeting or clothing); and
- begins to predict what comes next when patterns are extended.

3. **Geometry and Spatial Sense:** Geometry helps children systematically represent and describe their world. Children learn to name and recognize the properties of various shapes and figures, use words that indicate direction, and use spatial reasoning to analyze and solve problems.

The child:

- begins to recognize, describe, and name shapes (e.g., circles, triangles, rectangles—including squares);
- begins to use words that indicate where things are in space (e.g., *beside, inside, behind, above, below*);
- begins to recognize when a shape's position or orientation has changed;
- begins to investigate and predict the results of putting together two or more shapes; and
- puts together puzzles of increasing complexity.

4. **Measurement:** Measurement is one of the most widely used applications of mathematics. Early learning experiences with measurement should focus on *direct comparisons* of objects. Children make decisions about size by looking, touching, and comparing objects directly while building language to express the size relationships.

The child:

- covers an area with shapes (e.g., tiles);
- fills a shape with solids or liquids (e.g., ice cubes, water);

- begins to make size comparisons between objects (e.g., *taller than, smaller than*);
- begins to use tools to imitate measuring;
- begins to categorize time intervals and uses language associated with time in everyday situations (e.g., *in the morning, after snack*); and
- begins to order two or three objects by size (seriation) (e.g., largest to smallest).

5. **Classification and Data Collection:** Children use sorting to organize their world. As children recognize similarities and differences, they begin to recognize patterns that lead them to form generalizations. As they begin to use language to describe similarities and differences, they begin sharing their ideas and their mathematical thinking. Children can be actively involved in collecting, sorting, organizing, and communicating information.

The child:

- matches objects that are alike;
- describes similarities and differences between objects;
- sorts objects into groups by an attribute and begins to explain how the grouping was done; and
- participates in creating and using real and pictorial graphs.

Mathematics Manipulatives

GUIDELINES FOR CHILDREN USING MANIPULATIVES IN THE TEACHING AND LEARNING OF MATHEMATICS. Active, "hands-on, minds-on" learning involves the use of manipulatives. Manipulatives provide a concrete basis for understanding abstract concepts and are very effective teaching tools for all students. Most educators support the use of manipulatives to help students' conceptual understanding by aiding better internalization and visualization of concepts and ideas. The guidelines below offer some suggestions for management of materials appropriate for all levels of learning and interactions.

- Free time for exploration is necessary whenever a new material or manipulative is introduced. This is also appropriate for learning centers, as well as several moments prior to beginning a lesson.
- Arrange and prepare the materials beforehand according to the purpose of the lesson.
- Clear expectations must be provided for lesson goals and the use of materials.
- Specific directions concerning the purposes in using the manipulatives are imperative. Teachers and students must understand the purpose of the materials related to the lesson in order to make the connections from models to an internalized idea.
- Explicit guidelines must be established for what is acceptable and not acceptable behavior for using manipulatives.
- Teachers should model the use of materials and "think aloud" about what they represent.

RECOMMENDED MINIMUM MANIPULATIVE MATERIALS.

Kindergarten (Early Childhood)

Interlocking counting cubes (1,000)
Attribute blocks (four sets—60 each)

Pattern blocks (four sets—250 each with two mirrors)
Buttons, shells, keys, and other familiar objects for counting/sorting
Measuring instruments for time (demonstration clock)
Play money

Grade 1

Interlocking counting cubes (1,000)
Attribute blocks (four sets—60 each)
Pattern blocks (four sets—250 each with two mirrors)
Measuring instruments (to measure length, volume, mass, temperature, and time)
Play money

Grade 2

Interlocking counting cubes (1,000)
Base ten blocks (ones, tens, and hundreds for each child)
Attribute blocks (four sets—60 each)
Pattern blocks (four sets—250 each with two mirrors)
Measuring instruments, both metric and customary (to measure length, volume, mass, temperature, and time)
Play money
Two- and three-dimensional geometric models (two sets of common shapes and solids)

Grade 3

Interlocking counting cubes (1,000)
Base ten blocks (ones, tens, and hundreds for each child, one thousand block for each four children)
Pattern blocks (four sets—250 each with two mirrors)
Fraction models—circles, squares, bars, and/or rods
Measuring instruments, both metric and customary (to measure length, volume, mass, temperature, and time)
Play money
Two- and three-dimensional geometric models (two sets of common shapes and solids)

Grade 4

Base ten blocks or other place value models (ones, tens, and hundreds for each child, one thousand block for each four children)
Decimal models
Fraction models—circles, squares, bars, and/or rods
Measuring instruments, both metric and customary (to measure length, volume, mass, temperature)
Interlocking centimeter cubes (2,000)
Tangrams—one per child
Two- and three-dimensional geometric models (two sets of common shapes and solids)
Geoboards—one per child and one for teacher demonstration

TEKS for Pre-K–4

An understanding of the expectations for student achievement, as given by the Texas Education Agency (TEA), helps readers to approach the TExES in a competent and confident manner, ready to teach young children. For all grades Pre-K through 4, the introduction to the TEKS expectations in achieving mathematical learning states:

> *Problem solving, language and communication, connections within and outside mathematics, and formal and informal reasoning underlie all content areas in mathematics and that students use these processes together with technology and other mathematical tools such as manipulative materials to develop conceptual understanding and solve problems as they do mathematics. (TEA, 1997, p. A-1)*

> *Throughout mathematics in grades kindergarten through 2 students build a foundation of basic understanding in number, operation, and quantitative reasoning: patterns, relationships, and algebraic thinking; geometry and spatial reasoning; and measurement and probability and statistics. Students use numbers in ordering, labeling, and expressing quantities and relationships to solve problems and translate informal language into mathematical symbols. Students use patterns to describe objects, express relationships, make predictions, and solve problems as they build an understanding of number, operation, shape, and space. Students use informal language and observation of geometric properties to describe shapes, solids, and locations in the physical world and begin to develop measurement concepts as they identify and compare attributes of objects and situations. Students collect, organize, and display data and use information from graphs to answer questions, make summary statements, and make informal predictions based on their experiences. (TEA, 1997, p. A-1)*

> *Throughout mathematics in grades 3 through 5 students build a foundation of basic understandings in number, operation, and quantitative reasoning: patterns, relationships, and algebraic thinking; geometry and spatial reasoning; measurement; and probability and statistics. Students use algorithms for addition, subtraction, multiplication, and division as generalizations connected to concrete experiences; and they concretely develop basic concepts of fractions and decimals. Students use appropriate language and organizational structures such as tables and charts to represent and communicate relationships, make predictions, and solve problems. Students select and use formal language to describe their reasoning as they identify, compare, and classify shapes and solids; and they use numbers, standard units, and measurement tools to describe and compare objects, make estimates, and solve application problems. Students organize data, choose an appropriate method to display the data and interpret the data to make decisions and predictions and solve problems. (TEA, 1997, p. A-13)*

The curriculum and the learning expectations are presented in a spiraling effect. This means that each previous year provides a foundational basis for further concept development and elaboration for the following year.

Mathematics Standards and Sample Questions with Discussions

The standards (and competencies to which they relate) are initially stated with a brief elaboration that enhances the view of the role of the EC-4 teacher. Following each are sample questions for readers. Each section gives further discussion in the light of current relevant literature and research. Because some areas of the standards and competencies are very broad, the sample items attempt to capture the essence of the standard to its broadest scope and to assess the most important aspects of each standard.

Standards I Number Concepts, VII Mathematical Learning and Instruction, and VIII Assessment

The mathematics teacher understands and uses numbers, number systems, and their structure, operations and algorithms, quantitative reasoning, and technology appropriate to teach the statewide curriculum (Texas Essential Knowledge and Skills [TEKS]) in order to prepare students to use mathematics (Standard I). The mathematics teacher understands how children learn and develop mathematical skills, procedures, and concepts; knows typical errors students make, and uses this knowledge to plan, organize, and implement instruction; to meet curriculum goals; and to teach all students to understand and use mathematics (Standard VII). The mathematics teacher understands assessment and uses a variety of formal and informal assessment techniques appropriate to the learner on an ongoing basis to monitor and guide instruction and to evaluate and report student progress (Standard VIII).

Competency 012 (Mathematics Instruction): The teacher understands how children learn mathematical skills and uses this knowledge to plan, organize, and implement instruction and assess learning.

The EC-4 teacher plans appropriate activities for all children based on research and principles of learning mathematics. Instructional strategies that build on the linguistic, cultural, and socioeconomic diversity of children and that relate to children's lives and communities are employed. Developmentally appropriate instruction along a continuum from concrete to abstract and instruction that builds on strengths that address needs of the child is provided by the teacher. The teacher knows how mathematical learning may be assisted through the appropriate use of manipulatives and technological tools. It is important to motivate children and actively engage them in the learning process by using a variety of interesting, challenging, and worthwhile mathematical tasks and by providing instruction in individual, small-group, and large-group settings. Mathematics instruction uses a variety of tools (e.g., counters, standard and nonstandard units of measure, rulers, protractors, scales, stopwatches, measuring containers, money, calculators, software) to strengthen children's mathematical understanding. Appropriate learning goals based on the Texas Essential Knowledge and Skills (TEKS) in mathematics are developed while using these learning goals as a basis for instruction. The teacher helps children make connections between mathematics, the real world, and other disciplines. Various questioning strategies encourage mathematical discourse and help children analyze and evaluate their mathematical thinking. The teacher uses a variety of formal and informal assessments and scoring procedures to evaluate mathematical understanding, common misconceptions, and error patterns. It is important that the teacher understands the reciprocal nature of assessment and instruction and knows how to use assessment results to design, monitor, and modify instruction to improve mathematical learning for individual children, including English Language Learners. The teacher understands how mathematics is used in a variety of careers and professions and plans instruction that demonstrates how mathematics is used in the workplace.

Consider the following question:

Mrs. Jones was teaching her Pre-K class about volume, but she could not get students to understand that the amount of liquid in a cup was the same amount as when she poured the liquid into a flat bowl. What was happening? Select the *best* answer.

    A. The children are in the preoperational stage and do not have the ability to conserve yet.
    B. The children are in the preoperational stage and do not have the ability to transform yet.
    C. The children are in the preoperational stage and do not have the ability to classify yet.
    D. The children are in the preoperational stage and do not have the ability to seriate yet.

It is true that children are normally in the preoperational stage at this age. *Transformation* (*B*) refers to the ability to record a process of change. Even though children see a transformation occur (such as a line of coins, where the teacher moves or lengthens the row but does not add to the number of coins), they are unable to understand. The preoperational child will say that the lengthened row is a different row now rather than one that has been changed or transformed.

Reversibility refers to the inability to mentally cancel a change. Children at this age also experience this inability. *Seriation* refers to the ability to order things in a series according to increase or decrease in length, weight, or volume, so this would not be the right answer. This ability usually appears in the concrete operational level (7–11 years).

Classification is the ability to group on the basis of common characteristics or attributes. This allows a child to master ordering more than one object (A < B < C). This also appears at this age (7 to 11 years), although children in prekindergarten and kindergarten can form simple groups, usually on the basis of one attribute.

The *best* answer, however, would be *A*. Children below the approximate age of 7 in the preoperational stages do not have the ability to *conserve,* or see that the amount of something stays the same regardless of its shape or container (a clay ball flattened into a pancake). The lack of the ability to conserve also makes it difficult for young children to see that the amount of something is the same no matter the number of pieces into which it is divided (a candy bar divided into halves). The more that children work with materials such as water, sand, clay, rice, beans, paints, etc., the more they will understand conservation, reversibility, more/less, bigger/smaller, and the structures and meaning of numbers. The correct answer is *A*.

Teachers of young children must have a thorough understanding of intellectual growth expectations. Piaget believed that cognitive growth occurs as a progressive construction of logical structures that are constantly being modified and combined into more powerful logical structures. To the teacher this means that each and every child in that classroom is on an individually developing continuum. As children interact with their environment, they create internal representations that work to accommodate new experiences. It is the role of the teacher to plan and teach learning experiences that are appropriate for the developing stages of children. By observing and talking with children, teachers are better able to plan appropriate mathematical tasks that encourage progression along this developing continuum for individuals.

A brief review of Piaget's stages of cognitive development will help teachers understand mathematics educational theory for young children much more clearly. In the *Sensorimotor stage* (birth to age 2), children are egocentric and not aware of things outside their immediate environment. Learning involves pulling, pushing, turning, twisting, rolling, poking, and interacting with many different properties of objects. Children at this level require a rich environment with many stimuli. In the *Preoperational stage* (ages 2–6) children realize that objects exist outside the immediate environment. Learning involves discovering distinct properties and functions of objects as they compare, sort, stack, roll, distinguish triangles from squares, and begin to use some beginning abstractions to communicate (*That is a red square; The cat is under the table,* etc.). The ability to conserve often (but not always) begins toward the closing of this stage as students engage in a number of "dump-and-fill" play activities. These include exploration of space (going under chairs, into cabinets, etc.) and emptying and filling materials from areas such as cabinets and boxes. Children at this level should interact with a wide variety of objects, items, and materials (buckets, shovels, funnels, sand, water, etc.) to practice describing sorting, reversibility, and finding patterns based on attributes. During the *Concrete Operational stage* (ages 6–12), children complete the ability to conserve, begin to use symbols, and to classify with multiple attributes. They require experiences with touching, smelling, seeing, hearing, and performing. They begin to label and use symbols to describe and communicate as a form of internal representation. They must use hands-on tools to investigate. Children are progressing to abstraction, although moving to the *Formal Operational stage* (ages 12 and over) is *not* a guaranteed progression by a specific age (*as is the case in any of Piaget's stages*). The use of symbols and logical systems to build new knowledge is required. At this upper level children can interpret ideas, think independently, and combine new abstractions to create new ideas. Piaget suggests that there are four broad factors that are necessary and that affect the progression through these stages of cognitive development. They are (1) maturation, (2) physical experience, (3) social interaction, and (4) equilibration. Clearly, learning experiences for children through the age of 12 must involve objects, tools, interaction, reflection, and social interaction with materials for optimal cognitive growth. The EC-4 teacher knows that children best learn mathematical concepts by manipulating materials to observe what happens—individually and collaboratively. A key to EC-4 mathematics is planning *concrete* experiences that facilitate learning. A sound mathematics classroom learning environment and curriculum reflect this cognitive approach to learning.

Table 3.1   Common Mathematics Manipulatives

Name	Description	Concept Usage
Attribute blocks	color, shape, size, and thickness; five shapes, three colors—yellow-red-blue, large and small in size	classification, grouping, prenumber activities, symmetry, measurement, problem solving
Base ten blocks	wooden/plastic pregrouped/ trading models	help to create mental images and understandings of place value, operations, geometry, measurement
Calculators		problem solving, checking solutions, place value, number magnitude
Chips, trading	colored chips with assigned values two-sided, colored	place value for regrouping in carrying and renaming, fractions, number sense for decimals and operations, links blocks to algorithms
Counters/Tiles	many varieties such as plastic bears, frogs, chips, beans	prenumber activities, number sense, numeration

(continued)

Table 3.1   Continued

Cubes		
• Unifix	one side connects	can be used to develop one-to-one
• Multilink	all sides connect	correspondence, counting, sorting, basic
• Wooden	do not link	operations, geometry, spatial sense, algebra groupable place value
Cuisenaire rods	colored and length determine value	fractions, basic operations, logic, problem solving, area, perimeter, and more
Geoboards	square board with pegs— rubber bands used	area, logical thinking, number concepts, geometric figures, shapes, angles
Miras	reflective surfaces	symmetry, rotation, flips, and more
Paper folding	any area of paper	fractions, symmetry, recognizing polygons, and more
Pattern blocks	many shapes and colors—squares, triangles, rectangles, trapezoids, rhombuses, hexagons	fraction concepts, counting, sorting, matching, logical thinking, problem solving, symmetry

Consider the following question:

Ms. Mehrman wishes to foster critical thinking skills in her first-grade students. Using overhead attribute blocks, Ms. Mehrman places an attribute block on the overhead and has her students identify the four attributes (size, shape, color, thickness) of the block. She then asks the students to select a block that is "one different" from the beginning block (that is, it has only one attribute different from the original one). She places the new block next to the first one and begins to form a "train." The class identifies the four attributes of this new block and justifies that it is "one different" from the first block. The students are now asked to find a block that is one different from this second block, and the process continues. This activity would be most appropriate for developing students' understanding that:

A. there can be more than one answer to a question.
B. it is necessary to recognize the four attributes of each block.
C. the size of the attribute blocks may be large or small.
D. the thickness of the block is very important.

Students need to identify the attribute, but this activity requires a deeper level of understanding that fosters the development of critical thinking skills. Size is only *one* of the attributes. Thickness is only *one* of the attributes. Therefore, if Mrs. Mehrman puts up a large red block, students could select "one away" that was a blue, yellow, smaller, thicker, etc., block. The correct response is *A*. This activity will help students understand that there can be many correct answers to a question. This question requires children to engage in higher-order thinking. Too often, children think that there is only one right answer. This activity requires children to characterize each attribute block and consider which attribute block has only one attribute "different" from the block just played. There are many "correct" answers from which to choose. The correct answer is *A*.

Asking good questions is imperative for the teaching and learning of mathematics. Questions should pose thoughtful responses and reflection. Those types of questions move children from the knowledge and comprehension levels of Bloom's taxonomy upward to application, analysis, synthesis, and evaluation. Children should develop thinking that enhances their abilities to analyze, solve, and expand upon problem situations. Learning explorations and environments should provide many opportunities for learners to be safely challenged. In mathematics, "there should be explorations that have no answers, no precise answers, or that have many answers" (Troutman & Lichtenberg, 1999, p. 386). Timing is also a factor in better questioning. Asking thought-provoking questions, using appropriate wait time that promotes children's reflective thought, and asking children to elaborate and justify their responses helps encourage higher-order thinking.

Answering questions is not enough. It is through *communication* that mathematical ideas are organized, extended, clarified, and realized. Teachers should guide children in learning how to talk about mathematics in the classroom, and children should become comfortable and competent in expressing their mathematical ideas. Cobb and Lambert (1998) tell us that "Students who are involved in active discussions in which they justify solutions—especially in the face of disagreement—will gain better mathematical understanding" (p. 85). Thus it is through interaction that children begin to express ideas to peers, teachers, and others and learn to contemplate their own and others' responses. This can only occur in a risk-free learning environment where a teacher builds a sense of community through careful and reflective planning, questioning, and listening. Communicating mathematically also allows teachers to informally and formally assess understanding and progress. As children communicate mathematically, they better understand and self-assess their own abilities. They are able to hear explanations from other children on their own level that can enhance a teacher's explanation.

Consider the following question:

Ms. Ismail asks her fourth-grade students to discuss and then package color tiles into individual bags. There are 420 color tiles in the class set and 24 students in her class. How many color tiles will be in each student's bag? How many are left over? The students decide to divide 420 by 24 and get an answer of 17.5. They are not sure what the answer means. The *best* response for Ms. Ismail would be to:

A. have students recheck their answers.
B. ask students to discuss why they divided and what 17.5 means to this answer.
C. cut some color tiles in half.
D. ask students to round their answers.

Having students recheck their computations (Choice *A*) could improve computational accuracy but would not foster higher-order thinking. Having students use concrete objects to replicate the problem (*C*) might cause a deeper understanding, but without the teacher guiding the activity, students might not connect. Rounding the answer (*D*) has no application to this question. The teacher is asking students to assess their understanding of division and what the remainder means. She is encouraging students not just to give a set answer but to continue to question what the answer might mean to a real-life problem when something cannot be divided. The *best* response is *B*. Situations such as this one are important to address in the classroom. This provides the teacher with opportunities to informally assess the understanding of mathematical learning by allowing children to talk through their understanding. Children need activities that challenge their thinking and afford them experiences that help them to make sense of the mathematics that they are learning. The answer is *B*.

Table 3.2   Mathematics in Learning Centers

Center or Play Area	Mathematics Concepts	Manipulatives/Representations
Games, puzzles, and regular daily items	Grouping, counting, matching, patterning, ordering	Classification, numeral identification, logic, geometric forms
Housekeeping/Kitchens	Counting, measuring, one-to-one correspondence, estimation	Play money, numerals, labels
Water play/Sand table	Measuring, counting, conservation, estimation, positioning	Can draw numerals in sand, use measuring tools
Music/Puppets	Counting, one-to-one correspondence, patterning, classification	Create patterns with music, role play
Painting	Grouping, measuring, patterning, classification	Numeral writing, geometric designs
Woodworking	Measuring, counting, patterning, comparing size and shape, classification	Numeral writing, geometric designs, patterns
Block building	Counting, comparing size, one-to-one correspondence, classification, patterning, geometric shapes, positioning, estimation	Blocks as symbols, labels, can be used as many different representations

As with the vision of teaching and learning mathematics in today's classroom, assessment is also changing. Strict use of pencil-and-paper testing is no longer sufficient for mathematics. A variety of approaches to assessment are being implemented in the classroom setting, particularly alternative forms that provide a more complete and thorough picture of a child's level of mathematical understanding. Because children enter school with different levels of understanding and experiences with mathematics, assessment should be used to adapt instruction to children's needs. Interviews, checklists, and observations are more appropriate for assessing very young children. Writing and drawing in mathematics journals provides children with time for reflecting on the mathematics that they are learning and provides teachers with insight into children's thinking. *Performance tasks* that challenge children to perform or to apply their learning to new situations or events are used to reveal how children are learning and applying that learning to become successful problem solvers.

It is important to remember in assessment that, in early childhood classrooms, children may often have difficulty manipulating objects physically (the use of fine and gross motor skills). For example, a teacher may believe that a child really does understand a particular mathematics concept, yet an assigned task (e.g., cutting and pasting paper objects) is incorrectly completed. The EC-4 teacher must be aware that younger children cannot physically do some types of tasks easily, yet they can understand the concept. Knowing about the mental/physical gap helps a teacher to better assess the child's true understanding by using an informal approach to assessment (such as questioning or interviewing) rather than always relying on a set product. Mrs. Kay, for example, sits with her individual children at times and says, "Okay, I'm going to be the one with the pencil this time and you are going to tell me what to do." At other times, she asks partners to show each other how to work problems as she watches (Ashlock, 1990). Encouraging many forms of representations that reveal children's understanding of mathematics is important. Checklists, open-ended question responses, the use of rubrics, portfolios, student self-assessment, peer evaluation, and, as mentioned earlier, interviews and observations should all be a part of mathematics assessment.

Observation of children's learning mathematics informally provides teachers with unforeseen opportunities (teachable moments) to engage in questioning and probing into the child's thinking. These offer opportunities for meaningful learning. Teachers should not limit assessment to determining children's computation abilities or problem-solving skills. Teachers must also assess the child's attitude and mathematical thinking as applied to everyday problems. Much research has shown that attitudes and anxiety play a part in success. This seems to be more true for mathematics than many other subjects. Games that identify the strongest and weakest math students, for example, should be avoided with young children who are beginning to learn. Mathematics teaching, learning, *and* assessment must be inclusive of children of diversity, poverty, boys and girls, and those with special needs. For example, the female early childhood student must be observed in the Block Center as much as the family center. The most important type of assessment to determine and diagnose error patterns is to challenge the child to do a problem and observe the problem-solving strategies used by the child in working out a solution.

Consider the following question:

Ms. Baumbach is working with the entire first-grade class. She says, "I have put some pennies, nickels, and dimes in my pocket." She places her hand in her pocket. "I have put three of these coins in my hand. How much money do you think I have in my hand?" Many children are confused and begin voicing guesses. In order to facilitate problem solving in this situation, the teacher should *not*:

A. suggest an approach using trial and error.
B. suggest an approach that uses real coins.
C. allow students to verify their guesses.
D. ask an individual to come to the board and show how she got the answer.

The teacher wants her students to develop problem-solving skills. Trial and error (A) allows students to explore different possible solutions. These explorations foster development and logical reasoning and applying this reasoning to real-life situations. Using real coins (B) helps students to connect the problem to the real world. Students value money and want to become accurate when dealing with money. The use of actual coins makes the problem more pertinent to their everyday lives. Students need to verify their guesses (C), and this problem helps them develop understanding of the possible answers. This problem should help students realize that there are many possible and correct responses. Students need to develop several strategies to become good problem solvers, and A, B, and C are all positive ways to help children.

Teachers should always realize that when one child is working at the board, the remainder of the class is not. Because the question asks that we identify something that would *not* be helpful, the answer is D.

Along with more realistic or authentic lessons, another area of major importance in mathematics is problem solving.

Problem-solving means engaging in a task for which the solution method is not known in advance . . . problem-solving is an integral part of all mathematics learning, not an isolated part of the mathematics program. Students should have frequent opportunities to formulate, grapple with, solve complex problems that require a significant amount of effort. (NCTM, 1998, p. 76)

Teachers should carefully and reflectively select and plan learning experiences that are relevant and grade appropriate. Relevant problems are created that focus and motivate children to want to solve a problem because they can see a need or interest in their own lives and believe that they have or can acquire the skills to solve it. Young children should be introduced to problem solving in play. Ms. Clemens, for example, notices Shak and Brandy playing in the sandbox with cars. "Hm-m-m," she says. "It looks like it might be difficult to drive over to this side because your car might get stuck in the 'river.' What could you do? That's right! You could build a bridge. Which block shape would make the best bridge?" Teachers select grade-appropriate problem-solving challenges through the expectations of the TEKS. NCTM (1989) notes the importance of problem solving in mathematics by stating that it "should be the central focus of the mathematics curriculum. As such, it is a primary goal of all mathematics instruction and an integral part of all mathematical activity" (p. 23). However, problem solving is *not* just the traditional "story or word" problems at the end of the chapter in the textbook. Problem solving is a designated *process standard* (NCTM, 2000). Process standards are specific skills and strategies that are used to acquire and use mathematics content knowledge. Problem solving, therefore, is not a separate entity but is viewed as both a *skill* and an *attitude* that infiltrates the mathematics learning environment. Teachers who encourage their students to solve problems, who offer opportunities to apply strategies, who make students think, and who ask carefully worded questions (rather than simple recall questions) will provide their students with a rich problem-solving experience.

The NCTM Standards (1989) recommend that students develop and apply a variety of strategies to solve multistep and nonroutine problems. These strategies should include situations in which students "model situations using verbal, written, concrete, pictorial, graphical, and algebraic methods, reflecting on and clarifying their own thinking about mathematical ideas" (NCTM, 1989, p. 78). Additional recommendations include learning experiences that emphasize deductive and inductive reasoning methods, real-world relevancy, and the use of patterns and relationships to recognize, describe, analyze, and extend mathematical situations (NCTM, 1989). Strategies such as drawing a picture, looking for a pattern, systematically guessing and checking (trial and error), acting problems out, etc., must be taught so that children will be able to apply them independently.

It is the teacher who determines the learning environment in a mathematics classroom. This section reminds us that it is the role of the teacher to be the facilitator and a resource person and to provide opportunities to solve relevant problems through meaningful, concrete exploration. Teachers must always encourage children to gain new strategies in order to problem solve.

Standards I Number Concepts and II Patterns and Algebra

Standard I also overlaps with the competency below. The mathematics teacher understands and uses numbers, number systems and their structure, operations and algorithms, quantitative reasoning, and technology appropriate to teach the statewide curriculum (Texas Essential Knowledge and Skills [TEKS]). The mathematics teacher understands and uses patterns, relations, functions, algebraic reasoning, analysis, and technology appropriate to teach the statewide curriculum in order to prepare students to use mathematics (Standard II).

Competency 013 (Number Concepts, Patterns, and Algebra): The teacher understands concepts related to numbers and number systems and demonstrates knowledge of patterns, relations, functions, and algebraic reasoning.

The EC-4 teacher analyzes, explains, and describes number concepts (e.g., odd, even, prime), operations and algorithms, the properties of numbers, and models the four basic operations with whole numbers, integers, and rational numbers. Numbers are used to describe and quantify phenomena such as time, temperature, and money. The teacher applies knowledge of place value and other number properties to perform mental mathematics and computational estimation. The teacher illustrates relations and functions using concrete models, tables, graphs, and symbolic expressions. An understanding of how to use algebraic concepts and reasoning to investigate patterns, make generalizations, formulate mathematical models, make predictions, and validate results should be taught to students at this level. The EC-4 teacher knows how to identify, extend, and create patterns using concrete models, figures, numbers, and algebraic expressions and uses properties, graphs, and applications of relations and functions to analyze, model, and solve problems in mathematical and real-world situations. The teacher is able to translate problem-solving situations into expressions and equations involving variables and unknowns, and she or he models and solves problems with students, including proportion problems, using concrete, numeric, tabular, graphic, and algebraic methods.

Consider the following question:

Ms. Bell's first-grade class has surveyed the students at Washington Elementary School about their favorite soft drink from a list of Pepsi, Coke, Mountain Dew, and Sprite. A total of 42 students participated in the survey. Which would be the most appropriate graph to use to display this data?

A. A bar graph
B. A line graph
C. A circle graph
D. A pictograph

A line graph (*B*) is used to represent continuous data points. However, this problem deals with discrete and separate objects that have no connection. Each drink is a separate item that is not related or connected to any other drink. A circle graph (*C*) involves the understanding and application of degrees, ratios, and the use of protractors. These topics are covered in subsequent grade levels. Pictographs (*D*) are introduced later as another way to represent data. Students are then developmentally ready to code the data. Bar graphs (*A*) are appropriate for primary grades. (As an aside, when students are engaging with these types of activities, the teacher must include possible rationales for them [other than "isn't this fun to know" or "isn't this a fun activity?"] For example, fast-food restaurants clearly would be able to use this type of data to match customer preference; the school carnival committee could use this to provide drinks that people prefer; and so forth.) The correct response is *A*.

Students should develop organizational skills needed to properly handle larger quantities of data. Choosing an appropriate graphical representation is a fundamental requirement needed to present data in an accurate manner. Not only is it imperative for the teacher to model mathematical terminology, symbols, and communication, it is necessary for the teacher to provide active opportunities for children to do so.

Consider the following question:

Mr. Batiste distributes color tiles to each student in his kindergarten class. He asks the students to sort the tiles by color. Mr. Batiste sorts his set of color tiles on the overhead. When the students have completed the task, Mr. Batiste asks kindergartners to describe the data. Which of the following is the *best* description of Mr. Batiste's teaching objective?

    A. He wants to assess his students' knowledge of color.
    B. He wants to assess his students' ability to classify the color tiles.
    C. He wants his students to be able to discuss and explain the results of the sorting.
    D. He wants his students to work independently.

Color recognition is an important concept for kindergarten students to learn (*A*). However, it is not the *best* response. Sorting by color (*B*) is an important process for kindergarten students to learn. The ability to work alone is an important learning activity (*D*). However, this answer is also not the *best* answer. The *best* response is *C*. Mr. Batiste is encouraging his students to develop and use accurate mathematics vocabulary to synthesize the results of their sorting activity.

Let's try another question:

Ms. Ketkar has been working with her fourth-grade class on ordering decimals. To help students develop an understanding of the "size" of decimal values and to better help them "see" the decimals, Ms. Ketkar should use which of the following representations?

    A. An egg carton
    B. Cuisenaire rods
    C. Dot paper
    D. Centimeter grid paper

An egg carton (*A*) has 12 sections and would not be appropriate for fostering the development of the understanding of decimals that are based on powers of 10. Cuisenaire rods (*B*) are generally used when comparing and relating lengths. They are often used with fractions, area, and perimeter. Dot paper (*C*) is often used to help students develop spatial abilities. It is useful when asking students to do pictorial presentations of a concrete shape. The centimeter grid paper is based on 100 units, 10 rows and 10 columns (*D*). It provides a visual means of developing decimal notations. The correct response is *D*.

The development of number and numeration concepts must include the understanding of numbers, ways of representing numbers, relationships among numbers, and number systems. The knowledge and skills associated with number and numeration concepts is necessary for all students. Without a strong foundation in these areas, children will not achieve success and thrive in everyday mathematical situations. Children learn names of numbers first before ever understanding that a number symbolizes an amount. After learning the names and order of numbers, young children move to understanding one-on-one correspondence by using every opportunity in the classroom to touch and count. Mr. Jenson lines up students to go to lunch by touching them and counting, "One, two, three . . . ." He also asks students to put away materials by counting, for example "One block, two blocks, . . ." as appropriate. Providing a visual picture of the size of a number enables students to have a concrete method to show representations. Children must also learn to recognize and form the shape of numbers, or to write the name of numbers. As discussed with distinguishing and writing letters in the previous chapter, children should be given tactile experiences such as touching sandpaper numbers, stamping numbers, forming numbers in sand, shaving cream, or with clay, and so forth, remembering that some children do not develop fine-motor skills with a pencil for some time. From this basis, children must have learning experiences that foster the development of the meaning of operations and how they relate to each other along with the use of computational tools, strategies, and estimation abilities.

Howden (1989) believes good intuition about numbers and their relationships (number sense) may be developed by children through carefully planned learning experiences. Teachers who encourage good number sense teach common sense about numbers. It is not assumed that some children are good at mathematics and that some are not but that *all* children are capable of learning mathematics. Number sense strategies are taught and enhanced through activities that are logical, relevant, and set in real-world contexts. Estimation skills, for example, help children think about the correctness of their mathematics. Children should constantly be challenged to think about numbers: "Does this answer make sense? If so, why?" "Is this amount larger or smaller? If so, why?" Good number sense provides a foundation for developing all other areas of mathematics.

"Some surveys of adults reveal that mental computation and estimation are used as opposed to traditional computation" in everyday living (Carlton, 1980; Fitzgerald, 1985). Also, as the use of technology as a mathematics tool advances, the importance of estimation as a basic skill is even more critical because users must have an idea if their technological computations are "in the ball park." In the real world, a bank teller (or customer) who uses a calculator to quickly add deposits of $525.00 and $280.00 should know to recheck the figures if the calculator answer displays an answer of $1,505.00. Children should be experienced with the use, development, and application of estimation skills. NCTM (1989) states:

. . . (students) should be able to decide when they need to calculate and whether they require an exact or approximate answer. They should be able to select and use the most appropriate tool. Students should have a balanced approach to calculation, be able to choose appropriate procedures, find answers, and judge the validity of those answers. (p. 8)

Try this question:

For her first lesson on estimation Ms. Babinoux filled a glass jar with huge candy balls. She told children that the person who came closest to guessing the correct amount in the jar would win a prize. Children were excited to guess. Some children guessed a thousand and some children guessed ten. The closest person guessed 100 (there were 90 in the jar). She awarded the prize and then moved to some problems on the board. This focus was:

A. appropriate because it was relevant in showing students the value of estimation.
B. appropriate because it motivated students to use mathematics to get the prize.
C. inappropriate because students used no estimation strategies, so their answers were just "shots in the dark."
D. inappropriate because it is not age-appropriate to ask children to estimate.

It is certainly appropriate to have children begin to think about the logic of their answers through estimation, so the answer is not Choice *D*. The focus did motivate the students, but they did not use correct estimation skills to get the prize (*B*). This focus began the process of showing a rationale for having tools to estimate (*A*). It would have been very relevant had Ms. Babinoux immediately tied this to how and why we need to have estimation strategies to use in cases like this one (such as estimating how many candy balls are on the top row and how many possible rows there are in the jar and multiplying). Unfortunately, she did not use it in that manner. The correct answer is *C*.

By having a solid personal understanding of number and numeration concepts, teachers will be better prepared for planning appropriate learning experiences for students. Understanding number and numeration concepts means that teachers of young children should be competent in mathematics by having or developing a solid foundation of number sense and of basic computation of numbers themselves. Teachers may also review and test mathematical content by taking released TAAS/TAKS tests online. Any of the grade-level tests are good reviews. Readers are encouraged to seek additional resources at http://www.tea.state.txus/student.assessment/resources/release/index.html.

1. http://www.tea.state.tx.us/student.assessment/taks/index.html
   This Web site highlights the new student testing, TAKS, and provides a clear picture of which mathematics concepts should be taught and assessed at each grade level.
2. http://www.tea.state.txus/teks/111toc.htm
   This Web site highlights the student TEKS.

Consider the following question:

To aid her second-grade students in comparing fractions, which manipulative should Ms. Asif use to help her students "see" the size of the fractions?

A. Fraction strips
B. Base ten blocks
C. Egg cartons
D. Attribute blocks

Base ten blocks (*B*) would be more appropriate in activities involving place value or decimals. Egg cartons (*C*) would be appropriate for use with fractions with 12 as a denominator. Attribute blocks (*D*) would be appropriate manipulatives to use in activities that involve sorting and classifying. The fraction strips could be used with all fractions (*A*). (Fraction strips are a set of paper strips that are cut and shaded to represent the relation between and among wholes, halves, thirds, fourths, and other fractional parts of a whole.) The answer is *A*.

Try this one:

Ms. Garcia has been working with her kindergarten class on pattern recognition. To assess her students' understanding of patterns, she asks them the following question: "What would be the next number in this pattern? 1, 1, 2, 2, 3, 3, 4."

A. 5
B. 3
C. 4
D. 6

Five (*A*) is not in the pattern. Three (*B*) is not in the pattern. Six (*D*) is not in the pattern. Four is the correct response (*C*). The pattern begins with repeating sequential counting numbers. The answer is *C*.

To analyze data and to make accurate predictions, strategies are necessary. Activities should be selected to promote logical reasoning and the relationship between terms in a sequence. For the elementary teacher, it is imperative that children have opportunities to learn basic concepts of patterns and relationships to build on as they advance in study. In some subject areas, information can be learned in isolation, but mathematics is forever built upon a foundation of basics. Early experiences with patterns, functions, and relationships provide a foundational basis for later development of algebra and the study of solutions to equations. In later study, students begin to understand functions, reasoning about abstract objects, generalizations, and symbolic notation. These concepts underlie all areas of mathematics and the basis of mathematical communication. This is expressed in the following statement:

> *The search for and analysis of patterns and order are an integral part of doing mathematics, whether it is developing a computational algorithm, exploring properties of shapes, or figuring the solution to a probability problem. Children can learn the processes of doing mathematics as they learn mathematics content.*

However, the ability to reason is so important in this science of pattern and order that attention should be given explicitly to helping children develop their reasoning skills. (Van de Walle, 1998, p. 392)

Patterns are a way of helping children organize and order the world. Sorting, classifying, and ordering objects helps with patterns, geometric shapes, and data. Young children are able to identify patterns in their environment. Teachers should always encourage making generalizations about patterns by asking questions such as, "Tell me about that pattern on your sweater." "How do you know that it is a pattern?" "What is a missing part of a pattern?" "How would you make a pattern longer/different?" and "Can you clap this pattern after me?" Children should be encouraged to explore and model relationships using language and, later, notation describing their observations.

Many types of activities involving patterns (including echo patterns, patterns using stamps, stringing various objects, gluing or drawing patterned art projects, etc.) help to build logic and reasoning abilities in students. The early childhood class, for example, provides opportunities to string bead patterns, make trains, get in line in certain patterns, and so forth. Planning learning experiences that foster student growth in these areas are crucial building blocks to achieving success in mathematics. The early childhood teacher uses calendar time to show patterns of repeating days of the week. Older children keep weather patterns data or event patterns that lead into cause-and-effect or logical decision making. For example, "I predict that it may be cold again tomorrow, so I will need to bring my jacket." Pattern recognition also helps young children understand human behavior. ("Kevin is always talkative and lively, but today he is quiet, and when approached, snaps a bit. There is something different in his behavior pattern. Let's see if he is feeling bad.")

Try the following question:

Second-grade students are studying patterns. They notice that the sequence 2, 4, 6, 8, . . . has a pattern and that the values are increasing by 2. The sequence 5, 10, 15, 20, . . . is increasing by 5. These patterns help build the foundation for which math concept?

    A. Addition
    B. Fractions
    C. Algebraic thinking
    D. Subtraction

Addition (*A*) is not appropriate; no computation is required. Fractions (*B*) could be any number representing a part of a whole, without a pattern. Subtraction (*D*) is not appropriate; no computation is required. The correct response is *C*. This question demonstrates the importance of building a foundation for algebraic reasoning.

Two components of algebraic thinking for young children are (a) making generalizations and using symbols to represent mathematical ideas and (b) representing and solving problems. Learning experiences in which children make generalizations from observations about numbers and operations develop a foundation of algebraic thinking. The use of terminology such as *associative* and *commutative* is not necessary at this stage, but teachers should be aware of the algebraic properties used by young children and begin to draw attention to the concept. Studying patterns, functions, and algebra is the beginning of learning about the different uses of variables and how to solve equations.

Standards III Geometry and Measurement and IV Probability and Statistics

The mathematics teacher understands and uses geometry, spatial reasoning, measurement concepts and principles, and technology appropriate to teach the statewide curriculum (Texas Essential Knowledge and Skills [TEKS]) in order to prepare students to use mathematics (Standard III). The mathematics teacher understands and uses probability and statistics, their applications, and technology appropriate to teach the statewide curriculum (Standard IV).

Competency 014 (Geometry, Measurement, Probability, and Statistics): The teacher understands concepts and principles of geometry and measurement and demonstrates knowledge of probability and statistics and their applications (TEKS) in order to prepare students to use mathematics.

The EC-4 teacher applies knowledge of spatial concepts such as direction, shape, and structure and identifies and uses formulas to find lengths, perimeters, areas, and volumes of basic geometrical figures. Mathematical reasoning is used to prove geometric relationships, and the teacher uses translations, rotations, reflections, dilations, and contractions to illustrate similarities, congruencies, and symmetries of figures. Knowing measurement as a process, methods of approximation and estimation, and the effects of error on measurement are necessary. The teacher understands the use of numbers and units of measurement for quantities related to temperature, money, percents, and speed. The teacher has knowledge of conversions within and between different measurement systems. The use of graphical and numerical techniques to explore data, characterize patterns, and describe departure from patterns is known by the teacher. The theory of probability and its relationship to sampling and statistical inference and how statistical inference is used in making and evaluating predictions is important. The EC-4 teacher encourages mathematical arguments, making predictions, and drawing conclusions using summary statistics and graphs to analyze and interpret one-variable data. He or she knows how to generate and use probability models to represent situations and can teach students how to use the graph of the normal distribution as a basis for making inferences about a population.

Let's look at this question:

Ms. Fischer plans to introduce the concept of volume to her second-grade class. She wants her children to understand volume through exploration. Which would be the *most* appropriate for her to use?

A. Color tiles
B. A measuring cup
C. Pattern blocks
D. Attribute blocks

Color tiles (*A*) are used to represent two-dimensional situations. They are often used for perimeter, area, and multiplication arrays. Pattern blocks (*C*) are often used for two-dimensional activities such as tessellations and area. They also can be used effectively with fractions. Attribute blocks (*D*) are designed for activities using sorting and classifying. Volume is a *three*-dimensional quantity, and the measuring cup is the only three-dimensional object presented as a choice. The *best* response is *B*.

The application of mathematics to other curriculum areas and to the real world is a necessary and important component of the mathematics classroom. The value of connecting what children are learning in the classroom to its application in real-life situations cannot be overstated ("Why is it important, boys and girls, to have a correct lunch count? On a field trip we have 18 children who are on the bus. There are 21 children in our class. Should I tell the bus driver to leave now? Why or why not?"). ". . . (S)tudents should not only learn mathematics, they should also learn the utility of mathematics and the interrelatedness of mathematical ideas" (NCTM, 1998, p. 90). Most content areas have components or concepts that can be related to mathematics in some way. Teachers who focus upon these relationships use them to enhance mathematical appreciation and student growth. When mathematics is integrated with other subject areas, its value, understanding, and relevance are extended. Dump-and-fill activities, comparison books, and other activities in which students have an opportunity to see differences (prior to formal instruction) help young children begin to understand more/less, bigger/smaller, greater than/less than, and so forth. Setting up a class store is another easy way to have mathematics relate to the real world. This may also fit with a token economy management system, where children need to have so many play dollars or tokens to "purchase" a variety of reward items ("$10" for 10 minutes of free time on the computer, "$50" for being able to eat lunch with friends in the classroom on Friday, etc.).

A close *interdisciplinary relationship* exists between mathematics and science. Science often uses mathematics to explain and extend concepts. This link is through content and process. For example, much of science relies on patterns of data and measurement. It is also the use of data and statistics that help students clarify issues related to health issues in their personal lives and as consumers. Using survey data, children can also link data analysis and statistics to learn more about social studies. Map skills also require working with numbers. In turn, the use of ratio, proportion, and percents extends children's understanding of mathematics. Mathematical connections abound in other areas such as in music (patterns in rhythms and fractions) and in sports (measurement, geometry, data analysis and statistics, and much more). Teachers can also find an abundance of literary connections, including wonderful children's books about numbers and other mathematical concepts. Using a literature focus can help motivate and stimulate student interest in mathematics. Counting and shape books, rhymes, songs, and fingerplays complement learning mathematics and provide excellent focus activities for mathematics.

Children are motivated and interested when a story gives life to the mathematics they are learning. Let us look at some examples of activities that can spark interest in mathematics through language arts and reading. Dinosaur books such as *How Big Were the Dinosaurs* or *The Littlest Dinosaur* might be used to introduce a lesson on size or measurement, for example. A teacher may want to take a digital photo of something a child has created in the block center so that the child can describe it and/or tell a story about it ("This is my tower. I built it with cubes. Lots of people live here. There are some offices here, too."). Children who create a class survey, then write their own "story" about it are extending mathematics into language arts. For example, after graphing class shoes, Sara wrote, "There were fifteen kids who had tennis shoes on. Four had those kind of shoes with straps. They were girls. I think kids like tennis shoes best. People who make shoes ought to make mostly tennis shoes. I like tennis shoes best, too!" Using mathematics in applied situations leads to deeper understanding. Making tally charts and asking young children to explain them is also a way to have children understand the concept of one-to-one correspondence in naming numbers. At snack time, groups in Mrs. Barton's Pre-K class tallied choices of snacks to determine which was more popular, noting, "Ten friends like cookies best."

Answer the following question:

Which of the following activities would provide the best opportunity for fourth-grade students to apply measurement skills to a science context?

A. Investigating the habitat of butterflies
B. Determining the melting point of an ice cube
C. Exploring the properties of water
D. Investigating the properties of rocks and minerals

The investigation of the habitat of butterflies (*A*) would increase students' knowledge of butterflies but would not be a measurement activity. Learning about the properties of water (*C*) would not necessarily be a measurement activity but could be associated with volume. However, this is not the *best* answer. Determining the properties of rocks and minerals (*D*) is not necessarily a measurement activity but could be associated with volume. However, this is not the *best* answer. In order to determine the melting point, students would need to measure and record the temperatures preceding the melting point. *B* is the *best* response.

And this additional question.

Margie grouped her third-grade students in groups of four and gave each group a piece of yarn. She asked the students to make different closed figures with the yarn and to describe what they thought was happening to the area and perimeter of the shapes. She hoped that the students would discover which property remained the same, regardless of the shape. Which would remain the same?

A. The area of the figure
B. The perimeter of the figure
C. The length of the figure
D. The width of the figure

Area is the product of length times width ($A = l \times w$). As either the length or width is changed, the area (*A*), the space inside, will be different. Since the yarn is being used to make different shapes, the length (*C*) and width of the figure will change as the figure is changed. The width of the figure (*D*) will vary as the yarn is being moved to create new figures. The correct response is *B*. The perimeter is the distance around the figure. Although the yarn may change shape, the total length of the yarn (representing the figure's perimeter) remains constant.

Geometry helps students understand the three-dimensional world in which they live. Through the study of geometry, teachers must offer students ways to interpret and reflect on the physical environment with real and abstract methods. Learning activities should promote interaction with physical models, drawings, and software. These are exceptionally effective in helping children visualize geometric concepts.

> *Geometry and spatial sense are fundamental components of mathematics education. . . . Geometric representations can help students make sense of area and fractions; histograms and scatterplots can lead to insights about data; and coordinating graphs can be used to analyze and understand functions. Spatial reasoning is helpful in using maps, planning routes, designing floor plans, and creating art. (NCTM, 1998, pp. 61–62)*

Students must be encouraged to use geometric ideas in representing and solving problems in a variety of contexts. Geometric puzzles, geoboards, and blocks help children understand many-sided figures and circles. Geometry for young children should focus on manipulation. Primary children can construct many plane and solid figures from blocks, dominos, and even marshmallows or gumdrops connected with toothpicks. When children manipulate these objects, they see relationships much easier (two right triangles make a square, etc.). Hands-on and interactive experiences are the best ways to help children learn concepts and techniques that help them interpret their physical world. Children through fourth grade should be able to identify basic geometric shapes such as the circle, square, rectangle, triangle, quadrilaterals, pentagon (a 5-sided polygon), hexagon (a 6-sided polygon), octagon (an 8-sided polygon), and solid figures such as the cube, cone, pyramid, cylinder and so forth. When children are introduced to shapes in school, "bombardment" is the best instructional policy. The teacher, for example, may put on her hat with a circular brim and her apron with huge circles, while children work with paper plates and cut out circles from various materials in centers. Students come to the circle to sing a "circle song" and are served snacks that are circular (cross cuts of fruit, etc.). Basic concepts addressing symmetry, rotation, reflection, and transformation are also learned. Finding the perimeter (distance around) of figures and some area (surface measurement) measurements are taught in the primary grades.

Answer the following question:

Ms. Oar divided her first-grade students into groups of two. She asked each student to fold a piece of construction paper in half. On one-half of the paper each student was asked to construct a design using pattern blocks. When the students had finished their designs, the students switched places with their partners and were asked to replicate their partners' designs on the other side of the paper. This activity would be most appropriate for:

A. development of skills needed for repetition.
B. understanding that different students will have different designs.
C. development of spatial ability and awareness.
D. recognition of properties of polygons.

This activity helps students learn to duplicate and does not address higher-order thinking. This would not necessarily foster geometric understanding. This activity would help students notice polygons and their properties but would be *more* appropriate for development of spatial skills. The correct response is *C*.

Let's try another question:

Ms. Shanar wanted her first-grade class to develop an understanding of *nonstandard* measurement. She asked her children to measure the distance from the bottom of the classroom door to the doorknob. What would be an appropriate tool to use?

A. A paper clip
B. A pencil
C. A hula hoop
D. A color tile

A paper clip (*A*) would be too small and too difficult for first-grade students to try to use to measure a vertical distance. The hula hoop (*C*) is round and would not be appropriate for measuring a linear length. The color tile (*D*) is small. It would be very difficult for students to estimate the vertical distance using the color tile. A pencil would be the most appropriate item to use of the choices presented (*B*). It is longer than the paper clip and the color tiles and would be easier for the students to use to estimate the distance. The correct answer is *B*.

Measurement concepts include length, time, area, mass, and volume or capacity. See Table 3.4 to review measurement units, if needed. Measurement is used every day by children as they explore their environment and ask questions. "How tall am I?" "How long will it take to get there?" "How much longer till lunch?" "How much do I need?" "How far is it to my house?" Students need many experiences using standard and nonstandard measurement to foster their understanding of the physical aspects of the real world. A *nonstandard measurement* is any item that is used to measure other items. This might be a child's finger, a shoe, a book, a paper clip, or a pencil. Using such a nonstandard unit to measure another item, such as the length of a table, allows the child to grasp the concept using a repeated movement or a repetition of that unit. In other words, for the question "How long is the table?" children can use a book, placing the book on the table, making a mark and counting, "One." Then they can slide the book further along the table, make a mark and count, then repeat the procedure the length of the table while recording or counting the number of book lengths that are used to measure the table. While nonstandard measurement helps young children grasp the concept of repeated measurement, it also increases understanding of estimation skills.

The study of measurement is necessary for everyday life as well as for connecting other mathematical concepts and other content areas. It includes number operations, geometric ideas, statistical concepts, and notions of function (NCTM, 1998). Learning experiences should provide students with ample opportunities for selecting units and understanding appropriate measurement units and understanding the techniques, tools, and formulas of measurement. Other components of measurement study should include selecting and using benchmarks to estimate measurement (such as an inch is about as wide as an adult thumb) and scaling (making an object smaller/larger or drawing to scale). Older children will select and apply appropriate standard units and tools to measure length, area, volume, weight, time, temperatures, and the size of angles.

Teachers should carefully select learning experiences that foster student understanding of measurement and all associated aspects of applying measurement, including understanding that measurements can be approximations and that different units affect precision of measurement. Learning to

Table 3.3 Geometric Formulas and Measurement Units

P = Perimeter   A = Area   V = Volume   SA = Surface Area
(b = base, l = length, w = width, h = height)

Rectangle	▭	P = 2l + 2w	A = lw
Square	□	P = 4s	A = s²
Parallelogram	▱	P = sum of all sides	A = bh
Triangle	△	P = sum of all sides	A = ½ bh
Trapezoid	▽	P = sum of all sides	A = ½ h (b1 + b2)
Polygon	⬡	P = sum of all sides	A = depends on shape
Circle	○	C = 2πr or πd	A = 2πr²
Prism	△	V = Bh	SA = the sum of the area of each face
Cylinder	⬭	V = πr²h	SA = 2πrh + 2π²

MEASUREMENT UNITS

Customary | *Metric*

Length
12 inches (in) = 1 foot (ft)
3 ft = 1 yard (yd)
36 in = 1 yd
5,280 ft = 1 mile
1,760 yd = 1 mile

Length
1,000 meters (m) = 1 kilometer (km)
100 centimeters (cm) = 1 m
10 decimeters (dm) = 1 m
1,000 millimeters (mm) = 1 m
10 cm = 1 dm
10 mm = 1 cm

Area
144 square in = 1 square foot
9 square ft = 1 square yd
43,560 square ft = 1 acre (A)

Area
100 square mm = 1 square cm
10,000 square cm = 1 square m
10,000 square m = 1 hectare (ha)

Volume
1,728 cubic inches (cu in) = 1 cubic foot (cu ft)
27 cu ft = 1 cubic yard (cu yd)

Volume
1,000 cubic mm = 1 cubic cm
1,000 cubic cm = 1 cubic dm
1,000,000 cubic cm = 1 cubic m

Capacity
8 fluid ounces (fl oz) = 1 cup (c)
2 c = 1 pint (pt)
2 pt = 1 quart (qt)
4 qt = 1 gallon (gal)

Capacity
1,000 milliliter (mL) = 1 liter (L)
1,000 L = 1 kiloliter (kL)

Weight
16 ounces (oz) = 1 pound
2,000 lb = 1 ton (T)

Mass
1,000 kilograms (kg) = 1 metric ton
1,000 grams (g) = 1 kg
1,000 milligrams (mg) = 1 g

Temperature
32 degrees F = freezing point of water
98.6 degrees F = normal body temperature
212 degrees F = boiling point of water

Temperature
0 degrees C = freezing point of water
37 degrees C = normal body temperature
100 degrees C = boiling point of water

Time
60 seconds (sec) = 1 minute (min)
60 min = 1 hour (hr)
24 hr = 1 day (da)
7 da = 1 week (wk)
4 wk = 1 month (mth)
12 mths = 1 year (yr)
52 wk = 1 yr
365 da = 1 yr

select and use the most reasonable and appropriate unit of measurement is vital for understanding and application (e.g., "just a couple of blocks down the street," without this understanding can turn into a mile walk). The study of measurement is most effectively taught with the use of concrete materials. Children must have opportunities to handle measurement tools and apply concept knowledge to real-world, relevant situations (e.g., taking a teaspoon rather than a tablespoon of medicine). Children who measure the pet gerbil's cage for paper or the goldfish bowl for water, the bulletin board to put up new borders, space for a new center, and milk and cocoa in a kitchen center for chocolate milk, for example, are learning mathematics for everyday situations. Measurement is a fundamental concept for connecting mathematics with itself and to other content areas such as social studies, science, art, health, and physical education.

As mentioned, measurement concepts should first be taught with nonstandard units in order for children to grasp the general concept. The second step is to introduce standard measurement units and scales that are used in everyday life (such as inches, feet, yards, centimeters, meters, quarts, gallons, and so on). From this basic understanding, children should be able to understand the need for measuring with standard units and become familiar with standard units in the customary and metric systems. The third step in learning measurement is to carry out simple conversions such as from inches to feet or centimeters to meters within a measurement system. Most importantly, children should be able to understand such attributes as length, area, weight, volume, and size of angle and the appropriate type of unit for measuring each attribute (see Table 3.3). Providing a way for children to experiment with measuring is important for all grades and can be part of a kitchen, shop, garden, science, social studies, or growth center. Older elementary children will develop, understand, use formulas, and develop strategies for determining perimeter, surface area, and volume of solids.

Look at the following question:

Mr. Kurz is interested in having his second-grade class understand problem solving in real-world situations (determining the amount of decorative wall border needed for putting up a place for students' work). The children are asked to measure the width of their classroom using nonstandard measures. Stephen finds that the classroom is 36 shoes wide. Amy finds the classroom is 9 jump ropes wide. Which mathematical concept will the children apply to convert from one nonstandard measure to the other?

A. Metric measurement
B. Absolute value
C. Area and perimeter
D. Ratio and proportion

Response *A* implies the use of the metric measurement system with no connection to other types of measurement. Absolute value (*B*) applies to the distance from the origin and would be used if *direction* from the origin was being considered. Area and perimeter (*C*) relate to attributes of geometric shapes. Ratio and proportion (*D*) would provide a method of converting from one measurement system to another. The correct response is *D*.

Consider also the following question:

Ms. Rubalcava has placed 10 color tiles, 8 green color tiles and 2 yellow color tiles, into a paper bag. She tells her students that there are 10 color tiles in the bag and some are yellow and some are green. She shakes the paper bag and, without looking, picks one color tile from the bag. It is green. She asks the students to guess the color of the tile in her hand. She then opens her hand and shows the class the color tile. Ms. Rubalcava asks a student to record the color on the board with a tally mark. She places the color tile back in the bag and repeats the process 10 times. Her first-grade students help her tally her results. After the tenth pick, the tally is 7 green and 3 yellow. She asks the students to guess how many green tiles and how many yellow tiles are in the bag. She repeats the experiment and this time the tally is 9 green and 1 yellow. She repeats the process several more times and the students tally the data. Her purpose in this experiment is:

A. to help her students count.
B. to show the students that it is impossible to know how many green tiles and yellow color tiles there are without opening the bag.
C. to help students learn to organize and interpret data.
D. to better understand the concept of addition.

Even though the students do count the number of green tiles and yellow tiles (*A*), the object of this lesson is to develop an understanding of predicting how many tiles of each color are in the bag. Although the students will not know for certain how many green tiles and yellow tiles are in the bag (*B*) until all the tiles are shown, the students can learn how to give accurate predictions based on several repetitions. The object of the lesson is not to have students count the green tiles and yellow tiles (*D*) but to understand the concept of probability. The students will develop an understanding of how to collect data and why it is important to conduct several experiments in order to make a prediction. The correct response is *C*.

It is possible to help children to develop understanding of unknown situations. They can learn to form a rational basis to forecast accurate predictions when absolute certainty is not possible but when other necessary information is presented.

Probability and prediction is connected to data collection. Children are often interested in questions, such as "What is your favorite color?" "What kind of candy do you like the most?" and so forth. Inquiries such as these may be used to interest children in collecting information (data) and in developing how to best represent the findings of that data (graphing, charting, making a table). Teachers model these procedures with very young children as a class effort and gradually build a foundation of understanding. Older children enjoy conducting surveys that are part of their everyday lives. For example, they may wish to find out how many children prefer hamburgers or pizza in the lunchroom and how the cafeteria personnel use such data to plan for these preferences.

Try this one:

Mr. Webb's fourth-grade class has completed a unit on statistics. Frank, one of his students, wants to attain a 92 average for the five tests given each quarter. If Frank scored an 86 on his first test, a 96 on his second test, a 94 on his third test, and a 90 on his fourth test, what grade must Frank earn on his fifth test for a 92 test average?

A. 92
B. 93
C. 90
D. 94

For the goal average, there must be 460 grade points accumulated ($92 \times 5 = 460$). Frank must determine his current grade point by adding the four test sources ($86 + 96 + 94 + 90 = 366$). The difference will result in the needed test score of 94 ($460 - 366 = 94$). To check this, the sum of the five test scores, divided by 5, would result in an average of 92. The correct response is *D*.

In an increasingly technological world, it is imperative that students have experiences with concepts concerning data, statistics, and probability. Beginning in the primary grades, learning activities should include organizing data into categories, sorting experiences, and other informal activities that encourage refining questions and decision making. "Students can pose questions to investigate, organize the responses, and create representations of their data" (NCTM, 1998, p. 103). Building a foundation in the early grades with these types of activities allows students to further their understanding by interpreting data using methods of exploratory data analysis. Young children can question and gather data about themselves and their surroundings; sort and classify objects by attributes; represent data using concrete objects, pictures, and graphs; and discuss events related to their own experiences as "likely" or "unlikely" to happen (NCTM, 2000). Children might ask, "How many of us are wearing T-shirts today?" The results may be tallied and put into a chart, or a class picture graph may be created using a T-shirt as the displayed icon. Predicting the chances of an event can also be done with young children. "Do you think at least five people will score 100 on our spelling test on Friday? Why or why not?" Learning experiences based on data can help students to develop and evaluate inferences, make predictions, create representations, and stimulate communication. Along with these experiences, children need to understand and apply basic notions of chance and probability. The goal of a mathematics curriculum such as this is to produce students who are prepared for informed decision making. It is the responsibility of the teacher to provide such a learning environment that encourages and nurtures questions, interpretation, inference, and probability. Only through these efforts will mathematical literacy be achieved.

Standards V Mathematical Processes and VI Mathematical Perspectives

The mathematics teacher understands and uses mathematical processes to reason mathematically, to solve mathematical problems, to make mathematical connections within and outside of mathematical problems, and to communicate mathematically (Standard V). The mathematics teacher understands the historical development of mathematical ideas, the interrelationship between society and mathematics, the structure of mathematics, and the evolving nature of mathematics and mathematical knowledge (Standard VI).

Competency 015 (Mathematical Process): The teacher understands mathematical processes and knows how to reason mathematically, solve mathematical problems, and make mathematical connections within and outside of mathematics.

The EC-4 teacher understands the role of logical reasoning in mathematics, knows methods and uses of informal and formal reasoning, and applies correct mathematical reasoning to derive valid conclusions from a set of premises. The teacher applies principles of inductive reasoning to make conjectures and uses deductive methods to evaluate the validity of conjectures. Mathematical arguments and examples of fallacious reasoning are evaluated and recognized. The teacher understands connections among concepts, procedures, and equivalent representations in areas of mathematics (e.g., algebra, geometry) and understands how mathematics is used in other disciplines and in daily living. Manipulatives and a wide range of appropriate technological tools are known and used to develop and explore mathematical concepts and ideas. The teacher demonstrates knowledge of the history, the evolution of mathematical concepts, procedures, and ideas, and recognizes the contributions that different cultures have made to the field of mathematics and the impact of mathematics on society and cultures.

See how you do on the following question:

The students in Ms. O'Shea's fourth-grade class have completed studying addition, subtraction, multiplication, and division of whole numbers. To assess their understanding of whole number operations, Ms. O'Shea asks her students to mentally estimate the answer to the following question: 36×98.

It will be a number:
1. slightly less than 3,600
2. a lot less than 3,600
3. slightly more than 3,600
4. a lot more than 3,600

This question will help Ms. O'Shea assess her students' understanding of:
A. multiplying a whole number by 100.
B. multiplication as the inverse of division.
C. the fact that when you multiply, the product is always larger than the factors.
D. multiplication as a shortcut for repeated addition.

To obtain a product much smaller than the whole number multiplied by 100, the value of the factor must be closer to one. To obtain a product slightly larger than the whole number multiplied by 100, the factor has to be slightly larger than 100. To obtain a product a lot larger than the whole number multiplied by 100, the factor has to be considerably larger than 100. When a whole number is multiplied by a number slightly less than 100 (A), the product will be smaller than the whole number multiplied by 100. The closer the value approaches 100, the closer the product will be to that product. The answer is A.

Students need to be provided with opportunities to assess their own understanding of mathematical operations. Various activities should be used that present applications of mathematical operations in many contexts. Mathematical concepts should be explored in a holistic manner. Because one goal of mathematics instruction is computational fluency, children should have opportunities to master basic facts and operations and, as always, apply relevant experiences to real-world situations. Rarely does someone approach you in a conversation and ask, for example, for 21 to be divided by 7. Mathematics is normally based in some type of context. Understanding the meaning of arithmetic operations and how they are related is important.

"Children should be able to decide which mathematical operations (addition, subtraction, multiplication, division) should be used for a particular problem, how the same operation can be applied to other situations, how operations relate to one another, and what results to expect" (NCTM, 1998, p. 53). The meanings of addition and subtraction are the focus of Pre-K–2, while the meaning of multiplication and division is the focus of grades 3 through 5. Mental math skills are required learning experiences, although drilling students over and over again to memorize facts creates boredom rather than understanding. NCTM advocates the appropriate use of calculators and computers, but "when the instructional focus is on developing student-generated or conventional computational algorithms, the calculator should be set aside to allow for this focus" (NCTM, 1998, p. 51).

Consider the following question:

Ms. Ashman is teaching her class to do long division. This algorithm was introduced as follows.

```
16 | 89
    − 16    |
     73
    − 16    ||
     57
    − 16    |||
     41
    − 16    ||||
     25
    − 16    |||||
      9
```

Figure 3.1

This teaching approach emphasizes the process of division. Which approach is this?

  A. The quotient of the dividend and the divisor.
  B. Multiplication by the reciprocal of the divisor.
  C. The inverse operation of multiplication.
  D. Multiple subtractions of the divisor from the dividend.

Response *A* would use the standard algorithm for long division. Response *B* has no relevance to the question; it would apply to division with fractions. Division is the inverse of multiplication and could be used to check the solution. However, *D* is the correct response: Division is a shortcut for repeated subtraction. Groups of 16 are being removed from the original large group. Each tally mark represents the formation of a group of 16. *(89 is the dividend; 16 is the divisor, the answer is the quotient, and the leftover is the remainder.)* The answer is *D*.

Answer this question:

Ms. Sikes wants to incorporate calculators into her third-grade mathematics curriculum. She distributes calculators to each student. She asks students to enter the number 6,734 into their calculators. She then asks her students, in only one step, to have the number 6,704 show on the calculator display. Ms. Sikes uses this activity to develop her students understanding that:

  A. calculators provide correct solutions.
  B. calculators can be used for guess-and-check problem-solving strategies.

C. calculators can be used when an answer is needed quickly.

D. calculators can be used to help understand place value.

Using calculators to *check answers* will not help to develop higher-order thinking skills. Having the students skip count by 5s could help students recognize the pattern in a guess-and-check situation, but this is not relevant to this activity. Using the calculator to add the numbers would be using the calculator as a computation tool. This question assesses students' understanding of place value (*D*). The calculator would allow students the freedom to explore and to verify when they found the correct solution. The answer is *D*.

Texas strongly believes that technology needs to be incorporated into the mathematics classroom. Calculators provide a means for students to develop higher-order thinking skills in a noncomputational setting, because they allow children to focus on logic, reasoning, and estimation—rather than becoming bogged down by procedural computation. This may be doubly so for children with learning disabilities, since calculators may allow them to function very well in problem solving. Computers also provide motivating ways to reach children, although teachers should be aware that many programs offer only "worksheets on a screen." In contrast, Driscoll and Nagel (2002) describe a CD-ROM program that asks teams of children to express their categorization and classification strategies by putting together "things that go together" by clicking on them. Two trees (one big, one small) and three fish (one big, two small) are presented. At first the partners discuss the trees as one group and the fish as another, then the idea of *big versus small* categories emerge. These types of computer programs and many others add much to the mathematics classroom or a math center.

Teachers of mathematics are expected to maintain professionalism by staying knowledgeable and informed about current developments in the field of mathematics education such as new mathematical principles and standards, recent theories on learning and mathematics, instructional strategies, technology, and effective ways in which to implement these concepts. Workshops, journals, and the Internet help (NCTM Web site: www. nctm. org). By participating in professional development activities and using reflection, teachers are better able to gain ideas for interesting lessons and plan worthwhile mathematical tasks.

Consider the following question:

All fourth-grade classrooms are having a pet show next week. Mr. Messick is in charge of the show and needs to know about how many entry forms to print to send home. Mr. Messick gives his fourth-grade class the following problem to help solve this problem.

> *Seven children have pets at home. The mean number of pets per child is 2. How many pets does each child have? If there are 124 fourth-grade students, how many entry forms will need to be printed? Write several sentences explaining your answer.*

National curriculum standards recommend open-ended problems like this. Which of these statements best explains why?

A. Problems of this type are best solved by applying algebraic principles (solving for unknowns) to real-world contexts.

B. Open-ended problems like this allow for a variety of solutions and explanations and promote inquiry, reasoning, and communication.

C. In dealing with uncertainty, students have opportunities to collect and analyze data.

D. The teacher can use this problem for an easy assessment of the students' reasoning process and correct any misconceptions as there is only one correct answer.

Algebraic applications (*A*) would not be appropriate, as it is beyond the needs of this situation. This situation does provide an opportunity to collect and analyze data (*C*). It also provides for teacher assessment and methods of communication and verification. *B*, however, is the *best* response. The question provides children with an opportunity to apply classroom knowledge to real-life contexts. This is a major focus for student learning today. It is important that children learn mathematics with relevant, real-world application and contexts. In this situation, some children may have one pet, no pet, three pets, and so on. There is uncertainty of the exact number as in real life. Open-ended situations such as this model real-life situations. The answer is *B*.

It is very difficult to teach something that you may not remember or understand well yourself. Teachers must have achieved a level of competence and confidence in mathematics to successfully instruct their students. Obtaining a fourth-grade mathematics book or workbook and working all of the problems will help you assess any areas that may need review, or you may refer to the Web sites previously mentioned for review for a particular grade level.

DISCUSSION

In traditional mathematics instructional programs teachers taught by telling, and students learned by watching and listening to the teacher. Drill-and-practice followed direct instruction to determine if students could do what had been taught. Students were expected to replicate what they had seen the teacher do. This is not the view of mathematics instruction envisioned by mathematics education reform efforts. Reflected throughout the NCTM standards (1989, 1991, 1995, 2000) one finds a common theme—the learner is *active* and *interactive*. More hands-on, minds-on activities and lessons are promoted to accommodate and incorporate cognitive learning theories where children use exploration to build their own knowledge. A developmental or constructivist view of learning mathematics requires a significant change in how mathematics should best be taught and learned. Constructivism suggests that students begin learning by *doing*—"trying to make sense of unfamiliar situations, testing new ideas and conjectures, and even posing their own questions to answer" (Van de Walle, 1998, p. 39).

In the Texas classroom and on the TExES, the learner must be seen as *active*. The following is a list originating from the *Curriculum and Evaluation Standards for School Mathematics* document (NCTM, 1989) and discussed in Van de Walle (1998). These verbs reflect a more appropriate view of mathematics objectives in an active manner rather than a traditional view that encourages passive learners:

explore	predict	justify
formulate	solve	investigate
develop	verify	discover
construct	explain	describe
represent	conjecture	use (p. 13)

Classrooms that encourage the use of these terms will foster student achievement. The role of such a learning environment is to provide an exploratory setting, pose challenges, and offer the support that will encourage mathematical construction. Mathematics educators that subscribe to the constructivist view of teaching and learning mathematics acknowledge that learners must be actively engaged in activities that promote this role for the learner.

In 2000, NCTM produced a document that incorporated all three of its previous documents (NCTM, 2000). Two of its principles warrant special notice within this summary and discussion: the Teaching Principle and the Learning Principle. Let us review what we have learned in this chapter through these principles.

THE TEACHING PRINCIPLE

Effective mathematics teaching requires understanding what students know and need to learn and then challenging and supporting them to learn it well. (NCTM, 2000, p. 16)

"More than any other single factor, teachers influence what mathematics students learn and how well they learn it. Students' mathematical knowledge, their abilities to reason and solve problems, and their self-confidence and dispositions toward mathematics all are shaped by teachers' mathematical and pedagogical decisions" (NCTM, 1998, p. 30). This statement has serious implications and designated responsibilities for the classroom teacher. These components include analysis of and reflection on teaching and learning, *worthwhile mathematical tasks, the learning environment, and classroom discourse.*

Only through *thoughtful analysis* and *reflection* can teachers make the myriad of decisions surrounding successful teaching. Teachers must use their knowledge of mathematics, pedagogy, student learning, questioning, instructional strategies, and more to plan, teach, and assess the learning environment. Teachers apply all knowledge into practice within the classroom to determine a *learning environment* (Ball, 1993) for learning mathematics. Teachers who hold high expectations that all their children can learn mathematics (along with searching for exciting mathematics lessons) will result in children who enjoy math with a high sense of self-efficacy.

Using pedagogical content knowledge allows teachers to draw upon previous experiences and successes to apply to new situations such as determining *worthwhile* tasks (Shulman, 1986). Other factors, including *curriculum* and *learning goals,* help to shape the mathematical environment with the teacher as a co-learner (a vital role in constructivism). A crucial factor in the learning environment is the teacher's dispositions toward mathematics, learners, and mathematics education. Even young learners can "read" messages that teachers are not approaching a subject wholeheartedly—either because they don't like it or are unsure of math concepts themselves. There must be a "can-do" atmosphere that encourages student interaction and

discourse. The TExES mathematics class may remember Vygotsky's theory in which learning is enhanced through dialogue and social interaction. Teachers must also have knowledge of resources (curricular frameworks and guides, instructional materials, lesson plans, etc.) to help inform decision making and planning.

Teachers can provide classrooms that promote thinking, but it takes much more than worthwhile mathematical tasks and commitment to discourse. It takes deep insight about mathematics, about teaching, and about learners, coupled with a sound and robust mathematics curriculum and thoughtful reflection and planning. (NCTM, 1998 p. 33)

Teaching in the real world means being knowledgeable about many things. Children come to the classroom with diversity in prior learning: special needs; special talents; differences in culture, gender, socioeconomic backgrounds; and more. Each has his or her own perspective of the world, needs that he or she is seeking to be met, and informal experiences with mathematics. Awareness of each individual child's background and needs is crucial. The teacher must take responsibility for making sure that children who are differently abled have access to materials to help understand and the time to explore those materials—adapting instruction to the individual child. Mathematical challenges must also be created for gifted and talented children. Diversities and multicultural perspectives are celebrated. Teachers must accommodate learning for *all* children through planning, questioning, teaching, and assessing. Mathematics for young children is a natural way of beginning to explore their world. It is at the early childhood level that the playing field of diversities can best be addressed before the disparities widen. Girls, minorities, and children in poverty still often are not reaching their potential in mathematics due to bias. Teachers must provide learning experiences that give *all* children equal mathematical tools. Assessment in the classroom must focus on the child's understanding, thought processes, and attitudes about learning mathematics. Developing not only a positive attitude but also an excitement about the teaching and learning of mathematics in the classroom helps to promote and foster learning for all children. The following resources appropriately address this vision of teaching and learning in the Texas classroom (but should not be limited to these alone): the TEKS, the TAKS objectives, the NCTM Principles and Standards for School Mathematics (NCTM, 2000), selected district textbooks and developed curricula guidelines, other valuable Web site resources as listed at the end of this chapter, veteran colleagues and administrators, quality programs of inservice and workshops (many of which are offered in Texas through Regional Service Centers), reputable computer mathematics software and commercial learning programs, and activity sources that are learner centered.

THE LEARNING PRINCIPLE

Students must learn mathematics with understanding, actively building new knowledge from experiences and prior knowledge. (NCTM, 2000, p. 20)

This second vital principle involves learning. As we have emphasized, learning mathematics is viewed differently today than previously. It is believed that networks of knowledge create a structure of conceptual organization in learning. Old and new knowledge are connected, and children's *prior knowledge* and experiences effect new knowledge (Noddings, 1990). Teachers must consider this view in two ways. First, children may come to their class with rich and varied prior knowledge and experiences in mathematics or very little to no mathematical background. Second, teachers have a responsibility to each child to provide all the experiences and knowledge established by the TEKS in their grade level so that children can successfully move through the Texas curriculum.

The sense of a *mathematical community* is another perspective on learning mathematics (Lave, 1991). These perspectives blend to help create an active *community of learners* in the classroom where conceptual understanding thrives and procedural proficiency is present. Children must have opportunities to develop an appreciation and value for the usefulness of mathematics. In other words, students should (a) develop a disposition to see mathematical power, (b) become autonomous learners that analyze and reflect, and (c) develop the ability to

communicate mathematically. "To understand what they learn, [students] must enact for themselves verbs that permeate the mathematics curriculum: examine, represent, transform, solve, apply, prove, communicate" (National Research Council, 1989, pp. 58–59).

Children learn better through learning activities that are motivating and challenging within relevant, real-world contexts. This can be achieved through the use of manipulatives, technology and other mathematical tools, active discourse, and group collaboration. In order for teachers to be able to provide such a learning environment, Van de Walle (1998) presents seven strategies for effective teaching of mathematics.

1. Create a mathematical environment.
2. Pose worthwhile mathematical tasks.
3. Use cooperative learning groups.
4. Use models and calculators as thinking tools.
5. Encourage discourse and writing.
6. Require justification of student responses.
7. Listen actively. (p. 34)

The teaching and learning of elementary school mathematics now has a different profile. The roles of the teacher and the learner are different. It is now believed that teachers and students together share responsibility for mathematics learning (NCTM, 1998). Through careful, reflective planning, teachers are able to create learning environments that are challenging, motivating, and active communities of mathematical learning.

SUMMARY

Mathematics means much more than arithmetic. Most of us experienced mathematics learning in a much different way than we expect teachers to teach it today. It is more than practicing arithmetic, by working addition, subtraction, and multiplication and division problems on worksheets. Teaching and learning mathematics today is providing children with many varied opportunities to construct their own concepts of mathematics across all grade levels. For young children, each learner constructs knowledge based on experimentation and observations with real-world materials and situations. The role of the teacher is to provide a learning environment that fosters these experiences. Teachers support the language for the concepts that children are learning by using the correct terminology from the start and provide the time and materials that best represent a concrete concept. There must be time for hands-on manipulation for learners, and symbols should be introduced only after concepts are well understood by the children.

Early childhood is a perfect time for children to become interested in counting, sorting, building shapes, finding patterns, measuring, and estimating. Good mathematics instruction invites children to experience mathematics as they play, describe, and think about their world. Teachers have a duty to think carefully about how and what children will learn about mathematics in the lessons and centers they provide and also to monitor this learning carefully. Low-income groups often have difficulty in school with mathematics. Many young children come to school with informal mathematical abilities that can be nurtured in a safe learning environment, and motivation occurs when they can explore patterns, shapes, measurement, what numbers mean, and how they work. However, children need proper guidance to maintain this level of motivation and interest by effective teachers. These teachers interpret what children are doing and thinking and attempt to see mathematics from children's point of view. Teachers decide which concepts children are able to learn from their experiences, as lessons are planned that are developmentally appropriate and culturally considerate. Lessons that promote intellectual, social, emotional, and physical development encourage mathematical understanding in children. This type of teaching helps children to be self-motivated, self-directed problem solvers as they develop their first mathematics attitudes and abilities.

Learning environments must be created that encourage and motivate children to *want* to do mathematics and challenge them to represent and reflect on their mathematical thinking. This environment must be exploratory, offering children experiences with real-world items (such as items for shopping, money, sand, and water for measurement), blocks for construction, and other manipulatives that encourage experimentation. Learning centers are designated areas of a classroom in which the teacher has strategically provided opportunities for children to explore and experience mathematics (as well as other content areas) through different contexts, materials, and events. These are selected based on the teacher's goals for student learning and grade level appropriateness. Learning centers are effective across all grade levels. Through informal observations of children at play in or work in the centers, teachers are able to gain much insight into the levels of the mathematical understanding. Other learning centers for exploration and lessons are planned by the teacher that are developmentally appropriate based on these observations. Questions to ask children working with materials might include, "How tall is it? How much bigger is it? How do you know? Can you show me another way to do this? How are those shapes different?" Mathematics in early childhood cuts across many daily activities. Doing the daily calendar, talking about the weather, dividing items for tasting, and playing in the kitchen center all offer learning opportunities for young children. Playing with the sand and water tables, sorting (as children are putting away toys) or learning about exchange (in playing shopping or pretending to order and pay for items in a "restaurant") are important learning situations. In these early grades, mathematics should be seen as "how we use it" in the real world, not as a separate subject or entity.

It is important to continue to encourage this attitude of utility of mathematics. Using mathematics is apparent in daily activities as well as in other subject areas. If the class is studying shells or leaves, this is a perfect opportunity for the children to practice classifying, seriation, graphing, counting, measuring, and patterning. Classification skills develop from observation, reflection, and practice, and from discussion of different characteristics and attributes of objects. Children are able to distinguish shape, size, color, texture, and so on.

Seriation requires keeping in mind the characteristics of one element while comparing it to another element. Children compare objects very naturally: "My dessert is bigger," "This is heavier," or "Yours is taller than mine." Graphing develops from using pictographs to more sophisticated use of the coordinate system. Counting progresses through developmental stages for children. First, a child knows that each object must have a name (counting word); then the child knows that the list of names have an order; and then the child makes the connection between counting and number. Teachers encourage counting events at all times: "I have four children who are ready to go to lunch. Who will be number 5?" and so forth.

Measuring is based on the ability to *conserve.* Using the child's natural interest in size and shape to develop measurement concepts is important for the teacher.

Patterns are visual, auditory, spatial, numerical, or combinations of these. Skip counting is encouraged as children begin to count by twos, threes, fives, and so on. Children can make patterns with beads, blocks, tiles, pattern blocks, pieces of paper, shoes, their bodies, leaves, shells, flowers, seed, and many other items. They can recognize patterns on the calendar, in blocks, games, in the classroom, and in other contexts, materials, and events. Building on these experiences, **functions** are the patterns created when certain actions are performed on objects or numbers. These are the building blocks for developing algebraic concepts. This type of thinking is encouraged by scenarios like this one: if one child has two feet, two children have four feet, three children have six feet, and so on, as the pattern becomes a function.

Providing children with experiences where they use blocks to construct sets of objects and then think about the relationships that exist among the sets helps encourage the development of the concept of one-to-one correspondence (the concept that one object can be related to another object). Technology also offers a multitude of software choices outside drill activities that may be selected for use in the classroom to support instruction and encourage exploration and practice for developing children's understanding of mathematics.

Successful teachers build on children's everyday activities, incorporate their cultural origins, languages, integrate technology, and focus on strategies. They use a variety of instructional strategies, create meaningful contexts, and provide for active participation to help children learn, develop, and appreciate mathematics in their world. The NCTM Principles and Standards for School Mathematics and the TEKS for Texas schools offer guidelines for what mathematics is to be learned at different levels and the progression of that learning. Effective teachers remember that *how* mathematics is taught is just as important as *what* mathematics is taught.

A Snapshot
of Teaching Mathematics in the Elementary Classroom

CLASSROOM SCENARIO

The scenario exemplifies the vision of teaching elementary mathematics in the classroom according to national standards and state guidelines. Highlights of the scenario are represented in italics within parentheses. These comments explain why and how this type of lesson represents the "best" in teaching mathematics.

This third-grade class has been working on problems that involve separating or dividing. The teacher, Mr. Kaster, is attempting to provide the class with some early involvement with multiplicative situations (using multiplication). Simultaneously, Mr. Kaster wants to include experiences with contexts for deepening students' knowledge of and skill with addition and subtraction. This third-grade class has the knowledge and skill for performing addition and subtraction,

but their understanding of multiplication and division is still quite informal. There has been some development of the concept of fractions that connects to their ideas about division. The class has not yet learned the division algorithm (the conventional procedure for dividing).*

The twenty-five students in Mr. Kaster's third-grade classroom are planning to share a class treat.

(Mr. Kaster seized this "teachable moment" to engage the students in real-world, relevant problem solving.)

The problem involves 48 chocolate-iced cupcakes that were provided by a local bakery as a treat associated with the class field trip the previous day. Mr. Kaster has given the class the following problem: If there are 48 cupcakes for our class treat, how many can each child have?

(Mr. Kaster knows that this problem will most likely elicit alternative representations and solution strategies as well as different answers. This

*Adapted from NCTM Professional Standards for Teaching Mathematics, 1991, pp. 58–59

provides a wonderful opportunity for mathematics learning. It should additionally help the students develop their ideas about division, fractions, and the connections between them.)

The students are encouraged to think about the problem individually. After about 5 minutes, Mr. Kaster allows the students to form problem-solving groups.

(To promote collaboration and problem solving, Mr. Kaster has the students work in small groups of three and four to discuss their ideas about the problem. This is a routine practice for this class.)

While the students are working in small groups, Mr. Kaster walks around the room informally eavesdropping on the small group discussions.

(This is an extremely valuable method of informal assessment.)

While walking around the room of small groups working together, Mr. Kaster notices that one group immediately decides to represent the problem with mathematics manipulatives.

(Mr. Kaster always has various manipulatives available at the small group tables as well as all the full complement of manipulatives that are displayed in the Math Center of the classroom.)

Two groups chose color tiles to be cupcakes and began to represent the problem. Another follows, but selects pattern blocks. A fourth group begins to draw pictures of cupcakes. Group 5 works with paper and pencil and then sees that other groups have chosen different ways of representing the problem. They, too, select pattern blocks. After much discourse, group 6 scans the other groups to see what they are doing. This group decides to use pattern blocks. As one of the students is about to choose pattern blocks from the Math Center, another student rushes over and whispers in her ear. She then selects to use fraction circles.

As Mr. Kaster continues to facilitate the small group work, the leader of one group raises his hand.

(This is the system that Mr. Kaster has in place addressing small group discussions. Each member of the group has a role to fulfill. Roles are rotated periodically. Questions that arise must first be addressed in small group discussion. When there is a consensus that no solution is agreeable, only then and only the group leader may raise his or her hand to ask for help. This pro-

motes cooperative collaboration and learning within the groups as well as facilitating discourse and problem-solving skills.)

The student asks if they should include Mr. Kaster in the number of people having a cupcake. The other groups overhear this and readily agree that Mr. Kaster should have a treat, too. They agree to change the number of people from 25 to 26 to include Mr. Kaster.

After the groups have worked for about 20 minutes, Mr. Kaster asks if the children are ready to discuss the problem in the whole group. The groups seem to agree. Mr. Kaster asks who would like to begin.

(The teacher allows time for the children to develop their solutions independently, with a few others, and then involves the whole group. By asking who would like to share their solution, he encourages the students to take intellectual risks.)

Two boys, Juan and Mark, come to the front of the class. Using the overhead projector, they write:

$$
\begin{array}{r}
48 \\
-26 \\
\hline
24
\end{array}
$$

One explains, "There are 25 kids in our class plus Mr. Kaster makes 26, and so if we pass out 1 cupcake to each child, we will have 24 cupcakes left, and that is not enough for each of us to have a second cupcake, so there will be some leftover ones."

(Students are expected to justify their solutions, not just to give answers.)

Mr. Kaster and the students reflect on this solution that was presented. Mr. Kaster scans the class and asks if anyone has a comment or a question about this solution.

(The teacher solicits other students' comments about the boys' solution without labeling it right or wrong. As members of a learning community, Mr. Kaster expects the students to decide if an idea makes sense mathematically.)

One girl, Amanda, says that she thinks that solution makes sense, but that "8 minus 6 is 2, not 4, so the answer should be 22, not 24." She demonstrates by pointing at the number line above the chalkboard. Starting at 8, she counts back 6 from 8 to get 2 using a pointer. The two boys reflect on this information for a moment. The class is quiet.

Mr. Kaster waits.

Then Juan says, "We revise that. Eight minus 6 is 2."

Mr. Kaster listens closely but does not jump into the interactive discourse.

(The mathematical learning environment should be established as a "risk-free" atmosphere. Students should be encouraged to respectfully question one another's ideas. The boys "revise" their solution because they have been convinced by the girls' explanation. There is no sense here that being wrong is shameful.)

Another student remarks that their group had the same solution as the first one shared—one cupcake.

"Ashley?" asks Mr. Kaster, after pausing for a moment to look over the classroom of students. Mr. Kaster remembers that this group had a different approach.

Ashley states that her group may have found a way to give each student in the class more than one cupcake. Ashley coaxes another group member, Sam, to go to the overhead with her.

Using small color tiles on the overhead, the students demonstrate that each tile would represent a whole cupcake. The students proceed to divide the entire group of 48 cupcakes into two groups. One group represents the one student—one cupcake idea (26), while the other group (22) represents the leftover cupcakes.

(These actions demonstrate the same subtraction problem of the previous two boys that used the conventional representation of the problem.)

Ashley, "If we could cut these tiles in half, then each of us would get one whole cupcake and half of another one, we think." Sam and the rest of that group agree, "Each of us would get one and a half cupcakes."

Another student, Tom, suggests that since the color tiles cannot be cut in half, that they try to use the pattern blocks like his group had tried. The class agrees that this would be a good idea.

Tom joins Ashley and Sam at the front of the room. Using pattern blocks, the students demonstrate how 48 cupcakes minus 26 cupcakes leaves 22 remaining cupcakes to divide in half. Using the blocks by exchanging whole blocks (hexagon) for two pieces (trapezoids), they represent the 22 cupcakes as 44 half cupcakes. The group then proceeds to assign each of the 26 people with half a cupcake.

Mr. Kaster asks, "Do you have any leftovers?"

(The students work together to solve the problem. Sometimes they build on the solutions offered by classmates. Mr. Kaster gathers insights about students through close listening and observation [informal assessment].)

At times, Mr. Kaster takes the responsibility for pushing (facilitating) students' thinking forward.

"There are still 18 half cupcakes or 9 whole cupcakes leftover," replies Steve.

"What do the rest of you think about this?" asks Mr. Kaster.

(Mr. Kaster expects the students to reason mathematically.)

Several students give explanations in support of Steve's solution.

"I think that does make sense," says Mary, "but I had another solution. I think the answer is 1 plus one-half plus one-fourth." Mary is a member of the group that chose to use fraction circles to help in their small group discussion of the original problem.

(Students seem willing to take risks by bring up different ideas.)

After waiting for the class to have a time of reflection on Mary's comments, the teacher continues.

"I don't understand," Mr. Kaster says. "Could you show what you mean?"

(Mr. Kaster seizes the opportunity to extend the class's thinking about fractions through this real-world problem that has motivated and engaged all of the students into actively thinking mathematically using many approaches and representations of their thinking. This has been done throughout the use of manipulatives, conventional procedures, collaboration, and classroom discourse within a community of learners in a risk-free environment.)

This scenario is just one snapshot of the many ways that teachers of mathematics are able to develop rich mathematical learning environments in their classrooms. This exemplifies a learner-centered classroom. Teaching in this manner helps the teacher facilitate student understanding of mathematics. The use of *manipulatives*, small and large group collaborative discourse, and active hands-on, minds-on learning experiences help students to value mathematics as well as to develop conceptual understanding of mathematics. This empowers students to become mathematically literate and leads to successful student achievement and progress.

PRACTICE QUESTIONS

Select the best response to each of the following questions.

1. Mr. Morales asked his fourth-grade students to choose their favorite colors from a list of red, blue, green, and yellow. After the students had made their selections, the class tallied their data. Which type of graph would be the most appropriate to use for this information?
   A. A circle graph
   B. A line graph
   C. Box and whiskers plot
   D. A scatter plot

2. Ms. Maxwell wanted to help her second-grade students better understand place value. What would be a good manipulative to use?
   A. Cuisenaire rod
   B. Color tile
   C. Base ten blocks
   D. Attribute blocks

3. How many lines of symmetry does a rectangle have?
   A. One
   B. Two
   C. Four
   D. Six

4. Ms. Miller is using base ten blocks with her first-grade class to solve addition and subtraction problems. She asks her students to "show" her, using the blocks, the number 34. A possible solution is:
   A. 3 flats; 4 longs
   B. 3 flats; 4 units
   C. 2 longs; 14 units
   D. 1 long; 14 units

5. Alex spends approximately 45 minutes each school day on homework. If Alex continues to spend 45 minutes a school day on homework, how much time will Alex have spent after 15 days of school?
   A. 6.75 hours
   B. 10 hours, 25 minutes
   C. 11 hours, 15 minutes
   D. 11 hours, 45 minutes

6. Using the metric system, Mr. Coulter asks his class to estimate the length of their desk tops. A "reasonable" estimate could be:
   A. 60 cm.
   B. 60 mm.
   C. 60 m.
   D. 60 km.

7. Use the problem below to answer the question that follows:

$$+ \quad \frac{\rule{1cm}{0.4pt} \ \rule{1cm}{0.4pt} \ \rule{1cm}{0.4pt}}{\rule{1cm}{0.4pt} \ \rule{1cm}{0.4pt} \ \rule{1cm}{0.4pt}}$$

Use each numeral 0, 1, 2, 3, 4, and 5 once. Place a digit on each line so that you will have the largest sum possible.

This problem would be most appropriate for providing students an opportunity to use which problem-solving strategy?
   A. Working backwards
   B. Extending the problem
   C. Looking for a pattern
   D. Drawing a diagram

8. Before going on a field trip, Ms. Jurca must decide how many buses to request for all fourth-grade classes with a total enrollment of 315. She orders enough buses to transport all of the students. If each bus carries 60 students, how many empty seats will there be? A calculator is chosen by a fourth-grade student to help solve this problem. The student divides 315 by 60 for a solution of 5.25. The student is confused and asks Ms. Jurca for help. The teacher's best initial response might be to:
   A. ask the student to explain why he or she divided 315 by 60 and what that answer represents.
   B. suggest that the student use paper and pencil to check the answer.
   C. suggest that the next step should be to multiply and then subtract.
   D. explain that the answer 5.25 means that six buses will be needed to transport all of the students.

9. Children in Ms. Baker's fourth-grade class were asked to find the number of cats and dogs owned by the class. There was a total of 12 dogs and nine cats for the class. Ms. Baker wanted her students to use a pictograph to represent the data.

If a square represented three dogs and a triangle represented three cats, how many triangles should the students use to graph the data?

A. 4
B. 3
C. 7
D. 2

10. Ms. Martin is using rocker scales in her second-grade classroom. She has her students place objects of different weights on the scales. This activity could best be used to foster her students' understanding of:

A. how to weigh objects accurately.
B. how to predict which object is heavier.
C. how to find the total weight of objects.
D. how to better understand the concepts of less than and greater than.

11. The first step for the teacher to do when developing students' prenumber concepts is to:

A. spend class time working with concrete objects.
B. spend class time working with pictorial objects.
C. spend class time having students write their numbers.
D. spend class time having students recognize the words for the numbers.

A third-grade student is given 12 color tiles and is asked to create as many differently shaped rectangles as possible for each number from 1 to 12. Ms. Longino models these directions with six tiles, making two rectangles, as shown below. Use this information to answer questions 12 through 14.

12. Ms. Longino has chosen this activity to help develop her student's understanding of which of the following number concepts?

A. Percentages of whole numbers
B. Least common multiples
C. Factors of whole numbers
D. Numeration systems other than base 10

13. If during the activity, a student asks why a 4 × 3 rectangle and a 3 × 4 rectangle have the same shape, Ms. Longino may use this opportunity for a lesson on which of the following geometrical concepts?

A. Right angles and perpendicular lines
B. Properties of congruent figures
C. Properties of similar figures
D. Area and perimeter

14. Ms. Longino wants to encourage the application of higher-order thinking skills. Of the following questions, which would be the best question to ask at the end of this activity?

A. How many more rectangles could you make with 15 color tiles?
B. Which number from 1 to 12 made the most rectangles?
C. For any given number of color tiles, how could you determine how many rectangles can be made?
D. For any given rectangle, how can you determine the perimeter of the rectangles?

15. Ms. Jacob divided her second-grade students into groups of four and gave each group a copy of a grocery store advertisement. Students were asked to work as a group and plan a meal for four people that contained one item from each food group. Students were asked to ensure that the meal was nutritious and was the least expensive meal they could plan. Ms. Jacob's objective for this activity is to:

A. help students learn the food groups.
B. connect mathematics to real-world situations.
C. help students develop communication skills.
D. foster collaborative working groups.

16. Ms. DeVillier placed 60 color tiles in a bag: 20 red, 10 blue, 10 yellow, 20 green. She asked her third-grade students to construct a graph to accurately represent the ratios of the color tiles. The ratio of the area for the green tiles to the area of all the tiles should be:

A. 2:4
B. 1:2
C. 1:3
D. 3:1

Best Answers to Practice Test Questions Representing the Standards Listed

Be sure to look at the information that follows this section if you are unclear about these terms (for example, attribute blocks are described in Table 3.1, Common Mathematics Manipulations). Other terms are described in the Glossary.

1. A. *Circle graph:* This is the best answer to represent this type of data. A line graph indicates continuous data. A box and whiskers plot shows the shape of a data set. A scatterplot graph shows paired data values.

2. C. *Base ten blocks:* These are the best manipulatives for place value concepts. Cuisenaire rods may be used with fractions, ratio and proportion, measuring, and more. Color tiles may be used for counting, probability, fractions, and some place value. Attribute blocks would be used for sorting, classifying, and other activities.

3. B. *Two: Lines of symmetry divide the shape into mirror images.* A rectangle has two: one from side to side in the middle and the other drawn from end to end in the middle. Lines of symmetry may be formed when a shape is folded. From corner to corner would be a diagonal, not a line of symmetry.

4. C. *2 longs; 14 units.* This is the best answer. A long has a value of 10 units. Two longs would represent 20 units. Add the 14 units and the total number represented is 34. A flat has the value of 100 units.

5. C. *11 hours, 15 minutes.* The answer may be found by multiplying 45 minutes by 15 days and converting the total number of minutes to hours and minutes. This is done by dividing the product of 45 × 15 by 60 (minutes in an hour). The remainder is indicated as minutes leftover after making as many hours as possible.

6. A. *60 cm (centimeters).* This is the most reasonable answer. Millimeters are too small. A centimeter is about the width of the human little finger. A meter is comparable to a yard, and a kilometer is closest to a mile (though less than a full mile). Meters and kilometers are too large. (An inch is approximately 2.54 cm.)

7. C. *Looking for a pattern.* This is the best strategy to apply in a problem such as this. The other strategies are more appropriate when there is more information available. For example, if a few digits were placed in the problem, the work backwards would be appropriate. Extending the problem is not a good choice because there is not enough information provided. Drawing a diagram is not appropriate in this case.

8. A. *Ask the student to explain why he or she divided 315 by 60 and what that answer represents.* This teacher response exemplifies the constructivist approach to teaching mathematics. It allows children to reflect and justify their responses in order to make sense of the problem at hand. The other response choices here are not appropriate for a learner-centered mathematics classroom.

9. B. *3. This answer is best, as there are 9 cats.* The triangle represents 3 cats, so 9 divided by 3 = 3 triangles needed for the graph.

10. D. *How to better understand the concept of less than and greater than.* This activity is asking children in general to measure the differences in objects in relation to each other. Understanding the concept of less than and greater than is very well represented in this activity for second grade. Children are able to compare without using a specific measuring scale. The next step would be to ask children to "predict" which is heavier.

11. A. *Spend class time working with concrete objects.* Children are better able to understand mathematical concepts by first using concrete objects to manipulate. From there, learning progresses to pictorial or graphic, symbolic, and abstract.

12. C. *Factors of whole numbers.* As children work with the 12 tiles to make different rectangles, the results create rectangles of different dimensions that are multiplication arrays (1 × 12, 12 × 1, 2 × 6, 6 × 2, 3 × 4, 4 × 3). These represent the factors of 12.

13. B. *Properties of congruent figures.* By definition, congruent figures have the same size and same shape. Thus, 4 × 3 and 3 × 4 are congruent figures.

14. C. *For any given number of colored tiles, how could you determine how many rectangles can be made?* This question is the best answer because it challenges children to reflect, evaluate, and generalize the concept to another situation that allows many different responses. This has the children thinking beyond the usual recall of information.

15. B. *Connect mathematics to real-world situations.* It is extremely important that children learn and apply mathematics to real-world contexts to provide relevancy and to motivate children's problem-solving thinking.

16. C. *1:3.* Students need to develop organizational skills needed to properly handle large quantities of data. Choosing an appropriate graphical representation is a fundamental requirement that students need to present data in an accurate manner. This response gives the ratio of the area of all of the tiles to the area of the green color tiles. This is the correct response: There are 60 color tiles total and 20 of the 60 are green. (In this case, the ratio of the green tiles [20] to the entire group of tiles [60] is written $^{20}/_{60}$. This simplifies to $^1/_3$ and is written in ratio form of 1:3.)

CONTENT PRACTICE TEST

This section includes problems addressing various mathematical concepts to help refresh some basic mathematical thinking and procedures. Answer the questions below and check your responses with the answers. (For further review visit the Web sites previously listed and/or locate some mathematics textbooks to study.)

1. Which number is a prime number: 9, 21, 41, or 36?

2. Complete. _____ kg = 3,200 g

3. There are 32 employees at the office. Of the employees, 20 are women. What percent of the employees are women?

4. Multiply: $-5.2 \times + 2.6 =$ ___?___

5. Write in exponent form: $4 \times 4 \times 4 \times 4 \times 4$

6. Divide. $0.02 \overline{)1.576}$

7. What are the coordinates of point A?

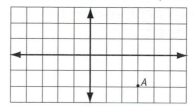

8. What is the LCM of 12 and 15?

9. Rosa spends $^1/_3$ of her allowance on lunch and $^1/_4$ of her allowance on entertainment. How much of her allowance is left?

10. What percent of 40 is 35?

11. Find the circumference.

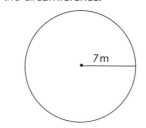

12. Find the volume.

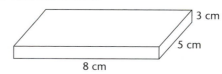

13. A sweater that usually sells for $29.00 is on sale for $26.10. What is the percent of decrease?

14. How tall is the house?

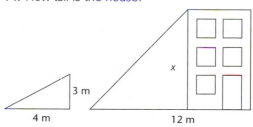

15. Subtract.

6 yds. 1ft.
-3 yds. 2ft.

16. What is the surface area?

17. Solve for *n*. $5n - 14 = -19$

18. Add. $5\frac{1}{6}$
    $+ 6\frac{5}{8}$

19. Round 68.0719 to the nearest tenth.

20. Jamyce has received grades of 89, 92, and 85 on 3 tests. What grade must she get on the next test in order to have an average of 90?

21. Subtract: $-6 - -5 =$ ____?____

22. Find the perimeter.

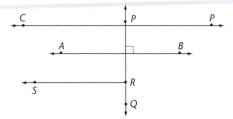

23. Which line is perpendicular to line AB?

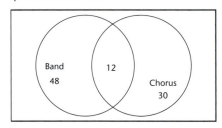

Use the Venn diagram below to answer questions 24–27.

24. How many students are in the band?

25. How many students are in the chorus?

26. How many students are in the band and the chorus?

27. How many students are in the band but not in the chorus?

28. How many square meters of carpeting are needed to carpet a room that measures 12 meters by 19 meters?

29. Which ratio is equal to the ratio 3:4?
    A. 4:3
    B. 6:7
    C. 15:20
    D. 20:15

30. Write as a percent: 3/8

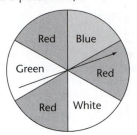

Use the spinner to answer questions 31-34. You spin the spinner. Find each probability.

31. P (red) (probability of hitting a red section).

32. P (not blue) (probability of not hitting a blue section). You toss a coin and then spin the spinner above. Find each probability.

33. P (head, red)

34. P (tail, red)

35. Find the permutation. There are 4 students and 4 chairs in a room. How many different possible seating arrangements are there?

36. Carrie used a 3-meter-long leash to tie her dog to a tree. What is the area of the circular region in which Carrie's dog can play?

Use the data below to answer questions 37–40.

85	75	70	70	70
100	90	85	90	65
70	90	80	65	85
75	100	75	95	95
65	90	90	85	90

37. The mode is _____ .

38. The range is _____ .

39. The median is _____ .

40. The mean is _____ .

41. Solve: $(6 \times 4) - (18 \div 3)$

42. Solve: $6(4 + 5)$

ANSWERS WITH PROCEDURAL RATIONALE

1. *41.* A prime number has only 1 and itself as a factor.

2. *3.2.* 1,000 g. in one kg.

3. *62.5%.* 20 is what part of the total, 32? Divide 20 by 32 for the decimal, .625. Change into a percent.

4. *−13.52.* The product in multiplication of a positive and a negative number will be a negative number.

5. *45.* The number of times the number is used as a factor determines the exponent.

6. *78.8.* The decimal point in the divisor and the dividend is moved two places to the left to make the divisor a whole number. Then division procedures are followed.

7. *(3, −2).* The first number in a coordinate pair represents the *x*-axis (horizontal) value, the second number is the *y*-axis (vertical) value.

8. *60.* The LCM is the least common multiple and is found by listing the multiples of 12 and listing the multiples of 15. Find the common multiple from the list that is the least in number.

9. *$\frac{5}{12}$.* Change $\frac{1}{3}$ and $\frac{1}{4}$ to have a common denominator of 12 ($\frac{4}{12} + \frac{3}{12}$), add to obtain 7/12. That subtracted from 1 (the allowance) ($\frac{12}{12} - \frac{7}{12}$) will be $\frac{5}{12}$.

10. *87.5 percent.* To find a percent of a number, divide 35 by 40. The decimal answer is then changed to a percent (.875 becomes 87.5 percent).

11. *43.96 m.* C = 2π r; (*pi* × radius); pi = approximately 3.14.

12. *120 cubic cm.* The volume is found by multiplying the measurement of each of the edges (8 × 5 × 3).

13. *10%.* Subtract the sale price from the original price ($2.90). Find what percent that is of the original $29.00 (Divide $2.90 by $29.00 to get .10, to become 10%.)

14. *9 m.* This is a proportion problem. The small triangle is similar to the triangle drawn from the building. Similar figures have angles and sides that are in proportion. The given ratios may be determined to be 3:4 and x (the unknown) is to 12. 3:4 as x is to 12. Cross products may be used to solve. (4x = 3 times 12 or 36). Solve for x.

15. *2 yd 2 ft.* The 6 yd. 1 ft. must be renamed as 5 yd 4 ft, as 1 yd is renamed (3 ft.) and added to the already 1 ft. Subtract.

16. *88 square cm.* Surface area is the sum of all the areas of each face of the figure. In this case there are 6 faces. Each is a rectangle. A = lw. (4 × 1, 4 × 1, 8 × 4, 8 × 4, 8 × 1, 8 × 1)

17. *−1.* Add 14 to both sides of the equation. 5n = −5. Divide both sides by 5; n = −1.

18. *$11\frac{19}{24}$.* To add unlike fractions, determine the least common denominator (24), then add. ($5\frac{4}{24} + 6\frac{15}{24} = 11\frac{19}{24}$).

19. *Zero is in the tenths place.* The 7 in the hundredths place determines that the zero be rounded up to 1. 68.1 is the answer.

20. *To obtain an average of 90 from four tests, a student would need a total of 360 grade points.* Add the first three scores to total, 266. Subtract this from 360 to get 94.

21. *−1.* To subtract −5 from −6 use the inverse of −5 which is a +5. Another traditional saying is to change the sign of the second number and add, when subtracting like signed numbers. To begin to teach students this concept, use a number line or use 2 color counters and teach making zero pairs (pairing a negative to a positive to make zero).

22. *38 cm.* Add the length of all four sides to determine the perimeter.

23. *Line PQ.* Perpendicular lines form a right angle at the point of intersection.

24. *60 (45 + 12).* This represents only the band members' set.

25. *42.* This set includes those that are members of the chorus and the band and only the chorus. (30 + 12)

26. *12.* This set is only those members that are in the band and the chorus.

27. *48.* This set represents the total of 60 minus those that are in both (12) totaling 48.

28. *228 square m.* To find the area for a rectangle, multiply the length by the width.

29. *15:20.* Two equivalent ratios make a proportion.

30. *37.5%.* 3 represents what percent of 8. 3 is divided by 8. That decimal quotient is changed to a percent.

31. $\frac{1}{2}$. There are three red sections on the spinner out of a total of six sections. 3/6 becomes $\frac{1}{2}$ in its simplest form.

32. $\frac{5}{6}$. There is only one blue section of the spinner and five that are not blue. 5 out of 6.

33. $\frac{1}{4}$. The probability of spinning a red is 1 out of 2 ($\frac{3}{6}$), for tossing a head is $\frac{1}{2}$. Multiply the two probabilities: $\frac{1}{2} \times \frac{1}{2} = \frac{1}{4}$.

34. $\frac{1}{4}$. Same as above.

35. *There are 4 choices for the first student. Once he sits down, there are only 3 choices for the second student. The third student has 2 choices. The last student has only 1 choice. Mathematically this is represented as $4 \times 3 \times 2 \times 1 = 24$.*

36. *28.26 square m.* The leash represents the radius of a circle. To find the area of a circle, multiply *pi* (3.14) times the radius squared.

37. *90.* The mode is the most often occurring number.

38. *35.* The range is the difference between the largest and the smallest numbers.

39. *85.* The median is the middle number. It is the average of the two middle numbers when the numbers are arranged in order.

40. *82.* The mean is the average. Total all numbers and divide by the number of numbers.

41. *18.* PEMDAS (Please Excuse My Dear Aunt Sally) This phrase represents the order of operations. Perform operations in parentheses first, then exponents, multiplications, division, addition, subtraction.

42. *54.* Same as above.

Table 3.4 Common Mathematical Difficulties for Children

Most difficulties that children have with arithmetic stem from a lack of understanding of important place-value concepts.

Place-Value Difficulties

- Associating place-value models with numerals
- Using zero when writing numerals
- Using regrouping concepts to represent numeral
- Naming place-value positions in a numeral
- Giving nonstandard place-value representations for a numeral

Addition and Subtraction Difficulties

- Identifying addition or subtraction situations
- Using counting to find basic addition facts with zeros in computations
- Using counting to find differences that are related to addition facts
- Regrouping when computing sums and differences
- When the two numerals in an exercise have a different number of digits
- A sum involving several addends or when a sum or difference involves large numbers

Multiplication and Division

- Identifying multiplication and division situations
- Determining the basic facts
- Using the basic multiplication facts to find related quotients
- Applying place-value concepts and basic facts to obtain products and quotients of multiples of ten
- Using zeros in a product or quotient
- Using the distributive property of multiplication over addition when computing products
- Regrouping when computing products and quotients
- Aligning partial products
- Solving word problems "when"

Rational Numbers

Difficulties associated with fractions
- Associating meaning with a fraction
- Using the equivalent fraction rule

- Applying appropriate uses of a common denominator
- Making appropriate interpretations for mixed numerals such as $2\frac{2}{3}$ or $5\frac{3}{8}$
- With the meaning of the operations

Difficulties associated with decimals
- Associating meaning with a decimal
- With place value and with the equivalent fraction rule
- With place value and with common denominators in addition and subtraction
- With the meaning of the operations and in distinguishing between various rules for the operations

Reading and writing difficulties
- Mathematical terms and symbols that are based on precise definitions are not generally learned in out-of-school environments.
- Sometimes words that have precise mathematical meaning are used ambiguously in everyday conversations.
- Mathematical words have other meanings in ordinary usage.
- Words are used inappropriately in mathematical context.
- The names and meaning of many mathematical symbols cannot be determined by looking at the symbols.
- Sometimes inappropriate or misleading visual models are given to illustrate the meaning of mathematical terms and ideas.
- Mathematical language is more concise than ordinary language.
- The organization of mathematical communications differs from the organization of ordinary reading materials.

(Adapted from Troutman & Lichtenberg (1999))

GLOSSARY

Acute angle. An angle that measures greater than 0 degrees and less than 90 degrees.

Acute triangle. A triangle that contains an acute angle.

Addend. A number that is added. In $5 + 8 = 13$, the addends are 5 and 8.

Adjacent angles. Two angles with a common vertex, a common ray, and no common interior points.

Algebra. A branch of mathematics in which arithmetic relations are explored using letter symbols to represent numbers.

Algorithm. A step-by-step procedure used to find a solution.

Angle. Two rays with the same endpoint. The endpoint is called the vertex of the angle.

Arc. Part of the circumference of a circle.

Area. The number of square units needed to cover a surface.

Associative property of addition. The sum is always the same when the addends are grouped differently. $(2 + 3) + 4 = 2 + (3 + 4)$.

Associative property of multiplication. The product is always the same when the factors are grouped differently. $(2 \times 3) \times 4 = 2 \times (3 \times 4)$

Average. A number obtained by dividing the sum of two or more addends by the number of addends. $(2 + 4 + 6 = 12 \div 3 = 4)$

Bar graph. A graph using vertical or horizontal bars to display numerical information.

Basic fact. A number sentence that has at least two one-digit numbers. Examples are: $7 + 1 = 8$, $15 - 8 = 7$, $9 \times 2 = 18$, $8 \div 4 = 2$

Bisect. To divide into two congruent parts.

Box and whiskers. A graph showing the shape of a data set.

Capacity. The volume of a figure, given in terms of liquid measure.

Circle. A plane figure with all of its points the same distance from a given point called the center.

Circle graph. A round graph that uses different-sized wedges to show how portions of a set of data compare with the whole set.

Circumference. The distance around a circle.

Commutative property of addition. Two numbers can be added in either order. The sums are the same.

Commutative property of multiplication. Two numbers can be multiplied in either order. The products are are the same. (2 × 4 = 8; 4 × 2 = 8)

Common denominator. A common multiple of two or more denominators. For $\frac{1}{6}$ and $\frac{5}{8}$, it would be 24.

Common factor. A number that is a factor of two or more numbers. A common factor of 9 and 6 is 3.

Common multiple. A number that is a multiple of two or more numbers. A common multiple of 2 and 3 is 6.

Complementary angles. Two angles whose measures add up to 90 degrees.

Composite number. A whole number greater than 1 that is not prime.

Cone. A solid with a circular base and one vertex.

Congruent. Having the same size and the same shape, as in a congruent figure.

Congruent angles. Two angles that have the same measure.

Conjecture. A well-thought out guess, prediction, or estimate.

Coordinate system. A graph with a horizontal number line (*x*-axis) and a vertical number line (*y*-axis) that are perpendicular to each other. The point of intersection is called the origin and labeled 0 on the graph. An ordered pair (*x, y*) is used to name a point on a coordinate system.

Counting. 1, 2, 3, 4 (naming sequence of numbers).

Cube. A rectangular solid with six congruent square faces.

Cylinder. A solid with two bases that are congruent circles.

Decimal. A number that uses place value and a decimal point to show tenths, hundredths, thousandths, and so on.

Dependent events. Events such that the outcome of the first event affects the outcome of the second event.

Denominator. The bottom number of a fraction, telling in how many parts the whole is divided.

Diagonal. In a polygon, a segment that connects one vertex to another vertex but is not a side of the polygon.

Diameter. In a circle, a segment that passes through the center and has its endpoints on the circle.

Difference. The answer for subtraction. In 16 − 9 = 7, 7 is the difference.

Distributive property of multiplication over addition. The product of a number and the sum of two numbers equals the sum of the two products. 3 × (4 + 2) = (3 × 4) + (3 × 2).

Dividend. A number that is divided by another number. For example in 36 ÷ 4 = 9, the 36 is the dividend.

Divisible. When one number is divided by another and the remainder is 0, the first number is divisible by the second number.

Division. An operation on two numbers that results in a quotient and a possible remainder.

Divisor. A number that divides another number. In the example 36 ÷ 4 = 9, the 4 is the divisor.

Endpoint. The point at the end of a line segment.

Equally likely outcomes. Outcomes that have the same chance of occurring in a probability experiment.

Equation. A mathematical sentence that uses the congruent sign ≅.

Equilateral triangle. A triangle with three congruent or equal sides and three angles of 60° each.

Equivalent fractions. Fractions that name the same fraction ($\frac{1}{2} = \frac{2}{4} = \frac{4}{8}$).

Even number. A whole number that is a multiple of 2.

Event. The particular outcome one is looking at in a probability experiment.

Expanded form. Expressing a number as factors. 325 = (3 × 100) + (2 × 10) + (5 × 1).

Exponent. A number that tells how many times the base is to be used as a factor or to be multiplied by itself. (In 2^3, 2 is the base, 3 is the exponent so it would mean 2 × 2 × 2).

Face. A flat surface of a solid figure.

Fact families. The related number sentences for addition and subtraction or multiplication and division that contain all the same numbers (for example, 2 + 3 = 5; 3 + 2 = 5; 5 − 3 = 2; and 5 − 2 = 3).

Factor. A number to be multiplied or a number that divides evenly into a given second number is a factor of that number. (in $2 \times 3 = 6$, 2 and 3 are factors of 6.)

Factor tree. A diagram showing how a composite number breaks down into its prime factors.

Factorization. Writing a whole number as a product of factors. (The factorization of 12 would be $2 \times 2 \times 3 = 12$.)

Frequency. The number of times a score appears in a list of data.

Function. For every input value there is one and only one output value.

Greatest common factor (GCF). The greatest whole number that divides two whole numbers. (The GCF of 24 and 32 is 4 evenly.)

Greatest possible error (GPE). The GPE of a measurement is equal to one-half the unit of measure.

Height of a triangle. The perpendicular distance from a vertex to the opposite side or base.

Hexagon. A polygon with six sides.

Independent events. If two events A and B are independent, then the probability that both will happen is $P(A) \times P(B)$.

Integers. The whole numbers and their opposites. . . . $-2, -1, 0, 1, 2$ . . .

Inverse operations. Operations that "undo" each other. Addition and subtraction are inverse operations. Multiplication and division are inverse operations.

Isosceles triangle. A triangle with two congruent sides.

Least common denominator (LCD). The least common multiple (LCM) of two denominators. (30 is the LCM of $\frac{1}{6}$ and $\frac{1}{15}$.)

Least common multiple (LCM). The smallest number that is a common multiple of two given numbers. (The LCM of 3 and 4 is 12.)

Line. A straight path that extends forever in both directions.

Line graph. A graph in which a line shows changes in data, often over time.

Line of symmetry. A fold line of a figure that makes the two parts of the figure match exactly.

Line segment. Part of a line with two endpoints.

Mass. The amount of matter that something contains.

Mean. The average of a set of numbers; the sum of the numbers divided by how many numbers there are.

Median. The middle number of a set of numbers after they have been placed in numerical order. (In the set [2, 3, 4], 3 is the median). If there are an even number of numbers, the median is the average of the two "middle" numbers.

Minuend. The number from which another number is subtracted. (For example, $14 - 8 = 6$, 14 is the minuend.)

Mode. The number that occurs the most frequently in a set of data. In the set [2, 4, 4, 3, 5] 4 is the mode.

Multiple. A multiple of a number is the product of that number and a whole number. Some multiples of 2 are 4, 6, and 8.

Multiplicand/multiplier. A number that is multiplied by another number. (In $7 \times 4 = 28$, the multiplicand is 7; the multiplier is 4.)

Numerator. The top number in a fraction that tells how many parts of the whole are being named.

Obtuse angle. An angle that measures greater than 90 degrees and less than 180 degrees.

Obtuse triangle. A triangle that contains an obtuse angle.

Octagon. A polygon with eight sides.

Odd number. A whole number that is not a multiple of 2.

Order of operations. When there is more than one operation and parentheses are used, first do what is inside the parentheses. Next, multiply or divide from left to right. Then add or subtract from left to right (PEMDAS or Please Excuse My Dear Aunt Sally).

Ordered pair. A number pair, such as (2, 3), in which the 2 (x-axis) is the first number and the 3 is the second number (y-axis).

Outcome. Any possible result in a probability experiment.

Parallel lines. Lines in the same plane that do not intersect.

Parallelogram. A quadrilateral (any four-sided polygon) with opposite sides parallel and congruent.

Pentagon. A five-sided polygon.

Perimeter. The sum of the lengths of the sides of a polygon.

Perpendicular lines. Lines that intersect at right angles.

Pi. The number obtained by dividing the circumference of any circle by its diameter. A common approximation for π is 3.14.

Pictograph. A visual representation used to make comparisons. A key always appears at the bottom of a pictograph or picture graph showing "how many" each object represents.

Plane. A flat surface that extends indefinitely in both directions.

Plane figures. Two-dimensional figures with flat surfaces such as squares, rectangles, hexagons, triangles, pentagons, and quadrilaterals.

Point. A location in space.

Polygon. A simple closed figure (square, triangle, hexagon, etc.).

Polyhedron. A space figure with all flat surfaces (faces).

Power of a number. A number found by multiplying the number by itself one or more times.

Prime factor. A factor that is a prime number. (The prime factors of 15 are 3 and 5.)

Prime factorization. A composite number expressed as a product of prime numbers. ($24 = 2 \times 2 \times 2 \times 3$ or $2^3 \times 3$).

Prime number. A whole number greater than 1 with exactly two whole positive factors: 1 and itself.

Probability. The chance that an event will occur.

Product. The answer in a multiplication problem. (in $36 = 4 \times 9$; 36 is the product.)

Proportion. An equality of ratios. ($\frac{1}{2} = \frac{4}{8}$)

Quotient. The answer in a division problem.

Radius. In a circle, it is a line segment that connects the center of the circle with a point on the circle.

Range. The difference between the highest and lowest values in a data set.

Ratio. A comparison of two or more values. $\frac{1}{2}$, $\frac{4}{6}$; or 1:2, 4:6; or 1 is to 2 as 4 is to 6.

Rational counting. The ability to order and enumerate objects in sets.

Rational number. Any number that can be expressed as a fraction a/b, where a and b are integers and b ≠ 0. Examples are: 3, $\frac{3}{1}$, $\frac{1}{4}$, .34, 56 percent, and so on.

Ray. Part of a line that has one endpoint and goes on and on in one direction.

Reciprocals. Two numbers whose product is 1. $\frac{2}{3} \times \frac{3}{2} = 1$

Rectangle. A parallelogram with four right angles.

Reflection. The mirror images of a figure that has been "flipped" over a line.

Remainder. The amount left over after a division problem. $\frac{18}{4} = 4r2$

Rhombus. A parallelogram with four congruent sides.

Right angle. An angle that measures 90 degrees.

Right triangle. A triangle that contains a right angle (90 degrees).

Rotation. The image of a figure that has been turned, as if on a wheel.

Rote counting. The naming of numbers in order without making any connection between numbers and sets of real-life objects.

Rounding. Expressing a number to the nearest thousandth, hundredth, tenth, one, ten, hundred, thousand, and so on as directed.

Scalene triangle. A triangle with no congruent sides.

Scatter plot. A graph showing paired data values.

Segment. Part of a line including two endpoints.

Similar figures Figures with the same shape but not necessarily the same size.

Slide. See *Translation*.

Solid figures. Three-dimensional figures such as cones, spheres, cylinders, cubes, prisms, and pyramids.

Sphere. A round, solid figure with all points an equal distance from the center.

Square. A rectangle with four congruent sides.

Statistics. A branch of mathematics that deals with the organization, description, and analysis of data.

Subtrahend. The number to be subtracted from another number. (In $15 - 8 = 7$, the 8 is the subtrahend.)

Sum. The answer in an addition problem.

Surface area. The sum of the areas of all the surfaces of a space figure.

Symmetry. A figure has line symmetry if it can be folded on a line so that the two halves of the figure are congruent (the same). The fold line is called the line of symmetry.

Translation. The image of a figure that has been "slid" to a new position without flipping or turning.

Trapezold. A quadrilateral with one pair of parallel sides. These sides are called the upper and lower bases.

Tree diagram. A diagram used to find the total number of outcomes in a probability experiment.

Triangle. A polygon with three sides.

Unit price. The ratio of the total cost to the number of units.

Variable. A symbol, usually a letter, that stands for an unknown quantity.

Venn diagram. A diagram that uses regions to show relationships between sets of things.

Vertex. The common endpoint of two rays that form an angle, or the point of intersection of two sides of a polygon or polyhedron.

Volume. The number of cubic units needed to fill a solid figure.

Weight. A measure of the force that gravity exerts on a body.

Whole number. Any one of the numbers 0, 1, 2, 3, ... There is no "largest" whole number. The smallest whole number is zero.

Zero property for addition and subtraction. For any number n, $n + 0 = n$ and $n - 0 = n$. Zero is the additive identity for addition.

Zero property for multiplication. For any number n, $n \times 0 = 0$.

REFERENCES

Ashlock, R. (1990). *Error patterns in computation on semi-programmed approach* (5th ed.). New York: Macmillan.

Ball, D.L. (1993). With an eye on the mathematical horizon: Dilemmas of teaching elementary school mathematics. *Elementary School Journal, 93*(4), 373–397.

Brooks, J.G., & Brooks, M.G. (1993). *In search of understanding: The case for the constructivist classroom.* Alexandria, VA: Association for Supervision and Curriculum Development.

Carlton, R.A. (1980, May). *Basic skills in the changing work world.* Monograph. Ontario, Canada: University of Guelph.

Cobb, P., & Lampert, M. (1998). *Communication.* Paper prepared for the National Council of Teachers of Mathematics. Reston, VA: NCTM.

Davis, R.B., Maher, C.A., & Noddings, N. (1990). Suggestions for the improvement of mathematics education. In R.B. Davis, C.A. Maher, & N. Noddings (Eds.), *Constructivist views on the teaching and learning of mathematics.* [Monograph Number 4]. *Journal for Research in Mathematics Education,* 187–191. Reston, VA: NCTM.

Driscoll, A., & Nagel, N. G. (2002). *Early childhood education, birth-8: The world of children, families, and educators.* Boston: Allyn and Bacon.

Fitzgerald, A. (1985). *New technology and mathematics in employment.* Birmingham, AL: University of Birmingham, Department of Curriculum and Instruction.

Howden, H. (1989). Teaching number sense. *The Arithmetic Teacher, 36*(6), 6–11.

Lave, J. (1991). Situated learning in communities of practice. In L. B. Resnick, J. M. Levine, & S. D. Teasley (Eds.), *Perspectives on socially shared cognition* (pp. 63–82). Washington, DC: American Psychological Association.

National Council of Teachers of Mathematics. (1989). *Curriculum and evaluation standards for school mathematics.* Reston, VA: Author.

National Council of Teachers of Mathematics. (1991). *Professional standards for teaching school mathematics.* Reston, VA: Author.

National Council of Teachers of Mathematics. (1995). *Assessment Standards for school mathematics.* Reston, VA: Author.

National Council of Teachers of Mathematics. (1998). *Principles and standards for school mathematics: Discussion Draft. Standards 2000.* Reston, VA: Author.

National Council of Teachers of Mathematics. (2000). *Principles and standards for school mathematics.* Reston, VA: Author.

National Research Council. (1989). *Everybody counts.* Washington, DC: National Academy Press.

Noddings, N. (1990). Constructivism in mathematics education. In B. Davis, C. Maher, & N. Noddings (Eds.), *Constructivist views on the teaching and learning of mathematics.* [Monograph Number 4]. *Journal of Research in Mathematics Education,* 7–18.

Shulman, L. (1986). Paradigms and research programs in the study of teaching. A contemporary perspective. In M. Wittrock (Ed.), *Handbook of research on teaching* (3rd ed., pp. 3–36). New York: Macmillan.

State Board for Educator Certification (SBEC). (2001). Certification strand for generalist early childhood fourth-grade. Retrieved May 22, 2001 http:/ /www. sbec. state. tx. us/ certstand/ genec_4. htm .

Texas Education Agency. (1997). *Texas essential knowledge and skills for mathematics*. Austin, TX: Author.

Texas Education Agency. (1998). *Texas assessment of academic skills mathematics objectives*. Austin, TX: Author.

Texas Education Agency. (2001). Curriculum guidelines for early childhood. Retrieved May 22, 2001 http:/ /www. tea. state. tx. us/ curriculum/ early/ prekguide. html.

Troutman, A.P., & Lichtenberg, B. K. (1999). *Mathematics, a good beginning*. New York: Brooks/Cole Publishing Company.

Van de Walle, J. (1998). *Elementary and middle school mathematics, teaching developmentally* (3rd ed.). New York: Longman.

RESOURCES

Artzt, A.F., & Newman, C.M. (1990). *How to use cooperative learning in the mathematics classroom*. Reston, VA: NCTM.

Baroody, A.J. (1993). *Problem solving, reasoning, and communicating (K–8): Helping children think mathematically*. Columbus, OH: Merrill.

Burns, M. (1985, February). The role of questioning. *The Arithmetic Teacher,* 14–16.

Burns, M. (1992). *About teaching mathematics: A K–8 resource*. White Plains, NY: Cuisenaire.

Carpenter, T.P., Carey, D.A., & Kouba, V.L. (1990). A problem-solving approach to the operations. In J. N. Payne (Ed.), *Mathematics for the young child* (pp. 111–113). Reston, VA: NCTM.

Eisenhower National Clearinghouse for Math and Science Education (http:/ /www. enc. org/). This Web site offers mathematics and science Internet links for teachers, stories, and ideas about mathematics and science teachers.

Fennema, E. (1973, May). Manipulatives in the classroom. *The Arithmetic Teacher,* 350–352.

Hart, L.C., Schultz, K., Najee-ullah, D., & Nash, L. (1992). The role of reflection in teaching. *Arithmetic Teacher, 1,* 40–42.

Hope, J. (1989). Promoting number sense in school. *The Arithmetic Teacher, 39*(6), 12–16.

Kamii, C., & Lewis, B.A. (1990, September). Research into practice: Constructivist learning and teaching. *The Arithmetic Teacher, 38*(1), 34–35.

Math Forum (http:/ /www. forum. swarthmore. edu/). This Web site includes classroom materials, online mathematics activities, software, articles, and more.

Mathematics Lessons Database (http:/ /www. mste. uiuc. edu/ mathed/ queryform. html). This lesson in mathematics and programs related to teaching mathematics.

National Council of Teachers of Mathematics (http:/ /www. nctm. org). This is the national organization responsible for the creation and publication of the mathematics standards.

Stenmark, J.K. (Ed.). (1991). *Mathematics assessment: Myths, models, good questions, and practical suggestions*. Reston, VA: Author.

Texas Education Agency. (1998). *TAAS Mathematics objectives and measurement specifications and the mathematics update 1998–1999: A guide to TAAS and the Texas Essential Knowledge and Skills (TEKS)*. Austin, TX: Author.

Thornton, C.A. (1990). Strategies for the basic facts. In J.N. Payne (Ed.), *Mathematics for the young child* (pp. 133–151). Reston, VA: NCTM.

Teachers are encouraged to seek additional resources for review at the following Web sites:

http:/ /www. tea. state. tx. us/ student. assessment/ resources/ release/ index. html. Teachers may review and test on mathematical content by taking released TAAS tests online. Any of the grade-level tests are good reviews.

http:/ /www. tea. state. tx. us/ student. assessment/ taks/ index. html. This Web site highlights the new student testing, TAKS.

http:/ /www. tea. state. tx. us/ teks/ teksfaq/ ch111. html. This Web site highlights the student TEKS.

A MATHEMATICS LESSON PLAN

BUILDING FRACTION CONCEPTS

Grade Level: Fourth

Main Subject Area: Mathematics

Integrated Subjects: Social studies, Art, and reading

Time Frame Constraints: 3–4 days

Overall Goal(s): To enable students to identify fractions and what they mean, to name parts of fractions, to determine the magnitude of fractions, and to recognize equivalent forms of the same fraction.

TEKS/TAKS OBJECTIVES:

§ 111.16. Mathematics: (013) (4.2) Number, operation, and quantitative reasoning. The student describes and compares fractional parts of whole objects or sets of objects.

§ The student is expected to:

A. use concrete objects and pictorial models to generate equivalent fractions;

B. model fraction quantities greater than one using concrete objects and pictorial models;

C. compare and order fractions using concrete objects and pictorial models; and

D. relate decimals to fractions that name tenths and hundredths using concrete objects and pictorial models.

§ 113.6. Social Studies, Grade 4; (11) Economics. The student understands the reasons for exploration and colonization. The student is expected to: (A) identify the economic motivations for European exploration and settlement in Texas and the Western Hemisphere;

§ 117.14. Art (b) Knowledge and skills; (4.2) Creative expression/performance. The student expresses ideas through original artworks, using a variety of media with appropriate skill. The student is expected to (B) design original artworks.

§ 110.6. English Language Arts and Reading; (b) Knowledge and skills; (15) Writing/purposes. The student writes for a variety of audiences and purposes, and in a variety of forms. The student is expected to: (A) write to express, discover, record, develop, reflect on ideas, and to problem solve.

OBJECTIVES:

• Students will draw their favorite types of pizzas on a piece of paper and divide it into fair shares.

• Students will observe the concept of "fair shares" and discuss various "fair share" situations.

• Students will, in groups, decide on their best definitions of division.

• Students will orally and on paper use "special names" that tell us how many parts make a whole (e.g., thirds, three parts, etc.).

• Students will recognize that the more parts that are needed to make a whole, the smaller the parts (by constructing and using fraction strips).

• Students will recognize that the numerator tells how many parts are being considered, and the denominator tells us how many parts are in a whole by drawing and labeling models.

• Students will recognize that equivalent fractions are another way of naming the same amount by constructing and manipulating fraction strips and manipulating two-colored counters.

• Students will draw a "newly invented" candy bar, design a wrapper for it and show division into ten "fair shares," with each labelled with its fractional name.

Sponge Activity: Students will draw their own pizza with all the ingredients they like.

Focus or Set Induction: The teacher will have a huge Hershey bar that is divided into squares. She will tell children that after the lesson they may have a piece, but that she wants to divide it now. She shows that she is giving one group about $\frac{1}{4}$; and another group $\frac{3}{4}$. If students do not start saying "that's not fair," then she should ask if it is fair. Then she will tell students that they will be talking about "fair shares" today. She will then ask them to draw a line on the pizza that they just drew in the sponge activity to show what would be a "fair share" of their pizza if there were two other friends coming for lunch (three altogether) Students should draw thirds.

MAKING CONNECTIONS:

1. **Connections to Prior Knowledge (using a literacy strategy):** Ask students what they already know about division. What is division

about? Ask groups to come up with their best definitions of *division*. Share each group's definition with the class and connect division to fractions. Relate that fractions are a division into equal parts.

2. **Cultural Connections:** Do you think that people around the world use fractions? If so, what are some ways (division of food, division of labor, etc.)? Teacher will also talk about how in most of Europe, up until the 1800s, a family's land always went to the oldest son. Was that a "fair" share for the rest of the children in family? However, what would happen if there were ten children and each got a fair share (families were big then) . . . then each of those children had ten children . . . then they each had ten? What would eventually happen to the land? How much land would a child eventually get? Many families wanted to try to keep their land in one piece. That's why the oldest son received the land, but the fact that people could not have a "fair share" of land influenced much of the immigration to the New World and to Texas (in the 1800s).

3. **Connections to the Community:** Ask students when they see their community using "fair shares." Is the street divided into equal lanes? When you order at a restaurant, do you get equal portions as the other diners for whatever you order? Wouldn't it be terrible if you went to McDonald's, and they gave your friend a whole burger and you only half for the same price (or you got five fries and they got fifteen)?

4. **Connections to Student Interests & Experiences:** See focus. Talk about other things we can divide to make fair shares with our friends or family.

ENVIRONMENTAL CONCERNS

Students need to be seated in small groups (three to four) at a table. Materials and supplies should be in the center of the table (paper, markers, fraction strips, two-colored counters).

Materials: Drawing paper, three large Hersey bars (or more, depending on class size), three or more same size bananas and oranges, knife, writing paper, overhead projector, blocks, markers, index cards with hole punched in top left-hand corner

Activities: *Guided Practice.*

I. **Area Model:** Teacher will draw a rectangle on the overhead and explain that this rectangle represents a "whole." Using this "whole," the teacher will draw a vertical line "halfway" through the rectangle. Class will discuss how many parts there are to the rectangle (two) and that the two parts are each "fair shares" (the same size). Using the rectangle as a reference, students will "say" the names of the parts: $\frac{1}{2}$, $\frac{1}{2}$ and the whole is $\frac{2}{2}$. Students will label each part ($\frac{1}{2}$, $\frac{1}{2}$). The teacher will ask children, "What do you think the bottom number is telling us?" and "What is the top number telling us?"

Teacher tells students that there is an easy way to remember how a fraction is written. She shows a banana in fourths and asks students to tell how many pieces are there (four). Then she tells children to write that number down (how many pieces make the whole) and put a line over it. Then she lifts one piece up over the remaining three pieces and asks children to tell how many pieces are on top (1). Now put a one over the four. She tells students that to identify fractions, we first count all the pieces that would make a whole or "fair shares", and that is called the *denominator*. Then we put down a line. Next we count the parts that have been raised up out of the whole (over the line), and that is the *numerator*.

The teacher will draw another rectangle, similar in size to the first rectangle, and ask for a volunteer to draw vertical lines so that there are three "fair shares." The class will discuss how many parts there are (three) and that each part is the same size. Students will also "say" names of the parts, using the area model as a reference; $\frac{1}{3}$, $\frac{2}{3}$, and the whole is $\frac{3}{3}$. The students will work in their groups and draw model for fourths, fifths, and sixths. Groups will share their area models with the class and explain why their models demonstrate the fractions and will "say" the names of their fractions. To discuss fractions larger than one, the teacher will show two models of the same fraction: for example, $\frac{1}{2}$, and students will discuss how many "fair shares" there are (four) and how to "say" the parts: $\frac{1}{2}$, $\frac{2}{2}$, $\frac{3}{2}$, $\frac{4}{2}$.

II. **Length Model:** Using the fraction strips, have each student make halves, thirds, fourths, fifths, and sixths—use a different color paper for each fraction. As students finish making "halves," ask them to write the fraction $\frac{1}{2}$; on each part of the fraction strip. Then, as a class, "say" the fraction names $\frac{1}{2}$, $\frac{2}{2}$. Do the same process for thirds, fourths, fifths, and sixths. Each student will have a set of fraction strips.

Literacy Connection: Ask the student to write comments about making the fraction strips. Ask them to write everything they can tell you about these fraction strips.

III. **Ordering Fractions:** Using their fraction strips, students, in groups, will take a piece of each different colored fraction strip (will be one from $\frac{1}{2}$, $\frac{1}{3}$, $\frac{1}{4}$, etc.), and they will be able to place, in order of increasing magnitude, the fractions $\frac{1}{6}$, $\frac{1}{5}$, $\frac{1}{4}$, $\frac{1}{3}$, and $\frac{1}{2}$. Students will then discuss $\frac{2}{3}$ and $\frac{2}{4}$, etc. In their groups, they will discuss the magnitude of fractions and why when the bottom number gets bigger, the piece gets smaller.

IV. **Set Model:** Using two-colored counters, ask students to "show" $\frac{1}{2}$, $\frac{2}{4}$, $\frac{3}{6}$, etc. (have students line them up so they can see equivalency). Discuss why if fractions can physically be grouped into smaller sets, the fractions can be simplified ($\frac{2}{4} = \frac{1}{2}$, $\frac{3}{6} = \frac{1}{2}$). If not, the fractions are said to be *relatively prime.*

Literacy Connection: Ask students to write a self-assessment about simplifying fractions. Students will write about what they learned with the Hershey bar. They will discuss what would happen if they divided the Hershey bar into four "fair shares." If they gave a friend two "fair shares" and the student kept $\frac{1}{2}$ of the Hershey bar, would they each have the same amount? Why or why not. Explain.

Independent Practice: Students will draw two pictures on one sheet of art paper. Students will "invent" a rectangular candy bar and design the wrapper for it. They will draw the bar itself and show how their new candy bar will be divided into ten "fair shares" (show their rectangle divided into ten equal areas). They also will mark each piece with the fractional name ($\frac{1}{10}$) and label each portion. Then they will discuss how many portions equal a whole and why.

What will children do if they finish early? Use a paper plate and demonstrate how to divide the area of the circle into three "fair shares."

Assessment: Teachers will assess students on their new candy bar. Design elements of the wrapper are to be completed only. Correct use of fractional names and "fair share" elements must be correct.

Closure: Teacher will show a PowerPoint presentation of various things in real life where fractions are used (bicycle spokes design, road sign that says $\frac{1}{2}$ mile to something, road line dividing road lanes, window panes, house construction, etc.). Teacher will give each student a piece of the Hershey bar and ask what he or she received ("a fair share").

Modification for a student with a learning disability in math (spatial skills): Ask the student to divide the rectangles into only two "fair shares."

Reflection: To be completed after teaching the lesson.

Developed by: Rena M. Shull, Ph.D., Assistant Professor, Rockhurst University, Debra Pellegrino, Ed.D., Associate Professor, Rockhurst University

DRAFT YOUR OWN MATHEMATICS LESSON PLAN

Title of Lesson: _____

Grade Level: _____

Main Subject Area: _____

Integrated Subjects: _____

Time Frame/Constraints: _____

Overall Goal(s): _____

TEKS/TAKS Objectives: _____

_____

_____

Objective(s): _____

_____

_____

Sponge Activity: _____

_____

_____

Environmental Concerns: _____

_____

_____

Rationale(s): _____

_____

Focus or Set Induction: _____

Making Connections:

1. Connections to Past or Future Learning _____

_____

2. Connections to the Community: _____

_____

3. Cultural Connections: _____

_____

4. Connections to Student Interests & Experiences: _____

_____

Materials: _____

_____

_____

Activities: Guided practice: _____

_____

_____

_____

_____

_____

_____

_____

_____

Independent practice: _____

_____

_____

_____

_____

_____

_____

_____

Assessment: _____

_____

_____

What will students do who finish early? _____

_____

_____

Closure: _____

_____

_____

Modification for Students with Special Needs: _____

_____

_____

Reflection: _____

_____

_____

OBSERVING MATHEMATICS EXPERIENCES/ACTIVITIES

During your visit to a classroom, use the following form to provide feedback as well as to reflectively analyze the room, the materials, and the teacher.

The Classroom Environment	Observed	Not Observed	Response
1. The teacher elicits prior student knowledge about mathematics.			If so, describe. If not, tell how she or he could have done so.
2. An appropriate and motivating focus is used to begin the lesson.			If so, describe. If not, what could be used?
3. The lesson includes manipulatives.			If so, describe the "tools of inquiry"/manipulatives used. If not, describe what type of manipulatives may have been appropriate for this lesson.
4. Children are given time to manipulate ("play with") concrete items/manipulatives prior to settling into the learning task.			If so, what was the effect? If not, what was the effect?
5. If manipulatives are used, for what percentage of the class do they seem effective?			If they were not effectively used, tell why you believe they were not and give ideas and proper time for effective use.
6. Children are allowed to use manipulatives during independent practice.			If so, about what percentage of the class continued to use them during this time? What was the result?
. A Math Center is a part of the room.			If so, describe what types of tasks were in the center. Do they appear to be motivating? Why or why not? If not, tell what type of center and tasks might be effective.
8. Mathematics tasks are integrated into other centers in the room.			If so, describe. If not, tell what type of tasks could be included.
9. The learning environment is student centered for mathematics.			If so, describe. If not, how could this be accomplished?
10. The learning environment is motivating for mathematics.			If so, describe. If not, how could this be accomplished?
11. The mathematics lesson is logically presented.			If so, describe. If not, how could this be accomplished?
12. The mathematics lesson is interdisciplinary.			If so, describe. If not, what other content could be included?
13. Real-life problems are used in examples or in work.			If so, describe. If not, what examples could be included?
14. Student-to-student interaction is a part of the lesson.			If so, describe. If not, tell why it should be.
15. Teacher-led consensus is part of the lesson.			If so, describe. If not, tell why it should be.

The Classroom Environment	Observed	Not Observed	Response
16. The teacher addresses children who are in transitional stages according to Piaget.			If so, describe. If not, how could the teacher do this?
17. Many types of visuals are available in the class (charts, checklists, strategies, etc.).			If so, describe. If not, what are some additions that would be beneficial?
18. The lesson is presented in a logical manner.			If so, describe. If not, what should be rearranged and why?
19. Math strategies were discussed by the teacher.			If so, describe. If not (and the lesson is appropriate), tell what and how strategies could be included.
20. Children are informally assessed.			If so, is it appropriate? If not, describe how it could be more effective. Were *all* children "checked for understanding"?
21. Children are formally assessed.			If so, is it appropriate? If not, describe how it could be more effective.
22. Children are authentically assessed.			If so, is this appropriate? If not, describe how it could be more appropriate.
23. The teacher is positive about mathematics.			If so, describe. If not, tell why it would be important.
24. The teacher involves all children in the lesson.			If not, who was left out? Why do you think this student(s) are left out?
25. An appropriate closure was made for this lesson.			If so, describe. If not, how could this have been accomplished?
26. You would have liked to have experienced this mathematics lesson as a child.			Tell why or why not.
27. This lesson is constructivist.			Tell why or why not.
28. You would have learned from this lesson.			Tell why or why not.
29. Modifications are made for some children?			If so, describe them and tell if they are effective. If not, what could be changed?

TEST YOURSELF ON MATHEMATICS

1. Ms. Burns is discussing the concept of time with her first-grade students. She asks her students to close their eyes and, when they think one minute has passed, raise their hands. Once students have raised their hands, they may open their eyes, but they are to remain quiet until everyone else has raised his or her hand. The purpose of this exercise is to:
   A. have first-grade students practice counting techniques.
   B. have first-grade students realize that there is more than one right answer.
   C. have first-grade students develop estimation skills with regards to time.
   D. have first-grade students realize that some students count faster than others.

2. Ms. Shelledy has placed her second-grade students in groups of four and has given each group a bag of color tiles, a piece of one-inch-square paper, and markers. She asks each group to separate the color tiles by color and then to make a bar graph to represent their data using the one-inch-square paper. Ms. Shelledy asks the groups to bring their graphs to the front of the classroom and discuss their graphs. The *main* objective of this exercise is to:
   A. learn how to work in cooperative groups.
   B. increase students' familiarity with using language to describe data.
   C. give students practice in creating bar graphs.
   D. increase students' ability to sort objects by attributes.

3. What number should replace the blank in the following number sentence?
   $35 \times \_ = 2{,}450$
   A. 60
   B. 70
   C. 75
   D. 80

4. Ms. Sewell distributes four-function calculators to her third-grade students and asks that they enter the number 7,346. She asks students what number they need to subtract from 7,346 so that they will have the numeral 7,046 on their calculator displays. The *main* purpose for this activity is to:
   A. increase the use of technology in the mathematics classroom.

   B. have students realize that calculators can be used to add or subtract numbers efficiently.
   C. increase students' understanding of place value.
   D. have students use mental computation.

5. In the empty box below, see if you can figure out the relationship and fill in the correct number in the empty box.

5	10
13	
21	26

   A. 5
   B. 6
   C. 16
   D. 18

6. Ms. McAninch took her first-grade class on a walk near the school. She asked her students to look at the buildings in the neighborhood and to see if they could identify shapes they saw. When the students returned to the classroom, they discussed the shapes they had seen. The *main* purpose of this activity was to have children:
   A. learn about the buildings in the neighborhood.
   B. connect mathematical shapes to the real world.
   C. learn that mathematics learning can happen outside of the classroom.
   D. see how many different types of buildings are in the neighborhood.

7. If a clock's hands have an angle of 269 degrees, it would show approximately how much of a turn?
   A. $\frac{1}{4}$
   B. $\frac{1}{2}$
   C. $\frac{3}{4}$
   D. 1

8. The fourth-grade students in Mr. Douglas' class were studying circles and learning how to construct pie charts. What would be the appropriate manipulative for them to use?
   A. Cuisenaire rods
   B. Base ten blocks
   C. Paper plates
   D. Attribute blocks

9. Look at the following letters and tell which has no line of symmetry.
   A. **C**
   B. **T**

C. X
D. L

10. Ms. Goyal groups her third-grade students into pairs. She distributes a pair of straws to each pair of students and asks them to "show her" an acute angle by arranging the straws on their desks. The best reason for having them work in pairs is to:
A. give students an opportunity to work with something unusual to make more of an impact.
B. give students an opportunity to collaborate and share their ideas about angles.
C. give students an opportunity to demonstrate and discuss a visual representation of an acute angle.
D. give students an opportunity to learn more about geometry.

11. On the following number line, which letter represents two-thirds?

A	B	C	D	E
0	.25	0.5	⁴⁄₆	1.0

A. A
B. B
C. C
D. D
E. E

12. Ms. Pellegrino groups her kindergarten students into groups of four and gives each group a balance beam and base ten blocks. She asks the students to place three units on one side of the scale and two units on the other side of the scale. The *main* purpose of this activity is to:
A. connect mathematics to science.
B. strengthen student understanding of the counting numbers.
C. develop the concept of inequality.
D. develop the concept of one-to-one correspondence.

13. A veterinarian had to prescribe medicine for a cat that weighed 12 pounds. How many ounces does the cat weigh?
A. 144 oz.
B. 192 oz.
C. 6 oz.
D. 1¾ oz.

14. Ms. Longoria asks her second graders to draw a picture of a square. Students then share their pictures with their classmates and discuss why they think their pictures represent squares. Ms. Longoria listens carefully to her students' responses, and when the class is through, she discusses

what the students have said and corrects misconceptions she has heard. This lesson would be most appropriate for:
A. students developing a visual representation of geometric shapes.
B. developing students' van Hiele levels of understanding.
C. helping students to articulate their responses.
D. assessment of students' understanding of squares.

15. Mr. Kahn asks his fourth-grade students to discuss multiplication. He distributes calculators to each student and asks them to multiply two counting numbers. The students discuss their answers. Mr. Kahn asks students to generalize the magnitude of their answers. The *main* objective for this activity is to:
A. give students practice with multiplication.
B. give students practice with calculators.
C. use technology in the mathematics classroom.
D. develop number sense concepts of magnitude.

16. If Ms. Hong offers her children the same types of candy from a bag, and there are 6 red pieces, 4 green pieces, and 9 yellow pieces, what is the probability of a child picking a yellow piece?
A. ⁹⁄₁₉
B. ⅑
C. ¼
D. ¹⁰⁄₁₉

17. Ms. Seo has her fourth-grade students working in pairs with pattern blocks. She ask them to build a square using the green triangles. She then asks the students to build a rectangle that is not a square with the green triangles. The *best* objective for this activity is to:
A. develop students' spatial skills.
B. help students distinguish between rectangles and squares.
C. familiarize students with pattern blocks.
D. develop students' ability with area.

18. The entire third grade at Oak Hill Elementary has been studying multiplication. Ms. Lewis discusses that four times five is the same problem as five times four. This example demonstrates:
A. the Commutative Property for Multiplication.

B. the Associative Property for Multiplication.
C. the Distributive Property.
D. Multiplicative Identity.

19. Mr. Donaldson has been teaching division concepts to his fourth-grade students. He arranges students in groups of four and distributes base ten blocks to the groups. He asks the groups to take ten units blocks and divide them equally into two groups. Then, he asks them to divide the ten blocks into five equal groups. Finally, Mr. Donaldson asks the students to divide the ten blocks into zero groups. The *main* purpose of this activity is to show that:
    A. division is making groups of equal size.
    B. zero can be divided by any number.
    C. it is not physically possible to divide a number by zero.
    D. when dividing by zero, there will be a remainder.

20. Miss Studer's kindergarten class is working in pairs to sort attribute blocks by large blocks and small blocks. When students have finished sorting their shapes, she asks each student to choose one large block and draw a picture of this shape on a piece of paper. The objective for this activity is to develop each student's:
    A. ability to make a choice.
    B. drawing ability.
    C. ability to transfer a design.
    D. ability to understand the meaning of *large*.

21. Mr. Erick's first-grade class is discussing their pets. Mr. Erick suggests that the class develop a graph of this data. He distributes Post-it® notes for the number of pets each child says that he or she has at home and asks them to write the pets' names and types of animal on their notes. Finally, he asks children to come to the front of the class and place their notes on a chart that has been divided into sections by types of pets that those in the class possess. The *main* purpose of this activity is to:
    A. find out about the types of pets the class possesses.
    B. connect the pet data to a graphical representation.
    C. connect students' personal data to the classroom.
    D. have students move around in mathematics class at a certain point, as is developmentally appropriate at grade level.

TEST YOURSELF ANSWERS AND RATIONALES FOR MATHEMATICS

Answer 1: This problem, even though it is easy to see, emphasizes that estimation skills help to build number sense for young children. It is increasingly important for teachers to help children "feel" the passing of time periods, as successful students throughout their schooling are able to gauge the passing of a certain amount of time to a particular task. For example, when a teacher says, "You have 10 minutes left to finish your work," successful students are able to estimate this and vary their work to fit the time allotment. The correct answer is *C*.

Answer 2: Students need practice using mathematical vocabulary to describe data. Explaining to others helps fix a concept in one's own mind. The correct answer is *B*.

Answer 3: One can work this problem by "trying out" or "plugging in" each of the answers or, better, by dividing 2,450 by 35. The correct answer is *B*.

Answer 4: Place value is the most difficult concept for elementary students. Activities are needed to help students understand it better. The correct answer is *C*.

Answer 5: The relationship is 5 numbers more for each set of numbers. Therefore, 18 would be 5 more than 13. The correct answer is *D*.

Answer 6: Connecting mathematics in the classroom to the real world allows students to concretely see that mathematics is a part of the everyday world—a strong rationale for learning geometry. The correct answer is *B*.

Answer 7: A clock represents a circle; $\frac{1}{4}$ of a turn would be 15 minutes and would be a 90 degree angle; $\frac{1}{2}$ of a turn would be 30 minutes and would be a 180 angle; $\frac{3}{4}$ of a turn would be 45 minutes and would be a 270 degree angle, and 1 turn would be a full hour (60 minutes) or a 360 degree angle. Because 269 degrees is almost 270, the answer is $\frac{3}{4}$ of a turn. The correct answer is *C*.

Answer 8: Paper plates are appropriate because of their circular shape. The correct answer is *C*.

Answer 9: The only letter that could not be "folded over" to have a perfect mirror image (or line of symmetry) is L. The correct answer is *D*.

Answer 10: Students solidify their knowledge through peer discussions. The correct answer is *B*.

Answer 11: A = zero, so this cannot be the answer. B = .25, or $\frac{1}{4}$, so this is incorrect. C = .5, or $\frac{1}{2}$, so this is not correct. The correct equivalent of $\frac{2}{3}$ is $\frac{4}{6}$, and one can also see that $\frac{4}{6}$ is placed about $\frac{2}{3}$s down the number line. The correct answer is D.

Answer 12: The scales are an authentic means to demonstrate equality and inequality. The correct answer is C.

Answer 13: We would have to remember that one pound equals 16 ounces. Then we can simply multiply 12 by 16 for an answer of 192. The correct answer is B.

Answer 14: Through appropriate questioning, students will develop to the next van Hiele level. The van Hiele Model, developed by Pierre van Hiele and Dina van Hiele-Geldof, is a five-level hierarchy of ways to understand geometric thought. The levels are sequential, and appropriate questioning can help students to move to the next level of geometric understanding. The correct answer is B.

Answer 15: *Magnitude of numbers* is a number sense attribute that students need to develop. One component of having number sense is *understanding the relative magnitude of answers*. Students need practice in determining the *reasonableness* of an answer, so students can ask themselves, "Is my answer 'in the ball park'? 'too big'? 'too small'?" Activities such as these can help build number sense. The correct answer is D.

Answer 16: Probability exercises help students decide how "probable" an event is—or how likely it is to occur. Since there are 19 pieces of candy and 9 are yellow, students should realize that the ratio $\frac{9}{19}$ describes the number of yellow pieces of candy in the bag. The child has 9 chances out of 19 of picking a yellow piece. The correct answer is A.

Answer 17: Spatial sense is an *intuition* about shapes and the relationship of shapes. Spatial sense can be developed by appropriate activities that help students experience these relationships. The correct answer is A.

Answer 18: Understanding that the Commutative Law applies to both addition and multiplication helps students develop an "ease" with computation; that is, they can see the relationship between numbers. The correct answer is A.

Answer 19: Using manipulatives to develop a conceptual understanding of division enables students to seek logical solutions to problems. The fact that we cannot physically "show" how to divide 10 objects into 0 piles means that this problem cannot be solved mathematically either. The correct answer is C.

Answer 20: Students need many experiences in transferring images. These experiences will help students develop their abilities to accurately represent what they see to images they can replicate. The correct answer is C.

Answer 21: Mathematics must be connected to the real-world experiences of students. These connections help students to "make sense of their world" by connecting the vocabulary of math to actual data. The correct answer is C.

4 Preparing to Teach Social Studies in Texas

Trenia L. Walker
Washington State University—Vancouver

Janice L. Nath
University of Houston—Downtown

The National Council for the Social Studies (NCSS) established a Task Force on Standards that defined socials studies as:

[T]he integrated study of the social sciences and humanities to promote civic competence . . . . The primary purpose of studies is to help young people develop the ability to make informed and reasoned decisions for the public good as citizens of a culturally diverse, democratic society in an interdependent world. (1994, p. 3)

This NCSS definition was adopted by the Texas Education Agency's (TEA) (1999) Social Studies Center (SSC) when creating its Texas Social Studies Framework. The aim of social studies, as noted above and according to both national and Texas state standards, is civic competence. Mike Moses, a former commissioner of education in Texas stated, ". . . we know that the goal of providing students with the knowledge and skills necessary to assume their roles as leaders in our state and nation in the 21st century rests primarily with the social studies" (TEA, 1999, unnumbered preface). In our classrooms and in the world beyond, we want people to learn to live and work together responsibly. Social studies instruction is critical—both for preparing students to become responsible, thoughtful, participating citizens, and to provide students with many of the basic skills that involve geography, economics, and other areas under the umbrella of social studies that they will need to function in our society today and in the future.

Often mathematics and reading programs are considered the basics in EC-4 education; however, a social studies program is also basic. The Texas Education Code (1995) §28.002 calls for each school district that offers kindergarten through grade 12 to include social studies as part of the required curriculum. This code also specifies that instruction in social studies will consist of Texas, United States, and world history. Economics, one of the traditional subjects in the social studies, is included as a part of the enrichment curriculum. The Texas Administrative Code §74.2 goes on to say that for elementary grades, "The district must ensure that sufficient time is provided for teachers to teach and for students to learn English language arts, mathematics, science, social studies, fine arts, health, physical education, technology applications, and to the extent possible, languages other than English" (Texas Education Agency, 1995).

While the state of Texas mandates the instruction of social studies in K–12 classrooms, teachers should truly appreciate the importance of the subject(s). As Parker (2005) points out:

Without historical understanding, there can be no wisdom. Without geographical understanding, there can be no social or environmental intelligence. And without civic understanding, there can be no democratic citizens and, therefore, no democracy. This is why social studies matters. (p. 4)

Regardless of their future career paths, students are citizens of our country and the world. Hopefully, each will be a *thoughtful* citizen who will contribute in positive ways to society. Students will also need to navigate in their city and state and, perhaps, through much of their country and the world through an understanding of geography. They will need to understand their personal and national economic situations; their rights and the rights of others; how other nations and beliefs affect this country; references to our history and that of others; how to resolve conflicts; and many other skills that social studies provide. For these reasons, it is vital that EC-4 teachers devote sufficient instructional time to social studies. A good social studies program will integrate opportunities to develop students' skills in many other subjects, including reading, writing, mathematics, science, music, and so forth (Chapin, 2006).

Let us now look at the requirements for social studies knowledge and skills that EC-4 teachers need—both in order to pass the test and to teach his or her students well. Table 4.1 compares the *teacher standards,* the *Texas Examinations of Educators Standards (TExES) test framework,* and the *Texas Essential Knowledge and Skills (TEKS)* for children. Notice the overlap in what both teachers and children should know and be able to do and what children

Table 4.1 A Comparison of Knowledge and Skills for Teachers and Students

Teacher Standards (What teachers should know and be able to apply)	*The TExES Framework* (What teacher test takers should know and be able to apply)	*TEKS Strands* (What EC-4 students should know and do)
Knowledge History Geography Economics Government	Social science instruction History Geography and culture Government, citizenship, and economics	**Knowledge** History Geography Economics Government Culture
Values Citizenship Culture		**Values** Citizenship Science, technology & society
Skills Research Intra- and interdisciplinary teaching Recent issues and developments in the field		**Skills** (based on the strands above)

should know and be able to do. If you become familiar with all of these areas, you will do well on the test *and* be knowledgeable for your students.

It is beyond the scope of this chapter to provide *all* the knowledge, skills, and other information necessary for EC-4 social studies. However, every attempt will be made to connect the areas shown in Table 4.1 and to provide basic knowledge in social studies. Because there are so many terms, dates, and important names, these will be bolded in the chapter rather than repeated in a glossary in this chapter. The social studies test framework for the Generalist EC-4 certification (as seen in Table 4.1) is made up of four competencies (numbers 016–019): (016) Social Science Instruction; (017) History; (018) Geography and Culture; and (019) Government, Citizenship, and Economics. The State Board for Educator Certification (SBEC) defines each of these competencies:

(016) Social Science Instruction. The teacher uses social science knowledge and skills to plan, organize, and implement instruction and assess learning.

(017) History. The teacher demonstrates knowledge of significant historical events and developments and applies social science skills to historical information, ideas, and issues.

(018) Geography and Culture. The teacher demonstrates knowledge of geographic relationships among people, places, and environments in Texas, the United States, and the world; understands the concept of culture and how cultures develop and adapt; and applies social science skills to geographic and cultural information, ideas, and issues.

(019) Government, Citizenship, and Economics. The teacher understands concepts and processes of government and the responsibilities of citizenship; knows how people organize economic systems to produce, distribute, and consume goods and services; and applies social science skills to information, ideas, and issues related to government and economics.

Elementary Social Studies Scope and Sequence in Texas

Traditionally, EC-4 social studies builds a foundation to support the learning that will occur in later grades. The **scope and sequence** of social studies programs reflects this goal. The *scope* of a program is the depth of the subject (or how far into the subject will you go). The *sequence* is the order in which the subject matter will be introduced. In Texas, generally, the scope and sequence of social studies is vertically aligned as follows:

Kindergarten: self, home, family, and classroom
  1st Grade: student's relationship to the classroom, school, and community
  2nd Grade: local community and impact of individuals and events on the history of the community, state, and nation
  3rd Grade: how individuals have changed their communities and world
  4th Grade: history of Texas from the early beginnings to the present within the context of influences of the Western Hemisphere

Following this type of scope and sequence allows teachers to begin social studies instruction by focusing on areas that are *familiar* to their students. In the earliest grades, for example, the focus is on students' personal knowledge and experiences that are closest to them (and, thus, more concrete). In later grades, instruction is expanded from close to more distant, either in time (historically) or in place (globally). For instance, one sees that a main focus in kindergarten is on family; therefore, students in subsequent grades may be asked to build on their understanding by learning about families in a previous century or from a distant land. This foundation building for learning subsequent topics is essential. The TEKS for children establish this foundation.

The TEA's Social Studies Center (2000) states that a comprehensive social studies program depends on the *integration* of eight strands listed in the TEKS. By providing teachers with such a guide, Texas hopes to ensure that students become responsible citizens in the 21st century and that they possess needed factual and conceptual knowledge, intellectual skills, and basic democratic values. The eight strands of the TEKS are: (1) History; (2) Geography; (3) Economics; (4) Government; (5) Citizenship; (6) Culture; (7) Science, Technology, and Society; and (8) Social Studies Skills. In the introduction to the TEKS statements, it is recommended that the skills listed in the geography and social studies skills strands be incorporated into the teaching of all the other essential knowledge and skills for social studies.

Let's look more closely at the test *you* will be taking. In the text that follows, each of the standards and competencies that make up Domain III (the social studies component) will be introduced with a statement that broadly defines what an entry-level EC-4 educator needs to know and be able to do. A descriptive statement will follow, explaining in more detail the knowledge and skills covered by the standard. We also show how content can be taught in appropriate ways for EC-4 students, along with sample questions of the type that might be found on the TExES. It is of value to learn these standards and competency statements well because they give solid hints about how to answer many of the pedagogy-type questions on the Generalist test. For example, the paragraph that summarizes Competency 016 tells us that Texas wants its teachers to know and use the EC-4 Social Studies TEKS to design instruction; thus, if a question on the Generalist exam asks what would be a good base for guiding one's social studies curriculum, knowledge of this competency would clearly point to choosing the TEKS as a good answer. The practice questions should also be used to organize your reading and review the content. Because the standards requiring specific knowledge (history, geography, economics, and government) contain *so* much information, they have been broken down into smaller, more manageable units. At the end of the chapter, you will find a sample lesson plan with an additional blank form to write your own. There is also a form that you can use to guide and inform your observations of a social studies classroom and more practice questions.

 # Standards I, II, and III Social Science Instruction

The social studies teacher has a comprehensive knowledge of the social sciences and recognizes the value of the social sciences.

The social studies teacher effectively integrates the various social science disciplines.

The social studies teacher uses knowledge and skills of social studies, as defined by the Texas Essential Knowledge and Skills (TEKS), to plan and implement effective curriculum, instruction, assessment, and evaluation.

Competency 016. (Social Science Instruction) The teacher uses social science knowledge and skills to plan, organize, and implement instruction and access learning. The beginning teacher:

- Knows state content and performance standards for social studies that comprise the Texas Essential Knowledge and Skills (TEKS) and understands the vertical alignment of the social sciences in the TEKS from grade level to grade level, including prerequisite knowledge and skills.
- Understands the implications of stages of child growth and development for designing and implementing effective learning experiences in the social sciences (e.g., knowledge of and respect for self, families, and communities; sharing; following routines; working cooperatively in groups).
- Selects effective, developmentally appropriate instructional practices, activities, technologies, and materials to promote children's knowledge and skills in the social sciences.
- Selects and uses appropriate technology as a tool for learning and communicating social studies concepts.
- Selects and uses instructional strategies, materials, and activities, including appropriate technology, to promote children's use of social sciences skills and research tools.
- Provides instruction that relates skills, concepts, and ideas in different social science disciplines.
- Helps children make connections between knowledge and methods in the social sciences and in other content areas.
- Uses a variety of formal and informal assessments and knowledge of the TEKS to determine children's progress and needs and to help plan instruction for individual children, including English Language Learners.

Implication of Child Development in Social Studies

As in other content areas, *age and developmental levels* play a large part in effective teaching and learning. This is particularly true in social studies, where children need a wealth of concrete and visual items to enhance their development of spatial skills and abstract ideas. The development of social skills and values also depends upon children's readiness. Teachers of very young children provide experiences that both tie children together as a group with their commonalities and also help children identify traits that make them unique. Early childhood activities that feature name games, focus on physical similarities and differences, and employ family-based themes are all a part of a good developmental social studies program.

Constantly creating situations in which social skills are enhanced is also an important developmental process. It is difficult to have a country in which values are a part of life because young children have few opportunities to express themselves, feel empathy, belong to a group, and practice other social skills—mostly because they sit all day in individual seats with little interaction. It is difficult to have democracy in a place where only authoritarianism is seen and where children have few choices and feel powerless. Even small activities, such as voting on tomorrow's snack from a menu of items, sharing in a group, choosing a center or project of their own, or deciding how to show mastery from a list of assessment items, help increase social studies elements in the classroom. Providing time for young children to **play** in social situations is also a huge step in this direction, are **directed** or **creative dramatics** (e.g., telephone conversations, pretending to be at the store, or doing chores). **Role-play** is also a part of communication, particularly with issues that involve emotions, empathy, and decision making. A teacher may ask for an ad-lib scenario, such as this:

> *Let's pretend that Roberto accidentally tore Janna's paper. How would Roberto feel? What could he say? What could Janna say? Let's have them show us how they would handle it in a positive way.*

Drama is also important in social studies, as children play parts in historical plays or skits and gain insight into historical characters by acting out written historical situations. These can be written by professionals, by teachers, or by children. **Mock trials** for many issues allow children to learn about our justice system as they simulate the courtroom and take on the roles of attorneys, judge, and jury. **Mock meetings** (e.g., town meetings and legislative sessions) help children understand ways for the public to be involved in local and national government. Creating formats for children to work in **cooperative groups** is perhaps one of the most important areas for children to practice social skills. Teachers who *structure* these groups well are not only teaching content but also helping children gain skills they need to get along in the real world, such as sharing; giving "I" messages ("I feel angry and hurt when you say things like that," rather than "You are so mean!"); learning to actively listen (maintain eye contact, let the other person talk without interrupting, then telling/restating what you think was stated by the other person); learning to give and receive praise; negotiating by taking turns; using a compromise. It is difficult for children to gain these skills if the teacher constantly resolves conflicts rather than allowing children to work through situations in which they can practice these skills themselves. Therefore, we can see that the EC-4 teacher is constantly teaching *social skills* parallel to teaching social studies knowledge and skills.

Consider the following practice question:

Ms. Landry noted that Black History Month was fast approaching. In her yearly plan, she had blocked out several lesson periods to focus on this topic in her diverse urban classroom. Which of the following instructional techniques would be her best choice for these lessons?

- **A.** Lecture
- **B.** Inquiry
- **C.** Cooperative groups
- **D.** Independent study

There are two key issues in this question—a diverse classroom and a focus on an event related to multiculturalism. Although you might have said that inquiry (*B*) is a worthy part of social studies instruction (and, indeed, it is), a teacher would want to use cooperative groups (*C*) to teach the principles of multiculturalism. This is *particularly* appropriate in diverse classroom settings. Manning and Baruth (2000) state that "research on cooperative learning and inter-group relationships has shown that students in cooperative learning situations develop great appreciation for cooperative-learning classmates" (p. 236). Telling, or lecture (*A*), reading about it during independent study (*D*), or even inquiry (*B*) are no substitutes for having students work together to accomplish goals with those who may be different from themselves. The *best* answer is *C.*

Technology as a Teaching Tool

One of the most important issues in social studies education today is the role of technology in teaching and learning. Technology has played a leading role in connecting the world in unprecedented ways. Instantaneous communication, access to media and popular culture, and globalization have contributed to the interconnectedness of the world. Social studies educators understand the role of technology in the world today and the possibilities for the future. Clearly technology has a role to play in contemporary social studies education.

There are many technologies that might be incorporated into the classroom: computers, television, videos, audio recordings, CD-ROMs, and other tools. Media such as CDs, VHS tapes, and DVDs offer many opportunities for students to experience cultures across time and distance. Teachers should always be sure to preview media before class presentation to ensure that they are age appropriate in overall content and language, interest, connection to the subject being taught, and presentation.

Computers have been placed in most elementary schools since the late 1970s. During those early days, they were primarily used to provide drill-and-practice opportunities for students. Students were presented problems and entered their responses; the computer would send back a graphic feedback (usually along the lines of a smiley face/sad face). Clearly, this use concerned educators who came to view computers as centers of busy work with the same limitations as a worksheet. While many of these drill-and-practice computer programs remain, there are many other computer applications that provide powerful classroom learning tools; some examples include:

1. **Word processing, database, and spreadsheet software.** These programs are nearly standard on all classroom and computer lab computers and can be used in the social studies classroom for collection and presentation of data and a variety of writing tasks.

2. **Problem-solving software.** These programs present complex situations in which students face a dilemma, choose from a number of possible alternatives, and arrive at a solution—thus encouraging active exploration and discovery. One of the most popular problem-solving programs for children in grades 3 through 8 is *Where in the World Is Carmen Sandiego?*

3. **Strategy and simulation software.** These programs place students into situations that are as authentic as possible. One of the most popular simulations is *The Oregon Trail.* It presents a series of decisions that pioneers faced in 1847 as they set out in wagon trains to find new homes in the Oregon Territory. For example, if a student decides to hunt or stop at a fort, they can lose time and may fail to pass through the mountains before the winter snows begin. This could lead to illness or not having enough food. With each decision, children are shown the consequences of their choices. Other popular simulation programs are: *SimAnt, SimCity,* and *SimEarth.* In each of these simulations, children are placed into settings in which they describe, create, and control a system. Popular strategy software titles include *Chess* and, for older students, *Civilization III.* In this game, players attempt to "dominate the world through diplomatic finesse, cultural domination, and military prowess." "The game is an addictive blend of building, exploration, discovery, and conquest. Players match wits against some of history's greatest leaders as they strive to build the ultimate civilization to stand the test of time." (*Civilization III* Official Web site, n.d.)

4. **Presentation software.** These programs are communication tools that combine video, graphics, animation, and text. These "authoring" programs enable students to organize and communicate information in more aesthetically innovative ways. Some of the most popular presentation software titles for students are *Flash, PowerPoint,* and *KidPix.* Social studies is a perfect place for students to begin whole class, small group, or individual presentations through the use of these tools.

5. **Web-based communication.** Classroom connections to the Internet are common today. With these connections, students can access and create:
   - Electronic mail (e-mail)/instant messages (IMs)/text messages
   - Newsgroups and Listservs
   - Web sites, using *Dreamweaver, Flash,* and *MS FrontPage*
   - Weblogs (blogs) (simple Web sites that contain personal writing space); students might read blogs that belong to others, including politicians or social activists, and/or create their own
   - Podcasts (broadcast files)—information is recorded, saved in a compressed file format, such as MP3, and uploaded to the Internet. Listeners can download and play files on an iPod or other portable media player.

Children can find and use **experts** as resources and "chat" with students in their school, city, state, country, and the world and participate in joint social studies projects with other classrooms in their school or elsewhere. E-mails, blogs, and podcasts can be used to gain and share information, to solve problems, to increase communication skills, to let others know their feelings on issues, and so forth. Students can gain online access to streaming television and radio programs from stations around the world. They might also use the Internet to access online newspapers from around the world in order to track current events from a variety of perspectives. The Internet should allow children to open the doors of their classroom and interact with people from all over the world—including experts and other students. Teachers should be reminded that they must always monitor electronic communications carefully.

Intradisciplinary and Interdisciplinary Issues

Traditional-style education emphasizes the "separate teaching of individual subjects"—language arts, mathematics, science, and social studies. These subjects are often divided into separate instruction time with very few interconnections. The limited number of hours in the school day often precludes all subjects from receiving equal instruction time, causing social studies educators to be particularly concerned. Maxim (1999) observes: "If social studies is somehow squeezed into the day's schedule, children are often led through a quick oral reading of a textbook section and a brief question-answer recitation period" (p. 23). To remedy these practices, teachers can seek **themes** and design **thematic units** (in order to **integrate subject areas** with social studies). These themes can cut across numerous disciplines, allowing for learning opportunities that are *deeper* not *wider*.

The National Council for the Social Studies (NCSS) (1994) has identified five key factors that make for powerful social studies teaching and learning:

1. Meaningfulness
2. Integrated
3. Value-based
4. Challenging
5. Student active

Maxim (1999) adds that "social studies appears to be the major area for blending subjects previously taught separately" (p. 24), and Berg (1988) answers the question of where social studies might fit into the integration of subjects. He states:

> *Right in the middle! A major goal of the social studies is to help students understand the myriad interactions of people on this planet—past, present, and future. Making sense of the world requires using skills that allow one to read about the many people and places that are scattered about the globe; to use literature to understand the richness of past events and the people who are a part of them; to apply math concepts to more fully understand how numbers have enabled people to numerically manage the complexity of their world. The story of humankind well told requires drawing from all the areas of the curriculum. (Berg, unnumbered pull-out section)*

When social studies is integrative in its treatment of topics, it can cut across disciplinary boundaries in both **intradisciplinary** ways (overlapping *within* social studies content such as geography and economics or history and government) and **interdisciplinary** ways (overlapping lessons between social studies and other content areas such as mathematics, science, language arts, music, art, etc.). Themes can span time and space and integrate knowledge, beliefs, values, and attitudes to action. This type of integrated instruction works to develop a knowledge of the evolution of the human condition through time, its current variations across locations and cultures, and an appreciation of social and civic decision making (NCSS, 1994). There are *six intradisciplinary* areas of social studies commonly found in the lower levels:

1. Geography
2. Anthropology
3. Sociology
4. History
5. Economics
6. Political science

How might planning such lessons work? An example of *intradisciplinary* integration (within the social studies disciplines) might be found in teaching the concept of families. For example, children might be asked to use historical thinking skills to compare what families were like long ago to now. They may use their knowledge and skills in sociology and anthropology to understand how the concept of family works in other parts of the world and use geography to locate those places. Families might be used to springboard discussion and to examine economics, which could, in turn, connect well with helping develop students' understanding of needs and wants (and other economic terms) and how those might change in various parts of the country and the world. Teachers who employ intra- and interdisciplinary themes can integrate in exciting ways for children.

Teachers who integrate across all subjects, or use *interdisciplinary* integration, will connect concepts across all content areas—not just within social studies. This is true across the curriculum, but social studies connects particularly well with language arts. Meaningful literature selections, especially mass-market books and trade books, can provide exceptional opportunities for students to develop the knowledge and skills that will help them examine their opinions and attitudes as they learn outside the textbook and worksheets. Thus, literature is an important tool in a social studies classroom because it can educate and entertain. According to Huck, Hepler, and Hickman (1993), "A history textbook *tells;* [but] a quality piece of imaginative writing has the power to make the reader *feel*" (p. 11). Student motivation may be increased vastly through the use of children's books with social studies content and themes rather than with a social studies textbook alone. Farris (2001) suggests that to "overcome flagging motivation often attributed to the student with learning disabilities, to challenge gifted readers, and to hook the child with ADD (Attention Deficit Disorder), lively children's literature books are the answer" (p. 333). Other researchers agree that reading social studies-based quality children's literature enhances a child's understanding of social studies:

> *Literary works are packed with conceptual knowledge about the human condition and can supply meaningful content for skill-building experiences . . . . Perhaps more completely and certainly more intensely than with textbooks, a creative teacher can use trade books to engage students in the pursuit of such citizenship competencies as processing information, examining other points of view, separating fact from opinion, and solving problems. (McGowan & Guzzetti, 1991, p. 18)*

Textbooks are primarily concerned with facts; whereas, literature is primarily concerned with feelings: compassion, humanness, misfortune, grief, happiness, and awe (Maxim, 1999). Unfortunately, social studies teaching and learning—more than any other subject—is dominated by textbooks (Loewen, 1995). Most of the criticisms aimed at textbooks (physical size and weight; prose style that is bland and voiceless; and excessive coverage of information that makes them boring) should really be about targeting the ways teachers use them (Maxim, 1999). Textbooks are *not* meant to be the entire social studies curriculum—only a single resource.

There are many books that can be used to develop social studies knowledge and skills. For example, a *mock trial* can follow the reading of the *Real Story of the Three Little Pigs* (or other fairy tales with similar plots). Offering readings with multiple perspective taking is a major goal of the social studies for children. Fairy tales from the past or from other cultures and/or countries can be analyzed and compared. These tales can reveal a great deal about the people who tell or write them. Themes around books such as *Everybody Cooks*

Rice (Dooley, 1992) or *Bread, Bread, Bread* (Morris, 1993) invite reading, tasting, and geographical curiosity. In a unit on the theme of homes, students might begin by reading *Houses and Homes* (Morris, 1992). Young children can orally describe, write about, and draw their own homes and those they find in their neighborhoods. From these tasks, they can investigate the concept of shelter in other parts of the world and discover why people have created different types of houses or shelters to match various conditions and environments. This will provide an opportunity to conduct some scientific investigations of building materials. Using spatial skills in a Block Center, children can also investigate how some structures are built, integrating mathematical knowledge and skills. Many other children's books investigate common but meaningful themes.

Other content areas (besides language arts) have the potential for connections with social studies. Music and art make social studies come alive for children. Health issues that people have faced in the past and today can be connected. Children can see the rationale behind mathematics skills when coupling them with social studies issues. Environmental studies also combine the subjects of science and social studies. This is true for most of the people-related topics in social studies. However, social studies makes a unique contribution to the curriculum through the following:

- It provides a forum for children to learn about and practice democracy.
- It helps children to explain their world in many dimensions, including environmental aspects.
- It assists children with positive self-development.
- It helps children acquire a foundational understanding of history, geography, biography, and the social sciences.
- It promotes a genuine sense of the social fabric.

Interdisciplinary education's greatest strength is its potential for helping children go beyond superficial knowledge. It enables them to develop an in-depth, multidimensional understanding of a topic. Why separate many topics into distinct subjects when they can be multiple dimensions of the same topic in many ways? By integrating subjects through themes, students become involved in activities that are ultimately more meaningful and powerful. Above all, social studies is the only curriculum subject with *people* constantly at the center of the subject matter (Ellis, 2006). Teachers who employ intra- and interdisciplinary themes can create much more stimulating lessons that help children go beyond the surface across the curriculum.

 Engaging *All* Students

Teachers need to have *more* than knowledge in their content; they must also have an understanding of their students. Four important areas of education have been identified by Grant and Vansledright (2001): (1) learners and learning, (2) content, (3) teachers and teaching, and (4) the classroom environment. Through these lenses, a useful framework for examining social studies classrooms can be viewed. Teachers are increasingly being confronted with a wide range of diverse students in their classrooms. Among today's students, there is growing ethnic and cultural diversity as well as significant differences in socioeconomic backgrounds and intellectual abilities. One of the biggest challenges for teachers is to design quality, thought-provoking, and engaging learning opportunities for *all* students.

The world inside classrooms reflects today's world. The current inclusion movement seeks to integrate *all* types of learners into the classroom. Although some may disagree with this idea, advocates (including those who write the TExES standards and competencies) "strongly believe that students with learning disabilities increasingly benefit both academically and socially from placement in the regular classroom" (Farris, 2001, p. 328). Inclusion might also extend to students identified as gifted. The classroom teacher has the task of reaching and teaching students along this "extensive continuum of skills and abilities" (Farris, p. 329). In a social studies classroom that reflects a wide range of abilities, teachers must change their methods. Instead of focusing on skills development and memorizing facts, teachers should "refocus on interdisciplinary teaching and theme-based units, student portfolios, and cross-grade grouping whenever possible while continually keeping the individual child in mind" (Farris, p. 330). Learning can often center on inquiry-based activities that develop higher-level thinking skills and interest for all.

Building Thinking Skills

The social studies classroom is an excellent place to provide students opportunities to develop thinking skills. Teachers and researchers often refer to thinking skills generically as "critical thinking skills." According to Sternberg (2003) there are three kinds of thinking students should learn: "creative thinking to generate ideas, analytical thinking to evaluate those ideas, and practical thinking to implement the ideas and convince others of their value" (5). These thinking skills correspond to the "higher levels" of Bloom's taxonomy of the cognitive domain, especially analysis, synthesis, and evaluation. Students who exercise analytical thinking skills will "analyze, critique, judge, compare and contrast, evaluate, and assess" (Sternberg, 2003, p. 5). Creative thinking assignments ask students to "create, invent, discover, 'imagine if,' 'suppose that,' and predict" (Sternberg, p. 5). Students who use practical thinking skills will "apply, use, put into practice, implement, employ, and render practical what they know" (Sternberg, p. 5).

Research has shown that students from about the age of five with both low and high abilities can learn skills associated with critical thinking (Swartz & Perkins, 1990). These researchers found that students of both low- to medium-ability thinking can improve in *all* subject areas, whereas the thinking of high-ability students can be improved in particular subject areas. Thinking skills instruction should be "embedded within the current curriculum" and used to "help students learn more and learn more deeply" (Johnson, 2000, p. 15).

Assessment and Evaluation

Students, parents, and teachers should all be constantly aware of a student's performance and progress. Informal and *formative assessments* provide information on an on-going basis. *Summative assessments* provide information on how a student has done on a particular set of objectives at the end of instruction. *Evaluations,* on the other hand, help the understanding of how well the student has done over a long period of time. Chapin (2006) explains that alone, a "score of a sixty or eighty tells little. It could be a 'good' score or a 'poor' score. The score has to be interpreted" (p. 104).

While both assessments and evaluations are useful in helping to explain student progress, assessments can also be exciting and meaningful learning activities. Designing these types of assessments can be more difficult for the teacher, but they will be much more authentic and motivational. At the beginning of any activity, teachers should provide clear expectations through goals and objectives to students, and provide them with several varied opportunities to demonstrate mastery. *Authentic or performance-based assessments* ask students to create "real world" products or to perform, not simply answer a set of questions. These can be particularly exciting in social studies. Examples of this type of assessment include: debates, Readers Theatre, dramatizations, songs or dances, posters, brochures, advertisements, cartoons, journal entries, and models, and so forth.

Reflective Teaching

As a *people-centered* subject, social studies often requires teachers to tackle controversial, often contradictory, issues such as conflict and respect. Savage and Armstrong (1996) write, "Teaching social studies is not for cowards" (p. 8). Social studies teachers "tend to be thoughtful people who have a point of view and who are willing to stand up for their commitments" (p. 9). These are important qualities and actions to model for students. Therefore, along with modeling respectful behaviors, social studies teachers must make many decisions daily regarding what roles will be taken in instruction. Essentially, they decide what *role* they will take and what role students will play during an activity to increase skills in interactions as well as in thinking. For example, teachers will be **experts** during direct instruction lessons, **consultants** or **facilitators** during cooperative group events, and **coaches** during inquiry and problem-solving activities.

Teaching decisions require **reflective practice**. The most effective teachers are those who regularly examine their own teaching. Grant and Vansledright (2001) believe that teachers should perform "regular examinations of and introspection into what, who, and how you're teaching, and why you choose to do what you do" (p. 265). They must consider how their beliefs and actions will influence their students and the subject(s) they teach. This is particularly true in social studies, where teachers may have strong beliefs and values that affect what occurs in the classroom—for example, they must be particularly careful of not including or over- or underemphasizing some perspectives because of their own biases towards some issues, especially those in cultural and political areas.

Part of reflective teaching involves keeping up with changing content and new social studies methods. EC-4 teachers are expected to engage in **professional growth** for social studies. Teaching a discipline such as social studies is not static but rather in a constant state of transformation—due to both the discovery of new knowledge and the changing political and cultural scenes. Texts are adopted for a number of years, so information can become outdated quickly. Teachers should be sure to **present *current* knowledge** and to make use of *current* events that touch the lives of their children. Teachers also cannot become complacent in their thinking about what, who, and how they teach, and they should update their knowledge and teaching methods to match children's needs and the changing times.

Teachers are professional educators and should make connections with others in their field. **Professional organizations** offer opportunities to interact with colleagues and gain insights into current research on teaching and learning strategies and tools for social scientists and for the classroom. Because it is imperative to keep up-to-date with the latest issues and trends in the field, teachers have numerous social studies resources that help them. For example, they can consult the monthly and quarterly *journals* published by NCSS—*Social Education* and *Social Studies and the Young Learner*. NCSS also publishes a monthly *newsletter* for members and maintains an online site at www. ncss. org that contains a great deal of information. There are also links to numerous listservs maintained by NCSS members where social studies educators may freely exchange information and ideas. There are a number of state and regional organizations that also provide professional development opportunities for social studies educators, and, of course, the Internet and other media are always at one's fingertips. The days of showing out-dated filmstrips on events, maps in which countries no longer exist, or amateur-like documentaries are gone. Resources now available for teachers (who make efforts to search them out) include vast amounts of resources, current lesson plans, up-to-date materials for children, and so forth.

Consider the following practice question:

Mr. Hood began to design a lesson on the history of the cattle kingdom era of Texas. He thought about how he could set up his lesson. What would be his best choice?

   A. After watching a film clip on the cattle drives, have students use their map colors to draw the main cattle drive trails.
   B. Integrate the lesson with mathematics, reading, and music.
   C. Have students read the chapter on cattle drives in their well-written social studies chapter on this topic.
   D. Invite a guest speaker from a local range to come in to speak with children.

Students should be given opportunities to make deeper connections with many topics so lessons will become less isolated and more meaningful. The *best* answer is *B*. Children should be able to relate the cattle drives to the economy of Texas to understand why the cattle industry flourished during this time period. Also, there were many songs that originated during this era, setting the stage for country and western music. Having students use map skills and seeing a filmstrip (Choice *A*) could be a part of the lesson, but failing to integrate other key information would make the lesson less meaningful. Simply reading a chapter (Choice *C*), would not make the connections needed for "big picture" understanding. Having a local rancher (Choice *D*) would be an excellent addition, although he or she might not be an expert on the history of this topic. The correct answer is *B*.

Standards IV and X History and Science, Technology, and Society

The social studies teacher applies knowledge of significant historical events and developments, as well as of multiple historical interpretations and ideas, in order to facilitate student understanding of relationships between the past, the present, and the future.

The social studies teacher understands developments in science and technology, and uses this knowledge to facilitate student understanding of the social and environmental consequences of scientific discovery and technological innovation.

Competency 017 (History): The teacher demonstrates knowledge of significant historical events and developments and applies social science skills to historical information, ideas, and issues.

The beginning teacher:

- Knows traditional points of reference in the history of Texas, the United States, and the world.
- Demonstrates knowledge of the individuals, events, and issues that shaped the history of Texas.
- Understands similarities and differences among Native-American groups in Texas and the Western Hemisphere before European colonization.
- Understands the causes and effects of European exploration and colonization of Texas, the United States, and the Western Hemisphere.
- Knows how geographic contexts and processes of spatial exchange (diffusion) have influenced events in the past and helped to shape the present.
- Demonstrates knowledge of the origins and diffusion of major scientific, mathematical, and technological discoveries and the effects of discoveries throughout history.
- Relates historical information and ideas to information and ideas in other social sciences and in other disciplines.
- Knows how to formulate historical research questions and use appropriate procedures to reach supportable judgments and conclusions.
- Understands historical research and knows how historians locate, gather, organize, analyze, and report information using standard research methodologies.
- Knows characteristics and uses of primary and secondary sources used for historical research (e.g., databases, maps, photographs, media services, the Internet, biographies, interviews, questionnaires, artifacts); analyzes historical information from primary and secondary sources; and evaluates information in relation to bias, propaganda, point of view, and frame of reference.
- Applies evaluative, problem-solving, and decision-making skills to historical information, ideas, and issues.
- Knows how to communicate and interpret historical information and ideas in written and graphic forms.
- Analyzes historical data (e.g., population statistics, patterns of migration, voting trends and patterns) using appropriate analytical methods.

Consider the following practice question:

Mrs. Scott is teaching her third grade students about the Underground Railroad. She wants to make sure the lesson is meaningful, so she plans to bring in a primary source. Which of the following would be considered a primary source?

 A. A biography of Harriet Tubman
 B. A wanted poster of Harriet Tubman from those times
 C. *Follow the Drinking Gourd*—a book, by Jeanette Winter
 D. The textbook chapter on the Underground Railroad

Choices *A, C,* and *D* are all examples of secondary sources since they report or summarize information "second hand." Other secondary sources might include reports from a newspaper or other media sources. Because these "reporters" or "summarizers" pick and choose their sources, social scientists caution that their viewpoints can sometimes be biased (for example, a history of the American Revolution written by an American author and another one written by a British author normally come from vastly biased perspectives). The answer is Choice *B* because this poster was an actual "witness to the events" of the times. Other primary sources might include letters, paintings (made during the times), photographs, diaries, autobiographies, and so forth that originate from people who actually lived "the event." The answer is *B*.

 # Teaching History

Of all six disciplines of the EC-4 social studies, history has long been dominant in the social studies curriculum. A question often asked is, *Why study history?* Ellis (2006) explains that our ". . . history is a fluid continuum. The present in which we live is also the future of the past and the past of the future" (p. 207). Stearns (1998) continues, noting that, "History should be studied because it is essential to individuals and to society." If we do not know where we have been in our past, it can be difficult to have a clear view of our future. While almost everyone agrees that history should be taught in the schools, there is a great deal of debate over what should be taught and to whom. Given the huge amount of history that exists for Texas, the United States, and the world, it is impossible to cover everything. Also, rote memorization of mere facts has proved to be insufficient. Students must go beyond simply knowing facts to being able to make sense of those facts and to use them to make good decisions as citizens. Research has shown that even the youngest children are constantly considering information and then constructing and reconstructing their understanding of things. Therefore, history teaching and learning is particularly appropriate for elementary school children because they are naturally inquisitive and can use accurate information and skill development to make sense of the people and events of the past to connect to their present. Everyone has heard that "history repeats itself." Without doubt, it is important that our children not make the same mistakes as others have before *and* also reach for the greatness of those who *have* been successful in raising mankind up in some manner. Also, as Ellis (2006) explains, "Children living in the present can benefit greatly from understanding the past—the sense of continuity, the inheritance, the traditions, the changes, and the reminders that are all around them" (p. 207).

The National Center for History in the Schools (NCHS) (1996) supports the idea that history at all levels, but especially for young children, *must* be meaningful.

> For young children, history—along with literature and the arts—provides one of the most enriching studies in which they can be engaged. 'What children of this age need,' Bruno Bettelheim has written, 'is rich food for their imagination, a sense of history, [and] how the present situation came about.' History enlarges children's experience, providing, in the words of Philip Phenix, 'a sense of personal involvement in exemplary lives and significant events, an appreciation of values and a vision of greatness.'

In order for students to develop a sense of history, they must consider events from a broader perspective.

Research has shown that children retain misconceptions that make sense to them somehow (Grant & Vansledright, 2001). This can also be true of their understanding of historical events. Events of the past are very complex, and children often oversimplify them. Therefore, it is important that they begin to develop an understanding of how the events of the past influence the present (cause and effect) and how our own past connects with that of others. According to Chapin (2006), this emphasizes the need to include, as a part of history instruction, a "wide array of knowledge from what are considered cultural areas: arts, literature, music, philosophies, religion, science, technology, and social and political knowledge" (p. 149). This will assist students in expanding their historical understanding.

As they broaden their understanding, students learn to think like historians (Wineberg, 2001). The NCHS (1996) explains that:

> *real historical understanding requires students to engage in historical thinking: to raise questions and to marshal evidence in support of their answers; to read historical narratives and fiction; to consult historical documents, journals, diaries, artifacts, historic sites, and other records from the past; and to do so imaginatively—taking into account the time and places in which these records were created and comparing the multiple points of view of those on the scene at the time.*

Historical thinking skills must be developed sequentially. The first step must be to know the facts about a particular person, place, or event. For example, how could someone argue who was the greater superhero—*Superman* or *Spiderman*—and present a valid case for their choice, *if* they had never heard of either? The same is true for history events and historical persons. A factual foundation must be present for any greater consideration and deeper understanding. This should remind you of Bloom's (1956) taxonomy, which says information and questioning begins with the knowledge level (recall of facts) but moves quickly to comprehension, application, analysis, synthesis, and evaluation. Having children use facts and information to make good decisions (the evaluation level) should be the goal in social studies.

The standards of history are somewhat similar across grade levels, although teaching methods and objectives may vary. For example, a third-grade class studying the community may use a computer to create a database of historical places in their community. This database might include pictures and descriptions of historic buildings, old homes, and other places of historical interest. Second-grade students may study older forms of transportation used in their communities (walking, horses, trains, and so on) and compare these to newer forms (cars and planes). They, too, could create a database for their information. This would allow children to categorize, arrange, sort, select, and display their information. Then they might predict what sorts of transportation would help people in their city in the future. These examples demonstrate how students could meet history standards in different ways.

Many times, teaching social studies, unfortunately, does not encourage students to connect their newly learned concepts with their lived experiences. This often leads students to justifiably ask why they should learn history when it has nothing to do with them. Most classroom experiences are determined by the content of textbooks rather than the pursuit of meaningful knowledge. According to Levstik and Barton (2001), history for primary grade-level students "rarely amounts to anything more than learning a few isolated facts about famous people connected to major holidays . . . . In fact, when asked why they think history is a subject at school or how it might help them, students sometimes can think of little, except that it might be useful if they were ever on *Jeopardy*!" (p. 14). The authors go on to explain that teachers must provide opportunities for students to make meaningful connections: "To get more understanding from history, teachers must begin with the concerns and interests of students and must help them find answers to questions that grow out of those concerns and interests" (p. 14). Students must begin to see social studies as patterns of human behavior from which much can be learned. History must be made to seem alive! For example, Ms. Hodges, in an inquiry model, asked her fourth-graders if they have ever heard the expression "your name is mud"? When some replied that they had, she asks if they could guess what the expression means and from where the expression originated. Ms. Hodges told students that she would answer any question they could formulate to find the answer, but she could only answer questions with a "yes" or "no." This caused students to think of their own questions and to also use the questions that others ask as resources to get to the answer (*Answer:* Dr. Mudd fixed the broken leg of John Wilkes Booth following President Lincoln's assassination. Most people thought for many years that Dr. Mudd was part of the plot to kill Lincoln and, in fact, he spent some time in prison. Because his name and reputation were ruined, even though he was finally proved innocent, the phrase became ingrained in American phraseology.) NCHS (1996) stresses that teachers should bring history alive by using "stories, myths, legends, and biographies that capture children's imaginations and immerse them in times and cultures of the recent and long-ago past" (p. 3). Documents, witnesses, and physical remains (**artifacts**) offer students clues to historical mysteries. Social studies teachers need to provide students with opportunities to apply critical thinking skills to organize and use information acquired from many of these resources and experts. They should seek out *many* ways for children to think at higher levels.

Distinguishing fact from opinion is one key thinking skill that students should develop. With this in mind, students must learn to differentiate between primary and secondary sources. **Primary sources** are first-hand sources; **secondary sources** use primary sources to deliver information at a later time. Secondary sources basically provide second-hand information. For example, suppose a car accident occurred in which a car hit another car from behind. A description of the accident given by an eyewitness to the police is a primary source because it comes from someone actually there at the time. The story in the newspaper the next day is a secondary source because the reporter, who interviewed the witnesses and wrote the story, did not actually witness the accident. The reporter is presenting a way of understanding the accident or an interpretation after talking to witnesses or others. Students should be able to locate each of these types of sources, be able to use them, and also understand that both sources can contain biased viewpoints, particularly secondary sources. In the example above, the eyewitness may have been hit by someone else in the past and embellished a bit because he or she is in sympathy with the driver who was hit (as could have been the reporter). Social studies teachers must teach children to analyze all such data for "spin," (or bias) of some kind. In this era, when even photographs and videos can be cleverly altered, it is most important for future citizens to be able to critically examine multiple primary and secondary sources to reach conclusions more truthfully. Children need to be able to carry out investigations—just like real historians.

Social scientists gather a great deal of facts and figures about people's activities. By organizing this data in different ways, they may observe certain patterns and relationships that will lead to useful conclusions. **Statistics** are numerical data that represent information about a given subject. There are many ways to display statistics, and these can be used in all areas of the social sciences. Graphs are a convenient way of organizing data. An economist could use a **line graph**

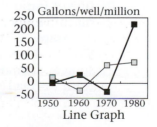

Line Graph

to show the change in oil production over time. A political scientist might present statistics in a **bar graph**. A **circle graph**, or **pie chart**, is an easy way to show the parts, or percentages, into which a total amount is divided. The full circle represents 100%, a half circle is 50%, and so on. Circle graphs could be useful for showing the percentage of the population of a large city that each of its ethnic groups represents. For young children, it might begin with percentages of each type of pet they have at home, type of lunch desired each day (and thus the importance of ordering food supplies correctly), or type of shoes worn. **Charts** and **tables** are also important means for organizing and displaying information. Children should be taught to read and interpret this information and to construct these types of graphs using keys. Most importantly, they should be taught how people use graphs to make decisions (for instance, a local pet store may look at the data and see that there is a large percentage of cats in the neighborhood, so stocking more cat supplies ensures that the store makes more money and local people can always find what they need).

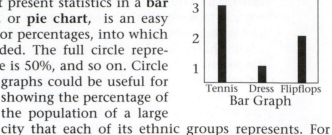

Bar Graph

Pie Chart

There are other visual means that are effective in EC-4 social studies teaching and learning. **Timelines**, for example, are graphic representations of a succession of historical events, constructed by dividing a unit of time into proportional segments. A timeline is an effective method of illustrating time spans between events. As children study the past, timelines help them put events into perspective by allowing them to "see" when important things happened (Maxim, 1999). Because young children relate to time *only* as it is meaningful to them, their first experiences in grasping prehistory experience is focusing on routines. Calendar time helps bring attention to the day of the week, yesterday, tomorrow, the seasons, and the routine of the day (in terms of teaching *after* and *before* and *sequencing* events). To help young children understand how things change with time, teachers can measure children's height throughout the year, keep a lost tooth chart, have a "baby versus now" photo board, and so forth. Maxim recommends that, for the very youngest students, teachers construct timelines on topics of immediate experience. Routines of their daily schedule can be illustrated on a beginning timeline. Research has shown that by fourth grade students will understand historical eras, sequencing major events over a period of time. For instance, cut-outs of symbols for major holidays in the United States or other events can be pinned or clipped onto a cardboard strip in sequence, or disks with pictures can be strung in order on a length of yarn. The students must decide which symbol comes first, second, and so on as they place the events in proper sequence. Children can also construct and illustrate a timeline of important events of their lives by drawing on a long strip of adding machine tape.

Maps are another visual means of representing information. Maps are used to show distances, strategic locations, boundaries, physical features, resources, climate, and so on. In order to effectively use maps, students must learn to "read" them. Learning to read maps is similar to learning to read the printed word. Children must learn to associate arbitrary symbols (a picnic table for a park, a star for a capital city, etc.) with something real in the environment. The "actual symbolic representation on maps is too abstract for kindergarten and early primary-grade children to use," notes Maxim (1999, p. 369); however, this does not mean that young children are incapable of using symbols of any kind as parents soon realize when they are passing the "Golden Arches" of McDonald's. There are a variety of social studies activities that will help students discover relationships between some physical aspect of their environment and its symbol. For example, children can informally play with blocks and other building materials. Playing with blocks will help children conceptualize space as they construct environments that simulate real locations ("In the Block Center today, boys and girls, I want you to try to 'build' our classroom'). Teachers might also take students on a class trip to take pictures around the school or neighborhood. These pictures can then be mounted on blocks of wood and children can be encouraged to play with them as they would their regular blocks to reconstruct their neighborhood. **Photographs** can be used to present visual data, and a number of schools are acquiring digital cameras that enhance technology connections. Teachers first take pictures of children in their environment to show them that familiar things can be represented by scale models. Teachers then point out that the pictures are small while the "real thing" is much bigger. Taking pictures of many of the things in the classroom and asking children to point to the real object leads children to understand that real things can be represented in much smaller ways. It is a smaller leap, then, for children to understand small map symbols. **Cartoons** are another way to develop symbolic understanding. Cartoons may be used to depict real people and to express all sorts of ideas and opinions. It is important to remind children that hurtful (or otherwise inappropriate) images or expressions should never be used. The most important thing to remember is to begin with symbols that are familiar to students or are seen often by children (e.g., the heart symbol in "I ♡ Texas," the international symbol for restrooms, or the symbol for "walk/don't walk").

Teaching standards ask that teachers not only know facts and provide meaningful activities but that they also know and have students involved in the **methods of historians**. Seefeldt (1997) states these methods as: (1) problem identification [i.e., investigators perceive that a problem is meaningful to them in some way]; (2) the ability to gather information from the past; (3) the ability to observe data carefully; (4) the ability to analyze data and make inferences; and (5) the ability to draw conclusions. Personal involvement in the problem-solving process will help students acquire a more balanced sense of history; that is, it is not only something one *knows* but also something that one *lives*. Children must be given opportunities to explore social studies rather than simply be exposed to it.

In summary, to develop our students' interests in history we must have a firm grasp of not only the content but also how to teach it (Maxim, 1999). Successful history teaching requires that teachers develop their knowledge of people, ideas, and events from the past for a foundation upon which to build exciting lessons. Knowledge of history will ultimately provide both teachers and students some insight for a better understanding of current problems and conflicts.

Given the extensive nature of the information that this standard covers, it will be broken down into the following headings and subheadings:

WORLD HISTORY

United States History and International Relations

Exploration and Settlement

National Unity

Regional Differences

Industrial Growth

Reform Movements

International Affairs

International Relations between the Superpowers

The Present

Texas History

Earliest Inhabitants

Early European Exploration and Development

Revolution, Republic, and Statehood

? Consider the following practice question:

What invention helped fire the sentiments that gave rise to the Reformation?

A. The pocket watch
B. The printing press
C. The cotton gin
D. The telescope

The Reformation began in 1517, when Martin Luther, a Catholic priest, challenged the authority of the Catholic Church. Word of Luther's challenge (or protest) against many church abuses that were occurring during this time spread quickly due to the printing press (*B*), invented in 1440. This, in turn, led to the birth of the Protestant religion (from protest) in which Luther's believers (and others later on) moved to a "Reformation" of church practices and beliefs. The pocket watch (*A*) was not invented until 1675. The cotton gin (*C*) was not invented until 1793, and the telescope (*D*) was invented in1608, but none of these would have a connection to religious reform. The correct answer is *B*.

KEY QUESTION: *What were the main events in World History?*

- Current paleontologists have located the remains of the first **homo-sapiens**, in Africa. Their existence has been dated from about 160,000 years ago. From there, civilizations migrated outward, eventually populating the world. An important concept in development of civilization is the move from hunting/gathering to the domestication of plants and animals. This allowed people to live in settlements rather than have to gather food in a nomadic life. As people remained together longer, languages, governments, economies, specialization of labor, and social networks began to form. These varied from place to place.

- Although evidence shows man to have been in the Middle East and Asia long before, from 3500 to 2000 B.C.E. (before Common Era/before Christian Era), river systems in the Middle East, India, and China saw the rise of **four major river valley civilizations.** One of the earliest was in the Middle East in the region of *Mesopotamia* (meaning "land between the waters") near present day Iraq. This land was part of the **Fertile Crescent** and was located between the **Tigris and Euphrates Rivers** and extending down along the Nile.

- Also in the Middle East, agricultural settlements along the **Nile River** in Egypt led to the creation of a major civilization in 3100 B.C.E. This began a period of rule by royal kingdoms, which lasted until the 900s B.C.E. Egyptians created a system of communication through written pictorial characters called **hieroglyphics.** We are able to read ancient hieroglyphics because of the discovery in 1799 of the **Rosetta Stone,** carved in 196 B.C.E. This stone contains text written by priests to honor Ptolemy, a pharaoh (a king of Egypt) and then to explain some governmental decrees. The same story was carved upon it in two languages (Egyptian and Greek) and used three scripts (hieroglyphic, demotic, and Greek).

- A third major civilization developed around the same time, 2600 B.C.E., on the coast of the Arabian Sea in present day Pakistan. This was the **Indus River Civilization.** Although they had a written language, it has yet to be deciphered; therefore, little is known about this civilization.

- The fourth major river valley civilization began in China, along the **Yellow River.** By 2000 B.C.E., the Chinese had discovered bronzeworking and were making tools and weapons from iron by 600 B.C.E.

- Around 2000 B.C.E. in what is now labeled as the Middle East, the Hebrews (later known as Israelites and Jews) brought **monotheism** (worship of one God) to the world. Other civilizations believed in **polytheism** (worship of many gods).

- Between 800 and 500 B.C.E., the Greeks formed dozens of independent city-states rather than a single nation. The Greek word for city-states is *polis,* which is where the word *politics* originates. The largest of the Greek city-states, **Athens,** formed a new type of governmental system in which the citizens (all free men) elected representatives to speak for them in deciding their laws. This was called *democracy,* or rule by the people. The **Greeks** are considered to have laid the foundation of Western Civilization. Greek writers and philosophers such as Socrates (470–399 B.C.E.), Plato (428–347 B.C.E.), and Aristotle (384–322 B.C.E.) are still influential in Western thought. Macedonia, north of Athens, produced Alexander (the Great), who conquered much of the land from Eastern Europe through much of India. His influence spread Greek ideas, including democracy, throughout his empire.

- As the Greek civilization declined, the new powerful civilization of **Rome** arose in the Mediterranean region. As Rome expanded its territory, a series of internal struggles began. Representative government **(the Republic)** started to fail and political power began to be concentrated in a single ruler **(dictatorship).** **Julius Caesar** was, perhaps, the most famous Roman ruler, followed by the first true dictator of the Roman Empire, **Augustus.** The **Roman Empire** lasted roughly from 31 B.C.E. until 476 C.E. and, at times, stretched north to the island of Britain (up to Hadrian's Wall near Scotland), west to Spain, south to Egypt, and also covered much of the Middle East. In 380 C.E. (Common Era/Christian Era/formerly, A.D.) Christianity was made the official religion of the empire by the **Emperor Constantine.** Rome fell in 476 C.E., most often accredited to the decay of values and morals, corruption in government, and sacking by several different Germanic barbarians tribes over the prior years.

- Advanced civilization has been tracked in China for over 4,000 years. The "golden age" of China, lasting almost a thousand years, loosely began in about 600 B.C.E. and was marked by modern papermaking, the compass, paper money, gunpowder, and the teaching of **Confucius** and **Buddha** (from China) and others who established the literary, moral, and religious traditions of Chinese society that would remain for centuries. Beginning about 200 B.C.E., **China** entered the first of its *four imperial dynasties*. The first emperor to unify the nation was from the *Qin* (Ch'in) dynasty. The name China is thought to have derived from the name of this dynasty, and it was during this period that the Great Wall was completed. The *Han* dynasty was one of the most prosperous, the strongest, and longest lasting of the Chinese dynasties, and it was during this time that the **"silk road"** caravan trade route to the West first opened due to the western expansion of the empire. The Sui, Tang, and Song dynasties followed, with the Tang dynasty often considered the high point in China's Golden Age. Peasant rebellions and military disasters destroyed the final dynasty in 906 C.E. China remained split into several independent states until a single Chinese nation emerged again in the 1200s under Genghis Khan and later Kublai Khan.
- In the Middle East a new faith, **Islam**, emerged in the 600s C.E. Founded by a wealthy merchant from Mecca, **Mohammed**, who, following a holy vision, spent his life spreading the message he received in the vision. Like Judaism and Christianity, Islamic faith has only a single deity. The word *Islam* comes from an Arabic phrase meaning "to submit to God." Followers of Islam, called **Muslims** (which comes from the phrase "servant of God"), follow teachings laid out in the Koran (Qur'an).
- After the fall of the Roman Empire, Europe began a period of decline from 500 to 1500 C.E. The beginning of the Medieval period (the term *Medieval* in Latin means middle ages) was known as the "Dark Ages" (476–1000), a time when it was felt that much ancient knowledge was lost, that little headway was made in civilization, and that it was dark because few written accounts survive (or were written) to enlighten us about these years.
- In Medieval Europe, there was no centralized government system. A system of small states with kingships ruled, allowing little mobility for serfs who were tied to the land. Wealthy landowners gave peasants their protection; in return these serfs had to work the land and give most of the products produced by their labors to the owners. This was called **feudalism.**
- In the years between 1095 and 1270, approximately eight Crusades were led by Christian kings and Popes against those (mostly Muslims) who held the Holy Land. Many reasons influenced Crusaders to "take the Cross": religious beliefs to recapture the Holy Land from Muslims or to gain salvation, overpopulation in areas of Europe, stepping stones to riches or nobility, desire to see military action, and so forth. The **Knights Templar**, who were warrior priests, were one group who fought in these wars.
- In England, citizens who had been ruled under an absolute monarchy begin to tire of kings who were wasteful and unjust. The **Magna Carta** (1215), imposed on England's King John by his barons, provided the first checks on the powers of the king. This document is considered to be the forerunner of constitutional law and our own Bill of Rights.

- **Marco Polo** was one of the first Europeans to travel through Asia on the Silk Road and to live for many years in China under the rule of Kublai Khan. He returned to write about many of the wonders he saw and experienced, and his maps spurred on other voyages and eventual discoveries.

- Toward the end of the Middle Ages, around 1300, a revival of culture and intellect began in southern Europe, being especially strong on the Italian peninsula. It eventually spread across Europe. This period, referred to as the **Renaissance** (meaning "rebirth" of classical ideas) lasted until approximately 1600. Artists such as Michelangelo and inventors such as Leonardo da Vinci, Copernicus (astronomy), and Newton (laws of motion) lead the way to new knowledge and "enlightenment."

- The **Protestant Reformation** began in 1517 when a monk named **Martin Luther** protested against the many abuses of the then powerful Catholic Church. He was excommunicated and founded the new Lutheran Church, which was the first of the protestant denominations.

United States History and International Relations

Consider the following practice question:

What document is known as the first document of American democracy?

A. The Articles of Confederation
B. The Constitution
C. The Mayflower Compact
D. The Federalist Papers

The Mayflower Compact was signed by the Pilgrim men aboard the Mayflower in 1620 before the colonists moved onto land at Plymouth. It was the official Constitution of the Plymouth Colony for over 70 years after its signing. In this document, the colonists agreed to govern themselves according to the will of the majority; thus, this compact is the first document of American democracy and the first America State Paper. The answer is *C*.

I. Exploration and Settlement

KEY QUESTION: *Who were the early European explorers in the Americas?*

- It is now accepted that **Leif Ericsson** and a small group of **Vikings** were the first Europeans to set foot on North America, probably as early as 1000 C.E. in present-day Canada.

- From the fifteenth through the seventeenth centuries, European nations explored and settled large parts of the New World. The Spaniards, landing first in the West Indies, established colonies in South America and Mexico. Later, in 1565, they explored much of Florida and founded a settlement at **St. Augustine.** Their explorations were motivated by the search for a route for Far Eastern goods, gold, the desire for territory, and the wish to convert native populations to Roman Catholicism.

- **Christopher Columbus** argued his case with *King Ferdinand* and *Queen Isabella* of Spain for sailing west to find the riches of the Far East markets. Columbus believed that the world was round rather than flat—a belief held by most during those times. In 1492, his three ships, the **Nina**, the **Pinta**, and the **Santa Maria** made landfall in the New World in the islands of San Salvador. Thinking that he had landed in India, he named the native tribes *Indians*. This was the first of four voyages. Although Columbus was not the first European to touch on the New World, his voyage opened doors to the wave of exploration and conquest by European nations.

- America was named for **Amerigo Vespucci**, who was said to have voyaged with Columbus and to have completed later voyages (which he mapped). Vespucci believed that Columbus had discovered a New World and, afterward, maps called this land "America."
- **Ponce de Leon**, a Spaniard, was the first European to set foot on land that is currently the *continental* U.S., as he explored Florida in 1513 looking for the famous "fountain of youth."
- **Vasco Nunez de Balboa**, a Spaniard, also sailed in 1513 and, after crossing land at the Isthmus of Panama, was the first European to see the Pacific Ocean.
- **Ferdinand Magellan's** ship (under the flag of Spain) was the first to sail around the globe in 1522.
- **Hernan Cortes**, a Spaniard, conquered the **Aztecs** for their riches in Mexico in 1519. Although the Aztecs were strong, they and their king, **Montezuma**, believed that Cortes was a part of an ancient prophecy, thus giving the Spaniards a great military advantage as they were first welcomed as gods.
- **Francisco Pizzaro**, a Spaniard, conquered the **Incas** in Peru and explored much of South America between 1531 and 1533.
- In 1527 **Cabeza de Vaca**, a Spaniard, accompanied by a small expeditionary force (including **Esteban**, an African slave), was the first explorer to land in Texas (having floated on a raft from a disastrous expedition in Florida). In 1536, four survivors finally found their way to Mexico City with mythical tales of Seven Cities of Gold.
- In 1539, **Hernando De Soto** explored much of what are now the southern states of the U.S. (Florida, Alabama, Georgia, the Carolinas, and Tennessee). De Soto claimed much land for Spain, including much of what is now considered "the South." He explored as far west as the Mississippi River.
- **Francisco Coronado**, a Spaniard, explored in 1540 much of what is now the states of Texas, New Mexico, Arizona, Oklahoma, and Kansas, also looking for the Seven Cities of Gold.
- **Giovannia da Verrazano**, sailing for France in 1524, and **Jacques Cartier**, a Frenchman, explored the upper New England coast and Canada for France in 1534. Cartier was searching for a Northwest Passage from France to the Far East. Although he did not locate a passage, he founded trade with Native Americans. This influenced France's interest in Canada through current times. Quebec remains a province of Canada where French is still the first language.
- The Spanish founded the settlement of **St. Augustine** in Florida in 1565 (which was to become the oldest settlement to be continuously occupied within the present day United States).
- **Sir Francis Drake** sailed along the Pacific Coasts of North and South America, and, on completing his voyage in 1580, was the first Englishman to circumnavigate the globe.
- **Sir Walter Raleigh** established the **first English colony** ("The Lost Colony") in America in 1587 on **Roanoke Island** in Virginia (named for Queen Elizabeth, who was known as the "Virgin Queen"). Supply ships

from England were delayed until 1590 and, when they returned, the colony was deserted. It is not truly known what happened to those early Roanoke settlers, but it is thought that most died and others were absorbed into local Native American tribes.

- By 1580, Spain had basically claimed as **New Spain** all of the land in what is now the southeastern, south central, and southwestern parts of the United States (in addition to most of South America). At this time, Spain was the most powerful country in Europe. However, England (under Queen Elizabeth) had many concerns and differences with Spain. In an effort to gain control over the seas, Spain sent a huge **Armada** of ships against England, which was defeated by a combination of Queen Elizabeth's navy and horrific weather in 1588. This defeat considerably diluted Spain's power and allowed England and France to become the leading imperialist nations.

- In the 1600s, the French and the English explored the wilderness lands of North America. The French founded colonies in Canada and all along the Mississippi River. They were more interested in staking claims to land and trading in furs and fish than in developing permanent settlements. French explorer **Samuel de Champlain** founded Quebec City in 1603 and built a fort to secure the territory in Canada. The French claim on lands in budding America and the increase in population of settlers expanding across the Appalachian Mountains caused clashes with the Native Americans. From 1756 to 1763, the British colonists in America faced the **French and Indian War**, which resulted in France losing all of its land east of the Mississippi River (except New Orleans) to the British.

- **Henry Hudson**, a English explorer, further investigated the Hudson Bay and Hudson River areas in 1609. Later, he laid claim to New Amsterdam (Manhattan) for the Dutch East India Company, but it was lost to the British several years later.

- **René-Robert Cavelier, Sieur de La Salle**, a Frenchman, explored the entire length of the Mississippi River from its source to the Gulf of Mexico in 1682 and claimed the land and river for France.

KEY QUESTION: *How did a desire for freedom influence daily life and government in early America?*

- **Jamestown**, named for King James I of England, was established in 1607 by merchants of the Virginia Company of London. The original colonists, 104 men, suffered terrible conditions, and many died. However, the strong leadership of **John Smith** (whose life was saved by **Pocahontas**, daughter of a Native American chief) kept the colony from collapsing. In 1612, **John Rolfe** discovered a new type of tobacco that could be grown in Virginia. This was the first major cash crop of the New World. The need for workers led to the first Africans being brought to Virginia. Initially, they were treated as **indentured servants** rather than slaves. An indentured servant was a person who agreed to work several years for a person or company in return for passage to America. Even though this colony was the **first permanent English settlement** in America, it is not as famous as *Plymouth Colony* because it did not open the doors to mass immigration from Europe (as did Plymouth).

- The desire for political and **religious freedom** brought many colonists to the New World. Pilgrims, Puritans, Catholics, and Quakers sought the right to worship without government interference.

- In 1620 the **Pilgrims**, a small group of religious separatists led by **William Bradford**, came to America on a ship named the **Mayflower**.

They had separated from the Church of England, at whose head was the king or queen, to return to the scriptures alone as a governing authority. Citing continued church corruption, they were persecuted for their beliefs in England. Prior to coming ashore in the New World, they drafted an agreement, the **Mayflower Compact**, committing the settlers of the **Plymouth Colony** in Massachusetts to self-government and majority rule. Thus, this Compact outlined the first form of **democracy** in America. This settlement marked the beginning of permanence and expansion on the North American continent. After the first hard year had passed, the Pilgrims celebrated the first **Thanksgiving** with the Native Americans who had been friendly towards them—the Wampanoag tribe. One Native American who was of particular help to the Pilgrims was **Squanto.**

- In 1629, the **Puritans**, a larger group than the Pilgrims who sought to "purify" the Church of England (but not necessarily separate from it), was led by **John Winthrop** to form a joint-stock company they called the Massachusetts Bay Company. A **joint-stock company** raises capital by the public sale of stocks in its company. King Charles I, happy to be rid of the Puritans, granted the group a charter to found a colony in the New World. Winthrop wanted to create a colony that would be a "city on a hill," a model for the world of what a Christian community ought to be. The Puritans carefully organized prior to their journey and settlement, which meant that the **Massachusetts Bay Colony** never went through the "starving years" that earlier colonies had endured in their first years.

- Puritan dissenters began to break away to form their own colonies. **Roger Williams** founded a colony in Providence in 1636, and **Anne Hutchinson** founded Portsmouth in 1638. They received a charter from Parliament in 1644 to combine their colonies into what would later become the state of Rhode Island. Connecticut was also founded by a Puritan dissenter, **Thomas Hooker**, in 1636.

- England also offered land grants to other religious groups. **George Calvert**, **Lord Baltimore**, a Catholic, was granted the first proprietary colony for Maryland in 1632. **William Penn** was given a land grant in what is now Pennsylvania to establish a colony for Quakers.

- **King Philip's War**—perhaps the most costly war in American history in terms of the percentage of lives lost—broke out in 1675 between the New England colonists and some of the local Native American tribes. Dwindling resources, including land, caused increased clashes between the cultures. Many other Native Americans fought with the colonists against Metacom, a Native American who took the English name of King Philip. Although the warring tribes were defeated, it took many years for the colonies to recover from this war.

- In 1692, Puritans in Massachusetts were shaken by the accusations of young girls in **Salem** who reported that they were being tormented by several witches who lived in the village. The **Salem Witch Trials** resulted in 20 executions, 19 by hanging and one crushing by rocks.

- By the 1700s, town meetings were conducted throughout the New England colonies. People voted, created their own laws, and sent representatives to colonial assemblies. **Individualism**, the belief in the dignity and worth of each person, had a firm religious and political base in the British colonies.

- Because many colonial economies experienced rapid growth, settlers worked hard to establish their own farms and businesses. Differing geographical and economic conditions led to three distinctive groups. The **thirteen original colonies** were divided into New England colonies, middle colonies, and southern colonies.

- The **New England Colonies** of Massachusetts, New Hampshire, Rhode Island, and Connecticut had poor soil and thus developed fishing, trading, whaling, and shipbuilding industries. The majority of those who settled here came from England.
- The **Middle Colonies** of New York, New Jersey, Pennsylvania, and Delaware grew large quantities of wheat and grain on family farms, established flour milling, and participated in some shipping and trading. Most of the settlers in this region came from England, Germany, Scotland, and France (and with some free Africans).
- The **Southern Colonies** of Maryland, Virginia, North Carolina, South Carolina, and Georgia had a climate and soil that favored the development of large plantations on which tobacco, indigo, cotton, and rice were grown. There was also some trading and shipping. These colonies were mostly settled by English, French, Scots, and slaves from Africa (on whom the economy of agriculture came to depend).

II. National Unity

KEY QUESTION: *What led the states to adopt a central government in 1790?*

- During the first half of the eighteenth century, England pursued a policy of **salutary neglect** and did not attempt to exercise much economic or political control over its North American colonies.
- In 1763, however, as a result of enormous debts arising from the **French and Indian War**, England decided to levy taxes on the prospering colonies.
- The **Stamp Act of 1765** was an English tax on newspapers and legal documents. Following colonial protests, this tax was repealed, but this was the seed of unrest that sparked the call of "no taxation without representation" for the colonies.
- In 1766, England imposed the **Townsend Acts**, which required new taxes on tea, glass, paint, and paper. Most colonial legislatures sent protests to the British Parliament. The British Crown initially responded by increasing the number of troops stationed in America. By 1770, tensions between colonists and soldiers ran high. In Boston, the hostility between the two groups led to an incident in which several colonists were killed, including **Crispus Attucks**, an African American. Samuel Adams called the incident the **Boston Massacre**. Parliament repealed all the taxes except the one on tea. This created a significant problem; if the colonies paid the tea tax they would, in effect, be confirming that England had the right to directly tax them. In 1773, a group of angry colonists (dressed up as Mohawk Indians) threw tea from British cargo ships into Boston Harbor. In response to the **"Boston Tea Party,"** England closed the port of Boston and severely limited self-government in Massachusetts. The fundamental disagreement was over England's taxation of the colonists without having been allowed representation in the British government.
- The British government (with King George III at its head) passed four acts, collectively known as the **Intolerable** (or the **Coercive**) **Acts** in response to the dumping of the tea: (1) the port of Boston was closed until the tea was paid for, (2) the Massachusetts royal governor was given

greater authority over the colonial legislature, (3) royal officials accused of a crime could be tried elsewhere, and (4) the Quartering Act required American colonists to house British troops.

- In 1774, Americans formed the **First Continental Congress** in response to the Intolerable Acts. Meeting in Philadelphia, its first act was to draft a petition to the British Parliament to protest the Intolerable Acts. In addition to their protest to England, they began to organize a militia to protect themselves. Up until this time, most colonists considered themselves **Loyalists** (or loyal to King George III). However, some were beginning to join groups such as the **Patriots**, rather than remain as "Englishmen." Committees of Correspondence were created to communicate throughout the colonies about events that had to do with the current politics.

- Initially the British government paid little attention to the First Continental Congress. By 1775 the British sent more troops to Massachusetts to arrest the leaders of the rebellion. **General Gage** led 700 British soldiers to Concord on a mission to search for and destroy a reported stockpile of colonial arms and ammunition. The Americans tracked the British troop movements and sent two riders, **Paul Revere** and **William Dawes**, to alert the countryside.

- When the British arrived at **Lexington**, they found a group of 70 American **Minutemen** (militiamen ready at a moment's notice) waiting for them on the village green. A British officer ordered the men to drop their weapons and disperse. The Minutemen held on to their weapons but did begin to leave the green. At the same time, a shot was fired. This was *"the shot heard 'round the world,"* marking the beginning of the Revolutionary War. Later that day, the American **Minutemen** drove the British from **Lexington** and **Concord**.

- A Second Continental Congress came together in 1775, and this Congress formed the **Continental Army** with **George Washington** at its head. This was a rag-tag army that used guerilla tactics on the British because of the poor odds.

- In June 1775, at the **Battle of Bunker Hill,** the Americans were driven back, but surprisingly, they inflicted huge losses on the British.

- In 1776, **Thomas Paine** published his famous pamphlet, *Common Sense,* which gave reasons why it was foolish to believe that Americans could reconcile with England.

- The Congress adopted the **Declaration of Independence** on **July 4, 1776.** In this declaration (mostly written by **Thomas Jefferson**), the basic principles of the United States government were set forth, along with the colonists' grievances and the reasons they were to be "freed" from England.

- George Washington, as commander of the Continental Army, after a year of losing battles and skirmishes to the British, managed to **cross the Delaware River** at night with his army and win the Battle of Trenton in New Jersey.

- In 1777, the Continental Army almost did not make it through the harsh winter at **Valley Forge.** There was little food, clothing, or shelter for soldiers. Morale was low throughout the winter. However Washington's strong leadership was able to keep the army together to continue the **Revolutionary War**, or the **War for Independence.**

- The French were very helpful to the emerging nation, sending ships, weapons, and officers such as **de Lafayette.**

- In October 1781, the **Battle of Yorktown**, the last major battle of the Revolutionary War, was won by the Continental Army, with help from the French. The British forces, under the leadership of **Cornwallis** surrendered.
- **Nathan Hale** spied on the British for the American army but was captured and executed. His famous last words were, "I only regret that I have but one life to lose for my country." **Benedict Arnold**, a high-ranking American officer, turned traitor to the young country during the war.
- In 1783, with the signing of the **Treaty of Paris**, the colonies had won the Revolutionary War and their freedom from England.
- One of the powerful symbols associated with the American Independence is the **Liberty Bell**. On July 8, 1776, the tolling of the Liberty Bell from Independence Hall in Philadelphia summoned citizens to hear a reading of the Declaration of Independence. In October 1777, when the British occupied Philadelphia, the Liberty Bell was removed from the city and hidden. It was feared that the British would have melted it down and used the iron for ammunition. The bell was returned to Philadelphia in 1778 when the British left the city. Despite a great crack in the bell, it was used throughout the period of 1790 to 1800 (when **Philadelphia** served as the nation's capital) to call the state legislature into session, to summon voters to turn in ballots, to commemorate George Washington's birthday, and to celebrate the 4th of July. The last time it rang was on the anniversary of Washington's birthday in 1846 when the final expansion of the crack made the bell unable to ring again.
- After the Revolutionary War, the colonies became independent states, joined together in a loose association under the first constitution of the United States—the **Articles of Confederation** (ratified in 1781). The Articles established a very weak central republican government (elected representation) with a Congress (but with only one governmental chamber [unicameral]). It could declare war but was not allowed to recruit an army. There was no executive branch, central federal judicial branch, or courts. States taxed each other's goods and used different monetary currencies.
- **Shays' Rebellion**, an uprising of debtor farmers in Massachusetts, showed the states how inadequate the Articles of Confederation were. The central government did not have the authority to put down the rebellion.
- In 1790, the site of the **District of Columbia (Washington, D.C.)** was designated as the nation's new capital city next to the Potomac River. **Benjamin Banneker**, an African American mathematician, surveyed the area and Charles L'Enfant was the architect and engineer who designed the plan for the city.
- Recognizing the many weaknesses of the Articles of Confederation, 55 delegates (now known as the "**Founding Fathers**") from the various states met in Philadelphia and eventually drafted the **Constitution of the United States**, adopted in 1790.
- The Constitution was the result of a series of *compromises* (called the **Great Compromise**). Among the most important of these were representation in the legislature and the method of electing the president. The debate over ratification divided the nation into Nationalists, or **Federalists**, who supported the Constitution and **anti-Federalists**, who feared that a strong central government might abuse its power and the

liberties of the people and the states. The Constitution consists of the **Preamble** or introduction, the **Articles** which explain the powers (and limits on power) of the federal government, and the **Amendments** that change or make explicit elements of the original Constitution.

- The Preamble to the Constitution reads:

  We the People of the United States, in Order to form a more perfect Union, establish Justice, insure domestic Tranquility, provide for the common defense, promote the general Welfare, and secure the Blessings of Liberty to ourselves and our Posterity, do ordain and establish this Constitution for the United States of America.

- There are seven **Articles** in the Constitution. The first covers the powers of the Legislature. Since this is the first Article, many Constitutional scholars believe that the Founding Fathers must have considered the powers of the Legislature extremely important. The articles specify the term of office for **Senators** (6 years), **Representatives** (2 years), and for **President** (4 years); provide for a **Supreme Court** (with 9 judges with lifetime appointments); and set up the **Electoral College** (a complex system for electing the President that provides for a balance of equality between all the states rather than the actual number of popular votes).

- There are **27 Amendments** to the Constitution. The first 10 of these are referred to as the **Bill of Rights**.

- The promise of a **Bill of Rights**, the first 10 amendments to the Constitution, allowed the anti-Federalists to accept the new government. Anti-Federalists wanted to guarantee that citizens would be protected from the new government, so they wanted many rights specified. These include: freedom of speech, press, religion, and assembly; the right to bear arms, to petition the government, due process in courts, and to a speedy and public trial; to not be forced to quarter soldiers in one's home; and protection from unreasonable search and seizure, self-incrimination, *double jeopardy* (to not be tried twice for the same crime), excessive bail, and cruel and unusual punishment. Finally, the 10th Amendment establishes the concept of **federalism**, which gives states all the powers not designated by the Constitution to the federal government. The **14th Amendment** abolishes slavery, the **15th** grants *all* U.S. (male) citizens the right to vote (including slaves), and the **19th** grants women the right to vote.

- In some ways, the **War of 1812** with England was a continuation of the Revolutionary War. The British and Americans had not finished with their differences. The British refused to abide by the terms of the Treaty of Paris (which had ended the Revolutionary War), and many British ships impressed, or kidnapped and forced thousands of Americans to serve on their ships. America declared war. In a major setback for the American troops, the British captured and burned down much of Washington, D.C. However, American troops successfully defended an attack on **Fort McHenry** in Baltimore. **Francis Scott Key**, a witness to this battle, wrote a poem to commemorate the event. This was set to music as "**The Star-Spangled Banner**" and became our national anthem. One of the most remembered events of this war was the victory at the **Battle of New Orleans** (in 1814) with **Andrew Jackson** commanding the U.S. troops. Although the war had already been declared over, the news had not reached the combatants there.

- "**The Star-Spangled Banner**" is our national anthem, but it has had potential rivals for this honor. One challenger is "**America the Beautiful**". In 1893, Katherine Lee Bates was inspired to write a poem about the sites she encountered on a cross country train trip. This poem was originally published on July 4, 1895, and was later set to music composed by Samuel A. Ward, who had been similarly inspired.

III. Regional Differences

KEY QUESTION: *How did the territorial and economic growth of the country lead to the war between the States?*

- During the first half of the 1800s, the United States acquired through wars, treaties, and purchases more and more land west of the original 13 colonies.
- In 1803, President **Thomas Jefferson** bought territory from the French. Know as the **Louisiana Purchase**, this nearly doubled the size of the United States. Jefferson sent **Meriwether Lewis** and **William Clark** to map out other parts of this purchase. They followed the Mississippi River and then continued west to eventually reach the Pacific Ocean in Oregon. A Native American woman, **Sacagawea**, helped to guide them. They returned in 1806, marking the beginnings of the covered wagons full of settlers who moved West to settle on their own land there.
- Protected from Europe by an ocean, American leaders continued to encourage territorial expansion on the North American continent and adopted a policy of neutrality toward foreign powers.
- In 1823, **President James Monroe** emphasized a policy of noninterference to warn European nations against intervening anywhere in the Western Hemisphere in his **Monroe Doctrine**.
- By the 1840s, people began to believe in **Manifest Destiny**, the idea that the United States was destined to expand from the Atlantic to the Pacific Ocean, and thousands of settlers began to cross the country in wagon trains.
- As the country grew and prospered, regional differences became more pronounced. The Northeast developed an industrial and trading economy. An **Industrial Revolution** (where mass production was being done with machines) began in the late seventeenth and early eighteenth centuries. Inventors such as **Eli Whitney** (who first patented the cotton gin), **Thomas Edison** (who experimented with early versions of electric lighting, the telephone, telegraph, electric railway, and an iron ore separator), and **Robert Fulton** (who invented the steamboat) helped begin the transformation from an agrarian to an industrial society. Finished products found markets easier when the **Erie Canal** (1825) helped open up the Midwest by creating a water route between the Atlantic Ocean and the Great Lakes.
- The South became increasingly more dependent on exporting cash agricultural crops such as cotton and tobacco to Europe, and the agricultural basis of their economy increasingly grew to depend on slave labor. In the West, cheap land encouraged smaller family farms.
- The growth of the railroad networks also helped homesteaders move West to work small farms of their own and to send goods back East. The completion of the *transcontinental railroad* from coast to coast in 1869 opened the country to the **Manifest Destiny**, or the dream of a country from the Atlantic to the Pacific.
- Regional differences, however, led to **sectionalism**, with Americans increasingly looking at issues in terms of what would benefit their own region. Northerners favored **tariffs**, or special taxes, on many imported

goods to protect their industries. Southerners, who imported more goods, opposed tariffs. Northerners favored the **National Bank**, which gave them a stable currency and investment funds. Westerners and Southerners favored state banks, which would give them easier credit needed in an agrarian society. Midwesterners wanted federal funds for the construction of roads and canals in order to get their products and produce to market more easily. Southerners favored the extension of slavery to new territories, something Northerners and Westerners both opposed. Growing sectionalism meant that Northerners and Westerners came to view any further extension of slavery as empowering the South at the expense of the slaves. However, many Southerners had heavily invested in slavery for their small or large farms (plantations) and felt that, in giving up their slaves, it would cost them their livelihood and land. Southern states used *slave codes* to designate the kind of work that each slave would do—house work, field work, and so forth. **Abolitionists**, particularly in the North, began to demand a complete end to (or the abolition of) slavery. **Harriet Beecher Stowe** wrote *Uncle Tom's Cabin,* which influenced many to become abolitionists. Some abolitionists began to help slaves escape through the **Underground Railroad**, the name for a series of safe houses in which people would help lead escaped slaves to the north and freedom. **Harriet Tubman**, an escaped slave, became a "conductor" on the Underground Railroad and was credited with freeing more than 300 escaped slaves. **Sojourner Truth**, another escaped slave, became a powerful and outspoken abolitionist.

- With the 1828 election of **Andrew Jackson**, sectional issues dominated national politics. A Westerner, Jackson antagonized Southerners by enforcing tariffs but also alienated Northerners by dismantling the National Bank. Under Jackson, the Indian Removal Act required that all Native Americans east of the Mississippi River be moved to west of the Mississippi. The Cherokee Nation was to be allowed to remain but, instead, Jackson had troops force march them to Oklahoma. This march, termed the **Trail of Tears** because of the sorrow and harshness of the 800-mile journey, left more than 4,000 Cherokees dead along the way.

- Several acts on the issues of slavery were instituted during the 1800s. The **Missouri Compromise** maintained the balance of free states versus slave states by allowing Missouri to come into the United States as a slave state and Maine as a free state. The **Kansas–Nebraska Act** allowed for these states, upon entering the United States., to choose for themselves. Sectional disputes further intensified when the Supreme Court, in the **Dred Scott Case**, invalidated compromises over the issues of extending slavery into new territories by providing that a slave would remain a slave, even if he or she was transported to a non-slave-holding state. The gap between the industrial North and agricultural South widened as each sought to control the central government.

- In 1848, when gold was first discovered in California at **Sutter's Mill** (near present-day Sacramento), the question of slavery in the Western territories became more critical. The **"forty-niners"** (those who rushed to California for riches) were a rough group, and California became a wild and lawless place during the **Gold Rush** years. As a result, many of the fortune seekers who wanted to move to California were often too afraid to bring their valuable slaves to the area, fearing violence and that the lure of gold would cause attempted escapes. These fears contributed to California's application for statehood as a free state in 1849. This posed a significant threat to the balance of free states and slave states in the United States.

- When **Abraham Lincoln** was elected president in 1860, the southern states felt that their interests were no longer represented by the federal government and withdrew, or **seceded**, from the Union.
- Under the leadership of **Jefferson Davis**, 11 states formed the **Confederate States of America** (the **Confederacy; the South**). The Confederate States were: South Carolina, Mississippi, Florida, Alabama, Georgia, Louisiana, **Texas**, Virginia, Arkansas, Tennessee, and North Carolina. The four slaveholding border states (Maryland, Delaware, Kentucky, and Missouri) and 19 other free states remained in the **Union** (the **North**).
- The **Civil War** began in 1861 when Confederate soldiers fired on federal troops at **Fort Sumter** in South Carolina. A *civil war* is fought between people who are citizens of the same country or live in the same area.
- The **Union,** or the North, had a decided advantage over the Confederacy, having twice the population of the South and three quarters of the nation's wealth. In addition, it had more factories and railroads.
- In July 1862, the first major battle of the war (the **First Battle of Bull Run**), fought on the outskirts of Washington, D.C., resulted in a victory for the Southern forces. **General "Stonewall" Jackson** led his Confederate troops against the poorly trained Union troops under the command of **General Irvin McDowell**. This led to a shake-up in command in the Northern forces. Lincoln had great difficulty finding someone to command the Union army. From 1862 to 1864, the succession of men Lincoln tried as commander of the Union army was as follows: **General George McClellan, General Ambrose Burnside, General Joseph "Fighting Joe" Hooker, General George Meade,** and finally **General Ulysses Grant.** Grant would win the war for the Union (the North)— **General Robert E. Lee** commanded the Confederate forces.
- Naval engagements were an important aspect of the Civil War. Early in the conflict, the Confederate navy achieved supremacy with their **ironclad** vessel—the *Merrimack.* Originally, the Northern navy had only wooden ships, which could not compete with the iron-plated ship. In 1862, the South's naval supremacy was ended by the North's new ironclad ship—the *Monitor.*
- In September 1862, the **Battle of Antietam**, technically a Northern victory, resulted in the bloodiest single day of battle in U.S. hisory. At the end of the day 22,726 lay dead, dying, or wounded. **General Sherman** undertook a "scorched earth" policy across the South, including the burning of Atlanta.
- Women participated in the war effort by working in factories or nursing (such as **Clara Barton**); a very few fought in the war and/or acted as spies.
- Perhaps the most famous battle of the Civil War took place July 1–3, 1863, at the small town of Gettysburg, Pennsylvania. In the **Battle of Gettysburg**, General Meade led 90,000 Union soldiers against General Lee's smaller Confederate contingent of 75,000 soldiers. Meade was severely criticized for allowing Lee to retreat with his remaining army back into the Confederacy, but the battle so weakened the Southern army that Lee never again attempted a serious invasion of the North. The **Battle of Gettysburg** was one of the costliest battles in history. When the fighting ended on July 3, 1863, there were 50,000 fallen

Americans from both sides on the battlefield. The battlefield cemetery was officially dedicated on November 19, 1863. President Abraham **Lincoln** delivered the dedication, beginning with "Four score and seven years ago our fathers brought forth on this continent a new nation, conceived in liberty and dedicated to the proposition that all men are created equal." In his relatively short speech, later referred to as the **Gettysburg Address**, he memorialized the Union dead and emphasized the power of their sacrifice. He placed the common soldier at the center of the struggle for equality, as he reminded the audience of the higher purpose for which their blood had been shed, so "that the government of the people, by the people, and for the people shall not perish from this earth."

- On January 1, 1863, Lincoln issued the **Emancipation Proclamation**, freeing the slaves in the Confederacy. Immediately, it freed only a few slaves, but it clearly established for the North that this was a war being fought not only to preserve the Union but also to eliminate slavery.
- By 1865, the Confederacy was defeated. **Confederate General Robert E. Lee** formally surrendered to **Union General Ulysses S. Grant** at **Appomattox, Virginia**, and the nation began the hard task of recovery. This recovery period was known as the **Reconstruction**.
- More than 618,000 Americans died in the course of the Civil War—more than all American Wars combined.
- **Abraham Lincoln** was assassinated by **John Wilkes Booth** at the Ford's Theater in Washington, D.C., only five days after Lee's surrender. It is theorized that the South would have been treated more positively in the Reconstruction era had Lincoln not been killed and **Vice President Andrew Johnson** not stepped into the Presidency.
- Southern states, such as Texas, voted mostly for Democrats up until the 1960s in response to the Reconstruction years. **John Tower**, who served in Congress for more than twenty years, was the first Republican senator to be elected since the Reconstruction.

IV. Industrial Growth

KEY QUESTION: *What were the effects of industrial growth on farms and cities?*

- **Reconstruction** hit the South very hard economically, as the North sought to punish the region for the war. Many Southerners lost their land because of the inability to pay taxes and produce crops (because of loss of life, limb, and slave workers), so even agriculture was depressed.
- In the South during the Civil War and **Reconstruction**, Blacks were given constitutional guarantees of freedom and protection through the **Emancipation Proclamation** and the **Civil War amendments to the Constitution** (13, 14, and 15). **Carpetbaggers** from the North came down to the South to take over land and businesses that could no longer pay their taxes and also to gain political power. **Scalawags** were White southerners with the same goals.
- As a result of the amendments, Southern states passed **Jim Crow Laws**, which legalized **segregation**, and other laws, labeled as **Black codes**, which succeeded in circumventing the amendments in order to deny Blacks the right to vote as well as other civil rights.
- Most Blacks in the South became **sharecroppers**, farming other people's land in exchange for a portion of their crops. Others became tenant farmers who leased land.

- Unlike Southern sharecroppers, Western and Midwestern farmers benefited from the rapid industrialization of the period. As agriculture became more mechanized, farmers were freed from backbreaking labor, but they felt they were still denied their fair share of the nation's wealth. Farmers often went into debt to purchase new equipment. Railroads charged them exorbitant rates to transport produce to markets, and middlemen siphoned off much of their profits. Therefore, farmers began to demand government regulation of railroad rates and cheap lending practices to ease their debts. They joined the **Grange**, a movement to press their demands for reform. They also formed the backbone of the **Greenback** and **Populist** political parties.

- In 1880, only one quarter of the population of the United States lived in cities, but by 1910, **urbanization** had almost doubled. Rapid technological advances of the industrial revolution fostered the development and expansion of industries. Scientific production techniques, such as the **assembly line**, transformed American industry, the economy, and society. **Henry Ford's** use of the assembly line to produce automobiles saw America go from four cars on the roads in 1895 to nearly five million by 1917. In 1916, while Ford was putting more cars on the road, the **Federal Aid Roads Act** established the framework for constructing a national network of highways. Americans became more mobile than ever before.

- Between 1880 and 1910, immigrants as well as farmers flocked to American cities to take jobs in the factories. They received low wages and worked under hazardous conditions. In 1911, a fire at the **Triangle Shirtwaist Factory**, in New York City, focused national attention on unsafe working conditions. Because the exit doors had been locked by management in order to keep out union organizers, 146 people, mainly women, died.

- To help workers, the **Knights of Labor** and other unions were started. **Samuel Gompers** founded the **American Federation of Labor** (AFL) in 1886. Members could vote to strike (stop working) or could appoint delegates to bargain for better wages and conditions.

- At the same time, industrial leaders, such as **Andrew Carnegie** and **Cornelius Vanderbilt**, created **trusts** to consolidate their control over America's steel and railroad companies. They virtually eliminated competition (created **monopolies**) so that they could set high prices and control the market for their products. These "**robber barons**" became active in state and national politics in order to impede attempts to regulate their industries.

V. Reform Movements

KEY QUESTION: *How did reforms change the life of Americans in the first half of the twentieth century?*

- From the turn of the century until World War I, members of the **Progressive Movement** sponsored legislation to improve the quality of American life.
- Reformers enacted pure food and drugs laws to protect consumers.
- The **Temperance Movement** began to gain support against drinking alcohol, but "bootleg" (illegal) alcohol continued to make its way into American homes and establishments. Temperance supporters hoped that **prohibition** (prohibiting the sale and consumption of alcohol) would solve the nation's poverty, crime, violence, and other social problems.

- Reformers like **Susan B. Anthony** supported women's efforts to gain the right to vote (or **suffrage**), which was finally granted in the **Nineteenth Amendment** in 1920.
- Women pioneers in male-dominated areas (such as aviation) furthered the position of women in society. In 1932, **Amelia Earhart** became the first woman to cross the Atlantic Ocean, flying from Newfoundland to Northern Ireland in 14 hours and 56 minutes. In 1937, she and one other crew member were attempting to circumnavigate the globe from west to east when her plane disappeared somewhere over the Pacific Ocean. What happened to Earhart remains a mystery today.
- The **NAACP** (National Association for the Advancement of Colored People) was founded in 1909 by **W.E.B. Dubois** and suffragette **Mary White Ovington.**
- Although slavery had ended, African Americans in the United States were still denied opportunities simply because of their race. There are many examples of those who overcame this discrimination. One is **Bessie Coleman**, born in Atlanta, Texas, in 1892. She was the first African American woman to become an airline pilot and the first American woman to hold an international pilot license. After being denied admission to American flight schools, Coleman studied French and, in 1920, traveled to Paris to attend flight school. Another African American pioneer, this time in the field of hair care and cosmetics, was **Madam C.J. Walker.** By 1917, hers was the largest business owned by an African American. According to many accounts, Walker was the first female American self-made millionaire.
- Child labor was outlawed and children were guaranteed schooling under compulsory education laws. **Jane Addams,** who lived in Chicago (and established Hull-House for immigrant children with working mothers), was instrumental in protecting children from child labor in the early 1900s. In the early 1920s she helped to found the American Civil Liberties Union, and was the first American woman to receive the Noble Peace prize.
- Many huge companies gained **monopolies** (owned all of the goods or services of a particular type). **Standard Oil** was one of the first monopolies. In 1904, under the leadership of **John D. Rockefeller**, the oil company controlled more than 90 percent of oil production in the United States.
- The government took on a greater role in regulating the economy. **Antitrust laws** were enacted to eliminate monopolies and regulate other unfair trade practices. The **Federal Reserve System** allowed the government to create a central bank that would control the monetary supply of the United States. This is still done partly by setting interest rates. At the time of publication, the current Chair of the Federal Reserve Board, Ben Benanke is fairly new, having been appointed in 2006. He replaced **Alan Greenspan** who was appointed in 1987 by President Reagan and who served almost 20 years.
- After World War I, Americans grew tired of reforms and wanted a **"return to normalcy,"** an era in which government would play a less important role in people's lives.
- In the "Roaring" 1920s, the economy boomed, and Americans devoted themselves to the making and spending of money. In this "frivolous era," of "flappers" and "speakeasies" (clubs where illegal alcohol was served), sports and film stars attracted national attention. Jazz music gained popularity. The novel, *The Great Gatsby* (1925) by F. **Scott Fitzgerald** came to symbolize the entire era.

- On "**Black Tuesday**," October 29, 1929, the **stock market crash** brought national prosperity and good times to a sudden and violent end. Stock prices fell rapidly, thousands of people lost their investments, and businesses and banks closed. The nation and the world were soon in the grip of the **Great Depression**, with millions of people unemployed. Families looked for public relief and charitable assistance. In the cities, "soup kitchens" and "bread lines" formed to feed the hungry.
- Rural areas were also hard hit during the Depression. One of the worst droughts in American history began in 1930. The region, stretching north from Texas into the Dakotas, came to be known as "**The Dust Bowl**." Overgrazing and overplanting, a steady decline in rainfall, and an accompanying increase in heat turned fertile farm regions into virtual deserts (desertification). Many farmers left their land in search of work. One of the classic portrayals of this period is **John Steinbeck's** novel, *The Grapes of Wrath* (1939).
- **President Franklin Delano Roosevelt (FDR)** proposed a **New Deal** to combat the effects of the depression. He proposed legislation to offer relief to the unemployed, to prevent economic abuses, and to reconstruct the economy with programs such as the **TVA** (Tennessee Valley Authority), Social Security, and regulation of Wall Street. Although FDR's legislative proposals eased some suffering, the Great Depression did not end until the country **mobilized** for World War II. American industry returned to full strength to manufacture the military machinery necessary for our entry into the war.
- The **Social Security Act** provided social insurance for the elderly and the unemployed.
- The **Security Exchange Commission (SEC)** was set up to regulate the stock market (on Wall Street).
- The **Works Progress Administration (WPA)** gave jobs to the unemployed.
- The **Tennessee Valley Authority (TVA)** put people to work building a series of dams that provided electricity to one of the most depressed rural areas in the nation.

VI. International Affairs

KEY QUESTION: *What are some key conflicts in which the United States participated?*

- The **Spanish-American War** was fought in part by **Theodore "Teddy" Roosevelt** (who later became president) and his **Rough Riders** in 1898, after Cuba asked the United States for help against Spain. The U.S. warship *Maine,* sitting in Havana harbor, exploded, which gave the United States the excuse it needed to fight against Spain. The results of the treaty, which ended this war, freed Cuba and gave the Philippine Islands, Guam, and Puerto Rico to the United States as a territory (which it kept until after World War II). The Philippines gained independence after WWII while Guam remains a U.S. territory and Puerto Rico is a commonwealth of the U.S. Roosevelt was instrumental in acquiring and building the strip of land in Panama that opened as the Panama Canal in 1914, and which was kept by the United States until 1999.
- In **1917**, **World War I** saw the United States fighting with the Allies (France, Great Britain, Belgium, Russia, Serbia, etc.) against the **Central Powers** (Germany, Austria-Hungary, the Ottoman Empire, and Bulgaria).
- In **World War II**, the **Allies** (France, the USSR, Great Britain, and many others) fought against the **Axis** (Germany, Italy, Austria, and Japan), beginning in Europe in 1939. Switzerland and others remained neutral.

The United States entered the war when Japan bombed **Pearl Harbor** in 1941. The war ended with victory for the Allies in 1945.

- The United States fought the **Korean War** from 1950 to 1953 after North Korea (with the help of some Chinese troops) invaded South Korea.
- **Vietnam** was a long war that began under President John F. Kennedy in the mid-1960s and ended under **President Richard Nixon.** Vietnam was divided into two parts, the South, which asked for help from the United States, and the North, under communist control. Initial arguments for the United States entering the war centered on holding the line of communism there rather than having South Vietnam fall and letting communism spread to other countries in the Far East (the **Domino Theory**). Although the United States was by far the more powerful nation militarily, the Cold War with China and the U.S.S.R. (Russia) seemed to hold the United States back from completing an all out victory. The American people began to tire of these types of politics and loss of American lives, and the United States eventually pulled out of the region, leaving Vietnam to the Communists. Many Vietnamese, fleeing from the Communists (some on overcrowded boats), immigrated or attempted to immigrate to the United States during this time.
- The **Cold War** basically ended in 1991 with the collapse of the communist government in Russia. Although there were complex reasons, many historians give much credit to President Ronald Reagan's policies against "the Evil Empire."
- The first **Gulf War (Operation Desert Storm)** began in 1990 and was a 42-day war (for the United States), in which the first President George Bush and 28 other nations came to the aid of Kuwait after it was invaded by Iraq under Saddam Hussein.
- The day after the attacks on the World Trade Center on 9/11/01, President Bush indentified the Saudi Arabian, Osama bin Laden, as the mastermind behind the attacks. Administration officials linked the airline highjackers to his Al Qaeda terrorist network. At the time, he and many members of Al Qaeda were believed to be in Afghanistan under the protection of the Taliban, a radical Islamic group. U.S. and British forces began an invasion of Afghanistan in October 2001 to capture bin Laden and overthrow the Taliban regime that had sheltered him. This began a new era of what President Bush referred to as a global war on terror in which American forces would confront threats to security before they reached the U.S. In 2003 a U.S. led coalition invaded Iraq to overthrow Saddam Hussein and make possible a democratic Iraq that could be a model for political change throughout the Middle East.

KEY QUESTION: *What was American foreign policy during the late 1800s to the mid-1900s?*

- From the 1890s to the 1940s, American foreign policy alternated between **isolationism** (retreat from international concerns) and **internationalism** (active involvement in world affairs). The United States also went through periods of **nativism** (a move to restrict immigrants) during the 1880s due to a large influx of immigrants from many countries. Nativism had appeared earlier in the 1850s after many Chinese immigrants came, particularly to work on building the railroads.
- **William Seward**, as Secretary of State in 1897, **purchased Alaska** and the Aleutian Islands from Russia, which turned out to be a huge economic profit for the United States when the discovery of **gold** caused a huge "rush" to that area in the 1890s.

- In the late 1890s, the United States adopted an activist foreign policy toward the Caribbean and the Pacific. It began to pursue a policy of **imperialism**, the political and economic control of other territories for purposes of prestige, power, and wealth.
- In 1898, the United States went to war to free Cuba from Spanish rule and to protect American trading interests. As a result of the **Spanish-American War**, the United States gained control of Puerto Rico, Guam, and the Philippines. Cuba was liberated but soon became an American protectorate.
- At the same time (1898), the United States annexed the Hawaiian Islands as a territory.
- In 1914, a Serbian separatist assassinated Austrian **Archduke Franz Ferdinand** and his wife in Sarajevo. Many historians have viewed this as the trigger for WWI. What had been an argument by Serbia wanting to separate (after having being annexed by Austria–Hungary) (along with military build up by many European countries and other causes) resulted in an escalation that would become **World War I.** European nations took sides and formed powerful alliances.
- The United States, under **President Woodrow Wilson**, tried to maintain a policy of **neutrality**, but in 1917 Germany's submarines sank unarmed American merchant ships and a British passenger ship, the *Lusitania,* killing 128 Americans among the 1,200 who died. The United States joined the **Allied Powers**—Great Britain, France, and Russia, among others—in fighting the **Central Powers**—Germany, the Austro-Hungarian Empire, and their allies.
- The **American Expeditionary Force (AEF)**, under the command of **General John J. "Black Jack" Pershing**, entered the war in the spring of 1918. He gained the nickname "Black Jack" when he led African American troops during his regular army days. Pershing eventually became the highest-ranking general in U.S. history.
- Several new weapons of war were tested during the **trench warfare** of World War I. Poison gas, rapid-fire machine guns, and the airplane are just a few of these weapons of devastation. The war had become a virtual **stalemate**, with neither side gaining ground, until America entered the war.
- The first major battle in which the Americans participated saw the defeat of the Germans at **Belleau Wood** (June 1918). The entry of America into the war was seen to turn the tide in favor of the Allies.
- When Germany accepted defeat in November 1918, both sides signed an **armistice.**
- In early 1918, Russia signed a separate peace agreement with the Central Powers and left the war because of the **Bolshevik Revolution** in October 1917. The communists, led by **V.I. Lenin**, took control of the country and killed **Czar Nicholas** and his family. This began the communist domination of Russia, which lasted more than 70 years. By the 1930s, it is estimated that Joseph Stalin's regime had killed and/or persecuted millions of Russians in **Gulags** (prisons for political opposition, usually found in areas such as Siberia).
- During the end of WWI at treaty making at the French palace at Versailles (**Treaty of Versailles**), President Woodrow Wilson put forth his idealist **Fourteen Points** to foster world trade and fair territorial settlements. These were ignored by the European powers who sought to severely punish the Axis powers. The United States never ratified the Treaty of Versailles due to Wilson's political miscalculations and subsequent stroke.

- Disillusioned with the peace-making process, Americans returned to an isolationist policy and rejected membership in the **League of Nations**, an international organization intended to settle international disputes peaceably.
- Without the American influence in the peace process, the Allied powers proceeded with their **reparations**, or payment for damages, which became the central focus of the Treaty. Almost immediately, Germans began to experience devastating economic hardships. It was not long until a charismatic leader, **Adolf Hitler**, emerged to rally the German people towards nationalist pride and against the countries who had demanded such staunch reparations.
- With the rise of several militaristic governments (**Adolf Hitler** and his **Nazi Party** in Germany; **Benito Mussolini** and the **Fascists** in Italy; and **Emperor Hirohito** and **Admiral Hideki Tojo** in Japan) the postwar settlements of the Treaty of Versailles did not last long. In the 1930s, these **Axis** powers began to absorb neighboring European countries (such as Czechoslovakia), while Japan invaded China. British Prime Minister, **Neville Chamberlain**, declared a policy of **appeasement** (giving in to demands and ignoring aggression in order to keep the peace) in response.
- **World War II** finally erupted for Europe in 1939, when German troops marched into Poland, violating their independence. The United States sided with the **Allies**, including France, Great Britain, and the Soviet Union against the **Axis** powers (Germany, Italy, and Japan) but remained neutral militarily.
- Following the 7:55 a.m. Japanese bombing of U.S. Pacific Fleet navy ships stationed in **Pearl Harbor**, Hawaii, on Sunday **December 7, 1941**, President Franklin Delano Roosevelt (FDR) declared that the United States would enter the war. In a little over an hour, Japanese planes had surprised and sunk eight battleships and three cruisers, killing more than 2,400 American sailors.
- American forces fought the war in both Europe (mainly on land) and the Pacific (mainly on the seas). The chief military planner for the United States was Chief of Staff **George C. Marshall**. The most decorated soldier of this war was a Texan, **Audie Murphy. Cleto Rodriguez**, another Texan, was a Medal of Honor recipient of Hispanic decent.
- In 1942–1943, the tide of battle in Europe shifted in favor of the Allies when the German offensive on the **Eastern Front** was stopped at **Stalingrad** by the Russian forces, and the Allied forces, under the leadership of **General George Patton**, recaptured North Africa.
- Hitler's **Final Solution** called for the extermination of Jews (and other "unsuitables" not of their "master race"). German Jews were the first to be sent to concentration camps. As Germany occupied other countries, Jewish citizens were identified and sent to concentration camps in southern and central Germany, Poland, and Austria. These camps (such as Dachau, Bergen-Belsen, Auschwitz, and others) were originally built as "labor camps" but became death/extermination camps. The **Holocaust** claimed the lives of six million Jews, almost two-thirds of Europe's Jewish population, and many others.
- On June 6, 1944, the commander of U.S. military forces in Europe, **General Dwight D. Eisenhower**, launched the Allied invasion—termed **D-DAY**—to liberate France from the Germans. The Germans had expected the invasion to come at the narrowest part of the English Channel and had not prepared extensive defenses on the beaches of

Normandy, where almost 300,000 Allied troops came ashore. The D-DAY Invasion proved to be one of the turning points of the war, although there were tremendous casualties.

- The land war in Europe ended on May 8, 1945 (**VE Day**), but continued in the Pacific against Japan until August of that year.

- The American strategy in the Pacific could be considered "island hopping." The U.S. Navy and the Marines battled the Japanese on island after island as they moved across the Pacific Ocean toward Japan. Two separate American operations were waged on the Pacific front: **General Douglas MacArthur**, based in Australia, moved from New Guinea to the Philippines, and **Admiral Chester Nimitz**, in Hawaii, directed American attacks on key Japanese-held islands. Primarily, the Pacific Campaign was waged by forces from the United States, Australia, and New Zealand.

- After Pearl Harbor, American anger, fear, and mistrust of the Japanese grew against those who were living in the United States, particularly along the Pacific Coast. FDR authorized **relocation camps** in the U.S. interior to intern citizens of Japanese ancestry who were living on the West Coast. More than 100,000 people of Japanese ancestry were identified, told to dispose of their possessions and taken to these centers. In 1944, their internment was upheld by the Supreme Court. Although most were released in 1945, few were ever compensated for their financial losses.

- As the Pacific front progressed, the Japanese lost four aircraft carriers (compared to one American carrier) in the **Battle of Midway**. This was the first defeat the modern Japanese navy had suffered, and it left the United States in control of the Central Pacific.

- Island fighting intensified as American forces advanced toward Japan. Week after week, the Japanese sent *Kamikaze* (suicide) planes against the American ships, sacrificing some 3,500 planes while inflicting great damage.

- In February 1945, the **Battle of Iwo Jima**, only 750 miles from Tokyo, was the costliest battle in the history of the Marine Corps. Nearly 26,000 Americans were killed in this battle. The battle is commemorated by a memorial statue in Washington, D.C., of Marines raising an American flag of victory on Mt. Suribachi.

- The **Battle for Okinawa**, 350 miles south of Japan, was another victory for American forces. The U.S. and its allies suffered nearly 50,000 casualties on land and sea before Okinawa was taken. Over 100,000 Japanese died in the battle. Many civilians were killed, and many others jumped over the island's cliffs after Japanese propaganda convinced them of the terror they would face under American domination.

- On April 15, 1945, President Roosevelt died during his fourth term in office. He was succeeded by his vice president, **Harry S. Truman.**

- In May 1945, American forces began a firebombing campaign on Tokyo itself. The **Doolittle Raid** was the first strike to reach the main islands of Japan. Some 80,000 civilians lost their lives from the firestorms started by the napalm dropped on the city by American bombers. Japan still did not surrender.

- In order to end the war and save what he believed to be thousands of American lives, President **Truman** made the decision to use two nuclear weapons against Japan. On August 6, 1945, an American B-29, the *Enola Gay,* dropped an **atomic bomb** on the city of **Hiroshima**. The explosion incinerated four square miles of the city, instantly killing more than 80,000 people. Many more survived to suffer the effects of radioactive fallout and to pass the effects on to their children in the form of birth defects. Japan still did not surrender. A second bomb was dropped on **Nagasaki** on August 9, 1945, inflicting another 40,000 deaths.

- **Emperor Hirohito** persuaded his ministers to surrender unconditionally on August 14, 1945. On September 2, 1945, on board the American battleship *Missouri,* anchored in Tokyo Bay, Japanese officials signed the articles of surrender.
- Germany was divided into **East** (Soviet-controlled) **Germany** and **West** (free) **Germany.** Its capital, Berlin, was divided into **sectors** for the Soviets, French, British, and Americans. East Germany and the Communist Sector of Berlin were cut off from the West until 1989.
- Over fourteen million combatants, not including civilians, lost their lives in World War II. A war crimes tribunal was set up in **Nuremberg** to bring Nazis who participated in crimes against humanity to trial. Hitler committed suicide in his Berlin bunker rather than face capture and trial.

VII. International Relations between the Superpowers

KEY QUESTION: *How did the United States react to Soviet expansion after World War II?*

- Since World War II until the end of this century, relations between the Soviet Union (the U.S.S.R.) and the United States have dominated world affairs. The two nations, along with their allies, kept their wartime pledge to create an international organization, the **United Nations**, to replace the disbanded League of Nations.
- In the late 1940s, the Soviet Union gained control of the governments of Poland, Bulgaria, East Germany, Rumania, and Czechoslovakia. The boundaries between communist-controlled countries and free nations became know as the **Iron Curtain.** In many areas, fences and walls were built to keep people from escaping communism. The **Berlin Wall**, the most famous of these, was finally torn down in 1989. German reunification was concluded in 1990.
- The United States responded with a **containment doctrine** to block further Soviet expansion and the **Truman Doctrine** to provide military and economic aid to countries threatened by **communism.**
- In 1947, the American government offered the **Marshall Plan** to all European nations, delivering assistance if they would work together to rebuild their economies after World War II.
- In 1949, the United States and its Western allies formed the **North Atlantic Treaty Organization** (NATO) to provide for a common military defense against the Soviet Union and its allies. In 1955, the Soviet Union responded by creating an alliance of its own—**The Warsaw Pact**—with the communist governments in Eastern Europe.
- The relationship between the two superpowers, particularly during the late 1940s and early 1950s, has been characterized as a **cold war**, a state of tension and hostility just short of war, in which both sides built up powerful arsenals of weapons (including nuclear weapons) and spied on each other to gain military and political advantages.
- The superpowers have also experienced periods of **detente**, or a relaxation of tensions. During such periods, summit conferences, cultural exchanges, and agreements such as the **Limited Nuclear Test Ban Treaty**, the **Helsinki Accords**, and the **Strategic Arms Limitations Treaties** (SALT) have taken place to bring down the level of fear of another world war.

- Perceiving Soviet threats to the **Third World** (the underdeveloped nations of Asia, Africa, and Latin America), the United States undertook policies of military alliances and economic and technical aid for "containment" in order to prevent a **domino effect** (the fall to communism of one country leading to the fall of its neighboring countries).

- In Asia, relations between the superpowers were severely strained when communist forces under the leadership of **Mao Tse Tung** won their civil war in China in 1949. The exiled Chinese government of **Chiang Kai Shek** moved its government to Taiwan (Formosa). The U.S. recognized the Chinese government in Taiwan but refused to recognize the existence of the mainland (Communist) Chinese government until 1979.

- In 1950, the United States fought the **Korean War** to prevent the further expansion of communism. The war ended with an agreement to divide Korea at the 38th parallel. Currently, there are two separate countries on the Korean peninsula: North Korea, which is communist controlled, and South Korea, which is democratic. The United States still maintains a strong military presence at the 38th parallel to enforce the division. North Korea is considered an ongoing threat to South Korea and the United States for its military threat and nuclear weapons program.

- In the 1950s during the Cold War, many Americans feared the threat of communism from *within* the United States, and Senator Joseph McCarthy led the country in attempting to find, label, and blacklist communists—those whom he saw as being American traitors and/or spies. Some were guilty and some were not, but many lost their jobs and reputations (**McCarthyism**). The **FBI** (Federal Bureau of Investigation) under **J. Edgar Hoover** helped investigate many of these cases.

- **Vietnam** (Indochina) had been a French territory until WWII. At the end of the war in 1945, communists tried to take over. By 1954, the United States was paying a major portion of the French war costs in Vietnam. When the French suffered their ultimate defeat in 1954, President Eisenhower was not prepared to commit U.S. forces to fight in Vietnam. An international conference held at Geneva divided the country at the 17th parallel. **Ho Chi Minh** gained control of **North Vietnam**, and the French continued to rule in the South. The agreement also stated that an election would be held within two years to decide the unification of the country. That election was never held. Instead, the United States took over for the French and installed a new leader in the South, **Ngo Dinh Diem.**

- In 1960, President Kennedy sent the first U.S. military advisors to Vietnam. The United States was there merely to advise the South Vietnamese military in their fight against the Communists in North Vietnam.

- On August 2, 1964, an American destroyer, the *Maddox,* was fired on by North Vietnamese torpedo boats in the **Gulf of Tonkin.** On August 4, the U.S. Navy sent another destroyer, the *C. Turner Joy,* into the Gulf with orders to fire at the North Vietnamese torpedo boats if they were fired upon. President Lyndon Johnson also ordered retaliatory air strikes on North Vietnamese naval bases.

- On August 5, 1964, **President Johnson** asked Congress to pass a resolution allowing him to take "all necessary measures to repel any armed attack against the forces of the U.S. and to prevent any further aggression." The resulting **Gulf of Tonkin Resolution** meant that the United States would become an active participant in the conflict. American combat forces in South Vietnam rose from 16,000 in 1963 to 500,000 in 1968.

- In 1968, the North Vietnamese launched the **Tet Offensive**, a series of attacks beginning unexpectedly during a major Vietnamese holiday (Tet—the Lunar New Year). The U.S. public, watching much of the conflict on the nightly television news, began to doubt whether the United States should remain in the war in Vietnam.

- Richard Nixon, running on an antiwar platform, won the election of 1968. Nixon announced the *Vietnamization* of the war (building up the strength of the South Vietnamese to defend their own country). Withdrawals of American troops began in June 1969. This did briefly quiet public protests against the war. However, in April 1970, Nixon ordered the secret bombing of parts of Cambodia where enemy forces were situated, attempting to allow time for the United States to withdraw. This was seen by some Americans, however, as widening the war into Indochina. News of the bombing led to widespread protests across the United States. On May 4, 1970, at **Kent State** in Ohio, members of the National Guard killed four students and injured nine others as they were protesting the war.

- The growing antiwar sentiment caused Congress to withdraw the **Gulf of Tonkin Resolution** in December 1970. Nixon, however, ignored the action. Then, in June 1971, the *New York Times* published a front-page story on the history of America's war in Vietnam. The feature was based on the findings of a top-secret Defense Department study—**The Pentagon Papers.** The report confirmed what the public had believed for a long time: the government had been dishonest, both in reporting the military progress of the war and in explaining its own motives for American involvement.

- During this period, the morale and discipline among American troops in Vietnam was rapidly deteriorating. The trial and conviction of **Lieutenant William Calley**, who was charged with overseeing the massacre of over 100 unarmed South Vietnamese civilians in the village of **My Lai**, attracted wide spread attention to the dehumanizing effects the war was having on some of those who fought it, particularly many of those who had been a part of a large military draft.

- Many Americans remain concerned about the thousands of soldiers who never returned from Vietnam. In 1995, the Pentagon reported that there are still 2,202 American soldiers missing in action (**MIA**) in Southeast Asia—1,618 in Vietnam. Far more Americans are still listed as missing from the Korean War (8,170) and World War II (78,750), but those missing in Vietnam seem particularly significant. This was partly due to the belief that U.S. soldiers were alive and being held as prisoners.

- In 1973, Henry Kissinger, Nixon's secretary of state, signed an agreement to end the war. Many prisoners of war (**POWs**) were finally released and returned home, but this was not until 1975 when U.S. involvement in Vietnam truly ended (with the famous helicopter evacuation of the remaining Americans and many Vietnamese from the American embassy in Saigon).

- In January 1975, forces from the North invaded South Vietnam. **President Gerald Ford** asked Congress for emergency aid for South Vietnam, but the request was denied. In April, the army of North Vietnam marched into Saigon, and the South fell.

- In Latin America, since 1959, the United States has been unable to oust the Communist regime of **Fidel Castro** in Cuba.

- In the Middle East, American recognition and support of Israel as a Jewish homeland in 1948 antagonized many Arab nations and jeopardized the flow of oil. In 1979, Iran held 63 Americans hostage for over a year.
- President Kennedy, after the disastrous **Bay of Pigs** invasion in Cuba, came very close to war with the Soviet Union when it was confirmed that the Soviets were furnishing Cuba with missiles as a staging area for them to reach the United States. Many nuclear fallout shelters were built in states that were within range, and children in schools practiced nuclear drills. Kennedy placed a naval blockade around Cuba and the missiles were removed.
- In 1987, **President Ronald Reagan** faced off with **Mikhail Gorbachev** (the leader of the Soviet Union) demanding that he "tear down this wall" (referring to the Berlin Wall separating East and West Berlin), meaning that the communist government should allow freedom in their country and in their other puppet states (such as East Germany). An arms race, the technological revolution in the United States, a lost war in Afghanistan, and other factors caused an economic collapse of the government in the Soviet Union, which dissolved itself in 1991, thus effectively ending the Cold War.
- In 1990, when Iraq invaded Kuwait, President George H.W. Bush's administration sent Iraqi leader, **Saddam Hussein**, an ultimatum to withdraw his troops. Hussein ignored the warning and, in January 1991, Operation **Desert Storm** was launched to liberate Kuwait. After fulfilling the mission, U.S. troops withdrew from Iraq.

VIII. The Present

KEY QUESTION: *What sorts of domestic issues has the United States faced in the last 40 years?*

- Since World War II, the U.S. government has been confronted with a variety of problems and challenges. Slowly, the nation moved toward becoming an integrated society. President Truman, for example, desegregated the armed services in WWII by executive order.
- In 1954, the Supreme Court declared segregation (the tradition of separate but equal) unconstitutional in <u>**Brown v. the Board of Education of Topeka.**</u> The principle attorney in the case was **Thurgood Marshall.** In 1967, President Johnson named Marshall as the first African American Supreme Court Justice.
- In 1955 in Montgomery, Alabama, a seamstress named **Rosa Parks** refused to give up her seat on the bus to a white passenger. The bus driver called the police, and she was arrested. News of her arrest spread rapidly and the National Association for the Advancement of Colored People (**NAACP**) quickly organized a boycott of the buses in Montgomery. They asked a young pastor named **Dr. Martin Luther King, Jr.** to lead the boycott. For 381 days, African Americans refused to ride the buses. The boycott remained nonviolent. In late 1956, the Supreme Court ruled in response to a lawsuit brought by one of the boycotters that bus segregation was unconstitutional. The Montgomery Bus Boycott proved that ordinary people could unite and organize a successful protest movement through **civil disobedience.** Dr. King wrote his famous Letter from the Birmingham Jail against racial segregation after one protest effort.

- When the Soviet Union launched **Sputnik** in 1957, President Eisenhower played an active role in establishing the **National Aeronautics and Space Administration (NASA)** and passing the **National Defense Education Act** to train more scientists and engineers.
- During the 1960s, Dr. Martin Luther King, Jr., helped make Americans aware of continuing racial injustices. The **Civil Rights Act** (1964), signed by President Johnson, sought to bring more equality to African Americans, especially in housing rights and in schools.
- Some African Americans did not feel that the Congress had done enough to remedy the centuries of segregation and discrimination. Angry rioters often took to the streets. There was a growing movement that believed that African Americans should take complete control of their communities. One of the movement's leaders was **Malcolm X.** His followers did not take the nonviolent approach that Dr. King's followers had used.
- Although Malcolm X was assassinated in 1965, racial tensions increased. In 1966, **Stokely Carmichael** issued a call for "**Black Power.**" Also in that year, **Huey Newton** and **Bobby Seale** founded a political party known as the **Black Panthers** to fight police brutality in predominantly African American neighborhoods.
- President Kennedy sent a bill to Congress in 1963 that would guarantee equal access to all public accommodations and gave the U.S. attorney general, Robert Kennedy, the power to file school desegregation lawsuits. To help persuade Congress to pass the bill, more than 250,000 people, including 75,000 whites, came to Washington. There, Dr. King delivered his most famous oration, the "**I Have a Dream**" speech. At that time, the **March on Washington** was the largest demonstration ever held in the United States.
- In 1963, President Kennedy was assassinated in Dallas. **Lyndon Johnson**, the vice president at the time, became the president. President Johnson continued to pursue Kennedy's civil rights agenda.
- In 1968, the United States lost two great civil rights figures. Both Dr. Martin Luther King, Jr. and **Robert Kennedy** were assassinated.
- Under President Johnson, Congress enacted the **War on Poverty** to provide job training and rebuild inner cities. It also passed **Great Society** legislation, such as **Medicare**, insuring the health of the elderly. Unfortunately the cost of the war in Vietnam was responsible for cutting the budget money available for many of Johnson's social programs.
- Congress responded by passing the **Civil Rights Act of 1964**, barring discrimination in housing and establishing the Equal Opportunity Commission.
- **President John F. Kennedy** and his brother, the attorney general of the United States, Robert Kennedy, were concerned with the needs of the poor. However, important domestic poverty legislation was passed only after President John Kennedy was assassinated.
- President Kennedy had vowed to put a man on the moon by the end of the 1960s. In 1969, President Nixon congratulated **Neil Armstrong** when he became the first man to walk on the moon. With the explosion of the space shuttle **Challenger** on January 28, 1986, American space programs underwent review for a period of time.
- Abuse of power became a major problem during Richard Nixon's presidency. Nixon and his advisors withheld and covered up information concerning a burglary at Democratic National Headquarters in the **Watergate** building complex during the 1972 presidential campaign.

The president and his aides had also used government agencies, such as the FBI and the IRS, for political purposes. When Congress took steps to impeach him, President Richard Nixon resigned from office.

- Through the efforts of **Rachel Carson** and others, America became aware of the need to clean up and preserve their environment. During the Nixon administration, Congress established the **Environmental Protection Agency** (EPA) and passed legislation to provide clean air and water.

- The economy has been a constant source of worry to American presidents. Under President Johnson, inflation increased at an alarming rate. Presidents Nixon, Ford, and Carter found it difficult to control inflation, especially because Arab oil policies raised the price of energy, thereby affecting the costs of manufacturing and transporting goods. Under President Reagan, inflation was finally halted, but the mounting **budget deficit** became a major problem. **Reagan**, however, had solidly contributed to the end of the Cold War by escalating the arms race with the Soviet Union, which ended in its collapse and opened up many other countries under communist rule (including East Germany).

- **George H.W. Bush** acted to stop the aggression of Iraq when it invaded Kuwait, sending troops (a good many of them were women) into **Desert Storm.**

- During his first term, President **Bill Clinton** was involved in a number of controversies, ranging from alleged wrongdoing in an Arkansas land deal known as "Whitewater" to charges of sexual misconduct. The strong economy and the lack of a significant Republican challenger resulted in Clinton's reelection in 1996. Clinton became the first Democrat since FDR to be reelected president. In December 1998, Clinton became the second president in the history of the United States to be **impeached**, or legally charged (with perjury). Like President Andrew Johnson, Clinton was tried and acquitted, so he did not leave office.

- In 2000, the Republican Party nominated **George W. Bush**, governor of Texas and son of former President George H.W. Bush. This resulted in one of the closest presidential elections in history. This presidential election was complicated by the media incorrectly proclaiming **Vice President Al Gore** as the winner, the withdrawal of an initial concession by Gore, butterfly ballots, hanging chads, a recount of votes in Florida, and several court challenges. Finally, Bush was declared the winner.

- In 1993, a terrorist bomb exploded in the parking garage of the **World Trade Center**, killing and injuring over 1,000 people in New York. Four Islamic militants were tried and convicted in this attack. In 1995, 168 people were killed and around 500 people injured when the **Oklahoma City Federal Building** was bombed. Timothy McVeigh was tried, convicted, and later executed for his role in the attack. His accomplice, Terry Nichols was convicted of conspiracy and sentenced to life in prison. Other terrorist attacks by Islamist militants have occurred on passenger ships, against U.S. embassies and a naval ship (the *U.S.S. Cole*), and in other places. On **September 11, 2001**, symbols important to the U.S. economy and the U.S. military—the twin towers of the **World Trade Center** in New York and the **Pentagon** in Washington, D.C.—were attacked by hijackers who flew commercial airplanes into the buildings. The twin towers collapsed and thousands died in what has been referred to as the worst act of terrorism in

American history. Passengers on another plane caused it to crash rather than have it hit another target in Washington, D.C. Advisors to President Bush have determined that **Osama Bin Laden** was the primary suspect in the attack.

IX. Holidays

KEY QUESTION: *What holidays do people celebrate in the United States and why?*

- **Martin Luther King Day**, celebrated the third Monday in January, honors the man who worked tirelessly for equal status for people of color, particularly African Americans. As the main leader of the Civil Rights Movement during the 1960s, he spearheaded nonviolent protests (sit-ins and marches) to help African Americans be treated as first-class citizens in America. Martin Luther King, Jr. committed his life to this cause (he was assassinated for his beliefs) and made it possible for many African Americans to obtain jobs, attend schools, and live in neighborhoods that were previously not open to them. His efforts sparked others in many communities and in other parts of the world to struggle for equality. The entire month of February is **Black History Month,** recognizing many other African Americans who have and continue to make contributions in many areas.

- **Chinese New Year** always occurs on the first day of the First Moon of the lunar calendar (usually between the end of January and the middle of February). Chinese families see the dinner on New Year's Eve as the most important family function of the year. As a time for renewal, every part of one's house must be cleaned, and poems (couplets) on long red paper are put by doors and windows to usher in the spring and good fortune. Debts accumulated during the year are settled by the last day of the year. Particularly important is the tradition of the Kitchen god, who during this time would give a report to heaven on the family. A ritualistic dinner of sweet and sticky rice cakes is an important way to send him off with a favorable report. All foods are prepared prior to the New Year to avoid having knives and other sharp objects "cut" the good luck of a New Year. New Year's Day brings red envelopes with good luck money for children, along with new clothes. Firecrackers, which drive away evil spirits, are heard throughout the first two weeks of the New Year. On the fifteenth day, the New Year's celebration ends with the First Moon and the Lantern Festival. In China, people go into the streets with lanterns for a parade—usually with Dragon Dances.

- **Tet** is the most popular Vietnamese holiday. It is celebrated during the full moon before spring planting (usually in January or February). Parades are held, and red and gold colors decorate homes to celebrate the lunar New Year. Everyone returns to their family homes for nearly a week to issue in luck for the New Year. Ancestors' spirits are believe to return, so graves are decorated with flowers, and those who have passed away are paid respect. Midnight on Tet is marked by gongs and drums and visiting friends. The **Moon Festival** is another popular holiday for the Vietnamese (in the eighth lunar month), particularly because children receive many gifts. Parades, drums, and dances are held, and moon cakes are eaten as the moon moves halfway down the sky.

- **Presidents' Day**, on the third Monday of February, honors, in particular, two of our most famous American presidents—**George Washington** (Revolutionary War commander, hero, and first president) and **Abraham Lincoln** (who preserved "the Union" of all of the states after the Civil War and who abolished slavery).
- **St. Patrick's Day**, celebrated on March 17, is the anniversary of the death of St. Patrick, the Irish patron saint credited with the conversion of many Irish to Christianity. In modern times on this day, "everyone is Irish," wears green, and generally celebrates Irish heritage.
- **Passover** is a Jewish holiday commemorating the Exodus of the Jewish people from slavery in Egypt. The Jews left so quickly after the pharaoh's release that they did not even wait for their bread to rise. For this reason, Jewish people avoid eating grain products and leavened bread products during this time.
- **Easter** commemorates the day that Christians believe Jesus Christ arose from the dead (the Resurrection) after being crucified and buried.
- **Texas Independence Day** is March 2. It marks the day in 1836 when Texas declared its independence from Mexico during the Texas Revolution.
- **San Jacinto Day**, April 21, commemorates the final Texas victory over Mexico under Santa Anna in 1835, which led to Texas becoming independent.
- **Cinco de Mayo** (or May 5) is the day Mexico won a victory over French troops in the Battle of Puebla in 1862, as France attempted to add Mexico to its empire under Napoleon.
- **Memorial Day**, celebrated in May, honors men and women who gave their lives in the service of our country.
- **Juneteenth**, on June 19, is also called Freedom Day or Emancipation Day and marks the day when African Americans in Texas finally heard in 1865 that they had been freed from slavery or emancipated.
- **Fourth of July** commemorates the date on which the Declaration of Independence from Britain was signed during the Revolutionary War in 1776.
- **Labor Day**, celebrated on the first Monday in September, honors America's work force.
- **Ramadan** is celebrated by Muslims throughout the world during the ninth month of the Islamic calendar. During this time, Muslims are required to fast from dawn to sunset each day to show their devotion to their religion, to impose self-control, and to experience empathy for those who live in poverty. It is a time to read the Qur'an (Koran), go to the mosque, give to charities, and come closer to goodness. Evening meals during this holiday are usually a time to share with family and/or friends. The Night of Power, the twenty-seventh night of the month, is especially holy and is remembered as the night when Mohammed received the first verses of the Qur'an. Many Muslims spend this entire night in prayer.
- **Rosh Hashana**, usually occurring between Labor Day and Discovery Day, begins the Jewish "High Holy Days." A ten-day celebration marks the Jewish New Year as a time to examine the past year and make new resolutions. Also known as the Feast of the Trumpets (because it begins with the blowing of a ram's horn), it ends with **Yom Kippur**, a day of atonement and fasting, when one is to right the wrongs that one may have committed during the past year. These are days for services, prayers, and introspection. The Shabbat is a day for prayers and services at a temple. It normally begins every Friday at sunset and finishes on

Saturday for Jewish worshippers. It is a day of rest and freedom from labors, and Orthodox Jews have specific restrictions. A Shabbat can also occur on particular holidays.

- **Halloween** falls on October 31 when many Americans dress up in costumes, and children receive candy as they "trick-or-treat" or attend parties. Some controversy in recent year has come about over this holiday because of its association with witchcraft and the occult, although others see it as traditional fun for children.

- **Dia de los Muertos** (Day of the Dead) is a Mexican festival on November 1 (All Saints Day) in which it is believed that those who have died "reunite" with their families. It is not like Halloween, a scary holiday, but a day on which the souls eat, drink, and are merry. Because of this, flowers, candles, and favorite foods and drinks are placed on graves, and skeletons of papier mâché and candies are found in homes and shops. After prayers for the dead, there are picnics and parties, but in the evening, bells ring all night to summon the spirits. Some relatives keep a night-long vigil.

- **Veterans' Day** is a day set aside on November 11 to honor all of those who have served the United States in the armed forces.

- The origin of the word **Diwali** comes from *Deepavali,* meaning "garland of lights." Many Indian Hindus and Sikhs see it as the beginning of a new year and/or a celebration of good over evil. The significance of the many small "Christmas-type" lights and candles displayed in many homes (along with fireworks in the community) represents light triumphing over ignorance. At temples, puja rituals (prayers) are part of the holidays, as is the cleaning of homes, special foods and sweets, and visits to family and friends. Diwali falls on the lunar new year, so the theme helps keep the idea of enlightenment aglow on the darkest night of the year.

- **Thanksgiving** commemorates the feast of the Pilgrims after a very hard first year in America. It was not until 1863 that this day became a national holiday. Our current holiday, set aside for the fourth Thursday in November, reminds us of the feast that was shared by Pilgrims and Native Americans after the first harvest in the new land.

- **Hanukkah**, or **Chanukah**, is a minor holiday for Jewish people. It is a festival, normally in late November or December, remembering the Jewish fight against the harsh Greek rule in Israel and the subsequent Temple rededication in Jerusalem in 165 B.C.E. On each of eight nights, a candle is added to the **menorah** (a special candelabra) to add to the evenings' remembrance of the events. The defiled temple was to be rededicated after the Jewish victory, but priests found only enough ritualistic oil to keep a light burning for one day. A miracle occurred, as this oil burned for 8 days—enough time to press and prepare more pure oil. Latkes (potato pancakes), jelly doughnuts, and other foods fried in oil are eaten during this time, and small gifts are given to family members. A game using a dreidel (a four-sided top) is often played. Jewish holidays fall on the same day according to the Jewish calendar, which is based upon the moon cycle, and is about 11 days longer. Therefore, the Jewish holidays do not occur on the same day each year on the standard calendar.

- **Christmas** is the most widely celebrated Christian holiday. December 25 is the day designated as the anniversary of the Nativity, or the birth of Jesus Christ. This national holiday is also associated with gifts brought to children by Santa Claus or St. Nicholas.

- **Kwanzaa** is celebrated from the day after Christmas to New Year's Day. Developed by Dr. Maulana Karenga, Kwanzaa introduces and reinforces seven basic values of African culture that contribute to building and reinforcing the family, the community, and culture among African American people (as well as Africans and those of African descent throughout the world). These values are called the *Nguzo Saba*, a Swahili term that includes unity, self-determination, creativity, collective work and responsibility, purpose, cooperative economics, and faith.
- **New Year's Eve** in the Western world occurs every December 31. Many parties are given to "bring in the New Year," and many people stay up until midnight to celebrate the change from the old year to the new. **New Year's Day** is January 1—a day for food and family.

X. Texas History Earliest Inhabitants

KEY QUESTION: *Who were the first Texans and in what activities did they engage?*

- Anthropologists believe that the first Texans, called **Paleo-Americans**, or Old Americans, crossed the land bridge connecting Asia and Alaska more than 37,000 years ago.
- These Old Native Americans of the Ice Age were hunters who roamed the High Plains of West Texas in search of ancient American elephants, mammoths, mastodons, ground sloths, and giant bison. These bison were twice the size and four times the weight of the modern buffalo. Eventually the Ice Age ended and the lush land of Texas became hotter and drier. Soon the animals that the Old Americans had depended on for food became extinct.
- Before the land bridge disappeared, around 7,000 years ago, a new group of humans made their way across it and eventually to Texas. These people of the Archaic Period were called **Amerinds.**
- These new people, like the Old Americans, were nomadic hunters and gatherers. The Amerinds of North America displayed almost identical racial or physical characteristics to each other, with only minor variations of height or color, but became differentiated culturally. They also split into linguistic stocks but through time lost even their mutual languages within each linguistic group. They made their tools and artifacts in different ways. The early Amerinds left twenty-seven different kinds of dart points on the Edwards Plateau alone.
- Culturally varied, speaking different languages, nomadic, and constantly impinging on each other, the hundreds of bands of Amerinds could only follow the oldest human logic: Many made war. Each new folk wandering from the north invaded already appropriated hunting grounds, and the first wars stemmed from the most logical of reasons, the defense of territory. But a constantly roaming and colliding people soon imbedded the idea and act of warfare deep in their cultural heart. Fighting became a central part of their lives; therefore, the center of society and the most important member was the warrior. Because the male warriors were too busy preparing for war and actually fighting, women performed most of the labor.
- The **Neo-American Age,** around 3,000 years ago, is marked by an "agricultural revolution." The people of this age began to domesticate crops, including maize (corn), beans, squash, tomatoes, potatoes, and cotton.

These people have been referred to as **Mound Builders** because of the burial and temple mounds they erected in the Piney Woods of East Texas.

- The largest group of these Mound Builders was the **Caddo Nation**, once the largest and most powerful Native American group in Texas. The Caddo settlements, mostly in East Texas, were relatively permanent. The Caddoan tribes hunted game as a supplement rather than a staple. They grew many varieties of crops and lived in villages made up of large timbered houses, which were domed and thatched. Because they were agricultural and war was no longer a central part of their culture, they were remarkably amiable to white men in the first years of contact—with disastrous results to their tribe. The Europeans brought with them diseases that had devastating effects on the tribes, which had little or no immunity to them.

- South of the Caddo nation, along the Gulf Coast, lived a number of smaller tribes. One of the most powerful was the **Karankawa**. These Native Americans inhabited an area from Galveston to Corpus Christi in a more nomadic way of life; that is, they were mostly hunters and gatherers.

- West of Karankawa country on a line ranging through San Antonio to Del Rio was the territory of a number of small bands of **Coahuiltecans**. Their territory was one of the harshest in the state. Because of the heat and the dry conditions, there were not enough game animals to support a hunting society. Farming was also futile in this area. These people learned to use almost every native plant that grew in South Texas. They made flour from agave bulbs, concocted "fire-water" from mescal and maguey leaves, and roasted mesquite beans. They also consumed spiders, ants, lizards, and rattlesnakes.

- The Jumano and Pueblo people both lived in far West Texas.

- The **Tonkawa** lived above the country of the Coahuiltecans, over the Balcones Escarpment. They ranged across the Edwards Plateau to the Brazos Valley. They lived by hunting, fishing, and gathering fruits, nuts, and berries. They lived on the edge of bison country in buffalo-hide tepees and used large domesticated dogs as beasts of burden. Horses and cattle, brought by the Spaniards in the 1500s, were still unknown to these early Indian tribes. The Tonkawas did not hunt or raid very far north of the Texas plains. They were relatively confined to the Edwards Plateau by another, fiercer tribe that commanded the largest buffalo territory—the Apache.

- The **Apaches** (or Lipan Apaches) inhabited the High Plains of Central Texas. Here there were millions of bison, elk, deer, and antelope. Each spring and fall bison congregated on the southern plains and grazed in a northward direction throughout the summer months. Anthropologists believe that the typical buffalo-hunting cultures of the Plains evolved first in Texas and then spread north.

- The **Plains Indians** centered their lives on the buffalo. The great hunts took place in the spring and fall, when small herds were surrounded by men on foot and shot with arrows until all the animals were killed. Immediately, the women set to work with their flint knives. Every part of the buffalo was used. Most of the meat was roasted and the intestines were cooked to provide a special treat. Some lean flesh was sun dried, or jerked, to be eaten over the winter. Some organs were cleaned and dried to be used as bags to store water. Bones were made into picks and other tools. Hides were dried for clothing, shelter, and blankets.

Apaches made teepees of buffalo skins and light frames of sotol sticks. These were flapped with bearskins for doors, and open at the top for escaping smoke. Fires were built in the centers and they were furnished with hide blankets. Four to twelve people lived in one teepee. The bison hides were tanned so fine that rain could not penetrate or stiffen them.

- In the hot months Apaches wore very little. In winter they wore deerskin shirts and heavy buffalo robes. Apaches possessed little besides their clothing, tools, weapons, and teepees. During the hottest months of the summer, the herds moved north to follow the grass and the rains, and avoid the blazing sun. During this period, the Apaches, still hunting on foot, were limited in their pursuit of the herds. Therefore they were forced to supplement their economy with other foods. They learned to domesticate crops by planting them in small patches along the infrequent rivers and streams. While these crops grew, Apaches settled down for long periods beside the waters. The Spanish called these semipermanent camps: *rancherias.*

- The **Comanches**, who became exceptional horsemen, dominated the Southern Plains of the United States, or what is currently the Panhandle of Texas. Originally, the Comanches migrated south because of the greater access to the mustangs that roamed wild. The warm climate and abundance of buffalo were additional incentives. Like many of the Plains Indians, Comanches were nomadic. The buffalo was extremely important to their way of life, providing them food, clothing, and shelter. They supplemented their meat diet through trade with agricultural tribes such as the Wichita and Caddo. Because of their trading skills, Comanches controlled much of the commerce of the Plains. The Comanches came to the Plains later than other groups, so they became accustomed to conflict. The Apaches and Comanches became mortal enemies.

  The most famous chief and warrior of the Comanche was **Quanah Parker,** whose mother, **Cynthia Ann Parker,** had been captured in a raid on Fort Parker. After many years, she was recaptured and returned to a white settlement, but she grieved for contact with her lost children.

- In the 1700s, missions were built with great walls to protect priests, settlers, and native converts from hostile tribes. In the 1800s, forts were established throughout much of Texas as protection for white settlers.

XI. Early European Exploration and Development

KEY QUESTION: *What was the primary function of the Spanish missions?*

- In mid-1519, sailing from a base in Jamaica, **Alonso Alvarez de Piñeda,** a Spanish adventurer, was the first-known European to explore and map the Texas coastline. This event marked the beginning of **Spain's rule** in Texas and the first of **six flags** that would wave over the state (Spanish, French, Mexican, Texan, Confederate, and United States).

- In 1528, **Cabeza de Vaca** was shipwrecked on what is today believed to be Galveston Island. His small band wandered the area for approximately six years, trading with the Indians of the region. He later explored the Texas interior on his way to Mexico City. Once there, he related a legend of the *Seven Cities of Gold.* **Esteban,** who traveled with him, was the first known African to set foot on the Americas.

- From 1540 to 1542, **Francisco Vasquez de Coronado,** a *conquistador* (or conqueror), led an expedition of more than 300 soldiers, Mexican

Indian allies, women, and priests through present-day New Mexico, western and northern Texas, and as far north as Kansas, searching for the cities of gold from the legend. Although he found no gold, he did strengthen Spain's claim on Texas. Coronado claimed for Spain all the territory he explored.

- Priests began to settle and build missions in the conquered territory so that they could "civilize" and convert to Catholicism the Indians of the area (and more firmly claim the land for Spain). The **first Spanish mission** was **Corpus Christi de la Isleta**, established near **El Paso** in 1682. The missions often had *presidios* (or forts) attached to them or nearby to help protect those who lived in the missions.

- The **French** claim to Texas rests on the explorer Rene-Robert Cavelier, **Sieur de LaSalle**, who set foot on Texas soil in 1685. He established **Fort St. Louis** inland from Matagorda Bay, after his ship ran aground with the remainder of 300 colonists with whom he started this disastrous journey. The colonists were beset by further hardships, and those who remained finally left to search for a way back to Louisiana. Two years later, LaSalle was killed by his own men. In 1689, Mexican explorer **Alonso de Leon** reached Fort St. Louis and found it abandoned. It is believed that Indians and disease destroyed the remainder of the French force. In 1995, a team of archaeologists from the Texas Historical Commission discovered *The Belle,* one of La Salle's frigates, in the waters of Matagorda Bay. In 1996, the exact location of Fort St. Louis was pinpointed near Victoria.

- Alarmed by the French presence in Texas and the French settlements in the nearby Louisiana area, the Spaniards established **Mission San Francisco de los Tejas**, in 1690 as the first East Texas mission.

- Throughout the 1700s, Spain established a number of Catholic missions throughout Texas to (1) spread Christianity, (2) establish permanent settlements for the indigenous people to be socialized, and (3) solidly lay claim to land for Spain. Missions were located near the major population centers of all the major Indian tribes of Texas, except for the Apaches of the higher plains. Most of these missions failed and were abandoned. However, one can still visit the Mission Trail in San Antonio where a number of mission churches are still in use. Mission San Jose still retains all of its defensive walls and outbuildings, so one can see exactly what an entire mission was like.

- European diseases such as measles and smallpox spread rapidly among the Indians and decimated their populations. By the end of the eighteenth century, the Caddo Indians had almost disappeared. Ironically, the diseases brought by Spaniards and Catholic priests of these missions exterminated the very people they had come to save.

- In 1718, the same year the French founded New Orleans, the tiny Spanish mission of **San Antonio de Valero (the Alamo)** was established. Viceroy San Antonio de Valero, for whom the mission was named, began to build a complex around his mission. For protection from the French and Indians, he established **Fort San Antonio de Bejar** (or Bexar) named for his brother.

- More and more people began to move to the San Antonio area. By 1726 there were two hundred men, women, and children, not counting Native Americans, living in the town of San Antonio.

- Other Spanish towns founded in this same time period are **Goliad** and **Nacogdoches**.

- **Jane Long** became known as the "**Mother of Texas**" because of the birth of her child on Bolivar Peninsula in 1821. She referred to herself as the first English-speaking woman to bear a child in Texas. However, the census between 1807 and 1826 reveals that several children were born to Anglo American women prior to this time.
- By 1800, Mexican colonization of the Rio Grande area affected Texas more than all the missions. This did three things: (1) Mexican cattle kingdoms entered North America; (2) it established land titles and other related Spanish laws in the region; and, finally, (3) it brought a new kind of settler to the area—the Mexican frontiersman who came to stay, unlike the priests and soldiers who came before them. Mexicans who moved to the area of Texas were called **Tejanos.**
- In 1821, the year Mexico gained independence from Spain, **Stephen F. Austin**, known as the "**Father of Texas**," received permission from the Mexican government to settle a colony of 300 families, now known as the "**Old Three Hundred**," in the Brazos River region in southeast Texas with special land grants. This was the first of the Mexican land grants to Anglos. Stephen F. Austin was continuing the work that his father, **Moses Austin**, a North American from Missouri, had begun the year before. Unfortunately Moses died before he could complete his plan. **Martin de Leon** was the only Mexican empresario to found a Texas colony. An **empresario** was someone who was granted land in Texas by Mexico in return for founding a colony. Most empresarios, like Stephen F. Austin, had brought settlers from the United States. De Leon's colony (near Victoria) was the only colony in which most families were Hispanic instead of Anglo American.
- Austin's settlement was the official beginning of Anglo American colonization in Texas. This trickle became a flood as Americans heard about the fertile land in Texas. **GTT** (Gone to Texas) was a sign left on many doors as settlers moved from other U.S. states and territories to Texas.
- Despite restrictions by Mexico, by 1836, there were between 35,000 and 50,000 Anglo settlers in Texas. By 1830, Mexico had become so concerned about the rapidly increasing numbers of Anglo American settlers that the Mexican government banned any further emigration into Texas by settlers from the United States. With the increasing Anglo population, a strain quickly developed in the relationship between the Texans and Mexico due to government, language, tariffs, corruption, and religion.

XII. Revolution, Republic, and Statehood

KEY QUESTION: *How did Texas ultimately break with Mexico and gain independence?*

- In the 1830s, Stephen F. Austin had become increasingly involved in the politics between Texas and Mexico, hoping that Texas would move to a more responsive and more central state government (rather than its state capital in Saltillo—over 500 miles away in the neighboring state of Coahuila). Traveling from Mexico City, Austin was arrested and thrown in jail without charges for almost a year. This further angered Texans. Early in 1835, Austin announced that he was convinced that war with Mexico was necessary to secure freedom.
- Growing tension in Texas was the result of cultural, political, and religious differences between the Anglo Americans and the Mexican

government. In response to the unrest, Antonio Lopez de **Santa Anna**, the president of Mexico, reinforced Mexican troops in Texas.

- Gonzales, a town in central Texas east of San Antonio, owned a cannon to protect itself from Native American attack. Mexico did not want the town to retain this weapon. A battle was fought at Gonzales on October 2, 1835, in which the Mexican forces were thwarted in their efforts to retrieve it. The famous Texas flag flying over Gonzales bore the words **"Come and Take It."** Although there were earlier minor skirmishes, the **Battle of Gonzales** is generally considered to be the first battle for Texas' independence.

- The Mexican dictator, **Santa Anna**, then gathered a substantial army to sweep through Texas. **General Sam Houston**, commander of the Texan army, ordered **William B. Travis** to the Alamo. There, Travis made a stand with about 189 men, hoping to give the Texans a chance to or- ganize more men for a stronger defense.

- The **Texas Declaration of Independence**, March 2, 1836, was produced, literally, overnight. Its urgency was paramount, because while it was being prepared, the Alamo in San Antonio was under siege by Santa Anna's army of Mexico. The Texas Declaration of Independence is sim- ilar to that of the U.S. Declaration of Independence. The declaration contains a statement on the nature of government, a list of grievances, and a final declaration of independence. Separation from Mexico was justified charging, among other things, that the government of Mexico had ceased to protect the lives, liberty, and property of the people.

- The **Battle of the Alamo** lasted 13 days, ending on March 6, 1836, with the deaths of all its defenders (numbering about 189). The mission was defended by Anglo-Texans, Hispanic-Texans, and others from the United States (and even a few from European countries) who had heard about the fight for freedom. The Mexican army of Santa Anna numbered 4,000 to 5,000 during its final charge. Among those killed were **David Crockett**, **Jim Bowie**, and **William B. Travis**. A small number of women, children, and slaves were spared by Santa Anna. Principal among them was the only adult Anglo survivor, **Mrs. Susanna Dickinson**, whose hus- band, Col. **Almaron Dickinson**, had also been killed in the fighting. These witnesses were told to spread the word of what had happened at the Alamo and to tell Sam Houston that resistance was hopeless. Santa Anna continued to sweep east towards Goliad.

- Texas had declared its independence on March 2, 1836, during the fighting at the Alamo. Delegates to the Convention of 1836 at Washington-on-the-Brazos had named **David Burnett** as the interim president until an election could be held. When this first election was held, **Sam Houston** became the first elected president of the Republic of Texas.

- A subsequent execution of **James Fannin** (who surrendered, fearing the same fate for his men as at the Alamo) and nearly 400 Texans who were holding the mission at **Goliad** on March 27, 1836, led to the battle cry of Texas' independence, "Remember the Alamo! Remember Goliad!"

- As Texans heard about the Mexican advance, many abandoned their property and belongings and headed quickly toward the safety of Louisiana, across the Sabine River border. This evacuation was called the **Runaway Scrape**. The flight was marked by lack of preparation and much panic. The people, mostly women, children, and the elderly, used any kind of transportation they had and many died on the run.

Often they were buried where they fell. This flight continued until the war was over, often just far enough ahead that Santa Anna's campfires could be seen at night.

- **The Battle of San Jacinto** was fought on April 21, 1836, near the present city of Houston. Santa Anna's entire force of 1,600 men was killed or captured by **General Sam Houston**'s army of 800 Texans; only nine Texans died. This decisive battle resulted in Texas' independence from Mexico. The **Treaty of Velasco** ended the revolution. Texas was now its own *independent country* (**The Republic of Texas**) and would fly its "**Lone Star**" **flag** for the next ten years before becoming part of the United States.

- Envoys from Texas had been meeting with officials from the United States well before the end of the war. The Texans wanted to join the United States once they gained independence from Mexico. However, when the war ended in 1836, many in the U.S. government opposed the annexation of Texas because it would have affected the balance of slave and free states. Representatives from the free states believed that Texas would certainly enter as a slave state, and the Congressional power of those from free states would be diminished.

- Five sites had served as temporary capitals of the country of Texas (Washington-on-the-Brazos, Harrisburg, Galveston, Velasco, and Columbia) before Sam Houston moved the capital to Houston in 1837. In 1839, the Texas Congress first met in the new town of **Austin**, the frontier site selected for the capital of the Republic of Texas.

- In 1845, **President James Polk** followed through on a campaign promise to annex Texas, and signed legislation making Texas a state. Texas was admitted as the 28th state on December 29, 1845.

- **Sam Houston** had commanded the Texas army during the Texas Revolution and had been president of the new country of the Republic of Texas. He also became governor of the state of Texas from 1859 to 1861 and U.S. senator after statehood was achieved.

- Even after the Texas Revolution, Mexico continued to dispute the independence of Texas, and several major incidents occurred where Texans and Mexicans engaged in battles and skirmishes. In 1842, Santa Anna sent a large force under **General Adrian Woll** that captured San Antonio. At the **Battle of Salado Creek**, **Colonel Mathew Caldwell** was successful in repelling the force. However, nearby another group from the LaGrange area was heavily outnumbered; the event became known as the **Dawson Massacre**, where a number of Texans fell and others were captured, many of whom died in Perote Prison in Mexico. Later that year, another group of Texas militia engaged a large Mexican force at the border of the Rio Grande (Mier City) and was forced to surrender. This became known as the **Mier Expedition** and led to the **Drawing of the Black Beans**. Prisoners who were captured were blindfolded and ordered to draw from 159 white beans and 17 black beans. Those who drew a black bean were executed.

- The **Mexican–American War** in 1846 ignited as a result of disputes over claims to Texas boundaries and continued border incursions. The outcome of the war fixed the Texas southern boundary at the Rio Grande River. 1848 saw the end of this war with the **Treaty of Guadalupe Hidalgo**, finally recognizing the annexation of Texas to the United States and ceding California and nearly all of the present-day American Southwest between California and Texas to the United States.

- Sixteen years after becoming a state, Texas seceded from the Union in 1861, following a vote by the Secession Convention to become part of the **Confederacy**. Governor Sam Houston was one of a small minority who opposed secession. Several Civil War battles took place in Texas (two at Sabine Pass, Galveston, and near the Rio Grande).
- The last land engagement of the Civil War was the **Battle of Palmito Ranch** in far south Texas in 1865.
- In 1866 the abundance of longhorn cattle in south Texas and the return of Confederate soldiers to a poor **Reconstruction** economy marked the beginning of the era of Texas trail drives to northern markets.
- The U.S. Congress readmitted Texas into the Union in 1870.
- The present Texas State Constitution was ratified on February 15, 1876.
- Altogether, six flags have flown over Texas: the Spanish, the French, the Mexican, the Texan, the Confederate, and the United States flags.

XIII. Inventions

KEY QUESTIONS: *What technological discoveries have affected America's history?*

- There have been many inventions that have changed the lives of Americans. Beginning with **Benjamin Franklin**'s experiment with a kite one stormy night in Philadelphia, **electricity** eventually became one of the most important inventions in history. In the mid-1800s, everyone's life changed with the invention of the electric lightbulb.
- **Gail Borden**, who came to Texas in 1829, was an inventor of many interesting items, but is best known as the father of the **modern dairy industry** (he patented the process for condensing milk in a vacuum).
- **Louis Daguerre** of France is, perhaps, the most famous of those who invented the **photographic** process in the mid-1800s.
- **Cyrus McCormick** invented the **reaper** in 1856, transforming the farm industry by allowing fewer people to produce more grain.
- During the 1800s in France, **Louis Pasteur** worked in several major areas that aided human beings throughout the world. The most important, perhaps, was the **germ theory** of disease. He also invented **pasteurization** to keep milk from souring and a vaccine for rabies.
- Early in the nineteenth century, the **automobile** changed people and society. The car gave people the freedom to move farther from their workplaces, which, in turn, gave rise to suburbs. Demand for cars resulted in a search for faster and cheaper ways to build them. **Henry Ford's assembly line** and **interchangeable parts** production for Model T cars changed the way the manufacturing industry operated. Support industries developed in response to the mass production of cars. Glass for windshields and rubber for tires were just two of these. Cars also made the construction of roads necessary. Road, bridge, and tunnel construction, in turn, produced new goods and services industries.
- **Joseph Glidden** was an inventor who changed life in Texas dramatically. In 1874, he patented **barbed wire** that was to bring to an end much of the open range ranching and the days of the cattle drives. This invention encouraged farming and smaller ranches to flourish.
- **Alexander Graham Bell** first patented his telephone in 1876.
- In 1920, KDKA in Pittsburgh was the first commercial **radio** station to go on the air. By the mid-1930s, almost every American household had

a radio. The first successful **television** transmission occurred in New York in 1927, although television sets in homes were not commonplace until the 1950s. These two broadcast technologies soon gave rise to the **advertising** industry.

- Advertising encouraged people to consume things, such as **household appliances**, which dramatically changed the twentieth-century lifestyle by eliminating much of the labor of everyday tasks. Engineering innovation produced a wide variety of devices, including electric ranges, washing machines, vacuum cleaners, dishwashers, and dryers. These and other products gave more free time, enabled more people to work outside the home, and contributed significantly to the economy.

- In the 1950s, **Jonas Salk**, an American, invented a vaccine for the terrible disease of **polio** that had left many Americans and people throughout the world with paralysis.

- The **computer** is a defining symbol of twentieth-century technology. It is a tool that has transformed businesses and lives around the world, increased productivity, and opened access to vast amounts of knowledge. Computers relieved the drudgery of simple tasks and brought new capabilities to complex ones. Engineering ingenuity fueled this revolution and continues to make computers faster, more powerful, and more affordable. The **Internet** is changing business practices, educational pursuits, and personal communications. It provides global access to news, commerce, and vast amounts of information.

- Perhaps the most amazing engineering feat of the twentieth century is the human expansion into **space**. Engineers have progressed from the early test rockets to sophisticated satellites. The development of space-craft has expanded the world's knowledge base and improved man's capabilities. Thousands of useful products and services have resulted from the space program, including medical devices, improved weather forecasting, and wireless communications.

- **Nuclear technologies**, although generally controversial, are among the most important achievements of the twentieth century. The harnessing of the atom has changed the nature of war forever. Nuclear technologies have also given us a new source of electric power and new capabilities in medical research.

Consider the following practice question:

Mr. McCarthy assigned his fourth-grade class a research project on the earliest immigrants of Texas. Which of the following groups were first?

A. Spanish
B. English
C. French
D. Amerinds

Europeans came to Texas beginning in the 1500s, more than 5,000 years *later* than the Amerinds. The Amerind nomadic hunters and gatherers came to Texas around 7,000 years ago. The correct answer is *D*.

Standards V and IX Geography and Culture

The social studies teacher applies knowledge of people, places, and environments to facilitate students' understanding of geographic relationships in Texas, the United States, and the world. The social studies teacher understands cultures and how they develop and adapt, and uses this knowledge to enable students to appreciate and respect cultural diversity in Texas, the United States, and the world.

Competency 018 (Geography and Culture) The teacher demonstrates knowledge of geographic relationships among people, places, and environments in Texas, the United States, and the world; understands the concept of culture and how cultures develop and adapt; and applies social science skills to geographic and cultural information, ideas, and issues.

The beginning teacher:

- Applies knowledge of key concepts in geography (e.g., location, distance, region, grid systems) and knows the locations and characteristics of places and regions in Texas, the United States, and the world.
- Understands geographic patterns and processes in major historical and contemporary societies and regions of Texas, the United States, and the world.
- Demonstrates knowledge of physical processes (e.g., erosion, weather patterns, natural disasters) and their effects on patterns in the environment.
- Knows how humans adapt to, use, and modify the physical environment and knows how the physical characteristics of places and human modifications to the environment affect human activities and settlement patterns.
- Understands the concept of culture and the processes of cultural diffusion and exchange.
- Understands the contributions of people of various racial, ethnic, and religious groups to Texas, the United States, and the world and demonstrates knowledge to the effects of race, gender, and socioeconomic class on ways of life in the United States and throughout the world.
- Understands similarities and differences in how various peoples at different times in history have lived and met basic human needs, including the various roles of men, women, children, and families in past and present cultures.
- Relates geographic cultural information and ideas to information and ideas in other social sciences and in other disciplines.
- Knows how to formulate geographic and cultural research questions and uses appropriate procedures to reach supportable judgments and conclusions.
- Understands research relating to geography and culture and knows how social scientists in these fields locate, gather, organize, analyze, and report information using standard research methodologies.
- Knows characteristics and uses of primary and secondary sources used for geographic and cultural research (e.g., databases, maps, photographs, media services, the Internet, interviews, questionnaires, artifacts); analyzes information from primary and secondary sources; and evaluates information in relation to bias, propaganda, point of view, and frame of reference.
- Applies evaluative, problem-solving, and decision-making skills to geographic and cultural information, ideas, and issues.
- Knows how to communicate and interpret geographic and cultural information and ideas in written and visual forms, including maps and other graphics.
- Analyzes data related to geography and culture using appropriate analytical methods.

Consider the following practice question:

Ms. Arcain is teaching her first-grade class about the environment. An important concept in this lesson is understanding resources. She wants to make sure that the students understand the difference between natural (renewable) and nonrenewable resources. For review, she asks students, "Which of the following is not a renewable resource?" Students should answer:

A. Water
B. Trees
C. Copper
D. Wind

Copper is a metal ore that is a nonrenewable resource. In other words, when it is used up, it is gone forever. Resources such as these are termed *limited resources*. The answer is *C.*

Teaching Geography

Geography does not simply begin and end with maps showing the location of all the countries in the world (Davis, 1992). In fact, such maps do not necessarily tell much. Geography should raise important questions about who people are and how they developed as individual societies and then provide clues to the answers. It is impossible to understand history, international politics, the world economy, religion, philosophy, or patterns of culture without taking geography into account. Unfortunately, students identify geography as a least favorite subject, just as they do history. Too often, teachers concentrate on recitation and memorization rather than allowing students to make meaningful connections between their lives and geography learning.

Traditionally, a central focus of geography has been on map reading and globe skills. Young children can begin to learn map skills, but globe mapping skills are not age-appropriate for Pre-K or kindergartners. For grades 1–3, globes should be used to pique curiosity and help children understand the physical roundness of the Earth (Seefeldt, 1997). However, young children, ages 5 to 7, are able to begin learning about symbols: something that represents another thing. This is a key concept in understanding maps and globes. Children can begin to learn about symbols by manipulating blocks to represent their classroom, as discussed earlier. Children might next work as a class to draw a representation of their classroom from a bird's view, developing symbols to represent desks, centers, the sink, the clock, and other features. They might compare this to a picture that they draw or a digital photo they take from their own desks to understand how a two-dimensional drawing can represent real life. From this point, students move to map their school, playground, and neighborhood. By third or fourth grade, students are ready to deal with landforms and other geographical features.

The concept of direction should follow the introduction of symbols. Prior to entering kindergarten, many children have only started to learn the basics of direction (left and right, up and down, in front of, beside, behind, etc.). Left and right may not come easy to children up until age nine. Many of the games and songs popular with very young children such as the *Hokey Pokey, Simon Says,* and *Mother May I* can be modified to help them with these specific concepts. Once students understand these simple directions they will be better able to understand **cardinal directions** (north, south, east, and west). *Simon Says* and *Mother May I* can be modified for older students with cardinal directions.

Meaningful connections can then be made ("It looks like we have a storm coming from the north. What do you think we should wear tomorrow?"). Once the concept of direction has been learned, students may be given opportunities to construct their own maps of their neighborhoods and other popular sites. Treasure hunts constructed by the teacher and by students offer enjoyable activities in constructing and following directions.

Many trade books can reinforce the concepts of maps and map skills. There are several works of fiction that deal with travel and treasure hunting. Trade books can also be used to help students gain understanding of other people and places in the world. For help in choosing appropriate trade books for geography and other social studies subjects, the National Council for the Social Studies annually reviews new trade books for children. The results are normally published in a special pull-out in the May/June issue of *Social Education.*

Materials for the Social Studies Classroom

There are a number of other materials that should be available for geography skills, for lessons, or to be placed in centers. A globe invites children to explore in primary grades. By the later grades, students should be able to answer questions placed in a globe center (for example, "Twirl the globe and stop it with one finger. In which hemisphere did you stop? If it is a landmass, what country is it? What do you think the weather is like there and why?"). Classroom maps for older children and age-appropriate map puzzles help children spatially in locating shapes of regions, states, countries, and/or water boundaries. Spatial skills are a prerequisite for success in geography, so teachers should work with children on these skills often.

Computer technology is also an important resource for the study of geography. Programs such as *Where in the World Is Carmen Sandiego?* ask students to combine geography knowledge and skills to problem solve. There are also many types of maps online, ranging from historical maps to the most current city street maps (that can be accessed through Web sites such as MapQuest). There are also interactive historic maps online. These maps offer students the opportunity to not only view maps, but, because they are interactive, students are free to navigate to other related information such as photographs and newspapers from a particular time or place. Bolick (2006) writes:

> Social studies educators have long taught with maps in the social studies classroom. The Information Age offers social studies teachers new and exciting methods for using maps to teach history. The Internet provides educators access to historical maps that traditionally have not been used in the classroom, as well as providing teachers and students the opportunity to interact with historic maps in new and innovative ways. (p. 137)

Students could draw map simulations on the computer with art software such as MS Paint. They could also physically construct landform maps out of materials such as salt, papier-mâché, or modeling clay.

Sand and water in a center is especially necessary for increasing physical knowledge of landforms. Adding props (that are safe and developmentally appropriate) such as houses, buildings, cars, trains, and so forth encourage children to build neighborhoods, farms, and cities as well as mountains, valleys, rivers, and so forth. Children should be allowed time to play in this type of center as well as to be directed to specific tasks at times. Teachers should ensure that sand stays moist for easy construction by adding water when needed. Children can also use the water to discover properties of erosion on the land. Sand centers can be constructed of anything that will hold well (rubber or plastic swimming pools, or even a large roasting pan for older children).

Blocks have been mentioned. Children should first be allowed to explore all of these materials and then gradually begin to construct increasingly complex forms found in their environment. For older elementary children, modeling clay should be used as a manipulative for landforms.

To connect places and people, props in a center provide for sociodramatic play as workers or community helpers (police hats, an astronaut helmet, doctor's bag, a chef's hat and kitchen items, etc.). These can be supplemented with other tools, play furniture, and clothes or uniforms of various jobs or of other eras. Other props for social studies skills might include play money and a cash drawer for economics, "store items," and doll families (of diverse ethnicities/skin colors, of various types of families, and of various ages, including grandparents). Seefeldt (1997) also suggests that books be put in a doll center for "reading babies to sleep."

The Art Center or art activities can also easily become integrated as a springboard for social studies by providing cultural items or artifacts. During the year, the teacher can insert artifacts into a center or show, for example, a piece of Native American pottery or jewelry, a mask, an ink drawing from Asia, or a picture of a clearly different era for students to interpret and use for inspiration. The Music Center or music activities may work similarly—as the teacher rotates recordings and instruments from various eras or cultures.

Picture files (actual or virtual) are one of the most effective tools for social studies. Teachers and/or students can gather many examples (and nonexamples) of a concept such as transportation (with pictures of cars, planes, cycles, trains, hot air balloons, skis, dog sleds, snowmobiles, etc.). Students can relate means of transportation to historic periods and geographic location. For example, cars have been in existence since the late nineteenth century but look very different today than they did then. In geography, a mountain picture file widens understanding of this concept by including pictures of volcanoes, forested mountains, snow-capped rocky peaks, island peaks, dry west Texas peaks, and villages in mountains in various countries.

Other resources may consist of community helpers. Speakers involved in jobs related to social studies, field trips, or having various vehicles come to school and (many more related activities) may provide a bridge to the real world from social studies.

Geography Content

In general, children are fascinated by our world. It is important that EC-4 teachers encourage this fascination among their students. Geography and culture offer many opportunities for children to explore their world and various peoples who inhabit it. The content in the geography competency (like the history competency) is fairly large. To make the geography content more accessible, it will be broken down into the following subheadings:

- The study of geography
- Climates
- Natural resources and the environment
- Texas geography

I. The Study of Geography

KEY QUESTION: *What are two major areas of the study of geography?*

- Geography studies both our planet and the people who live on it.
- There are two main branches of geography—physical geography and cultural geography. **Physical geography** focuses on the Earth and its physical

environment. Changes in the Earth's crust have created mountains, plateaus, and other landforms. Factors such as weather, earthquakes, and volcanic eruptions continue to alter these landforms. Also included in physical geography are soils, vegetation, climate, and resources, and anything that pertains to our land, water, or atmosphere.

- **Cultural geography** studies how human groups have lived and changed in relation to the physical environment. Cultural geographers have defined various useful concepts to aid them in this study. One such concept is **population density**, or the average number of people living within a given amount of space, such as a square mile. Urban areas, or cities, are more densely populated than rural areas. **Migration** is another important concept, since it refers to the movement of groups of people out of (**emigration**) or into (**immigration**) different regions. How people use and transport resources and themselves is also part of cultural geography.

- Physical geography also involves describing position through **absolute location** (precise points on a map or grid) and **relative location** (the ability to express a location in relation to other sites—such as San Marcos is about 25 miles south of Austin) (Brophy & Alleman, 1996). Absolute location is related to **latitude (parallels)**, or the horizontal lines of the Earth's grid that are set up like rungs of a ladder to measure how far north or south from the Equator a location is. The **Equator** is a *parallel line* that cuts right through the center of the Earth horizontally and has a location of 0° (zero degrees). Absolute location also requires the measure of **longitude (meridians)**, or the vertical lines of the Earth's grid that stretch "long-ways" from the North Pole to the South Pole. These measure how far east or west a location lies from the **Prime Meridian** (Greenwich, England), which also has a location of 0°. **Time zones** are associated with longitude and change at every fifteenth meridian (there are 24 time zones altogether). The continental United States has *four time zones* (Eastern, Central, Mountain, and Pacific), each an hour later as one moves from the east coast towards the west. Absolute locations are measured in **degrees** and **minutes** north or south and east or west (for example, Houston is located at the coordinates 29° 45'; North latitude and 95° 23'; West longitude).

- The world is divided into **four hemispheres** (or half spheres) based on these absolute locations: the **Northern** Hemisphere (the half of the Earth above the Equator; the **Southern** Hemisphere (the half of the Earth below the Equator); the **Eastern** Hemisphere (the half of the Earth to the east of the Prime Meridian); and the **Western** Hemisphere (the half of the Earth to the west of the Prime Meridian). North America lies both in the Northern and Western Hemispheres.

- There are **seven continents** (or large land masses): North America, South America, Asia, Africa, Antarctica, Australia, and Europe.

- There are **five oceans**: Atlantic, Pacific, Indian, Arctic, and Antarctic (also known as the Southern Ocean). Smaller regions of the oceans are seas, gulfs, and bays. A *sea,* generally salt water, is a smaller body of water usually surrounded by the larger waters of an ocean. For example, the Bering Sea near Alaska is surrounded by the Pacific Ocean, and the North Sea near the United Kingdom is part of the Atlantic Ocean. A **gulf** or **bay** is also part of an ocean but it is surrounded on three sides by land. The Gulf of Mexico and Galveston Bay are examples.

- **Relief maps** have *raised* features to show elevation. **Topographic maps** show detailed elevations using varied colors (and other details) but are flat maps.

- The geography of the United States is a result of changes mainly caused by plate tectonics, volcanic activity, and glaciers over millions of years. When viewing a topographical map of the United States from the east coast to the west coast, the land that borders the Atlantic Ocean and south around the Gulf of Mexico coastline is mostly coastal plains (primarily lower, flat land). The **Appalachian Mountains** appear next, stretching from the south in Alabama to the Canadian border in the north. This geography caused the New England area and the southeastern states to be settled first, until a way over the mountains (the **Cumberland Gap**) was widened by **Daniel Boone**, an American explorer, in 1775. These mountains open out further west to miles and miles of Great Plains, covering most of the middle of the United States, and stretching from Texas to the Canadian border. In early history, it was in this area where the great buffalo herds roamed (along with many Native American tribes), because this rolling plain was once covered by lush grasslands. The **Mississippi**, North America's greatest river, runs through this plain from north to south, ending in a large delta area near New Orleans. A **delta** is an area of silt in which a river meets the sea. This deposit usually forms the Greek letter *D*—which is a triangle. These plains are finally broken by the Rocky Mountains, running from their small beginnings in Texas to Canada. On the west side of the Rocky Mountains, a great strip of desert stretches from Arizona northward. The high desert area is caused by other ranges of mountains that line the Pacific coast in the west (the **Sierra Nevadas**, and further north, the **Cascades**). When moisture from the Pacific Ocean hits these mountains, it moves upward, cools, and drops most of its precipitation on the west side of these mountains, thus preventing much rain from reaching the other side.
- The **Hawaiian Islands**, our fiftieth state, are the tips of high ocean volcanoes.
- Huge **glaciers** cut deep lakes and valleys in the northeastern and northwestern parts of the country (such as the **Great Lakes**).
- High mountain ranges were the result of shelves of rock coming together and being forced upward (**plate tectonics**).

- Some educators suggest that the combined physical and cultural study of places be coupled with **nine basic human activities:**
    1. Protecting and conserving life and resources
    2. Producing, exchanging, and consuming goods and services
    3. Transporting goods and people
    4. Communicating facts, ideas, and feelings
    5. Providing education
    6. Providing recreation
    7. Organizing and governing
    8. Expressing aesthetic and spiritual impulses
    9. Creating new tools, technology, and institutions
    (Hanna et al., as reported in Brophy & Alleman, 1996, p. 118)
- Other areas of **cultural geography** include the development of political systems (for example, how physical factors such as mountains and rivers help set the boundaries of nations), the development of economic systems (for example, how the amount of rainfall in an area helps determine its economy), transportation, languages spoken, and the geography of natural resources (for instance, how the presence or absence of resources affects population distribution). **Cultural diffusion** discusses how the exchange of ideas, thought processes, inventions, beliefs, agricultures, etc., spread as groups of people come into contact with other groups physically (or through technology).

Let's try another question:

Ms. La asked children to tell which part of the map is the compass rose. What did children tell her?

A. The compass rose is A.
B. The compass rose is B.
C. The compass rose is C.
D. The compass rose is D.

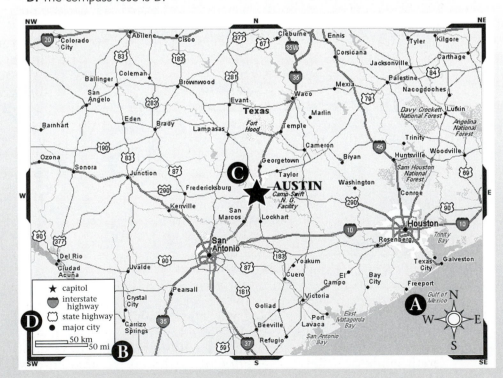

The map scale (as labeled B) on this map gives the reader a clue as to the correspondence of length on a map to real life. For example, one inch on a map may equal 50 miles. A capital city on a map (shown here labeled C) is usually shown with a large star. A map key or legend (labeled on this map as D) shows all of the symbols used on a map and can also contain the map scale and other information needed to interpret the map. The **compass rose** (as is marked A) gives the reader the **four cardinal directions** (north, south, east, and west) and often the **intermediate directions** (northeast, northwest, southeast, and southwest), so the reader can understand the map's orientation. The answer is *A*.

II. Climates: How and Why They Differ

KEY QUESTION: *What are the types of climates?*

- Wherever people live, climate has an important effect on the way of life. It influences the clothing worn, food grown, housing constructed, and transportation used.
- **Climate** refers to average weather conditions *over a long period of time*, taking into account temperatures, wind, and amounts of **precipitation** (rain, sleet, snow). Wind and ocean currents affect climate as do landforms (such as high mountains) and proximity to the coast.
- **Weather** is the atmospheric conditions *during a short period*; weather may change from day to day.
- To a large extent, climate depends on the amount of the sun's heat that reaches a place. Because the Earth is tilted as it **revolves** (goes around the sun), the strength of the sun's rays varies in different parts of the Earth and at different times of the year.
- When the Earth is tilted closer to the sun, the rays are stronger and that hemisphere experiences summer. In the winter, that same hemisphere will be tilted away from the sun, and the sun's rays will not be as warm.
- The Earth is divided into three general regions of climate: the **polar regions**, the **temperate regions**, and the **tropics**.
- The rays are least strong on the **polar regions**, around the North and South Poles. Polar climates (within the **Artic** and **Antarctic Circles**) are extremely cold with light precipitation, usually in the form of snow. As only mosses and small plants can live on the frozen ground, the area is unsuitable for agriculture. Polar regions are sparsely populated. In their winter, these regions are so tilted away from the sun that they receive only a few hours of light during the day. In their summer, there are only a few hours of dark, because the Earth is tilted so far towards the sun.
- The middle regions between the poles and the equator are **temperate zones.** Temperate climates normally do not have extremes in temperature and are characterized by four distinct seasons. Crops can be grown for a good part of the year. Climatologists identify four kinds of temperate climates: **marine, continental, desert,** and **mountain.**
- The **marine climate**, which is found near seacoasts, is mild with moderate to heavy precipitation in all seasons.
- The **continental**, or Mediterranean, climate of inland regions is characterized by hot summers, mild to cold winters, and light precipitation.
- The **desert climate** is hot and dry with scarce precipitation.
- The **mountain** or highlands climate tends to be cool with moderate precipitation. Nearby places in a highlands region may have rather different climates if they have different elevations or different positions relative to prevailing winds.

- Most of the world's population is found in temperate zones, where the climate is favorable for mental and physical activity, and natural resources for agriculture and industry are accessible.
- The **Equator** is an imaginary circle on the surface of the Earth, equal distance from each pole and dividing the Earth into northern and southern hemispheres. This marks the widest part of the Earth.
- The **Tropic of Cancer** is an imaginary horizontal circle around the Earth (latitude) north of the Equator (23.5N) that marks the northern boundary of the tropics. This line crosses Mexico, the Caribbean Sea, the Sahara Desert of Africa, central India, Southern China, and the Pacific Ocean just north of Hawaii. Below this line, the climate is normally hot all year round because of its short distance to the Equator. The **Tropic of Capricorn** is an imaginary circle (latitude) south (23.5S) of the Equator that marks the southern boundary of the tropics. This line crosses south central South America, Southern Africa, the island of Madagascar, the Indian Ocean, central Australia, and the Pacific Ocean just south of Tonga. Above this line, the climate is normally hot all year round because of its short distance to the Equator.
- The sun's rays are most strong and direct in the **tropics**, the area near the equator. **Tropical climates** are almost unchanging—very hot, humid, and wet. Jungles and rain forests with their abundant plant life are difficult to clear for agriculture. There are arid areas in the topics as well. The tropics are also not heavily populated.

III. Natural Resources and the Environment

KEY QUESTION: *What are the basic types of natural resources?*

- Any material supplied by the Earth that people can put to use is called a **natural resource**. Resources can be a "pull factor" that attracts people to an area. Lack or loss of resources can be a "push factor," meaning that people want to leave an area in which they originally settled. There could also be other economic, environmental, or social reasons that serve as push factors, but resources are an important factor.

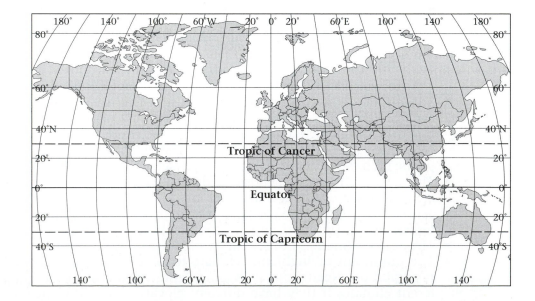

- **Renewable resources** are those that can be replaced in the foreseeable future. For example, forests can be replanted after trees are cut, and a water supply in a certain area is replenished by rain.
- Examples of **nonrenewable resources** are minerals in the Earth's crust. Metal ores (iron, gold, silver) and fossil fuels (coal, oil, natural gas) are among the most important minerals in today's world.
- Researchers are working to find substitutes for some metals that may be used up and to find new energy sources to lessen our dependence on fossil fuels.
- A region's economy develops, in part, according to its available resources. **Arable land** (land suitable for farming) and arid fertile soil are needed for an agricultural economy to succeed. In forested areas, the lumber industry is important, as is mining in regions with mineral deposits.
- People usually settle in areas in which water is available. Fresh water is needed for both home and industrial use. The process of using water to turn wheels and generate electricity is known as **hydroelectric power.** Waterways serve as important transportation routes for ships carrying raw materials and manufactured goods. **Port cities** develop where there are good harbors or waterways.
- Wherever people live and work, they affect the air, water, soil, and mineral resources. Dirty (**polluted**) air and water are often unsafe for living things. Industries sometimes pollute rivers, lakes, and oceans by dumping toxic (poisonous) wastes. Oil spills are another hazard for plants and animals.
- Most air pollution is caused by exhaust from automobile and industrial emissions. In addition to polluting the air, some smoke can combine with moisture in the air to form acids. These acids return in precipitation (**acid rain**) to pollute the land as well as bodies of water. Air pollution is dangerous to health and may cause severe respiratory problems. Local health departments and a federal government agency, the **Environmental Protection Agency** (EPA), monitor air and water and track down polluters. The government also protects the environment by banning the use of cancer-causing chemical pesticides and regulating vehicle exhausts.
- Pollution remains one of the world's most serious problems. Our industrialized societies throughout the world must learn to take responsibility for the environment.

IV. Texas Geography (see www.tsha.utexas.edu/tools)

KEY QUESTION: *What are the four geographic regions in Texas?*

- Texas is currently the second largest state in both population and in territory. The largest state in terms of population is California, and Alaska is the largest state in terms of territory.
- With an area of 267,339 square miles, Texas is larger than most nations and contains every major landform: mountains, plains, plateaus, lakes, rivers, hills, and so forth.
- There are four major land regions in Texas: the **Gulf Coastal Plains**, the **North Central Plains**, the **Great Plains**, and the **Trans-Pecos Region.**
- The **Gulf Coastal Plains**, an immense lowland area in the southern and eastern portions of Texas, covers about one third of the state. The Gulf of Mexico provides a long border to the south. Two large port cities are

Houston and Corpus Christi. Houston began its growth as a port city and currently, the Houston Ship Channel, a 52-mile inland waterway, connects Houston to the Gulf of Mexico. The port is ranked first in the United States in foreign waterborne commerce, second in total tonnage, and sixth in the world.

- The **Piney Woods** makes up the eastern section of the **Gulf Coastal Plains.** The area of vast pine forests and the lands immediately to the west are suitable for diversified farming and livestock.

- The **Valley,** located on the south/southwest border with Mexico and bordering the Gulf of Mexico, makes up the southern section of the **Gulf Coastal Plains.** Cotton, vegetables, and citrus fruits (such as grapefruit and oranges) are among the notable crops grown in the area. Crops can grow all year in this area. The **Rio Grande River** marks the border with Texas and Mexico.

- At the western edge of the Gulf Coastal Plains, stands a line of southward and eastward facing hills. These balcony-like hills, called the Balcones Escarpment, mark the boundary between lowland and upland Texas and the beginning of the **North Central Plains.** Part of this region is hillier and rockier than the rest of the Great Plains that extend into northern Texas. This area is often called the Hill Country. Most of the land in this area is used for raising cattle.

- An **aquifer** is an underground geological formation that is water bearing or that stores and/or transmits water. The largest of these, located in the North Central Plains, is the Edwards Aquifer. The **Edwards Aquifer** has been designated as one of the most productive aquifers in the world. It is designated by the EPA as a "sole source" drinking water for the 1.5 million people of San Antonio and the Austin–San Antonio corridor. The aquifer is also vital to the agricultural and light industrial economy of the region. Springs flowing from the Comal and San Marcos Springs provide water for the tourist and recreation industry.
- The **Great Plains** region extends into the northernmost areas of Texas, including the Panhandle. This region depends on irrigation from underground water supplies and much of this northern area is flat. Some of the areas of the Great Plains offer grasses, weeds, and trees suitable for raising cattle, sheep, and goats.
- The **Trans-Pecos** region is located in the west/southwest corner of the state where many **mountains and basins** are found. The region is rocky and very dry. With the recent discovery of groundwater reserves there is some limited agriculture production: cattle, cotton, and alfalfa. This region contains most of the state's mountains and best scenery. **Guadalupe Mountains National Park** and **Big Bend National Park** are two such areas.
- Texas has several of the largest urban areas in the United States: Houston, the Dallas/Fort Worth metroplex, and San Antonio are in the top ten, and Austin and El Paso are in the top twenty.
- The **capital** of Texas, **Austin**, is located roughly in the middle of the state in an area known as the Hill Country.

 # Culture

The increasing cultural diversity of the United States challenges educators to understand differing values, customs, and traditions and to provide responsive multicultural experiences for all learners. Currently, one in four Americans is of African, Asian, Hispanic, and/or Native American ancestry. By the year 2050, that number will be one in three (Duvall, 1994, p. 2).

Teachers must work harder than ever before to educate the diverse children of today's classrooms. According to the Houston Independent School District (H.I.S.D.) Web site, there are 91 different languages spoken by students in the city schools in Houston, Texas. Each of these children comes to the classroom bearing his or her cultural norms that may or may not agree with those found in the United States.

Traditionally, the United States tried to create unity through the public education system by assimilating students from diverse racial and ethnic groups into a single *melting pot* of "American culture." Of course, assimilation requires some self-alienation (denying who you are in order to become someone else). Once everyone was assimilated, all cultures should *melt* together. While the United States is one nation by borders, sociologically we are far from it. Educators can work with children and their families better by gaining an understanding of cultural, ethnic, racial, socioeconomic, and individual differences, especially in light of the wealth of cultural diversity of the nation that increases daily. Although having everyone feel that they are truly American is extremely important, the **"salad bowl" theory** offers a model for having children retain their heritage and, at the same time, add American heritage. In this theory, various ingredients are mixed together, but the flavor of each ingredient retains its individual flavor.

These issues of multicultural education are different from those of global education. Generally, multicultural education references those who live in America and the many cultures here. **Global education**, on the other hand, looks at the connections between *Americans* and the other people in the world. These two entities are not mutually exclusive. They both stand for freedom and universal values, "essential concepts in today's ethnically polarized and troubled world" (Massialas & Allen, 1996, p. 191). Both multicultural education and global education are necessary components of a new multidimensional citizenship that is developing in the world today.

According to Chapin (2006) multidimensional citizenship requires more than just knowledge. Multidimensional citizenship "calls for viewing problems from a global perspective using critical thinking skills." It also involves a commitment to the following convictions:

1. We are all global citizens who share a responsibility for solving the world's problems and for creating the world we desire.
2. We are all members of the family of humankind. We are responsible for understanding and caring for people of cultures different from our own.
3. We are stewards of Earth, which is our home and life-support system. (Chapin, 2006, p. 240)

Instruction should incorporate a global perspective on, for example, ecology, resources, cultures, and human choices. Children should be shown that nations and people depend on each other for survival. A change in a Pacific current, such as El Niño, can have ramifications for the entire world. Limiting oil production in the Middle East can automatically cause concern for the rest of the world; the record-setting gas prices in the United States were one consequence. These were nothing in comparison to the gas lines experienced in the United States, Europe, and many other parts of the world when the flow of oil was disrupted in the 1970s. The stock price drop of over 10 percent in the Hong Kong market in 1997 immediately affected all the stock markets of the world. It is difficult, if not impossible, to find any major event in any area of the world without implications for the rest of the world.

One way that students might learn about the others who have lived across space and time from them is through fables and folktales. Traditional tales exist in every culture. Often these stories began in ancient times and have been passed down from generation to generation through oral retellings. The same basic story often exists in many different cultures. For example, there are many versions of the Cinderella story that are told in countries around the world.

Myths are some of the oldest examples of traditional literature. These are stories that tell of the origins of the world and of nature. The best-known ancient mythologies were created by the Greeks, Romans, and Norse. **Epics** are long stories that are grounded in mythology. These stories always have a human hero who ultimately triumphs over evil. Examples of epics include *Beowulf* and *The Odyssey*. **Legends** are stories that are supposedly based on real individuals or events. There is a mix of realism and fantasy in these stories. The tales of King Arthur are an example of a legend. **Tall tales** are much more exaggerated and often humorous versions of legends. Some of the most popular tall tales have been about **Johnny Appleseed** (who planted apple trees across the west), **Pecos Bill** (who perfected cowboy skills), and **Paul Bunyan** (who was a larger-than-life lumberjack). **Folktales** are another kind of traditional literature with strong appeal for children. Some reasons for this appeal, according to Lynch-Brown and Tomlinson (2005), may be because the stories are humorous, filled with action from beginning to end, and clearly address issues of justice by rewarding the good and punishing the bad. Some examples of folktales are

Goldilocks and the Three Bears, the *Three Little Pigs, Puss in Boots,* and so forth. Although the terms *folktales* and *fairy tales* are often interchanged, they are not the same thing. While **fairy tales** share characteristics of folktales, they also contain elements of magic and fantasy (fairy godparents, witches, spells, enchantments, and so on), while folktales do not. Examples of fairy tales include *Hansel and Gretel, Sleeping Beauty, Snow White, Rumpelstiltskin,* and so on. The most famous collection of fairy tales was published in Germany by two brothers, **Jacob and Wilhelm Grimm. The Brothers Grimm** began collecting fairy tales from across Germany and France in 1803. Between 1812 and 1857 they published seven volumes for a total of 211 fairy tales.

Another type of story with culturally educative value for children is the **fable.** These are stories, typically containing animals as actors that teach strong moral lessons. Lynch-Brown and Tomlinson (2005) write that these stories have, throughout history, appealed to both adults and children and as a result, were the first type of traditional story to appear in print. The best-known collection of fables is **Aesop's Fables. Aesop** (620–560 B.C.E.) was a slave and storyteller who lived in Ancient Greece. He traveled across the region repeating fables such as *The Ant and the Grasshopper, The Hare and the Tortoise, The Town Mouse and the Country Mouse, The Boy Who Cried Wolf,* and so forth. His fables have been translated into many of the world's languages.

Using traditional literature will help children learn lessons about life, moral values, and others. This is a critical component for developing cultural awareness, and teachers should see value in offering their students the opportunity to gain this type of insight.

Teachers who make a difference in the lives of children recognize the potential for success for *all* children. Gay (1991) explains that, "The primary message from previous research on cultural diversity and learning social studies is that cultural socialization affects how students learn" (p. 154). For the social studies classroom, this means that the most important responsibility that the teacher has is to create a classroom environment that respects and supports the unique backgrounds of all children. There are some things to consider that will help develop this type of classroom:

1. Cultural perspectives must be integrated into the total social studies curriculum. Teachers should not rely on special days or holidays, weeks, or months (such as Black History Month) to incorporate multicultural perspectives.
2. Understand the existence of the "hidden curriculum" that focuses overwhelmingly upon events around Western European experiences. There are many groups who traditionally have been relegated to the margins of U.S. history. These people deserve to be recognized in the main "texts" of history. Even language can create this concept. For example, there would not have been any cave children if there had been only cave<u>men</u> in our history.

The social studies curriculum should include the contributions of the many cultures to American life. Much of the strength of this nation derives from the diversity of its ethnic heritages and cultural origins.

One difference in children is gender. Stanford (1996) discovered that two major patterns emerged in student–teacher interactions and gender discrimination: (1) teachers give boys more attention, both positive and negative; and (2) boys demand more teacher attention. Although differences in gender success have narrowed (and some believe it has even reversed), Stanford recommends several things for the teacher to do in the classroom. These include: becoming conscious of the attention they give each gender in classroom interactions; modeling gender equity by providing an equitable environment; and selecting nondiscriminatory curricular materials that contribute to a sense of gender equity in the classroom. The contributions of women to the life, culture, and development of this nation must not be overlooked, nor merely relegated to Women's History Month in March.

Consider the following practice question:

Mr. Chancellor's fourth-grade class was studying the geographic regions of Texas. Students first investigated the different regions and then, in small groups, designed travel brochures for their region. For the group assigned the Valley region, what characteristic of the region should they emphasize?

A. Orange and grapefruit production
B. Mountains
C. Pine forests
D. Cattle, sheep, and goat ranching

Mountains are found in the Trans-Pecos region (Mountains and Basins) of West Texas; pine forest are found in the Piney Woods region along the border of Louisiana in East Texas and the eastern part of the Coastal Plains; and sheep, cattle, and goat ranching are predominant in the High Plains. Oranges and grapefruit grow in the most southern part of Texas—in the warm Rio Grande Valley near the Gulf of Mexico and the border of Mexico. The answer is *A*.

Standards VI, VII, VIII Economics, Government, and Citizenship

The social studies teacher knows how people organize economic systems to produce, distribute, and consume goods and services, and uses this knowledge to enable students to understand economic systems and make informed economic decisions. The social studies teacher knows how governments and structures of power function, provide order, and allocate resources, and uses this knowledge to facilitate student understanding of how individuals and groups achieve their goals through political systems. The social studies teacher understands citizenship in the United States and other societies, and uses this knowledge to prepare students to participate in our society through an understanding of democratic principles and citizenship practices.

Competency 019 (Government, Citizenship, Economics) The teacher understands concepts and processes of government and responsibilities of citizenship; knows how people organize economic systems to produce, distribute, and consume goods and services; and applies social science skills to information, ideas, and issues related to government and economics.

The beginning teacher:

- Understands the purpose of rules and laws; the relationship between rules, rights, and responsibilities; and the fundamental rights of American citizens guaranteed in the Bill of Rights and other amendments to the U.S. Constitution.
- Understands fundamental concepts related to life in a democratic society (e.g., importance of voluntary participation and the expression and tolerance of differing points of view, roles of public officials).

- Knows the basic structures and functions of local, state, and national governments and their relationships to each other and knows how people organized governments during the early development of Texas.
- Understands the key principles and ideas of the U.S. and Texas Declarations of Independence, Constitutions, and other significant political documents.
- Understands basic economic concepts (e.g., economic system, goods and services, free enterprise, interdependence, needs and wants, scarcity, roles of producers and consumers), knows that basic human needs are met in many ways, and understands the value and importance of work.
- Understands the characteristics, benefits, and development of the free-enterprise system in Texas and the United States and knows how businesses operate in the U.S. free-enterprise system.
- Demonstrates knowledge of patterns of work and economic activities in Texas and the United States, past and present, and knows how a society's economic level is measured.
- Understands the interdependence of the Texas economy with those of the United States and the world.
- Relates information and ideas in government, citizenship, and economics to information and ideas in other social sciences and in other disciplines.
- Knows how to formulate research questions related to government, citizenship, and economics and uses appropriate procedures to reach supportable judgments and conclusions.
- Understands research in government, citizenship, and economics and knows how social scientists in these fields locate, gather, organize, analyze, and report information.
- Knows characteristics and uses of primary and secondary sources used for research in government, citizenship, and economics (e.g., databases, maps, media services, the Internet, biographies, interviews, questionnaires); analyzes information from primary and secondary sources; and evaluates information in relation to bias, propaganda, point of view, and frame of reference.
- Applies problem-solving, decision-making, and evaluation skills to information, ideas, and issues related to government, citizenship, and economics.
- Knows how to communicate and interpret information and ideas related to government, citizenship, and economics in written and graphic forms.
- Analyzes data related to government, citizenship, and economics using appropriate analytical methods.
- Knows how to apply skills to foster good citizenship (e.g., negotiation, conflict resolution, persuasion, compromise, debate).

Consider the following practice question:

Ms. Thompson wants her kindergarten class to understand the importance of rules. How can she best communicate this idea to her students?

A. Require that students memorize her list of five posted classroom rules.
B. Bring a newspaper to class and have students talk about what the president does as chief executive.
C. Ask students to help develop a set of classroom rules.
D. Ask the principal to explain the school's rules to the children.

The best answer would be to ask students to help develop a set of classroom rules (*C*). Creating rules and practicing the use of authority help develop a child's understanding and ownership of justice and fairness. Once children have experience in rule making, they may then relate their experiences to understanding how rule making and enforcement occur in the adult world (Chapin, 2006) (*B*). Memorizing (*A*) or telling (*D*) does not create understanding or ownership. The correct answer is *C*.

According to educational researchers (Martorella & Beal, 2002), elementary schools are excellent educational environments for developing good citizens. This is because elementary schools are relatively small, and the people in them (administrators, staff, teachers, and students) often form a close community. All of these people become concerned citizens of their classrooms and their schools. Students and teachers are concerned not only with the school's policies and programs but also with the physical appearances of their individual classrooms and the common areas of the building and surroundings.

Teachers should use this sense of caring to foster students' active involvement in their school community. Democratic classrooms are essential to encourage and model activism. In such an environment, teachers begin to teach responsibilities with classroom jobs and rules that allow children to take responsibility for their own behaviors. A simple definition of *democracy* is "rule by majority or a government of the people." In a classroom setting, democratic ideals such as respect and cooperation are central. Students should play an active role in establishing their goals and rules. On the first day of school, EC-4 teachers should involve students in establishing classroom rules. This will give the students a sense of involvement and ownership in their new community.

Playing an active role in establishing classroom rules will also give students the opportunity to understand one of the fundamental principles of democracy—that rights come with responsibilities. Democracies are characterized by hard choices, and choices become difficult when they cause one's values to conflict. For example, if we value freedom, we must also value justice and responsibility (one is free to speak but not to yell "fire" in a crowd if there is none). Values can sometimes be hard to reconcile; however, students must learn this most central feature of democracy. Personal choices are most often based on values. In a representative government like that of the United States, people elect representatives that share their values. Therefore, it is essential that children begin to identify and develop their own personal values. Economic concepts could also help children begin to identify personal values. A main concept in economics, for example, involves a "lesson" in hard choices—cost and benefit. Children should ultimately understand the importance of making decisions that provide the greatest benefits. A key factor in teaching these concepts is that children cannot learn them from reading a text during social studies time. They must experience them in classrooms in which principles are alive and well every day.

The remainder of this section contains content information for government, citizenship, and economics necessary for EC-4 teachers preparing to teach social studies.

 ## Government Content

The subject of "government" analyzes and compares different types of political systems. Political scientists try to understand decision making in politics and how individuals and groups obtain and use political power. Political systems and concepts are broken down into the following subheadings:

- Foundations of government
- Writing the constitution
- Development of federalism
- Election processes
- Symbols of the United States
- Texas government
- Symbols of Texas

I. Foundations of Government

KEY QUESTION: *What fundamental ideals are expressed in the Declaration of Independence?*

- Any group of people living and working together needs certain laws and services. A **government** acts on behalf of the group, making and enforcing laws and providing for other needs. A democracy does so with the consent of those who are governed. Sovereignty in a democracy, therefore, lies with the people (**popular sovereignty**). The U.S. Constitution provides for majority rule but protects the rights of the minority. **Due process** is forever present to guarantee that the individual is protected through a system of rights in the court system and cannot be arbitrarily punished.
- **Political science** studies how different types of governments function.
- Governments can be classified by how many people take part in the decision-making process. In a **monarchy**, one person (such as a king, a queen, a shah, or an emperor) usually inherits ruling power. An *absolute monarch* has complete authority to govern. A *constitutional monarch* has limited power and must work with other government officials. Constitutional monarchies still exist now in several Europe countries where the king or queen is more of a figurehead; an elected parliament makes most major governmental decisions.
- In a **dictatorship**, or **totalitarian** government, the government is totally controlled by one person or a small group who maintains power by force rather than through democratic principles. Extensive control is exercised over people's lives, and all other political parties are disallowed; thus many freedoms are often curtailed. Dictators often rise to power during times of national unrest. Hitler rose to power in Germany and Mussolini in Italy in the years preceding World War II. Saddam Hussein was a dictator in Iraq, and Kim Jong Il currently controls North Korea.
- In an **oligarchy**, a small, very powerful governing class rules. This type of government could have been found in South Africa prior to 1994. Until that time, the Black African majority was ruled by a smaller group of white Western Europeans (Apartheid).
- **Communist** governments seek, but have rarely succeded, to establish a classless society in which everyone has common ownership of the means of production. **Karl Marx**, a nineteenth-century German political economist is most associated with explaining the concept of communism.
- In a **democracy**, all of the people take part in governing the country. Ancient Greece was an example of a **direct democracy** because *all* of its citizens (free males) met to make decisions. The United States is a **representative democracy** in which the people elect representatives, such as the members of Congress, to carry out the work of the government.

The belief in a republican government (or government headed by elected officials) is why the United States is referred to as a **republic** (as found in the pledge to the flag: "I Pledge Allegiance to the flag of the United States of America and to the *Republic* for which it stands, one Nation under God, indivisible, with liberty and justice for all.").

- When the 13 original colonies decided to free themselves from British rule, the writers of the Declaration of Independence expressed a political philosophy of **individualism** that is still basic to American government today. "Rugged individualism" emerged from those who moved into the New World and carved out the land self-sufficiently as individuals or as families.

- One of the tools that governments (and, of course, businesses) use is **propaganda.** Propaganda is a strategic technique used to persuade another person to believe or act upon an idea. By using certain symbols or words in vague generalities, a good propagandist can make people feel angry, sympathetic, apathetic, or any number of emotions. This technique was used often by Hitler's government to cause people to feel patriotic. Other techniques of propaganda also include *name-calling, scapegoating* (falsely labeling individuals or a particular group of people as the reason something bad occurs), *band wagoning* ("get on board" because it is the "in" thing to do), using testimonials or *endorsements* of famous people, and *stacking the deck* (only offering biased reasoning from the opinions that propagandists endorse). Other important concepts to understand are **point of view**, or the perspective from which something is told (ownership), and **frame of reference**, which is a structure of concepts, values, customs, and/or views by which an individual or group perceives or evaluates data, communicates ideas, and regulates behavior. Historians recognize that history is, by and large, written by those who "win." Therefore, it can be a biased prospective, not taking into account the perspectives of those who did not win or survive. Thus was the case with Native Americans, for example, who for many years were stereotyped as savages in western movies. The pendulum then swung to view them as a "perfect" culture—at one with nature. Careful study, without bias, finally allows good historians to view these cultures on an individual basis, seeing that some Native American tribe maintained advanced civilizations that were model societies (although their ways were not Westernized), while other groups kept slaves, used human sacrifice, and treated women and enemies viciously.

- The philosophy of the Bill of Rights emphasizes the equality of all people and the right to "life, liberty, and the pursuit of happiness."

- The U.S. government exists to protect these rights, and the power of the government comes from the consent of the people. If the government ignores the people's will, the people have the right to elect new officials.

II. Writing the Constitution

KEY QUESTION: *At the Constitutional Convention, what compromises were required?*

- Five years after the American Declaration of Independence was written, the first national constitution governing the United States was approved, or ratified, by all of the states. This document was known as the **Articles of Confederation.**

- These Articles created a *central government* but with very limited powers. This government could not make laws without unanimous state agreement, nor could it settle conflicts between states. There was no president or national court system. It soon became clear that these weaknesses had to be corrected.
- In 1787, 55 delegates from all the states, referred to as the **Founding Fathers**, met at the Constitutional Convention to develop a new system of government.
- A debate about the nature of representation of individuals and of states was settled by the **Great Compromise**: a two-chamber or **bicameral** Congress was created, consisting of a **House of Representatives** (the number of representatives is determined by state population) and a **Senate** (only two representatives from each state).
- The new **U.S. Constitution** also provided for shared power and responsibilities in three ways: (1) a **separation of powers** that defines three branches of government with distinct powers; (2) a system of **checks and balances** that allows each branch to oversee the other two; (3) a **federal system** that divides governing power between the national government and state governments.
- The three branches of the federal government are the (1) **legislative branch**, which includes the *two* houses of Congress (the House of Representatives and the Senate) and makes the laws; (2) the **executive branch** whose main power resides with the president who executes or carries out the laws; and (3) the **judicial branch**, which includes the Supreme Court and lower federal courts who interpret, according to the Constitution, the meaning of the laws.
- **George Washington** was elected the first president of the United States under the new constitution and served for two terms, followed by other Founding Fathers, **John Adams** and **Thomas Jefferson**.

III. The Development of Federalism

KEY QUESTION: *What is federalism and how does the federalist system provide for the sharing of power between the states and the federal government?*

- **Federalism** refers to a type of democracy in which there is shared power between the national and state governments. After much debate between the Founding Fathers, the **Federalists** (those who favored the ratification [adoption] of the Constitution and the idea of shared powers) and the **anti-Federalists** (those against ratification and who favored states rights more), the Constitution was finally approved by the required number of states in 1788.
- Because the anti-Federalists were concerned that the Constitution did not provide strong enough guarantees of state power or of individual liberties, the Federalists promised to pass a Bill of Rights during the first Congress.
- The first ten amendments to the Constitution are called the **Bill of Rights**. Nine of these placed limits on Congress by forbidding it to infringe on certain basic rights: freedom of religion, speech, assembly, and the press; immunity from arbitrary arrest; of life, liberty, or property taken for a crime without due process of law; speedy public trial by jury; no excessive bail or cruel and unusual punishments; and others. The Tenth Amendment reserved to the states all powers except those specifically withheld from them or delegated to the federal government.
- Thus far, there have been a total of 27 Amendments to the Constitution. The **Thirteenth Amendment** prohibited slavery in the United States. The

Fifteenth Amendment guaranteed the right to vote to all men, no matter their race. The **Nineteenth Amendment** guaranteed the right to vote to all citizens, including women. The **Twenty-fourth Amendment** declared poll taxes and similar measures designed to prohibit people from voting were unconstitutional. The **Twenty-sixth Amendment** gave 18-year-olds the right to vote.

- These amendments were proposed following one of the two methods outlined in the Constitution: (1) an amendment must be proposed by two-thirds of both houses of Congress or (2) by two-thirds of the state legislatures. Approval by three-fourths of the state legislatures is needed for the amendment to be ratified (passed).
- Powers given specifically to the national government, such as establishing post offices and coining money, are **delegated powers.**
- Other powers—those not specifically granted to the national government and not denied to the states—are called **reserved powers.** Examples would include the administration of education and the regulation of police forces.
- **Concurrent powers,** such as tax collection, are shared by both the national and state governments.
- Because powers are divided in various ways, no group or part of government can become too powerful (**checks and balances**). These checks and balances include: (1) the president's ability to **veto** laws passed by the Congress (or legislature); (2) the Congress being able, by vote, to override a presidential veto; (3) and the president making appointments to the Supreme Court when a place is open, but the Congress must approve nominees. The Supreme Court can also rule on laws passed by both the Congress and the president as unconstitutional. The principles of the Constitution encourage national, state, and local governments to work together to serve the American people.

IV. The Election Process

KEY QUESTION: *How does the method for electing the president differ from the way in which members of Congress are elected?*

- Elections and voting are the foundations of U.S. democracy.
- On the federal level, voters elect the president and members of Congress.
- At the state and local levels, voters cast ballots for governors, mayors, state legislators, and city or town council representatives.
- Voters also have opportunities to express their opinions on laws and amendments. Any citizen eighteen years of age or older may register to vote.
- Political parties are not provided for in the U.S. Constitution. However, political differences, beginning early in our history, brought about a two-party system: the Democrats and the Republicans (in more recent times). Despite the strength of the two parties, the history of the United States is filled with third parties (or independent parties) that have achieved limited and temporary successes. The most successful third-party candidate was **Theodore Roosevelt.** His Progressive, or "Bull Moose Party," won 27.4 percent of the vote in the 1912 election.
- Today, **Democrats** usually favor a strong federal government involved in economic and social issues. **Republicans** usually want less federal involvement in the lives of individuals and businesses and greater state responsibility.
- The parties nominate candidates for various public offices.
- In most states, **primary elections** are held to choose **presidential candi-**

dates. In these preliminary elections, voters from each major political party select delegates who will, in turn, decide on the parties' candidates for president. These delegates generally pledge to vote for a particular candidate at the parties' national conventions.

- Presidential elections are held every four years. According to the Constitution, the president must be a natural-born citizen of the United States, be at least 35 years old, and have been a resident of the United States for 14 years.

- Citizens do not directly elect the president or vice president. Rather they choose electors to represent them in the **Electoral College.** This system was set up to avoid having the states with the most popular votes due to their great populations (such as New York and California) always deciding the presidency. In this system, because each state has a number of electors equal to the total number of its senators and representatives, both population and equality count (much like the makeup of the two-house [bicameral] Congress). In most states, the electors are usually pledged to vote for the candidate who won the popular vote in their state. There have been three instances where the person who won the popular vote did not win the presidency. In 1824, Andrew Jackson received more popular votes and more electoral votes than did John Quincy Adams. However, while he did receive a plurality of the votes, he did not receive a majority. This meant that the election had to be decided by the House of Representatives. The House voted for Adams. In 1876 Samuel Tilden received more popular votes than his opponent; however, Rutherford B. Hayes won the election by one electoral vote. In the 2000 election of President George W. Bush, Albert Gore, Jr. received a majority of the popular vote but not the electoral votes needed to win.

- To be elected, a presidential candidate needs a majority of electoral votes. If no candidate receives a majority, the president is chosen by the House of Representatives (this happened in 1800 and 1824), and the vice president is chosen by the Senate.

- The **House of Representatives** has 435 members. This total is divided or apportioned among the states *according to population*. Representatives serve two-year terms.

- The Speaker of the House succeeds the Vice President, should anything happen to the President and the Vice President.

- There are 100 **senators,** *two from each state.* Senators are elected for six years, with a third of the Senate being elected every two years.

- Both senators and representatives are elected by direct popular vote.

- **Laws are made** by the two houses of Congress and signed by the president in the following manner: (1) an elected representative (from the House of Representatives *or* the Senate) proposes a **bill;** (2) legislative committees review the bill; (3) both Houses vote on the bill; (4) if approved by both the House and the Senate, the bill goes to the executive branch [president or governor, if it is a state bill]; (5a) if the president [or governor] signs, the bill it becomes law, (5b) if the president [or governor] vetoes the bill, it is dropped *or* Congress can override the veto with a two-thirds vote to make it a law.

V. Texas Government

KEY QUESTION: *How is the Texas government similar to the U.S. government?*

- After Texas became independent of Mexico, **Sam Houston** became the first president of the Republic of Texas (following **David Burnett** who was ad interim president during the Texas Revolution when Texas was not yet its own country). The second elected president of the Republic, **Mirabeau B. Lamar** (1838–1841), is called the "Father of Education in Texas."

- **Lorenzo de Zavala**, a prominent politician in Mexico in the government of Santa Anna, immigrated to Texas when it became clear to him that Santa Anna was not going to abide by the Mexican Constitution of 1824. In 1836, he signed the Texas Declaration of Independence from Mexico and was also elected vice president of the Republic of Texas.

- The last president of the Republic of Texas was **Anson Jones** (1844–1846).

- When Texas became a state, 10 years after independence, the first governor of the state was **James Pinckney Henderson** (1846–1847).

- In 1874, the election of **Richard Coke** began a Democratic party dynasty in Texas that continued unbroken for more than 100 years. Many of the states in the South felt that the Republican party of Lincoln and Johnson (during Reconstruction following the Civil War) had been harsh and punishing.

- In 1888, the dedication of the present **state capitol** in **Austin**, made of pink granite from the Hill Country of Texas, and largely financed through the XIT Ranch, ended seven years of planning and construction.

- **James Hogg** took office as the first native-born governor of Texas in 1891.

- **Miriam A. "Ma" Ferguson** was the second woman to serve as a governor in the United States. Because of the date of elections in Texas, she was technically the first woman elected to that office. She served from 1925 to 1927 and again from 1933 to 1935.

- The present Texas State Constitution was ratified on February 15, 1876.

- Currently, the Texas Legislature convenes in Austin for no more than a 140-day regular session every odd-numbered year (unless special sessions are called).

- There are three branches in the Texas government (as in the federal/U.S. government): (1) the executive branch [the governor], (2) the legislative branch [the Texas Senate and House of Representatives], and (3) the judicial branch [Court of Criminal Appeals and the Texas Supreme Court for civil and juvenile cases].

- The **governor** of Texas is elected to a four-year term in November of even-numbered, nonpresidential-election years. There is no limit on the number of terms a governor may serve.

- The governor may call additional 30-day special sessions in which the legislature may consider *only* the subjects submitted to them by the governor.

- A statewide elected official, the **lieutenant governor** is the presiding officer of the senate and serves a four-year term. In Texas, the governor and lieutenant governor do not run on a combined ticket as do those who seek the offices of president and vice president in the United States. Therefore, it is fairly common for the governor and lieutenant governor to be from different political parties.

- The **Texas Senate** consists of 31 senators elected to four-year overlapping terms of office with no term limits. The lieutenant governor serves as president of the Texas Senate.

- The **Texas House of Representatives** consists of 150 representatives elected in even-numbered years to two-year terms of office (also with no term limits). At the beginning of each regular session, the House elects a speaker from its members to serve as the presiding officer.

- The **Legislative Budget Board** (LBB) primarily develops recommendations for legislative appropriations and performance standards for all agencies of state government. The LBB also prepares fiscal notes and impact statements that provide the Legislature with information and analysis on bills being considered for enactment.

- The **State Auditor's Office** (SAO) functions as the independent auditor for Texas state government. The SAO reviews state agencies, universities, and programs for management and fiscal controls, effectiveness, efficiency, performance measures, and statutory compliance and compliance with administrative rules and regulations.
- Among other Texas firsts, in 1972 **Barbara Jordan** became the first African American woman from a southern state to serve in the U.S. House of Representatives. She represented Houston's eighteenth Congressional District. When she died in 1996, she was buried in the Texas State Cemetery, becoming the first African American woman to be interred there.
- In 1981, **Henry Cisneros** became the first person of Hispanic background to be elected mayor of a large U.S. city. At the time he was elected as mayor of San Antonio, it was the ninth largest city in the United States.

VI. Texas State Symbols

KEY QUESTION: *What are the symbols of Texas and the main features of Texas?*

- State Capital: **Austin** (named after Stephen F. Austin who gained land grants for the first group of American colonists in Texas ("The Old Three Hundred")
- Motto: **Friendship**, coming from the original word for Texas (*Tejas*), which is what the Caddo Nation called its tribes—friends.
- State song:

   ### Texas, Our Texas*

   Texas, our Texas! All hail the mighty State!
   Texas, our Texas! So wonderful so great!
   Boldest and grandest, Withstanding ev'ry test;
   O Empire wide and glorious, You stand supremely blest.
   Refrain:
   God bless you, Texas! And keep you brave and strong,
   That you may grow in power and worth,
   Thro'out the ages long.

   *Words by Gladys Yoakum Wright and William J. Marsh. © 1925 by William J. Marsh. Copyright renewed 1953 by William J. Marsh. Used with permission of Southern Music Co., San Antonio, Texas

- State bird: the **mockingbird**
- State flower: the **bluebonnet**, the brilliant blue wild flower that covers a great part of the state in the spring, giving some fields almost the allusion of being a lake of blue
- State tree: the **pecan tree**, which can grow in all counties in Texas and is native to 150 counties
- State pledge: **Honor the Texas flag. I pledge allegiance to thee, Texas, one state under God one and indivisible.**
- State flag: the "**Lone Star**" flag was adopted in 1839 as the flag of the Republic of Texas. When Texas became a state, the Lone Star flag remained the state flag. Its colors are "Old Glory" red and blue (the same colors as the U.S. flag) and white, representing bravery, loyalty, and purity.
- Nickname: the **Lone Star State** (after the flag)
- State mammals: **longhorn** (large); **armadillo** (small)
- Highest mountain: **Guadalupe Peak** in the Guadalupe Mountains of West Texas

- Largest Ranch: **King Ranch**
- Borders: **New Mexico** (northwest), **Oklahoma** (north) (Red River), **Arkansas** (northeast), **Louisiana** (east) (Sabine River), **Mexico** (west) (Rio Grande River), **Gulf of Mexico** (south)
- Longest river: **Rio Grande River**
- **U.S. presidents from Texas:** Lyndon B. Johnson (LBJ), Dwight Eisenhower, George W. Bush (although he was governor of Texas, he was not born in Texas)
- **Mission San Jose:** known as Queen of the Missions was founded during the mission period of Texas. It is located in San Antonio and was built so well that it was practically impregnable. Even today one can view much of the practical yet beautiful work that went into its construction. All of the outer walls, dwellings, workshops, and mill are still intact (as well as the church which is still in use).
- **San Jacinto Monument:** the world's tallest memorial column was built on the land where the Battle of San Jacinto was fought (which brought Texas independence).

 # Citizenship

Many of the important decisions affecting our lives are political decisions. Citizenship is a very important concept, especially when you have a government ruled by the people, as we have in the democratic republic of the United States. Thomas Jefferson believed that people must be educated to assume this "office of citizen." What are the rights and responsibilities of citizenship? The state of Texas reinforces the importance of educating for citizenship. According to the Texas Education Code (Texas Statues, 1995), Chapter 4.001 Public Education Mission and Objectives:

> *Objective 5: Education will prepare students to be thoughtful, active citizens who have an appreciation for the basic values of our state and national heritage and who can understand and productively function in a free-enterprise society.*

Unfortunately, interest in citizenship seems to be waning as evidenced, in part, by the voting rate. According to the census bureau, voter turnout for the November 2004 presidential election was 64 percent of registered voters, and this number did not include those of voting age and eligibility who are not registered to vote. For the Congressional election in November 2002, only 42 percent of citizens who were eligible to vote actually did. Maxim (1999) explains that "to most students and adults, the study of the institutions and processes involved in these matters is confusing and uninteresting" (p. 302). Richard Brody (1989) is convinced that apathy toward civic life (the public life of a citizen) is the result of a failure of civic education; "Americans fail to see connections between politics and their lives because they have not been taught that the connections exist and are personally relevant" (p. 60). Maxim (1999) also notes that democratic education has traditionally studied the structure and functions of government without regard to how they affect one's life. Essentially, democratic education was equated with democratic knowledge. Barber (1989) argues, however, that, "if democracy is to sustain itself, a richer conception of citizenship is required" (p. 355). Barber calls this richer concept *strong democracy* and describes it as follows:

If the point were just to get students to mature into voters who watch television news diligently and pull a voting machine lever once every few years, traditional civics . . . would suffice. But if students are to become actively engaged in public forms of thinking and participate thoughtfully in the whole spectrum of civic activities, then civic education and social studies programs require a strong element of practical civic experience—real participation and empowerment (p. 355).

Thus the role of citizens in a strong democracy "includes real, active participation in civic processes (such as helping with a local effort to provide shelter for the homeless) and institutions (such as volunteering to lead a group of Girl Scouts)" (Maxim, 1999, p. 302). Active participation of informed and responsible citizens is the ultimate goal of democratic education. Students should also learn of figures in history who have exhibited these elements of "good citizenship." One example is **Florence Nightingale**. She was born into a wealthy British family living in Italy in 1820. During these times, nursing was not a distinguished occupation; therefore, Nightingale's decision to become a nurse met with the intense disapproval of her family. She also became an advocate to correct the appalling level of care for poor and indigent people. In 1854, she and a staff of volunteer nurses went to Turkey to care for British troops wounded in the Crimean War becoming known as the "lady with the lamp." As a result of this experience, Nightingale wrote a 1,000-page report to Queen Victoria and the Royal Commission on the Health of the Army, which ultimately resulted in the creation of an Army Medical School and a major overhaul of army medical care. An example of good citizenship from an American citizen is **Helen Keller**. Born in 1880, many people know her only as a deaf–blind scholar; however, she was also an important activist for people with disabilities, for women's suffrage, the working class, and other causes.

In order to effectively participate in a strong democracy, citizens must be able to think critically in order to make reasoned decisions and to work out societal problems as part of their civic responsibilities. Productive thinkers are those who: (1) possess knowledge on which to base thought, (2) can represent information from several points of view and understand multiple perspectives, (3) have the motivation to use the thinking skills acquired, and (4) can combine thought processes into strategies to solve problems. In order for students to become productive thinkers, they must be challenged to make their *own* meanings, not merely to remember the meanings of others. In addition, good and thoughtful citizens should: (1) understand laws and know the process for changing them, when needed, (2) understand political issues and participate in voting for their best representatives, (3) monitor their representatives' performance, (4) understand the tax structure, and, (5) when needed, be able to participate in other civil duties (such as jury duty, etc.).

The words *discovery learning, inquiry, problem solving, inductive thinking, thinking,* and *thinking skills* all refer to the processes that people use to discover knowledge, make decisions, and solve problems. Rather than being given answers in social studies, it is a more active process to have students actively seek them out on their own. Our knowledge about subjects can change, fade, or become obsolete; whereas, our ability to think remains constant. Productive-thinking strategies allow us to acquire necessary knowledge and apply it thoughtfully. One of the goals of social studies education is to foster effective higher-order thinking skills that are needed outside the classroom by all members of society, particularly when it relates to citizenship. This can be expanded by careful instructional decisions on the part of the teacher by including student active strategies such as debate, mock trials, role play, and other hands-on/minds-on thinking models.

Economics

Consider the following practice question:

Mrs. Laine created two chocolate "factories" role plays in her fourth-grade classroom. In one, she placed four "employee" volunteers: a mixer (a person whose job was to take the chocolate out of its container and mix it), a pourer (who would take the bowl and pour the chocolate into a mold), a baker (who would put the chocolate into the oven and take it out), and a wrapper (who would wrap the chocolate in a special foil). In the other was a sole proprietorship, where a lone owner did all the jobs. Mrs. Laine provided mixing bowls, forms, and aluminum foil so students could pretend to be doing their jobs. When Ms. Laine called, "go," each "factory" went to work to produce as many chocolates as they could in a specific length of time. The assembly line won. In the next round, however, she had the mixer "go home sick." The assembly line stalled because no one else knew this jobs and the sole proprietorship won. Mrs. Laine was teaching that:

A. blue-collar workers are often in assembly-line positions.
B. specialization of an assembly line also requires cross training.
C. the demand of a product increases the price.
D. it would be better to have a corporation.

Mrs. Laine wanted to show children that an assembly line works very well, but it can come to a halt if only one worker knows each job because of too much *specialization*. The best idea is to have *cross training* for an assembly line. The answer is *B*.

Economics focuses on the production, distribution, and consumption of a country's goods and services. Economic factors have an important influence on how people in a society live. The economics standard is broken down into more manageable segments:

- Types of economic systems
- Consumer influence
- Structures of business
- Government revenues and expenditures
- Business cycles and government regulation
- International economics
- Economics of Texas

I. Types of Economic Systems

KEY QUESTION: *What is the role of the government in the three different types of economic systems?*

- **Economics** is the study of the ways in which goods and services are created, distributed, and exchanged.
- The **standard of living** of a society is the material well-being of its members. The United States has one of the world's highest standards of living in the world.
- Societies must make decisions about what and how much to create in the way of goods and services.
- Societies also must decide how its goods and services are distributed. The ways in which these decisions are made depend upon the type of economic system.

- There are **three major types of economic systems:** communism, socialism, and capitalism. There are also traditional economies, as seen (now rarely) in some native groups, who have economies that produce and distribute goods through old customs and beliefs.
- **Communism** is one of the three major types of economic systems. In this system the government owns all businesses and makes all production decisions. All citizens are supposed to share equally in the country's wealth. Communist economies are often planned economies with set national goals for different areas of the economy. For example, many communist countries focus on a high military budget. Cuba and China are currently communist economic systems.
- **Socialism,** a second type of economic system, is based on the idea of a cooperative society in which wealth is more equally distributed and basic social needs are taken care of through the government (mostly through a system of very high taxes). The government controls some basic industries and public utilities, whereas other businesses are owned by individuals. Socialist governments provide many social welfare programs such as health care and aid to the poor. Sweden is highly socialist; Great Britain is somewhat less, but still, socialist.
- **Capitalism,** as is found in the United States, is a third type of economic system in which *individuals* basically control the means of production, distribution, and exchange. The government usually does not interfere much in business. Capitalism is a **free-enterprise system** or **market economy** because, with the exception of some limitations imposed by the government, citizens may engage in whatever business they choose and may produce and charge what they want, to the extent of supply, demand, and price that the market will allow.
- Most modern countries have mixed economies that emphasize one system but use elements of others. For example, the United States has a capitalist system. However, because of the complex nature of our society, the government needs to exercise some control over business and industry. There are also government-owned and operated enterprises in the United States, including the Postal Service, the public schools, some railroad lines, and social welfare projects such as public housing developments, Medicare, and Social Security.

II. Consumer Influence

KEY QUESTION: *What is the relationship between the price of and the demand for a product?*

- A **consumer** is an individual who buys or uses goods and services for personal **wants** (would *like* to have an item) and/or **needs** (*needs* something for survival).
- Consumers buy more of some products and services than others. The ways in which consumers spend their money (**demand**) influence producers' decisions about which goods to make or which services to provide (**supply**). When the supply of a particular good or service is low, the price normally rises. When the supply of a particular good or service is high, the price normally goes down.
- Businesses that make **goods** (concrete products to sell) or provide **services** (work done for someone, such as computer, car or home repair; medical care; teaching; or consulting) must always consider supply and demand in order to make a profit. Thus, if the market is saturated with an item or a service, a company will not be able to charge very much

for it (unless, for example, everyone wants it and has money to buy it), and salaries for the service will drop.

- **Supply** is the amount of available goods and services. The development of **assembly lines** has meant faster production of goods and also standardized products. An assembly line is an arrangement of machines, equipment, and workers for a continuous flow of pieces in **mass production** operations, where everyone has a specialized job. However, the assembly line can stop if the division of labor is too **specialized** (each worker only knows a specified part of a job), and one link of the assembly line is sick or away. All assembly lines should use some amount of **cross training** in order to maintain production levels.

- **Demand** is how many people want to buy the product or service. Goods and services can be sold at different prices. Usually, prices affect demand. An increase in price normally results in a decrease in demand. A lower price usually means a greater demand. However, this relationship is not *always* true.

- The demand for some goods and services is not greatly affected by price. For example, the demand for milk or bread does not change much, even if prices go higher. The demand for these products is said to be **inelastic.**

- In contrast, the demand for video recorders or computers is greatly increased when the price drops. The demand for these products is **elastic.**

- Businesses study the changes in supply and demand for their goods and services to determine an **equilibrium point**—the price at which consumers will buy exactly the amount supplied by the producer.

- When there is overproduction, a **surplus** is created, and the saturation of the market causes demand and price to fall. When there is underproduction, a **shortage** occurs, and prices rise.

- Because of the importance of consumers, businesses try to gain favor for their goods and services through advertising. Consumer protection groups, like **Nader's Raiders** founded by **Ralph Nader**, check the safety and reliability of products and services and the accuracy of the claims in advertisements.

III. Structures of Business

KEY QUESTION: *What three elements are needed for the operation of any business?*

- To create goods or services, a business needs three things: (1) natural resources or land, (2) labor, and (3) capital goods. These things are known as **factors of production.**

- **Natural resources** are materials that can be found in nature. Metal ores, water, wood, and land are examples of natural resources.

- **Labor** is the human activity that is required to produce goods or services. Labor can be classified into two types: blue-collar and white-collar. *Blue-collar workers* are manual laborers, such as construction workers, electricians, or factory employees. *White collar workers* are employed at desk jobs in offices; examples include lawyers, bankers, and journalists.

- **Capital** is wealth used to produce more wealth. Machinery, tools, and equipment are examples of capital. Money also is capital if it is producing more wealth, as in interest-paying savings accounts. Money can be used to buy other capital or to buy natural resources or labor.

- **Business** is any activity in which goods and services are exchanged for profit.

- Businesses are organized in different ways as sole proprietorships, corporations, or conglomerates.
- A **sole proprietorship** is a business owned by one person. Today, sole proprietorships make up over 75 percent of U.S. businesses. About 8 percent of U.S. businesses are *partnerships,* in which two or more people are owners and operators.
- A **corporation** is a business that is licensed, or chartered, by state or local governments. Corporations are owned by people who buy shares (stock) in the business. Stockholders receive *dividends,* or earnings from the business, based on the number of shares they own. Stockholders elect a board of directors to make decisions for the business. About 17 percent of U.S. businesses are corporations.
- Labor Unions are formed by many workers in a particular industry or service to protect the rights of their members against the owners or management. Teachers in some states can belong to a labor union. The largest labor union in the United States is the **AFL-CIO** (American Federation of Labor-Congress of Industrial Organization). **Cesar Chavez** organized Mexican American migrant and other agricultural workers in California into the United Farm Workers Union to remedy their harsh working conditions and low wages.
- A **conglomerate** is a corporation that owns or controls companies in many fields.
- Unions must also be careful not to price their companies out of business with demands. Union workers can agree to **strike**, or refuse to work and protest on picket lines.
- **Profit** is the excess of income over all costs that a business has in producing its goods and/or services, including the interest cost of the wealth invested. This is the money made after all expenses.
- **Need** is a specific quantity of a specific good for which an individual would pay any price. These are the basic goods and services a person *must* have for day-to-day survival.
- **Scarcity** occurs when there is an insufficient supply or amount of something needed. The availability of a good will effect the price consumers have to pay.
- **Price** is the amount of money, or other goods, that you have to give up to buy goods or services.
- **Barter** is an exchange of goods for goods, without using money.
- **Free enterprise** is a system in which sellers and buyers are free to own property and engage in commercial transactions with little or no government regulation.
- **Laissez faire**, which loosely means "hands-off," is a doctrine of government noninterference in the economy except as necessary to maintain economic freedom.
- **Interdependence** is a term used to describe how one industry depends on the work of another. For example, the building of a house requires several goods and services. Lumber mills, window manufacturers, and so on supply the goods to construct a house. Architects and construction workers provide some of the services required to build a house.

IV. Government Revenues and Expenditures

KEY QUESTION: *What are two main sources of government revenues?*

- The U.S. government raises and spends billions of dollars each year. To pay for its activities, the government accumulates **revenue** (income), mainly through a variety of **taxes**.

- The **personal income tax** brings in the most money. This is money that every citizen who works must pay (usually as a deduction from his or her employment check). The rate of tax is based upon one's income. Those who have a low income pay fewer taxes than those who are the middle and higher income brackets. There are **deductions** that many can make (for example, how many dependents a worker has).
- The second largest amount of revenue comes from **social insurance taxes** such as that for **Social Security** (a proportional tax taken out of payroll). In turn, those who have paid into Social Security receive retirement and other benefits such as disability, spousal survivorship if needed.
- Substantial amounts of revenue also come from corporate income taxes, **excise taxes** (taxes on nonessential items [such as tobacco]), customs duties and **tariffs** (charges levied on imported items), state income taxes, school and property taxes, highway tolls, fines, licensing fees, and sales taxes. Texas does not, at this time, have a state income tax.
- In recent years, government expenditures have been greater than revenues (or it has spent more than it takes in); this results in a **budget deficit.** The accumulated total of these deficits is called the **federal debt.**
- To get some of the money it needs, the government also borrows money through the sale of **bonds.**
- The largest government expenditures are for payments made directly to Americans in the form of Social Security and Medicare benefits (for older citizens), federal retirement pensions (for government employees), unemployment compensation, and social welfare programs.
- **Defense** is the second-largest spending category.
- Interest paid on the federal debt is the third-largest cost and will continue to be a major expense for many years. Economists and government officials propose different ways to reduce the debt: reducing government spending, raising taxes, or a combination of both of these approaches.
- The government also spends money on public health programs, job training, research, veterans' benefits, and payments to state and local governments to operate publicly funded programs.

V. Business Cycles and Government Regulation

KEY QUESTION: *What methods do the government use to fight inflation?*

- Most countries experience periodic changes in their economies.
- The movement from one level of economic activity to another and back again is known as the **business cycle.**
- When the economy moves down from prosperity to **recession**, production decreases and unemployment increases.
- A very bad recession, such as the one the United States experienced in the 1930s, is called a **depression.** In a depression, unemployment is rampant and there are few goods to buy because so many commercial enterprises go out of business.
- Another condition that has an adverse effect on the economy is inflation. **Inflation** is a general rise in prices. People can buy less with the same amount of money. The real value of the dollar declines.
- During periods of recession or depression, the government tries to stimulate the economy with public works projects and low-cost business loans. The government has also examined **trickle-down economics** as a way of getting the economy to recover. The government de-

creases taxes and increases benefits for companies and business so that they can hire more people and make more goods. In that way, the employment rate increases, so that workers can find jobs and begin to buy goods again.

- The government can also influence business cycles through monetary policy. The **Federal Reserve System** (or "The Fed"), consisting of 12 regional Federal Reserve Banks, is a regulatory agency with the power to supervise the country's banks and adjust the money supply. The Fed can lower the amount of cash reserves banks must keep, making more money available for loans. Raising the reserve limit decreases the amount of available money.

- The Fed can also adjust interest rates. Higher interest rates mean fewer people and businesses will want to take out a loan, or if they do, they have less money left over to spend. In this way, the Fed can shrink the money supply to combat inflation.

- The government makes decisions affecting the economy by studying various statistics called **economic indicators**. The **Consumer Price Index** (CPI) is a way of measuring the dollar's value. The CPI is the *average* price of essential goods and services, such as food, housing, and transportation.

- Another important economic statistic is the **Gross Domestic Product** (GDP). The GDP is the value of all goods and services produced *within* a country in a year. The components used to calculate the GDP are: personal spending (food, clothing, etc.), government expenditures (defense, roads, schools, etc.), investment spending by individuals and businesses (houses, buildings, inventories, etc.), and net exports. From this, the cost of all imports is subtracted, and this figure is the U.S. GDP. The **Gross National Product** (GNP) is the sum of all goods and services produced by U.S. citizens—no matter where they are produced. For example, if a U.S. factory operates a plant in Mexico, then the profits that the firms earn would contribute to the GNP of the United States. This same factory would contribute to the GDP of Mexico.

VI. International Economics

KEY QUESTION: *Why are protected markets created?*

- Most Americans wear clothes, drive automobiles, consume some foods, or use radios, televisions, or other electronics that were manufactured in other countries.

- As the leading trade nation, the United States **imports** (brings in) and **exports** (sends out) billions of dollars of goods annually. The combination of imports and exports makes up a country's **balance of trade**. A country has a favorable balance of trade when it exports more than it imports. If a country imports more than it exports, then it has an unfavorable balance of trade.

- Imports mean a greater variety of goods and allow consumers to purchase some products at lower prices. Currently, **NAFTA** (the North American Free Trade Agreement) between the United States, Canada, and Mexico eliminates many tariffs to promote trade. However, some U.S. industries complain that they cannot compete with foreign manufacturers that are able to produce and sell goods more inexpensively than U.S. companies, particularly because of cheaper labor in foreign countries.

- The United States exports many goods that other countries do not make or cannot produce as cheaply. Many of this country's industries—especially agriculture—depend on exporting for a large share of their profits.
- Although exports increase sales and provide employment for U.S. workers, heavy exports of some goods can sometimes keep prices high at home.
- Countries trade with one another for their mutual economic benefit. However, most countries find it necessary to regulate foreign trade to protect their economies. If the U.S. imposed no limits on imports of certain products, many American businesses would be forced to close because other countries can produce these products so cheaply. Special taxes, or **tariffs**, are therefore sometimes imposed on certain foreign goods to make them more expensive so people might choose to buy American-made products instead. When tariffs are used to make foreign goods more expensive than similar items made at home, then a **protected market** is created. However, if restrictions that trading partners impose on one another become too severe, both countries can suffer economically.
- Sometimes countries prohibit their usual trade with each other because of a political conflict. A ban that is imposed on trade because of foreign policy is called an **embargo**.

VII. Economics of Texas

KEY QUESTION: *What are the major economies of Texas?*

- Until recently, the Texas economy was land-based and colonial in structure. Texas produced, processed, and shipped its agricultural and mineral products to outside markets. Texas was dependent on external demand and the prices paid for its cotton, cattle, or petroleum.
- The first real economy in Texas was created by southern planters and was based on large slave plantations. Cotton helped shape Texas history as a major **cash crop** (agricultural crop destined to be sold rather than used by the farmer). As early as the times of Stephen F. Austin's original colony, the leading export was **King Cotton** (called so because it was the "king" of crops and very valuable). Cotton was barged down Texas rivers to the Gulf of Mexico to be shipped to Europe or the United States. This crop was the heart of the economy during the era of the Republic of Texas and early statehood. After the Civil War, the plantation system was replaced with sharecroppers. In the early 1900s, the **boll weevil**, a type of beetle, inflicted serious damage on Texas cotton crops. In 1904, an estimated 700,000 bales were lost to the boll weevil at a cost of approximately $42 million. The boll weevil caused a steady drop in Texas cotton yields over a thirty-year period. The economy has diversified, but cotton is still an important part of the Texas economy. Texas harvests still account for a third of the total cotton production in the United States.
- The **cattle kingdom**, inherited from the Mexicans, spread across the entire American West in the late nineteenth century. Initially, the cattle business involved rounding up open range and stray cattle and driving them north to Kansas railheads. The demand for beef created a link between the western frontier and the industrial marketplace. Like King Cotton, the cattle kingdom drew people and money from outside the state and involved agricultural products shipped to distant markets.

- By 1866, cattle had replaced cotton as king in Texas. The abundance of longhorn cattle in south Texas and the return of Confederate soldiers to a poor Reconstruction economy marked the beginning of the era of **Texas trail drives** to northern markets. Cattle that sold for $4 a head in Texas, brought $30 to $40 in the North.
- **The King Ranch**, which takes up much of the land between Corpus Christi and Brownsville, Texas, was established by Richard and Henrietta **King** as one of the largest ranches in the world. Their new breed of cattle, the Santa Gertrudis, was particularly suited to the Texas range.
- In the 1880s the **XIT Ranch**, owned by a syndicate, covered portions of three million acres and 10 Texas counties and was the largest fenced ranch in the world. The sale of the land financed the construction of the state capitol building in Austin, the largest state capitol in North America. This building is second in size only to the national capital in Washington, D.C.
- For much of the twentieth century, **petroleum** was the basis for the Texas economy. From the first major oil discovery at **Spindletop**, near Beaumont (by **Pattillo Higgens**, the prophet of Spindletop, who initiated the search in the area, and mining engineer Captain **A. E. Lucas**, who brought in the first "gusher" in 1901), Texas and the production of crude oil have been synonymous. Between 1900 and 1901, Texas oil production increased fourfold. In 1902, Spindletop alone produced just over 17 million barrels, 93 percent of the state's production. The massive amounts of money involving oil production brought great prosperity to the entire state.
- After World War II, the U.S. market sought cheaper oil in the Middle East. However, the oil embargo by the Organization of Petroleum Exporting Countries (**OPEC**) in 1973, a year after Texas reached its peak in oil production, caused an economic boom during the 1970s as prices were driven upward.
- This boom, of course, was followed by the bust of the 1980s when, in 1986, the price for West Texas crude fell below $10 a barrel. In 1981, the petroleum industry contributed 27 percent of the state's **gross state product** (GSP). Ten years later, in 1991, the industry contributed only 12 percent to the GSP.
- In recent years, the **Texas economy** has diversified from oil and natural gas production, although Texas is still about third in U.S. production. Agricultural goods (with cotton and cattle still coming first, followed by citrus and other vegetables and grains grown in the valley near Mexico) are still important. This area of the economy depends on the **crop yield**, or the amount of an agricultural product that can be grown or produced *and* actually sold (due to factors such as weather, pests, and so forth). **Computers** and **electronic products** are now Texas' largest export. The communications equipment industry is very important to the Texas economy. This industry is composed primarily of establishments that manufacture telephone, radio and television broadcasting, and wireless communications equipment. The import/export industry in Texas contributes greatly, due to a great number of deep-water ports along the Gulf and its large international airports. The economy and the population of Texas continue to grow due to the warm climate, the favorable taxation, and the lower cost of land and housing in Texas.

Consider the following practice question:

Ms. Henning's fourth-grade class is ending its unit on the different economies of Texas. To insure their understanding, Ms. Henning asks them the following question:

Which of these is not one of the major economies of Texas?

A. Tourism
B. Oil
C. Cattle
D. Cotton

Remember to read the question carefully. We are looking for the answer that is *not* a major part of the Texas economy. Oil, cattle, and cotton have been and continue to be important economies for the state of Texas, now adding technology as a major contribution. Although some areas of Texas do enjoy a great deal of tourism (San Antonio, South Padre Island, etc.), it is not a major economic factor. The *best* answer is *A*.

SUMMARY

As you have gathered by now, many of the competencies covered in the social studies section of the TExES overlap in their coverage. This makes organizing these principles an important consideration as you prepare to take the TExES Generalist. Knowledge of both the TExES social studies competencies and the social studies TEKS for children is incredibly important on this test—along with knowing how to *teach* them. Understanding the interrelatedness of the TExES standards, the competencies, and the TEKS should facilitate your study of the types of social studies questions that may appear on the TExES Generalist. Hopefully what you gain here will help you to easily move from a preservice teacher into your role as a knowledgeable classroom teacher (or from an "out-of-state" teacher to a Texas teacher).

Teachers today have the tremendous responsibility of shaping the future through their work with children. This is an awesome responsibility, since our children today will become tomorrow's voters and leaders. Thinking of education merely in terms of the present is no longer sufficient. It is important for all teachers to have a vision of the future for the children they teach—and for the country and world in which we all want to live. This vision should reflect a teacher's passion to work with children and give purpose and direction to their decisions about good social studies instruction. We hope that you will carry this vision throughout your days as a teacher of social studies.

REFERENCES

Barber, B. (1989). Public talk and civic action: Education for participation in a strong democracy. *Social Education, 53,* 355.

Berg, M. (1988). Integrating ideas for social studies. *Social Studies and the Young Learner, 1,* unnumbered pullout section.

Bloom B. (1956). *Taxonomy of educational objectives, handbook I: The cognitive domain.* New York: David McKay Co Inc.

Bolick, C. (2006). Teaching and learning with online historical maps. *Social Education, 70(3),* 133–137.

Brody, R. (1989). Why study politics? *Charting a course: Social studies for the 21ˢᵗ century* (pp. 59–63). Washington, DC: National Commission on Social Studies in the Schools.

Brophy, J., & Alleman, J. (1996). *Powerful social studies for elementary students.* New York: Harcourt Brace College Publishers.

Chapin, J. (2006). *Elementary social studies: A practical guide* (6th ed.). Boston: Allyn & Bacon.

Civilization III Official Web site. (n.d.). Retrieved December 6, 2006, from www. civ3. com

Davis, K. (1992). *Don't know much about geography: Everything you need to know about the world but never learned.* New York: William Morrow

Dooley, N. (1992). *Everybody cooks rice.* New York: Scholastic Books.

Duvall, L. (1994). *Respecting our differences: A guide to getting along in a changing world.* Minneapolis: Free Spirit Publishing.

Ellis, A. (2006). *Teaching and learning: Elementary social studies.* Boston: Allyn and Bacon.

Farris, P. (2001). *Elementary and middle school social studies: An interdisciplinary approach.* Boston: McGraw-Hill.

Gay, G. (1991). Culturally diverse students and social studies. In J. Shaver (Ed.), *Handbook of research on social studies teaching and learning* (pp. 144–156). New York: Macmillan.

Grant, S., & Vansledright, B. (2001). *Constructing a powerful approach to teaching and learning in elementary social studies.* Boston: Houghton Mifflin Co.

Huck, C., Hepler, S., & Hickman, J. (1993). *Children's literature in the elementary school.* Boston: McGraw Hill.

Johnson, A. (2000). *Up and out: Using creative and critical thinking skills to enhance learning.* Boston: Allyn & Bacon.

Levstik, L., & Barton, K. (2001). *Doing history: Investigating with children in elementary and middle schools.* Mahwah, NJ: Lawrence Erlbaum.

Loewen, J. (1995). *Lies my teacher told me: Everything your American history textbook got wrong.* New York: New Press.

Lynch-Brown, C., & Tomlinson, C. (2005). *Essentials of children's literature.* Boston: Pearson Education.

Manning, M., & Baruth, L. (2000). *Multicultural education of children and adolescents.* Boston: Allyn and Bacon.

Martorella, P., & Beal, C. (2002). *Social studies for elementary school classrooms: Preparing children to be global citizens.* Upper Saddle River, NJ: Merrill Prentice Hall.

Massialas, B., & Allen, R. (1996). *Crucial issues in teaching social studies K–12.* Belmont, CA: Wadsworth Publishing Company.

Maxim, G. (1999). *Social studies and the elementary school child.* Upper Saddle River, NJ: Prentice-Hall.

McGowan, T., & Guzzetti, B. (1991). Promoting social studies understanding through literature-based instruction. *The Social Studies, 82,* 16–21.

Morris, A. (1992). *Houses and homes.* New York: Harper Collins.

Morris, A. (1993). *Bread, bread, bread.* New York: Harper Trophy.

National Council for the Social Studies. (1994). *Expectations for excellence.* Washington, DC: Author.

The National Center for History in the Schools. (1996). *National standards for history.* Los Angeles: Author.

The National Center for History in Schools (n.d.). Retrieved December 6, 2006 from http://nchs. ucla. edu/

Parker, W., & Jarolimek, J. (2005). *Social studies in elementary education* (12th ed.). Upper Saddle River, NJ: Prentice-Hall.

Savage, T., & Armstrong, D. (1996). *Effective teaching in elementary social studies.* Englewood Cliff, NJ: Prentice-Hall.

Seefeldt, C. (1997). *Social studies for the preschool-primary child* (5th ed.). Upper Saddle River, NJ: Merrill.

Social Studies Center (2000). *Texas social studies framework.* Retrieved on January 14, 2007, from http://socialstudies. tea. state. tx. us

Stanford, B. (1996). Gender equity in the classroom. In D.A. Byrnes & G. Kiger (Eds.), *Common bonds: Anti-Bias in a diverse society* (pp. 79–94). Olney, MD: Association for Childhood Education International.

Stearns, P. (1998). *Why Study History.* Retrieved December 6, 2006, from American Historical Association [AHA] Web site: http://www. historians. org/ pubs/ Free/ WhyStudyHistory. htm

Sternberg, R. (2003). What is an 'expert student?' *Educational Researcher, 32*(8), 5–9.

Swartz, R., & Perkins, D. (1990). *Teaching thinking: Issues and approaches.* Pacific Grove, CA: Midwest Publications.

Texas Education Agency [TEA]. (1999). *Texas social studies framework Kindergarten—Grade 12: Research and resources for designing a social studies curriculum.* Austin: Author.

Texas Education Agency. (1995). Retrieved May 14, 2007, from http:// tlo2. tle. state. tx. us/ statutes/ docs/ ED/ content/ htm/ ed. 002. 00. 000028. 00htm

Texas Statutes/Education Code [TEC] (1995) *Chapter 4.001 Public Education Mission and Objectives.* Retrieved May 14, 2007, from Texas Statutes Education Code Web site: http:// tlo2. tlc. state. tx. us/ statutes/ edtoc. html

Wineberg, S. (2001). *Historical thinking and other unnatural acts: Charting the future of teaching the past.* Philadelphia: Temple University Press.

A SOCIAL STUDIES LESSON PLAN

Constructing and Using a Timeline

Grade level: Third

Main Subject Area: Social Studies

Integrated Subjects: Language Arts/Reading, Art

Time Frame/Constraints: Two social studies class periods

Overall Goal(s): To help children understand, use, and create a timeline.

TEKS/TAKS OBJECTIVES:

§ 113.5 **Social Studies** (b) Knowledge and Skills (1) History, (3) (b) create and interpret timelines;

§ 117.11 **Art** (b)(1)(A) identify sensory knowledge and life experiences as sources for ideas about visual symbols, self, and life events;

§ 110.5 **English Language Arts and Reading** (b)(7)(B) read from a variety of genres for pleasure and to acquire information from both print and electronic sources (2-3); (d)(12)(D) use multiple sources, including print such as an encyclopedia, technology, and experts, to locate information that addresses questions (2-3).

Objectives: Students will view out-of-order events and write corrections on a sheet of paper.

Students will view a PowerPoint presentations and, as a whole class, put various scenes from a person's life back in order and label them.

After viewing a timeline from the activity above, children construct their own timelines about important events in their lives on adding machine tape.

Students will, as a whole class, help the teacher explain the uses of a timeline.

Pairs of students will construct timelines of the main events of an important person's life.

Each student will explain one or two of these events to the class.

Sponge Activity: Teacher has children look at a timeline on the overhead where the dates and simple school events during the year are placed out of order and asks children to see if they can see anything wrong and, if so, how would they fix it (write on a sheet of paper).

Environmental Concerns: Partners will need to have space to work together on their timelines.

Focus: Discuss and show the correct timeline of school events from the sponge. Ask children if they think it is easier to think about and remember events when they are in order or out of order. The teacher shows a PowerPoint presentation of pictures (a baby, a toddler, an elementary student, a middle school student, a high school graduation, a college graduation, an adult holding a baby, an old person, etc.) which are out of sequence, all with the years the pictures were taken shown below the picture (the teacher may have pictures and a timeline of her own life to share, if desired). The teacher asks children if this is a good way to show the person's life and why or why not. The children are asked to help the teacher put them in order, label the pictures, and reconstruct a good timeline to go with the pictures. Show the "redesigned" PowerPoint presentation in order and discuss the difference from the first showing. Show an example of a constructed timeline of these events (and include pictures on the timeline, if possible, by shrinking them and placing with the year and the event).

Rationale: Events take place in a certain order of time. A timeline is a good tool to logically understand, record, and remember the order of events (sequencing). Cause-and-effect can often be established by looking at a timeline. Show children a short timeline of four events in which this is the case (could be a classroom issue, a school issue, or a real or "made-up issue" to illustrate the point). For example, it could be as simple as: *Carrie called Brandi a name on Monday, and Brandi called Carrie a name on Tuesday. There was hitting between the two girls on Wednesday and the teacher called the girls' parents, who came to school on Friday. There was no television or video games for the girls for the next month at home.* (Teacher should quickly construct a timeline with the main events and ask students to show how a timeline can show cause and effect, or even prediction.)

MAKING CONNECTIONS:

1. **Connections to Past or Future Learning:** How many of you have seen a timeline in your social studies book before? What was the topic? What did it show? Why do you think the book authors put in it your social studies book? What did it help you understand?

2. **Connections to the Community:** Do different groups in your community have a calendar of events? This is like a virtual timeline in "real time." Are they different for different groups of people? Are different groups of people in your community more interested in certain events (for example, who might have Cinco de Mayo on their timeline of events)?

3. **Cultural Connections:** When we study other parts of the world and history, it can sometimes seem like a puzzle because, at the same time something important is happening in one part of the world something important is also happening in another part of the world; it is difficult to see that without timelines.

4. **Connections to Student Interests & Experiences:** Have you ever heard anyone tell a story or seen a movie that did not tell everything in order? How difficult was it to understand when your mind had to go back and forth to try to make sense of things? (Teacher could actually tell a story with several events out of order to make this point.)

Materials: Adding machine tape, colored pencils, PowerPoint presentations, simple biographies, bookmarked Internet sites of currently "popular" people, card paper for accordion timelines

Activities: Guided Practice: As an example, the teacher shows another simple biography/ timeline of an important person (depending on the time of year choose Martin Luther King, George Washington, etc.) on a PowerPoint presentation. The class will brainstorm important events that may have happened in their own lives (year they were born, the year [or age] when a sibling was born, learning to ride a bike, traveling to a special place, starting school, going to first grade, playing on a team, going to second grade, etc.). Students are given two strips of adding machine tape (one for a draft).

They are asked to draw pictures of the important events and label them in order of the year and/or age they were when the event happened. **Independent Practice:** Partners will pick from a menu of interesting people and design an accordion timeline (strip of paper folded into four sections) of the major events of the life of the person whom they select, based upon a short (or prepared) biography or bookmarked Internet site. Each partner will explain one or two important events on the timeline orally to the class.

Assessment: *Informal*: Teacher will check for understanding by questioning students' on their personal timelines and after the oral presentations of events from biographical timelines. *Formal*: Students must include at least four major events on their "famous person" timelines (40%); events must be in correct sequence (40%); drawn picture must be representative of the event (10%); and dates must be included (10%).

What Will Students Do Who Finish Early?
Have students go to the computer and look up timelines of their favorite Harry Potter characters at http://www.hp-lexicon.org/timelines/timelines_char.html or look up Harry Potter's timeline at http://www. hp-lexicon.org.timelines/timeline_harry.html (or another current movie with a similar Web site).

Closure: Students will share their personal timelines with a partner, pointing out one or two of the most important events. The teacher will ask students what makes a timeline correct and useful.

Modification for Students with Special Needs: Sara's partner (who is currently working with the speech therapist) will present orally for her partnership.

Reflection: To be completed after teaching the lesson.

DRAFT YOUR OWN SOCIAL STUDIES LESSON PLAN

Title of Lesson: _____

Grade Level: _____

Main Subject Area: _____

Integrated Subjects: _____

Time Frame/Constraints: _____

Overall Goal(s): _____

TEKS/TAKS Objectives: _____

_____

_____

Objective(s): _____

_____

_____

Sponge Activity: _____

_____

_____

Environmental Concerns: _____

_____

_____

Rationale(s): _____

_____

_____

Focus or Set Induction: _____

_____

_____

Making Connections:

1. Connections to Past or Future Learning _____

_____

2. Connections to the Community: _____

_____

3. Cultural Connections: _____

_____

4. Connections to Student Interests & Experiences: _____

_____

Materials: _____

_____

_____

Activities: Guided practice: _____

_____

_____

_____

_____

Independent practice: _____

_____

_____

_____

_____

Assessment: _____

_____

_____

What Will Students Do Who Finish Early? _____

_____

_____

Closure: _____

_____

_____

Modification for Students with Special Needs: _____

_____

_____

Reflection: _____

_____

_____

OBSERVING SOCIAL STUDIES EXPERIENCES/ACTIVITIES

During your visit to an EC-4 classroom, use the following form to provide feedback as well as to reflectively analyze the room, the materials, and the teacher.

Name: _____ Grade Level Observed:_____ Date(s)_____

Title or Short Description of Lesson or Activity:_____

	Observed	Not Observed	Response
1. The seating arrangement is flexible (students remain in straight rows).			Describe the arrangement. What are some advantages and disadvantages?
2. A center is designated for role-play and simulation activities. This could include costumes, props, a variety of types of currency from the U.S. and other countries, and other materials related to social studies.			If so, describe. If not, describe what a Social Studies Center might include.
3. There are images placed around the room that depict people who have exhibited courage and/or good citizenship.			If so, describe. If not, describe images that might be included and why?
4. There is a Geography Center.			If so, describe. If not, describe what this type of center might look like.
5. There are materials, such as modeling clay, papier-mâché, and salt, available for hands-on use by students to construct geographic landforms.			If so, describe. If not, what materials could be added?
6. There are graph paper, markers, colored pencils, and other map-making tools available for student use.			If so, describe. If not, what materials could be added?
7. There are geography manipulatives such as maps, puzzles, and globes available for student use.			If so, describe. If not, what could be added?
8. If there is no Geography Center are these types of activities integrated within other centers or areas of the classroom?			If so, describe. If not, what could be changed?
9. There are numerous picture files available for students depicting people, places, and events from other times and places.			If so, describe. If not, what files could be added?
10. There are trade books that support the teaching of social studies in the class library.			If so, describe. If not, what titles might be included?
11. The class library contains biographies, factual stories of places and events, and cultural narratives.			If so, describe. If not, what titles might be added?

	Observed	Not Observed	Response:
12. The class library contains traditional literature, such as myths, epics, legends, tall tales, folktales, fairy tales, and fables.			If so, describe. If not, what titles or types of books might be added?
13. There are artifacts, images, and/or other resources from other cultures or societies displayed in the classroom.			If so, describe. If not, what could be added and why?
14. Displayed artifacts, images, and other materials are positive depictions that are attractively displayed.			If so, describe. If not, give ideas for what could be added or omitted and why.
15. Social studies topics are connected to other social studies areas in an *intra*disiplinary way (for example, geography and economics).			If so, describe. If not, give ideas for what areas could be logically connected?
16. Social skills are a part of a lesson.			If so, describe. If not what skills could be appropriately included?
17. There is a current events reader, such as *Weekly Reader,* in the classroom.			If so, describe how it is used. If not, describe how this type of resource might be used.
18. Technology is available in the classroom.			If so, describe any links to usage with social studies. If not, in what ways could technology be logically added?
19. There are advanced technological tools available for teacher use (overhead computer projector, document camera, digital camera, etc.).			If so, describe how they are used. If not, how might they be incorporated?
20. Students have the opportu-nity to use various technologies in classroom presentations.			If so, describe. If not, how could they be incorporated?
21. Students use presentation tools in an effective manner.			If so, describe. If not, how could this element be included?
22. There are electronic media, such as a television, VHS and/or DVD player, a cassette and/or CD player, in the classroom.			If available, describe. If not, what could be added?
23. The social studies text and other instructional materials used are up to date.			Describe if so, or if not, tell in what ways they are dated.
24. The social studies textbook and/or other instructional materials used shows different genders and cultures.			If so, describe. If not, what is not included?

	Observed	Not Observed	Response:
25. The teacher's media library contains films, music, and other recordings for social studies.			If so, describe. Are these available for student use? If not, what titles might be included and tell how they might be used to further students' knowledge and skills in social studies?
26. There are student-created recordings in the media library.			If so, describe. What is the value of having these in the media library?
27. tudents use the computers primarily for word processing and for Internet research.			If so, describe.
28. arious software titles are available for student use.			If so, describe. If not, what titles might be appropriate and why?
29. Students make decisions in their classroom on major and/or minor issues (assignments, rules, etc.).			If so, describe. If not, what are some choices that the teacher could give to them?
30. he lesson begins with a motivating focus.			If so, describe. If not, what could be used?
31. he lesson is presented in a logical manner.			If so, describe. If not, what could be rearranged and why?
32. he activities are motivating.			If so, describe. If not, explain why not.
33. The activities involve higher levels of thinking.			If so, describe. If not, what could be added?
34. The teacher uses an appropriate closure to end the lesson.			If so, describe. If not, what could be added?

TEST YOURSELF FOR SOCIAL STUDIES

1. Mrs. Wickcam had her fourth graders design questions for an interview to find out information on the Vietnam War from their grandparents or others of that generation. Mrs. Wickcam is having her students do:
   A. qualitative research.
   B. quantitative research.
   C. inquiry.
   D. survey.

2. Mr. Jackson asked students to find how much rainfall parts of West Texas received for the last year. Students are most likely to find this information in:
   A. an atlas.
   B. periodicals.
   C. an almanac.
   D. a gazetteer.

3. The children in Mrs. Momin's third-grade room have been asked to describe some of the cities, the rail system, and the temples of Japan. They are being asked to describe:
   A. a region.
   B. physical characteristics.
   C. human characteristics.
   D. location.

4. Mr. Poteet's children are asked to show the largest natural region in Texas on a large classroom map. To what region should they point?
   A. Mountains and Basins
   B. Great Plains
   C. (North) Central Plains
   D. Coastal Plains

5. Ms. Baba called on Jamie to tell the class about topography. Which of the following is *not* a part of topography?
   A. Glaciers
   B. Rivers
   C. Plateaus
   D. Dams

6. Fourth graders were asked to guess at the climate of a city if it was located as follows: ocean, short coastal plain, mountains, city. They should answer that it would probably be:
   A. very wet.
   B. very cold.
   C. very dry.
   D. very hot.

7. Mrs. Day wanted Julia to point to the country of Panama and tell the class what type of landform was located there. Julia pointed Panama out on the large map and told them that it was a(n):
   A. mesa.
   B. fjord.
   C. isthmus.
   D. delta.

8. Ms. Klein's class was involved in an activity in which she divided the class into two groups. One group was labeled "the settlers" and the other was labeled "the Texas Native Americans." The question they were to answer was, "Who should have the land?" Each group was to research the conflict between the two groups during the 1800s and come up with reasons why their group should have the land. One group would present their reasons, while the other listened, followed by the other group presenting their reasons. After the initial presentation, each group would gather again to decide any rebuttals, and in a second round, present them to each other. After this presentation, each group was to go back and see if they could develop a compromise(s) for the situation with which they felt both sides could live. Each group presented their compromises, then went back to their groups to discuss whether or not they could accept what was offered. Finally, each group told what they could or could not accept to the other. This social studies activity is a(n):
   A. oral history.
   B. case study.
   C. learning center.
   D. conflict resolution debate.

9. Ms. Alvados wants her second-grade children to look up Web sites related to their local community. One of the *first* things she should do is:
   A. go online and look at the sites and bookmark them, if necessary.
   B. have children do a search on their own to see how many sites come up.
   C. ask the technology specialist to go online to see what is available.
   D. examine the URL address.

10. Mr. Kahn showed his students the following map and asked, "Who can tell me what city is located at 29° 45'; North latitude

and 95° 23′; West longitude?" What is the answer?

A. Shanghai, China
B. Mexico City, Mexico
C. Karachi, Pakistan
D. Houston, Texas

11. On a map, Ms. Lymes asked children to identify the mouth of a river. Which letter below should they pick?

A. A is the mouth.
B. B is the mouth.
C. C is the mouth.
D. D is the mouth.

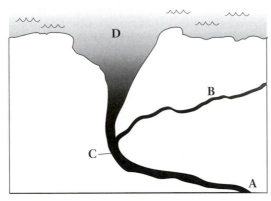

12. Mrs. Delgado's class was studying the ranching days of Texas. Mrs. Delgado asked students to identify the largest Texas ranch that had covered all or parts of ten Texas counties. They should answer:

A. the King Ranch.
B. the XIT.
C. the Waggoner Ranch.
D. the JA Ranch.

TEST YOURSELF ANSWERS AND RATIONALES FOR SOCIAL STUDIES

Answer 1: *Quantitative research* (B) involves "quantities" of numerical data. Students might examine statistical information, for example, on how many men were drafted for this war and how many volunteered. *Inquiry* (C) refers to the

way that many social scientists go about completing a study. This involves developing a question and a hypothesis, collecting and analyzing data, drawing conclusions, and developing a generalization. For example, Mrs. Wickcam might ask students to investigate the question of whether or not this was a popular war. Students might hypothesize it was not. They might gather data on war protests, etc., and conclude that, although many Americans may have thought that the Domino Theory (when one country is taken over by communism, others nearby will "fall") was worth fighting for, by the end of this war, most Americans did not feel that it had been worth the many American lives lost. Students might generalize that wars cannot be continued or won if they are not seen as important by most Americans. Although a survey (D) can be conducted orally, a *survey* usually gives category choices rather than has the participant talk at length about a question. The answer is *qualitative research* a type of research that uses methods such as interviews, observations, questionnaires, etc., to collect data that is *in words* rather than numbers.

Answer 2: *Periodicals* (B) are sources such as magazines and newspapers. A *gazetteer* (D) deals with population and related statistics. An *atlas* (A) contains maps. Sometimes one finds rainfall maps in an atlas that is a generalization for the area, but normally one would look in an almanac (C) for specific information for a particular year. An *almanac* is a yearly account of information such as rainfall and other weather trends, ocean tidal tables, sunrise/sunset tables, information on moon phases, planting guides, and a host of other information (both scientific and folk). The answer is C.

Answer 3: These terms all have different definitions. A **region** (A) is an area that is different from another, differentiated by either physical differences (such as a mountain region versus a coastal region) or by differences in culture and language (for example, the Southwest U.S. is a region known for its cowboy culture). If students had been asked to describe the many islands of Japan, the rivers, and/or Mount Fuji, they would have been describing the **physical characteristics** (B), which can also include other landforms, climate, and so forth. **Location** (D) refers to the place where something is situated on the Earth, normally using the **grid system** of latitude (parallels) and longitude (meridians). Students are being asked to describe *human characteristics,* which include all of the things that change a place through *people's* actions. The answer is *C.*

Answer 4: Texas is divided into four natural regions, as listed above. The *Mountains and Basins* area (located in far West Texas and containing El Paso) is the smallest region (*A*). The (North) *Central Plains,* is located along the border of Oklahoma, and is the second smallest (*B*). The *High Plains* runs from the Panhandle of Texas (in the north) down through much of the Hill Country in the middle of Texas. This is the next largest region (*C*). The largest region, however, is the *Coastal Plains* (*D*), which encompasses all of East Texas and stretches along the coast of the Gulf of Mexico through the Valley. The answer is *D.*

Answer 5: *Topography* is defined as all of the landforms in a region and may include hills, mountains, valleys, peninsulas, plains, lakes, and so forth. Choice *D* (dams) is a man-made addition, so it is not a part of the *natural* topography. The answer is *D.*

Answer 6: We would not be able to tell if the climate would be cold (*B*) or hot (*D*) without first knowing the latitude. However, we could guess that the climate would be very dry (*C*) because, most often, moisture-laden winds from the ocean blow across the coast and up the mountains. At this point, the air cools and moisture condenses and turns to rain. Thus, most of the moisture usually falls on the "ocean side" of the mountains, and there is little moisture left by the time the winds arrive on the other side of the mountain, where the wind also warms up. That is why we see the coastal side of California as more lush and fruitful and, on the other side of the mountains, Arizona as mostly desert. The answer is *C.*

Answer 7: A *mesa* (*A*) is a landform that means "table" in Spanish. Mesas look like steep hills but are completely flat on top and are mostly found in the Southwestern United States. A *fjord* (*B*) is a landform that is a *very* deep bay leading out to the ocean with mountains around three sides. These are formed by glaciers cutting the land through to the sea and are found in colder areas of the world such as Norway, Alaska, and New Zealand. A *delta* (*D*) is a landform that is formed by a river throwing out its silt for many years where it meets the sea. The letter "D" in Greek looks like a triangle, and a

delta forms a huge triangle at the mouth of a river such as the Nile or the Mississippi. An *isthmus* (*C*) is a landform that is only a sliver of land connecting two greater masses of land. Thus is the case where North America and South America are connected in Panama. There is a theory that there was, at one time, an isthmus between Alaska and Asia across the Bering Sea that ancient peoples and animals walked across. The answer is *C.*

Answer 8: All of these activities are excellent for teaching social studies. However, *oral histories* (*A*) have students read or listen to *first-hand accounts* or gain first-hand accounts through interviews of people about an era of history or an event. A *case study* (*B*) centers on a person, place, or problem to show a particular example of something under study. For example, students might do a case study on the Mount St. Helen's eruption to show what happens to people during such a disaster by collecting video clips, statistics, oral accounts, and so forth. *Learning centers* (*C*) are small established areas where students go to reinforce information, gain enrichment, and so forth. For example, Mrs. Klein has a Texas Revolution Center where children have pre-arranged tasks such as arranging representative pictures of each event of the Texas Revolution on a timeline, listening to songs from that era as well as more modern songs like "The Alamo," identifying where the major events took place on a map, matching heroes of the revolution with their deeds, and so forth. However, the activity described in the question is a *conflict resolution* debate because students are working on a compromise. The answer is *D.*

Answer 9: To be sure that the sites are safe for viewing for young children, the teacher should first go online to look at the sites and bookmark them, if needed (*A*). It might be interesting for children to see how many sites come up in a search and have them select the best sites, but a teacher must be very careful that none of these are "adult" sites. It is also necessary for a teacher to identify the purpose of a Web site and determine if the Web site will match his or her goals and objectives. This can be done by looking at the URL address (*D*) to see the expertise of the author, the date the information was entered on the site, etc., to help establish any bias in information. As children grow, they can be taught these skills as well. The teacher might do this in collaboration with the technology specialist in his or her school, but it is still the responsibility of the teacher to make sure that the sites match the curriculum and that they are safe for children. The answer is *A*.

Answer 10: Remember a memory model for latitude (it is like the rungs of a "*lat*ter" or ladder [they go horizontally across the world]). They also tell us how far north or south from the Equator a place is located. Longitude measures distance east or west from the Prime Meridian in Greenwich, England, so longitude lines run "longwise." Therefore, the city that matches Mr. Kahn's question is Houston, Texas (*D*). Shanghai, China (*A*) is located at latitude: 31° 14'; North and longitude: 121° 27'; East. Mexico City, Mexico (*B*) is located at latitude: 19° 28'; North and longitude: 99° 09'; West; and Karachi, Pakistan (*C*) is located at latitude: 24° 51'; North and longitude: 67° 02'; East. The answer is *D*.

Answer 11: Letter *A* shows the *mouth* of the river, or its *beginning.* Letter *B* shows a *tributary* (or another smaller river or stream that connects with the main river. Letter *C* shows the *channel* of the river, and *D* shows the *delta* (or the end of a river, which dumps silt out into the ocean or gulf in the form of a Greek letter *D*. The answer is *A*.

Answer 12: The *King Ranch* (*A*) was originally smaller (covering about 800,000 acres) than the XIT (*B*), but the King Ranch (located west of Corpus Christi in South Texas) has remained in tact so is the largest today. The *XIT,* was located in the Panhandle and owned by a syndicate of investors. During the 1800s, it covered about 3,000,000 acres and was the largest ranch in Texas during its time—prior to much of its land being sold to finance the state capital building in Austin. The *Waggoner Ranch* (*C*) and the *JA Ranch* (*D*) were also both large ranches but not nearly to the extent of the XIT or the King Ranch. The answer is *B*.

5 Preparing to Teach Science in Texas

Mary E. Wingfield
University of Houston

Lynn S. Freeman
University of Houston–Victoria

This chapter contains information about science in the elementary classroom. A brief introduction to science education provides the theoretical basis for the state's standards. Then, each of the science standards and relevant practice questions will be discussed. A model science lesson and evaluation by standards, a resource list, and references are presented, followed by another lesson plan, a form to draft your own lesson plan, an observation sheet, and more practice questions.

According to the National Science Education Standards (National Research Council, 1996), "Lifelong scientific literacy begins with understandings, attitudes, and values established in the earliest years" (p. 114). Therefore, teachers of elementary-school-aged children must remember to foster a sense of wonder, design investigations, ask questions, and promote curiosity. Today's science teachers benefit from newly designed curriculum materials and kits that include developmentally appropriate manipulative materials. Textbooks are no longer viewed as tools for memorizing definitions but as one of many resources available for information. Finally, appropriate instructional strategies should be employed that encourage inquiry, problem solving/higher-order thinking, cooperative learning, and concept attainment.

Science education reform efforts have relied on research studies from the National Science Teachers Association, the American Association for the Advancement of Science, and the National Science Foundation. The effort to improve science education has resulted in the establishment of new state guidelines and National Standards. Texas teachers see these reform efforts detailed in the Texas Essential Knowledge and Skills (TEKS) for science for each grade level (access at http://www.tea.state.tx.us/teks). The format of the TEKS reflects national reform efforts through its introduction at each grade level. One example notes that "In kindergarten, science introduces the use of simple classroom and field investigations to enable the development of students' skills of asking questions, gathering information, communicating findings, and making informed decisions. Using their own senses and common tools as a hand lens, students make observations and collect information. Students also use computers and information technology to support their investigations" (TEA, Chapter 112.2 (a) 1). Texas children are evaluated on their knowledge of the elementary TEKS in the TAKS test (Texas Assessment of Knowledge and Skills).

The TAKS test focuses on an understanding of scientific processes, the nature of science, and the content strands of life, earth, and physical science. Correlations with the National Standards, TEKS, and district guidelines ensure that students are benefiting from a concerted effort by numerous scientists and science educators to provide meaningful, inquiry-based, student-centered, "hands-on" science instruction. The next section of this chapter highlights each of the eleven Texas science standards for the Generalist EC-4 TExES (Competencies 020–023).

 # Standard I Science Instruction

Competency 020: The science teacher manages classroom, field, and laboratory activities to ensure the safety of all students and the ethical care and treatment of organisms and specimens.

The beginning teacher considers safety considerations as essential in the hands-on science classroom of today. Curiosity and immaturity combine to present hazards with even the most common materials. This standard requires that the teacher knows and understands safety regulations and guidelines, procedures for responding to an accident in the laboratory, including first aid, legal issues associated with accidents, potential safety hazards, and modification of equipment for students with special needs. In the classroom, the teacher employs safe practices by arranging the space for storage, traffic flow, and access to each student. The teacher is responsible for reading the Materials Safety Data Sheet (MSDS) and other chemical labels and for ensuring that safety equipment, including an eye washer, a fire blanket, and a fire extinguisher, is available. The teacher needs to check all materials prior to use and must create an environment where rules and safety procedures are important. Potential hazards in the field, including insect bites, poisonous plants, and allergies, require planning and preparation. They should not, however, be used as an excuse for avoiding field investigations listed in the TEKS grade level. Finally classroom pets are a wonderful way to promote responsibility and encourage scientific observations. Considerations must be given to the possibilities of allergies, appropriate instruction in care and treatment, and extra supervision to ensure the careful handling of animals.

Consider the following practice question:

Ms. Davis, a third-grade teacher, intends to continually reinforce the importance of safety in the science classroom and makes sure that:

A. safety rules are posted in the room.
B. the class previews each activity together to identify potential hazards.
C. signed safety contracts are required at the beginning of the year.
D. safety is part of each student's grade.

The teacher realizes that even if grades are used (*D*), safety rules are posted (*A*), and safety contracts are signed at the beginning of the year. (*C*), students will need *constant* reminders for all activities because they may include specific hazards. The correct answer is *B*.

Laboratory safety begins in the planning stages, where activities need to be evaluated and risks minimized. Plastic containers are substituted for glass; food allergies are considered; and appropriate management, preparation, and proactive measures are employed. However, accidents can happen even in the most carefully planned instruction. Therefore, safety procedures must be practiced.

In 1965, the Texas Board of Health adopted standards for eye and face protection. Later, the U.S. Congress passed the Occupational Health and Safety Act (OSHA) and in 1986, Texas enacted the Texas Hazardous Communication Act (HazCom). These acts govern how employees (and students) must be informed of potential risks involved in handling scientific materials and how materials that may harm the environment are to be disposed of. This information is found on the **Material Safety Data Sheet (MSDS)** for every chemical substance with which employees (and students) come into contact, including cleaning agents, laboratory chemicals, and other products. Schools *must* keep an up-to-date record of all MSDSs for every chemical on site. This record is displayed in a centralized location and available for inspection.

Safety equipment should be available in every room. Even with proper use of safety goggles and safety glasses, an emergency eye washer (either fixed or portable) is essential in case of eye contamination from chemicals or foreign material. Fire extinguishers, fire blankets, and practiced procedures of "stop-drop-and-roll" are necessary whenever flame or heat is used. The use of personal protective equipment (goggles); proper storage, use, and disposal of materials; and the need for a safety contract and clearly posted rules are all included in this competency.

Numerous sources are available for additional safety information. Each campus should have a copy of the **"Texas Safety Standards"** (http://www .utdanacenter.org/sciencetoolkit/safety). Then click on *Texas Safety Standards for Kindergarten-Grade 12*. The major safety points to remember include:

- Obtain and review all state and district guidelines and policies.
- Provide appropriate safety instruction, including a safety quiz and safety contract for students and parents to sign.
- Instruct students on proper use of safety equipment—goggles, fire extinguishers, etc.
- Provide practice sessions for safety rules and procedures.
- Identify potential hazards and provide appropriate safety precautions before each activity.
- Instruct students to immediately report any personal injury, damaged equipment, and hazard potentials.
- Do not permit students to handle science supplies or equipment until they have been given specific instruction in their use.
- Prevent loose clothing and/or hair from coming into contact with science supplies, chemicals, or equipment.
- Instruct students in the proper care and handling of classroom pets and organisms.
- Expect the unexpected, never taking hazards for granted.

Try the following practice question:

After using cabbage juice, vinegar, lemon juice, egg white, and baking soda to identify acids and bases with litmus paper, the teacher should:

A. dismiss students to their next classes immediately.
B. instruct students to return unused chemicals to their original containers.
C. instruct students to clean work surfaces and wash their hands.
D. have students move away from tables so that the teacher can clean the area properly.

The *best* answer is *C.* Returning unused chemicals to original containers (*B*) might lead to contamination. Other labeled containers should be used to store unused chemicals. Answers *A* and *D* fail to promote safety consciousness and appropriate practices, leaving little responsibility to students (although answers *C* and *D* list two appropriate procedures for chemical use with children). The correct answer is *C.*

Standard II Using Science Tools, Materials, Equipment, and Technologies

Competency 020: The science teacher understands the correct use of tools, materials, equipment, and technologies.

The beginning teacher knows and understands concepts of precision and accuracy in the process of data collection. The teacher can use grade-appropriate equipment and technology for gathering, analyzing, and reporting data. This includes the use of the International System of Measurement (i.e., the metric system) and the ability to perform conversions within and across measurement systems. Scientific communications include the teachers' ability to organize, display, and communicate data in a variety of ways (e.g., charts, tables, graphs, diagrams, written reports, and oral presentations).

Consider the following practice question:

After providing laboratory equipment for her fourth-grade students, Ms. Estrada notices that the triple beam pan balance is not even. She should:

A. instruct students to add a few gram masses until the balance is even.
B. use that balance for only weighing large objects because it is not accurate.
C. level the balance by using the adjustment dial.
D. use a different balance.

The triple beam balance has an adjustment dial that balances the pan with the beam masses. Adjustment is necessary after the balance has been relocated. Answers *A* and *B* might work as solutions, but they do not model the importance of accuracy in science. Option *D* is unnecessary. The correct answer is *C*.

In the collection of data through observations, scientists use many tools. Magnifying lenses, microscopes, telescopes, and measuring devices (e.g., Pyrex beakers, graduated cylinders, and balances) would be included in a science classroom. Equipment for the EC-4 classroom needs to be developmentally appropriate. For example, **double-pan balances** in early grades are used to indicate less-than and more-than relationships with regard to weight. Teachers must also be familiar with the correct terminology and use of the equipment so they can instruct their students. For instance, a liquid tends to adhere and curve upward on the sides of graduated cylinders. Teachers should know that measurements must be taken by reading the bottom of this curved liquid, called a **meniscus**, in order to obtain an accurate measurement.

Try the following practice question:

Mr. Landry starts a lesson on the proper use of a microscope and *first* has children:

A. identify the parts of the microscope: the stage, eyepiece, and arm.
B. make slides to view under high magnification.
C. explain the difference between high- and low-power magnification.
D. predict the total magnification power of the instrument.

The students need to correctly identify and name the parts of the microscope. This procedure facilitates subsequent important instructions for microscope use. Although *B*, *C*, and *D* might be appropriate at some point in the lesson, the students would need the microscope terminology to use and follow directions. The correct answer is *A*.

Data collection and interpretation are included in this standard, and the teacher is expected to promote scientific communication through graphing. The third- and fourth-grade TEKS include the following student expectations related to scientific inquiry: "construct graphs, tables, maps, charts to organize, examine, evaluate information" and "analyze and interpret information to construct explanations from direct and indirect evidence" and "communicate valid conclusions."

Students will be able to interpret graphs if they have had experience in constructing them. Teachers should provide numerous opportunities for students to collect and organize data. Bar graphs are used for data of groups, sets, or categories. Early grades often collect categorical data and organize bar graphs, for example, for types of weather, car and bus riders, favorite foods and clothing, pets, and birthday months. *Line graphs* are useful for comparing two sets of continuous numbers and finding the relationship between those data. Technology can also be used to collect data on simple spreadsheets and design graphs, and students can communicate results using presentation software.

Consider the following practice question:

Mr. Gray's paper recycling project allowed the third graders to collect data. Children presented the information each week as pie charts showing percentage of mass recycled per class. At the end of the year, the children wanted to know how the percentage for their grade had changed throughout the year. How should the data be represented?

A. Pie chart
B. Line graph
C. Bar graph
D. Data table

The *pie chart* (A) was used per week for results, but this format would not show change over time (only percentages of a whole). A *bar graph* (C) would best show categories on the *x*-axis (i.e., types of paper recycled such as newspaper, copy paper, etc.). A *data table* does organize data, but this format does not have visual impact to depict changes throughout the year. The correct answer is a *line graph.* The manipulated variable on the *x*-axis (**horizontal**) would be numerical and continuous (weeks per year), and the responding variable on the *y*-axis (**vertical**) would be the third-grade percentage each week. A line graph would clearly depict the relationship between these variables, and the trends of increasing or decreasing recycling would be evident and visual. The correct answer is *B.*

Let's look at the *pie chart* used by Mr. Gray's students to show the percentage of weight recycled each week by each class. Note that weekly data would best be represented as the *pie chart* in Figure 5.1.

In order to organize and analyze information, data are often recorded in tables. A *data table* is organized lists of information or observations that should be titled and labeled for clear understanding (an example is shown in Table 5.1).

This information can be visually represented on a line graph (as in Figure 5.2) because the data for both variables (time and population) are continuous and numerical.

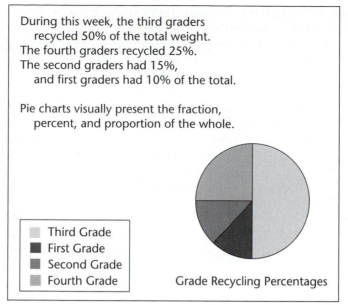

During this week, the third graders
   recycled 50% of the total weight.
The fourth graders recycled 25%.
The second graders had 15%,
   and first graders had 10% of the total.

Pie charts visually present the fraction,
   percent, and proportion of the whole.

Third Grade
First Grade
Second Grade
Fourth Grade   Grade Recycling Percentages

FIGURE 5.1 Pie Chart

TABLE 5.1   Yearly Catfish Population in Big Star Lake

Year	Catfish Population
1999	550
2000	800
2001	1200
2002	700

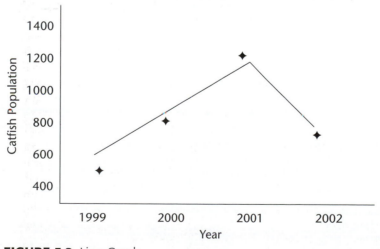

FIGURE 5.2 Line Graph

The **manipulative variable (MV)** is always plotted on the *x*-axis (horizontal), and the **responding variable (RV)** is plotted on the *y*-axis (vertical). Line graphs allow us to determine increasing and decreasing trends (e.g., the catfish population increased from 1999 to 2001) and to determine data values that fall between collected data points on the graph line. For example, what was the population halfway in-between 1999 and 2000? (The answer is 67.5.) Teachers should ask many questions, including which year had the highest catfish population, the lowest population, and so forth. They can also ask the students to: (1) identify patterns and trends—which year looks different than the rest, (2) make inferences—explain what happened to the population between 2001 and 2002, and (3) make predictions—what do you think will happen to the population in 2003? Thus, the line graph is the best format to depict the annual data for fish in a nearby lake for Mr. Gray's class.

Try the following practice question:

During a kindergarten science lesson on animals, Ms. Lowe gave each student a box of animal cookies and asked them to sort the animals by shape. These animal data could be visually represented best as a:

A. data table. **C.** pie chart.
B. line graph. **D.** bar graph.

The categorical data (type of animal) would be the manipulative variable (MV) on the *x*-axis (horizontal), and the number of that type would be the responding variable on the *y*-axis (vertical). A data table (*A*) could list this same information, but it is not visual. A line graph (*B*) is used for continuous, numerical data. A pie chart (*C*) helps to show data collected as parts of a whole. The bar graph would clearly show which type of animal was most represented and which was least represented. The correct answer is *D*.

FIGURE 5.3
A graph in progress

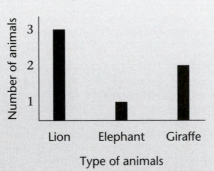

Finally, this standard on tools, equipment, and technologies includes emphasis on measurement and the metric system.

Consider the following practice question:

A first-grade teacher wants to introduce measurement to her students. She gives each group of students five objects to observe and asks them to compare the objects to a:

A. metric ruler.
B. standard ruler.
C. student's shoe.
D. yard stick.

First-grade students should use measurement aids without numbers to compare and develop *greater than* and *less than* concepts. Upper-grade students would use standard measurement tools—*A, B,* or *D*—where divisions and markings are clearly understood and are appropriate for the task. The correct answer is *C.*

Scientists use measurement to quantify their observations. For example, an observation of a "large" butterfly has no frame of reference, but a butterfly with a 4-centimeter wingspan is more specific. Scientists are careful that the measuring instrument is appropriate for the task. For example, a graduated cylinder with 1 milliliter markings is more accurate than a beaker with 50 milliliter lines. **Graduated cylinders** are designed and manufactured specifically for liquid measurement. Measurements are often repeated and averaged to increase their validity and reliability.

The *International System of Units* or the **metric system** was adopted internationally for use in 1960. All but two countries quickly made the conversion to the metric system, and this system is used internationally for commerce and scientific work. The metric system was designed to relate mass, distance, and volume for pure water. A cubic box that is one centimeter on each side has a volume of $1 \times 1 \times 1 = 1$ cubic centimeter (volume = length $\times$ width $\times$ height). The amount of water that would fill such a box is defined in the metric system as one milliliter, and it has a mass of one gram (at standard temperature and pressure).

The metric system makes use of base units—**gram** for mass, **meter** for length, and **liter** for volume. Prefixes (e.g., kilo-, deci-, milli-) modify the base units. Converting within the metric system is as easy as adding a zero or moving the decimal point, because each prefix represents a factor of ten. The

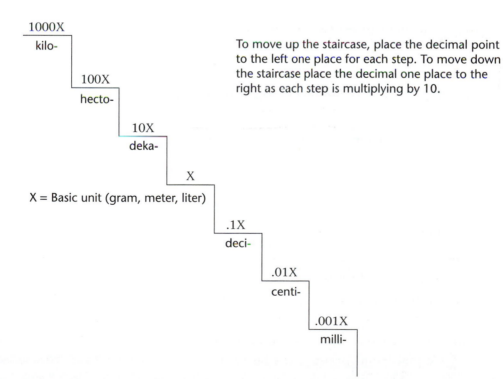

FIGURE 5.4 Metric Ladder

staircase depicted in Figure 5.4 is a visualization of how these prefixes are related. To help you remember this order, you might use a memory model for the first letter of each word (King Henry danced [a] dizzy, crazy minuet) or one of your own.

For example, since there are 10 millimeters in each centimeter, 10 centimeters in each decimeter, and 10 decimeters in a meter, there are 1,000 (10 × 10 × 10) millimeters in a meter. A kilogram is a measure of mass that represents 10 hectograms, 100 dekagrams, and 1,000 grams.

Try the following metric conversions:

_____ centiliters = 4 liters (L)   27 meters = _____ millimeters (mm)

_____ dekagrams = 50 grams (g)   5 liters = _____ centiliters (cl)

_____ kilometers = 140 hectometers (hm)   .05 kilometers = _____ meters (m)

_____ centigrams = 75 dekagrams (dcg)   65 kilograms = _____ dekagrams (dcg)

Answers: 400 centiliters = 4 liters; 5 dekagrams = 50 grams; 14 kilometers = 140 hectometers; 75,000 centigrams = 75 dekagrams; 27 meters = 27,000 millimeters; 5 liters = 500 centiliters; .05 kilometers = 50 meters; 65 kilograms = 6,500 dekagrams. Also note the abbreviations used.

Several common but important measurements and their metric values are listed below:

- Boiling point of pure water at sea level: 100 degrees Celsius (212 degrees Fahrenheit)
- Freezing point of pure water at sea level: 0 degrees Celsius (32 degrees Fahrenheit)
- Normal human body temperature: 37 degrees Celsius (98.6 degrees Fahrenheit)
- Distance from the sun to the earth: 149,637,000 kilometers (93,000,000 miles) (Conversion factor, 1 mile = 1.609 km)
- Weight of 10 pound bag of potatoes: 4.54 kg (Conversion factor, 2.2 pounds = 1 kg)
- 15 gallon tank of gasoline: 56.775 liters (Conversion factor, 1 gallon = 3.785 liters)

Try the following practice question:

Mrs. Henry is teaching her third-grade students to measure mass in the metric system. Which of the following measurements represents the smallest mass?

A. .045 grams
B. 78 milligrams
C. .009 kilograms
D. .333 hectograms

The least amount of mass cannot be determined until all choices are converted to the same unit. For example, one yard is more than 27 inches, even though the number 27 is greater than the number 1. "Apples" must be compared to "apples" to make a comparison. Converting all the choices into grams would yield (A) .045 grams, (B) .078 grams, (C) 9 grams, and (D) 33.3 grams. Clearly, .045 grams is the least value. The correct answer is A.

Standard III Science Inquiry

Competency 020: The science teacher understands the process of scientific inquiry and its role in science instruction.

The beginning teacher understands that the type of scientific investigation used depends on the questions to be answered. The teacher understands the use of technology in scientific research and the principles and procedures used in conducting descriptive studies, controlled experiments, and comparative data analysis. The teacher links prior knowledge and experience to the investigations and focuses inquiry-based activities from questions and issues that are relevant to the students. The teacher models the processes of scientific inquiry by using combinations of the following:

- *Asking a scientific question, formulating a testable hypothesis.*
- *Selecting appropriate equipment and technology for gathering information.*
- *Making observations and collecting data.*
- *Organizing, analyzing, and evaluating data to find trends and patterns and making inferences.*
- *Communicating and defending a valid conclusion about the hypothesis under investigation.*

Consider the following practice question:

Mr. Lopez has completed a fourth-grade unit on the environment and intends to assess students' ability to use higher-order thinking skills to draw conclusions based on experimental data. Given a graph of alternative fuels and the resulting air pollution, the students would be able to:

A. evaluate which alternative fuel would be best for the environment.
B. describe the process of measuring resulting air pollution.
C. predict what new alternative fuel will be invented in the future.
D. list three alternative fuels.

As this is an evaluation-level question, the student is required to use knowledge and synthesis to think at a higher level. Correctly reading the graph could include answer *D*, but the listing task requires only the lowest level of knowledge. Basing the conclusions from the graphed information, in this case, would not enable the student to describe the process (*B*) or to predict (*C*) future events. The correct answer is *A*.

Science teachers are able to promote scientific attitudes related to inquiry and skepticism through careful investigations and analysis of results. Challenging students to: (1) make predictions; (2) develop research questions; (3) form hypotheses; (4) conduct descriptive, experimental, and correlational investigations; and (5) correctly analyze the results enables them to become problem solvers and critical thinkers. Questions from all levels of Bloom's taxonomy allow students to use the knowledge of facts and vocabulary to build comprehension through explanations in their own words and applications of the knowledge in other contexts. Higher levels of thinking include analysis—taking apart, comparing/contrasting; synthesis—putting together, designing/creating; and evaluation—recommending/judging based on selected criteria. Assisting students in developing higher-order thinking prepares them for the level of scientific literacy they would need (for example, to read a newspaper story about a new medical discovery [or diet drug] and be able to question the report's authors, their sources of information, the investigation's methods, and the interpretation of the data). In an effort to promote the science educational reforms that produce a scientifically literate society, students need authentic experiences with critical thinking and analysis in real-world contexts. Teachers should promote conversations between young scientists to encourage them to see each other as resources and demonstrate that more is learned when scientific information is shared.

Try the following practice question:

During a second-grade science lesson about states of matter and heat, Ms. Curtis allows children to observe the physical changes of an ice cube placed in a sunny spot on the playground. Which of the following questions regarding the melting of the ice cube would be most effective in encouraging students' use of higher-order thinking skills about the effect of heat on matter?

A. What is the amount of time it takes for the ice cube to melt?
B. What would happen if the ice cube were placed in the shade?
C. Why does the melted liquid look bigger than the original ice cube?
D. What is the temperature of the sunny spot?

Making predictions would require students to use their observations to hypothesize about the amount of heat and the effect of the heat on the ice cube in the shade. Although the time (*A*) and temperature (*D*) could be recorded, these answers do not require higher-order thinking. Choice *C* would allow students to make predictions but does not directly involve the effect of heat on states of matter. Making use of students' questions is a good way for teachers to advance higher-level thinking and problem solving. Teachers should be flexible, continuing the investigations and promoting student inquiry. The correct answer is *B.*

Consider the following practice question:

Mrs. Glenn, a first-grade teacher, wants her students to understand the scientific process of classification. She provides a container of different rocks to each group of students. What question should she first use to direct her students?

A. How many rocks does your group have?
B. Can the rocks be sorted into two groups? Explain the grouping of each rock.
C. Can you predict where each of these rocks came from?
D. How can you find more about each rock?

Although choices *C* and *D* might be interesting and appropriate for instruction, the objective is to practice classification. Choice *A* requires a response based on low-level knowledge, one that does not require classifying. The correct answer is *B.*

Teachers realize that scientific inquiry is promoted through the practice and use of science process skills. Each of the TEKS grade levels begins with an emphasis on science process skills that can be used in the classroom on a daily basis.

The **basic science process skills** include:

- **Observing:** Using the five senses to describe objects and events. Observations can be qualitative (e.g., color, shape) or quantitative (e.g., length, mass, volume).
- **Classifying:** Sorting objects or events into groups based on common characteristics or attributes.
- **Measuring:** Determining the length, volume, mass, temperature, or area to describe and quantify objects.
- **Communicating:** Sharing observations and explanations of objects or events with others.

The **integrated process skills** include:

- **Inferring and predicting:** Explaining or drawing conclusions about an object or future event based upon observations.
- **Using variables:** Studying effects of manipulating and controlling variables.
- **Representing data:** Organizing observations and measurements to make data useful.
- **Experimenting:** Using the process skills necessary to ask a question, plan an investigation, collect data, and form a conclusion.

All children can use their curiosity to observe the natural world around them. Children must be encouraged to use their senses to make observations and gather data. When children are able to use their own senses to gain information, they remember it much longer than they would if it had simply been told or read to them. Science with the senses literally comes alive. Even Pre-K and kindergartners routinely communicate selected weather conditions at calendar time, classifying their results and representing the data through pictures or graphs. Teachers can often integrate these skills throughout other content areas by infusing prediction into a reading assignment, measuring into a mathematics lesson, or observation in the fine arts and P.E.

Consider the following practice question:

The second-grade TEKS (2.7A) expects children to "observe, measure, record, analyze, predict, and illustrate changes in size, mass, temperature, color, position, quantity, sound, and movement." The teacher supplies thick and thin rubber bands stretched over cardboard box lids. The students design a controlled experiment with a testable hypothesis to find out if sound produced by plucking the thick and thin rubber bands is different. The experimental design must include all of the following *except:*

A. manipulative variables—thick and thin rubber bands.
B. responding variables—same or different sounds heard.
C. controlled variables—same-size box lids, and same person plucking each rubber band with the same force.
D. a diagram for data.

Although a diagram or visual organizer could be a part of the lab, the actual experiment must include *A, B,* and *C.* Controlled experiments should also be repeated and the data averaged when necessary. The correct answer is *D.*

Scientists use specific processes and criteria to investigate and interpret the natural world. This procedure is called the **scientific method**, and it involves seeking observable evidence in a systematic process. This process begins with **observations** that can be gained from the senses and/or enhanced through technology. For example, a thermometer provides a quantitative measurement rather than a vague sense of feeling hot or cold.

For scientists, observations lead to questions about "why?" or "what if?" These questions lead to the examination of existing knowledge on the subject in order to learn more about the phenomena they are questioning. This research step is important because the problem may have already been studied or an answer discovered, or new findings could lead the scientists toward a possibly different **hypothesis** or "educated guess" about the solution. The **experiment** is a means of comparing an unknown set of circumstances to one that is known or controlled. A **variable** is a factor that affects the outcome of the experiment. **Manipulative variables** are able to be changed—such as changing the thick rubber band to the thin one to see what new outcome in sound will occur in the preceding question. An ideal experiment tests only one variable at a time and compares the result to a **control** setting (where the variable is not present or consistent). This method helps to clarify or examine the outcome, identify possible cause-and-effect relationships, and make predictions for further study. After a hypothesis has withstood repeated testing and experimentation, the hypothesis can be called a **scientific theory**—a general explanation of a group of related phenomena.

Teachers should continuously use events and activities that stimulate students' questions and curiosity. Students should have opportunities to explore these events. Sometimes this exploration can be unstructured and more like play. Instructional structure is needed at other times. This format is conducive for the investigation procedures described above. This instructional approach is often called **inquiry-based** or **discovery**. Its goal is to foster engagement, scientific thinking processes, and student-generated generalizations.

Consider the following practice question:

Third-grade students notice that recently planted bushes near the edge of the playground are all brown. The teacher uses their observations to promote inquiry about plant growth and environmental conditions. What step should they take next to follow the scientific method?

A. Research the plant type to determine its ideal growing conditions.
B. Write a report for the school newspaper about their observations.
C. Formulate a testable hypothesis or an educated guess.
D. Plant some new bushes and add water daily.

The students' observations lead to questions, and now they must undertake research to narrow their possible explanations. Then they can form a testable hypothesis (*C*) and set up an experiment in which water, soil conditions, sunlight, and/or temperature can be investigated. The cause of the plants' condition may not be a matter of water (*D*), and their scientific reporting (*B*) should be undertaken after they have tested their hypothesis. The correct answer is *A*, research what they can find out about the situation first.

Standard IV Teaching Science

Competency 020: The science teacher has theoretical and practical knowledge about teaching science and about how students learn science.

The beginning teacher knows the developmental characteristics of students and how that influences science learning. The teacher understands the importance of play for the Pre-K child at a water table and the need for manipulatives and concrete experiences for the young child. Teachers use developmentally appropriate methods to plan and implement inquiry-based science programs. They establish a collaborative scientific community that supports actively engaged learning and make accommodations for the needs of all students. Teachers must use strategies that assist students in the development of content-area vocabulary; word meaning in content-related texts; and comprehension before, during, and after reading content-related texts. Teachers must understand common student misconceptions in science and learn theories about how students develop scientific under-standing. In the classroom, teachers will sequence learning activities in a way that allows students to build upon their prior knowledge and challenges them to expand their understanding of science. This can be done through lab and field investigations that promote curiosity, openness to new ideas, and skepticism. Teachers will use a variety of instructional strategies to ensure all students' reading comprehension of content-related texts. They will assist students in locating and retaining content-related information from a range of texts and technologies. Teachers will also help students to locate the meanings and pronunciations of unfamiliar content-related words through dictionaries. Teachers will respect student diversity and use questioning strategies to move students from concrete to more abstract understanding. As a facilitator, teachers will expect students to be active participants through individual, small group, and whole-class strategies. Working with others provides a model of the scientific community where researchers often communicate and share findings.

Consider the following practice question:

Ms. Peters has been teaching her second-grade science unit on dinosaurs by reading about dinosaurs and having students color pictures. After all, she says, there are really no hands-on approaches to studying dinosaurs because they aren't around anymore. Which activity would be *least* consistent with developments in science education about how students learn science?

   A. Include hands-on experiments about fossils—pressing shells in play dough for example.
   B. Include hands-on measurement activities to compare dinosaur size to animals of today—lifting strings with helium balloons to show and compare the heights of some dinosaurs, for example.
   C. Include use of computer technology to visit an archeological site.
   D. Show the movie *Jurassic Park*.

The hands-on activities (*A* and *B*) are developmentally appropriate and in keeping with research about how second graders—who are concrete learners—would best learn. Choice *C* stresses tech-nology, and a computer archeology site would provide a visual of authentic science—opportuni-ties for career discussions and connections of relevance to the real world. Showing a video (*D*) is not the best choice, as it is passive, and students may not be involved. The correct answer is *D*.

Understanding how students learn and making modifications in instructional strategies are hallmarks of an effective teacher. Learning theories from *Piaget, Bandura,* and *Vygotsky* provide the teacher with a theoretical framework and tools for success in the classroom. Most preservice programs require an educational psychology course, and the early childhood focus usually outlines the *stage theory* of Piaget's cognitive development. From sensorimotor to preoperational stages, language development is rapid, because speech is used to express understanding of observations of children's worlds. The concrete operation stage is characterized by **conservation**—the ability to hold or save a mental picture (a short wide jar holds the same amount as a tall thin one) and ability to *reverse* physical change. It is important to realize that children in the elementary grades need hands-on experiences and manipulative materials because they are concrete learners and often unable to visualize an abstract concept. Piaget's final period of formal operations from age 11 through adulthood is a period when students are able to solve problems in a logical and systematic way and to think abstractly. Using the scientific method independently, they can then design experiments and refine the skills taught in earlier grades. According to Piaget, children acquire physical knowledge, logico-mathematical knowledge, and social knowledge through the interactions with their environment. Teachers of young children should provide stimulating, concrete experiences and promote problem-solving activities to enhance knowledge development.

Vygotsky, who theorized about the role of cognitive development in social interactions, developed the *Zone of Proximal Development* concept—an area of cognitive development that can be enhanced with instruction that presents ideas and materials that are just ahead of the child's current cognitive status. Both Piaget and Vygotsky stress the importance of the *construction of knowledge* by the learner. Unlike a blank slate to be filled by the teacher, the child comes with experiences and prior schema (sometimes misconceptions) that need to be challenged.

The instructional strategy of the *learning cycle* fits the view of constructivists' learning theory. Often described as the "5Es," the steps are:

Engage

Explore

Explain

Elaborate

Evaluate

First, the teacher gains attention and uses a focus to introduce the lesson. Asking questions generates curiosity about the concept, **engages** the learner, and can be a means to assess prior knowledge. Using a *KWL chart* (what I know—what I want to know—what I learned), for example, the teacher can *identify concepts and misconceptions*. Next, students **explore** the materials—a natural response that encourages curiosity and stimulates more questions. As a facilitator, the teacher challenges students' observations and *prompts discussions*. In the third step of **explaining**, it is the teacher's role to define vocabulary, clarify results, and help draw conclusions. The **elaboration** step allows the student to use and transfer the concept knowledge in a new way. These are usually the extension activities or try-at-home examples that students design on their own. Finally, **evaluation** includes the numerous ideas and examples in Standard V that follows.

In the classroom, there are numerous programs and opportunities to include technology and enhance learning. The videodisc format of *Windows on Science,* information searches on the Internet, CD-ROM and simulation activities, data collection and participation in programs like the international GLOBE (http://www.globe.gov/fsl/workshop/registration.p) all help to compress or expand time and space while ensuring safety and availability of experiences. Teachers and students may also use simple database programs to organize information and word processing or visual presentation software programs to report and share results.

Consider the following practice question:

Ms. Helms recognizes that her students are struggling with a social studies chapter and the concept of community when one student declares, "Look, it's like the ants in our ant farm. Some work, some take care of the young—but together, everything can get done." Ms. Helms's *best* response is:

A. "Good point. But ants are animals, and people are people."
B. "Well, yes, how else can you compare these two systems?"
C. "Well, yes, but ants are just acting out of instinct."
D. "Good point. But we're studying social studies now—not science."

Using an ant farm in the first place was a great science lesson for Ms. Helms' students. Integrating the concrete example as a model for the abstract concept of community is developmentally appropriate and cognitively beneficial for the students. Higher-order thinking through analogies establishes more cognitive connections for the students. Answer (D) does not promote interdisciplinary learning. Answer (A) and (C) do not enable students to make connections in learning. The correct answer is B.

Standard V Assessment

Competency 020: The science teacher knows the varied and appropriate assessments and assessment practices to monitor science learning.

*The beginning teacher knows the relationship between curriculum, assessment, and instruction and understands the importance of monitoring and assessing students' science knowledge and skills on a regular, ongoing basis. In the area of assessment, the teacher knows the importance of validity, reliability, and absence of bias. Also, the teacher knows the purposes and uses of various types of assessments, including **diagnostic** (before), **formative** (during), and **summative** (after). Teachers know strategies for assessing students' prior knowledge and can use assessment to inform instructional practice. They share evaluation criteria with students and engage students in meaningful self-assessment. In the classroom, the teacher can use formal and informal assessments of science performance, including rubrics, portfolios, student profiles, journals, and checklists and can base decisions regarding instructional content, methods, and practice on information about students' strengths and needs gathered through assessment.*

Consider the following practice question:

Second graders are learning the scientific process in TEKS 2.10, in which they are expected to describe and illustrate the water cycle. The teacher provides numerous hands-on activities for students to observe evaporation, condensation, and precipitation related to the water cycle. She asks questions during the activities and reteaches when necessary. How should the teacher grade the students on their understanding of the objective?

   A. Give one final written test with matching items.
   B. Have students write definitions of the vocabulary.
   C. Use a rubric that contains knowledge and skills attained.
   D. Have students do a self-assessment.

The teacher should grade students' understanding of the objective through multidimensional means (rather than by a single attribute [*A*]). Although definitions might be part of the instruction, they do not allow the student to "describe or illustrate" or show understanding of the water cycle (*B*). The rubric contains the knowledge and skills attained and can be used to grade students on their activities, questions and answers, cooperative group participation, and understanding. Self-assessment (*D*), though desired, does not allow for a grade. The correct answer is *C*.

Reform efforts in science education include mandates for instruction and for assessment. We cannot continue to evaluate students with one unidimensional measurement. Knowledge and understanding should be assessed through *formal* and *informal* means. *Authentic assessment* includes observations by the teacher with a shift from a behavioral to a cognitive view of learning. Teachers should use tasks that represent meaningful instructional activities that tap productive thinking and problem-solving skills. Children should be encouraged to collect their work over time and develop portfolios or presentations of their knowledge. With multiple learning styles comes assessment through audio, visual, tactile, and kinesthetic means. Student performance of the water cycle could include a skit of a water drop, the sun, a cloud of water vapor, a thundercloud full of water, rain, and all the processes of evaporation, condensation, and precipitation clearly represented through materials, songs, and hand motions.

Standard VI History and Nature of Science

Competency 020: The science teacher understands the history and nature of science.

The beginning teacher knows the limitations of the scope of science and the use and limitations of physical, mathematical, and conceptual models to describe and analyze scientific ideas about the natural world. He or she knows that science ideas and explanations must be consistent with observational and experimental evidence but realizes that science is a human endeavor influenced by societal, cultural, and personal views of the world. Teachers understand that scientific theories are constantly being modified to conform more closely to new observational and experimental evidence about the natural world. They understand how logical reasoning is used in the process of developing, evaluating, and validating scientific hypotheses and theories. They appreciate the principles of scientific ethics and the role of publishing and peer review in the development and validation of scientific knowledge. Teachers understand the historical developments of science and respect the contributions that diverse cultures and individuals of both genders have made to the body of scientific knowledge. In the classroom, teachers can analyze, review, and critique the strengths and weaknesses of scientific explanations, hypotheses, and theories using scientific evidence and explanation. Viewing science as a way of knowing, they can provide students with opportunities to examine types of questions that science can and cannot answer. They can use examples from the history of science to demonstrate the changing nature of scientific theories and knowledge. They can analyze ways in which personal or societal bias can affect the direction, support, and use of scientific research and design instruction that accounts for the contributions of individuals from a variety of cultures.

Science is often viewed as a body of knowledge that resulted from years of experiments. Formal science training often included the memorization of endless concepts, terms, and formulas. Today, science education is viewed as a verb—as a way of thinking and acting and as an expanding body of knowledge that cannot possibly be memorized. In fact, estimates of the knowledge explosion predict that scientific information doubles every two to five years. Teaching your students how scientists developed their experiments and analyzed their results will be more useful than simply memorizing a definition that they may not understand. Learning about the people involved in the production of scientific knowledge will give students a sense of career awareness. They need role models, guest speakers, and diverse cultural examples to make science come alive. Learning about the struggles of science will teach lessons of persistence, patience, and the excitement of discovery.

Numerous resources are available for the teacher to integrate the history and nature of science into the classroom. The National Public Radio presentations of Dr. John Lienhard's "Engines of Our Ingenuity" are broadcast twice daily and are available from the Web site at http://www.uh.edu/engines. A simple Web search of "scientists" gives links to women in science at http://www.astr.ua.edu/4000WS/4000WS.html, to African Americans in the sciences at http://webfiles.uci.edu/mcbrown/display/faces.html, and to numerous pages on **Albert Einstein** (theory of relativity), **Thomas Edison** (electricity), **Sir Isaac Newton** (laws of motion), **Madame Curie** (radioactivity), **Antonio Novello** (first Hispanic surgeon general), **Mae Jemison** (first African American woman in space), **Dr. Daniel Hale Williams** (African American doctor who performed the first successful heart surgery), **Louis Pasteur** (pasteurization), **Barbara McClintock** (only woman to win an unshared Nobel Prize in Physiology or Medicine for genetic research), and others.

Students should know that **Lewis Latimer**, the son of slaves who escaped to freedom in Boston, drew the patent for **Alexander Graham Bell's** original telephone and he himself invented the carbon filament for the incandescent electric light. They should realize that **Charles Drew**, another African American, was a pioneer researcher in the area of blood plasma preservation, saving thousands of soldiers' lives in World War II through establishment of blood banks. Yet he died from loss of blood following a car accident near a hospital that admitted only whites. We can have a greater appreciation for the contributions to science made by people who overcame discrimination. Women like **Rachel Carson**, who wrote *Silent Spring* in 1962, testified before Congress and withstood the attacks of the chemical industry who denounced her as a hysterical woman for her attention to environmental issues. Women like **Sally Ride**, who became the first U.S. woman to go into space, serve as examples for females in the classrooms today.

Standard VII Personal and Social Decision Making

Competency 020: The science teacher understands how science affects the daily lives of students and how science interacts with and influences personal and societal decisions.

The beginning teacher knows the role that science can play in helping to resolve personal, societal, and global challenges. The teacher understands how human decisions about the use of science and technology are based on factors such as ethical standards, economics, and societal and personal needs. Teachers understand the properties of natural ecosystems and how natural and human processes can influence changes in the environment. They know about concepts related to changes in populations and to characteristics of human population growth that impact consumption on the renewal and depletion of resources. Finally, they understand that scientific concepts and principles relate to personal and societal health, including the physiological and psychological effects and risks associated with the use of substances and substance abuse. In the classroom, the teacher can use situations from students' everyday lives to develop materials that investigate how science can be used to make informed decisions. They can apply scientific principles to analyze factors that influence personal choices concerning fitness and health and factors that affect the probability and severity of disease. They can demonstrate how factors such as population growth, use of resources, overconsumption, technological capacity, poverty, and societal views can influence changes in the environment. They can demonstrate how science can be used to make informed decisions about societal and global issues through the analysis of advantages and disadvantages of a course of action.

Understanding the relationship between science-technology-society (STS) helps students to appreciate the need for science in their daily lives. If they can observe the pollution problems from automobiles (technology) and realize that government decisions about air quality and emissions testing are possible societal responses, they can use their science information to make informed decisions. Older elementary students should be encouraged to collect newspaper articles about current STS issues in their community and in the world. Cutting down the rainforest, using land indiscriminately for oil exploration, transporting oil in tankers that spill and pollute the oceans, overpopulation, and overconsumption are current events issues that strongly impact the future. Students can access data collected from other students throughout the world—or establish their own research sites. The international GLOBE program (http://www.globe.gov/ghome/educators.html) trains teachers to work with their students in authentic inquiry. Activities from tracking El Niño temperatures, tree budding times, acid rain values, and global warming conditions can be accomplished by classroom "scientists." Teachers can also choose numerous texts that emphasize STS issues, including *Investigating and Evaluating STS Issues and Solutions* (Hungerford et al., 1997), that enhance critical thinking and problem-solving strategies by providing sample vignettes to analyze and rubrics that identify skills. Hopefully, these same students will become knowledgeable citizens of the future who can make better choices about environmental policies, land use, and government regulations.

 # Standard VIII Physical Science

Competency 021: The science teacher knows and understands the science content appropriate to teach the statewide curriculum (Texas Essential Knowledge and Skills) in physical science.

The beginning teacher has a basic understanding of physical science concepts and processes. These include properties of objects and materials; concepts of force and motion; concepts of heat, light, electricity, and magnetism; as well as conservation of energy and energy transformations. In the classroom, the teacher conducts demonstrations and facilitates experiments and experiences that promote understanding of these ideas.

In order to teach effectively, the teacher needs an understanding of the science concepts and definitions presented to the student at each grade level. A review of the TEKS for science at http://www.tea.state.tx.us/teks, teachers' manuals, and curriculum guides is a good place to start. Other resources include textbooks, dictionaries, CD-ROM encyclopedias, and Internet searches for key terms. Although TEKS at all grade levels begins with a stated emphasis on: (1) classroom and field investigations, (2) scientific inquiry, (3) critical thinking and decision making, and (4) tools and process skills of science, they also include examples of developmentally appropriate concepts and content. Stated concepts at lower grades may be studied again in upper grades in greater depth in a spiraling curriculum. For example, kindergarten TEKS states that the student is expected to "record observations about parts of plants including leaves, roots, stems, and flowers." The seventh-grade student also studies plants but is expected to "identify that radiant energy from the sun is transferred into chemical energy through the process of photosynthesis."

The following are examples of science concepts included in the TEKS for grades K–4:

- Kindergarten: Studies **changes** (weather, seasons, life cycles); explores the **natural world** (rocks, soil, water); and observes and describes **living organisms** (plants, animals).
- Grade 1: Studies **sources of water** (streams, lakes, oceans); compares *characteristics of living organisms*; identifies and tests ways that *heat* may cause change; manipulates objects to show relationship between **parts to the whole** (for example, a flashlight needs batteries to make it "whole").
- Grade 2: Collects information using **tools** including meter sticks; describes and illustrates the *water cycle*; demonstrates change in *motion* by applying force (push or pull); studies functions of *plant and animal parts*.

- Grade 3: Studies the sun and planets in our *solar system;* investigates *magnetism* and *gravity;* observes **states of matter** (solids, liquids, and gases); compares *adaptations* and *needs* of organisms, including habitat.
- Grade 4: Constructs *complex systems* (an electric circuit); draws conclusions using *fossils;* identifies the sun as a major source of energy; studies **properties of matter** (such as density); observes **patterns in nature** (such as metamorphosis, weather).

The following provides key science ideas selected from concepts included in the elementary TEKS.

Physical Science: Key Ideas

- All **matter** is made of particles called atoms. Matter is anything that occupies space and has mass. *Mass* and weight are not the same. **Mass** is the amount of matter in an object. **Weight** refers to the gravitational force between objects and the Earth (or another planet). For example, a person who weighs 130 pounds on Earth would weigh 275 pounds on Saturn but only about 18 pounds on the moon. **Density** is the ratio of mass/volume and helps explain how objects sink or float.
- **Matter** is found in three states—solid, liquid, and gas. Matter converts from one state to another by heating or cooling. When materials are heated, the **molecules** (combinations of atoms) move faster and spread farther apart so that the material expands. When cooled, material contracts. **The Law of Conservation of Matter** states that in ordinary chemical reactions matter is neither created nor destroyed but only changed from one form to another. All the existing molecules recombine into new combinations.
- **Atoms** contain protons and neutrons in the nucleus and electrons outside the **nucleus** (the core of the atom). Elements are composed of the same kind of atoms. Each element has a different number of protons and electrons. Compounds have combinations of two or more kinds of atoms.
- **Mixtures** are not chemical combinations and can be physically separated. In a **solution** the substance that dissolves is the **solute**, and the substance that does the dissolving is the **solvent**.
- **Energy** is defined as the ability to do work. Energy can be changed from one form to another. Stored energy is **potential energy**. When stored energy is released, it is changed to **kinetic energy** or motion energy. Kinetic energy depends on the mass and the speed of the object.
- The following **forms of energy** exist: *light, heat, sound, chemical, nuclear* or *atomic, mechanical,* and *electric.* Physical interactions typically convert one form of energy to others. For example, a flashlight converts electrical energy to light and heat energy. An automobile engine converts the chemical energy in fossil fuels to mechanical energy (chemical→mechanical).
- **Electricity** is a form of energy from electrons that provides light and heat. Two types of electricity are **static electricity** (when two materials rub together, and electrons are transferred) and **current electricity** (when electrical energy flows through a conductor in a circuit). **Conductors** are materials that allow the energy of electrons to move easily. **Insulators** are materials that resist the electrical flow of energy.
- **Heat** is a form of energy that transfers from one object to another by **conduction** (contact among moving molecules in solids), by **convection** (contact among moving currents of liquids and among gases), or by **radiation** (waves from the sun or other sources).

- **Magnets** exert a force (a push or a pull) within a region called a *magnetic field*. The **Law of Magnetic Attraction** states that two unlike poles attract each other, and two like poles repel each other. An **electromagnet** is a coil of conducting wire wrapped around a metal core. As electric current flows through the wire, the core becomes a temporary magnet.

- **Newton's** three **Laws of Motion**, established in the 1700s, state that an object at rest remains at rest unless a force acts on it to move it. That is, all objects have inertia—the tendency of an object to resist a change in the state of motion (**First Law of Motion**). This rule explains the importance of seat belts in auto accidents. **Acceleration** is any increase or decrease in the speed or direction of an object. It is related to mass and force in the following equation: F = ma (force = mass × acceleration). When forces are exerted on something, the greater force "wins." The **Third Law of Motion** states that for every action there is an equal and opposite reaction. This rule explains the forces operating in rocket, auto, and boat engines. Newton's laws opened the door for scientists to determine other laws that control our world.

- **Velocity** relates the speed and direction of a moving object. **Speed** is the distance an object moves in a given period of time.

- **Gravity** is the force that pulls (attracts) all physical objects toward each other.

- **Work** is force multiplied by the distance an object moves. In the metric system, force is measured in **newtons**. Thus, work is measured in **newton-meters**, more commonly called **joules**.

- **Simple machines** change how work is done by increasing/decreasing the amount of force or speed of force applied, changing the direction of the force, or transferring the force from one place to another. Examples of simple machines include *levers*—three classes of which differ by position of the fulcrum; *pulleys*—fixed and movable; *wheel and axle; inclined plane; wedge;* and *screw*. **Compound machines** contain one or more simple machines.

- **Waves** are described by their wavelength (frequency), speed, and amplitude. The electromagnetic spectrum is an arrangement of light and other electromagnetic waves of different frequencies. The **visible spectrum** includes the seven colors of light. These are red, orange, yellow, green, blue, indigo, and violet. **Opaque** objects are the color of light reflected; a **transparent** object is the color of light transmitted. Smooth surfaces reflect light waves. Light waves often bend (are refracted) when passing through one material to another. Laser light is an intense, narrow beam of light of one wavelength.

- **Sound** is created by the vibrations of a material and is transmitted via a material medium that can be a solid, liquid, or gas. Sounds are described by their pitch and intensity.

Consider the following practice questions:

Using a relevant application for science knowledge, Mr. Allen explains that the construction of homes built in the southern United States differs from those built in the northern United States in many ways. The placement of the heating/air-conditioning vents in Texas homes and buildings is usually in the ceiling because:

A. cold air is less dense than warm air, and conduction can occur.

B. warm air needs to be forced to circulate to the ceiling.

C. warm air is less dense than cold air, so it doesn't move.

D. cold air is denser than warm air, and convection can occur.

Cold air is denser (thicker) than warm air and will sink to the floor as the warmer air rises, producing a convection current that moves air within the room. If the cold air was released from floor vents, the air would not circulate because the warmer, lighter air would remain warmer near the ceiling. Using knowledge of density and convection in a real-world context shows students that science is relevant to their lives. The correct answer is *D*.

In order for a force to move an object, there must be an unbalanced force applied so that the force is stronger in one direction than in the other. What will happen if two people are pulling at opposite ends of a rope (as in a game of tug-o-war) and the stronger person is pulling with a force of 5N while the smaller person is pulling with a force of 3N?

A. Both people will fall down.
B. The smaller person will be pulled towards the stronger person.
C. The stronger person will be pulled towards the smaller person.
D. A net force of 2N will be applied in the direction of the smaller person.

The unbalanced force will result in a net force of 2N in the direction of the greater force (the stronger person). Therefore, *B* is the correct answer.

Standard IX Life Science

Competency 022: The science teacher knows and understands the science content appropriate to teach the statewide curriculum (Texas Essential Knowledge and Skills) in life science.

The beginning teacher knows and understands the fundamental concepts and processes of living systems, including the ideas that different structures perform different functions, that organisms have basic needs, and that organisms respond to external and internal stimuli. Important life science concepts include an understanding of the life cycles of organisms, the relationship between organisms and the environment, and how species and populations evolve and adapt over time. The teacher provides activities and examples and describes stages in the life cycle of common plants and animals. Through observations, students identify adaptive characteristics and explain how adaptations influence the survival of populations or species. Students compare inherited traits and learned characteristics and explain how hereditary information is passed from one generation to the next. Students also analyze the characteristics of habitats within an ecosystem and identify organisms, populations, or species with similar needs, and analyze how they compete with one another for resources. The following provides more explanation of these ideas.

Life Science: Key Ideas

- **Living things** are able to reproduce, grow, respond to change, excrete and secrete waste, and die. Living things **adapt** (change) to the unique conditions of their environment. They interact with and affect their environment, and the environment affects living things. Living things inherit and transmit the characteristics of their ancestors.
- Living things are classified in one of **five major kingdoms: animals, plants, protista** (including viruses and slime molds), **monera** (including blue-green

algae and bacteria), and **fungi** (including various types of fungus). The kingdoms are further classified into increasing smaller groups, including **phylum**, **class**, **order**, **family**, **genus**, and **species** (then varieties and hybrids). For example, a dog's classification is:

Kingdom—Animalia
Phylum—Chordata (animal with backbone)
Class—Mammalia (animal with body hair)
Order—Carnivore (animal that eats meat)
Family—Canidae (animal with dog-like features)
Genus—Canis
Species—familia

- All plants and animals are made of **cells**. Each cell is surrounded by a **cell membrane** that controls what enters and exits the cell. Plant cells have a **cell wall** (an outer, rigid covering). Cells are controlled by the **nucleus** that contains chromosomes made of the genetic codes called **DNA** (deoxyribonucleic acid). Cells obtain energy to do processes through an energy reaction involving **ATP** (adenosine triphosphate). Cells undergo the processes of **mitosis** producing two new identical cells. **Meiosis** in sex cells produces two new cells with half the original chromosomes. Groups of cells that work and function together are tissues. A group of tissues working together is called an **organ**. And a group of organs working together are called a **system**.

- Living things reproduce in two ways: *sexually* and *asexually*. **Asexual reproduction** occurs in simpler species (yeasts, bacteria, etc.) when one organism produces new offspring. **Sexual reproduction** occurs with male and female organisms and enhances variation in the genetic diversity, which enhances the long-term survival of the species.

- Plants undergo several life processes. **Photosynthesis** is very important because it is the sole chemical process that captures, converts, and stores solar energy. Further, it is the source of oxygen in the atmosphere. Photosynthesis involves the ability of green plants with chlorophyll to trap the sun's energy, take in carbon dioxide and water, and produce food (carbohydrates) and oxygen. Plants, just like animals, undergo respiration using oxygen and releasing energy and carbon dioxide as byproducts. Plants also use the processes of **digestion** to break down and use nutrients, the process of **transpiration** (the evaporation of excess water through stomata in leaves), and **capillary action** (the transportation of materials within the plant parts).

- Plants have behavior and structural **adaptations** for survival in their environment and for various other functions. Major structures for growth include: **roots** (for anchoring the plant and for taking in nutrients from the ground), **stems** (for support and transportation of nutrients), and **leaves** (for the ability to make food and oxygen). Major structures for flowering plants' reproduction include the **stamen**, **pistil**, **petals**, and **sepals** on the flower. Fertilized egg cells from the ovary divide and multiply, eventually forming **seeds**. Each seed consists of stored food, a seed coat, and the tiny plant called an embryo. Seeds need favorable conditions to germinate and grow. Temperature, water, and air are all external variables that affect seed germination and plant growth. These factors and sunlight affect plant growth.

- Animals are commonly divided into two groups—animals with backbones, called **vertebrates**, and animals without backbones, called **invertebrates**. Only the chordate phyla have backbones and include classes of fish, mammals, reptiles, birds, and amphibians.

- The vast majority of animals are invertebrates and include the phyla of arthropods (insects, crayfish), mollusks (clam, oyster, snail), echnioderms (starfish, sea urchin), annelids (earthworms, leech), aschelminths (hookworms, pinworms), platyhelminths (tapeworm—a parasite living and feeding in its host), coelenterates (jellyfish, coral), and poriferans (sponges).

- **Insects** have three body parts—*head* (with pair of antennae), *thorax* (with three pair of legs and two sets of wings), and an *abdomen*. Some insects undergo complete **metamorphosis** with four stages of change—egg, larva, pupa, and adult. Other insects undergo *partial metamorphosis* with three stages—egg, nymph, and adult. Some insects are social and live in colonies with genetically defined, specialized roles (bee societies include the queen, drones, and workers).
- **Spiders** (class arachnida) are not insects; they are arthropods with eight legs.
- **Fish** breathe through gills located on each side of the head that exchange the dissolved oxygen in the water and release carbon dioxide, a byproduct of cell respiration. Fish are cold-blooded animals with fins; their body temperature is the same as that of surrounding water.
- **Amphibians** (including frogs, toads, and salamanders) live in water in young stages but live on land near water as adults.
- **Reptiles** (including turtles, snakes, and alligators) are cold-blooded, breathe through lungs, and have rough, thick, dry skin.
- **Birds** have porous or hollow bones that make them lighter and able to fly. They are warm-blooded, which means that their body temperature remains the same regardless of the temperature around them. Many birds migrate or move throughout the year because of unfavorable weather conditions. Egg incubation is the process of adults' sitting and warming the eggs until they hatch.
- **Mammals** have hair (even a whale has a few bristles), have lungs for breathing, are warm-blooded, and usually have live young that are fed milk through mammary glands. Mammals have many adaptations for living in different environments. Some of those adaptations are very similar from animal to animal and some are very different. Bats use a guided flying process, detecting objects through sound echolocation. Whales, dolphins, and porpoises have lungs but live only in oceans. Some mammals (e.g., woodchucks) hibernate all winter. Others (e.g., bears and skunks) have a long winter sleep during which inactivity and slowed breathing allow survival using stored food during harsh weather.
- **Man**, a mammal, has used other animals to do work and to provide food and clothing. Man has also tried to protect animals that are **endangered** (few in number) and has worked hard to prevent *extinction* (no longer exist on this planet). Man's activities have resulted in many endangered and extinct plants and animals. Climatic changes have also resulted in extinction of many plants and animals.
- The human body is made of millions of tiny cells that undertake specialized work. Five main types of **tissues** include: muscle, nerve, epithelial, connective tissue, and blood. The main *body systems* include: skin, skeletal, muscular, digestive, circulatory, respiratory, excretory, nervous, reproductive, and endocrine.
- Three main areas of the body are the head, or *cranial cavity,* that holds the brain; the chest, or *thoracic cavity* that includes the heart and lungs; and the *abdominal cavity* that contains the stomach, intestines, liver, pancreas, kidneys, bladder, and reproductive organs.
- The human **heart** is strong muscle tissue that acts like a pump by contracting and relaxing. It has two sides separated by a wall called the *septum*. It has four chambers—two *atria* and two *ventricles*. The right atrium receives blood from the veins and pumps it into the right ventricle where it is then pumped into the lungs to exchange carbon dioxide (a by-product of cell respiration) for

oxygen (necessary for respiration). The blood returns to the left atrium and is pumped to the left ventricle and into parts of the body through a large artery. The heart, arteries, and veins along with small, branching capillaries make a closed **circulatory system**.

- The **respiratory system** includes the nose, nasal passages, throat (pharynx), windpipe (trachea), voice box (larynx), bronchi, bronchial tubes, alveoli (clusters of little air sacs), and the lungs.
- Knowledge of genetics, antibodies, vaccines, and immunity continues to give us new procedures to protect us from bacteria and viruses. The history of medicine provides examples of how scientists obtain, modify, and advance their knowledge.

Try the following practice questions:

Ms. Garcia's third graders are studying animal habitats and food chains. She wants her children to know that the herbivores in an ecosystem depend upon which of the following organisms for their survival?

A. Carnivores
B. Omnivores
C. Producers
D. Decomposers

In a food chain, **producers** (plants) make their own food for energy. **Consumers** either eat the producers and/or other consumers to obtain energy. They are classified as **herbivores** (plant-eaters), **carnivores** (meat-eaters), or **omnivores** (eating both animals and plants). For example, the hamburger and bun that you eat (consumer-omnivore) came from a cow (consumer-herbivore) that ate grass (producer). The grass trapped the energy of the sun in order to grow and this energy is passed throughout the food chain. The correct answer is C. Organisms survive in their environments because of inherited traits and learned behaviors.

Which of the following characteristics of a dog is most likely inherited from its parents?

A. Obesity
B. Limping
C. Fur color
D. Ability to catch a ball

Although a dog may exhibit all of the characteristics listed, only fur color would be *inherited*—passed on through the genetic material of the parents. The correct answer is C.

Standard X Earth and Space Science

> **Competency 023: The science teacher knows and understands the science content appropriate to teach the statewide curriculum (Texas Essential Knowledge and Skills) in Earth and space science.**
>
> *The beginning teacher knows and understands the properties of Earth materials as well as changes in the Earth system. Students should participate in investigations of properties and uses of rocks, soils, and water. They could describe characteristics of weather and collect data with simple weather instruments. The teacher assists students with models that demonstrate changes in the earth's surface due to earthquakes,*

weathering, glaciers, etc. Finally, the teacher can describe the basic characteristics of the sun, moon, and stars—especially the position of the planets in
relation to the sun and the consequences of the moon's orbit around the
earth (phases of the moon each month), the **Earth's orientation** (23 degree
tilt) and movement around the sun, and the **Earth's rotation** (spin) on its
axis (day, night, seasons). The Earth's tilt increases the amount of sunlight
striking the sections of the Earth that tilt toward the sun and decreases the
amount of sunlight in those sections tilted away from the sun. As the Earth
moves (**revolves**) around the sun every 365 days, the sections receiving
more-direct and less-direct sunlight change and reverse. The combination of
tilt, revolution, and energy transfer act together to cause weather changes
and seasons. The Earth's rotation on its axis moves a given position on the
Earth's surface into the path of sunlight and then away from that path.
Sunrise, day time, sunset, and night are the result.

Earth Science: Key Ideas

- The solid section of the Earth contains four major layers. The **inner core**; the **outer core**; the **mantle**, consisting mainly of rock; and the **crust**, which is the thin (3 to 30 miles) outer layer on which life exists.

- There are three basic types of rocks found on Earth—**igneous** (rocks formed from cooled magma such as granite), **sedimentary** (rocks formed by pressing soft sediment such as sandstone), and **metamorphic** (rocks formed from other types of rocks that have been heated and pressed such as marble). All are formed of one or more minerals. The rock cycle is a description of the mixing and changing of rock material found in the Earth. These changes result from heat, melting, cooling, chemical reactions, and pressure. Rocks are classified by physical characteristics and rated by hardness (on the **Mohs scale**), luster, and specific gravity.

- **Continental drift** refers to the theory that all land masses were once joined together as a single unit called *Pangaea* and have since moved as separate continents. The evidence includes the apparent "puzzle-fit" of the current continents, the similarity in fossil record among continents, climate, and mountain range locations.

- Studies of the age and appearance of the ocean floor helped scientists form the theory of **plate tectonics**, explaining that the upper layer of the Earth's surface is made of approximately twenty huge plates that move in different directions causing spreading, colliding, and fracture/fault boundaries.

- **Earthquakes** and **volcanoes** occur most often at plate boundaries as the plates push against each other. Volcanoes can arise from these pushing forces, forming shield, cone, and composite cones and releasing hot, molten rock materials as well as sulfurous gases as soot and dust particles. Earthquakes also can result from plate pressure. Their intensity is measured by a seismograph and compared on the Richter scale.

- Other Earth processes that cause change include the formation and **movement of glaciers** and **weathering** by **wind erosion**, **water erosion**, and *freezing* and *thawing*. Ancient glaciers are responsible for cutting deep gashes in the Earth's surface, sometimes hundreds of miles long, that can fill with water (such as the **fjords** in Norway and Alaska or lakes and valleys in other areas).

- Earth's **atmosphere** is divided into several layers. The **troposphere** (where we live) consists of 78 percent nitrogen, 21 percent oxygen, and 1 percent other gases, including helium and carbon dioxide. The next layer is the

stratosphere with its ozone layer that absorbs the sun's ultraviolet radiation, a health risk to many living things. The next layer is the **mesosphere**, followed by the **ionosphere**, and finally the **thermosphere**.

- The **water cycle** consists of the movement of water between the Earth's surface and the atmosphere. The water cycle includes **precipitation** (rain, snow, sleet, hail, etc.), the collecting and falling of rain and snow from clouds to the Earth as a liquid; the movement and accumulation of surface and ground water in streams, lakes, underground tables, rivers, and oceans; **evaporation** from the water's surface due to heat or wind; and **condensation** of water vapor in the air to water droplets due to cooling. The Earth's surface, land forms, air temperature, and wind (caused by uneven heating of land and water surfaces) all contribute to our climate and weather conditions.

- Our planet is just one of eight in our **solar system** that also includes *moons* (natural satellites that orbit a planet), *asteroids* (space debris that drift around the sun particularly between Mars and Jupiter), *comets* (space debris believed to consist of rock, ice, dust, and gases which presents with a vapor tail), and *meteors* (space meteroids that enter the Earth's atmosphere, creating a shooting, or falling, "star" as they burn). In orbit around the sun are Mercury, Venus, Earth, Mars, Jupiter, Saturn, Uranus, and Neptune. The sun is a star, radiating energy (heat and light). Our solar system is part of the Milky Way galaxy—one of many galaxies in the universe. Our **moon** is a satellite of our planet that revolves around the Earth and reflects the sun's light. The moon has phases each month (new, waxing crescent, first quarter, waxing gibbous, full, waning gibbous, last quarter, waning crescent, and new), depending on its position.

Consider the following question:

In which of these ways can volcanoes build up new land?

 A. Add heat to expand the Earth's surface.
 B. Create gases and water vapor.
 C. Change the type of rock on the Earth.
 D. Add lava to the Earth's surface.

Volcanoes can form new land through the process of eruption of lava (molten rock) that cools. The correct answer is *D.*

Try this practice question:

Which of the following factors causes seasons on Earth?

 A. The Earth's rotation on its axis and size of the sun
 B. The Earth's magnetic field and distance from the sun
 C. The size of the solar system in relation to the sun
 D. The tilt of the Earth's axis and its orbit around the sun

The seasons of the Earth are a result of its tilt on its axis and its orbit around the sun. When the sun's rays are more direct on the Northern Hemisphere, it experiences summer and the Southern hemisphere is in winter. The reverse happens when the sun's rays are more direct on the Southern hemisphere (summer) and less direct on the Northern Hemisphere (winter). The correct answer is *D.*

Standard XI Unifying Themes

> **Competency 020: The science teacher knows unifying concepts and processes that are common to all sciences.**
>
> *The beginning teacher knows that scientific literacy relates not only to facts and information but also to understanding the connections that make this information useful and relevant. The teacher knows how the concepts and processes listed below provide a unifying framework across science disciplines:*
>
> - *Systems, order, and organization*
> - *Evidence, models, and explanations*
> - *Change, constancy, and measurements*
> - *Evolution and equilibrium*
> - *Form and function*
>
> *Teachers realize that systems and subsystems can be used as a conceptual framework to organize and unify the common themes of science and technology. They know that patterns in observations and data help to explain natural phenomena and allow predictions to be made.*
>
> *In the classroom, the teacher can apply the systems model to identify and analyze common themes that occur in physical, life, Earth, and space sciences. They can analyze a system (the ocean, a cell, a flashlight) and general features of a system (input, process, output, feedback). They can analyze the interactions that occur between the components of a given system or subsystem and can use the system to model and analyze the concepts of constancy and change.*

Consider the following practice question:

A new fourth-grade teacher is overwhelmed with the curriculum guides, time demands, and preparation for all the content areas of a self-contained classroom. The teacher proposes the following solution at a team meeting.

    A. Have the principal hire a science specialist.
    B. Have all the fourth-grade teachers share ideas and develop integrated units.
    C. Have all the fourth-grade teachers concentrate only on TAKS content areas.
    D. Have guest speakers come in more often.

The fourth-grade TEKS require students to "identify patterns of change such as in weather, metamorphosis, and objects in the sky." An integrated unit about weather could include science process skills of observation and data collection, organizing, and reporting. It could also engage students in writing, reading, and research (language art requirements). Fiction and nonfiction trade books could also be added for the students' enrichment. The data collection and graphing provide authentic opportunities in mathematics and the social studies for investigations of science careers, severe weather's impact on society, and climates and conditions around the world. Science is a part of our daily lives and its integration with other content areas can only help students to learn more. Although speakers (*D*) and specialists (*A*) could often be used for additional instruction, the self-contained classroom teacher best knows how to maximize effective content connections. The correct answer is *B*.

In the classroom, interdisciplinary emphasis (between content areas—e.g., science and math are discussed in the AIMS program at http://www. aimsedu.org) enables the teacher to reinforce learning and fit curricular pieces together. Science should also have an intradisciplinary focus (not just separate life, Earth, and physical) that is relevant and meaningful.

A TExES Science Lesson

In the classroom, a teacher facilitates the following long-term investigation of mealworms. Your task is to analyze and evaluate this student-centered science activity for its compliance with the standards. The results will yield examples of the unifying concepts of systems, change, properties, patterns, models, and survival, all embedded within the format of this investigation.

MEALWORM INQUIRY PROJECT *Focus:* Children will be given a "critter" population (5 to 10 mealworms). Their task is to diligently observe and record what they see and learn. This population will change over the next few weeks.

Directions to the students: You will need a wide-mouth, transparent container with a small amount of dry oatmeal. The critter population should be maintained at room temperature and sustained with a small slice of apple or potato. The slice should be changed regularly. Because the population cannot escape, a lid is not needed. The population might, however, be transferred temporarily to a flat surface (like a shoebox lid or wax paper) for easier study. The critters are not harmful; they do not transmit disease. They are, however, fragile and must be handled with care. The log/diary will be submitted for grading after at least six weeks of observation.

The log should:
  A. contain a minimum of two to three observation entries per week, noting changes and/or behaviors of the critters. The observations should be dated and organized into a systematic format of your choice.
  B. reflect an "inquiring mind." Communicate questions, feelings, speculations, predictions, and intuitive leaps that you experience as you are, indeed, thinking about what you see.
  C. communicate evidence of informal "sciencing." Devise and try simple experiments. Report what you tried, what happened, and what you learned. You should also communicate ideas you would like to try but could not, given consideration of the animal, safety, time, and/or equipment.
  D. contain a number of simple, labeled drawings that visually communicate observations.
  E. contain a one- to two-page summary of what was observed and what was learned about these critters. A small group will meet and report/share findings in order to coordinate a master report to be presented to the class.

Lesson Evaluation Using the Standards

The critter assignment is inquiry based and student centered—encouraging higher-order thinking as well as promoting curiosity and independent student "sciencing." Obviously, the basic science concept of metamorphosis is investigated as well as basic needs requirements and care for living things. Use of laboratory and instructional materials is encouraged and metric rulers, scales, and magnifying lenses are all available. The assignment addresses safety with regard to the harmless nature of the critters and the materials used for observation. The science process skills are emphasized as observations are used to make and test hypotheses. Students must take measurements to collect and organize data and, finally, to present findings through scientific communication.

The assignment is authentic and parallels how scientists would approach the process of learning about the natural world. The observations lead to experimental designs with testable hypotheses that can be repeated. Students can find out if the critters prefer light or dark, respond to sound, and eat more oatmeal or cornflakes. Students can also answer other original questions. The assignment stresses interdisciplinary learning as it integrates language arts through journal writing and reporting, mathematics through measurement and graphing, and fine arts through drawings with details.

Recent developments and research in science education have reinforced the use of discovery, inquiry, cooperative group reports, science process skills, and the use of technology for research. Mealworm information can be found online at: http://www.reachoutmichigan.org/funexperiments/quick/eric/mealworm.html.

REFERENCES

Hungerford, H. R., Volk, T. L., & Ramsey, J. M. (1997). *Science-technology-society. Investigating and evaluating STS issues and solutions*. Stipes Publishing.

National Research Council. (1996). *National science education standards*. Washington, DC: National Academy Press.

Texas Essential Knowledge and Skills (TEKS) access at http://www.tea.state.tx.us/teks

RESOURCES

Information for science teachers working with students with disabilities includes:

- Visit your regional service centers for viewing assistive technology.
- Review Ed Keller's Internet page: Strategies for teaching science to students with disabilities: http://www.as.wvu.edu/~scidis
- Write for information from:

SAVI/SELPH Center for Multisensory Learning
Lawrence Hall of Science
University of California
Berkeley, CA 94720

Additional safety information can be obtained from: http://www.utdanacenter.org/sciencetoolkit/safety/texas_safety.php.

American Chemical Society
1155 16th Street NW
Washington, DC 20036

Texas Department of Health
Occupational Health Program
1100 West 49th Street
Austin, TX 78756

Flinn Scientific Inc.
P.O. Box 219
Batavia, IL 60510

A SCIENCE LESSON PLAN

Title of Lesson: Camouflage (How Organisms Utilize Camouflage for Survival)

Grade Level: Third or Fourth

Main Subject Area: Science

Integrated Subjects: Science, Mathematics, Language Arts/Reading Technology

Time Frame/Constraints: One science period

Overall Goal(s): To help students understand how important camouflage is for animals' survival and how environmental changes can cause animals to change and/or become endangered.

TEKS/TAKS OBJECTIVES:

§ 112.5.3.9. (3.9) **Science:** Science concepts. The student knows that species have different adaptations that help them survive and reproduce in their environment. The student is expected to: (A) observe and identify characteristics among species that allow each to survive and reproduce; (B) analyze how adaptive characteristics help individuals within a species to survive and reproduce; (3.10) Science concepts. The student knows that many likenesses between offspring and parents are inherited from the parents. The student is expected to: (B) identify some inherited traits of animals;

§ 110.5. **Language Arts:** English Language Arts and Reading (b) Knowledge and skills; (1) Listening/speaking/purposes. The student listens attentively and engages actively in various oral language experiences. The student is expected to: (E) listen responsively to stories and other texts read aloud, including selections from classic and contemporary works (K–3); (4) Listening/ speaking/communication. The student communicates clearly by putting thoughts and feelings into spoken words. The student is expected to: (B) clarify and support spoken messages using appropriate props, including objects, pictures, and charts (K–3); (14) Writing/purposes. The student writes for a variety of audiences and purposes and in various forms. The student is expected to: (A) write to record ideas and reflections (K–3); (B) write to discover, develop, and refine ideas (1–3); (C) write to communicate with a variety of audiences (1–3); and (D) write in different forms for different purposes such as lists to record, letters to invite or thank, and stories or poems to entertain (1–3).

§ 111.15. (3.13) **Mathematics:** Probability and statistics. The student solves problems by collecting, organizing, displaying, and interpreting sets of data. The student is expected to: (A) collect, organize, record, and display data in pictographs and bar graphs where each picture or cell might represent more than one piece of data; (B) interpret information from pictographs and bar graphs;

§ 126.2. **Technology:** Technology Applications (5) Information acquisition. The student acquires electronic information in a variety of formats, with appropriate supervision. The student is expected to: (A) acquire information including text, audio, video, and graphics.

Objectives: (Note: As a discovery lesson, the teacher should not give the objectives to the students until after students are able to go through discovering the concept.)

- Students will watch a puppet demonstration on "hungry birds" and participate in a relay to collect "worms" (yarn pieces) of different colors.
- Students will listen to *How to Hide a Meadow Frog.*
- Students will classify data and compare graphic results with other groups.
- Students, in groups, will search in magazines and on the Web for camouflaged animals to construct a poster of at least 8 animals (4 examples and 4 nonexamples).
- Students will write at least four sentences in a paragraph describing his or her camouflaged animals using correct terminology of predator/ prey. Students will predict the survival of a camouflage/noncamouflage organism.
- Students will orally present their posters.
- Students will watch a PowerPoint presentation, try to find camouflaged animals, and vote on the best camouflaged animal.

Sponge Activity: Children quickly draw their favorite bird.

Environmental Concerns: Lesson plan is written in the 5E's (constructivist's framework). Needs to be a nice day with dry ground. (Safety issues: check outside area for glass or other dangerous items on the ground; explain relay rules— no pushing; one "worm" only per turn).

Rationale(s): There are many, many animals that live in our neighborhoods—even if we live in a city. Many other animals live in the rural areas of Texas. One way that they stay alive is by blending in with their environments so no one sees them easily. We must be careful about animals' environments.

Focus or Induction Set: The teacher should go outside prior to the lesson and scatter the "worms" (yarn pieces) on the grass. Using a bird puppet, the teacher should question students about why the puppet "is crying" (it is hungry and needs to look for food). On a KWL chart, the teacher should quickly write down what students know about the diet of birds and how baby birds are fed (making sure *worms* is on the list). The teacher asks children to pretend that they are birds and go outside and find some food. The teacher then sets up relay teams of three or four members to go outside to hunt for food. Because the little bird is a puppet, the teacher should tell students that he likes "yarn worms." Students run the relay quickly for the previously scattered "worms". (The discovery should be that children realize that predators cannot see prey that is the same color as the environment—but this should come out later.)

Making Connections:

(Give after the concept has been discovered.)

1. **Connections to Past or Future Learning:** Do you see or hear the word *camouflage* related to man in anyway? Show pictures of soldiers and equipment from Iraq with camouflage uniforms, and ask why they think the army selec-ted these types of uniforms.

2. **Connections to the Community:** What animals live in your neighborhood? Are they easy to see or not?

3. **Cultural Connections:** Can you think of any cultures that use camouflage and why? (Tribes in rainforest areas are hunters, and they don't want their prey to see them flee; they do not have grocery stores to do shopping, so they must hunt for everything they eat; many tattoo their bodies in patterns).

4. **Connections to Student Interests & Experiences:** What type of camouflage would you wear if you wanted to hide in your room? On the playground? Why?

Materials: Multi-colored yarn "worms"—2-inch pieces (50 each). Try to have one set of worms that matches the color of the ground); party hats for beaks, markers, graph paper, nature magazines/pictures with animals.

Activities: Guided Practice:

EXPLORE: Have each team organize their data showing the number of each different color worm and make a graph. Have groups share and compare graphs noting how they are the same and different. Make a class graph with all the data and do more comparison of each group's graph.

EXPLAIN: (concept introduction, terminology) Using the class graph, explain that there were 50 of each color worm that were scattered in the habitat and discuss the conditions of the habitat—green grass, partially brown dirt areas, and so forth. Read the book *How to Hide a Meadow Frog* and explain the terminology *predator/prey, endangered/extinct.* Explain how the green and brown worms were able "to hide" in the habitat and, therefore, are better able to survive and reproduce. The yellow, red, and blue worms were more obvious and hunted to the point of being endangered or extinct.

ELABORATE: (concept application—camouflage works in nature as well as in the colored yarn activity online). In groups, have students cut out pictures from nature magazines or print pictures that show examples of animals using camouflage and nonexamples of animals not camouflaged and paste them on a poster.

Independent Practice: Each student writes a short paragraph about their animal, including where it lives, what preys on it, how it protects itself through camouflage, and why it is more likely to survive than the nonexample. Each paragraph should contain at least four sentences and include the words *predator* and *prey*. Each group shows and orally describes their poster.

Assessment: Each student must have at least two pictures in his or her "square" (an example and a nonexample). Each student should write a short paragraph about their camouflaged animal (including where it lives, what preys on it, and how it protects itself through camouflage). Each student gives correct information orally about his or her animal and why it is more likely to survive.

What Will Students Do Who Finish Early? Students will go to the following Web site and pick out a camouflaged animal, print out the information for the chosen animal, and follow the directions for coloring: http://www.enchantedlearning.comcoloring/camouflage.shtml.

Closure: Prepare a PowerPoint presentation that shows a number of camouflaged animal pictures and have students try to "Find the Critter" (similar to http://www.longhorncattle.com/camo2.html). Students will vote on the best camouflaged animal.

Modification for Students with Special Needs: Bianna will only write two sentences for credit.

Reflection: To be addressed after teaching the lesson.

DRAFT YOUR OWN SCIENCE LESSON PLAN

Remember that discovery lessons should be taught often in science. When using discovery, be sure to think of the 5 E's and deliver instruction so that Explanation follows Exploration.

Title of Lesson: _____

Grade Level: _____

Main Subject Area: _____

Integrated Subjects: _____

Time Frame/Constraints: _____

Overall Goal(s): _____

TEKS/TAKS Objectives: _____

_____

_____

Objective(s): _____

_____

_____

Sponge Activity: _____

_____

_____

Environmental Concerns: _____

_____

_____

Rationale(s): _____

_____

_____

Focus or Set Induction: _____

_____

_____

Making Connections:

1. Connections to Past or Future Learning: _____

_____

2. Connections to the Community: _____

_____

3. Cultural Connections: _____

_____

4. Connections to Student Interests & Experiences: _____

_____

Materials: _____

_____

_____

Activities: Guided practice: _____

_____

_____

_____

_____

_____

_____

_____

_____

_____

Independent practice: _____

_____

_____

_____

_____

_____

_____

_____

_____

Assessment: _____

What Will Students Do Who Finish Early? _____

Closure: _____

Modification for Students with Special Needs: _____

Reflection: _____

_____

OBSERVING SCIENCE EXPERIENCES/ACTIVITIES

During your visit to an early childhood classroom, use the following form to provide feedback as well as to reflectively analyze the room, the materials, and the teacher.

	Observed	Not observed	Response
1. Science lessons are taught (integrated) with other content area on a daily basis.			If so, about how much time is spent on science? If not, why do you think they are not integrated?
2. The science lesson is clearly inquiry based.			If so, was it effective? If not, what could change to make it effective?
3. A demonstration was included in the lesson.			If so, describe. Was it effective? If not, what type of activity might be included?
4. A hands-on lab was included.			If so, describe. Was it effective? If not included, how did children participate?
5. Safety issues were discussed prior to the lesson (if inclusive of a lab).			If so, describe. If not, what should have been included?
6. Lab materials were ready for students.			If not, what was the result?
7. The teacher demonstrated the process for a lab.			If so, was it effective? If not, what could change to make it effective?
8. The teacher had written guidelines for the lab for students.			If so, were they effective? If not, what could change to make them effective?
9. The lab had an assessment component.			If so, was it effective? If not, what could change to make it effective?
10. The teacher monitored students during the lab.			If so, what was the result? If not, what was the result and what should change?
11. Formative assessment was conducted.			If so, was it effective? If not, what could change to make it effective?
12. The seating arrangement allowed for all children to be able to see any demonstrations.			If not, what should change to make it more effective?
13. There are Science Centers in the room that include hands-on materials for free experimentation in science.			If so, describe. Do they seem interesting and appropriate? If not included, or not interesting, what materials and activities could be included?
14. Long-term Science Centers are set up in the classroom (aquariums, terrariums, insect metamorphosis, etc.).			If so, describe and tell if they are well cared for and well presented. Do children have a part in their care? If not a part of the classroom, what could be added?

	Observed	Not observed	Response
15. A classroom pet or other animal is set up in the classroom.			If so, describe. Do children have a responsibility in the care? If so, is it appropriate? Why or why not? If not, what type of classroom pet would be easy to add?
16. If a classroom pet or other animal is available, there are rules for its care posted or known by all children.			If so, describe. If not, what should be added?
17. Science safety equipment is readily available for teacher and student use.			If so, describe. If not, what should be added?
18. The environment of the classroom during science is one of encouraging <u>multiple</u> answers.			If so, describe. If not, what could be changed?
19. Higher-level questioning was a part of the science lesson.			If so, describe. If not, what should be added?
20. An exciting focus opened the lesson.			If so, describe. If not, describe one that could have been employed.
21. Trade books and other reading materials on science (both factual and "sci-fi") exist in a classroom library.			If so, describe. If not, what materials could be included?
22. All science equipment in the room is set up safely for use (no unsecured electrical cords, materials are easy to reach, etc.).			If so, describe. If not, describe how the room could be made safe.
23. Technology is integrated with the science lesson.			If so, describe. If not, how could this change?
24. Technology is available for students' use in science lessons or in science centers.			If so, describe. If not, how could this change?
25. The science lesson took into account children's developmental levels according to Piaget (for example, with issues of conservation, reversibility, transformation, concreteness, etc.).			If so, describe. If not, what aspects should be addressed?
26. The teacher involved *all* children in the lesson.			Describe the balance of involvement. If not all were involved, what kinds of children were not?
27. The teacher was positive about science.			If so, describe. If not, tell why it's important to be positive.
28. There was student-to-student interaction during the lesson.			If so, describe. If not, tell why it would be important to have this type of interaction.
29. An appropriate closure is used to end the lesson.			If so, describe. If not, what could be used?

TEST YOURSELF ON SCIENCE

1. Sound travels fastest in which medium?
   A. Iron
   B. Air
   C. Water
   D. Vacuum

2. Which of the following statements about isotopes is *false*? Isotopes are:
   A. atoms whose nuclei have the same number of protons.
   B. atoms whose nuclei have different numbers of neutrons.
   C. atoms whose atomic weight is the same.
   D. atoms whose atomic number is the same.

3. Which chemical element is common to marshmallows, diamonds, and charcoal?
   A. Silver
   B. Nitrogen
   C. Water
   D. Carbon

4. Coral is found in warm ocean waters and provides protection and habitat for many ocean organisms. Coral is classified as a(n):
   A. animal.
   B. shell.
   C. plant.
   D. rock.

5. The Earth's atmosphere is a mixture of gases structured in layers. The layer of the atmosphere where most of the Earth's weather occurs is called the:
   A. stratosphere.
   B. troposphere.
   C. mesosphere.
   D. thermosphere.

6. Which of the following statements about the sun is *false*?
   A. The sun, the closest star, is 93 million miles from the Earth.
   B. The sun is made of magma and hot gases.
   C. The sun's energy reaches Earth through radiation.
   D. The sun is a fusion reactor in which hydrogen fuses to form helium.

7. The history of space exploration has yielded knowledge and prompted questions about our place in the universe. Which U.S. space program in the 1960s and 1970s focused on investigating the moon?
   A. Viking
   B. Pioneer
   C. Apollo
   D. Sputnik

8. Reptiles have dry scaly skin while amphibians have moist smooth skin. Which of these animals is an amphibian?
   A. Lizard
   B. Python
   C. Iguana
   D. Salamander

9. Which of the following statements about water is *false*?
   A. About 40 percent of water in the water cycle is new each year.
   B. About 70 percent of the Earth's surface is covered with water.
   C. About 55 percent of the average human adult is made of water.
   D. About 1 percent of the Earth's water is fresh and drinkable.

10. Which of the following is not classified as a simple machine?
    A. Inclined plane
    B. Pulley
    C. Electromagnetic door bell
    D. Wheel and axle

TEST YOURSELF ANSWERS AND RATIONALES FOR SCIENCE

Answer 1: The correct answer is *A*. Iron is a solid. Sound travels as a vibration faster through solids because the molecules are more closely packed. Sound does not travel in a vacuum because there are too few molecules to transmit the vibrations.

Answer 2: Statement *C* is false. Isotopes are atoms whose nuclei have the same number of protons (and hence the same atomic number) but have a different number of neutrons, thereby changing the atomic weight. Therefore, the correct answer is *C*.

Answer 3: The correct answer is *D*, carbon. The element carbon is present in the listed substances, but silver and nitrogen are not. Water (a combination of hydrogen and oxygen) is a compound, not an element.

Answer 4: The correct answer is *A*, animal. Coral is a simple, delicate animal that secretes and lives inside a hard limestone coating made from calcium in seawater.

Answer 5: The correct answer is *B,* troposphere. The layers of the Earth's atmosphere from the surface outward are: troposphere, stratosphere, mesosphere, and thermosphere.

Answer 6: Magma is hot, melted rock. The sun, the nearest star, is a hot mass of glowing gases. The correct answer is *B.*

Answer 7: The Apollo program put Neil Armstrong and Edwin Aldrin on the moon in 1969. The unmanned Viking program landed on Mars in 1976, and the Pioneer program circled Venus. Sputnik was the Russian program that launched the first man into space in 1961. The correct answer is *C,* Apollo.

Answer 8: The correct answer is *D,* salamander. The other animals are reptiles with dry skin.

Answer 9: The correct answer is *A.* There is no "new" water in the water cycle. The amount of water on the Earth is fixed, but it is recycled through evaporation, condensation, precipitation, and accumulation.

Answer 10: The inclined plane, pulley, and wheel and axle are simple machines. They change how work is done by decreasing the amount of the force required. The doorbell uses electromagnetism. The correct answer is *C.*

6 Preparing to Teach Art in Texas

Sara Wilson McKay
North Texas State University

Janice L. Nath
University of Houston–Downtown

As long as art is the beauty parlor of civilization, neither art nor civilization is secure.

John Dewey, 1934, p. 344

This chapter addresses the art standards of the EC-4 comprehensive exam. These standards range broadly to include art objects and their relationships to their makers and their cultures. As Dewey points out in the quote above, the role of art should not be limited to what is beautiful. Rather, art plays a considerable role in how civilizations perpetuate themselves. Accordingly, this exam explores more than just what young students construct in the classroom. Even at the early childhood and elementary levels (EC-4), students are expected to engage with ideas about how art is created; art histories of diverse cultures; and analysis, interpretation, and evaluation of works of art.

Art in the early childhood classroom plays an important role in the learning and development of young children. Gardner (1983) maintains that art allows perception, awareness, judgment, and the expression of ideas to occur in ways that are not purely linguistic or mathematical (such as in reading, writing, science, and technology). These alternative ways of knowing may be most visible in young children who are not always able to clearly express themselves verbally (Wright, 1997). Early childhood specialist Malaguzzi (1993) identifies a stumbling block in early education, citing that spoken language is increasingly imposed on children through imitative mechanisms that are typically devoid of meaning. In contrast, Malaguzzi advocates that children learn best through strong imaginative processes linked to their experiences and to the problems of these experiences. Art, especially when it is integrated into a learning program rich with problem-solving projects, involves precisely the kind of imaginative processes advocated for the early childhood classroom. Wright continues by suggesting that art provides "a powerful means with which to promote future-oriented learning, particularly for young children, because [it] involves nonverbal, symbolic ways of knowing, thinking and communicating" (p. 365). Through art, young children play active roles in the processes of discovery, self-awareness, personal communication, social interaction, perception, skill use, analysis, and critique. These goals for young children in art are consistent with the standards for the visual arts addressed in the EC-4 comprehensive TExES exam. The understanding of artistic development as a domain of human growth, like development in the cognitive or social domain, points to the important role of early childhood professionals (Kindler, 1996). This crucial role is underscored by the clear standards EC-4 teachers are expected to meet.

Consistent with the design of the previous chapters, this chapter is structured with an overview of the various art standards that are, in turn, correlated to the Texas Essential Knowledge and Skills for Fine Arts. Each is followed by a discussion of the competencies. Additionally, for each standard, there are sample items with responses. A sample lesson plan, a sheet for drafting your own plan, and an observation sheet are also included.

TEKS-Related Correlations

There are five art standards for the EC-4 comprehensive exam and, in the past, the art section has comprised roughly 11 percent of the test. Statistically, this is an area that has been an obstacle for many test takers due, perhaps, to the incredible breadth of what is included in the term *art* and a general lack of emphasis on these areas throughout the present educational system. This may be the case because of the fear expressed by John Dewey in his quote at the beginning of this chapter. Generally, people approach art without keeping in mind all that it does for people. Rather, they assign art a role, such as decoration, and forget to ask for what else it could be important, especially for young children. Thus, in addressing these standards, you will find that they go beyond a single limited view of art; therefore, a broad perspective about art will help in thinking about these proficiencies. Additionally, these standards are in line with the Texas Essential Knowledge and Skills (TEKS) for Fine Arts for students and are therefore essential knowledge for early childhood teachers as well.

The TEKS for Fine Arts are designated in four basic strands:

- *Perception:* The student develops and organizes ideas from the environment.
- *Creative Expression:* The student expresses ideas through original artworks, using a variety of media with appropriate skill.

- *Historical/Cultural Heritage:* The student demonstrates an understanding of art history and cultures as records of human achievement.
- *Critical Evaluation:* The student makes informed judgments about personal artworks and the artworks of others.

The TEKS chapter 117 for Fine Arts goes on to say:

> *Four basic strands—perception, creative expression/performance, historical and cultural heritage, and critical evaluation—provide broad, unifying structures for organizing the knowledge and skills students are expected to acquire. Students rely on their perceptions of the environment, developed through increasing visual awareness and sensitivity to surroundings, memory, imagination, and life experiences, as a source for creating artworks. They express their thoughts and ideas creatively, while challenging their imagination, fostering reflective thinking, and developing disciplined effort and problem-solving skills. By analyzing artistic styles and historical periods, students develop respect for the traditions and contributions of diverse cultures. Students respond to and analyze artworks, thus contributing to the development of lifelong skills of making informed judgments and evaluations.*

In the discussion of the various standards outlined below, watch for correlations among these TEKS strands and what the test covers. You will definitely see significant overlaps, which require a broad understanding of what art is.

Standard I Perception in Art

(Note: Competency 024 applies to all art standards.)

The EC-4 teacher understands how ideas for creating art are developed and organized from the perception of self, others, and natural and human-made environments.

The EC-4 teacher assists students in their ability to perceive and reflect on the environment. The teacher uses correct terminology for the art elements (i.e., color, texture, shape, form, line, space, value) and the art principles (i.e., emphasis, contrast, pattern, rhythm, balance, proportion, unity) in order to help students analyze art and their environment. The teacher constructs art lessons that foster creative thinking and problem-solving skills. The EC-4 teacher also plans lessons that encourage observation and reflection on life experiences, and s/he identifies visual symbols that can be analyzed and compared in both natural and human-made subjects.

This standard relates directly to the first of the TEKS, requiring teachers to emphasize *student perception* of their environment for both art-making and evaluation of art. It requires that teachers understand the value of multisensory experiences for EC-4 students and necessitates that teachers know that life experiences and imagination are sources for artistic creation. Along with Gardner's theory of multiple intelligences, perception often governs young children's views of reality and can be the basis for their developing logic (Wright, 1997). The early childhood teacher who is knowledgeable of this standard understands the important role of perception in education and knows that the basic elements of art and principles of design help students gather and assess what is perceived. Because this standard requires knowledge of the elements and principles of art, teachers should know how to recognize the relationships among these elements and principles in works of art.

Consider the following example:

The following reproduction of Marcel Duchamp's *Nude Descending a Staircase* (1912) best shows:

A. texture. **C.** balance.

B. movement. **D.** line.

Test taker 1 answered *C*, claiming the reproduction has equal amounts of visual weight on each side. Test taker 2 answered *B*, because her eye went from the top left corner to the bottom right and that showed her movement. Test taker 3 answered *D*, because she saw a lot of lines. Test taker 4 answered *B*, because of the title of the work "*Nude Descending . . .*". Test taker 5 also answered *A* because he knows paintings sometimes have texture.

To answer this question correctly, a limited knowledge of the elements of art and the principles of design would be helpful. Choice *A* is not correct because the reproduction shows no *tactile* evidence that one area is rough and another area is smooth. Although the test taker was right to think about some paintings and sculptures having *texture*, he should have looked closer to support his decision with visual evidence. Choice *B*, *movement*, is supported with visual evidence and the test taker stated it well by identifying how her eye reacts when looking at the reproduction. Noting that her eye moved from one side to the other gives the test taker visual evidence for her answer (not to mention the title of the artwork). Choice *C* is a valid choice, but is it the *best* choice? This is an asymmetrically *balanced* artwork but when looking at this work of art, do you feel an *overwhelming* sense of balance? When a question asks you for what it shows *best* it is looking for what is overwhelmingly exemplified: Keep this in mind. Choice *D* actually falls in the same category as Choice *C*. A reproduction that best shows the *use of line* (*D*) would most likely consist primarily of clear, overt lines, not ambiguous lines that are hard to follow. If they are hard to follow or hard to identify, they might be suggesting something else is important (such as in this case with the emphasis on movement). The correct answer is *B*.

1950: 134–59. Duchamp, Marcel, "Nude Descending a Staircase, No. 2" Philadelphia Museum of Art. The Louise and Walter Arensberg Collection. Used with permission.

In order to be able to address this standard about perception, we need to pay special attention to what art encompasses. In one respect, art uses a common language called the *elements of art* and the *principles of design*. Below you will find definitions of the major building blocks of art and descriptions of how they can be arranged in a composition. There is also a chart that may be helpful in trying to understand how an artist uses various elements of art in order to achieve certain principles of design. For example, using conflicting shades of color might suggest contrast in a design, whereas using similar shades of color might suggest unity in a design. This is just an example of the kinds of things to look for when one analyzes a work of art structurally.

The Elements of Art

Line: The path of a moving point, a mark made by a tool or instrument as it is drawn across a surface.

Shape: A two-dimensional area that is defined in some way, perhaps with an outline or solid area of color. Shapes may also be *implied*.

Form: Objects that have three dimensions (length, width, and depth) and therefore have mass and volume.

Space: Shapes and forms exist in space. On a flat surface, artists can employ various means to imply the illusion of three-dimensional space, such as modeling to show volume, objects diminishing in size as they move to the background, overlapping, and showing more detail and brighter colors in the foreground with duller colors and less detail in the distance.

Texture: The way a surface feels or appears to feel if you could touch it.

Color: The aspect of objects caused by the varying quality of reflected light. Color is possibly the most expressive element of art but the most difficult to describe. Colors appeal directly to our emotions and can stand for ideas and feelings.

Value: The relative lightness or darkness of a work or part of a work, whether in color or in black and white.

The Principles of Design

Rhythm and Movement: The repetition of visual elements such as shapes, lines, or spaces. Visual rhythm creates the sensation of movement as the viewer's eyes follow the "beats" through a work of art.

Balance: The arrangement of elements in works of art. This may be symmetrical, asymmetrical, or radial.

Proportion: The relative size of one part to another.

Contrast: The degree of difference between colors, shapes, tones, or other elements in a work of art.

Variety: Combination of elements using diversity and change. Too much sameness might be dull; thus, artists add variety to their work to make it more interesting.

Unity: Allows the viewer to see a complex combination as a complete whole. If all the parts are joined together in such a way that they appear to belong to a whole, the work of art will be unified.

Emphasis: Center of interest in a picture; the focal point. Artists generally designate the most dominant part of the work by using some of the elements above to emphasize the most important point.

The chart in Figure 6.1 (adapted from Mittler, 1994) is helpful when looking at an artwork in order to determine how a composition is arranged. Use this chart to organize your thoughts about the artist's techniques.

FIGURE 6.1

| | | Principles of Art (how the artist organizes the work) | | | |
		Unity	Variety	Balance	Emphasis
Elements of Art (building blocks)	Color				
	Line				
	Shape				
	Texture				
	Value				

And now, let's try this:

In a kindergarten class, how can a teacher best relate art to daily life?

- **A.** Have an Art Center in which students draw whatever they feel in their journals.
- **B.** Ask students where they see art in the world.
- **C.** Give students 15 minutes of free art time at the end of the school day.
- **D.** Ask students to describe aspects of their environment in terms of colors, shapes, and light.

Choice *A* is not appropriate because there is no specific assignment that asks students to look at their surrounding culture in the form of daily life. Similarly, Choice *C* gives children no direction in using that free time. Consequently, there would be very little learning about the relationship of art to daily life. Choice *B* is a good question; however, for kindergartners it is too broad and vague. This question would allow students to use their homes, the outside world, school, etc., to identify art. The problem, however, lies in the fact that these choices might overwhelm a kindergartner, who would not know where to focus first. With the prompting of various settings and good questions, teachers might be able to salvage this choice and get to larger connections of art and daily life, but this is not the *best* answer. The most specific way to address the connection between art and life with kindergartners is to use the informal way of describing art suggested in Choice *D*. This choice is the most concrete answer which is needed to let children's imagination expand. Plus, the variety of answers inherent in the question means that discussion of possible student responses will yield a rich understanding of the multiple ways art is reflected in daily life. The *best* answer is *D*.

Standard II Creative Expression in Art

The EC-4 teacher understands the skills and techniques needed for personal and creative expression through the creation of original works of art in a wide variety of media and helps students develop those skills and techniques.

The EC-4 teacher demonstrates a basic understanding of techniques used to create various forms of art, including drawing, painting, printmaking, construction, ceramics, fiberart, and electronic media. The teacher is also able to help students use the art elements and principles in making art in various media and understands age-appropriate activities. The EC-4 teacher helps students see their artworks as personal expression and based on relevant ideas in students' lives (i.e., ideas, experiences, knowledge, and feeling). Also, the EC-4 teacher helps students differentiate between copy art and original works of art, focusing on the use of critical and creative thinking while making art. The teacher also demonstrates safe and appropriate use of materials and equipment.

This standard basically corresponds to the second point of the fine arts TEKS that pertains to creative expression. This requires that teachers know how to differentiate between two-dimensional and three-dimensional forms of art and are familiar with the qualities and uses of various media used to produce artworks (i.e., paint, crayon, chalk, clay, etc.). The EC-4 teacher knows how the art elements and principles are used to create art in a variety of media. The teacher also understands the ways personal, social, and political ideas are expressed through works of art and encourages the use of experience, memory, and imagination as sources for making original art.

Consider the following example:

Third-grade students are exploring pattern and repetition in art. How might a teacher best extend this knowledge from two-dimensional media to three-dimensional media?

A. Let students make prints from Styrofoam plates.

B. Have students experiment with weaving by making bracelets.

C. Ask students to create shoebox houses and decorate the outsides with patterns they draw.

D. Have students make a whistle out of clay.

Choice *A* is incorrect because printmaking is a two-dimensional medium. Choice *C* is a poor choice since students merely apply flat (2-D) designs on top of a 3-D model, therefore they don't use pattern and repetition in the construction of the three-dimensional part of the artwork. Choice *D,* while definitely a three-dimensional product, makes no mention of how pattern or repetition might be used in constructing the artwork. Had there been mention of using Pre-Columbian patterns on the whistles, it may have been a stronger answer, but as it stands, weaving is the most direct translation of repetition and pattern from two dimensions to three dimensions. The *best* answer is *B* because the motions of weaving will reinforce the idea of repetition in making various patterns in the bracelets, which are three-dimensional. The correct answer is *B.*

In addition to needing to know the basic vocabulary of art, the teacher should be familiar with ways of *art-making* for the classroom and the fact that visual creations are forms of communication. In general, one should be mindful of what is required of the student and whether the emphasis is on process or product. An art project that results in 24 identical Valentines, although popular *not* for educational reasons, is also not an appropriate art-making activity if there is no individual input from the student. "Recipe-oriented" art activities that require children simply to do what the teacher does (or wants) do not allow children to develop artistically (Szyba, 1999). Additionally, some students may not be able to relate to the relevance of particular products due to their own living conditions. In trying to conceptualize appropriate art-making activities, think through the following techniques that, when paired with solid content and student input, will be strong activities where the students' process is augmented and the students' communication is enhanced. In working with young children, teachers should welcome, even encourage, conversation among the children as they are working and praise original ideas, hopefully motivating each child to find his or her own way of working with the art material and/or the problem posed (Szyba, 1999). The following are ways of **art-making.**

Drawings: Making marks on a flat surface of material, usually paper. Contour drawings trace the outside edge of an object, and gesture drawings are quick drawings to get the idea of an object. Use charcoal (black chalk-like substance), colored chalk for paper (not for chalkboards), conte crayons (available in black, brown, and sienna), pen and ink, pencils or wax crayons, and pastels (similar to chalk but finer and available in a wider range of colors).

Paintings: Usually more color-dependent than drawings. Use oils (slow drying, so not used in *early* childhood), acrylics (quick-drying, water-soluble), tempera (used in schools, dries quickly, opaque, inexpensive, water-soluble), and watercolor (transparent, used with soft brushes).

Printmaking: An original artwork made in multiples. Images are raised or scratched into a surface (like scratch-foam, linoleum, wood blocks, potatoes, or erasers) and ink is rolled onto the surface. Either the raised part or the non-scratched part is then pressed or stamped onto paper or fabric. This can be repeated. Fingerprints are also a basic form of this artform.

Collages: Paper, fabric, and various other materials are combined to adhere to a surface. Making collages is *not* just cutting things out of a magazine and pasting on what you like. They involve placement and thought about the other elements of art and principles of design and usually revolve around a central idea.

Sculpture: Free-standing, three-dimensional, and able to be viewed from all sides. These include carving (stone or wood cut or chipped to create a form), modeling (clay shaped into a form—ceramics), casting (a form is created, a mold is made, and then it is filled with melted metal or plaster), and assembled (different materials are collected and joined together to create a form).

Fiberarts: Use of textiles, fabrics, yarns, threads, etc., to produce weavings, quilting, needlework, basketry, and fiber sculpture. Fiberarts also can include spinning of yarn and thread from raw materials.

Electronic media: Technology-assisted image making. This may include draw-and-paint software programs as well as more sophisticated software such as Adobe Photoshop. Issues such as copyright and originality are explicit when working with this kind of media and should be taught to children.

General age-appropriate art-making activities include:

Kindergarten:
- Spontaneous drawing and painting
- Scribbling and naming scribbles
- Combinations of ordinary things to design imaginative places (Szekely, 1999)
- Use and identification of primary colors
- Choices of color based on emotional appeal, not realism
- Identification and use of patterns and textures

First and second grades:
- Use of different kinds of lines, spacing, shapes
- Building forms with clay or wood to develop concepts
- Using more realistic color
- Mixing of colors in painting
- Repeating shapes in a rhythmic flow
- Creating patterns
- Making rubbings of various textures

Third and fourth grades:
- Making lines with a variety of tools
- Contour drawing and gesture drawing
- Understanding of shading concept
- Realization of various points of view
- Recognizing emerging themes like permanent vs. temporary or natural vs. man-made (Miller, 1999)
- Mixing colors and shades
- Using a compass for radial balance
- Organizing compositions using the principles of design (Linderman, 1997)

These guidelines do not suggest that there are no exceptions to these activities; they are provided for general age-appropriateness. However, the most important component in designing art-making activities for students should emphasize strong content, individuality, thoughtful process, and open criteria. This allows children to be successful in their attempts at visual communication.

Now, try your hand at this assessment item:

Which of the following techniques would be best for showing pattern and creating texture in a first grader's artistic composition?

A. Crayon rubbing of the bottom of student's shoe and printmaking using small found objects

B. A tempera painting using primary colors

C. Perspective drawing showing depth

D. Sculpting a figure out of wire

Rubbings (*A*) show patterns and textures, and printmaking lends itself to making patterns because you can use the prints again and again. If enough paint was used in a tempera painting one might get some texture, but a painting could have primary colors without having patterns. Perspective drawings (*C*) are too advanced for first graders and wire sculptures (*D*) show neither texture nor pattern. Therefore, the *best* answer is *A*. Based on what we learned about pattern and texture from the elements of art and the principles of design, crayon rubbings and printmaking with small objects are the most age-appropriate activities because both incorporate pattern and texture into the activity. The correct answer is *A*.

Standard III Appreciation of Art Histories and Diverse Cultures

The EC-4 teacher understands and promotes students' appreciation of art histories and diverse cultures.

The EC-4 teacher describes, compares, and contrasts art of different periods and cultures and explores reasons why different cultures create and use art. The teacher can describe the role of art in everyday life and is able to describe the main idea in works of art from various periods and cultures. The EC-4 teacher is aware of the role of art in storytelling and documenting history and can describe the role of art in different careers. The capable teacher is able to demonstrate how ideas have been expressed using different media in various cultures and at different times.

The capable teacher meeting this standard understands the characteristics of a variety of art forms of *multiple* cultures both from Western and non-Western traditions. This standard requires that teachers know characteristics of art from various historical periods, including various reasons cultures created and used art and continue to do so. Teachers are knowledgeable about careers in the arts and they understand the various **roles of art** (e.g., *storytelling, documentation, personal expression, decoration, utilitarianism, inspiration,* and *social change*) in different cultures.

This standard directly relates to the historical/cultural heritage strand of the fine arts TEKS. The teacher's understanding of the roles of history and culture and their relationships with art is intrinsic to being able to help students experience and explore diverse cultures through the arts. Meeting this standard entails inquiring into art and its origins and seeking connections across cultures. Early childhood educators advocate that developing art appreciation in young children deepens their understanding of the world and enriches their daily lives (Epstein, 2001). Even simple discussions with children about the choices involved in designing a storybook or the design of tiles on the floor develop young children's ability to discuss art in the context of their cultures (Johnson, 1997). These kinds of discussions reinforce the value of talking with even the youngest of learners about art in their daily lives as well as art they see from various cultures.

Consider the following example:

Use the reproduction of *Green Coca-Cola Bottles* (1962) by Andy Warhol to answer the next question.

A third-grade teacher wants to show that art can reflect a society's beliefs. In the context of this painting, the teacher could *best* do this by asking the students to suggest why:

A. the Coke® bottles are full.
B. there are seven columns and 16 bottles in each row.
C. the artist chose Coke® bottles as his subject and the bottle is repetitive.
D. the artist didn't use Pepsi® cans.

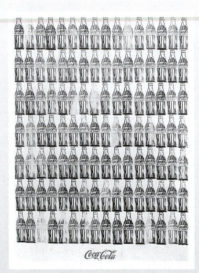

First, let's look at the suggestion the students might give. Choice *A* focuses on a detail of the artwork that is more of a descriptive fact than something to be interpreted about society. If, however, one of the bottles was deliberately empty or half-full then this might be interesting question, but, as it stands, it gains the student no insight about social beliefs. Choice *B* is the same situation as *A.* Choice *C* has students consider what repetition might represent. This allows students to interpret multiple possible meanings from this overwhelming element in the artwork. The entire artwork consists of repetition and is, therefore, important to interpret for social beliefs that may be expressed through repetition. Choice *C* similarly asks students to interpret the other main feature of this work of art, the subject matter. This entire work of art uses Coca-Cola® as its subject matter. It is appropriate, then, to ask questions about the significance of this choice. One test taker understood the importance of subject matter choice for artists such as Andy Warhol (who focused on consumerism) to gain the correct answer from this knowledge. Choice *D* asks students to essentially exchange apples for oranges, Coca-Cola® for Pepsi®. Although this may be interesting, the shift to consider Pepsi® in place of Coke® does not significantly shift the social beliefs being communicated in this work. Therefore, answer *C* is the best answer.

Andy Warhol 1928–1987, Green Coca-Cola Bottles, 1962
Oil on canvas. 82½ × 17 in (209.55 × 144.8 cm)
Whitney Museum of American Art, New York. Purchased with funds from the
Friends of the Whitney Museum of American Art 68.25.

Teachers should recognize art, regardless of whether it is labeled "fine" or not, as a product of its culture. Independent of exclusive criteria, art reflects its producing culture in the questions it asks, in what it holds up as art, and in what content it chooses to represent. An understanding of the relationship between art and culture is probably one of the most important things the EC-4 teacher can pass on to young students, as it is an understanding that results in the creation of a window into others' worlds. In order to have some sense of the historical events that are contemporaneous with the developments and movements in art, Table 6.1 presents a very brief overview of a primarily Western history of art (but with many non-Western references), which is organized to show how art reflects principal social and cultural ideas of its time. This overview is in no way meant to represent all that is "important" about art and history. Rather, it is intended to provide a way of recognizing the manifestation of social and historical issues in the art of a particular culture.

Table 6.1 Western History of Art—Overview

Period/Style	Social Issues and Historical Events
Paleolithic (25,000 B.C.E.): First examples of pigment being placed on a surface (cave drawings). Abstract sculptural figures in stone.	"Magical" explanations for natural phenomena, including procreation. Shelter limited to cave dwellings or other preexisting natural forms of protection.
Egyptian (3000 B.C.E.): Proportion in figurative art—rigidity reflects the strength of Pharoahs.	Development of pyramids. Pharaohs are divine and immortal, and the focus is on life after death.
Greek Art (500–325 B.C.E.): Art and architecture reflect concerns with order and rationality. Unparalleled naturalistic style in sculpture.	Beginning of Western culture as we know it. Human body elevated to highest ideal. Gods given human form and human weaknesses. Advent of philosophy, democracy, medicine, geometry, algebra, and astronomy.
Roman Art (500 B.C.E.): Contributed realism in figurative sculpture and painting. Massive temples, baths, and other government buildings decorated with reliefs and other sculpture. The triumphal arch celebrated victories of war.	Took over Greek and Etruscan culture and adopted it. The idea of republic develops further.
Asian Developments (1200–300 B.C.E.): Animal style prevalent in early bronzes. *Pi* disc reveals Chinese desire for unity. In India, dome-shaped shrines house relics of Buddha.	Development of Confucian principles for living. Advent of Taoism, Chinese philosophy. Birth of Buddha in 537 B.C.E. Rise of Buddhism, with its belief in reincarnation and Nirvana.
Byzantine Art (to 1000 C.E.): Domed churches; mosaic becomes highly developed art form. Naturalism and realism are totally lost.	Beginning of Byzantine culture, Eastern Orthodox religion. Gradual decline of Western (Roman) empire. Muslim empire gains strength.
Romanesque Architecture (1000–1200 C.E.): Developed in Spain, using very thick, strong walls, and repetitive arches.	Many medieval people travelled (particularly on pilgrimages) across Europe, spreading the style for churches and monasteries.
Gothic Art (c. 1300): Pointed arch introduced, along with buttress system, lending extraordinary height to the interior. Images mostly religious; reflects religious stories and stories of major events. Architecture "carries the eye up" to God.	Abbot Suger of St. Denis equates light in architecture with ethereal presence.
Developments in Islam and Asia (600–1100): Principal form of Islamic architecture is the mosque, featuring a tower (minaret) used in calling to prayer.	Islamic empire expands from 662. Crusades begin.
Renaissance (1350–1650): Ever-increasing naturalism (*David, The Mona Lisa*) religious themes (Sistine Chapel, various Madonnas), linear perspective invented; exactness and order is reborn from the classical Greek and Roman times. The importance of the individual is emphasized. Exploration takes these new ideas to Germany and the Netherlands.	Humanism: A philosophy that emphasizes the value of each person; no limits to arriving at the level of genius. The popes commission artworks that reflect balance, serenity, perfection, and beauty. Trade and the printing press encourage intellectual freedom and exploration. Important artists were Michelangelo, Leonardo da Vinci, Raphael, Titian, Botticelli, and Donatello.

(continued)

Table 6.1 Continued

Art in China: Landscape painting is held as pursuit of the founding principle of the universe and is therefore the highest artform. Exiled artists make political art showing bamboo that will bend but not break under Mongol rule and orchids that flourish without soil around their roots.	Marco Polo visits China in 1275. Mongol ruler Kublai Khan rules as a tyrant and forces artists into exile. In 1368, Mongols are overthrown.
Pre-Columbian Art: Olmec (**1500 B.C.E.–300 C.E.**) focused on pyramids and large stone statues. In Mayan (300–900 **C.E.**) culture, narrative relief sculpture dominates. Aztecs (1300–1500) celebrate calendars with connections to nature and body systems.	Because of European exploration during the Renaissance, Hernán Cortes conquered the Aztecs in 1519. This art is termed "Pre-Columbian" because it predates the "discovery" of it by explorers in the age of Columbus.
Baroque (1600–1700): Most notable for its theatricality and drama in art that is achieved by use of light and monumentalizing and elaborate ornamentation. Rembrandt, Van Dyck, Frans Hals, Vermeer, and Rubens are noted painters as is Bernini in sculpture.	To combat rising Protestantism, the Vatican intended to turn Rome into the most magnificent city in the world and demanded that religious art "speak and impress" the masses with its grandness. Art became a commodity to the large group of middle-class bourgeoisie, especially in Northern Europe.
Rococo (early 1700s): Curvilinear style of the Baroque is modified and refined to be more delicate. Painting and sculpture begin to reflect sensuality and extreme ornamentation was the norm in most art forms.	Decadence of France under Louis XVI and Marie Antoinette, who lead needlessly extravagant lives. Aristocratic values at their crest.
Romanticism (1750–1850): Color and expression of subject matter reign supreme. The worship of nature is foremost. Painting shows passion of subject. In landscape painting, human's insignificance in the face of the infinite is called the "sublime."	Individuality and the power of the individual mind become prevalent social themes. Writings by Thoreau and Emerson contribute to renewed interest in nature.
Realism (1850–1900): Romantic idealism fades in favor of depiction of reality—the "here and now"—where real ordinary things and people become worthy subjects.	The advent of democracy, developing science, and photography brings about new vision of society. Social inequities examined in art and literature. Marx writes the *Communist Manifesto*.
Impressionism (late 1800s): Marks the beginning of modern art. Focuses on the pleasures of life, backing off from Realism and Social Realism. Leisure is the main subject. Optical mixing is interesting and the "fleetingness" of a moment becomes key to represent. Often associated with "dots" of light colors, Manet, Monet, and Renoir were of this period.	Progress of industrialization creates a "leisure class." Artists have the sole occupation to observe the habits of a city and comment on their observations with flair.
Post-Impressionism (late 1880s): No dominant visual style, but there is an increase in the expressive possibilities of color. They critique modern life and the elitist qualities of the Impressionists. There is a new emphasis on space and form. Van Gogh, Gauguin, and Cezanne represent this style.	Travel to the outskirts of cities and even islands is possible. The World's Fairs in Paris create impetus for social critique of the elite.
Cubism (early 1900s): Trying to see the three-dimensional world in two-dimensional terms. Emphasis is on trying to see the world in terms of the cylinder, the cone, the sphere, and the cube. Picasso painted and drew many works of this type but is also considered a modernist.	Much industrial progress is seen in the first airplane flight, first radio transmission, and the opening of the Henry Ford plant. Also Einstein's theory of relativity in 1905 brought up a new notion of time and space.
Futurism (1910s): Champions speed, motion, energy, and the machine. Painting and sculpture show movement.	WWI begins and there is a celebration of the new science of the twentieth century.

Dada (1920s): Art reflects a nihilistic point of view and a horror of war. Nonsensical juxtapositions of ideas attack tradition of Victorian values and challenge the status of art's sacred or precious images.	WWI ended with nearly everyone feeling the effects of great loss. Women's suffrage gains strength in the United States.
Surrealism (1930–40s): More positive than Dada; exploration of dream images and incorporation of chance events into compositions. The most famous of these artists are Salvador Dali and Miró.	Theories of Freud and his "dreams" and the significance of the subconscious are explored by the Surrealists. The Great Depression takes place and Hitler begins to rise to power.
Abstract Expressionism (1950s): Energetic use of line and color along with the ability to document the actions of the artist. Jackson Pollack represents this period.	In response to WWII with the Holocaust and the atomic bomb, artists turn inward to abstract representations of feelings. The center of the art world moves from Paris to New York.
Pop Art (1960s): Art reflects more humorous, less serious approach. Common images from popular culture, advertising, television, magazines abound. The transformation of the commonplace into the monumental is a dominant theme.	Postwar United States is very commercialized and consumer oriented. Fast food is inaugurated with McDonald's and the TV dinner. Artists such as Andy Warhol used a photo-like technique to emphasize consumerism.
Minimalism (1970s): Artists seek to simplify in the face of the excess of 1950s culture. The notion of space and the material presence of shape and form are key in what some term "hard edge."	With the beginning of the space race at the Soviet launch of Sputnik, schools and art take a back seat to the basics approach to life.
Postmodernism (1960–present): Pluralistic art incorporates diverse ideas and cultural values. Art reflects new and old technologies intermixed; reevaluation of traditional canons of art history, particularly roles of women artists. The question of identity is key along with other social and political issues.	The Civil Rights movement, the military involvement in Vietnam, the assassination of Martin Luther King, the feminist movement, the AIDS epidemic, and the collapse of the Berlin Wall all signify the pluralistic state of current society.

Source: Adapted from Sayre (1997).

The most important element in thinking about art and culture is to be aware of the ever-reflective relationship of art and the society that produces it. In relating art and its culture to young students, one should be sure that children can relate aspects of their own culture (the world around them) to the cultural aspects of the artwork in question. Also, students should be asked to look at their own surrounding culture to identify possible sources of art, (but teachers must be sure that this is specific and appropriate for each grade level). Young students have varying understandings of what culture is as they go through various grade levels, depending on their focus. For example, in general, second graders are going to be less aware of fashion trends than sixth graders, simply because of how these two groups think about their surrounding society. Kindergartners will more likely focus on their immediate family as culture, whereas fourth graders can begin to generalize to the state and national levels. This varying understanding of culture is important to remember in making age-appropriate cultural connections to artworks.

Try the following item:

A fourth-grade class is studying masks from a West African tribe. The teacher explains that the symbols and colors of the masks have different meanings depending on the ceremony for which they were created. Masks celebrating a good hunt have different symbols and colors than masks celebrating a birth in the tribe. Which of the following activities would be the *most* appropriate and effective art activity for supporting students' understanding of this subject?

A. Students design their own symbols based on those found on African masks.
B. Students make a mask in the African style based on their own important ceremony.
C. Students make a detailed copy of an African mask and then paint it.
D. Students make Mardi Gras masks, using symbols from African masks.

Choice *A* is incorrect because it does not make the connection of important cultural symbols to a ceremony. Rather, it devalues the African symbols by encouraging students to fabricate their own. Likewise, Choice *D* devalues the symbols by transferring them to a nonrelated event, Mardi Gras. Choice *C* does not challenge students to make any connection through the replication of these masks. It is simple copying, which rarely serves any educational purpose. Choice *B* is the *best* choice. Good rationales for choice *B* are that it incorporates students' experiences as well as some African history; it encourages students to personalize this knowledge; and most of all, it creates understanding about why African masks are important to tribes. Additionally, this choice stresses the importance of ceremony and ensures that students understand West African culture before making their own masks. The *best* answer is *B*.

Standard IV Analysis, Interpretation, and Evaluation of Art

The EC-4 teacher understands and conveys the skills necessary for analyzing, interpreting, and evaluating works of art and is able to help students make informed judgments about personal artworks and those of others.

The EC-4 teacher assists students in developing skills necessary to analyze, interpret, and evaluate works of art as well as the visual world around them (visual literacy). The teacher also helps students to substantiate their understanding and interpretations by determining and describing their own personal criteria for interpreting and evaluating the main idea in artworks.

This standard directly relates to the fourth strand of the art TEKS—focusing on critical evaluation. Today's highly visual world requires that even young students are able to process and make meaning from the barrage of images that make up our image-laden culture. Because of this, **visual literacy**—or the ability to make meaning from what is seen—requires that young children be given the tools needed to create meaning from the bombardment of imagery, be it television or the Internet, in order to become critical citizens. The tools required to accomplish such a task relate directly to the development of higher-order thinking skills in the visual realm. The conscientious early childhood teacher uses all of this knowledge to encourage critical thought.

In the early childhood classroom, critical evaluation requires that teachers develop meaningful art experiences for young children. They should avoid potentially harmful activities that require children to work with preformed objects (like templates or coloring book pages) that subliminally tell children there is only one best way to create or interpret (De la Roche, 1996), but teachers must engage children with genuine interest through their responses. Respectful responses to young children's observations about artworks of adults and the artworks of their peers teach children to value the aesthetic concerns of others. These aesthetic observations can stem from easy conversations about common objects such as cups or chairs (for example, "Why is one more comfortable to hold or to sit on? Which one is nicer to look at?") Obviously, there are no "right" or "wrong" answers to either of these questions, but these types of questions give students the tools to justify their own critical responses in positive ways. Additionally, discussions about which of the child's artworks should be kept or discarded help young children articulate their own value systems and their own criteria for evaluating art—again, a transferable skill to our own consumer culture, which often preys on children's inability to discern what they like and why (Johnson, 1997).

Consider the following example:

A third-grade teacher wants to encourage students to apply skills of interpretation and aesthetic awareness in a visual context. Which of the following activities would *not* be effective and appropriate for achieving this goal?

A. Asking each student to write a short poem and then to create a small drawing that expresses the feeling of the poem.

B. Showing an artwork to the class and then having each student write a story that he or she thinks the artwork is telling.

C. Having students look at two portraits in two widely differing styles and then discuss what mood is expressed in each portrait and how the mood was created.

D. Having each student complete a coloring sheet.

Then have children critique each other on how well the directions were followed.

Choice *A* requires students to interpret their poems by translating the ideas in their poems into a visual form. It follows that students would then need to aesthetically evaluate their artwork to see if they adequately expressed the intended emotion. This activity achieves the teacher's goal. Choice *B* clearly allows students to construct their own meaning or interpretation of the artwork by evaluating the work aesthetically. Choice *C* asks students to evaluate moods and compare and contrast. It takes these skills into the visual realm by asking students to tell how, in each painting, that mood was created. This also clearly achieves the teacher's objectives. All three of these options allow room for students to interpret, or draw their own meaning from, the visual art in some way. However, Choice *D* offers an activity that has no creative value. It must be said that a teacher's goals may sometimes include following directions, but this is not an activity that enhances interpretation and creativity.

Any standard that addresses higher-order thinking skills requires a quick review of Bloom's taxonomy in terms of art that outlines levels of critical-thinking skills:

- *Knowledge,* in which students recall art terminology, titles, dates, and such; recognize, name, identify, label, define, examine, show, and collect information.
- *Comprehension,* in which students explain, describe, translate, interpret, and summarize collected information.
- *Application,* in which students go beyond the concept or principle they have learned and *use* that principle or technique. Here they can think creatively, make preferences, and project ideas. They can experiment, predict, imagine, and hypothesize as they attempt to solve problems.

- *Analysis*, in which students make connections and establish relationships, categorize, compare and infer, classify and arrange, and organize and group information.
- *Synthesis*, in which students critically design, plan, combine, construct, and produce something original.
- *Evaluation*, in which students critically examine their own work and the work of others as they learn to criticize, judge, appraise, and make decisions.

Art in the early childhood classroom is a wonderful way to build skills in each of these critical thinking categories. Critical evaluation for students (as the TEKS advocate) requires that teachers be confident interpreters of works of art, taking into account important contextual information about the art in question. Teachers who critically challenge their students must also approach art critically. They must take on the responsibility to elevate art instruction beyond the level typical of "holiday art" or take home projects that all resemble the teacher's model. In fact, there is an art criticism model in use in many early childhood classrooms that help teachers do just that. The *Feldman Model of Art Criticism* suggests four steps to engage with works of art meaningfully: *Describe*—observers take visual inventory of a work of art, *Analyze*—observers think of how the parts relate to the whole, *Interpret*—observers create possible stories and meanings from visual evidence, and *Evaluate*—observers think through the "whys" of the artwork, ultimately developing their own criteria for judgment about the work of art (Feldman, 1992). There are obvious correlations among Bloom's higher level thinking and Feldman's steps for art criticism. Look for such correlations in Table 6.2.

Table 6.2 Sample Questions to Stimulate Higher-Order Thinking

Recalling (Knowledge and Comprehension)—generally straightforward questions
(NOT usually higher-order thinking skills)

	Example Questions
Naming:	What is the title of this painting?
Listing:	What do you see at the top, bottom, and sides of the painting?
Describing:	What are the figures in the boat doing?
Matching:	Which picture goes with the word *sad*?
Defining:	What is meant by *cool* colors?
Observing:	What is the woman wearing on her head?
Identifying:	Which building is the lightest value of blue?
Counting:	How many apples are in the still life?
Completing:	This type of artwork is called (sculpture, landscape painting, portrait painting, and so on).

Processing (Application and Analysis)—open-ended questions
(some are geared more to higher-order thinking than others)

	Example Questions
Comparing:	How is this mask like (or unlike) that mask?
Explaining:	Why did the artist place the horizon so high (or so low)?
Inferring:	From looking at these paintings, what can we infer about space and diminishing sizes?
Sequencing:	Arrange the paintings in order, from those with the brightest and most intense colors to those with the dullest colors.
Classifying:	Which sculptures of figures are most realistic? abstract? expressive?

Explaining cause and effect:	How did the artist use repetition and pattern to emphasize the face?
Contrasting:	How does the texture on the helmet differ from the fur collar?
Making analogies:	Can you think of another artist (or culture) who produced art similar to this piece?

Application (Synthesis and Evaluation)—hypothetical questions and personal interpretations (higher-order thinking skills)

	Example Questions
Forcasting:	If this artist had lived fifty years longer, how do you think his or her style might have changed?
Predicting:	Which artist, in this group of six, do you think will be best remembered for his or her technique in a hundred years?
Judging:	Which painting do you think shows the most artistic merit?
Imagining:	How do you imagine this artist would have painted a horse? Would he or she have used the same style and technique as in painting this landscape.
Applying:	How would you paint a cubist picture of a penguin?
Hypothesizing:	How do you think this sculpture would have looked if the artist had painted it with bright colors?

Source: Adapted from Herberholz & Herberholz (1998).

In thinking through some of these questions, the key to determining whether higher-order thinking skills are employed is to look for the kind of student action required. Those that require children to go beyond mere copying, describing, and naming to a level of application, synthesis, and evaluation are going to be more effective in addressing higher-order thinking skills.

Now let's try an assessment item to see whether the relationship of art to higher-order thinking skills has been clarified:

A fourth-grade teacher shows students a painting of a serene landscape and then a wild abstract gestural painting. Which of the following questions about these two pieces would *best* promote students' use of higher-order thinking skills?

 A. Have you ever seen these paintings before, and where did you see them?
 B. Are the colors used in the second painting also used in the first painting?
 C. How does each artwork make you feel, and why does the painting make you feel that way?
 D. What would you name each of the paintings?

Choice *A* is merely a recalling exercise. Choice *B* is a comparison question. Choice *D* might require some degree of creativity in coming up with the titles, but there is no place for the student to explain the name that was created. Choice *C* asks students to account for their feelings, thereby requiring the most student action. Thus, Choice *C* is the *best* answer because of the kind of effort required by the student.

Standard V Cognitive and Artistic Development

The EC-4 teacher understands how children develop cognitively and artistically and knows how to implement effective, age-appropriate art instruction and assessment.

The EC-4 teacher is able to evaluate and assess curricula and instruction in art as well as the skills and abilities of individual students. The teacher is able to address the strengths and needs of each child and monitor and encourage growth of students' thinking in art. Teachers recognize and utilize the valuable interdisciplinary structure of the early childhood classroom, keeping in mind stages of mental, social, and physical development. Teachers also engage in professional development in art, including most recent research and contemporary practices about art teaching at the early childhood level. This also requires that teachers are able to communicate effectively about the value of quality art programs in the EC-4 curricula.

This standard is basically the rationale for why the TEKS in the fine arts were deemed necessary to develop and are worthwhile to teach. Teachers who meet this standard know about children's stages of development (cognitive intellectual, social, emotional, and physical) and how these apply to art. They also know how to determine appropriateness of curricula and art activities while showing relevance of these skills in other content areas. Successful EC-4 teachers are aware of **Discipline-Based Art Education (DBAE)**—discussed later in this chapter—and its goal of applying learning from the arts across the curricula. Effective assessment and management of all students in the art curriculum is also a necessity. Knowledge of professional development sources for art education is also important. The Texas Art Education Association (TAEA) (http://www.coe.uh.edu/taea/), the Center for Educator Development in the Fine Arts (CEDFA at http://finearts.esc20.net/), and art links on http://dept.houstonisd.org/curriculum/finearts/htm/links.htm) are extremely useful resources for the EC-4 teacher.

A teacher's ability to teach the TEKS to students in the best manner possible requires that he or she knows the most current developments in the field. The recent development in art education, DBAE, is a good example of how the four strands of the TEKS are met through its shared emphasis on art-making, art history, art criticism, and the philosophy of art. Clearly, this initiative incorporates all four strands of the TEKS.

Again, Gardner's theory of multiple intelligences confirms the early childhood teacher's knowledge of sound art instruction for the young child. There are multiple forms of cognition—visual and spatial being two of them. Art instruction that is mindful of this strengthens cognitive growth across the board (Wright, 1997). Logically, what follows is an *interdisciplinary* approach to learning through the arts. This means applying these very same standards in the realm of art, with an eye for making many possible connections between art and other subject areas. Connections to the arts should figure prominently in any cross-curricular endeavor because thematic links transport the arts into everyday experiences (Pitri, 2001). In terms of the TEKS, cross-curricular connections ask that children put their knowledge of the arts to work reinforcing their learning. Perception skills are aligned with skills in language arts, for example. Creative expression becomes art-making with a purpose, and mathematics skills are necessary for many types of art and graphic design. Historical and cultural heritage take on a broader significance by virtue of their connections with other social studies. Drawing significance from links among other subjects requires critical evaluation.

Consider the following example:

Which statement reflects current thinking about art education in the elementary school?

A. Developing students' technical skills by having them select and then work with a single art medium for an extended period of time.

B. Developing students' drawing skills by having them view and attempt to copy reproductions of drawings by famous artists.

C. Developing students' knowledge of art history by having them focus on important periods of artistic achievement before moving on to other areas (e.g., perceptual awareness).

D. Developing students' critical skills by encouraging them to reflect on their own artwork in the act of creating what they have done so far to guide what they do next.

Choice *A* exemplifies past modes of art education where the emphasis was on technical product. However, current thinking of art education in the elementary school values *process* over product. The emphasis in Choice *B* on drawing by copying does not allow students to develop cognitive skills at the same time. Current thinking in art education emphasizes purposeful art-making. Choice *C* is a partial component in current thinking in art education because there is an emphasis on art history in addition to art criticism, aesthetics, and art-making. This choice strays from current thinking in the field by separating out history from perceptual awareness, etc. This choice does not support integrated art education that is emphasized in the field. Choice *D* encourages critical thinking by having students engage in reflective art-making where they are able to compare what they did with what they are doing now. This kind of art education is congruent with teaching students art in ways that make them critical and reflective about their own activities (which current thinking supports). The best answer is *D*.

Discipline-Based Art Education (DBAE)

As mentioned earlier, current thinking in art education is characterized by what is known as Discipline-Based Art Education (DBAE) in which art education incorporates four strands of art: *art history, art-making, art criticism,* and *aesthetics* (or the philosophy of art). Consider the diagram in Figure 6.2 (adapted from Wilson, 1997).

DBAE is:

- different from past approaches to art education that generally focused on students' free expression and art-making;
- not a set curriculum but rather a set of principles based on the domains or disciplines that contribute to creating and understanding art: art criticism, art history, art-making, and aesthetics (the philosophy of art); and
- a holistic, comprehensive, multifaceted approach to art education focusing on artworks at the center of thematic inquiry and instruction.

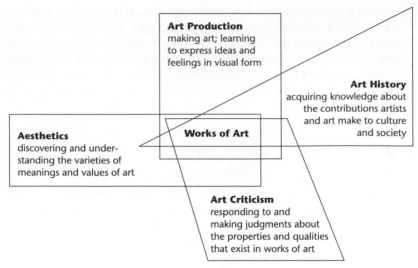

FIGURE 6.2 Discipline-Based Art Education Model

Through DBAE, students:

- make art;
- view and study art (original and reproductions);
- respond to and discuss art;
- speculate about meaning and value in art;
- read and write about objects that have cultural significance;
- develop multiple skills and capacities for making art and responding to art; interpreting, and evaluating their own art and the art of others;
- view and study works of art from many cultures and times, including fine arts, folk arts, and applied arts; and
- learn how art relates to the rest of the school curriculum, how art influences culture, and how culture influences art.

From the preceding lists it is easy to see how easily DBAE mirrors and incorporates the TEKS for art. Curricula should enable children to develop their creative abilities for making art (also called **studio art**); to understand art's cultural and historical context and the contributions that artists make to society (**art history**); to respond to and evaluate the qualities of visual imagery (**art criticism**); and discover and understand the varieties of meanings and values of art (**aesthetics**). DBAE uses adult role models from each of the art disciplines as sources for ideas and methods. This enables the teacher in a DBAE classroom to provide students opportunities for a much wider encounter with art than has traditionally been the case in art programs that only emphasize production activities. Through cumulative learning, students in grades K–12 are able to experience art at many different levels with increasing competence and sophistication.

It is key to recognize the important role that *works of art* play in DBAE; they are at the center of this approach to art education and are the link between the four art disciplines. Works of art are selected for study because they have relevance to both the actual communities and the communities of interest in which students live. Students are encouraged to create works of art in which the themes and topics and subjects and ideas found in the works of artists are adapted to children's interests and the interests of contemporary society.

Through this process, DBAE has acquired a depth that is lacking in much of contemporary education. DBAE encourages inquiry, knowledge, competence, caring, freedom, well-being, and social justice, which some educational reformists cite as the "moral purpose" necessary for reform (Fullan, 1993).

Appropriate student activities in a DBAE format include the following questions, some of which obviously should be reworded for use in a particular grade-level.

Art-Making

- What might have been the sources of the artist's visual idea, and how are these eventually manifested in a given art object?
- What are the steps involved in working in a given medium to make it ready for the artist to use?
- What are the impacts of work habits on the production of art objects?
- Is the artistic impetus or idea a new one; is it a variation on an old or established idea; or does it build through elaboration or revision of other works or traditions?
- What processes does the artist appear to utilize in order to work out a visual solution?
- How might the creative work of artists depend upon the character of their lived experiences?

Art Criticism

- What is the subject or theme of the work, and what does the work say about the intentions, interests, or social or political concerns of the artist?
- What are the significance and meaning of the objects, nonobjects, or visual effects in the work, and how do the visual and tactile elements contribute to an effective and meaningful statement?
- What do critics say the work means, and how is the work regarded overall in the development of the artist and of other artists?
- How do different audiences relate to or interpret this work and how does its context influence its meanings?
- Does this work sustain attention and involve active discovery of new things?

Art History

- Where, when, why, and by whom was the work made?
- What are the traditional meanings of the objects and symbols in the work?
- What are the distinguishing characteristics or qualities that identify the work and relate it to other works of art?
- Who and what in the artist's life affected him or her most?

Aesthetics

- How can we assign value to what various perceivers say about works of art?
- Should artworks that are deemed sacred, privileged, or private by groups within one culture be publicly displayed by another culture for all to see?
- To what extent should a viewer substitute his or her own personal perceptions, ideas, and judgments for expert and academic testimony?

- Is the alteration of a work of art the destruction of an existing work of art or the creation of a new one?
- Should we honor the deathbed request of an artist who wants his or her unsold works destroyed?
- Do citizens have the right to remove public artwork, paid for through taxes, if some members of the public find it offensive? Who decides? What arguments would make the case one way or the other? (Dobbs, 1998)

These questions should help in understanding the goals of DBAE. In general, we can characterize current thinking in art education as a shift from product to *process,* an emphasis on *connected, integrated learning* in and through art and a *multifaceted approach* to art education.

Interdisciplinary connections are key to making art education in the early childhood classroom meaningful. As Howard Gardner suggests in his *Frames of Mind* (1983), students who engage with the arts have the opportunity to be smart in different ways because of the different perspectives that art encourages. Consider the following:

> *The arts contribute to an overall culture of excellence in a school. They are an effective means of connecting children to each other and helping them gain an understanding of the creators who preceded them. They provide schools with a ready way to formulate relationships across and among traditional disciplines and to connect ideas and notice patterns. Works of art provide effective means for linking information in history and social studies, mathematics, science and geography . . . opening lines of inquiry, revealing that art, like life, is lived in a complex world not easily defined in discrete subjects. (Gardner, 1993)*

Because our lives do not naturally fall into 50-minute segments during which we focus on one subject at a time, it is important that teachers integrate multiple disciplines in their instruction, with an eye on making learning more meaningful for students (Cornett, 1999).

It is imperative, moreover, that teachers focus on the word *meaningful* used in Cornett's sentence. Teachers should be cautioned that artworks should not be used merely to illustrate topics and concepts (Wilson, 1997). Critical-thinking skills in the arts are transferred to other subjects (Boyer, 1995) and should be recognized and used as such. Projects or assignments that are purported to be interdisciplinary but only address the educational objectives of one subject matter are not using the arts meaningfully. In successful interdisciplinary connections, students are *challenged* in a subject area and in art. Look for this dual feature in the following interdisciplinary examples. In evaluating the artistic component, bear in mind the other standards already addressed as guidelines. The greatest issue with regard to interdisciplinary art is that there should be some openness to allow *for more than one way* to produce an assignment, even though criteria are set and will be used for assessment.

Relating Language and Art

- Write poems and stories and create artworks to complement them or vice versa.
- Make paintings, drawings, and murals that reflect books that you have read.
- Play a game that practices different types of language usage, such as using gestures, action words, or facial expressions, instead of words, to suggest

a mood or feeling. Practice drawing these gestures, actions, and expressions.
- Create puppets that offer opportunities for interpretations and expressions of ideas, thoughts, and feelings.
- Draw, rather than write, a book report.
- Dramatize a book in dance using costumes, music, and art.
- Make art using news articles as the impetus.

Relating Science and Art

- Study and draw the anatomy, structure, and workings of natural forms such as the human figure (or part of the body such as a hand, foot, ear, etc.).
- Make sculptures using the principles of balance, gravity, and kinesthetics.
- Design touch pictures and feeling boxes (pictures and boxes made from various textures and materials).
- Design and build bridges and buildings.
- Study how scientists use various chemicals to clean and restore paintings and sculptures (such as the Sistine Chapel).

Relating Mathematics and Art

- Draw pictures that show mathematical problems and solutions that involve weight, balance, measurement, and geometry.
- Introduce games that offer visual and spatial planning such as chess and checkers. Relate spatial planning to drawings.
- Create optical art by dividing spaces on paper.
- Use mathematical tools such as rulers and compasses to create drawings and designs.
- Engage in art activities that require measurement and planning such as weaving and architectural models.
- Use technology to create graphic arts.

Relating Social Studies and Art

- History becomes alive through art. Visually interpret (that is, draw, sculpt, or paint) historical events or developments.
- Study the history of a country (or a state) through artists' paintings.
- Draw and compare similar artifacts of various cultures.
- Create maps of a city as seen through the eyes of an architect and a city planner. (Linderman, 1997)

Many teachers, in examining the TEKS, wonder how to include art when they must teach so many other requirements for state testing (TAKS). As the demands on educators' time and other expanding responsibilities encroach, teachers must see interdisciplinary learning and art inclusion as a solution instead of cutting out one area in preference for another (Dobbs, 1998). The end result is stronger learning in both the arts and the subject area because learning will have to be cognitively transferred from one domain to another within the same lesson, thus it requires the student to be more fully engaged in the learning process. In addition adding art creates a motivating classroom experience.

One last assessment item:

A teacher wants to link his or her second-grade science curriculum with art. The best example of a lesson that would accomplish this goal would be:

A. Children make a papier mâché mobile of the solar system.
B. Children draw, color, and label the stages of metamorphosis of a caterpillar into a butterfly.
C. Children enlarge and paint encyclopedia drawings of flowers and diagram their parts.
D. Children imagine an animal to which they assign certain characteristics and create a three-dimensional habitat for it.

While students may enjoy doing both Choices *A* and *B*, these are not the *best* answer. Choice *C* clearly promotes little learning in either science or art. Little is gained in the process of copying. Both *A* and *B* result in students' most likely creating relatively similar products. This aspect is completely avoided in Choice *D*, wherein students creatively design animals with characteristics that require them to practice their knowledge of adaptation and animal habitats in a creative process. Certainly, it is excellent to give students hands-on activities to reinforce learning such as in Choices *A* and *B*, but be careful to differentiate between a hands-on activity and an interdisciplinary lesson. Because Choice *D* involves critical application of both scientific and artistic knowledge, this choice is the *best* interdisciplinary lesson. The answer is *D*.

SUMMARY

This chapter has explored the foundations of art education within the context of the EC-4 TExES exam. The hope is that the components discussed here will help you understand the five standards for the Visual Arts section so you will put them to good use when you enter the early childhood classroom. This chapter should serve as a review for the comprehensive exam but, more importantly, should be useful in the classroom setting. The standards addressed here are not meant to stand outside of classroom practice. Rather, these strategies are solid ways to ensure that art plays an important role in your curriculum.

Early childhood educators have identified ten distinct barriers to establishing a strong base for later learning in the arts for young children. They are: (1) succumbing to stereotypes, (2) assessing children's work in terms of personal ability, (3) reducing art to following instructions, (4) concentrating on precociousness, (5) searching for exotic materials, (6) forgetting who creative teaching is for, (7) avoiding the fine arts, (8) believing that creativity and chaos are synonymous, (9) failing to teach techniques, and (10) neglecting professional development in the arts (Jalongo, 1999).

Given the discussion of this chapter, do not let these factors be barriers to your students' future learning in the arts. Use your knowledge to break down these barriers and open up the role that art can play in your early childhood classroom.

Art should play a crucial role in your curriculum development for many reasons, including those rationales given within the discussion of the various standards. However, let's return to Dewey's words, from the beginning of this chapter, about art ensuring civilization. In particular, contemplate the following association of art and democracy:

If democracy is a fundamental value of this country, art must play a central role in education. It is art that encourages critical thought and respect for diverse points of view. It is art that practices novel solutions to age-old problems and encourages freedom of expression. It is art that allows us a window of understanding into those around us. The practice and study of art enacts democracy where diversity is valued and respect is instilled even in the earliest learning years.

Seriously consider the role art can and should play in your early childhood classroom. Democratic civilization is not secure without it.

REFERENCES

Boyer, E. L. (1995). *The basic school: A community for learning*. Princeton, NJ: The Carnegie Foundation for the Advancement of Teaching.

Cornett, C. E. (1999). *The arts as meaning makers: Integrating literature and the arts throughout the curriculum*. Upper Saddle River, NJ: Prentice-Hall.

De la Roche, E. (1996). Snowflakes: Developing meaningful art experiences for young children. *Young Children, 51*, 82–83.

Dewey, J. (1934). *Art as experience*. New York: Perigee Books.

Dobbs, S. M. (1998). *Learning in and through art: A guide to discipline-based art education*. Los Angeles: The Getty Education Institute for the Arts.

Epstein, A. S. (2001). Thinking about art: Encouraging art appreciation in early childhood settings. *Young Children, 56*, 38–43.

Feldman, E. B. (1992). *Varieties of visual experience*. New York: H. N. Abrams.

Fullan, M. (1993). *Changing forces: Probing the depths of educational reform*. London: Falmer.

Gardner, H. (1983). *Frames of mind: The theory of multiple intelligences*. New York: Basic Books.

Herberholz, D., & Herberholz, B. (1998). *Artworks for elementary teachers: Developing artistic and perceptual awareness*. Boston: McGraw Hill.

Jalongo, M. R. (1999). How we respond to the artistry of children: Ten barriers to overcome. *Early Childhood Education Journal, 26*, 205–208.

Johnson, M. (1997). Teaching children to value art and artists. *Phi Delta Kappan, 78*, 454–456.

Kindler, A. M. (1996). Myths, habits, research, and policy: The four pillars of early childhood art education. *Arts Education Policy Review, 97*, 24–30.

Koster, J. (2001). *Bringing art into the elementary classroom*. Belmont, CA: Wadsworth Thomson Learning.

Linderman, M. G. (1997). *Art in the elementary school*. Madison, WI: Brown & Benchmark.

Malaguzzi, L. (1993). History, ideas, and basic philosophy. In C. Edwards, L. Gandini, & G. Forman (Eds.), *The hundred languages of children* (pp. 41–90). Norwood, NJ: Ablex.

Miller, S. A. (1999). Shape it! Sculpt it! *Scholastic Early Childhood Today, 13*, 46.

Mittler, G. A. (1994). *Art in focus*. New York: Glencoe.

Pitri, E. (2001). The role of artistic play in problem solving. *Art Education, 54*, 46–51.

Sayre, H. M. (1997). *World of art*. Upper Saddle River, NJ: Prentice-Hall.

Szekely, G. (1999). Designing BRAVE new worlds. *Arts & Activities, 126*, 46–47.

Szyba, C. M. (1999). Why do some teachers resist offering appropriate, open-ended art activities for young children? *Young Children, 54*, 16–20.

Wilson, B. (1997). *The quiet evolution*. Los Angeles: The Getty Education Institute for the Arts.

Wolfensohn, J., & Williams, H. (1993) *The power of the arts to transform education*. Los Angeles: J Paul Getty Trust.

Wright, S. (1997). Learning how to learn: The arts as core in an emergent curriculum. *Childhood Education, 73*, 361–365.

AN ART LESSON PLAN

Title of Lesson: Night Skies and Art

Grade Level: Third (or Fourth)

Main Subject Area: Art

Integrated Subjects: Science, Music, History, Language arts

Time Constraints: Three integrated periods

Overall Goal(s): To introduce children to the idea of nature and science as part of the fine arts and to become familiar with the style of one famous artist (Van Gogh).

TEKS/TAKS OBJECTIVES:

§ 117.11. **Art** (b)(3.1) Perception. The student develops and organizes ideas from the environment. The student is expected to: (A) identify sensory knowledge and life experiences as sources for ideas about visual symbols, self, and life events; and (B) identify art elements such as color, texture, form, line, space, and value and art principles such as emphasis, pattern, rhythm, balance, proportion, and unity in artworks. (3.2) Creative expression/performance. The student expresses ideas through original artworks, using a variety of media with appropriate skill. The student is expected to: (A) create artworks based on personal observations and experiences; (B) develop a variety of effective compositions, using design skills; and (C) produce drawings, paintings, prints, constructions, ceramics, and fiberart, using a variety of art materials appropriately. (3.3) Historical/cultural heritage. The student demonstrates an understanding of art history and culture as records of human achievement. The student is expected to: (A) compare content in artworks from the past and present for various purposes such as telling stories and documenting history and traditions; (B) compare selected artworks from different cultures; and (C) relate art to different kinds of jobs in everyday life. (3.4) Response/evaluation. The student makes informed judgments about personal artworks and the artworks of others. The student is expected to: (A) identify general intent and expressive qualities in personal artworks; and (B) apply simple criteria to identify main ideas in original artworks, portfolios, and exhibitions by peers and major artists;

§ 117.12. **Music** (b) (3.5) Historical/cultural heritage. The student relates music to history, to society, and to culture. The student is expected to: (A) identify aurally-presented excerpts of music representing diverse genres, styles, periods, and cultures; (C) describe relationships between music and other subjects;

§ 112.5. **Science** (b) (11) The student knows that the natural world includes earth materials and objects in the sky;

§ 110.5. **English Language Arts and Reading** (b) Knowledge and skills; (1) Listening/speaking/purposes. The student listens attentively and engages actively in various oral language experiences. The student is expected to: (B) respond appropriately and courteously to directions and questions (K–3); (C) participate in rhymes, songs, conversations, and discussions; (D) listen critically to interpret and evaluate; (E) listen responsively to stories and other texts read aloud, including selections from classic and contemporary works; (2) Listening/speaking/culture. The student listens and speaks to gain knowledge of his/her own culture, the culture of others, and the common elements of cultures. The student is expected to: (A) connect experiences and ideas with those of others through speaking and listening; (3) Listening/speaking/audiences/oral grammar. The student speaks appropriately to different audiences for different purposes and occasions. The student is expected to: (C) ask and answer relevant questions and make contributions in small or large group discussions; (4) Listening/speaking/communication. The student communicates clearly by putting thoughts and feelings into spoken words. The student is expected to: (A) use vocabulary to describe clearly ideas, feelings, and experiences; (17) Writing/grammar/usage. The student composes meaningful texts applying knowledge of grammar and usage. The student is expected to: (C) compose elaborated sentences in written texts and use the appropriate end punctuation; (D) compose sentences with interesting, elaborated subjects;

§ 113.5. **Social Studies** (14) Culture. The student understands the importance of writers and artists to the cultural heritage of communities. The student is expected to: (A) identify selected individual writers and artists and their stories, poems, statues, paintings, and other examples of cultural heritage from communities around the world; and (B) explain the significance of selected individual writers and artists and their stories, poems, statues, paintings, and other examples of cultural heritage to communities around the world.

Objectives: Following a fieldtrip to the planetarium (if possible) or after viewing a teacher-created planetarium (in a small tent or projected onto the ceiling), students, as a whole class, will review their experiences.

Students will listen to four songs with lyrics about stars, and participate in a whole class discussion about them.

Students will view various artworks based upon the night sky as they listen to classical music will follow. A whole class discussion.

Students will listen to a Native American legend on the origin of stars, discuss history of man's fascination with the night sky, and view aboriginal cave drawings.

Students will complete an original painting based upon Van Gogh's style and title it.

Students will complete a "museum guide description" for their painting, accurately describing it with five sentences and with the use of five new vocabulary words.

Students will participate in a museum "walk-about".

Sponge Activity: Students will listen to the following songs: (1) "When You Wish Upon a Star"; (2) "The Impossible Dream" ("The Unreachable Star"); (3) "Swingin' on a Star"; and (4) "Starry, Starry Night."

Environmental Concerns: A fieldtrip to the planetarium increases interest. Obtain permission from the principal, the museum, and parents early. If a fieldtrip is not possible, the teacher can create a planetarium in a small tent to be set up in the classroom and/or put florescent objects on the ceiling (or fix major stars to the ceiling) and create a "planetarium" by darkening the lights. Give special directions for safety in darkened area.

Rationale(s): Many famous artists and artworks deal with night. Many composers and poets have written songs and poems inspired by the night sky. Throughout history people have looked up to the night sky and been inspired, both in the fine arts and in science, to capture the way that the night sky makes us feel.

Focus or Set Induction: Ask children to tell what all four songs from the sponge activity had in common (they are about stars) and which song they liked the most and why. As children listen to classical music ("Eine Kleine Nachtmusik" ["A Little Night Music"] by Mozart, "The Planets" by Gustav Holst, and "Thus Sprach Zarathustra [2001: A Space Odyssey Theme"]) show them the following artworks: *Starry Night* and *Starry Night over the Rhone* by Vincent Van Gogh, *Landscape with Stars* by Henri-Edmond Cross; photo images like http://www.diana.dti.ne.jp/~show-g/m083. jpg and http://www.diana.dti.ne .jp~show-g/m051.jpg from *Art of the Night Sky* Web site; *Midnight Sky Style* by David Robinson (modern day) at http://www.yessy.com/art/ paintings/landscapes_nature/skyscapes/night_ sky.html?view=277076; *Moon Through Tree Branches* by David Hayward at http://www.yessy .com/art/paintings/landscapes_nature/skyscapes/ night_sky.html?view=379913; Jewelry Lapis Bracelet *Night Sky* at http://www.novica.com/ itemdetail/index.cfm?pID=110075; and Glass art (*Night Sky from Jupiter*) at http://jermanartglass. com/nitesky_jupiter.jpg.html. Ask children to discuss: (1) what types of art they saw (paintings, photos, jewelry); (2) what other types of art there might be related to the night sky; (3) which is their favorite artwork and why. Ask students to: (1) examine the Van Gogh paintings more carefully and describe what they see; (2) tell which type of music they think goes best with the Van Gogh pictures and why; (3) discuss in what time period they think each piece of music was written and the artwork was created; (4) learn vocabulary that describes these two paintings (silhouette, bold, swirling, marbled, vivid, fanciful, churning, or others); (5) what they think Van Gogh might have been thinking when he painted the pictures.

MAKING CONNECTIONS:

1. **Connections with Past or Future Learning:** Ask children what they already know about stars and if they have seen artwork that focuses on the night sky.

2. **Connections to the Community:** Talk about where you can go in Texas to view the night sky very well (e.g., a planetarium [in various cities]; NASA [in Houston]; or an observatory [in the Davis Mountains]).

3. **Cultural Connections:** Tell students a Native American legend about the stars. Show an aborigine petroglyph from Australia (see http://googolplex.cuna.org/12433/5spot/story.html?doc_id=893 or http://www.space.com/scienceastronomy/060605_rock_art.html)

4. **Connections with student Interests & Experiences:** What can you recognize in the night sky? What types of occupations do you think use both astronomy and art? What movies have you seen that show stars?

Materials: Four songs: (1) "When You Wish Upon a Star"; (2) "The Impossible Dream" ("The Unreachable Star"); (3) "Swingin' on a Star"; and (4) "Starry, Starry Night"

Pictures/Artworks: (1) petroglyph; (2) *Starry Night* by Vincent Van Gogh; (3) *Starry Night over the Rhone* by Vincent Van Gogh; (4) *Landscape with Stars* by Henri-Edmond Cross; (5) Photo images; (6) jewelry. Need Internet.

Other: Native American legend of stars; white art paper; black construction paper; temperas paint or other liquid water color (needs to be a paint that stays vivid); foam shaving cream; cardboard scrapers; pencils; trays slightly larger than art paper; combs, popsicle sticks, scissors; other art supplies (for free choice); example of a "museum description"; short history of Van Gogh that is age appropriate; finished model of marbling technique

Activities: Guided Practice: Play four songs with lyrics and discuss. Show artworks, listen to music, and discuss; make connections. Read students an art museum description of several paintings and discuss the elements of Van Gogh's paintings in terms of descriptions of this type. Give a short history of Van Gogh and tell why he is a famous artist. Children can select from a variety of materials to complete their Van Gogh-style paintings (crayon-resist, etc.). Give directions for one idea such as a teacher demonstration of marble printmaking (www.princetonol.com/groups/iad/lessons/middle/marbling.htm). In a tray a bit larger than the art paper you wish students to use, squirt out foam shaving cream about 10" thick and use your hand to level it out (the teacher may want to have several trays ready up to this point). Then put watercolor paint (Prang temperas are good or other liquid watercolor

paints) on top of the foam in various colors that students choose (usually limit to three colors); teachers or students can do it. Students use a Popsicle stick or other instrument to swirl paint as desired, trying to keep the paint on the surface rather than pushing it down into the foam. Have students lightly press their papers on top (do not press all the way to the bottom) (foam can be reused for 5 or 6 prints). Use a piece of cardboard to scrape foam off the paper (the design will stay), then put aside to dry. Have students use a sheet of black construction paper the same size as the background paper to draw their landscape, and use a comb or other instrument dipped into paint to scratch designs into the landscape and/or heighten sky effect on the background. Cut out landscape and, when the background is dry, paste the landscape on top of the background sky. Students may also want to enhance with colored glue, stamps, and so forth. Show an example. The teacher will discuss options of other materials for choices so as to encourage a variety of approaches and creativity.

Independent Practice: Students will complete a painting loosely based on Van Gogh's style, title it, and write a museum description that includes why it is similar in style to Van Gogh's work.

Assessment: Individuals must complete their paintings, title them, and write descriptions of them (as per a museum guide) to be placed below their paintings. The descriptions should contain at least five sentences that accurately describe the students' individual paintings and contain five new art vocabulary words. Descriptions should include a reference to the style of Van Gogh.

What will students do who finish early? Go to bookmarked Web sites to view other artworks based on the night sky. Students may also write a short story about what is occurring in their artworks.

Closure: Art museum "walk-about."

Modification for Students with Special Needs: Carrie has difficulty holding regular brushes, so hers will need to be wrapped in foam rubber.

Reflection: To be completed after teaching the lesson.

DRAFT YOUR OWN ART LESSON PLAN

Title of Lesson: _____

Grade Level: _____

Main Subject Area: _____

Integrated Subjects: _____

Time Frame/Constraints: _____

Overall Goal(s): _____

TEKS/TAKS Objectives: _____

_____

_____

Objective(s): _____

_____

_____

Sponge Activity: _____

_____

_____

Environmental Concerns: _____

_____

_____

Rationale(s): _____

_____

_____

Focus or Set Induction: _____

_____

_____

Making Connections:

1. Connections to Past or Future Learning: _____

_____

2. Connections to the Community: _____

_____

3. Cultural Connections: _____

_____

4. Connections to Student Interests & Experiences:

_____

_____

Materials: _____

_____

_____

Activities: Guided practice: _____

_____

_____

_____

_____

_____

_____

_____

_____

_____

_____

Independent practice: _____

_____

_____

_____

_____

_____

_____

_____

_____

_____

_____

_____

_____

Assessment: _____

_____

What Will Students Do Who Finish Early?

_____

_____

Closure: _____

_____

Modification for Students with Special Needs: _____

_____

Reflection: _____

_____

OBSERVING ART EXPERIENCES/ACTIVITIES

During your visit to an early childhood classroom, use the following form to provide feedback as well as to reflectively analyze the room, the materials, and the teacher.

	Observed	Not Observed	Response
1. Art is a part of a thematic lesson or unit.			If so, describe. If not, what connections to other content could be added?
2. A variety of art materials is available as free choice.			If so, describe. If not, what could be added?
3. Children are encouraged to use a variety of materials.			If so, describe. If not, what could the teacher provide?
4. Children are asked to talk about artwork that is shown by the teacher.			If so, describe. If not, what could the teacher do to encourage discussion?
5. Children are asked to talk about their own artwork.			If so, describe. If not, what could the teacher do to encourage this?
6. A variety of artwork is exhibited (sculpture, prints, collages, crafts, jewelry, etc.).			If so, describe where and how. If not, what changes could be made?
7. Example art that is shown to children is of high quality (a clear print, large slide presentation, etc., where details can be noted).			If so, describe. If not, what changes should be made?
8. Art is connected to technology in some manner.			If so, describe. If not, how could it be integrated?
9. Children have sufficient time to *think* about an art project.			If not, describe how long they were given. What was the result? How long do you think they might need?
10. Children have sufficient time to *complete* an art project.			If not, describe what was the result? How much longer do you think they might need and why?
11. Teacher directs children in art activities with specialized art vocabulary.			If so, describe. If not, what opportunities were missed to do so? What vocabulary could be added?
12. There is discussion about what students are trying to communicate in their art.			If so, how was this led by the teacher? If not, what could be encouraged and how?
13. Teacher provides structure for children to view and discuss their art and that of peers.			If so, describe. If not, describe a possible scenario.
14. Teacher exhibits well-known artists' work or other appropriate examples in a lesson.			If so, describe. If not, give ideas for what could be added?
15. Teacher exhibits art examples from various cultures, genders, time periods, and age groups.			If so, describe. If not, give ideas for what could be added in a developmentally appropriate way.

	Observed	Not Observed	Response
16. Higher-level questions are asked about art.			If so, describe. If not, give ideas for what questions could be added to encourage higher-level thinking.
17. Teacher encourages reflective evaluation on artworks.			If so, describe. If not, what could he or she do differently?
18. The teacher models new techniques in art (versus asking children to copy his/her example).			If so, describe and tell if it is effective. If not, what was the effect on student products?
19. The environment is accepting of children's efforts in art.			If so, describe. If not, give ideas for what could be changed in a developmentally appropriate way
20. An Art Center is provided.			If so, describe. If not, give ideas for what could be included in a developmentally appropriate way.
21. The Art Center has rotating tasks.			If so, describe. If not, tell why not and what seems to be an effect of this.
22. Children are allowed age-appropriate independence for choices in the Art Center to elicit creative expression.			If so, describe. If not, what is the effect? What could be changed?
23. Other centers have integrated tasks or materials connected with art.			If so, describe. If not, what centers could be integrated with art and how?
24. The teacher monitors art projects, discussing progress and giving suggestions.			If so, describe. If not, what is the result?
25. Effective assessment is given.			If so, describe. If not comment on what assessment could have been used and why.

TEST YOURSELF ON ART

1. Mrs. Nomeni wants to include an art activity in her third-grade science class. What would be the *best* activity from those listed below?
   A. Draw a picture of the class experiment from an illustration in their books.
   B. Draw a series of pictures of what happened in the experiment that was conducted in class.
   C. Color and label a worksheet on the experiment.
   D. Draw a picture of something that impressed them about the experiment in class; then tell or write about the drawing.

2. Mrs. Henderson taught her third graders a thematic lesson on animals. As part of the integration, she had children create an animal of their choice from clay. First, however, she showed children a number of pictures of animal sculptures in various styles and had children compare and contrast these. She discussed with students the prices of some of the sculptures that were for sale and talked about making a living as an artist. Next she gave students the clay and asked them to create their animals, noting that they had 20 minutes to work on their projects. At the end of the lesson she was disappointed in their work; she felt she had provided a good lesson. What element had she *not* considered?
   A. Motivation
   B. Knowledge
   C. Problem-finding and production
   D. Immersion and incubation

3. Mr. Kendricks had his fourth-grade class think about landforms that involved water (lakes, rivers, oceans, creeks, etc.) in his social studies time. He had students, in groups, draw and color a picture of each of these concepts. What would be the *best* preactivity he could include for student success on this project?
   A. Creating a concept web with the whole class brainstorming and organizing ideas and descriptions about these concepts
   B. Reading a story to the class about a child's adventures on a boat
   C. Asking children to close their eyes and imagine they are aboard some type of craft on each of these water forms and to describe how they think it would feel as they float along
   D. Asking children who have seen each of these forms to describe the concepts and their experiences

4. Ms. Tomás wants to integrate an art activity into her kindergarten class. What would be the *best* activity for her to put in a center?
   A. Have children sort cards with primary colors.
   B. Have children sort the work of several different artists.
   C. Have children sort art of different historical periods.
   D. Have children sort concepts illustrated by different artists in different times.

5. The Pre-K teachers met at the beginning of the year to talk about the supplies they would need to order to complete the units they planned to teach. They discussed the art activities that they wanted children to complete, how age appropriate they were, and how they would fit into their goals and objectives. What area is the *most* crucial to discuss before ordering?
   A. How much children would be motivated by the activities
   B. How much money they have in their budget
   C. Safety and disposal
   D. Establishing good rules for working with art this year

6. Mr. Kim wanted to set up a good art evaluation plan for students in his self-contained elementary classroom. What would be *best* for him to use?
   A. Test scores
   B. Rubrics
   C. Checklists
   D. Portfolios

7. At Thanksgiving, Ms. Ortiz decided that her first-grade students would integrate a creative art project by painting a pumpkin that they would cut open later. Students would then count the seeds, bake the seeds, and sample them. She provided them with orange, brown, green, and black paints and paper. This could *best* be described as:
   A. an excellent integration because it has students focus on the details of the pumpkin for later

B. not an open-ended use of art
C. a motivating focus activity
D. a project that is not time efficient

8. Mr. Howell wanted to introduce his third graders to rhythm and movement, balance, proportion, contrast, variety, unity, and emphasis. These concepts make up:
   A. The principals of design
   B. The elements of art
   C. The ways of art-making
   D. Discipline-Based Art Education

9. Which of the following is *not* true?
   A. Red + yellow = orange
   B. Blue + red = violet
   C. Blue + yellow = green
   D. Yellow + black = brown

TEST YOURSELF ANSWERS AND RATIONALES FOR ART

Answer 1: Choices *A* and *C* are mindless; they involve copying—a lower level activity. Choice *B* is better, but basically involves only recalling the steps. Choice *D,* however, requires the learner to select a meaningful part of the experiment and describe its meaning after the illustration is completed. This would be beneficial to both art and science and would involve a higher level of thinking. The *best* answer is *D.*

Answer 2: Koster (2001) tells us that there are seven points to consider in the creative process: (1) motivation, (2) problem-finding (3) knowledge, (4) skills, (5) immersion, (6) incubation, and (7) production. Mrs. Henderson gave them motivation (*A*) and knowledge (*B*) through the integrated lesson. There was some problem-finding (*C*) in her discussion about making a living selling art, and children had products—although lacking. However, she allowed barely any time at all for *immersion* and *incubation.* It is believed that without time, the production will never be a true work of art and that children will always believe they are not capable of good art. Creativity in any area (music, language arts, science, etc.) must always include time to think deeply about ideas (Koster, 2001). The correct answer is *D.*

Answer 3: All of these activities could add some interest to the lesson. However, we are looking for the *best* one for a *successful project.* The activity that would most help students with their drawings is Choice *A*—creating a concept

web. A web would include details and descriptions of each landform. For example, the "bubble" for oceans on the concept web might have spokes with words such as *most of the Earth, waves, tropical, blue, green, Artic, fishing, big ships, whales, and hurricanes.* For lakes, the spokes might be *huge (like Great Lakes), shipping, small, enclosed (landlocked), waterskiing,* and *fishing.* These details would help children both in social studies and in art. Reading a story such as the one described (*B*) does not include all of the concepts needed for the assignment. Choice *C,* imagining, would be a good activity, but probably would not provide many of the details needed for a successful drawing. Choice *D* provides an element of "connecting children's background experiences to new learning," which is stated as a good practice numerous times in the competencies; however, children probably have not seen all of the concepts that are needed in this lesson. The best answer is *A.*

Answer 4: Age appropriateness is important in every content area, including art. Choices *C* and *D* would be a bit too difficult for kindergarten children without quite a bit of prior instruction. Choice *A* would be an activity that would help students to learn their colors. To really *integrate* art, however, Choice *B* would be the *best.* For example, the teacher could select pictures of an animals to sort, done in various mediums (paintings, ink drawings, watercolors, sculptures, cave paintings, etc.) or different types of transportation or landforms—whatever was being learned. Sorting concepts with artworks increases students' vision of the concepts and shows a wide range of how artists depict them. The best answer is *D.*

Answer 5: It would be good to look at *all* of these areas prior to making decisions. Teachers should always consider children's motivation (*A*) and classroom management (*D*) with special areas such as art—in which children may ruin clothes or cause possible concern with materials and tools. Of course, the budget is the determining factor in ordering supplies (*B*), although many times caregivers can contribute art supplies that are not within a budget. However, a *crucial* discussion before ordering supplies should be safety and disposal issues. Teachers can consult the *MDSS (Material Data Safety Sheet)* required by schools and most often used for science, but it should also tell about the safety of art materials as well. There are *many* safety issues for teachers to think about with art supplies (Koster, 2001): The need for storing particular supplies in a safe place for young children, the air quality of a classroom (to avoid fumes), reading warning labels to determine safe use guidelines, identifying possible toxic poisons, changing quality as art materials age, risk of misuse for younger children, and so forth. Younger children are particularly at risk because they often experiment orally (putting things in their mouths), and their physical and mental development can cause them to misuse products and tools because of lack of control. Another concern is the health status of children in the class who may have particular allergies (although teachers may not know this at the time of their discussion), but teachers must concern themselves with chalk dust, for example, when using pastels, with skin allergies with paints and clays, and other toxins that may cause difficulties. A final safety concern that teachers need to consider is to check the school's fire code or other safety codes prior to displaying any art in classrooms and in the halls. The answer is *C*.

Answer 6: The best way to evaluate children in art would be through portfolios (*D*), which could contain all of the other assessment instruments listed and others (test scores, rubrics, checklists, task assignments, self-evaluations, anecdotal records, products, and so forth). The portfolio lends itself not only to teacher evaluation but to student self-evaluation and reflection. The answer is *D*.

Answer 7: This lesson could contain a very good integration of art (*A*), as well as a motivating focus activity (*C*), and a time-efficient project (*D*) (although we don't have any information to support this choice—either positive or negative). However, the problem is not with the activity but with the art element. This is not an open-ended activity. Children cannot be very creative because they are being given a limited amount of materials with which to work. Teachers should introduce various techniques and art supplies and then allow children to select how they would represent the subject (perhaps in a collage, in a pencil drawing, or with chalk) if they want children to be creative. The answer is *B*.

Answer 8: Mr. Howell is introducing the *principals of design* (*A*). The *elements* of art (*B*) consist of color, form, shape, space, line, texture, and value. *Ways of art-making* (*C*) include drawing, painting, printmaking, collage, sculpture, fiberarts, and electronic media. *Discipline-Based Art Education* (DBAE) (Choice *D*) is an approach to teaching the four stands of art together: art history, art-making, art criticism, and aesthetics. The correct answer is *A*.

Answer 9: Choices *A*, *B*, and *C* are all true. *D* is not. Therefore, the answer is *D*.

7 Preparing to Teach Music in Texas

Janice L. Nath
University of Houston–Downtown

Teachers who will take the Generalist test should be familiar with many aspects of music, as the state of Texas has established music standards for all ages of children. Under each music standard Texas has provided information that includes *Teacher Knowledge* (what teachers should know about music) and *Application* (what teachers should be able to do when teaching music at their particular grade level). These standards are given in this chapter, but they can also be downloaded in chart form from http://www.sbec.state.tx.us/SBECOnline/standtest/standards/ec4music.pdf.

Many of you are probably wondering why the state of Texas requires elementary teachers to know about teaching music, as you may have grown up in (or are teaching in) a school where there is a special teacher for all music classes. You may not realize that there are *no* specialized music teachers in many Texas schools, particularly in the lower grades. Therefore, if any music is to be taught in those schools, it is you—the regular classroom teacher—who will be responsible. It would be a terrible thing, I hope you will agree, for children to grow up without learning about music—both in the sense of appreciating the wide range of music the world has produced and in learning the songs and music that bind our culture. You may be the one person who opens the door for a child's love for music, special musical talents, or even a career in music. Therefore, our state wants to offer students the opportunity to have a teacher who can bring music into each Texas classroom, even if a district is not able to provide a music specialist for each school.

This chapter is not only written to help those teachers who have had little, if any, music training but also to provide a good review for those who may have had some experience with music. Let us take a closer look at the standards that will be tested here.

Standard I Visual and Aural Knowledge

(Note: All music standards are covered under Competency 025.)

The music teacher has a comprehensive visual and aural knowledge of musical perception and performance.

The EC-4 teacher, in addition to other subject areas, should know and understand the standard terminology used to describe and analyze musical sound. Thus, he or she should be able to identify and interpret music symbols and terms, use standard music terminology, and identify different rhythms and meters. In addition, she or he should be able to identify vocal and instrumental sounds and distinguish among timbres; recognize and describe the melody, harmony, tempo, pitch, meter, and texture of a musical work; and identify musical forms. Teacher knowledge should also include how to demonstrate musical artistry both through vocal or instrumental performance and by conducting vocal or instrumental performances. The teacher should be able to perceive performance problems and detect errors accurately.

There are many concepts in music that you should know as a beginning teacher of young children—because you may be required to teach music as one of your subject areas. The main concepts taught through fourth grade include duration, rhythm, pitch and melody, form, dynamics, tempo, instrument families, and timbre and tone color.

Duration

One of the first concepts about which young children learn in music is **duration** of sound—that is, there are *long sounds* in the world all around us (sirens, mooing cows, etc.), and there are also *short sounds* (jackhammer, clicking sounds of a computer keyboard, etc.). These variations of length of sound (or duration) are also found in music and can be represented by symbols or *musical notes*. Each symbol, or written musical note, represents a certain length (or count) that the sound should last. The longer the count or length held, the "less darkened, encumbered, or decorated" a note is when written. For example, the symbol for the longest tone in music is called a **whole note** and looks like a hollow circle—almost the same as the letter "O." If we were to sing one tone or note ("la-a-a-a," for example), while we slowly counted to four in our heads, that would be about the length of a whole note's duration. To begin to teach very young children this concept, you may want to begin with long animal sounds and have them "sing" whole notes.

O   **O**   **O**   **O**
Moooooo!   Moooooo!   Moooooo!   Moooooo!

There is an easy connection in determining duration of musical notes to mathematics (fractions, to be exact). If the whole note gets four equal counts in a certain piece of music, then we would read the next shorter tone as getting two counts. The symbol for this tone is called a **half note.** If you divided the whole note that you sang before into two half notes, they would sound like "La-a" "La-a" (if we counted 1-2 in our heads for the first "La-a" and 3-4 for the second "La-a"). Half notes are described as hollow circles with a stem. The half note tones can then be divided into shorter **quarter notes,** which would be sung or played as "La," "La," "La," "La," as each receives one short count (1, 2, 3, 4). The quarter note looks like a half note with a stem, but the circle is filled. To continue to teach young children about the length of sound here, you may want to have them continue with less sustained animal sounds.

(The sheep says in half notes:)   Ba - a   Ba - a   Ba - a   Ba - a

(The hen says in quarter notes:)   Cluck! Cluck! Cluck! Cluck! Cluck! Cluck! Cluck! Cluck!

We can continue to divide these length or duration symbols into eighth notes, sixteenth notes, and so on, each getting half as much time as the note before. The shorter the note, the more that it is darkened in and the more "flags" it has attached. Let us see how this might look in music. As you sing "La" to yourself, hold each note as long as the count below it shows.

A whole note

O
1-   2-   3-   4
La-   a-   a-   a!

Half notes

1-   2   3-   4
La-   a!   La-   a!

Quarter notes

La!   La!   La!   La!
1   2   3   4

Eighth notes

La! La!   La! La!   La! La!   La! La!
1   &   2   &   3   &   4   &

To continue to explain this concept to children, you could compare a whole note to a telephone ring or siren. The half notes are similar to the length of a grandfather clock's "bonging." The quarter notes are like a clock ticking or a car blinker, and the eighth notes are like someone typing fast on the computer. You can see how these symbols work in the song "Old MacDonald" below. Try singing the song by counting the numbers below rather than the words and you will have an idea of how the shape and design of the note tells you how long to hold it.

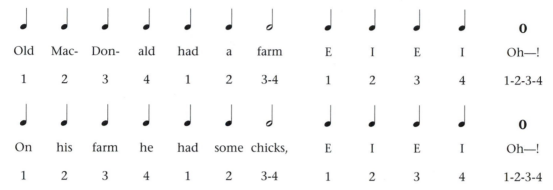

Old	Mac-	Don-	ald	had	a	farm	E	I	E	I	Oh—!
1	2	3	4	1	2	3-4	1	2	3	4	1-2-3-4

On	his	farm	he	had	some	chicks,	E	I	E	I	Oh—!
1	2	3	4	1	2	3-4	1	2	3	4	1-2-3-4

There is also a symbol for when *no* music should be played or sung—the **rest.** When you see a rest symbol, it means to "rest" your voice or instrument by *not* singing or playing for a certain time period. Rest symbols (or notations of silence) correspond to the values of musical notes so we see: (1) whole rests, (2) half rests, (3) quarter rests, (4) eighth rests, (5) sixteenth rests, and so forth. Again, these symbols indicate a period of time when there is no sound for an established duration. Each rest appears very different from the others, unlike the notes we saw earlier to which flags and darkening are added as the note gets shorter in length or duration. Rests with their counts are shown below. Remember that there will be a length of silence for each rest, according to its value.

whole rest	half rest	quarter rest	eighth rest
1-2-3-4	1-2 3-4	1 2 3 4	1&2&3&4&

One important thing to remember in teaching the duration of notes and rests is that the sound (or, in the case of rests, *no* sound) occupies the entire space in time until the next note or rest value is written. If one is singing or playing a whole note with the value of four counts, for example, each count must be equal—including the last count. One cannot count, "One—two—three—fo- One—two—three—fo—One. . . ." It must be, "One—two—three—four—One—two—three—four. . . ."

Rhythm

The concept of **rhythm,** or sound organized in time, is an important one in music and strongly relates to the discussion above. If you have ever marched, played a "pat-slap" game, chanted while jumping rope, or participated in a rap, you have experienced the beat, or pulse, of music. This pulse of the music can be easily felt through toe-tapping or dancing and is, perhaps, the most fundamental, though not the whole concept of rhythm. For example, sing the words to "Baa Baa, Black Sheep" and tap your foot at the same time. You will experience a very *steady beat* in sets of 2s (count "1, 2" over and over as you hum the tune). Notice that each set is divided by a bar. The distance between bars, in music, is called a **measure** and separates sets of beats into groups—in this case, sets of 2 beats per measure.

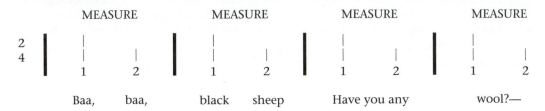

In "Twinkle, Twinkle Little Star," there is a steady beat, or foot tap, in sets of four.

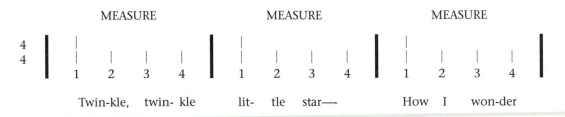

In most Native American music, there is a very steady pulse of four beats. In stereotypical Native American music, such as we hear in Wild West cartoons, a very *strong beat* comes on the first of the four beats (ONE-two-three-four, ONE-two-three-four). Think of the drum beat associated with stereotypical Native American music and see if you can tap it out below. In *authentic* Native American music this loud-soft-soft-soft rhythm is not so distinct.

The beat changes, however, in "On Top of Old Smoky" and "Happy Birthday." When you toe-tap to either song, you should feel beats in sets of three with a very *strong beat* on the first beat (ONE-two-three, ONE-two-three). This is a rhythm also seen in many waltzes.

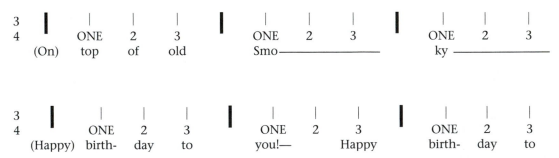

Try tapping or patting each of these songs to see if you feel the beat. Another type of music that has a strong beat is a march. This type of music is easy for many people to follow, as in a marching band or military group, because it helps people to walk in time together: "left, right, left, right; 1,2,1,2." "Yankee Doodle" is a march that demonstrates this beat. Try to move your feet to feel this rhythm as you count to the melody.

One	Two		One	Two		One	Two		One	Two
Left	Right		Left	Right		Left	Right		Left	Right

| Yankee | Doodle | | went | to town, | | riding | on a | | po- | ny |

One way to see if you are keeping the beat regularly is to set a **metronome.** This is an instrument that sounds like a loud clock and "ticks" to the beat that a composer has written or a musician has selected for each piece of music. It takes the place of a director when playing or singing alone, so that one does not inadvertently speed up or slow down the music. Thus, a singer or instrumentalist can be sure to practice the correct beat in a very *steady* manner throughout a piece of music.

Now that you have a "feel" for what beats are all about, how do composers tell players or singers to play what they intended? At the beginning of each piece of music, as shown below, you will see the **meter** sign that indicates how many beats per measure the composer desires. This is indicated by two numbers that are one on top of the other called the **time signature.** The number on top of the time signature indicates how many beats there are per measure, or, for our purpose, divided "foot tap or pat/clap sets." The bottom number tells what kind of note gets one beat. For example, a "2" on the bottom means that a half note gets one beat, but a "4" on the bottom would mean that a quarter note gets one beat. There can be many combinations, but here we will deal with only the most common time signatures. Let us look at the following signatures written below.

4 There are four equal quarter notes to a set in a measure (1-2-3-4; 1-2-3-4).
4 The 4 on the bottom indicates that a quarter note gets one beat (or think math again . . . a 1/4 of a whole note gets a beat = a quarter note).

2 There are two even quarter notes to a set (1-2; 1-2), as in a march.
4 A quarter note gets one beat.

3 There are three even quarter notes to a set (1-2-3; 1-2-3), as in a waltz.
4 A quarter note gets one beat.

If we now combine the two concepts discussed above, we can see that the notes have a *value length* (duration) and the composer can arrange a *set of notes* together. When we tapped the beat of "Baa, Baa, Black Sheep," we were in $\frac{2}{4}$ time, "Twinkle, Twinkle Little Star" was in $\frac{4}{4}$ time, and "On Top of Old Smoky" and "Happy Birthday" were both in $\frac{3}{4}$ time. A question in the exam may ask you to determine "time" or meter for a familiar piece of music.

Sometimes music changes time signatures in the middle of a song. If you see measures that look like the ones below, you can see that the beat pattern changes. Using time signature changes is the way in which composers tell us that the beat of the song should change, for example, from a waltz beat to a march beat. This does not happen very often in popular vocal music, but we frequently see, hear, and feel the change in instrumental music.

Time signature change

We have spent some time talking about the beat or pulse and the duration of notes and silence, but another element that contributes to rhythm is the patterns of accented and unaccented sound that occur in music. We can also find these in poetry. For example, in "Jack and Jill went up the hill," there is a heavy accent on the words Jack/Jill/up/hill with other less accented words between, although there is still a steady 1-2/1-2 beat that we can tap. The same occurs in music. This concept might be compared to our heart providing a steady, consistent beat, while we go about running, jumping, stopping, stepping, and so forth. In music, all of this organization of sound is **rhythm.**

Children seem to develop musical abilities as they mature. By about age 7 to 9, rhythmic coordination improves dramatically, and by the fourth grade, most children should be able to discriminate among elements of duration (length of sound) and meter. The ability to *perceive,* recall, and reproduce musical elements precedes the child's ability to read, or decode, and make sense of rhythmic phrases and other musical features. To help children learn about rhythm, first promote the natural tendencies of children in rhythmic play when they are moving to the music, then use direct music instruction to teach the elements of rhythm. Thus children should first internalize "how the music feels" before they are introduced to the process of decoding music symbols. Clapping to music or having students listen to a beat that you play will help them "feel" the rhythms. Relating words to rhythm is also helpful, as you have seen above. All words have a rhythm, so select words to match rhythms you wish to teach. For example, say the following words in a rhythmic pattern—"Hou-ston, Dal-las, Wich-i-ta Falls!" This activity also helps young readers with determining syllable division. Can you perceive the rhythm of each word and of the phrase as a whole? Model such patterns often, then ask students to echo or clap what they hear. This is an excellent way to introduce the idea of rhythm, and young children love pat-clap or echo games and will follow along easily. As with the psychomotor domain, it is best to break instruction and performance into small tasks. As children grow in their abilities with rhythms, ask students to differentiate between rhythm patterns and explain their thinking or sort out several patterns. At first, discriminate rhythm examples within songs children know rather than using abstract or unknown music.

National and state standards tell us that children should be able to create, notate, and perform simple rhythmic patterns. Another good way to help children understand and perform the concept of rhythm is to have rhythm instruments available. Instruments can be genuine or can be created from anything that students can beat, rattle, or shake to the beat. Some typical instruments for beginning rhythm activities might be rhythm sticks, hand drums, bongos, maracas, guiros (ridged gourd instruments), jingle bells, tambourines, claves (hardwood sticks), sand blocks, wood blocks (hardwood blocks with a hardwood striker), slit drums, cowbells, hanging cymbals, finger cymbals, triangles, resonator bells, and glockenspiels or xylophones. As an aside, some of these instruments can be rather expensive, but this is an excellent time to begin to teach children the value of taking care of instruments and treating them with respect. Computers and other technologically based devices, including keyboards, sequencers, synthesizers, and drum machines, can also be used. Having a variety of instruments gives students choices in improving and/or creating their own sound composition.

 ## Pitch and Melody

The next concept or idea you will need to know (and teach) is, "How do you know what tone to sing or play?" This question is related to another beginning musical concept for younger children: *Some sounds are high, and some are low.* Again, this is a concept that you would first want to compare with sounds that are familiar to children. For example, a mouse usually has a high "squeak" while a cow has a low "moo." High and low sounds go together to form a **melody.** When you hum a tune, you have hummed the melody, or the tones or pitches that are put together to create a unique piece of music that is recognizable as a particular song. Thus, if asked to sing or hum "Mary Had a Little Lamb," you are humming or singing the melody of that song. The melody may have other parts of music that are added, but if these *other* parts were played or sung alone, we would not be able to recognize it as a particular song. Think of the melody as the "main plot" of a song. As in a story, there can be many details that you could add in the telling; but if you were to tell these details alone, no one would be able to follow the storyline. Also, as in literature, there may be a **musical theme.** A melody may, thus, have a pattern that occurs several times throughout a piece of music. This is usually recognized at once and serves to bring the piece of music together as a whole. If you know the popular instrumental song "The Entertainer," you will quickly catch the idea of theme and of how the same patterns are repeated to create a theme.

A good way to begin to teach children about melody is to have children move their hands up and down as they sing a melody, or they may draw a graphic representation. For example, a part of the melody of "Jingle Bells!" (Jingle bells! Jingle bells! Jingle all the way!) might be drawn like this:

Jingle bells!   Jingle bells!   Jin- gle all the way!

Each musical **note,** or symbol of sound, not only shows us length (as discussed above in duration) but is also given a name from the musical alphabet based on its tone—or how high or low the sound should be. The musical alphabet only uses seven letters *A* though *G,* then repeats itself in tones higher or lower. An *octave* is a set of eight tones from a named tone (such as a C note) to the same tone (C), only higher or lower. For example, sing the first two notes of "Somewhere over the Rainbow," and you have an octave. If you can, go back now and hum all the notes in between step by step. You will find that, altogether, you have hummed eight notes. An octave can be from any starting note, but must end on the same one eight tones higher or lower (for example, C, D, E, F, G, A, B—to a higher C; C/C is an octave). A piano and a harp are two instruments with a great number of octaves.

But how do you know what key or string to play? The answer is where a note is located on a musical staff. The name of a note is related to the place where it is found on a **musical staff** (the five lines and five spaces on which all music is written). There are a treble staff and a bass staff in music. The staff for high notes/sounds is called the **treble** and is marked by a **treble clef** symbol, while the staff for low notes/sounds is marked by the **bass clef.** Normally (but not always), the melody is written on the treble clef. If you are singing a part written for a **soprano** (high voice) or **alto** (mid-high voice), usually for a female or young boy's voice, or if you were playing an instrument with a high sound (such as a flute, a violin, or a clarinet), the music is read from the treble clef. If you have a male mid (**tenor**), mid-low (**baritone**), or very low (**bass**) voice or are playing an instrument with a lower sound (such as a tuba, trombone, or string bass), music is read from the bass clef. Instruments like the piano, with many pitches available (both high and low), use both the treble clef and the bass clef. In simple music, we may only see the staff with the melody on it. When other notes are added in a more complicated piece for harmony, there is a staff of music for treble and one for bass—each marked with its clef sign. Naturally, since these staffs are written one on top of the other, the treble clef (for high sound) is on top, and the bass clef (for lower sounds) is on the bottom. Note the symbols for each clef:

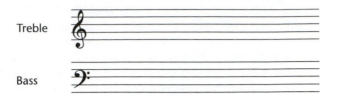

Treble

Bass

Again, part of understanding how music is produced involves understanding the relationship of size, length, and tension to sound. The higher the sound, the smaller and shorter the vocal chords, instrument, or strings, and vice versa. Children's voices are high because their vocal chords are still very small. If you are playing an instrument that has both high and low notes, such as the piano, two clefs are presented—the treble on top and the bass clef on the bottom. If you open up the top of a piano, you can see that the high notes are played by a hammer striking shorter, thinner strings. If you also look at the strings of a guitar, you will see that the higher notes (treble) are played by the fingers strumming the thin strings, while the lower notes (bass) are played on thicker strings. The same is true with a harp. The lower the note, the longer and thicker the string. Tension is also considered in pitch. When a trumpet or trombone player wishes to play a higher pitch, he or she blows air through tautly stretched lips but produces lower tones by blowing through relaxed the lips. A singer also uses tension. For example, note the tension of your vocal chords increasing as you singer higher and higher. **Pitch** is caused by vibrations of the materials of the instruments or by the vocal chords. The higher the pitch, the faster the vibrations. The lower the tone, the more slowly the vibrations move.

Music is designed so that pitch is easily "read." Each musical note written on a staff has a particular *pitch,* or tone of sound, that is high or low and that is associated with its name. For our purposes, we will only learn the names of the notes where the melody is often found—the treble clef. Beginning music students have always remembered the names of the notes written on the treble clef by two easy methods. The notes arranged in between the lines of the treble clef spell "FACE" (from the bottom up). The notes arranged on the lines of the treble clef are EGBDF ("Every Good Boy Does Fine" or "Every Good Boy Deserves Fudge") from the bottom up. By remembering these placements on a staff, you can easily read the name of the note. Vocalists can read, then remember, and sing the correct pitch, while instrumentalists play the note by reading it from the staff. Remember that these five lines and four spaces are known as a musical staff. There are also notes above and below the staff, continuing in the order of the musical alphabet. Look at each staff below.

Note names in spaces	Note names on lines	Together
0 E	F	0 E F
0 C	D	0 C D
0 A	B	0 A B
0 F	G	0 F G
	E	E

You may have heard the song "Do, Re, Mi" from the *Sound of Music* or heard someone sing a *scale* (the eight notes of a musical octave) "do, re, mi, fa, sol, la, ti, do," where each note gets progressively higher. You can also sing or play back down each scale. Many music texts teach students to sing using the concept of these tone names first rather than notes.

Steps, leaps, and repeated tones are important concepts in music. When you hear a **scale** (do, re, mi, fa, sol, la, ti, do) and back down or part of a scale (do, re, mi), you are hearing an example of notes or tones arranged in **steps**— that is, the sound moves from one note to another without skipping a tone. However, if a tone *does not* change its pitch, it is called a **repeated tone**, such as you hear in the first few notes of "Jingle Bells" ("Jingle Bells, Jingle Bells . . ."). Sing this first line of the song. Note that your voice does not change its tone at all—that is, your voice does not go up or down. This is a repeated tone.

There is another way that tones are arranged—in **leaps**. When tones leap, the pitch moves up or down, but it skips tones in between as it moves. As you continue to sing "Jingle Bells", the next few words go "Jingle all . . ." This line of music has a high leap, then a low leap ("Jingle all"), then ends in steps with the words ("the way"). Think about how this whole first line of music puts together *repeated tones, leaps,* and *steps* to form a *melody*. The following may help you to see that visually.

repeated tone	repeated tone	repeated tone	repeated tone	repeated tone	repeated tone	repeated tone	leap	leap	step	step
Jin-	gle	bells!	Jin-	gle	bells!	Jin-	gle	all	the	way!

Music also can be arranged in half steps or tones. When you see a piece of music that has a symbol known as a **flat** (♭) or a **sharp** (♯), the composer means that your voice or instrument should only move up a half step or tone for *sharps* or move down a half step or tone for *flats*. When a composer wants to indicate a *flat* or *sharp* in the middle of a piece of music, it is called an *accidental*. Note how the following accidentals (in this case, *sharps*) are written in this example:

C   E   D♯   E   D♯   E   G   D   C   E   D♯   E   D♯ E
You do the Hokey Pokey, and you turn yourself about

A composer can also indicate a sharp or flat *every* time a particular note is played or sung in his or her piece of music by placing a flat or sharp symbol at the very beginning of a piece of music on the line or space of the note desired where the note(s) is normally written. In the next example, we see that the composer wants us to play or sing a B *flat* every time we come to a note on the B line. In the second of these examples, we can see that the composer asks us always to play a *sharp* when we come to F notes, as a sharp symbol has been placed on the line where the high F is normally found (EGBDF). If we skip down to the second line of music on the next page, we can see that the composer chose to put three *flats* into this composition. By looking at the lines and spaces, we can see that we have a flat on the line where B is located ("Every Good Boy . . .") and the spaces where A and E are (F<u>A</u>C<u>E</u>) located.

Therefore, when we are reading this music and we come to B, A, and E, we would automatically play or sing half steps or tones instead of whole steps.

All B notes should
be B flat

All F notes should
be F sharp

In this same example, the composer begins with three flats. He or she can change this in the middle of a piece of music as well. In other words, the composer may say, "I want this music to start out with all B flats, but in the middle, I want to change to all B flats plus all E flats. This would be called a **key change**, and it makes a difference in the sound of the music. The music can change from no flats at all to one to seven flats or no sharps at all to one to seven sharps (one half tone up or down for each note in the musical scale—A, B, C, D, E, F, G). A key change usually creates an emotional surge in music. The staff below shows a key change from three flats to one flat.

Key and *key changes* are important concepts for other reasons. Have you ever started to sing a song and found that the tone on which you started made it impossible to hit the high notes (or maybe the low notes) as you continued singing along? This is a fairly common occurrence in singing "The Star-Spangled Banner." What did you do? Usually, if you were singing alone, you probably began again—either on a higher note or lower note, which would have helped you hit those notes that you could not sing the first time. This whole concept is related to the *key* in which a song is played or sung. You may have seen a movie where a singer is trying out for a part, and she or he asks the piano player to accompany him or her in a certain key ("Can you play it in C?"). Almost all simple children's songs are written in the keys of C, F, or G. These keys are the most popular because they offer easy accompaniment on many instruments and the voice range is fairly good for singing.

All of the arrangement of the tones that we have discussed creates a melody. Again, melody is a sound pattern that often allows us to easily sing or hum along with a piece of music or to recognize a particular composition when we hear it played.

 **Form**

Music is written with an overall plan, structure, or **form**. The elements that help shape music into forms are repetition, contrast, and variation. For example, a **melody pattern** is one that can be heard to be repeated several times throughout the music. We use the letters of the alphabet or even shapes to help us identify form, where contrasting parts of music are heard. For example, a song might have an ABA pattern or an ABAB pattern:

One can see this very easily in simple popular songs that have verses but come back to one chorus or *refrain* (part of the song that repeats). Looking again at "Jingle Bells," we know that the song begins with one melody pattern (A) and ends with a different melody pattern in the refrain or chorus (B), thus the form is AB:

A   Dashing through the snow, in a one horse open sleigh
O'er the field we go, Laughing all the way
Bells on bobtails ring, Making spirits bright;
Oh, what fun to ride and sing a sleighing song tonight!

B   Oh, Jingle Bells! Jingle Bells! Jingle all the way!
Oh, what fun it is to ride in a one horse open sleigh!

"Oh, Susannah!" is another good example of a song with a different form. It is written in *AAB* form, where there the pattern is three sections; the first and second verses repeat the same melody, while the ending verse (refrain or chorus) is different.

A   Oh, I come from Alabama with my banjo on my knee
I'm going to Louisiana, my true love for to see.

A   Oh, it rained all day the night I left, the weather was bone dry
The sun so hot, I froze to death, Susannah don't you cry.

B   Oh, Susannah! Don't you cry for me,
For I come from Alabama with my banjo on my knee.

"The Bear Went over the Mountain" is a simple example of ABA:

A   The bear went over the mountain,
The bear went over the mountain,
The bear went over the mountain,
To see what he could see.

B   To see what he could see,
To see what he could see.

A   The bear went over the mountain,
The bear went over the mountain,
The bear went over the mountain,
To see what he could see.

Music can be written in any of these combinations (even adding other forms such as C, D, etc.). A **rondo** refers to a musical form that has different sections and where the A pattern is repeated after each different section.

When singing or playing songs with repeated *forms*, we often see repeat signs. A **repeat sign** (:‖) is a handy symbol that tells the musician when to go back and play or sing a passage again. The musician either goes back to the beginning of the music and repeats all of it *or* finds this sign (‖:) and begins from that point again.

Why would form be important to know as a musician? First of all, it is very useful for singers. If a singer masters the melody of one section, such as the melody of *form A* in "Oh, Susannah!" above, and knows that the next verse is exactly the same form, then he or she can easily repeat the melody. It is also easier to "sight read," or sing without the help of a musical instrument, when that form appears. For instrumentalists it is the same. However, knowing form really helps musicians memorize their music. In instrumental music, form can be of great importance in arranging more sophisticated orchestra pieces.

Teaching children about melody is much like teaching rhythm. By about age 8 children should be able to have a fairly stable tonal recall ability. To help children learn about melody, first promote the natural tendencies of children in known and invented melodies, then use direct music instruction. Model melody patterns often, then ask students to copy what they hear—as in echo melody games. As with rhythm, break instruction and performance down into small tasks. Ask students to differentiate between melody patterns and explain their thinking, and help them sort out several patterns. Again, when giving direct instruction on melody, isolate examples of melody within songs children know rather than offering examples with which they are unfamiliar. Have them recognize the same melody pattern played on different instruments. Encouraging students to invent short melodies and write them down where someone else could read them helps children understand the decoding process. Learning to match the exact pitch of a song is usually the last element of acquiring a song (as you may well know from trying to sing along with your favorite vocalists on the radio). Begin with concentration on words, then melody contours, and finally work on matching exact pitches.

Dynamics

We are not yet through with the way we decode written music. There are some other very important ways that a composer shows us to how read music. For instance, another question (when we want to play or sing) is, "How loud or soft should the whole piece or a particular part of the music be?" Composers indicate volume by writing terms or abbreviations of those terms into a piece of music. They are usually seen in italics and in Italian, so if you speak that language, you are already ahead in knowing about **dynamics** (how loud or soft the music should be). The most common words relating to dynamics, or volume, are *forte, mezzo forte, mezzo piano,* and *piano.* The symbols for those are **f** *(forte),* **mf** *(mezzo forte),* and in contrast, **mp** *(mezzo piano),* and **p** *(piano),* and they are simply written right under or, in some cases, above the notes of the music. *Forte* means forceful, loud, or with strength (as in "that is really my forte" or my strength). *Mezzo* is "medium" or "between" two sounds (as in a mezzanine, or the floor in a building "between" two floors), so *mezzo forte* is medium loud or medium forceful. *Piano,* on the other hand, indicates softness, so *mezzo piano* means to play or sing in a medium soft manner. What would you think *ff* or *pp* would be? Exactly! Doubly loud or *very* soft! If you think of most music that you know, you will realize that a song does not stay at one level of sound, but changes *dynamics* within the song just as a "dynamic" speaker would vary his or her voice rather than remain monotoned. There is a way to indicate this in music as well. The composer simply uses **crescendo** (gradually become louder) or *decrescendo* or *diminuendo* (gradually become softer) or the symbols for these words. A teacher may say that children should think of the small end as the smaller sound and the large end as the larger sound. These symbols have the same meanings in mathematics. Look at the notation mark in the following example:

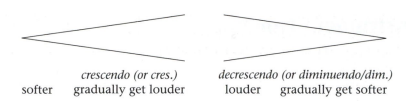

	crescendo (or cres.)	decrescendo (or diminuendo/dim.)
softer	gradually get louder	louder gradually get softer

The sound on this end should be **less than** the other end.

The sound on this end should be **greater than** the other end.

The sound on this end should be **less than** on the other end.

Another way to indicate a change in volume is with an *accent mark*. When an accent mark is used below a note, that note should be stronger or louder or more forceful than the sounds around it. Think again of the stereotypical Native American drums where the **accent** is on the first beat or note.

ONE two three four   ONE two three four

 ## Tempo

Another Italian lesson comes with determining the **tempo**, or speed, of the beat—that is, how fast or slow the music should be played. Some terms that you might encounter are *largo* (very slow, as most *large* things move slowly), *adagio* (slow), *andante* (walking speed, not fast, or "my aunt walks not *too* fast") or *moderato* (moderate). In contrast, *allegro* (quick or merry), *allegretto* (very lively), and *presto* (very fast, as when you are pressed to hurry) are all terms that show when the beat should be played quite rapidly. Sometimes music speeds up during the song. Thus, it might be marked *accelerando* (get faster gradually, as in accelerating) or vice versa with *ritardando* (or slow down gradually, or retard your speed).

Yet another type of contrast in music is indicated by more Italian terms. For example, you may want to sing or play smoothly (*legato*) with a blended connection between notes, or a musical piece may require distinct precision in a way that each note is *detached* or *separated* (**staccato**). For example, in "Row, Row, Row Your Boat," the first part of the song is often sung or played smoothly with connection between notes (*legato*). Contrast that sound with the "Alphabet Song" (A, B, C, D, E, F, G . . .) where the voice or instrument clearly separates notes (*staccato*), much like a prancing horse.

Let's look at how many elements are combined now to allow us to read music. Here we have a song written in *treble clef* with one *flat* (B^6) with *three beats* per measure. It is to be played at a *moderate speed* and *loudly* in the second measure. The melody notes read: GFA, CAG.

Instrument Families

Elementary students usually begin to identify musical *instruments* of bands, orchestras, and even of other lands both visually and *aurally* (or by their unique sound). One way of identification involves classifying or grouping musical instruments into families. The **percussion** family of instruments, for example, are those that are played by beating, shaking, scraping, or striking. Drums, tambourines, rattles, rasps, triangles, and xylophones are some examples. The piano, too, is often classified as a percussion instrument because the player's fingers strike the keys and, in turn, small hammers inside the piano strike the strings to make sound. Many of the percussion instruments are used to keep a strong beat in music such as the strong beat you hear when drums are played in rock and roll bands, the strong beat of Native American music, or the big bass drum being struck as a marching band goes by. These are instruments that are very old in the history of civilization, probably because many are easily constructed. They are often the first instruments that children learn to play, for most have just one tone (known as unpitched instruments), although instruments such as timpani drums and xylophones do have many tones and are known as pitched instruments. Using unpitched percussion instruments, children are able to easily learn to read the rhythm and length of notes first—before they must worry about reading the names of notes for a melody.

Another group of instruments is known as the **woodwind** family. At one time all of these instruments were made of wood, although now you find these made of plastic and metal. Woodwind instruments are played by blowing air into a tube such as in the clarinet, oboe, saxophone, bassoon, pan pipes, English horn, flute, piccolo, and so forth. Many (but not all) of these instruments have a mouthpiece where a sliced piece of reed is fastened. This reed vibrates as the wind passes down through the tube to create a unique sound.

The **brass** family, obviously, has instruments that are made of tubes of brass. These long metal tubes are curled around and around, usually ending in a "bell" shape that "flowers" to the outside. The brass players make sounds by "buzzing" their lips inside the small, bell-shaped mouthpiece and moving a slide or pushing on valves to create different pitches. The trumpet, trombone, French horn, and tuba are all examples of brass instruments.

The last family is called the **strings.** String instruments include the violin, viola, cello, and string bass. Of course, all of these have strings and many are played with a bow that is drawn across them to vibrate the strings, thus creating the sound.

Another important concept to review when thinking about instruments is how the pitch is created for each instrument. The guideline is that the *smaller the instrument, the higher the sound.* Therefore, the small flute makes a much higher sound than the much larger tuba. To hear many instruments, go to http://www.dsokids.com/2001/instrument.chart.htm.

Timbre and Tone Color

Each instrument has its very own characteristic sound, "voice," or **timbre.** A bell, for example, has a ringing sound that it does not share with other instruments. Another name for this individual sound is **tone color.** Individual singers also have their own tone color, as most have a unique sound that is theirs alone (although we have all tried to imitate the tone color of our favorite popular singers—usually in the privacy of our showers). Combinations of instruments often create a unique sound as well. The choice of how a composer puts sounds together is as important as the artist's selection of colors. In Native American music one often hears a combination of drums, rasps, rattles, and flutes that, when heard together, almost always creates a mental picture of this culture. The same is true of country and western music with guitar and fiddles, or Spanish music with castanets and guitars. Also, there are many special instruments that have very unique sounds that are often associated with one particular area of the world. The samisen from Japan is one such instrument; the bagpipes from Scotland are another; and the didgeridoo from the Aboriginal people of Australia is yet another example. There are many such unique instruments from Africa and other areas of the world.

All of the elements that we have spoken about up to this point—*tempo* (speed), *dynamics* (loudness), *meter* (beat), *key,* and *choice of instruments* affect the overall **mood** of the music or the feeling that a piece of music creates for the listener. A lullaby, for example, makes us feel quiet and gentle, while a march or rap song makes us feel excited and ready to move our feet. Each person may have a different reaction to the same composition, just as we may react differently to books, movies, and other art forms. However, it is not difficult to explain certain feelings when hearing certain types of music. The brooding mood of bagpipes accompanying "Amazing Grace" contrasts with the toe-tapping happiness of the fiddle in "Turkey in the Straw." Great compositions or even popular songs often have contrasting moods within the same piece as the elements discussed above work together. Emotion is the true power of music.

Another way that mood is created in music is through use of what we term *key.* There are two major divisions in Western music (versus music from the Far East)—major and minor keys. Most Western music is written in major keys. The main difference when you hear a song written in a **minor key** is that it often sounds "bluesy" or sad. Two famous examples that you may know that are written in minor keys are "When Johnny Comes Marching Home Again" and "Summertime." **Ballads,** or songs that tell stories, are often (although not always) set in minor keys, especially when they tell sad stories.

When one instrument plays or one voice sings a main melody, it is called a **solo** performance, even though an instrument or instruments may *accompany* it in the background. Elvis Presley was, perhaps, the most famous *solo* male vocalist of the 1950s, although he was always accompanied by a guitar or group of musicians. The only time a solo singer or **chorus** (a large group of singers) has no instrumental accompaniment is when an arranger indicates that the voices should be **a cappella,** or for voices *alone* with no instrumental accompaniment. When there are two or more musical instruments playing different pitches together, when one instrument is playing different pitches at the same time (such as the piano, autoharp, or guitar), or voices are singing different parts, harmony is created. **Harmony** means that two or more different tones are being played or sung together. When instruments of a band or orchestra are playing together or a choir of *many* people are singing different parts together, the harmony is usually very rich because there are many tones being played at once. A barbershop quartet usually has a four-part harmony. When three or more pitches are played together, we call this a *chord.* When a singer is accompanied by a guitar, autoharp, or piano, you are most likely hearing chords of a harmony being played.

There are other ways to create harmony. An *ostinato* is created by singing or playing a rhythm pattern over and over again throughout a song, normally as a part of the background. For example, in "Frère Jacques" ("Are You Sleeping?"), one voice or part can sing the lyrics of the whole song, while a second, ostinato voice sings the following words and melody over and over again, "Are you sleeping? Are you sleeping?" throughout the song—even though the main voice continues with the rest of the song. *Partner songs* also add harmony. This occurs when two different songs are sung or played together. A famous example of this is "Scarborough Fair" by Simon and Garfunkel. Two different songs are actually being sung at the same time, yet they blend together well. Singing or playing *rounds* is a very easy way to create harmony as well. This occurs when one group of musicians begins a song, and others wait to start until the group before it has finished the first musical phrase. There can be three to four groups waiting to sing at different starting points in a round. Most of us have sung "Row, Row, Row Your Boat" in a round. In a *counter melody,* a song is sung or played, but a different melody is also being played or sung at the same time. If you know the famous "The Stars and Stripes Forever" march, you may recall the end of the piece where the very high piccolo trills a counter melody against the main melody as it continues.

The terms above also affect the **texture** of music—that is, how one voice (or instrument) alone sounds versus how different voices (or instruments) sound together. The quality produced by the number and kinds of instruments put together (or instruments and voices) also refers to texture. You can think of musical texture just as you might think of the weave of a cloth. Some weaves are thick and sturdy, while others are thin and delicate—and everywhere in between. The same is true of the texture of music.

Another term that you may need to know relates to music belonging to particular cultures—**musical conversation.** In African American spirituals, one may often hear a solo voice ask a question or make a statement while the refrain/chorus comes behind to answer or reinforce it. In "Deep River," for example, the musical question asked is, "Oh, don't you want to go to the Gospel feast, that Promised Land, where all is peace?" The answering phrase comes next, "Deep River, my home is over Jordan . . . I want to cross over. . . ." A well-known musical conversation asks, "I looked over the Jordan, and what did I see?" "Comin' for to carry me home. . . ." The answer is, "A band of angels comin' after me. . . ."

All of the terms we have discussed in this section help us to begin reading music. There are many, many more terms in music, but these are the basics to help you begin. It is easy to access a number of other musical terms by typing in "music+theory" in a search engine on the Internet. For example, go to www.essentialsofmusic.com and select the glossary to find definitions and play-back examples. In the next section, we will look at some elements that will help teach children music and help us to be better teachers of music.

First, test your knowledge on some sample questions from this section:

Mrs. Cottle had her first-grade students first clap their hands to a song, then stand up and walk in time to the music. She was trying to teach them about:

- **A.** timbre.
- **B.** dynamics.
- **C.** rhythm.
- **D.** instrument families.

Answer *A* cannot be the answer because timbre distinguishes the way one instrument or voice sounds different from another. A tuba has a different timbre (a very different sound to our ears) than a violin. Answer *B*, dynamics, refers to how loud or soft music is played or sung, so this cannot be the answer. Answer *D* cannot be the answer because there was no mention of the different instruments being played here. Answer *C*, however, is correct. Having children clap or walk to music is a very good way to have them feel the rhythm of a piece of music. They would hopefully begin to feel the beat, an element of rhythm. The correct answer is *C*.

Ms. Botetourt wanted to teach her children about music with a strong beat. She selected a march to demonstrate two strong beats per measure, a Native American piece to demonstrate four strong beats per measure, and a waltz. How many steady beats per measure does a waltz have?

   A.   5   **B.**   1   **C.**   8   **D.**   3

A march demonstrates *two* strong beats per measure, as it helps people (particularly in the military) keep together in marching. Since we only have two feet, a march has a beat for each: left, right, left, right; 1, 2, 1, 2. Native American music is often presented with a very strong ONE-two-three-*four* (4) beat, while a waltz has *three* strong beats per measure or set, often with a very strong first beat (ONE-two-three, ONE-two-three). The correct answer is *D* (3 beats).

Students in Mr. Spellman's class were given a writing assignment to describe a *churning sea-coast*. He had waited for a rainy day for this assignment to set the mood. In addition, he put on a piece of music to heighten the effect. Before having students write, he asked, "Listen to how the composer used the string family and the percussion family to create a swirling, crashing mood. What instruments do you think you hear from the percussion family here?"

For what type of instruments were students suppose to listen?

   A. Instruments such as the tuba and the trumpet.
   B. Instruments with strings like the violin and the cello that are often (although not always) played by drawing a bow across the strings.
   C. Voices accompanied by woodwind instruments.
   D. Instruments that are struck, beaten, shaken, crashed, or scraped, such as the timpani drum, cymbals, bass drum, and triangle.

Answer *A* is not correct because the tuba and trumpet are members of the musical instrument family that are all made of *brass*. Answer *B* is not correct because, though he was probably going to ask them next about the string family instruments, he asked *first* about the percussion family instruments. Answer *C* is wrong because, although it mentions a family or instruments, it does not discuss the type of instruments in that family, *and* Mr. Spellman does not talk about voices. Answer *D* is correct because instruments in the percussion family are those that are played by striking, beating, shaking, or scraping. Many orchestras use percussion instruments such as the timpani drums and cymbals to indicate dark, brooding power such as in a storm. Cymbals often imitate the sound of crashing lightning, while the triangle can be struck lightly to sound like raindrops. The correct answer is *D*.

Standard II Singing and Playing

The music teacher sings and plays a musical instrument.

> *The early childhood teacher must know methods and techniques for singing or for playing a musical instrument and must be able to sing or play an instrument while demonstrating accurate intonation and rhythm.*

This standard also overlaps with Standards I and III, as the teacher must first understand all of the information contained within those two standards so that the information and knowledge contained there can be applied to either playing an instrument or singing. Note however, the important message of this standard: The teacher is expected to sing *or* play with his or her children often and in a way that maintains an accurate pitch and correct beat of the music. You may not have had the opportunity to take music lessons or be a part of a band or choir, but that does not mean that it is too late for you to learn to read music in order to sing or play an instrument. In days long past, there was often a piano in every elementary classroom, and the teacher played while children gathered around to sing. Excellent recordings (often, *karaoke*-style) and "easy" instruments have replaced this concept in many classrooms. Again, Texas expects you to be able to sing *or* play in order to teach children about music! One suggestion, if you do not already play an instrument that is conducive to accompaniment, invest in an autoharp or guitar. An *autoharp* is a stringed instrument that is very easy to play—you simply push down buttons that, in turn, create chords for harmony. Then, simply strum for accompaniment. A guitar is a bit harder, as you must learn which strings to press to create chords for accompaniment, but both are excellent instruments for the classroom. It does take practice to feel comfortable, but the rewards of singing with your children and adding the harmony of an instrument are great. Both instruments offer the opportunity for children to gather in front of you or in a circle where you can easily see them. With knowledge of only a few chords, you can sing and play a large variety of easily learned children's songs. You should pay close attention to the information in the other standards for information on singing and/or playing an instrument.

 # Standard III Music Notation

The music teacher has a comprehensive knowledge of music notation.

The EC-4 teacher must know how to read, recognize aurally, interpret, and write standard music notation. This includes use of clefs, keys, and meters.

You have been introduced to these concepts in Standard I in reading, interpreting, and writing music notation. Please review each, as this overlap indicates that they are of particular importance. The other emphasis in this standard, however, is recognizing musical concepts when you hear them—that is, aurally. Of course, that would be difficult to determine in a paper-and-pencil test, but as a teacher of musical concepts, you should be able to point out the concepts given in Standard I, such as texture, mood, beat, and so forth, as you listen to music with children or as they sing or perform for you. For example, as they sing, you should be able to say, "Children, if you will *crescendo* (get louder gradually) right at this point in the music, it will give more power to the song," or as you listen to the song "Memories" from the musical *CATS!* together, you should be able to say, "Boys and girls, doesn't that *key change* in the middle just work to give you goose bumps! What a wonderful technique by the composer!" Begin to listen to music with a musician's ear and notice each of the concepts discussed in Standard I so that you can bring them to the attention of children. Music book series often group several examples of these concepts on tapes or CDs. This makes it easy for you to hear and teach examples to your children.

Generalists are not responsible for Standard IV.

Consider the following questions:

Ms. Glymph examined the sheet music that she wanted to teach her class for the PTO program next month.

This is   my country!   Land of my   birth!

1. How does the dynamics symbol of this first line tell her it should be sung?
   A. Slowly
   B. Rapidly
   C. Loudly
   D. Softly

2. How many beats per measure does this song have, and what note receives one beat?
   A. Two per measure and a whole note receives one beat.
   B. Four per measure and a quarter note receives one beat.
   C. Four per measure and an eighth note receives one beat.
   D. Two per measure and a whole note receives one beat.

3. For how many beats would the word *birth* be held in this line?
   A. One
   B. Two
   C. Three
   D. Four

In question 1, she would look for the dynamics symbol written in line with the notes that are affected. This is an *f,* or *forte,* so the song would begin loudly (*C*). In question 2, she would look at the time signature. In this music, it is 4/4. The top number tells her that there are four beats per measure and the bottom of the time signature tells her that a quarter note gets one beat (*B*). In Question 3, the measure with *birth* is represented by a whole note. In this song, a quarter note gets one beat, so a half note receives two beats, and a whole note receives four beats (*D*). Children would hold *birth* for four full beats.

Standard V Texas and American Music History

The music teacher has a comprehensive knowledge of music history and the relationship of music to history, society, and culture.

The EC-4 teacher should know how music can reflect elements of a specific society or culture and be able to analyze various purposes and roles of music in society and culture. Being able to recognize and describe the music that reflects the heritage of the United States and Texas is an important element in this area. Teachers should also know various music vocations and avocations.

Why should every child know about music? It is a universal human experience, although individuals and cultures certainly react to music in their own unique ways. Consider that humans may be somehow "wired" for music, since music has been a part of man's life since the beginnings of history. Music was often a means to preserve history and stories orally as well as to entertain. It was (and still is) used to honor people, places, events, and ideas. Music motivates people to do things such as support a cause, fall in love, worship, or even march into war. Music is used as comfort or to express joy, laughter, nonsense, yearning, anger, sorrow, protest, and celebration. In fact, music can be associated with and can express every human emotion. Just think about how bland your favorite movies would seem without the sound track enhancing the emotions that are being acted out. Imagine the emptiness of a wedding, graduation, or other ceremony that did not have traditional music as an accompaniment. We find that the rhythm of many kinds of labor has also been expressed through music—as well as the joys of play and diversion after work was done. People have used music to express traveling to new places and experiencing new things but also to remind them of their homelands and their lives before. Many different cultures of people share and express their music in distinctive ways and celebrate their traditions and holidays in song and dance. Music helps to unify people as a culture. To understand this musical part of a people is to understand them better as a whole.

The same can be said in reference to historical times. By analyzing instruments and the expressions of music from different periods of history, we can understand more easily the people who lived in those times. For example, is the music heavy and angry, or is it delicate and light? Does the music tell us that people danced and sang—or marched to war? Are the words set to music carefree, romantic, sad, fearful, or purposeful in some other way? Is the majority of the music of a population or period of time patriotic in nature? Elements such as these can tell us much about a society or culture and its times. But music can also transcend cultures, times, and ages. Good music may be enjoyed for centuries and by many different cultures throughout the world, thus becoming an instrumental or vocal *classic.* Thus music could almost be considered a universal human endeavor, because so many people of the world have created and enjoyed some type of music and musical traditions.

Texas Music

One requirement noted by this state standard asks you to teach children about our state and national music. As you drive through Texas today, scan radio stations and listen to the many kinds of music that the people of Texas love. Texas music is truly a reflection of the many cultures that exist here today and the rich history of Texas.

The first people of America and Texas were Native American tribes. We know little about some of these tribes, but others still exist today and have recordings and videos of song and dance. Although each Native American nation has developed its own unique music, musical instruments of Native Americans often include various drums, handmade flutes, and rattles. Voices often accompany songs and dances in sing-song chanting in their tribal languages. Generally, there is a strong beat. Native American songs exist for almost every aspect of men's and women's tribal life—work, planting, hunting, social dances, celebrations, and other rituals of a people. Honor songs are sung to pay special homage to those who are deserving. Much Native American music deals with the forces of nature, myths, legends, and the spiritual aspect of life. Although there has been some melding of Native American music with more modern music, by and large this music has remained unaffected by other cultures.

Following along through the history of Texas, we note the exploration and settling of Texas by those from Spain, and later Mexico. During these early days when the flag of Spain, then Mexico, flew over Texas, religious festivals were held throughout the year honoring the saints and events found in the Roman Catholic religion—the religion of those of European descent living in Texas at that time. Many of these continue throughout Texas today, particularly in communities with Hispanic traditions and ties. *Las Posadas,* for example, commemorating Mary and Joseph's search for shelter in Bethlehem, is a popular combination of religious and mariachi-style music that remains as a part of San Antonio's December celebrations. Barges carrying performers of the pageant and of many other groups cruise the river singing Christmas songs. Mariachi music, typically joyful and exuberant, is very typical of Mexico and is heard often in Texas communities throughout the state. Musicians in traditional black and silver Mexican cowboy (charro) costumes stroll and sing in Spanish to the accompaniment of guitars, violins, guitarrons (bass guitars), and trumpets. They often sing *corridos* (Mexican folk ballads), *rancheras* (ranch songs), and *boleros* (romantic songs), often with much harmony. Many schools and several universities in southern Texas offer study in mariachi music. *Conjunto* music is also a sound heard often in Texas. Created by the working class along the border in the early 1900s, it is a bright and happy sound of Mexican-style music that has borrowed both its main instrument (the accordion) and some of its style (polka) from the Texans of German descent. With *conjunto* as its roots, the more modern *tejano* music today is defined as current popular Hispanic-style music (rather than a very specific type of sound). Made famous by the tragic death of its star, Selena, it has gained considerable following in the past few years. One can hear all of these types of Hispanic-based music often in Texas, but the focus of the Hispanic community in Texas often centers on El Cinco de Mayo, a holiday celebrating a battle won in Mexico's fight for independence. During this holiday, there is a great deal of music and folk dancing, and grand balls are held in some parts of Texas.

Music was an important part of the lives of the early settlers and colonists from the United States and the Texas Revolution as well. It is said that Texans went into the Battle of San Jacinto (the battle that won Texas independence) singing "Will You Come to the Bower?"

Early settlers who came from the United States to Texas brought ballroom dancing that was mixed with folk dances from the many European countries of their ancestries. During the early 1800s, upper-class circles of early Texas colonists and officials in the Mexican government attended sophisticated balls, while *fandangos* were street entertainment with music, dancing, and other activities. At *shindigs,* settlers with little or no formal music or dance instruction attempted polkas and schottisches, dancing in an even more informal and frolicking way. In the formal dances of higher circles, groups danced to figures or quadrilles in the European style, and reminders about what to do next were often called out to the dancers. Over time, the person responsible for this became "the caller," and dancing depended less and less on the formal steps—thus merging into the style that we know as the *square dance.* One folk dance that was popular during this part of Texas history was the *play-party game.* Dancing to instruments was not considered proper among some religious leaders and groups, so the accompaniment to dances was sung or called, and the dance itself was called a "game." This "game" also had to serve when little or no music was available. Quite often in the early years of Texas there might have been only a single fiddler at a function. The World Champion Fiddlers' Contest in Crockett, Texas, shows how important this type of musician was to the roots of Texas music.

Although Texas now boasts several of the nation's largest urban areas, much of Texas still has deep roots in its cowboy heritage and music. This was music first sung and played by cowboys on the many cattle drives that originated on the ranges of Texas and moved north to Kansas railroads and markets in the mid-1800s. After the Civil War, many settlers had moved west from southern states, bringing traditional music of the South with them (ballads, hymns, and minstrel songs). Adaptations of these old songs of life on the range formed the basis of western swing in the 1930s, creating the roots of our modern country-and-western music. To go with this music, folk dancing in Texas developed its own style. The Cotton-Eyed Joe, for example, is a popular dance step that many Texans still learn. As radios became available, the traditional dances began to fade, replaced by the more popular American dances and music of the times during War War II. Later rock-and-roll moved to the popular front. However, country-and-western music and dance has always been a part of many Texas communities and has made a resurgence since the 1970s with popular country singing stars topping the charts. Several popular movies featuring country-style line dances and songs that have a more rock-and-roll rhythm have helped to keep this music in the hearts and minds of many Texans.

In the later part of the 1800s, many Germans began to leave Europe, fearing the rising militarism of Prussia and desiring to own land of their own. With them they brought their own unique music. Today, the *ohm-pa-pa* of German music is heard throughout many parts of central Texas, the area most settled by these groups. During the mid-1800s festivals centered around the homes and communities of German immigrants. In New Braunfels today, *Wurstfest* is always held in October and features German music, dancing, and food. The polka-style music, played most often by small brass bands in German communities, is also still heard in many Texas Czech communities.

Texans also hear and enjoy music that has its roots in African American cultures. You may have heard the expression "King Cotton" in reference to Texas prior to the Civil War. Many parts of eastern and central Texas were optimum for growing cotton, and because Texas was a Southern slave state, many African Americans were brought here as workers. With them, they brought their music. After *Juneteenth,* when Union forces brought the news to Texas that the slaves had been freed, many of these emancipated slaves began to look for work. Theirs was a hard life, and most went into either sharecropping or became migratory workers. All hoped to find a place where discrimination and racism were not part of their day-to-day existence. The *blues,* the sound that emerged from these times, was a way for these people to express extreme feelings of sorrow, dejection, suffering, and, yet, even hope and humor. During the early 1900s African American composers contributed greatly to other genres of music. Scott Joplin from Texarkana, known as the "King of Ragtime" for his "Maple Leaf Rag," pioneered the energizing, lively sounds of ragtime. Jazz followed and formed a backdrop for rhythm-and-blues and rock-and-roll. This led the way for R&B performers such as Texas-born Janis Joplin in the 1960s.

Attending festivals throughout the state gives Texans an opportunity to hear music and see dancing from many Texas immigrants' historical backgrounds. The Lebanese-Syrian festivals in Austin, the National Polka Festival in Ennis, and the Greek Festival in Houston are only a few events at which the sounds of the cultures that make up Texas can be heard. In addition, certain cities and towns highlight other music. The Texas Folklife Festival is, perhaps, the most inclusive of all the festivals and is held annually at the Institute of

Texas Cultures in San Antonio. Round Top is home to a renowned Classical Festival each year, Palo Duro Canyon hosts the outdoor musical "Texas" each summer, and the musical extravaganza "Fandangle" is performed at Fort Griffin in Albany, Texas. Several cities host excellent jazz festivals, including San Antonio, Corpus Christi, and Houston. Houston also has an excellent opera season, and famous musicals can be seen in most larger cities and/or on many university campuses throughout Texas.

Here are some of the many other famous singers and composers from Texas who have contributed to Texas and American music.

Tex Ritter	Roger Miller	Trini Lopez	Buddy Holly
Gene Autry	Kris Kristofferson	Roy Orbison	ZZ Topp
Dale Evans	Freddie Fender	Lyle Lovett	Johnny Mathis
Willie Nelson	Waylon Jennings	Selena Quintania Pérez	
Beyoncé	Geogre Strait	Tanya Tucker	

The state song, **"Texas, Our Texas,"** can often be heard and/or sung during morning announcement times, at assemblies, at some football games, and at other opening ceremonies at many Texas schools and community events. Texas teachers should learn it in order to teach it to children and to help them understand the respect that Texans hold for their state's symbols.

American Music

National and state standards ask that students relate music to history, society, and culture. Because we can say that music is often a reflection of the times in which it is produced, it is helpful for you to know not only about the genres of American music but also about the period in history from which they come and what was happening in America during those times. Little is learned when a teacher just says, "Here is a song from—(colonial America or from another culture or another country)." The investigation of what makes that particular piece so unique is what will bring children to better understand a historical period or culture—ours and that of others.

American music has a long history that parallels much of European musical history as well as the course of events that shaped our country. The first Pilgrim colonists were a very religious people who thought of music mainly for the part it could play in religion. They used only a few traditional English hymn tunes to sing a number of psalms. However, as the colonies quickly became settled, America took three turns in its music—one direction for the more cultured and wealthy; another direction for those many pioneers who lived more isolated, rural lives; and yet another for the slaves who were brought here early in our nation's history.

Where cities prospered, Americans integrated popular European music and dances into their colonial life. Many of the wealthier class listened to and danced European-style minuets and gavottes, mainly to the tunes played on harpsichords. The English and American aristocracy wished to replicate life they remembered from European courts on their plantations and by holding balls in flourishing urban areas. This type of music was from the Baroque era and would last almost until the Revolutionary War. In Europe during this time, Bach wrote many of his fugues (mainly for organ). Handel wrote his oratorio, *The Messiah*. An *oratorio* is an opera without costumes, scenery, or action and is normally religious in nature. Vivaldi also wrote the set of four works known as *The Four Seasons*. You may have seen Baroque architecture that exuberantly "fills every space" with movement. Baroque music is very much the same in nature—highly ornate. This music was usually characterized by a single mood. If the work began with a mood such as sorrow or joy, that single feeling was maintained throughout most of the work.

Settlers soon began to move out from the East Coast into small and isolated rural homes (where not even a tavern supported music). In their own homes they sang folk ballads from their original homelands—mostly without accompaniment. If there was a musical instrument, it was probably a fiddle, a mouth harp, or a homemade lute.

Slaves were brought to America very early in its history and from many different African areas and countries. Slaves were forced to adapt to an unfamiliar world that led to a difficult new way of life, a new language, and a new religion. Music became a way of life as slaves united the many cultures and sounds they brought from various parts of Africa and used music to pace their work, communicate, express feelings, and sing songs of worship and of hope. Often, one singer would start a song and others would answer (*field hollers* or *cries*) or join in on the refrain after a verse was sung. This music was mainly unaccompanied—sung with voice only (*a cappella*). *Spirituals,* religious songs that were really folk music in nature, first developed as work songs and later combined with impressions of hymns. Spirituals often retold Bible stories in a dialect more common to slaves and ex-slaves. *Spirituals* were eventually accepted into the general population and sung by Americans of many cultures, becoming widespread with the popularity of religious camp meetings in the later 1800s.

Let us return to the early days of America again to look at a different type of music. In the early days of America, England sent troops to its colonies. For the military, music was mostly from fife and drum during this time, but with the coming War for Independence against England, popular American songs such as "The Liberty Tree" (America's first patriotic song) and "Yankee Doodle" came to the forefront. "Yankee Doodle," a mockery used by the British to make fun of the "backwoods" colonists before and during the war, became so much a symbol of defiance and pride that it was practically the national anthem for years following the Declaration of Independence. As the United States became more settled and people began to travel along established trails, rivers, canals, and seaport, many public houses, inns, or taverns began to appear. These provided a place besides church to go where people could hear and share music together. People also gathered together to celebrate festive occasions, and dance was often a part of those occasions. Folk dances of America developed during this time were the *play-party game* and *square dance* (discussed earlier in Texas music). *Long-ways* and *circular formation* dances (such as the Virginia Reel) developed, along with other round dances in which the general movement of all partners goes around the room (such as in the polka or schottische). **Square dancing** is seen very much as a true U.S. folk dance.

For those who remained in touch with the culture of Europe, the Baroque era in Western music was followed by the Classic Period (1750–1820), whose main composers were Mozart, Haydn, and Beethoven. As during the Baroque period, most of these works were commissioned by the wealthy in Europe. The main composers were influenced by popular tunes of the times. A characteristic of this music is a range of emotions and themes displayed in each piece rather than maintenance of one mood throughout. The **symphony**, emerging from this period, was an orchestral work of four movements typically lasting from 25 to 45 minutes, with a fast section, slow section, dancelike section (like a minuet), and an emotional, fast end. *Chamber music,* using only a small number of instruments, also emerged from the aristocrats' or merchant classes' musical evening's entertainment. The signers of our Declaration of Independence probably attended dances where the popular dance sounds of Mozart were played.

As time marched on in Europe, the age of Romanticism in music (1820–1900) was full of uplifting aspirations and beautiful ideals. Music was no longer written just for commission but to fulfill an inner need of self-expression—particularly of yearning love. Also, composers began to look at national feelings—both their own and that of other countries—and draw on folk songs, dances, legends, and history. Indeed, there was a great individuality of style based upon the concept of nationalism in many works of famous composers of that time such as Tchaikovsky and Chopin. *Program music,* based on a story, legend, or scene, was a popular style, as we see in Tchaikovsky's *Romeo and Juliet.* Interest in formal music boomed in the United States, as concert halls (such as Carnegie Hall) were built in many larger cities in the later part of the century.

A more informal type of musical entertainment began during the early 1800s in the United States, termed the *minstrel show,* and it became an important type of entertainment for a number of years. During these shows, comedy, dances, and songs were performed first by white entertainers with black face makeup but later on by African Americans. Dances were normally jigs and clog dances that later developed into **tap dancing**—another truly American form of dance. Accompaniment was often played by the fiddle, tambourine, and banjo, whose rapid, upbeat sounds subsequently influenced ragtime. As these programs became more elaborate with many performers, this type of entertainment eventually changed to *vaudeville.*

During the mid-1800s, a famous composer was working on a style of music that belonged to the United States alone. *Stephen Foster* wrote folk songs that articulated the U.S. character and spirit of work and the home. Much of his work vocalized plantation life and the life of African Americans during these times. Unfortunately, the United States became embroiled in the staggering Civil War just following this time period. From the Civil War, we remember marching songs such as "The Battle Hymn of the Republic" (from the North) and "Dixie" (from the South). Beginning in the very late 1800s reasonably priced, wholesome popular music and stage dance was presented in vaudeville shows such as the Ziegfeld Follies. Songs that were carefree and innocent, such as "A Bicycle Built for Two," were written and performed during this period when the United States was mostly at peace. *Victor Herbert,* sometimes called the father of popular music, wrote light operettas such as "Babes in Toyland" up through 1920. The marches of *John Philip Sousa* from this period, including "The Stars and Stripes Forever," also became world famous.

The years of the 1900s to the present have seen many styles of music. This was the age when the United States, like other nations, was changing from a rural, agricultural country to urban, industrial centers. The symbolism and expressionism created in modern art during this period was often mirrored by concert composers, as they experimented with unconventional, dissonant sounds and rhythms. *George Gershwin* and *Aaron Copland,* who composed during this time, are two of the most famous U.S. composers. Gershwin, with his "Rhapsody in Blue," bridged popular music (jazz) with music for the concert hall. Copland, with his nationalistic agenda, wrote expansive music representing areas of the United States and American life that is still popular with adults and children today ("Billy the Kid," "Appalachian Spring," "The Red Pony," etc.). Spirituals were also changing to become *gospel songs.* These newly composed religious songs were more upbeat, with lively voices full of movement, accompanied now with instruments and (often) hand-claps.

Jazz, an American sound created from predominately African American roots, probably began early in the 1900s. The contributing elements were slavery and the hard life after Reconstruction. The heart of jazz lies in *improvisation* (creating music on the spot), *syncopation* (an "unexpected accent"), and *call and* *response* (where a voice or instrument is answered by other voices or instruments). The main styles of jazz included *ragtime* (player piano sound), the *blues, Dixieland,* and *boogie-woogie* (with its "walking bass" sound). In the 1920s many young people danced the Charleston to some of these sounds. In the 1930s radio brought music into U.S. homes throughout the country and allowed many people to hear more popular music. *Swing* (big band sound) of the World War II years, *bebop* or *bop,* and *"cool"* jazz of the early 1950s continued the jazz heritage. The years during World War II were filled with popular songs remembering those who waited and worked on the home front but portraying a clear determination to win the war. Glitzy musical movies with song and dance boomed during this era, too, as a way to escape from the hardships of the war and the Depression that had preceded it. U.S. musical theater boomed through the new genre of *musical plays* of Rodgers and Hammerstein II (*Oklahoma, South Pacific, The King and I, Carousel, The Sound of Music,* and others). In the 1950s Leonard Bernstein became king of this genre by writing *West Side Story.*

The late 1940s also saw *rhythm-and-blues* emerge from the African American communities, with artists such as Little Richard and T-Bone Walker. Later, *country-and-western* from rural communities appeared, along with *rock-and-roll.* In the mid-1950s songs like "Rock Around the Clock" and stars such as Buddy Holly (from Lubbock, Texas) and Elvis Presley rocketed rock-and-roll to the top of popular music. *Rhythm-and-blues* (R & B), however, remained the main source of movements in pop music throughout the century. These genres influenced the evolution of *rock.* The event that ensured that rock would remain as an influential popular style was the first U.S. tour of the Beatles in the mid-1960s. Television programs like *Ed Sullivan* and *American Bandstand* also brought not only music but the faces of popular singers to the U.S. public, eventually leading to the development of music videos like those shown now on MTV. Along with the more electric sounds of *rock* (*classical rock, psychedelic rock, acid rock*) came the folk influence of many of the protest songs of the "atomic age" and the Vietnam war. Softer folk songs of these times were reflected by such artists as John Denver who often sang about our states in such songs as "Country Roads" and "Rocky Mountain High." The reverberations of R&B and gospel united somewhat to produce the popular music called *soul* from the African American community. The 1970s saw a returned interest in partner dancing with the *disco beat,* and *country rock* became popular in some areas of the United States. *New wave, reggae,* and *heavy metal* sounds continued into the 1990s, and *rap* emerged as a hard, angry, chanting sound from urban African Americans. As music of this century moved from *jazz* to *rock* and *rock* to *rap,* melody became ever less important than the beat. Most popular music genres of this period have not lasted long, so it will be interesting to see what the "new modern style" will be.

Other more regional styles of music are a part of our national music history as well. Until recent times, the isolation of the Appalachians and other eastern mountain regions kept their *folk music* pure and uncorrupted by other types of music. The stringed dulcimer accompanies most of these songs, which have an Old English or Scottish sound, while the *bluegrass* sound of this region has a faster, upbeat mood with banjos, guitars, and other instruments. Cowboy and Native American music were previously discussed in the section on Texas music. *Cajun music* from Louisiana is another unique type of U.S. music. Cajun's sad ballads are grounded in the forced migration of the Acadian French from Canada by the British, while the more exuberant sounds of their dance songs came from the mix of those who settled there long ago (from France, Africa, and the Native Americans of the area). The accordion, fiddle, and lyrical mix of French and the local dialect has a sound that is unique. *Hawaiian music* is another type of indigenous music that belongs to the native islanders of our 50th state. In old Hawaiian music, chants with heavy rhythms were accompanied by percussion instruments such as a hollow gourd (*ipu*) or bamboo sticks (*pu'ili*), although the more modern sound comes from a coupling of the Portuguese guitar (now the ukulele), steel guitar, and missionary hymns. Current trends combine traditional folk songs of the islands, modern instruments, and themes of life surrounded by water and the beauty of nature all around. The native dance, the hula, can be slow and graceful, fast and furious, or light and comical. Native Hawaiians love their children to be included in music, and there are many charming hulas for children that can be brought to our classrooms.

Each of the genres and composers discussed above—and many that have not been—is described at length in music books and on the Internet. In fact, much of the information for this standard comes from an excellent source, *The Handbook of Texas Online* (www.tsha.utexas.edu/handbook/online/index.html). It is important, however, for you to *hear* these different sounds. As a teacher of music and as an American, you should try to learn and understand our country's musical styles and history for all the richness music offers. Music in the United States will continue to change, but we should try to understand this part of our history and culture well.

As a note, when tragedy struck as a result of terrorists' actions in New York, Pennsylvania, and Washington on September, 11, 2001, it was our patriotic songs such as "God Bless America," "America the Beautiful," "The Star-Spangled Banner," and others that helped to unite us as a nation. Every child in Texas deserves to feel that bond of belonging through knowing and being able to sing these American songs.

As a teacher, one should note that some religious affiliations maintain their Constitutional right for their children not to stand for the *Pledge of Allegiance,* considering it nationalism (in which they do not believe). This extends to teachers not requiring these children to stand for our national anthem, "The Star-Spangled Banner," or to sing other patriotic songs. Parents who belong to these affiliations will let you know. Other children should be reminded of the respect that stopping activity, standing, etc., shows for our national anthem in particular.

Musical Careers

Yet another element of this standard, and another rationale for teaching music, is teaching students about the many areas of employment that involve music directly and indirectly. Certainly, children should understand that people can grow up to become music educators/teachers of general music, to play a particular instrument, or to be a member of a band or choir, but they may not realize that there are many other occupations in which music is the focus. Some of the following could be leisure or volunteer activities listed below, but many are also employment opportunities for the future:

Member or director of a: symphony, stage band, chamber orchestra, band pit orchestra, or popular music band.

Member or director of vocal work or dance in a(n): chorus, choir, musical, opera, ballet, folk dancing group, or other performance show, or as a choreographer. (Musicians might work or enjoy performing in city or national organizations, religious institutions, theme parks, cruise ships, restaurants and private parties, weddings, radio, television, or movies.)

Employment in the recording industry such as: composing, publishing, as a member of a road crew, in law, in studio technology, as an arranger, as a coach, as an equipment engineer, or as a composer for background music in television, radio, or movies.

Employment in technology: software designer, electronic instrument designer, sound manager, or producer.

Other areas might include: composer, music historian, professional music critic, disc jockey, instrument maker or repairer, music therapist, music store owner, college professor, advertising (jingles), or tuner.

There are many areas that could involve music both recreationally and as a way to make a living.

Standard VI Evaluating Musical Performances

The music teacher applies a comprehensive knowledge of music to evaluate musical compositions, performances, and experiences.

In this competency, it is important for teachers to know and understand the criteria used to evaluate and critique musical performances and experiences. Therefore, they must be able to recognize accurate pitch, intonation, rhythm, and characteristic tone quality. Teachers should also be able to diagnose performance problems and detect errors accurately. Finally, they should be able to integrate music with other subject areas.

Teaching Children to Sing

As the music teacher of younger children, a goodly number of your activities will involve children in singing. Here are some tips that you may want to use in teaching children to sing—and, it is hoped, to sing well. The first goal in music is to have children participate. Shyness or other reluctance is often overcome by providing inviting activities in a pleasing environment with musical games and lightness, rather than forcing children to "perform." Songs should be selected in which children can find an interest and that they easily handle within their small voice ranges (i.e., songs where the pitches are not so far apart and notes are not very high or very low). If a song can be integrated with other topics, that often creates interest as well, but one of the most compelling ways to involve young children is to use songs in which their names are inserted in some way. Children (and the teacher) are usually more confident in a circle, where closeness gives the confidence to sing out. Treat the introduction of a song as you would a motivating introduction to a new book by setting the stage or a mood of inquiry. Memorize the song so you will be able to maintain eye contact. Then, introduce the whole song as it is supposed to be, so children catch the exact spirit of the music. Don't forget that songs often introduce new vocabulary or words that, when sung, may not sound like spoken words. Explain new vocabulary, and talk to children about the importance of pronouncing consonants clearly (e.g, the third line of "Silent Night" is *not* "all is Sprite" but "all is bright").

When seriously teaching a song, use your voice *without* accompaniment first. If you find it difficult to sing melodies, use a tape or a CD as you sing along. It is important that students at some points have a good model to imitate (sometimes adult and sometimes children's voices). Imitation is the main way children learn to sing. Give the correct beginning pitch (using a key on an instrument, if needed, a pitch pipe, or your voice) and begin the song. Then repeat the song several times during the introduction phase, so that children are not only introduced to the song but so they also "get well acquainted" with it. Even though you may feel it is monotonous, don't hesitate to keep songs going for young children through many repetitions—sometimes singing, sometimes humming and doing motions if applicable. Repetition, however, does not always work without other motivation to keep children involved. The teacher who creates a reason for listening to the music (by asking questions about the music to heighten perception, playing a game, using dramatization, etc.) will find that students remain interested. The younger the child, the better to teach by rote (imitation) *only* and use short repetitive songs, chants, echo songs, or poems in which only one or two things change in each verse, and children's names are inserted often. Again, much repetition will help children learn to sing a song and enjoy many types of music. Young children do not value the unfamiliar in music—either in singing or instrumentals. Yet, if they don't hear certain types of music or sing certain songs often, they will not be familiar with (or value) those forms.

Songs that combine movement and motions are developmentally good for children (see section on Teaching Children to Move). Songs can be used to enhance concepts, teach directions, and so forth. Do not be concerned with singing or listening to *many* songs during music time. Most children will be more satisfied with one or two songs or musical activities that they find gratifying rather than glossing over many "half-tasted" experiences or practicing for very long periods of time. Let the mood of children be your guide when possible, as they will gain more from the experience. If they are getting too active, use a "quiet song" to bring down the level of activity—or invigorate a waning time with an exciting, active song. Also, do not be worried that very young children do not sing along all the time. A music listening center may encourage young children to listen or sing quietly on their own. We may not be sure how very young children are truly reacting in many ways to music. They may want to get up and leave a singing circle or move in different ways. Do not be too concerned, as they may just be discovering and reacting in a different way than we might expect. They may also be singing alone or at home.

There are some other factors that can encourage children to sing better as they grow. One common quality error in singing well occurs because the vocalist cannot sing whole phrases without breaking for a breath. During the learning process, have students read or speak sentences, noting where they should finish and take a breath, then do the same by singing. Finally, move to having children sing whole phrases. Because it is also very important that a singing voice project out to the audience, have older children repeat this process to someone across the room to encourage projecting one's voice as it remains controlled. However, forced projection can result in an unpleasant tone quality with younger children, so it would be better to emphasize breath support and use of breath. This will eventually lead to more natural projection. During any musical performances requiring projection, use a larger group of children or have a microphone available rather than force projection. It is also very important for students who are performing to stand or sit straight with both feet on the floor in order to get a full breath of air. If standing, children should also be straight, perhaps with one foot slightly in front of the other and resting on the ball of the foot with the chin tilted at a lower angle. This will help them to learn to control their breath from the diaphragm rather than the chest, so they can hold notes out for extended periods or sing whole musical phrases or sentences rather than gulp for air in the middle. Some voice trainers suggest that singers draw in air for singing as if sipping through a straw, filling their rib cages well with air, then exhaling as if they were blowing to cool some hot food. Children should not tense up when singing but keep their shoulders relaxed. Doing some stretching exercises helps the whole body become ready to contribute. Singing with a tight jaw is also not desirable, so exercises are beneficial that have students begin a yawn or slow repetition of vowels and try to sing in a relaxed way.

Very young children should not always be expected to sing a tune on correct pitch, but by about the age of 7, they should begin to grow into this ability. If they are not able to do so, there are several things that might help. Young children tend to sing loudly, sing as they speak (using a speaking voice), or even shout rather than use the light voice that a child should have while singing. Singing on key can be improved by practicing with the Kodaly system of Curwen hand signals indicating on which tone the singer should be. In this system each note has a hand signal that represents its tone and name. A teacher can have students match their voices to the tone indicated by the hand signal (you may have seen this in the old movie *Close Encounters of the Third Kind*, as scientists matched hand signals to the famous five tones played as communication by the spacecraft). Having children listen to recordings of children's voices singing (rather than adults all the time) and having children sing more softly should also help. Echoing pitch games with speaking and singing will also help, as will playing tapes of familiar voices in the school speaking and singing (for example, other teachers they know, the principal, friends, etc.). Playing a pitch on an instrument, having the student "think the correct pitch," then having the child sing, can be helpful, too. Having those who use their speaking voice (rather than a singing voice) imitate other sounds, such as animals, sirens, or trains, along with a range of human sounds (whispers, hisses, hums, or shouts) develops a more flexible singing voice and an increased range.

As mentioned, *diction* is also an important part of singing. If you hear children singing in a shrill or throaty manner, it may be because of faulty diction. Have students work on uniform production of vowel and consonant sounds. Articulation helps the listener understand. Sometimes teachers will present a song at such a fast-paced tempo that it is difficult for students to understand the words or carry the melody well. Also, have children practice singing words or phrases with pure vowels so that they can feel how their tongue operates if they are to sing clearly. Just as practicing an instrument is important in mastery, so is practicing singing correctly. Again, by selecting songs that have a small range of tones, rather than very high to very low, children can often grasp those "middle" sounds. Sometimes we laugh about family or peers who are "tone deaf," but some of our young singers will be, too. They may just need attention to tone and practice. Discuss with them the importance of being a good listener so that they can be a good "repeater" of things they hear. Train students to watch the teacher for hand directions, especially if you should be working on a program presentation. Tape and play many sounds for children to listen to and identify. Echo games are a must for practicing various pitches and diction. If a child has continued problems with tone, it is also worth checking medical records to see if there is any reason this should be occurring. Telling a child he or she cannot sing or should not try to sing (unless, of course, there is a temporary or permanent medical condition) can create a stigma carried through life, diminishing the joy that singing can bring.

Teaching Children to Move

Development in the *physical domain* is another rationale for having a music program. Children, through musical response, learn how to control their bodies and refine large and small movements with the body and the voice. By using movement, many areas are heightened: dramatic response, imagination, and spatial perception. When songs are selected with simultaneous movements in a group, for example, students become more aware of the space around them, of their balance, and so forth. A teacher should realize, however, that developing physical skills takes time and much repetition for young children, especially to fine tune various movements. Finger plays and playing correct rhythms with percussion instruments require a great deal of repetition to coordinate eye/hand or finger control. These are an important part of development, without doubt, for young children, and music can make it an enjoyable process. Remember that young children are individual in their stages of development in the physical domain and that very young children may have some difficulty with movements such as skipping to music. Although most mid-elementary children can skip and hop, they may still have difficulty with control in dance steps until the later elementary years. Offer opportunities for both structured music and for free creative movement. Be certain that plenty of safe space is provided for freedom of movement. Also, without setting limits on most movements, set limits on behavior before movement activities that would make movement lessons disintegrate. Demonstrate many movements to children to give them guidance and choices—swaying, creeping, galloping, rocking, whirling, and so forth—both with and without various types of music. When asking children to move, they should *hear* the music before they can respond. This allows them to imagine and make judgments on what their movements could be before they actually try it. Brainstorming ideas about "what the music is asking us to do" also aids in creativity. Again and most importantly there should be opportunities for many *types* of movement: finger plays, singing games, and creative and free responses. At times, children should be encouraged to "do what they feel like" to the music. Those who do *feel* the music will, and other children may look to see what the teacher is modeling. Therefore, the teacher should be a participant, too. At other times, you as the teacher may make suggestions, such as, "Can you feel the heavy sounds? Can you move slowly like an elephant?" Provide opportunities to move in games or with groups as well as individual opportunities.

Standard VII Planning and Implementing Effective Music Lessons

The music teacher understands how to plan and implement effective music instruction and provides students with learning experiences that enhance their musical knowledge, skills, and appreciation.

Teachers should know and understand the content and performance standards for music that comprise the Texas Essential Knowledge and Skills (TEKS) and the significance of the TEKS in developing a music curriculum. They should be able to use the TEKS to develop appropriate instructional goals and objectives for student learning and performance and provide students with multiple opportunities to develop music skills specified in the TEKS. By knowing the appropriate sequencing of music instruction and how to deliver developmentally appropriate music instruction, teachers should be able to provide students with an experience that is delivered in developmentally appropriate ways that encourage active engagement in learning and make instructional content meaningful. Teachers should know a variety of methods for developing an appropriate and effective curriculum and lesson plans for the music class and be able to adapt their instructional methods to provide appropriate learning experiences for students with varied needs, learning modalities, and levels of development and musical experience. Also, teachers should know learning theory as it applies to music education and be able to provide instruction that promotes students' understanding and application of the fundamental principles of music. They should understand the importance of helping students develop music skills that are relevant to their own lives and provide each student with opportunities to contribute to the music class by drawing from their personal experiences. Teachers should provide each student with varied opportunities to make music using instruments and voice, to respond to a wide range of musical styles and genres, and to evaluate music of various types. Teachers should provide each student with a level of musical self-sufficiency to encourage lifelong enjoyment of music and be able to use varied materials, resources, and technology to promote students' creativity, learning, and performance. Teachers know strategies and benefits of promoting students' critical-thinking and problem-solving skills in relation to music and can provide students with frequent opportunities to use these skills in analyzing, creating, and responding to music. While the teacher knows procedures and criteria for selecting an appropriate repertoire for the music class, she or he should teach students to apply skills for forming and communicating critical judgments about music and musical performance using appropriate terminology. Using technology and various other materials and resources available for use in music education is an important part of a teacher's knowledge base. Teachers should help students develop an understanding and appreciation of various cultures through instruction related to music history and discussion of current events related to music that ties music to the past and present. They should also incorporate a diverse musical repertoire into instruction, including music from both Western and non-Western traditions. While knowing appropriate literature to enhance technical skills, teachers should also know the value of and techniques for integrating music instruction with other subject areas. Promoting music can be an integral element in students' lives, whether as a vocation or as an avocation, and encouraging students to independently pursue musical knowledge should be a part of a teacher's mission in music. Finally, teachers should be aware of and teach students proper health techniques for use during rehearsals and performances.

National standards for music suggest that there are four basic strands in which children should be involved in music: perceptions, creative expression, historical and cultural heritage, and critical evaluation. However, *involvement* is the key for children in each case at this age, because they learn by *doing*.

Music in the Domains

Although good music instruction works to support all major domains (the physical, the emotional, the social, and the cognitive), the domain most touched, perhaps, in music is the *affective*—that of feeling, emotions, and appreciation. The five stages of the *affective domain* are: (1) *receiving* (actively attending), (2) *responding,* (3) *valuing* (demonstrated by individual choices made), (4) *organization* (ranking in importance), and (5) *characterization by value* (acting consistently with one's values). You may easily see how this might work in the music classroom. Initially, in order for children to learn to love, appreciate, and critique music, they must first be given numerous opportunities to listen or actively attend, then respond. Because children will develop feelings about the many types and facets of music (through either good or bad examples), the teacher should be sure that encounters with music are positive in all ways possible. Teachers should also provide students with effective tools for judging the value of music. If they cannot actively talk about and use the elements, structure, and effect of a variety of musical examples (presented in Standard I), it will be difficult for them to evaluate and value choices.

Other domains are also part of music. The *cognitive domain* in music involves the acquisition of musical theory, history, and so forth, while the *physical domain* centers on both body movement and motor skill development (both large and fine). Music enhances athletic skills of growing children through movement. Musical finger plays and movement games should be a part of the physical and spatial development of every early childhood classroom, as children progress from common movements such as patting or clapping to the imitation of other animals or inanimate things to role-play and, finally, to organized musical games. Music provides a backdrop for kinesthetic learners by coupling learning to their developmental processes. Older elementary children should not be denied the kinesthetic modality either. The following example is a "silly song" that represents both the use of music as a memory model for remembering land forms concepts and a song that has students access kinesthetic movement to help in the learning process. It is written to "If You're Happy and You Know It."

> I'm a mountain and I know it, climb my rocks! (Children first make a "peak" with their hands, then do a "climbing motion" with their hands.)
>
> I'm a mountain and I know it, climb my rocks! (Repeat motions.)
>
> I'm a mountain and I know it, and I've got steep sides to show it. (Children form a peak with their hands, then with their right hands point to the left "steep side.")
>
> I'm a mountain and I know it, climb my rocks! (Repeat first motions.)
>
> I'm a plateau and I know it, flat on top! (Children form a "table top" plateau with their hands and arms.)
>
> I'm a plateau and I know it, flat on top! (Repeat motions.)
>
> I'm a plateau and I know it, and I'm flat on top to show it. (Children form a "table top" plateau with their hands and arms and "smooth" the flat top.)
>
> I'm a plateau and I know it, flat on top! (Repeat first motions.)

Other verses and motions might include:

I'm a peninsula and I know it, I stick out! (Children form a "peninsula" by sticking an elbow out to the side.)

I'm a hill and I know it, round on top! (Children form "hill" above head with hands.)
I'm a valley and I know it, a deep "V"! (Children form a "V" by crossing their forearms almost at the elbow in front of them.)

Social skills develop when children are engaged in the many musical activities involving groups or partners. The teacher should be a sharer and co-experiencer of each activity, but the learner him- or herself must listen, react, create, and perform to gain. All children have the potential to develop their skills and their appreciation for music, given opportunities by a Texas teacher.

Remember Your Pedagogy

For successful experiences, all music should be age appropriate in terms of ability and subject matter *and* in terms of intellectual development, social development, and physical development. As a reminder, an important part of learning theory tells us that stages of each domain are not always tied to an exact age, so students may move through stages of these domains at different rates. In addition, the zone of proximal development theory (where children can function with help from an adult or capable peer) should be a part of music planning as well; we want to challenge young children with music rather than overwhelm them with concepts and skills that they cannot yet handle. Many concrete and manipulative experiences combined with visuals should be an important part of music instruction. Remember also that some movements that older children can accomplish to music are not appropriate for the coordination of the young child. On a serious note, teachers must consider that much of our popular music today no longer contains lyrics or messages appropriate for children. Listen to *all* songs that you will play in class carefully. You do not want children to hear some songs or repeat lyrics that would lead an angry parent and/or administrator to your doorstep. Children should be allowed to bring their own music to share, but do establish parental knowledge and rules for appropriateness. Select a variety of music throughout the day, even though children will or may already have begun to develop preferences. Although certain types of music are not appealing to young children, your opinion matters, so if you also indicate distaste in certain music, young students may imitate your modeling.

When teaching music, foremost, do not forget other pedagogy from your *PRR (Professional Roles and Responsibilities) TExES*. Provide a classroom that is warm and open and that invites discovery, creativity, and improvisation. Establish rules and routines that help students become accepting of each other during performances, and give directions that show respect for instruments, equipment and each other in movement. Positively encourage children always, especially in performance and creative areas. Provide for continuity and relevance for young children by sharing music from their home/community/culture. Plan and follow lesson plans (both long-range and daily), as you would with other subject areas, that help students understand the objectives and the rationales for a musical experience. Download and use the music TEKS as a guideline for preparing goals and objectives for which you are responsible at the grade level in which you teach. Texas expects that you will do this for *every* subject, including music. Allow for both whole-class and individual experiences and for integrating other arts and subject areas whenever possible. Give children opportunities to explore varied sounds. Provide them with thinking at all levels—particularly at higher levels. Such activities at the synthesis level might include creating musical introductions and accompaniments to stories or poems, improvising or writing short songs or simple operettas, designing new musical accompaniments to songs children already know, designing a new movement to a certain song, creating their own instruments, and so forth. Make judgments in terms of your objectives on how well children are progressing and use those assessments to reflect upon how it will impact what you do the next time in class.

There are other important reasons for teachers to understand the basics of music for the elementary classroom. The greatest potential for developing and encouraging musical interests and skills lies in the years of early childhood and elementary school. Also, multiple intelligence research identifies *musical* intelligence as one of several intelligences. As such, those children who have talent and intelligence in music should be provided a way "to shine," as they develop their talents more fully in the classroom. For other students, we know that to offer experiences in an intelligence area such as music, according to recent brain research, is to develop new physiological pathways. Children who learn best in kinesthetic or tactile ways also often "shine" during music classes, although, again, all children's skills in these areas can be enhanced. Music is one subject that can be developed both for playing, movement, and singing skill, as well as for appreciation. In the early childhood years, a tremendous amount of musical growth can occur—*if* that growth is nurtured by a caring teacher.

Music is emotional in nature, and teachers can take advantage of that aspect. As with the background music to movies, classroom music can heighten students' experiences with certain subject areas such as writing and reading literature, or it can encourage a student to "be a part" of another land or era. For example, playing Native American music in the background as students enter their social studies classroom can set a mood for the day's lesson on the various tribes of Texas and can continue to involve students as they work on an independent project later in the hour with Native American music as a backdrop. Playing a focus song to lead into an activity can create considerable interest or can close a lesson in a way that helps the lesson linger in the minds of students. For instance, a teacher who was planning a "science-heavy" unit on the Titanic might open or close with the popular theme song from that movie to connect science to the reality of human tragedy. And what student could not write a more vivid descriptive piece or poem on spring, for example, with Vivaldi playing softly in the background? Many songs can be found to introduce specific topics or concepts. Because music touches the emotions so easily, it can be used by a creative teacher to enhance the mood of the classroom and as an aid to increase creativity and learning across the curriculum. Often, music text series seek to combine works of art and poetry with works of music. This helps to further develop the affective domain, as students can relate to how a painter suggests feelings and emotions with color, lines, and shapes . . . to how a poet does the same with words . . . to how a musician does so with many variations of sounds.

Music Connections

Music has also been tied to learning in different subject areas in other ways. You may have grown up with songs, for example, that helped you remember the alphabet, seasons, holidays, and sequencing of letters and numbers. This will be investigated in detail in a moment. You have already seen reasons why *mathematics* has a direct tie with music, particularly when looking at fractions.

The study of the production of sound can easily be tied to *science* lessons, and, in *social studies,* there are many small and well-written operettas published for children about various historical periods. These provide students with motivating preludes to find out more about these times and persons.

Multicultural studies and music go hand-in-hand when boys and girls begin to learn about people around the world. Simple songs written in other languages, may, for example, be a child's first experience with foreign language; they also help a child understand that many peoples throughout the world are the same in that they express similar feelings (and often do so through music). Music tells us much about the peoples of the world as well as the different regions of the United States. Music provides exciting differences for a child to see from place to place and from era to era, depending on who writes it, who performs it, for what occasions music is made and performed, and the different instruments and ways of singing that exist. The state music standards in almost every grade level require students to investigate diverse cultures by playing or singing songs or participating in musical games of other cultures. For young children, this aspect of introducing other cultures is extremely inviting. For example, a unit on Japan can include a "tea party" with traditional music of the country playing in the background as students sip their tea, learn about the new country, and create a haiku. Other multicultural experiences and events should often include music.

Very compelling is the fact that music provides a very safe way of *reading* for students—as children follow along with choral lyrics. In this "low-risk" read-along situation, music can add to student confidence, and literacy is promoted through voice/print pairing.

Music, when played as a backdrop for reading or drama as a mood setter can enhance student creativity in dramatic roles. A play can be enhanced when students, using simple instruments, create a musical motif for each character. The matching musical motif is played each time the character enters or speaks. As the story becomes more involved and exciting, so does the instrumentation.

Art and music often fit together naturally, as the teacher selects background music that relates in some way to an art project while students work, or the teacher may ask students to "let the music tell them" what to paint or draw. Art is often combined as a part of music texts as a way for students to understand comparisons between art and musical elements such as texture, shape, and line.

Music also helps us to learn facts and acts as an aid to memory. Governmental processes, grammar, and math concepts have been set to music as an entertaining way for countless students to remember specified material (for example, how a bill goes through Congress). Many of you may still be able to name all the states by singing a song such as "Fifty . . . nifty . . . ". Such productions as *Schoolhouse Rock,* for example, provide many songs about facts on social studies, grammar, money, multiplication, and science (to order, go to http:// disneyvideos.disney.go.com and search for schoolhouse rock, or see lyrics at www.schoolhouserock.tv). For example, one song, *Conjunction Junction*, tells students, "Conjunction Junction, what's your function? Hooking up words and phrases and clauses." Music can also be used as a memory model for students, as the teacher finds or composes words to popular melodies (or helps students create their own) that relate to a subject at hand. Many of you already know how a certain song or piece of music triggers a memory of a place, a date or time period, or a particular person. As a memory model for students, the teacher finds or makes up words to songs (as noted earlier in the song, "I'm a Mountain and I Know It . . ."), particularly popular melodies, that relate to a subject at hand. These lyrics can be quite serious or very silly. For example, a fourth-grade classroom was being observed while taking a test. Earlier, the student teacher had taught her students a song that she had made up to help them remember simple machines and their functions. Students did very well on the test, but interestingly enough, there was quite a bit of humming of the "machine song" going on in the classroom that day, as students "accessed" their lyrics and, thus, their definitions. Older elementary students also love to create these types of lyrics related to the various curriculum areas and put them to popular melodies, rap rhythms, and so forth, while younger children love to sing these types of songs because the melody is often already familiar. Do remember, however, that students coming from *outside* the United States may not readily know these tunes. You may need to teach the originals first.

Having students create their own music as an activity, of course, involves having them work at the *synthesis* level—a higher-level of thinking. For example, in composing, students can create various rhythms or construct sound stories around a theme (holidays, a person, a trip, feelings, or another concept), in which sounds that represent the theme to the child are collected on tape. A "sound tape" of human vocalizations (hums, whispers, hisses, sighs, shouts, etc.) that students write and record makes an interesting composition. They may create a poem or story backdrop (for example, a sound tape for each animal in a rain forest book), lyrics and/or melodies, short operettas, chants, raps, or hand, body, or dance movements of their own.

A methodology, *Suggestopedia*, created by Bulgarian Georgi Lozanov, has been used since the 1970s in teaching foreign language in an accelerated manner. In this technique, Baroque music is used to relax the mind, as his research shows that a tense mind closes in learning languages. However, with music, learning in a new language can be easily accepted—for mental barriers are less taut. Using the Suggestopedia techniques, the teacher often uses music in tandem with guided visualization or imaging. A scene is read containing a considerable amount of contextual clues along with known vocabulary. From this, students are able to gain understanding into the new vocabulary in a relaxed manner. Carrying this idea a step further into our elementary classrooms, new vocabulary in many different subjects may be "Greek" to our students, so the same method can be applied in various areas of study. For example, in a modified version of Suggestopedia, a teacher may play one of the many "nature" CD selections that are available of rain forest sounds combined with relaxing music. She or he asks students to relax, close their eyes, and "take a journey" into the rain forest. As the music plays, the teacher softly delivers a script that is full of contextual clues with new vocabulary words embedded within. New vocabulary and concepts are shown in boldface:

> Close your eyes and relax and come with me now to the rain forest of Central America. The first thing that overwhelms our eyes here is the green **vegetation**— the incredible number of growing plants! Everywhere you look the **vegetation** is so green, and many of these plants have beautiful flowers. This green **vegetation** grows all year long—because the location is so warm and **humid**—that is, sticky and damp. About nine feet of rain falls here every year! How **humid** it is here! I am already sweating and my clothes are sticking to me. Most places in Texas receive only about one to two feet of rain each year. There is so much rain in the rain forest that it cannot evaporate, so the **humidity** (or moisture in the air) remains high all the time. Think about how it feels in Texas in the summer on a day when the **humidity** is high—you feel sticky, sweaty, and damp. In the rain forest, there is even more **humidity**! That's one reason for so much green **vegetation**. The **vegetation** gets so much moisture. Also, the **vegetation** never freezes like it does in many parts of Texas. It is so warm here, so the **vegetation** grows and grows and grows! That is why, when we look down upon the rain forest from

*above, we view a "sea of green." So much **vegetation**! If we look closely, as we enter the rain forest now, we can see that we are standing in the **understory** of the **vegetation**. It is not like a **jungle** as I thought it would be from some movies, it's a forest. A **jungle** is difficult to walk through because it is choked and tangled with undergrowth. In fact, here in the **understory** of the rain forest, there is almost no **vegetation**—most of the plants grow thickly above us. I can see why! It's so dark here on the **understory** floor—a little like a basement under the other stories of a house—the **understory**. There is very little light here because the **vegetation** growing above us almost covers the sun! Look down and we can also see why there is little **vegetation** on the forest floor or the **understory**. The soil is clay—it is not a rich soil at all like a **jungle** would have! Reach down and take some soil from the **understory** in your hand. You could almost make a little clay bowl out of it, just like we mold clay in our art class. All around us in the **understory** there are roots. . . . (the teacher would continue to introduce the **canopy** layer and the **emergent** tree layer as the tape or CD continues to play.)*

Speech and music also go hand-in-hand, as the spoken word has rhythms of which the child is not often aware. Singing, chanting, and rhyming words in the context of music help the child develop better speaking skills and understanding of pronunciation. Encouragement of experimentation of all types of verbal sounds helps the child to become more sensitive to his or her own speaking voice and develop that voice in a more dynamic manner.

Music can also be a mood adjuster for behavior. Teachers who have students enter a classroom where calming music is playing can often feel a difference in the way the class begins to focus. Conversely, music can invigorate a class after a long period of academic work or can help relieve some of the stress accompanying long test periods. Cute musical transitions have always been used by kindergarten teachers to move students from one activity to another, but clever teachers in all grades may find that age-appropriate music creates the perfect routine for changing activities or moving to new work areas in a more conducive manner. Very young children will need the consistency that certain songs can give, so teachers establish songs that build familiar routines for them during the day. Use familiar music before going on, so that they feel safe in branching out to explore the new.

Thinking about music can give children enjoyable ways to develop and reinforce thinking skills. Music can be a higher-level thinking activity in and of itself, as students compose or create their own compositions or think about sound in creating their own instruments. Boys and girls can analyze and evaluate music to determine their reasons for liking or disliking a song or composition and can interpret what a composer is trying to say through music. After comparing and contrasting, they can choose meaningful alternatives. Older elementary students can investigate music in association with other activities and happenings. Thus, music becomes an integral part of students' lives in many areas—rather than, "It's time for music class now!"

? *Try this practice question:*

For one musical activity, Miss Larson wanted a permanent Music Center in her early childhood class. She and a friend built a huge three-sided box that was comfortable enough for one or two students. The open side pushed up against the wall, so that when Miss Larson wanted to change the center, she could just pull it out from the wall. Light inside was provided by several holes in the top. Inside she placed only one or two instruments at a time (some with multiple tones capability, some that were monotoned). For example, one week she placed two drums inside, each with a different tone, while the next week she set up resonator bells (bells with three pitches and of three different sizes) and a mallet inside. Sometimes instruments were homemade (a durable box with seeds that could be shaken) and sometimes they were ordinary items (pot lids). She gave directions, mostly focusing on the care of the instruments. This center was:

A. inappropriate because children do not know what to expect or do with the instrument(s) because no proper instruction has been given.
B. inappropriate because young children cannot be expected to take care of the instruments when they are not in sight of the teacher, and they already have a chance to play with ordinary things at home.
C. appropriate because it provides time and space for young children to spontaneously explore and create music.
D. appropriate because young children need to have private time and the center is constructed so as to combine music with time away from others.

Answer *A* is not correct for young children because, at times, they should be able to experiment independently in music. We would not select *B* either, because we expect that children will take care of the instruments, and, as music teachers, we continuously instruct and enforce this concept. An important part of experimenting with sound is discovering what the environment has to offer (*C*). We cannot be sure that students have the opportunity at home to experiment (*B*). *D* is incorrect because the center is constructed to ensure that students are insulated when they are noisy (which we would expect here) rather than creating private time. Let's return to *C*. *C* is correct, as this type of center provides an inquiry-based time and space for young children to perceive information about the instrument (that is to experiment for data), analyze, and to come to some conclusions on their own. As new instruments are switched, they apply learned information to the new experience. Too many instruments at once would be overwhelming to the young child and would not give the child an opportunity to focus. An activity that should follow would be to have children make their own instruments, some of which may find their way to this center.

Let's try another question:

Mrs. Bradford's social studies class has been working on a unit on Africa for almost two weeks. Students have read about the continent of Africa, researched it on the Internet, seen videos, worked on art projects, and focused on African music as well. Tomorrow Mrs. Bradford will give a test on this unit.

On this day, she first had children put away their things and relax. She put on a CD softly in the background entitled "African Safari" and proceeded to involve the class in a Concept Development model. She first asked students to brainstorm all the words that they could think of when they heard the word "Africa" and felt the music playing. As students thought of words, she wrote them on the board. Among the many examples that students contributed were:

drums	plains	tigers	singing	flutes
lions	safari	chants	many tribes	cheetahs
hunting	elephants	waterfalls	flamingos	Nile
ivory	gold	Lost Cities	desert	jungle
homemade instruments	big cities	colonies	many countries	
"The Lion King"	dancing in the villages	big mountains		

As the music was replayed, she asked her cooperative tables of students to classify the terms on the board into groups that belong together for whatever reason they think. Then, they were to label these groups with a name. They could also add any terms that they had left out that might belong in their categories. One cooperative group came up with the one of the following classifications and labels:

African Music	**They added to this category:**
handmade instruments	hunting dances
drums	story dances
flutes	masks
dancing in the village	chants
singing	

Other categories emerged into land forms, African animals, and so forth. As each group read their categories, the class was asked to add anything else that came to mind about Africa. Mrs. Bradford then asked each cooperative table to select one category and create two to four sentences using all of the words they listed. The cooperative group that selected African Music wrote, "In lots of villages in Africa, instruments like drums and flutes are handmade. The village uses these when they sing and dance. Lots of African music is just voices chanting without any music. The people there sometimes wear masks to act out stories—like a hunt."

The music added all but which of the following important elements to this lesson?

    A. triggered memories of what students had seen about Africa in movies, videos, photos, etc., so it acted as a part of scaffolding and tapping past experiences.
    B. added another modality to the lesson.
    C. added interest to the lesson, so it helped with motivation.
    D. helped to increase students' ability to read music.

The Concept Development model is an excellent way for teachers to determine what students know about a concept as a class. It is also helpful to begin teaching a lesson on a new concept. It helps a teacher determine prior knowledge so that students are not bored by the reteaching of information they know. As in this case, it is also extremely useful as a review for a unit test so students can self-monitor what they have gained prior to testing and the teacher can see what she or he might need to reteach. The music gives this lesson an added dimension in all of the areas mentioned in *A, B,* and *C.* In addition, if the teacher puts the same music on during the test, Suggestopedia experts believe that students will be able to access much more information. Although this model helped to increase vocabulary that has to do with some musical terms (drums, chants, etc.), there is nothing in the lesson that deals with decoding music. The correct answer is *D.*

Technology and Music

Technology has opened the doors wide to engage students in music. Not only does advanced technology in listening allow us to hear music more clearly than ever before but also, as mentioned earlier, it allows students to hear their own music immediately, make judgments, and make alternative decisions to refine their performances. Electric instruments and sound equipment allow for amplification and purer sound. Music created totally through the use of synthesizers (electronic devices that create sounds) or music/sounds that are altered in some way by electronic devices is termed *electronic music*—rather than music played on electronic instruments such as the electric guitar or other amplified instruments. Music synthesizers that allowed sounds to be produced in almost any way a composer desired became available in the

1950s. Through the next decades computers made the process of composing easier and easier. Software programs work with computers to create sounds similar to almost any musical instrument, to save a composer's music and recall it for editing later on, and so forth. These are all excellent technology packages for budding musicians. Still other software packages teach students how to read music easily. Although working with MIDI (Music Instrument Digital Interface) is sometimes complicated, it can open a whole new world of possibilities with synthesizing. To hear what MIDI can do, go to the following website and select from the types of music that you would like to hear: www.phiharmonia.co.uk/thesoundexchange/sound_samples/sample_libraries/phrases. Companies such as eJamming offer the online or in-class ability to play music with others in real time with MIDI instruments. Do not forget the Internet as a source for many types of music, biographies of composers, music history, and other pertinent information.

Resources

One question that you must be asking if you do not have a considerable background in music is, "How will I know what to teach and where will I get ideas?" Many schools have music book series such as Silver Burdett, McGraw-Hill, etc., although you may have to share one set per grade level. These series may come with student texts at all levels of elementary music instruction. Some investigation as to where these series might be found in your building or district may be in order, but it will be worth it for your students. Teachers' editions offer clear examples of appropriate scope and sequence, along with many valuable activities. Most importantly, if these series are provided by your school, they often come with excellent, high-quality recordings (with both children's and adults' voices), written music for accompaniments or classroom instruments, charts and other visuals, and cross-indexes for convenience.

The TEKS (Texas Essential Knowledge and Skills) for music students is also a guide for teaching scope and sequence of skills and is a *requirement* for teachers to follow in Texas. There are TEKS expectations and elements for teachers in music (under Fine Arts) for young and elementary school children by grade level and these can be accessed online. Again, TEKS for music are available for downloading at http://www.tea.state.tx.us/rules/tac/chapter117/index.html. National Music Standards for young children are also available at http://www.menc.org/publication/books/prek12st.html.

Libraries can also be important places for you to find music resources. You can find song and musical activity books, books about young musicians, biographies of famous composers, and recordings to check out for many age levels. Most university libraries have sets of teachers' editions and/or examples of student texts of music series from major textbook publishers to investigate.

People can also add much to your music program. The school district in which you work may have a musical specialist who oversees many schools. Other teachers in your school may also be a source of ideas and materials. Be sure to ask your principal about other teachers in your building who could become musical resources to you. It is most important for you to maintain a schoolwide network for the music program as well. Other teachers may want to share in various aspects of a program or performance, so be sure to communicate what is happening musically in your school. Other district schools (especially "feeder" schools) can be a resource for sparking interest in music for students, as you invite musical groups from intermediate, middle, and high schools to perform in your elementary school or class. Musical interest can be ignited in your children, as they see teachers in upper grades conducting exciting performances with older children. Be sure to inform your children and their parents about musical performances in your district or community that provide a source of interest and entertainment. Most school bands and choirs perform concerts and musicals during various times of the year, so making sure that you are a part of the information network (and can pass this information on) should be part of your commitment to music and your community. A quick guide to musical events around the state along with other information can be found at www. texasmusicguide. com. Also, parents can be excellent resources for musical experiences—as well as people from the community who take an interest in children and music. Ask parents through notes, emails, or calls, and be resourceful in your community in searching for professional or amateur musicians who might add to the musical experiences of your children by volunteering in some way.

For teachers, the Internet offers a wide variety of resources—from finding suitable materials for any type of music desired, to finding organizations for music teachers, to locating quick examples of instrumental sounds. The Texas Music Educators site at www.tmea.org and the Texas Music Teachers site at www.tmta.org are two such sites that provide information and links to many other sites. The Internet has a great variety of "click on" songs and musical pieces from all eras. Musical histories and biographical information on great composers can be found at a moment's notice, and online music stores offer all types of musical recordings as well as books and sheet music. There are also a number of tapes and CDs suitable for these grade levels available from retail stores, school supply catalogs, or teachers' stores.

There are several journals that may act as resources of interest to teachers of music: *American Suzuki Journal, British Journal of Music Education, General Music Today, Canadian Educators Journal, Kodaly Envoy, Music Educators Journal,* and the *Orff Echo.* As with all subject areas, music has organizations to which teachers belong—both national and state—many of which publish good resource journals or offer beneficial conferences. The Texas Music Teachers Association (www.tmta.org), the Texas Music Educators (www.tmea.org), and the Music Teachers National Association all have Web sites for membership and information and act as good resources. Http://www.nats.org is the site for the National Association for Teachers of Singing. Http://www.isd77.k12.mn .us/music/k-12music is an excellent site with many other links to organizations that may be useful. Be creative and persistent in your Internet searches, and you will find what you need. Sites do change, so if any sites listed in this chapter are no longer found, try looking through a modified search by name or subject.

The Home, Community, and Music

One accepted element of pedagogy asks that the teacher seek to link the culture of parents and the community with instruction. This would also be true with the music curriculum as a scaffolding issue—that is, children will first relate to the type of music with which they are familiar. In planning, therefore, look carefully at the culture of the community and its unique engagement with music. In Texas, for example, we mentioned that there are rural communities that are of German and Czech descent whose children grow up learning to polka, while in other communities, children can two-step with country-and-western music almost before they begin school. Young African American children in many communities may have considerable experience with gospel music, while young Hispanic students may know the sounds of *tejano* very well. Of course, there are communities and individuals everywhere in between who relate to *many* types of music. One mission of schools is often seen as "supporter of a culture." Therefore, the mission of music in schools is not only to expose boys and girls to a wide variety of music but to help students develop musical skills and songs that they can enjoy in their own world—that of their community's culture along with that of family and friends. Again, it is important for teachers to know what musical events are offered in the community around the school and capitalize on the connections. Parents are more likely to support programs with which they are comfortable musically, although most want their children to have a well-rounded education in music as well. Most young children love to perform, so school programs offer an excellent bridge to draw parents to the school. You may even have parents who are knowledgeable and willing to help with your programs—a great resource!

Health and Safety in Music

There are some issues to which teachers must attend in music regarding the health and well-being of their students. Most importantly, if a teacher is lucky enough to have a classroom or school set of recorders (beginning instruments that look much like a clarinet), much care must be taken to ensure that these instruments are thoroughly cleaned in order to avoid having bacteria build up inside from warm breaths and to stop the passing on of germs and illnesses if children must share. Make sure to use a sanitizer that does not react with plastic. We know that germs can be easily spread through hand contact, so when children will be holding hands during musical activities or trading rhythm instruments, cleaning hands prior to and after the activity may save children passing colds and other germs during epidemic times of the year.

The loud volume of music can also be of concern. The hearing of children should be considered, especially those who are forced to continuously sit next to speakers or loud instruments. Another safety issue concerns instruments that are played with mallets or strikers. Provide strict rules about the appropriate use of these on the instruments for which they were designed only.

During musical movement exercises, song games, or dances, the teacher is responsible for making sure that space is cleared so that students do not trip over desks or other items as they become involved. Special concern for children with exceptionalities, particularly those with physical challenges, should be made here. Finally, if students are going to be on stage or use risers for special programs, establishing rules and practicing moving on and off are musts for safety.

Special Needs Children at Music Time

Classrooms may have children who are differently abled that are a part of the classroom all day or may be mainstreamed for some subjects by reason of Public Law 94–192. If a child has been placed in a regular classroom for music as a part of the "least restrictive environment," teachers should make sure that they include those children and modify their objectives, if applicable, on their IEP (Individual Education Plan) as required by law so that these students can participate to the fullest of their abilities. Learn as much as you can about the child and his or her abilities and needs ahead of time and do not be afraid to call on the help of specialized teachers and parents as resources. If a child is coming to a self-contained classroom only for music, be sure to have music times set out clearly to work in coordination with the schedule of the special needs teacher. Your manner of acceptance and welcome will be the model for your students to follow.

Many children with mental differences or learning disabilities may need special attention in the music class regarding introductions to the instruments, as the sounds may startle, cause sensory "overload," or confuse them. Because music is emotional, these students may sometimes overreact during listening times to certain pieces or instrument sounds. Note short attention spans and be ready to change approaches if a child becomes too excitable or too bored. Clear structure and repetition (if children are unable to read long passages) is also a necessary part of instruction for some children with special needs, even in music class. Try to begin and end the class in a routine way (perhaps with one particular welcome or greeting song and a particular farewell song). Work on small portions of music at a time with immediate feedback to help eliminate failure. Establish clear signals to end music, as some students may become so involved that they do not stop. Children should be expected and encouraged to participate to the fullest of their abilities and praised well and often for their efforts.

For students with hearing difficulties, the teacher of music must go to further lengths to help in relating the lesson visually, through vibration in a tactile manner (by having students touch) and kinesthetically (through motions). Seating is especially important for these children so that they may see visuals, feel vibrations, and catch the rhythms of movements. Many may not be totally impaired, so seating close to the music source or having a non-pitched instrument close to an ear may be vital—though it may depend on whether their hearing loss involves clarity or loudness (frequency) difficulties. Individual modification may need to be made for distortion in hearing devices for music and group singing. Be certain that students can see your face and speech movements during all instruction and singing, and use clear, distinct articulation. If a child has near or total impairment and signs, signing lyrics is also encouraged. Often these children face speech difficulties, too, so help in language development (diction, rhythm, etc.) is important in music class.

Students who are visually impaired may be able to participate fully in most lessons, although lessons that focus on listening and rote learning of songs *along with* tactile aids for some activities will increase learning. Children with visual difficulties may need physical guidance in any movements to music. If not fully impaired, large visuals in black and white or large-print song books may be provided. If students are learning Braille, see if there is a way to obtain Braille song books so they can follow along with the words. When entering the classroom for music, always warn these students of new placements of sound equipment or instruments or of the fact that you have moved chairs in anticipation of an activity.

Children who are orthopedically challenged may need help with alternative movements, if applicable to the lesson, but they can often participate in most other ways. Sometimes the class can be very helpful in creating a design that helps these students move about and participate more easily. Watch phrasing of words used in movement activities so that *all* children can participate, depending on the particular circumstances. Provide *alternatives* for movements such as "Stand up and walk around in a circle" in classrooms with children in wheelchairs, for example. When playing rhythm instruments, special accommodations may be needed to help children hold a mallet or stick in some way.

Musically gifted students also require special attention. Some larger school districts have magnet schools for musically talented children, although most are left to the school or classroom teacher. Be sure that you are providing opportunities for these children to work at their levels through enrichment experiences.

There are other special needs and combinations of special needs not covered here. Students who have learning disabilities that affect other subject areas will have the same difficulties in music classes (reading, sequencing, etc.). One important thing that teachers need to remember is that by law (PL 94–192), documentation needs to be provided for evaluation purposes on objectives set by the ARD (Admission, Review, and Dismissal) team. Continue to seek out resources to help with each type of need, and remember that each child is truly an individual and will have needs specifically for the extent to which he or she can participate. Music may offer children with special needs an avenue of communication not open to them in many subject areas. It is often a nurturing force in their lives as well as an expressive one.

Consider the following practice question:

Ms. Mitchell told students that tomorrow would be a special writing day. They were going to experience "a concert" in class, then become *music critics* by writing about what they judged to be good or poor quality for two of the four pieces they would hear. They would choose two and evaluate what they heard, what they liked, what they didn't like—and why.

"To go to a concert," she told them, "tickets must be purchased. During certain times of the day today, you can to go back to the 'ticket booth' desk in the back of the room and select your seating for tomorrow's concert from the seating chart map. You will each get an envelope with 'money' for a seat." All envelopes contained different amounts of money, so students would have to make a decision on where they could buy their seat based on the money in their envelopes. As students purchased tickets, Ms. Mitchell put their names on those tickets in order to hand out tickets quickly the next day.

Ms. Mitchell went over the expectations for concert behavior: Wait for the usher to seat you, no changing seats because each person has paid for a particular seat, no talking once the concert has started so all can hear, no getting out of one's seat during the music (and if you are not seated by the time the concert begins, you may not go in until there is a break) because it will be dark, and show one's appreciation by clapping (and calling out "bravo" if the performance was very, very good). She also told them about the sequence of events for the orchestra: warm-up of the musical instruments at the beginning, applause at the entry of the concertmaster (first seat violinist), tuning of the instruments, entry of the conductor (applause), possible entrance of soloists; applause of the end of each piece, and applause at the end of the concert with standing ovations reserved for outstanding performances. She also reminded them of some longer pieces that they had already listened to in class that had different movements with silence in between. She laughed in telling them that sometimes audience members who don't know the music well start clapping between the movements—and the music is not really over yet! A good guideline, she noted, is to wait to see if lots of others begin applause, and if still unsure, wait until the conductor actually steps down. She also told them that they should look particularly nice tomorrow. Although everyone who attends concerts does not dress up, it does show respect for the performers to look nice. Refreshments would be served during intermission (with conversation), so all those who followed the rules would have something at that point. Finally, she quickly went over a bit of information on the composers that they would hear.

The following day, Ms. Mitchell had students line up at the door and gave out their tickets with "programs." She had two students role-play ushers, who seated students in their correct seats for the concert. She then introduced the music and had several students role-play the entrance of some of the orchestra members, and, finally, she had students listen to two exciting pieces of music. Punch and cookies were served at intermission, followed by "flashing of the lights," reseating, and the playing of two other pieces of music. At the end of the concert, Ms. Mitchell asked students to quietly return to their own seats to review the elements needed for critiquing and begin the writing process, as she replayed the selections. This music class contributed the *most* to:

A. introducing students to some of the great composers.
B. having students understand concert etiquette.
C. having students use thinking skills of comparing and contrasting.
D. the integration of mathematics and writing.

Standard 7.10s asks Texas teachers to teach concert etiquette. Role-play is the perfect introduction to a real concert. It is hoped that one field trip might include a musical performance of some type. Ms. Mitchell has also integrated this into her writing class, as she is asking students to compare and contrast the different pieces of music so choice C would be a good *second* choice. Although this lesson does integrate some math and writing (*D*), the main focus is music. The music that she selected for listening could be from the great composers (*A*) but could also be chosen more for the enjoyment of this grade level. The emphasis here, however, was on the concert etiquette. Role-play might include any one of the many types of concerts that children might attend: symphony orchestra, chamber orchestra, recitals, choral and/or church music, operas, or ballet. The correct answer is *B*.

Generalists are not responsible for Standard VIII.

Standard IX Assessment

The music teacher understands student assessment and uses assessment results to design instruction and promote student progress.

The teacher knows the skills needed to form critical judgments about music. He or she knows techniques and criteria for assessing students' musical knowledge and skills and can use multiple forms of assessment and knowledge of the music TEKS to help determine students' progress in developing those music skills and understanding. Continuing, the teacher uses an understanding of ongoing results of assessment to continuously develop instructional plans. The EC-4 teacher can use standard terminology in communicating about students' musical skills and performance and can give constructive criticism when evaluating skills or performances. Meaningful prescriptions to correct problems or errors in musical performances can be easily offered.

The state provides several ways of knowing what is expected of children in Texas EC-4 classrooms. Teachers can use these guidelines to assess if their children are receiving the information and experiences needed to meet these expectations and how well children are achieving in this area. For example, the online *Texas Music Curriculum Guidelines* for 3- and 4-year-old children show that: Children should express themselves through singing and movement and by playing simple instruments. Children should learn to experiment with music concepts, volume, tempo, and sound. They should also begin to appreciate different types of music.

The child:

- participates in classroom music activities.
- begins to sing a variety of simple songs.
- begins to play classroom instruments.
- begins to respond to music of various tempos through movement.
- begins to distinguish among the sounds of several common instruments.

As another example, the TEKS for fine arts can be downloaded at www.tea .state.tx.us/rules/tac/chapter117/index.html. The following example shows some of the expectations for kindergarten (other grade levels can be found there as well).

Knowledge and skills:

1. *Perception. The student describes and analyzes musical sound and demonstrates musical artistry. The student is expected to:*

   A. *identify the difference between the singing and speaking voice, and*

   B. *identify the timbre of adult voices and instruments.*

2. *Creative expression/performance. The student performs a varied repertoire of music. The student is expected to:*

   A. *sing or play classroom instruments independently or in a group, and*

   B. *sing songs from diverse cultures and styles or play such songs on musical instruments.*

Teachers should be sure that they are using these Texas expectations for their grade levels to design short- and long-range music plans to include all of the TEKS at their grade level because teachers are accountable in this area. Using these as a base, teachers can also assess if children are receiving opportunities in all areas and measure the quality and quantity of the experiences. Criteria for judging individual achievement should be built into plans, as with other subjects that are taught. As children participate in experiences, plans should either reflect progression or reteaching of information and/or skills in music.

 ## Assessment and Evaluation

What areas should be included in music assessment and evaluation? Information on *all* the domains on which music touches may be included: (1) development of *physical skills* based on the ability to sing, play, and move at expected levels along with observed growth in perception through sensory responses or the ability to respond to musical differences; (2) growth in conceptual/*cognitive* development or thinking skills related to the elements of music, history of music, and so forth; (3) growth in the *affective domain* in terms of musical participation (both planned and free), musical preferences, creativity, and expressiveness; and (4) growth in the *social domain,* the interpersonal skills, and communication gained through musical participation.

Some responses to music are *overt* (or observable) but, more often than not, *covert*—that is, they take place inside the individual through the affective domain. For that reason, assessment and evaluation present some difficulty for teachers in music. However, teachers need to be able to communicate to children and their parents about student growth in music—as would be the case with other subject areas. With Pre-K and kindergarten children this can be challenging because of widespread developmental differences. Young children do not respond well to paper-and-pencil testing, and children often know and can do much more than they can verbalize. However, parents appreciate and expect teachers to inform them about strengths in musical areas (for example, can a child coordinate a marching beat, does the child have good short-term memory in repeating rhythms, does the child have an excellent sense of imagination in creating new sounds, does he or she have a clear, pleasant singing voice, and so forth). These and other factors that the teacher can glean from music class are also hints that may help a teacher understand how the student is developing in other subject areas. Supporting budding talent may also be a joint venture at home, if parents know their child is interested and/or talented.

As with other subject areas, teachers may evaluate the child in music *diagnostically* (to examine specific problems), *formatively* (over a period of time), and *summatively* (at the end of a specified period of time). Anecdotal records or observation sheets are favored by many teachers in music (especially for special needs children), while others use checklists or rating scales that can help more with issues of quality. Singing and using both directed and improvisional movement-to-music activities provides a way for the teacher to see what children are hearing and then translating into observable movements. A portfolio of audio- or videotapings may also be used to show development. Oral questioning provides a great deal of information. Paper-and-pencil sheets on the elements of music might be used for older students as they are asked to begin learning to read and write music. Excellent performance in music does involve a degree of talent, and some children may have the talent to become world-class performers, while others simply do not. However, because instruction and training can make a difference in how children appreciate music all their lives, teachers must be careful to use assessment in music in ways that are helpful and not hurtful. For that reason, we must use music terminology mentioned in the standards above with constructive criticism such as, "Listen carefully to the pitch that you hear now and try to match your voice carefully to it. Now try to make your voice go up just this much more (show hand signal)" or "Your audience will really appreciate hearing rising dynamics during this part because it makes the piece more powerful," rather than general comments such as, "You are hurting my ears today!" or "Can't you sing louder there?" Teachers alone may be responsible for children's loving or hating music. Teachers can affect children's desire for participation in music for the rest of their lives through the use of critique and assessment.

Assessing learning in music can be both written and performance based, but having children become good judges of music, including their own, is the best way for them to gain a lifelong appreciation of music. In addition to a teacher's assessments, children should critique their own performances by listening to their own tapes and by listening to many sources. Let them tell you, the teacher, how to make their performance(s) better. Here are some questions that may help young critics begin to think critically (depending on the instance):

Was your musical performance played/sung on key?

Was/were your instrument(s) in tune?

Did your choice of instruments fit the music well?

Did your piece or performance fit together with its forms?

Did your piece/performance project a mood (how did you feel when you performed it)? If so, did it succeed? How well?

How resourceful were you in creating a unique piece?

Was the tempo/speed of the music correct to easily sing or play along?

Was the tempo consistent or regular if so written?

Was your choice of dynamics correct to express what the composer wanted?

Was your sound too loud or too soft to be effective?

Were the lyrics expressive?

Was there enough variety in the music to make it interesting?

What are some ways that you could have sung/played this song differently?

What else could you or the composer/performer of a piece have chosen or done to make the music better?

The same questions could be asked of many selected examples of music that a teacher introduces, including questions such as why a particular piece of music was interesting—with the criteria centering on the musical elements and what these elements do for music (e.g., intensifying and declining dynamics, feelings of tension and release, introduction and climax and closure, elegance and appeal of the notes of the melody). Focusing on these elements will help students become excellent critics. It is difficult for children to understand how to describe their feelings without excellent modeling, however. The teacher should remember to carefully model often what she or he hears in music in order for children to be comfortable in their own assessments.

 # Standard X Professional Responsibilities

> **The music teacher understands professional responsibilities and interactions relevant to music instruction and the school music program.**
>
> *Teachers must know the legal and ethical issues related to the use or performance of music in an educational setting and be able to comply with copyright laws to make appropriate and ethical decisions. They must be able to comply with federal, state, and local regulations concerning the use or performance of music. In another area of professional responsibility, teachers must know strategies for maintaining effective communication with other music educators, the value of continuing professional development in music education, and the types of professional development opportunities that are available to music educators. Knowing strategies for and maintaining communication with students, parents/caretakers, and others in the schools and community about the music program and its benefits are also a part of being an EC-4 teacher (previously discussed in Standard VII).*

Copyright Laws and Music

All teachers are tempted at times to take care of their needs for copies of sheet music or recordings easily and quickly. However, copyright laws help composers, musical artists, recording studios, and music publishers make their living. Without royalties, no money is received from their work. Some music is not copyrighted, but if a work is, the teacher must follow guidelines stated in laws. Most modern works are copyrighted, *even if not* specifically marked.

The following guidelines may help you understand copying music. Teachers are allowed to copy a single copy of a book chapter, article, short story, essay or poem, chart, graph, diagram, cartoon, or picture, but making multiple copies is a bit more complicated. Teachers can make multiple copies on a one-time basis but not more than one copy per student, and the copyright must be included. This must also meet a brevity test. Copying music, too, falls into this category. A music teacher can copy a part of a musical work (one per student) but not the whole work (no more than 10%). The teacher must also not take more than one short poem, article, story per author (or two excerpts) or take more than three items from a collected work. Copying should not be for more than one course per term, or there should be no more than nine instances of multiple copying per class term. When in doubt, buy multiple copies, or request permission, as the composer, publisher, or recording company can seek monetary damages. If you have just made the decision to use an item based on its value to the lesson and could not expect to get permission quickly, then you may follow the guidelines above. You may also make "emergency" copies to replace purchased copies that are not available for an impending performance. A music teacher may make some alterations to music and copy them, but not so much that the fundamental nature of the music or lyrics is changed. When using copyrighted music, teachers may record student musical performances and retain them for evaluation and rehearsal purposes *only*. One sound copy *only* of a copyrighted piece of music may be made and retained for rehearsal, exercise, or examination purposes, if already owned by the teacher or the school. A music teacher may not make copies that would, in essence, create his or her "own music series or book" or replace collective works. The copyright must always appear on the copy. Students or teachers may not include copyrighted songs or music on a Web site without permission. When adding any music to technology-based projects, permission must be obtained, if copyrighted. These serve as only very brief guidelines, and, as we know from the legal battles in which Napster (a company who allowed music to be downloaded from the Internet) engaged, legal issues change. Most of those involved in music are very glad for teachers to use materials, but they must be given the chance to agree. Several Web sites such as www.law.cornell.edu/cgi-bin/empower (then search for music) and http://library.austin.cc.tx.us/gen-info/copymusic.html or www.music.indiana.edu/music_resources/copy.html give more complete details of copyright laws and information on how to obtain permission to copy. When in doubt, be sure to check the details.

In addition to these laws, there may be other local policies and regulations that might affect performances in music. If you plan on children performing in another area outside of school, you need to check carefully to make sure you have followed local guidelines. Communicating with parents and your school district about what music will be performed and in what context is also an important part of musical performance, as parents and the district have the right to exclude their children from certain types of musical performance. If you are planning a large performance, it is better to know sooner rather than later that a number of children may not show up at the performance or that your selections must be changed at the last moment.

SUMMARY

With the information offered here, you should have a good grasp of what you might need to pass most TExES questions about teaching music. Learning musical terms will get you started in teaching music, should you not have a specialized music teacher in your building. Even if you have never played an instrument (or have had others request of you, *"Please* don't sing!"), you should be encouraged to bring music to the classroom. Children honestly do not care about the quality of your voice (although they will also need to hear good models during your time with them), but they *will* learn to be embarrassed by their voices if you show embarrassment over yours. However, children react positively to an enthusiastic singer, even if the voice is less than professional, and they will join in at a moment's notice. In the push for good test scores many schools without music teachers may encourage teachers to drop everything but "the basics." As a creative teacher, however, you should be encouraged to use music in every way to support and enhance basic subjects rather than treat them as separate areas—for the many reasons stated in this chapter. Music is a lifelong joy for most human beings and can be more appreciated and enjoyed if there is some sort of background for understanding.

There is *much* more to be learned about music and many more musical terms. This introduction, however, can help you through the basics. It is difficult to only *talk* or *read* about these terms and genres. Listen when your radio is on at home or in the car for the musical terms and types of music that you have read about here and try to seek out as many examples as you can. If you are the only music teacher your children have, we hope this chapter will encourage you to teach music in the best ways possible—for your children! Enjoy musical times with your children—it will make your day much richer, too!

A MUSIC LESSON PLAN

Cattle Trails in Texas

Grade Level: Fourth

Main Subject Area: Music

Integrated Subjects: Social Studies, Reading, Math, Art

Time Constraints: 3 hours (Music, Social Studies, and Reading)

Overall Goal(s): To familiarize students with an era of Texas history and representative music of this era to appreciate the past and present work in an important area of the Texas economy.

TEKS/TAKS OBJECTIVES:

§ 117.15. **Music** (b)(4.5) Historical/cultural heritage (A) identify aurally-presented excerpts of music representing diverse genres, styles, periods, and cultures; (C) perform music representative of American and Texas heritage; (D) identify connections between music and other fine arts; (2)(A) sing or play a classroom instrument independently or in groups (B) sing songs from diverse cultures and styles or play such songs on a musical instrument; (4) create simple accompaniments; (1)(A) categorize a variety of musical sounds, including children's and adults' voices; woodwind, brass, string, percussion, keyboard, and electronic instruments; and instruments of various cultures;

§ 111.16. **Math** (a) (2) make estimates . . . ;

§ 117.14. **Fine Arts** (2)(B) design original artworks; (4)(B) interpret ideas and mood in original artworks;

§ 110.6. **Reading/LA** (8)(C) read for varied purposes such as to be informed, to be entertained . . . ; (b)(9)(A) develop vocabulary . . . ; (15)(D) write to entertain such as to compose humorous poems . . . :

§ 113.6. **Social Studies** (b)(4)(B) explain the growth and development of the cattle . . . industries.

Other objectives may also be met.

Objectives: After observing a map of the major cattle trails in the 1800s, students will pick one trail and estimate the length of time it took for the drive from Texas; students will write their estimates on a card that the teacher will pick up later.

Students will complete a "quick draw" as they listen to "On the Trail" (*Grand Canyon Suite*) and participate in a discussion on its mood. Students will only have 5 minutes after the music has finished to complete their drawing.

Students will share their quick draw with a partner and evaluate the mood captured with the music.

After viewing Western art, students will identify connections of music to art.

Students will listen to, read, and sing three songs from the trail drive days.

Students will view (and listen to) a PowerPoint presentation of instruments (guitar, banjo, fiddle, and harmonica) that come from this era and will discuss orally the tone, color, and texture of these instruments.

Students will read a short selection from the perspective of a young person during this era.

Students will select and use rhythm instruments as they sing the songs again and orally make judgments of created sound.

Students will complete a four-line verse to the melody of a traditional song (one of the three from above) with a minimum of two pairs of rhymes.

Students will listen to a current country music selection and compare and contrast traditional trail music with the modern selection (using a Venn diagram).

Sponge Activity: Students view trail maps of major Texas cattle trails, pick one, and estimate how long it would have taken from start to finish. Students will write their estimates on "pick up cards."

Environmental Concerns: Teach during Rodeo Week (if relevant to a school). Integrate three periods back to back. Could also add more mathematics with measurements for cooking "trail menus."

Rationale(s): The cattle industry in Texas set up an important economy and had a considerable effect on music in Texas and the West that continues today. Many of the songs that came from this era are considered American "classics" that many Texans (and other Americans) know and sing. Western music continues as a considerable industry today but has its roots in this era.

Focus or Set Induction: Give students the actual mileage of the trail drives and the average miles per hour and have them refigure their estimates. Teacher will pick up cards and acknowledge the children who came closest. Students listen to "On the Trail" from the *Grand Canyon Suite* and quick draw what they hear/see in their minds. Go back and discuss the instruments used, the mood of the music, how it was achieved. Students will show their drawings to a partner and discuss how well the artist captured the mood of the music. While the teacher repeats the music, show students some "cowboy art" (posters such as "Lifetime in the Saddle," "Horse Roundup," "Place in the Sun" [and others by Jack Sorenson], and pictures of sculptures by Remington, and/or other oils and photographs) and briefly discuss the style and mood of these works of art. Tell students about the Cowboy Artists of America Museum in Kerrville, Texas.

MAKING CONNECTIONS:

1. **Connections with Past or Future Learning:** What famous movies or television shows have you seen about cattle drives? Have you been to a rodeo? What kinds of music do you hear associated with these? Do people still do this kind of work with cattle? Is the cattle industry still a major economy of Texas? Why do you think singing was a part of trail drives?

2. **Connections to the Community:** Does your community have a rodeo? Have you ever seen (or seen on the news) one of the trail rides from many parts of Texas that end in Houston to kick off the rodeo? (There are excellent pictures of this at http://www .photohouston.com/texas-cowboy-pictures/ cowboy-photography-stock-photos.html.) Have you listened to any modern country music? Is there a country radio station in this area? Do you think that there are many current songs about driving cattle? Why or why not?

3. **Cultural Connections:** The first Texas cowboys were *vaqueros*. *Vaqueros* (or "cow men") came from Mexico to Texas to work on ranches owned by Spaniards and Mexicans before the Texas Revolution. Much of the dress we associate with cowboys originates from these *vaqueros*.

4. **Connection to Student Interest and Experiences:** Many dude ranches still exist (some in Texas) where you can go on trail rides or

cattle drives. Many Texas communities have rodeos. Many schools have a rodeo day or week. Many Texans enjoy modern-day country music. Have you participated in any of these? Have you seen the award ceremonies on television for country music artists? What did you like about any of these experiences?

Materials: Trail drives map, cards for estimation; *Grand Canyon Suite;* Western art posters, photos, sculpture, and/or other art; art paper; real instruments or pictures of them (guitar, banjo, harmonica) and sounds of each instrument; sheet music of three traditional songs (and CD, if needed); list of new vocabulary words; PowerPoint presentation of instruments; reading sheets; rhythm instruments; current popular country song on a young person's experience of a trail drive.

Activities: Guided Practice: Students will listen to and sing three songs from sheet music from the cattle drive era of Texas history ("The Old Chisholm Trail", "Bury Me Not on the Lone Prairie," and "Get Along Little Doggies"). The teacher will introduce vocabulary that is not familiar, and all will discuss the message of each song. Students will return to the map from the sponge activity and trace the "Old Chisholm Trail." The teacher will discuss the guitar, fiddle, harmonica, and banjo with students and explore why these may have become popular instruments in Western music. The teacher will show a PowerPoint presentation of these instruments (with each instrument playing alone). Discuss the tone color of each and their texture together. In paired reading, students will read a short description of a young person on a cattle drive. Students will discuss, select, and use rhythm instruments that they feel will enhance the songs and use those in singing the songs once again. Students will orally judge if the instruments helped to enhance the song or not and explain why or why not. Ask students to think and tell which instruments, in general, seem to best represent Western music, how certain instrument sounds cause us to think of the West, and which of the three songs they liked best and why.

Independent Practice: Students will compose a four-line verse (that could have been from the era and that can be sung to the melody of one of the songs learned). The teacher should review rhymes and have students pick out some rhymes in the songs. Be sure to have students write on their papers which song the verse matches. Invite students to share their verses.

Assessment: Individuals will participate in singing and playing rhythm instruments (checklist), participate in discussions (checklist), play an instrument (checklist), and complete a four-line verse that matches the rhythm of one of the three traditional songs from above with at least two sets of rhymes.

What Will Students Do Who Finish Early? Students will expand their "quick draw" artwork into an art composition, search on the Internet for trail drive vacations, or create their own new trails for a cattle drive from their town or city to a market.

Closure: Students will listen to a current country song and they, as a whole class, will use a Venn diagram to quickly make comparisons. Ask children if they like current country songs, and which country songs they might know. Ask if the themes are the same or different from the "old style" cowboy music. The teacher may want to bind children's verses for the classroom library and to sing with the melodies later on.

Modifications for Students with Special Needs: Tomás has hearing difficulties and will be placed closer to the music sources.

Reflection: To be completed after teaching the lesson.

DRAFT YOUR OWN MUSIC LESSON PLAN

Title of Lesson: _____

Grade Level: _____

Main Subject Area: _____

Integrated Subjects: _____

Time Frame/Constraints: _____

Overall Goal(s): _____

TEKS/TAKS Objectives: _____

_____

_____

Objective(s): _____

_____

_____

Sponge Activity: _____

_____

_____

Environmental Concerns: _____

_____

_____

Rationale(s): _____

_____

_____

Focus or Set Induction: _____

_____

Making Connections:

1. Connections to Past or Future Learning: _____

_____

2. Connections to the Community: _____

_____

3. Cultural Connections: _____

_____

4. Connections to Student Interests & Experiences: _____

_____

Materials: _____

_____

Activities: Guided practice: _____

_____

_____

_____

_____

_____

_____

Independent practice: _____

_____

_____

_____

_____

_____

_____

Assessment: _____

_____

_____

_____

_____

What Will Students Do Who Finish Early?

_____

_____

Closure: _____

_____

Modification for Students with Special Needs: _____

_____

Reflection: _____

_____

OBSERVING MUSIC EXPERIENCES/ACTIVITIES

During your visit to an EC-4 classroom, use the following form to provide feedback as well as to reflectively analyze the room, the materials, and the teacher.

Name: _____ Grade Level Observed: _____ Date(s): _____

Title or Short Description of Lesson or Activity: _____

	Observed	Not Observed	Response
1. All children are encouraged to participate in musical experiences.			If so, describe. If not, what children were left out and how could they be encouraged?
2. Ample space allows children and adults to move around freely and safely during a musical experience (if applicable).			If not, what could be changed?
3. A center is designated for *listening* to music.			If so, describe. If not, describe one that could appropriately and easily be included?
4. A center is designated for other musical experiences (creating instruments, exploring sounds, etc.).			If so, describe. If not, describe in detail at least one center that could be easily included.
5. If there is no designated Music Center, music activities are integrated within other centers.			If so, describe. If not, describe exactly how music could be included in other centers.
6. If there is music-related equipment freely available to children, the equipment is developmentally user friendly.			If so, describe. If not, what could be added?
7. The regular classroom contains technology related to music (e.g., electronic keyboard, software for music on computer).			If so, describe. If not, what could be easily included?
8. The regular classroom contains rhythm instruments (rhythm sticks, hand drums, tambourines, triangles, etc.).			If so, describe. If not, what could be added?
9. Children use rhythm instruments and/or wind instruments during the day.			If so, describe. If not, when could the teacher easily add this element?
10. If children use rhythm instruments or wind instruments, the teacher discusses elements of proper use (care of the instruments, safety, sanitation). Are expectations for use posted?			If so, describe. If not, what could be added?
11. The teacher encourages *creativity* with music in some way.			If so, describe. If not, how could the teacher encourage creativity?

OBSERVING MUSIC EXPERIENCES/ACTIVITIES

	Observed	Not Observed	Response
12. If music is available for free listening, there is a variety of music/sounds available for free choices.			If so, describe. If not, what could be added?
13. Music is integrated during whole group time in a developmentally appropriate way.			If so, describe. If not, how could this be accomplished?
14. Music is integrated during circle time in a developmentally appropriate way.			If so, describe. If not, give ideas for how it could be done.
15. Music is integrated during independent and/or teacher-led small group time in a developmentally appropriate way.			If so, describe. If not, give ideas for how this could be accomplished.
16. Music is used as a memory model for children.			If so, describe. If not, give some ideas on how this could be incorporated.
17. Children are comfortable singing and singing with motions without prompting.			If so, describe. If not, how could the teacher better encourage this?
18. Children are comfortable dancing or participating in gross-motor movement with music.			If so, describe. If not, how could the teacher better encourage this?
19. Movements for dance or other musical participation are modeled by the teacher.			If so, describe. If not, what changes could be added?
20. Movements for dance or other musical participation movements are physically developmentally appropriate.			Explain why or why not, if applicable.
21. Listening to music is used for a reward at times in a management plan.			If so, is it appropriately done? If not, how might it be added?
22. The teacher offers a *variety* of musical experiences during the day.			If so, describe. If not, what could be added?
23. There is a set of publisher-prepared music books for each classroom or for each grade level in this school.			If available, describe. If not, describe any written music materials the teacher uses.
24. There is a set of publisher-prepared tapes/CDs or other listening materials for each classroom or for each grade level.			If available, describe. If not, describe any listening materials that could be added.

	Observed	Not Observed	Response
25. The teacher uses standard musical terminology to describe and analyze musical sounds (makes references to musical symbols, terms, rhythms, meter, mood, texture, etc.).			If so, describe. If not, describe when and what language/terms could be used.
26. The teacher engages children in learning to *read music* in some way.			If so, describe. If not, could he/she do so? Why or why not?
27. The teacher teaches children a new song.			If so, is it taught effectively? If not, how could she/he be more effective?
28. If music is integrated with other subject areas, the connection is a logical one.			If so, describe. If not, how could this be more logically connected?
29. Children are assessed on their skills or knowledge of the musical element of the lesson or experience in an appropriate way.			If so, describe. If not, what type of assessment could be appropriate?
30. The music/songs are age appropriate.			Why or why not? Describe.
31. The teacher includes hand actions with appropriate songs.			If so, what is the result? If not, what could be included?
32. The teacher discusses new vocabulary or articulation of words in a new song.			If so, describe. If not, what descriptions or vocabulary could be included?
33. The teacher discusses issues of quality of singing (appropriate volume for young voices, proper projection, breathing through a phrase, proper position, etc.).			If so, describe. If not, what are some appropriate additions?

TEST YOURSELF ON MUSIC

1. The symbols underneath the musical staff above tell the musician to:
   A. play or sing this piece of music loudly.
   B. play or sing this piece of music softly.
   C. gradually increase the volume of the instrument(s) or voice(s), then decrease the volume.
   D. gradually decrease the volume of the instrument(s) or voice(s), then increase the volume.

2. Ms. Thomas was using the school's set of fourth-grade music books with CDs to teach her class a song. Halfway through the song, the music was marked *a cappella*. This means that:
   A. the song should become a duet.
   B. all sound should become *andante*.
   C. voices should stop singing and only the instruments should be heard.
   D. the instruments should stop playing and only the voices should be heard.

3. Ms. Miller's third-grade class was reading a story about two children in the 1800s who were taken on a cattle drive from Texas to the market in Kansas City. Ms. Miller realized that this was a perfect time to teach children some of the more well-known songs from this era, so she began to search for them. She was able to find three ("The Old Chisholm Trail," "Oh, Bury Me Not on the Lone Prairie," and "Get Along Little Doggies"), but only in one book in the local library. She found the lyrics on some Web sites, but she wanted the written music so students could see the melody lines. The songs in the book that she found also had chords marked where she could play along with her guitar or autoharp. Which of the statements below would be correct?
   A. She could legally make a copy for each child in her class this year.
   B. She could not legally copy these pages for her students.
   C. She could legally copy one song for her class.
   D. She could legally make a copy for all of the third-graders for this year, because all the third-grade teachers share lessons.

4. If a musician wanted to indicate that no music should be played or sung for a moment, which symbol would be used:

5. Ms. Phan often plays particular instrumental music as focus and/or closure activities in her social studies class when she talks about various cultures. For example, when her lesson is about Japan, she plays a CD with the sound of the *samisen*, and when she talks about Australia, she pulls up some *didgeridoo* music from the Internet. She always asks children to discuss how the sound of that country's instrument has its own characteristics. This element of music is called:
   A. harmony.
   B. timbre.
   C. mood.
   D. texture.

6. The state song in Texas is:
   A. "Texas, Our Texas."
   B. "The Eyes of Texas Are Upon You."
   C. "Deep in the Heart of Texas."
   D. "The Yellow Rose of Texas."

7. A type of true American dance that developed from formal European quadrilles is:
   A. tap dance.
   B. square dance.
   C. fandango.
   D. hula.

8. What type of music depends on *improvisation*, *syncopation*, and *call and response*?
   A. Swing
   B. Classical rock
   C. Gospel
   D. Jazz

9. Stereotypical Native American music is often played with a drum and is written as follows:

   The symbol underneath the first beat of every measure is called a(n):
   A. repeat sign
   B. crescendo
   C. accent mark
   D. staccato mark

10. Mrs. Ganesh asked her children to identify the melody from "Rudolph the Red-Nosed Reindeer." It is:
    A. ABCA
    B. AABA
    C. ABCD
    D. ABBA

TEST YOURSELF ANSWERS AND RATIONALES FOR MUSIC

Answer 1: The musical symbols underneath this staff have to do with *dynamics* (how loud or soft music is to be played). These symbols reflect a *crescendo* (<) followed by a *decrescendo* (>). These notations indicate that the musician should first begin to *increase* the volume, and then *decrease* the volume; therefore, Choice C best describes the notation. If the composer had wanted to play or sing the whole line *loudly* (A), he/she would have written an **f** for *forte* at the beginning. If he or she wanted the line to be played or sung softly (B), the composer would have written a **p** for *piano* (soft). Had he or she wanted to decrease the volume then increase the volume (D), the notation would have been ><. The answer is C.

Answer 2: A *duet* (A) is a song for two voices or two instruments only, just as a *trio* is for three, a *quartet* is for four, and so forth. *Andante* (B) is a musical notation, indicating *tempo* (or speed) and meaning that the music should be played not so fast or about "walking speed" (versus *largo*, which is *very* slow; *adagio*, which is slow; *allegro*, which is quick; or *presto*, which is *very* fast). *A cappella* refers to voices only. The answer is D.

Answer 3: Copyright law is important in sheet music and in copying recordings. There are several issues at stake when copying written music. The law allows a teacher to copy up to no more than three items from a single work, so she is safe in this respect; therefore, Choices B and C are not true and can be eliminated. She can copy, but she is only allowed to copy *for one class*, so we must eliminate D. Her situation meets the guidelines that say if a teacher decides that an item is very valuable to a lesson and it would be impossible to get permission before the lesson is to be taught, a teacher can copy for one time only. She can copy for this instance (A), but if she wants to use these songs next year, she would have to seek permission if there is a copyright. The answer is A.

Answer 4: Choice A is a symbol for the *treble clef*, which would mean that higher instruments and higher voices would read the music from this staff (versus the bass clef, which is for lower voices or instruments). Choice C are *eighth notes*, which means a voice or an instrument would play or sing very short sounds at that particular pitch. Choice D is a *time signature* that shows four beats per measure (from the 4 on the top) with a quarter note receiving one beat (from the 4 on the bottom). Choice B is a *half rest*. A rest means that no voice or instruments should play or sing. Because this is a whole rest, there should be no sound during the entire measure. The answer is B.

Answer 5: **Harmony** (A) refers to two or more different tones being played together. Although there *may* be harmony in the music she plays, she is asking for special distinguishing characteristics of each instrument. *Mood* (C) is made up of many elements of music (*tempo* [speed], *dynamics* [loudness], *meter* [beat], *key*, and choice of instruments) that affect the overall "feeling" generated by the composer to the listener. Although the selections that she plays may also have "a mood" (for example, bagpipes can have a very sad mood or a rousing military mood), she wants to narrow down the characteristic sound of each instrument. *Texture* (D) refers to how the sounds of different voices or instruments are "woven" together to create a piece of music. Again, in the question she is asking for children to talk about the very specific characteristic sound (or voice) of an instrument that is not shared with any other instrument. This is known as the *timbre* of an instrument. The answer is B.

Answer 6: "Texas, Our Texas" is the state song (A). The words can be found in the social studies chapter of this book. Choices B, C, and D are all popular Texas songs, but they are not the official state song. The answer is A.

Answer 7: Although tap dance (A) is considered a true style of American dance, it developed as a part of minstral shows. Fandangos (C) and shindigs were dancing *events* in the early settlers' days of Texas—rather than a type of dance. Hula is the original dance of the native Hawaiian people, but it is based upon Polynesian (not European) roots. Choice B, square dancing, is considered a true American style of dance that originated from European formal figure dances, such as the quadrille and the minuet. Early on, reminders about which figure came next were often "called out" in America, leading to the role of a "caller" in square dancing. Gradually, the music changed, and the dance depended more on following the caller versus memorizing the exact order of the figures, leading to what we know now as the American square dance. The answer is *B*.

Answer 8: Swing (*A*) is associated with the "Big Band" sound during and right after World War II, and is normally played as written. Early rock (or rock-and-roll) follows an exact written form rather than improvisation, although in later psychedelic rock and acid rock, improvisation was used. Gospel (*C*) was a forerunner of jazz and sometimes used call and response, but the *best* answer is jazz (*D*). The heart of jazz is improvisation (or creating music on the spot), call and response (where one instrument or voice will answer or echo another), and syncopation (an "unexpected" accent). The answer is *D*.

Answer 9: A repeat sign (*A*) tells the musician to go back and repeat a section of the music again and is written as ":ǁ". A crescendo (*B*) may look similar to the symbols shown, but a crescendo would stretch under several notes in a measure, indicating a gradually increasing volume. A staccato mark (*D*) is written as a period underneath a note, showing that that particular note would be played *very* short. Choice *C*, an accent mark, is correct. This means that the note under which the accent mark is written should be heavily emphasized (played or sung harder). The answer is *C*.

Answer 10: Form refers to the repetition, contrast, and variation of a piece of music. The following shows the repetition of the melody two times, a contrasting section, and a repetition of the original melody for a form of AABA.

A
    Rudolph, the Red-nosed Reindeer,
    Had a very shiny nose,
    And if you ever saw it,
    You would even say it glows.

A
    All of the other reindeer,
    Used to laugh and call him names,
    They never let poor Rudolph
    Join in any reindeer games.

B
    Then one foggy Christmas Eve,
    Santa came to say,
    "Rudolph, with your nose so bright,
    Won't you guide my sleigh tonight?"

A
    Then how the reindeer loved him,
    And they shouted out with glee,
    "Rudolph, the Red-nosed Reindeer,
    You'll go down in history."

8 Preparing to Teach Health and Physical Education in Texas

Mel E. Finkenberg
Stephen F. Austin State University

Janice L. Nath
University of Houston—Downtown

John M. Ramsey
University of Houston

Domain V of the Generalist EC-4 Test Framework addresses "Fine Arts, Health, and Physical Education." This chapter focuses upon two of these areas: health and physical education. As is the case with art and music, many schools have a specialist for young children who may coach and may teach health while many other schools must rely on the self-contained teacher (especially for health). Therefore, Texas requires all EC-4 teachers to be tested on these standards. Because many colleges and universities do not require course work in these areas, this portion of the test has been an obstacle for many test takers. However, as a result of the passage of Texas Senate Bill 19 in 2001, it is hoped that needed attention has been placed on these two areas for teachers of young children. Senate Bill 19, authored by Senator Jane Nelson, requires school districts to provide daily physical activity as part of their physical education curriculum for children in grade 6 and below. Such activity must involve physical exertion of an intensity and for a duration sufficient to provide positive health benefits to students.

Studies consistently conclude that U.S. children are at risk due to the lack of health and fitness education opportunities provided in schools. The "fattening" of America can be directly linked to the diminished emphasis on physical education, particularly in the elementary schools where values can be established early. The document entitled *Healthy People 2000: National Health Promotion and Disease Objectives* was released as a governmental strategy to improve the health of *all* Americans, although a majority of the 300 target goals are specifically directed toward improving the health status of U.S. children and youth. New objectives (*Healthy People 2010*) include increasing the quality and years of healthy life.

The release of the Surgeon General's report of physical activity and health (U.S. Dept. of Health and Human Services, 1996) documented many health benefits achieved through moderate and regular activity. The report showed that people of all ages benefit from regular physical activity. Never before, however, has a body of research been compiled to show such a strong need for activity and fitness in the lives of our youth, and research since this time strongly supports this premise. Activity programs are an absolute requisite for healthy youngsters. Yet helping children to become more active adults is not the only area educators view as important. Educators also believe that emotional development, safety, violence prevention, and other health-related issues can make a difference in a healthy life for children.

Consistent with the design of the previous chapters, this chapter is structured with an overview of the various standards and competencies within the health and physical education components of Domain V. These have, in turn, been correlated to the Texas Essential Knowledge and Skills (TEKS) for health and physical education. Additionally, sample items with discussion, a lesson plan (and form for writing your own plan), and an observation form are offered.

Standards are broad statements that present the main idea of the knowledge and skills expected of a beginning educator. Each standard contains a list of specific knowledge and skill statements (the competencies) that further explain the focus and requirements of each standard. The standards and their knowledge and skills statements are fundamentally based on the TEKS, the statewide curriculum for Texas public schools. In the discussion of the standards and competencies outlined below, correlations between standards, the competencies, the TEKS, and the content of the Generalist examination will become apparent.

Many of the attitudes and values of lifelong mental and physical health for children are related to Bloom's (1956) affective domain. The **affective domain** influences lifelong learning and consists of the following levels:

1. **Receiving or attending.** The learner must first be ready, able, and motivated to receive and attend to information (i.e., listen, be aware of, observe, recognize, realize, be tolerant of).
2. **Responding.** The learner has to become engaged with the information in some manner (i.e., respond, cooperate, appreciate, comply, discuss).
3. **Valuing.** The learner selects the information and expresses a value about it (i.e., appraise, assess, evaluate, critique).
4. **Organization.** The learner places the value of the information in an order of importance (i.e., demonstrate, perform, uphold, engage in).
5. **Characterization.** The learner chooses to take the information and makes it part of his or her life or a part of his or her character (Bloom et al., 1956, in Cruickshank, Jenkins, & Metcalf, 2002).

A teacher must be certain that he or she plans health and physical education lessons with consideration of this domain in mind. For example, if a teacher wanted children to appreciate eating in healthy ways, children must first *receive* or *attend* to a rationale for the concept (self-esteem is connected to weight, mobility, health deterioration, dental decay, and so forth) and receive information on how this can be accomplished. Teachers might have children respond to the information, for example, through a tasting fair of healthy snacks, by designing a survey that shows which healthy foods are best liked, and by working comparison problems of the calories and food value of healthy snacks with nonhealthy snacks so that children become engaged with the concept. Learners may next be asked by a visiting nutritionist to "prepare a healthy meal or snack tray" by gluing cutout pictures of healthy foods from a variety of food items onto a paper plate and explain why they selected each. Just as a teacher is requested to extend the knowledge and comprehension levels of thinking to higher levels in the cognitive domain, the teacher should go beyond just having children *attend* in this domain. Children should have opportunities to role-play, choose, discuss, and be actively involved and thoroughly engaged with these concepts. It is only after children *receive/attend* and *respond* that learners begin to value a concept. EC-4 teachers should always remember that children learn these types of health lessons and gain positive attitudes *throughout* the year. If only a few days are spent on a unit in any health area (nutrition, safety, stress, or so forth), the information and ideas will seem disjointed and unimportant. Teachable moments that reinforce health issues occur daily. A teacher should take full advantage of those moments (in addition to integrating health lessons with other subject areas) to bring the health issues discussed in this chapter to the forefront. Children revisit important topics in a spiraling curriculum throughout the early childhood and elementary years, establishing positive ways of growing into healthy lifestyles.

 # Standards I and II Health

Competency 026: The health teacher applies knowledge of both the relationship between health and behavior and the factors influencing health and health behavior. The health teacher plans and implements effective school health instruction and integrates health instruction with other content areas.

A beginning teacher understands health-related behaviors, ways in which personal health decisions and behaviors affect body systems and health, and selects strategies for reducing health risks and enhancing wellness throughout the life span. The teacher also demonstrates knowledge of major areas in health instruction, including body systems (e.g., structures and functions of various body systems), illness and disease (e.g., types of disease, transmission mechanisms, defense systems, disease prevention), nutrition (e.g., types of foods and nutrients, maintenance of a balanced diet), stress (e.g., effects of stress, stress-reduction techniques), and fitness (e.g., components of fitness, methods for improving fitness). Understanding and teaching about substance use and abuse (including types and characteristics of tobacco, alcohol, and other drugs and of herbal supplements) are also expected of the beginning teacher, as is understanding the influence of various environmental factors (e.g., media, technology, peer and other relationships, environmental hazards) on individual, family, and community health. He or she should also understand types of violence and abuse (including causes and effects of violence and abuse and prevention). The Texas teacher is expected to select and use instructional strategies, materials, and activities to teach principles and procedures related to safety, accident prevention, and response to emergencies. EC-4 teachers should apply critical-thinking, goal-setting, and decision-making skills in health-related contexts and understand the use of refusal skills and conflict resolution to avoid unsafe situations. They should select and use instructional strategies, materials, and activities to help children build healthy interpersonal relationships (e.g., communication skills), demonstrate consideration and respect for self, family, friends, and others (e.g., practicing self-control) and understand the roles of healthcare professionals, the benefits of health maintenace activities, and the skills for becoming healthwise consumers. The teacher also applies knowledge of health content and curriculum, including the Texas Essential Knowledge and Skills (TEKS), and plans and implements effective, developmentally appropriate health instruction, including relating the health-education curriculum to other content areas.

Choosing a Healthy Life

Consider the following question:

Ms. Vasquez teaches elementary health and physical education. Her programs include a variety of personal health and safety skills. She has planned a unit in nutrition, focusing on healthy snacks. Which of the following activities would be most appropriate for this course?

A. Have students read from short "canned" skits (written by professionals) to other students about healthy snacks.
B. Have students write paragraphs about what constitutes healthy snacks.
C. Hold a directed discussion in which children are led to discover the nutritional contents of a variety of their favorite snacks.
D. Divide the class into collaborative groups and have each group choose a different snack to present a nutritional report about what they have learned.

The correct answer is *D* because presenting findings through collaborative groups involves each learner in active discussion of what constitutes healthy snacks. This option allows students to be active participants in the determination of nutrition concepts. Although each of the remaining options may meet the instructor's objective, *D* is the superior choice due to the active participation and knowledge construction of the learners.

This practice question relates to the health education component of the TEKS, whereby learners acquire the health information and skills necessary to become healthy adults and learn about behavior in which they should and should not participate. To achieve that goal, learners need the following understanding: (a) learners should first seek guidance in the area of health from their parents; (b) personal behavior can increase or reduce health risks throughout the lifespan; (c) health is influenced by a variety of factors; (d) learners can recognize and utilize health information and products; and (e) personal/interpersonal skills are needed to promote individual, family, and community health.

Let's try another practice question:

Mr. Harris teaches elementary health and physical education. He wishes to teach health and safety skills that relate to the well-being of students, friends, and family. Which of the following instructional units would promote self-responsibility as it relates to family and friends?

A. Personal hygiene
B. Exercise and fitness
C. First aid
D. Nutritional needs

The key phrase in this assessment item is "health and safety skills that relate to the well-being of students, friends, and family." Although Choices *A, B,* and *D* relate to personal health and safety, they do not specifically correlate with others involved in the application of health and safety principles. The use of basic emergency aid procedures as identified in Choice *C* could directly affect the well-being of others, including friends and family. Further, these skills imply and develop decision-making and problem solving skills that foster healthy interactions and promote learners' interpersonal skills. The correct answer is *C*—first aid.

Although many learning experiences related to caring for personal health take place in the home, sometimes children do not learn good personal health and safety patterns from parents and families. Teachers can therefore ensure that children are taught, encouraged, and reinforced with activities that maintain a lifestyle of appropriate personal health and safety.

Some believe that basic health is too personal to include in an educational curriculum. However, health education may never reach some young students at the time it may be needed. Elementary and middle school children have many questions and concerns about such personal health matters as skin care, hair care, dental hygiene, and many other personal health matters. Apart from the formal learning and experiences that take place in a health instructional program, older elementary children often turn to less reliable sources of information such as popular magazines, product advertisements, radio and/or television, and peers. These sources may be biased or inaccurate.

Texas Senate Bill 19 also encourages districts to utilize the Coordinated Approach to Child Health program (CATCH), which is designed to prevent obesity, cardiovascular disease, and Type II diabetes in elementary children. CATCH offers a successful blend of physical education, classroom curriculum, nutrition awareness, student-directed activities, and physical education equipment designed to promote and maintain cardiovascular health in children grades K through 5. CATCH began as a research study founded by the National Heart, Lung, and Blood Institute. Its purpose was to establish the direct link between school health and physical education in developing healthier behavior among children in grades 3 through 5. Now expanded to cover grades K through 5, CATCH remains the largest and most rigorous school-based health promotion study to date. With more than 600 school programs, CATCH continues to impact students long after they complete the coursework. Published in the *Journal of the American Medical Association* (JAMA), results indicate that student intake of total fat and saturated fat was reduced while the intensity of physical activity performed both inside and outside school increased (Luepker, Perry, McKinlay, et al., 1996).

CATCH encourages kids to:

- move, run, jump, and dance as they participate in moderate to vigorous physical activities using a variety of equipment;
- develop good nutrition habits as they learn to recognize and monitor their fat and salt intake; and
- declare themselves "smoke-free!"

The four components of CATCH are the classroom curriculum, physical education, the school food service, and the family partnership. Teachers and staff are trained to implement and coordinate these components. These intervention strategies were shown to significantly increase the intensity and duration of physical activity and decrease the energy intake from fat and saturated fat in intervention school lunches.

School Health Facilities

Maintaining a healthy life also includes having regular medical and dental preventive care. Some children may have their first experience with healthcare in school. Children need to know enough about their bodies to tell the nurse, for example, exactly "where it hurts" and/or what symptoms may be present. A teacher should schedule a tour of the clinic facility or nurse's office early in the year, especially for younger children, as it could be a scary experience if the first visit is when the child is sent there ill. Teachers should ask the nurse to visit the class so young children know him or her better and understand the role the nurse plays in their healthcare. (Other healthcare workers can also be asked to visit.) Many teachers place appropriate real or play medical equipment in a "Doctor's Center" so that children can become familiar with these. In addition, teachers can provide stories that describe examination procedures, use puppets to role-play medical or dental procedures, or stage phone practice to call for help in an emergency. All young children can learn about emergencies and how to call for help at school or away from school. The school nurse also serves as a resource and teacher for many health issues.

As an aside, the EC-4 teacher is often the first to see underlying illness or health issues, as she or he is most often with children during many waking hours. The EC-4 teacher must be vigilant as an advocate for any health issues that are noticed, including abuse.

Nutrition

Consider the following practice question:

Mrs. Cleary, an elementary school teacher, is concerned about the eating habits of her students. Which of the following dietary guidelines should be stressed to elementary school students?

- **A.** Eat a variety of foods from the basic food groups that contain adequate starch and fiber.
- **B.** Eat primarily proteins and avoid carbohydrates.
- **C.** Eat what you like as long as you exercise and take vitamins.
- **D.** Eat only foods low in fat.

The correct choice is *A* (eat a variety of foods from the basic food groups that contain adequate starch and fiber). This response supports a balanced diet. It is important to promote positive nutritional habits at the elementary grades because it is difficult to change eating patterns once they have been established.

Poor nutritional status may result in several problems. Although *under-nutrition* can be a problem, in the United States the more common malnutrition problem is **overnutrition**, with about 17 percent of adolescents being overweight (Gill, 2007). Obese children are likely to be at risk of chronic disease later in life and are likely to suffer emotional stress as well. Healthy eating habits are best begun at an early age. In other words, the best way to maintain ideal weight and eat well throughout life is to learn how to eat and exercise early in life. Teachers should help parents teach their children proper eating habits and exercise. Of all the habits of living, the most important to good health is eating properly.

Teaching young children about food choices can begin with experimentation. The EC-4 teacher may offer a variety of healthy snacks, even using the opportunity to integrate social studies by a cultural or "theme" tasting ("Today, boys and girls, we are going to visit Hawaii. Let's look on the map to see where Hawaii is and why these wonderful fruits grow there . . ." as the teacher offers fresh pineapple chunks, mango, banana, passion fruit juice, and so forth). Cultural lessons can accompany these lessons with information on why, when, and with what (forks, knives, and spoons; chopsticks; fingers) foods are eaten in different cultures and why the food is a good choice. Because very young children cannot yet classify a number of ideas, it is suggested that children be asked to classify food into categories that are easier to sort (such as milk products, eggs, vegetables, breads, meat, fruit, and nuts). Later they can be introduced to the food pyramid with the number of recommended servings (bread, cereal, rice, and pasta at the bottom with the most servings allowed; fruit; vegetable; dairy products; meat, poultry, fish, dry beans; and, with minimum servings, fats, oils, and sweets). This pyramid plays a major role in helping students understand how they can choose a healthy meal by selecting different proportions from different parts of the pyramid.

Parents can be used as a resource to reinforce trying foods at home and promoting healthy eating. Teachers should also remember to send a list of foods home that will be offered in class for tasting due to the possibilities of food allergies or cultural or religious desires for children not to eat certain items. At school, children should never be forced to eat what is offered in class. However, presenting foods in enticing ways should encourage children to try them. Teachers who reward young children with praise may also encourage others. Rothlein (cited in Brewer, 2001) suggests that only small amounts should be offered and the color, texture, and shape should be discussed. The teacher should also be a role model, and he or she should keep trying, despite children's reluctance. If reluctance is encountered, the teacher should try to determine if another way of serving a food would be acceptable (for example, raw carrots versus cooked carrots). The teacher may want to plan activities that integrate food preparation with other content (for example, have young children count out 6 raisins to form "a smile" on their snack plates). When children are involved in the preparation of foods, they are often more eager to try something new.

Healthy Relationships

This standard is addressed in a variety of components of the TEKS. Learners are expected to know healthy ways to communicate consideration and respect for self, family, friends, and others. Learners are expected to demonstrate skills in respectful communicating; describe and practice techniques of self-control such as thinking before acting; and to express needs, wants, and emotions in appropriate ways. Emphasis is placed on teaching children the skills necessary for building and maintaining healthy relationships. Children are expected to learn to identify characteristics needed to be a responsible family member or friend, to list and demonstrate good listening skills, and to demonstrate critical-thinking, decision-making, goal-setting, and problem-solving skills for making health-promoting decisions. Elementary school children should also be equipped with conflict resolution skills.

Despite a teacher's best efforts, conflict is often present in the schools. Conflict resolution represents a range of important skills for children to learn. Students should be made to understand the sources of conflict and instructed on how to better manage it. Three primary main conflict management techniques include:

- Avoiding the conflict. This means walking away from a fight or not acting in a way that will provoke another person.
- Defusing the conflict. Adding humor to the situation or using delaying strategies can help defuse the conflict.
- Negotiation. This management technique means trying to find a way to compromise about the conflict.

Family members and teachers are especially important role models. Yet the media also offers many roles to children. Many American children spend more time watching television than they do working on schoolwork. Television has the potential to be a powerful educational medium. It is also apparent that violence on television can provide violent or aggressive models for children. Teachers should provide as many other positive role models as possible to counter this effect (good literature, resources in the community, and others).

The issues of peer pressure, popularity, and high-risk behaviors impact even young children as they watch how others dress, what they say, and how they act. Children need to know that rejection is an unfortunate but inevitable part of life. It can be disappointing but should not be devastating. Part of good mental health is resiliency. Children must acquire knowledge and the ability to set limits, communicate effectively, and employ refusal skills. These basic skills are necessary to help students deal with daily pressures. Remember that peer pressure is not always a negative influence. Pressure to behave in a health-enhancing fashion can go a long way in helping a child. It is also essential that children understand that parents and other family members are not always opposing forces. Peers do not *always* lead children astray. However, teaching children about what qualities make a good friend who would make a positive impact on their lives should also be a part of the EC-4 health curriculum.

 # Teaching About Illness and Disease

By understanding the difference between sickness and health in persons of all ages, learners will be able to explain ways in which germs are transmitted, methods of preventing the spread of germs, and the importance of immunization. In this way, they will be able to identify causes of disease other than germs (such as allergies and heart disease) and explain how the body provides protection from disease. They should then be able to apply practices to control the spread of germs in daily life such as hand washing and skin care, noting that the skin is our body's major protector from germs. Teachers should schedule the *time* for healthy routines (such as always washing hands before eating and after visits to the restroom). The teacher can also be a role model whenever he or she has an opportunity with Think-Alouds ("I have a bit of a cold today, boys and girls. I am not going to come close to you to try to keep you from getting it," or "Excuse me a moment . . . I am starting to cough, so I am just going to get a tissue."). Teachers themselves should be very cautious with germs. If a teacher must aid a child in blowing a nose, for example, he or she should always wash his or her hands immediately afterwards. Gloves should be available and worn for cleaning up any bodily fluids as per *universal precautions*. Tables where young children work should be cleaned often, as should toys and manipulatives.

Teaching children about the symptoms of common childhood afflictions can also be a good idea. Head lice, ringworm, pink eye, and other maladies may become less shared and less of a stigma if children understand how they occur and how they are cured (if handled in a matter-of-fact way). A teacher may also need to discuss HIV and AIDS. Depending on the age level, children may want to talk about it to help alleviate fears that people can contract AIDS from being around or touching someone with the disease. Certainly, children's fears need to be answered by teaching them that one cannot contract HIV/AIDS other than from infected blood, from intravenous needles often associated with drug use, from a mother with HIV to a baby in the womb or through nursing, and from unprotected sex. The EC-4 teacher must be appropriate in what she or he tells children with regard to age but should answer children's questions, for they see and hear much about disease and may understand very little.

Consider the following practice question:

Ms. Jackson has noticed that a number of her third-grade students have been coming to school with colds and flu-like symptoms. Which of the following strategies would be most useful for helping students understand self-responsibilities as they relate to friends and family?

A. Students will keep a log of their personal health attributes on a daily basis and discuss the logs each Friday.

B. Students will work in groups to discuss communicative and noncommunicative diseases and how they are transmitted.

C. Students will interview parents and friends in order to determine their health status.

D. Physicians and other healthcare practitioners will be invited to discuss with the students the health hazards they present when they come to school ill.

While maintaining health logs and discussing them with the class is a useful tool for assessing health status (*A*), it does not lend itself to assisting learners in developing self-responsibility. Choice *B* will give students the requisite information needed for preparing them to understand concepts and issues of health and self-responsibility; this is the correct choice. Choice *C* also does not provide the learner the opportunity to promote interpersonal well-being. Choice *D*, although having the potential for providing learners with a cognitive basis regarding health and safety issues, is not structured to provide the learner the opportunity to promote interpersonal well-being. The correct answer is *B*.

Substance Abuse

It is important to remember that individuals make choices about their health behavior. This requires teaching about decision making. Teachers must also enhance learner skills so that children can carry out healthy behaviors. For example, a fourth grader who is deliberating about trying tobacco or another harmful substance must be shown choices in order to make good decisions and provided with occasions to practice the skills to avoid drug abuse. Bandura's (cited in Eggen & Kauchak, 2001) social learning theory is conducive to building these skills. For example, Bandura would suggest that the fourth grader who is contemplating drug use must: (1) understand what methods must be done to avoid it, (2) believe that he or she will be able to use the methods, (3) believe that the method(s) will actually work, and (4) anticipate a benefit after achieving the behavior. Social learning theory posits that children can learn these concepts, in part from watching others and, with practice, can develop the necessary skills required for any particular behavior.

The key focus for teachers is to select learning strategies that have proven effective, provide background information, assist in decision-making skills, support personal and social skill-building, and allow opportunities for practice. One activity is unlikely to fulfill all of these qualifications, so careful planning is required to accomplish this task.

Healthy Communication

Students develop many different relationships throughout their elementary school years. For instance, relationships with family members, same-age friends, relatives, and teachers begin to change as children progress through school.

Although speech develops in most children in predictable developmental sequences, communication as a skill does not come naturally to all children. Effective communication includes a range of skills that must be learned. A person's ability to communicate can have a direct effect on self-esteem and the quality of relationships with others. Besides helping a child's self-esteem, good communication skills are important to help a child succeed in the classroom and beyond. Success in school depends on listening and speaking skills as much as on intellectual ability.

One important area in communications is the ability to recognize facial expressions and emotions. EC-4 teachers may use a number of activities to help emotional awareness (identifying emotions when given pictures of faces, creating collages to represent a particular emotion, drawing, storytelling, questioning, and presenting good literature models). A record of what emotions each child is able to easily identify should be maintained. Teachers should also record whether children can identify the possible causes of emotions. Lack of emotional intelligence (Goleman, 1995) has been linked to adult failure in many ways. To help this area teachers should provide opportunities for students to work together in pairs, small groups, and teams. Providing roles in co-operative education situations and focusing on a social skill of the day can help children become aware of verbal and nonverbal behavior (Kagan, 1992).

Consider the following practice question:

All of the following are characteristics of good communicators, *except*:

    A. People are sensitive to the needs of those with whom they communicate.
    B. People are assertive without being aggressive.
    C. People withhold their own opinions from the conversation.
    D. People use "I" statements.

Three of these choices are appropriate communication skills. However, children should be taught that their opinions make important contributions to communication (*C*). When children first enter school, they are very self-centered and more concerned about their own needs. They rarely identify with the needs and characteristics of others. As they continue in school, they begin to develop an increasing awareness of others. As they age, children begin to redirect their personal concerns to intellectual concerns and group activities. They begin to expend more energy on friendships and the community around them. In this process, they need greater communication skills. The correct choice is C.

Refusal Skills

Refusal skills are part of good decision making. Children need good refusal skills when it is necessary to say "No" to an action or remove themselves from a potentially harmful situation. Any situation that threatens personal safety or health, tempts children to break laws or norms, detracts from personal character, asks students to disobey parental rules, or results in loss of self-respect calls for strong refusal skills.

Catchy slogans and signing pacts have been criticized because they do not strengthen self-concept, social skills, and prosocial behaviors. Teachers should concentrate on these areas with particular attention to those children exhibiting difficulty in the areas mentioned above and offer opportunities for children to role-play various situations to practice these skills.

Try this practice question:

Mrs. Smith's health class is discussing a model for using communication skills. In practicing refusal skills Jake responds to pressure to use the drugs by stating, "No, thank you." Which of the following is the *best* assessment of this refusal strategy?

A. Saying "No, thank you" is inappropriate because there is no need to thank people for an invitation to misbehave.
B. It's a good response because you are being polite.
C. It doesn't match his nonverbal communication.
D. It's a good response because it's short.

Students should be taught that in order to develop good refusal skills, they should:

- Employ assertive behavior. This allows others to know that you are in control of your behavior and the situation.
- Use body language that matches your assertive verbal behavior. Body language indicates that you are sincere. Students should make it clear that they do not desire to engage in unsafe situations.
- Avoid potentially harmful/dangerous situations.
- Be a positive role model. Children should act and talk in a manner that commands respect.

You don't have to say "No, thank you." There is no need to be polite when placed in a situation that may be unsafe. Choice *B* is not correct because it is not an assertive response. We have no information on Jake's nonverbal behavior, so choice *C* is incorrect, and simply having a short answer does not make it the best response. The correct answer is *A*.

Teaching About Violence

Violence as the answer to conflict has become all too common. Nowhere is the magnitude of the concern about the growing rate of violence reflected more urgently than in Goal 7 of the *Goals 2000: Educate America Act* (1994). Students attending schools in which violence occurs will likely not focus on meeting rigorous standards, not perform at high academic levels, or complete schooling. Students and teachers concerned more about their personal safety than about education cannot concentrate on teaching and learning. Violence and abuse in schools is not unique to public schools or urban centers. No geographic region is excluded. The public's concern about discipline and violence in schools is well warranted.

It is the responsibility of educators to help prevent violence. Violence prevention means two things: reducing our children's risk of facing violence in the future and preventing the immediate threat of violence to our children now. As a teacher, you should recognize that there are behaviors and strategies that can help you safeguard yourself and the students in your classroom. Characteristics of teachers whose classrooms have been identified as relatively violence free include:

- developing positive relationships with students in the classroom and in the community;
- taking preventive action by creating classroom environments in which the teacher is clearly in control;
- knowing how to diffuse a confrontation; and
- insisting on backup support when necessary.

Various programs exist that endeavor to teach children how to manage anger and conflict. These programs typically share the following ideas:

- Conflict is a normal part of human interaction.
- When individual prejudices are explored, students can learn how to appreciate people whose backgrounds are different.
- Disputes need not have winners and losers.
- Children who learn how to assert themselves nonviolently can avoid becoming bullies or victims.
- Children's self-esteem is enhanced when they learn how to build nonviolent, nonhostile relationships with their peers.

A recent and unsettling phenomenon has recently been seen in children and young adults, particularly in urban areas; that is, they are avoiding reporting harmful behaviors of others, including the witnessing of serious criminal activity at times. Because of heightened security issues in and out of schools, it is imperative that children be taught the difference between just "tattling" and that of reporting important information. Many teachers handle tattlers as pariahs or ignore tattlers altogether, perhaps contributing to this behavior. Some children see allegiance to their culture and/or friends as more important than to society as a whole or to authority figures. Teachers must reinforce problem solving with others but also help children understand that sharing the types of information that could be harmful to others (or even themselves) is essential. Teaching these skills in role play, discussing the differences in tattling versus telling, and taking children's reports as serious when needed are all ways to increase children's confidence in coming forward when there is serious concern.

Incorporating the above principles in the health education curriculum is essential. Research has shown that comprehensive school health education is effective in influencing youth's behaviors and establishing a pattern of healthy behavior in the future.

 # Stress

Let's try a practice question:

Joey, a fourth grader, is having trouble coping with stressful situations in school and at home. This unresolved stress has caused him to become angry with his friends for little reason. What would be the *best* thing the teacher could do to help him?

- **A.** Have him begin an exercise program immediately.
- **B.** Discover his sleeping habits and see if he needs more sleep.
- **C.** Analyze his diet and make recommendations for a diet that will help reduce stress.
- **D.** Seek help from the counselor in the school.

Let's examine the alternative responses. Although it is true that exercise can reduce stress levels (*A*), it is apparent that there are a number of factors contributing to the child's demeanor. Exercise, while a valuable tool, will not necessary provide the results anticipated. Thus, response *A* is not correct. Although sleeping habits can impact behavior, there is nothing to indicate that the child's stress is a manifestation of lack of sleep. Answer *B* does not provide a comprehensive solution or one that the teacher could control. The same can be said for answer *C*. Typically, stress and the hostile behavior exhibited by students are a manifestation of several factors. The answer is *D*—seek help from a counselor. Although a teacher can try other stress-reducing strategies, the role of the counselor in schools is to provide professional help for individual students, advice for teachers and guidance for parents, and perhaps, explore testing or provide mini-lessons about various emotion-based topics. The correct answer is *D*.

Consider another question:

Members of a fourth-grade physical education class were running relay races. One boy exclaimed, "I was so afraid that I would drop the baton that I started sweating a lot, and my stomach felt funny. I was afraid that I'd let the team down." This statement best reflects the knowledge of what principles and practices needed by teachers?

- **A.** Teachers need to be aware that a learner's motivation is best gauged by stress symptoms and measures the learner's level of motivation.
- **B.** Teachers need to recognize signs of stress demonstrated by learners, and they should use opportunities like this to teach coping skills that can be used by students.
- **C.** Physical education instruction should include skills that are stressful during the early learning phases of motor activity.
- **D.** Physical education instruction should include stressful situations to match those encountered in the learner's nonschool environments.

One of the unique advantages of physical education is that it provides the opportunity to view students in a variety of stressful situations. Teaching students that stress is a natural outcome of being placed in the competitive situation described is an excellent introduction to teaching students how to cope with stress. As a result, Choice *B* is correct. Motivation and stress are not necessarily related to successful achievement of motor skill development, so *A* is incorrect. Providing stress during the early stages of skill development, as in Choice *C*, will result in frustration on the part of students. Teaching motor skills should result in a balance between mild stress and success. Item *D* is not correct, since the goal is to use these situations to teach students coping skills, not to purposefully create stressful environments. The correct answer is *B*.

It is possible to teach children skills in *coping* (the ability to deal with problems successfully) and *decision making* (a process in which a person selects from two or more possible choices) through instruction in physical activity. Specific strategies for teaching children coping skills include:

- admit that the problem exists and face it.
- define the problem and decide who owns it. (Is the problem theirs, or does it belong to others?)
- list alternative solutions to the problem.
- predict consequences for oneself and others.
- identify and consult sources of help.
- experiment with a solution and evaluate the results.

Young children can formulate these into the following steps:

RED LIGHT: Stop! Calm down . . . and think before you act.

YELLOW LIGHT: Say the problem and how you feel. Set a positive goal. Think of lots of solutions. Think ahead of the consequences.

GREEN LIGHT: Go ahead and try the best plan (Goleman, 1995).

When making decisions, students should definitely consider each of the following steps:

1. Gather information.
2. Consider the available choices.
3. Analyze the consequences of choices.
4. Make a decision and implement it.
5. Evaluate the decision and begin at step one with a new plan if the decision did not yield positive results.

The use of "challenge" activities such as climbing walls, rope courses, and other physically demanding activities have recently gained impetus because of their value in teaching both coping and decision-making skills. Teachers must remember that young children are still egocentric in development, and children in poverty may not have the ability to navigate through decisions involving long-term goals. Teachers should help young children begin making decisions that deal with short-term goals first. Children who are never allowed or offered choices in a classroom never have the opportunity to practice making decisions.

 # Technology and Health

The technology revolution has had a dramatic impact on our ability to teach youngsters concepts related to health and fitness. An example is the use of heart rate monitors that permit children to gain a greater understanding of the cardiorespiratory system and the establishment of cardiorespiratory fitness. Another example is the use of video cameras to allow a child's performance to be filmed for immediate self-assessment. Audiovisual aids add another dimension to teaching concepts and are excellent for reinforcing learning. The Internet allows children access to a great deal of health-related fitness information and to set up interdisciplinary studies across distances to gather health-related data, share active games, and so forth. The Internet also provides teachers with the opportunity to communicate with others and to share their ideas and questions.

Technology also brings numerous products to consumers' attention. Teaching children about being a smart consumer of health products helps them understand that they must read labels, gather more information at times, and be constantly alert for false advertising. For example, having learners create their own "cure all" or "miracle weight loss" products along with a label and advertisements (which can be filmed) helps children understand this phenomenon.

Safety

The need for safety and efforts to provide it have been part of people's lives since the beginning of human existence. Although the hazards have changed over time, the fundamental problem is the same. Ever since humans sought shelter and developed weapons to protect themselves, the anticipation of danger and the ability to overcome it have been major keys to safety and survival. Instruction in safety and injury prevention is an important component of an elementary school curriculum. The leading cause of death among children ages 1 to 14 is unintentional injuries. Each year over 3,000 children between the ages of 5 and 14 die from unintentional injuries (e.g., garage doors, swimming pools, transportation incidents, accidental poisoning, etc.). Over half of these fatalities result from motor vehicle accidents (in which many children were not wearing seatbelts). For this reason, safety instruction cannot be ignored.

Attitude formation begins early in a child's life and has a major impact on safety behavioral patterns. Although innumerable factors influence attitude formation, the actions of parents and respected adults, including teachers, is a major force, particularly among children in the primary grades.

For health education to be effective in the elementary school, it is important that the school program be coordinated with health-promotion activities throughout the schools and community. Messages delivered in a consistent fashion and from several sources (teachers, parents, school staff, community leaders, and peers) are more effective in changing behaviors.

The elementary school teacher's responsibility is to instill in pupils those attitudes that encourage them to act to protect their own safety, that of their families, and that of society. Safety education is not only training in conservation of life and the prevention of accidents but also instruction in how to be a good citizen. Other responsibilities of the teacher are to guide learners in molding sound values, to direct their thinking and decision making, and to help them regulate their behavior. According to the TEKS in health education, teachers should direct children's understanding of the health information necessary to become healthy adults and to learn about behaviors in which they should and should not participate. To achieve that goal, students should understand the following: (a) students should first seek guidance in the area of safety from their parents; (b) their own behaviors throughout their lifetimes can increase or reduce safety risks; (c) a variety of factors affects and influences safety; (d) students can recognize and use safety information and products; and (e) personal/interpersonal skills are needed to promote individual, family, and community safety.

What safety issues are important for a teacher to include in his or her class? Fire, traffic, sun, water, gun, poison (including another person's medications), and human predator safety are all issues of which children should be aware. Several of these can scare and worry children, so a teacher must be careful to balance information in a way that is completely age appropriate. Drills (fire, violence or lock-downs, and bad weather) should be practiced until they become matter-of-fact. Instead of lining up in the routine way during the year, teachers can occasionally say, "Today, when we line up to go the library, we are going to do our fire drill line-up, so listen for my 'three bells'," or "When we come in from recess today, I want you to practice the lock-down routine," or "When we line up outside our classroom, let me see everybody practice the bad weather position." Outside resources such as fire departments and police departments can provide instruction in many of these areas. If outside resources are not available, EC-teachers must still provide instruction. "Stop, drop, and roll," exiting an area before calling 911, designating a gathering spot, and, of course, not playing with fire should be a part of all children's knowledge for school and home. Traffic safety instruction can include areas on the playground and in centers where children pretend to be vehicles or "drive" small toy vehicles according to traffic rules. In Texas, young children need to learn about outdoor safety due to the direct sun and what measures to take to prevent skin cancer. Texas teachers should also be cognizant of sunburn and heat stroke when children are engaged in outdoor activities. Children should also be taught about strangers through role-play, games, or puppet play. Many videos and police departments deal well with "good touching" versus "bad touching." Guidelines should be communicated to children and parents to help latchkey children be more safe (such as Internet and phone rules of never giving out one's name, parent's name, or address) (Brewer, 2001). Teachers and parents should be careful about labeling children's clothing and materials on the outside to prevent a predator from easily identifying a name and calling out to a child.

Consider the following practice question:

An elementary teacher, Mrs. Santos, wishes to promote an understanding of community safety among her children. As the lesson is introduced, several children tell her that some children display unsafe behaviors while riding their bicycles to and from school. For example, they do not wear protective gear and weave in and out of traffic. Mrs. Santos would like her students to understand their roles and responsibilities in helping to ensure community safety while children are riding their bicycles.

Which of the following activities would be most appropriate for this purpose?

A. Making a list of inappropriate behaviors and the safety problems these behaviors cause.
B. Writing a letter to school and city officials as well as the local police informing them of the bicycle safety problem and asking for assistance in eliminating the problem.
C. Suggesting to the well-behaved students that they avoid streets in which students practicing unsafe bicycle riding behavior is displayed.
D. Starting a telephone campaign to report the unsafe bicycle riders to the appropriate officials.

Let's examine the alternatives. Choice *A* is not the correct answer, since it does not address the standard targeted in this question; that is, it does not address promoting an understanding of community safety among the students. Choice *B* is the correct choice. By writing a letter to important community members, the learners are demonstrating an understanding of the concepts and issues of community health and safety and applying this understanding to the well-being of people collectively. By selecting this choice, the elementary teacher demonstrates that she understands community health and safety issues and fosters learner understanding of the related responsibilities. Choices *C* and *D* are not correct, since these result in a failure to apply the concepts related to community health. Read the question very carefully to be sure you note nuances such as community versus personal safety. The correct answer is *B*.

Try another practice item:

During a discussion about community health in Ms. Arevalo's third-grade class, several children said that they often see others playing in an abandoned building known as a hangout for drug users. Ms. Arevalo would like her students to have an understanding of their own roles and responsibilities in helping to ensure community safety. Which of the following activities, suggested by the students in response to the situation, would be most appropriate for this purpose?

A. Suggesting to the students that they find a new place to play.
B. Making a list of the negative outcomes that could happen as a result of playing in an abandoned building.
C. Having students picket the abandoned facility in order to bring attention to it.
D. Making public officials aware of the dangers and possible hazards resulting from the abandoned building and asking them for their assistance.

Suggesting to children that they find a new place to play (*A*) helps to promote issues of health and safety but does not promote the well-being of people collectively. The same is true for Choices *B* and *C*. The correct choice, therefore, is *D*. By making public officials aware of the potential dangers and hazards, learners are better able to understand their roles in community safety. This promotes the idea of a responsible community; that is, if a situation is harmful and we do nothing and someone is hurt, we, too, are responsible to some degree. The answer is *D*.

The common thread interwoven throughout lifestyles and habits is that good health is often a choice, not chance. Children make daily choices about their health and, in doing so, establish early patterns of behavior. The learner who doesn't wear a seatbelt is at greater risk of injury. The learner who elects not to wear protective equipment while riding a bicycle also increases risk. The learner who refuses to wear eyeglasses exacerbates his or her vision problem. The injured child incurs medical costs for his or her parent(s) or may even become dependent upon the state healthcare system. Choice of lifestyle impacts those around us.

In contrast, learners who learn to brush and floss their teeth early are less likely to develop dental problems. Children who eat healthy snacks and remain within defined weight limits are less likely to suffer the many health problems associated with obesity. This reduces healthcare costs for all and places the family in a preventive mode rather than a treatment mode. Children must understand that in these and many other ways they are responsible for their health status. It is essential that they also know this responsibility is easily carried out if they make healthful decisions—decisions that are often simply a matter of applying common sense and information that they learn.

Standards I–VI Physical Education

Competency 027: The physical education teacher understands principles and benefits of a healthy, active lifestyle and motivates students to participate in activities that promote this lifestyle. He or she demonstrates competency in a variety of movement skills and helps students develop these skills. The teacher uses knowledge of individual and group motivation and behavior to create and manage a safe, productive learning environment and promotes students' self-management, self-motivation, and social skills through participation in physical activities. The EC-4 physical education teacher uses knowledge of how students learn and develop to provide opportunities that support students' physical, cognitive, social, and emotional development and provides equitable and appropriate instruction for all students in a diverse society. Using effective, developmentally appropriate instructional strategies and communication techniques to prepare physically educated individuals is also a requirement.

> *The beginning teacher applies key principles and concepts in physical education (e.g., cardiovascular endurance, muscular endurance, flexibility, weight control, conditioning, safety, stress management, nutrition) and their significance for physical activity, health, and fitness. The teacher must also apply knowledge of physical education content and curriculum, including the Texas Essential Knowledge and Skills (TEKS), and of children in early childhood through grade 4 to plan and implement effective, developmentally appropriate physical education activities. The EC-4 teacher also knows and helps children understand the benefits of an active lifestyle, and he or she modifies instruction based on individual differences in growth and development. The Texas teacher applies knowledge of movement principles and concepts to develop children's motor skills and selects and uses developmentally appropriate learning experiences that enhance children's locomotor, nonlocomotor, body-control, manipulative, and rhythmic skills. The teacher is able to select and use instructional strategies to promote children's knowledge and application of rules, procedures, etiquette, and fair play in developmentally appropriate games and activities. The teacher designs, manages, and adapts physical education activities to promote positive interactions and active engagement by children. Finally, the teacher evaluates movement patterns to help children improve performance of motor skills and to integrate and refine motor and rhythmic skills.*

These standards are related to the component of the physical educational TEKS that states that learners acquire the knowledge and skills for movement that provide the foundation for enjoyment, continued social development through physical activity, and access to a physically active lifestyle. The goal is for the learner to exhibit a physically active lifestyle and understand the relationship between physical activity and health throughout his or her life. In elementary school, children learn fundamental movement skills and begin to understand how the muscles, bones, heart, and lungs function in relation to physical activity. Identifying personal fitness goals and beginning to understand how exercise affects different parts of the body are an important part of the instructional process.

Children should learn how to identify components of health-related fitness, including identifying sources of health fitness information about appropriate clothing (including safety devises and equipment) and safety precautions in exercise settings.

Try this practice question:

The fourth graders at Moses Elementary School are learning about the risk indicators related to a healthy lifestyle. Which of the following factors would these students learn about that contribute *least* to an unhealthy lifestyle?

A. High blood pressure
B. Watching television and playing video games
C. Diets high in unsaturated fats, lack of exercise
D. Smoking

Watching too much television and playing videogames (*B*) concerns health educators, but this item does not mention a specific amount of time spent at these activities. Careful scrutiny of this question should make Choice *B* the apparent choice. Each factor cited in Choices *A, C,* and *D is* a risk indicator that contributes to an unhealthy lifestyle. The correct answer is *B.*

Recently, many elementary school physical education programs have incorporated more health-related aspects of human wellness into their curricula. The excessive number of overweight or undernourished children has created a need for programs that help children assess their eating habits and plan effective weight-control programs. Problems related to stress management and alcohol and drug consumption have prompted the physical education profession to redefine and emphasize new aspects of physical fitness. This new direction and emphasis toward a positive state of well-being has created a need for programs that help children understand how their bodies work, how they can monitor body changes, and how they can design personal fitness programs for improving and maintaining optimal levels of health.

Health-related physical fitness includes aspects of physiological function that offer protection from diseases resulting from a sedentary lifestyle. Such fitness can be improved and/or maintained through regular and moderate physical activity. Specific components of health-related fitness include cardiovascular fitness, body composition, strength and endurance, and flexibility. Currently, experts (Pangrazi, Corbin, & Welk, cited in Brewer, 2001) recommend that children be physically active at least 60 minutes everyday. If particular grade levels do not schedule recess every day or employ a specialized physical education teacher for classes, the classroom teacher must fulfill this responsibility through directed and nondirected play, a regular exercise program, and movement activities in the classroom during the course of the day.

Cardiovascular fitness offers many health benefits and is often seen as the most important element of fitness. It includes the ability of the heart, the blood vessels, and the respiratory system to deliver oxygen efficiently over an extended period of time. In order to develop cardiovascular fitness, activities must be **aerobic** in nature (i.e., activities that are continuous and rhythmic in nature, requiring that a continuous supply of oxygen be delivered to the muscle cells). Activities that stimulate development in this area are jogging, biking, rope jumping, aerobics, and swimming.

Body composition is an integral part of health-related fitness. It is the proportion of body fat to lean body mass. Attaining physical fitness is made more difficult when an individual's body composition is high in body fat.

Another component of health-related fitness is **flexibility,** the range and ease of motion of a joint. The amount of flexibility depends upon the structure and nature of the joints involved, the nature of the ligaments surrounding the joint, and the extensibility of the muscles connected to the joint. Through stretching activities, the length of the muscles, tendons, and ligaments can be increased. Flexibility is important to fitness; a lack of flexibility can create health problems for individuals. For example, people who are flexible usually have good posture and may have less lower-back pain. Many physical activities demand a range of motion to generate maximum force such as serving a tennis ball and kicking a soccer ball.

Muscular strength and endurance are the other components of health-related fitness. **Muscular strength** is the amount of force that a muscle or group of muscles can exert. When muscular strength is desired as a training outcome, it is necessary to move near-maximum workloads with minimal repetitions. **Muscular endurance** is the ability of the muscles to continue to function over a long period of time. To develop muscular endurance, a low-resistance, high-repetition workload is suggested. For most, a balance of the two workloads is probably the most useful. Climbing or pulling exercises and jumping rope are particularly effective for children's strength.

It is important to distinguish between health-related fitness and skill-related fitness. The focus of **health-related fitness** is to help youngsters understand how much activity is required for good health. Emphasis is placed on the process of *activity* and *participation* rather than on the product of high-level performance. **Skill-related fitness** on the other hand, helps *improve performance in motor tasks* related to sports and athletics. The ability to perform well is influenced to a significant degree by predetermined genetic characteristics. If skill-related fitness is taught in elementary school, it should be accompanied with an explanation about why some children and adults perform well with a minimum of effort whereas others, no matter how much they practice, never excel in certain areas. This may be due to height, body type, length of specific bones, or other factors but should not keep a person from enjoying a particular activity.

Once children are personally convinced that exercise is important for their own well-being, there is a good chance that physical activity will become a permanent part of their daily lives. It also appears that once a child's lifestyle moves in this direction, he or she will begin to modify his or her diet and other health factors to complement this positive and healthy way of living.

Consider the following practice question:

Mr. Pollack has his students find their heart rates after walking around the gymnasium for 3 minutes. They rest for a few minutes. Children are then to jog for 3 minutes and take their heart rates at the completion of the jog, followed by having them jump rope for 3 minutes and finally by having them sprint for 3 minutes. After each activity, students take their heart rates again. What is the most likely reason for doing this lesson?

A. To identify what types of activities place greater demands on the heart.
B. To complete a variety of cardiovascular activities in one session.
C. To maintain aerobic capacity for 12 minutes.
D. To identify how to measure heart rate effectively during a workout.

It is important for learners to understand that different activities place different demands on the heart. Having learners see the importance of the effect of different types of activities on the cardiorespiratory system is a valuable tool for understanding the concepts underlying the components of health-related fitness (*A*). There is little to be gained by completing a variety of cardiovascular activities in a single session (*B*). Although an activity may be conducted for a significant length of time (*C*), it is the intensity of the activity that determines whether it is aerobic in nature. The walking phase of this activity does not constitute time spent in the *aerobic phase,* which is defined as when the cardiorespiratory system is able to meet the demands of the body's muscles and tissues with an adequate supply of oxygen. Learning how to take one's heart rate (*D*) is an important skill, but not the most likely reason for this lesson. The answer is *A*.

Physical activity positively impacts the growth and development of children. Research supports the value of an active lifestyle for optimum growth and development. As clearly documented in the Surgeon General's report on physical activity and health (U.S. Dept. of Health and Human Service, 1996), there is an identifiable correlation between the incidence of health disorders and a sedentary lifestyle. Lifetime participation in physical activity often depends on early participation and gratification gained from such participation. Developing motor skills at an early age provides the tools needed to be physically active throughout life. A teacher's job is to integrate exciting activities in which children are physically active and in which they want to participate.

Despite the national interest in physical activity, the focus has not trickled down to elementary school children since only 8 percent of nationally surveyed elementary schools provide for *daily* physical education (National Center for Chronic Disease Prevention and Health Promotion, 2000). Only about one-third of our children participate daily in school physical education programs nationwide. The need for activity as an integral part of children's lifestyles and their education is strong. Participation in physical activity is more important than the concern to train children to pass fitness tests. Programs that focus on activity give all youngsters the opportunity for success and long-term health. Physical education programs must be designed to teach children how to live an active and healthy lifestyle. Teachers should advocate for children in support of such schoolwide programs.

Consider the following practice question:

During a fitness unit, students were required to keep a daily journal of activity and food consumed. These journal entries could benefit participants by which of the following?

A. Teaching students the importance of daily exercise for all people.
B. Teaching students how to monitor weight gain/loss by diet.
C. Teaching students the importance of diet and exercise as a lifetime commitment to better health.
D. Teaching students that diet is not a primary consideration in maintaining fitness.

It is critical that students are made aware at an early age of the benefits of a lifelong commitment to the combination of physical activity and nutrition (*C*). As we age, the need for regular physical activity and a focus on proper nutrition becomes more evident and more critical. Choice *A* is not correct, since daily activity is desired, but not viable in many cases. Participation in moderate physical activity three to five times weekly will provide many health-related benefits. Monitoring weight gain and loss, as in Choice *B*, is not meaningful unless children are taught the significance of weight gain and loss. Muscle weighs approximately 2.5 times the amount that fat weighs. As a result, weight gain does not always indicate a problem. If the ratio of percent fat to lean body mass (muscle) decreases, we are more fit. This is an important concept for children to understand. Choice *D* is incorrect. Diet is an essential component of fitness. The answer is *C.*

 # Movement

The TEKS guidelines in movement relate to skill development and developmentally appropriate activities. In the early years of elementary school, the emphasis is on applying movement concepts and principles to the learning and development of motor skills. Learners are first taught to demonstrate competency in fundamental movement patterns and proficiency in a few specialized movement forms. As children mature, they are expected to demonstrate appropriate use of levels in dynamic movement situations such as jumping high for a rebound and bending knees and lowering the center of gravity when guarding an opponent. Smooth combinations of fundamental motor skills such as running and dodging and hop-step-jump as well as attention to form, power, accuracy, and follow-through in performing movement skills are emphasized. Controlled balance on a variety of objects such as balance boards, stilts, scooters, and skates are objectives of this standard, as are simple stunts that exhibit agility such as jumping challenges with proper landings.

Teaching physical skills is related to the psychomotor domain. The **psychomotor domain** consist of the following levels:

1. **Perception.** Sensory cues are used to focus on how to perform a skill (i.e., the learner pays attention to, notices, recognizes, senses, perceives, or detects).
2. **Set.** Think of "ready, set, go!" *Set* means that a learner becomes prepared (not only physically but mentally and emotionally) to do a skill (i.e., the learner is ready, prepared, takes steps, and desires).
3. **Guided response.** This is the phase where a learner tries a skill as the instructor observes and coaches (i.e., the learner tries, performs, practices).
4. **Mechanism.** The learner practices enough to become proficient (i.e., the learner improves, increases skills).
5. **Complex or overt response.** The learner can now use the skill very proficiently (i.e., the learner masters, excels, perfects).
6. **Adaptation.** Now, the learner can perform new skills from the one learned by modification (i.e., the learner adapts, adjusts, accommodates).
7. **Origination.** The learner can create new skills that are based on the original skill, yet are completely original (the learner produces, originates) (Bloom et al., 1956, cited in Cruickshank, Jenkins, & Metcalf, 2002).

Try this practice question:

Lyn Addis teaches elementary physical education. Her program includes the skills of games, sports, and sequential gymnastics. Which of the following represents the appropriate sequence for kicking?

A. Kick the stationary ball, kick a rolling ball while running, kick a rolling ball from a stationary position.
B. Kick a rolling ball while using a running approach, kick a rolling ball, kick a stationary ball, kick action without the ball.

C. Kicking leg action without a ball, kicking a stationary ball, kicking a rolling ball, kicking a rolling ball while using a running approach.

D. Kick a rolling ball, kick a rolling ball while running, punting.

Kicking a stationary ball, kicking a rolling ball, and kicking a rolling ball while using a running approach (A) are techniques used to develop the skill of kicking in a sequential manner. Choices B and D involve initiating the development of the skill using an advanced approach. This can lead to frustration on the part of the learner. The correct choice is C. Using a kicking leg option without a ball allows for the establishment of the correct mechanics.

Fundamental skills are those utilitarian skills that children use to enhance the quality of life. This group of skills is sometimes labeled basic or functional. Fundamental skills are basic attributes that help children function in the environment. Related to this experience is the opportunity to learn basic concepts about stability, force, leverage, and other factors related to efficient movement. Understanding genetic diversity among people, such as muscle type, cardiorespiratory endurance, and motor coordination is requisite for helping students evaluate their physical capabilities. These *basic* or *fundamental skills* are divided into three categories—locomotor, nonlocomotor, and management skills.

Locomotor skills are used to move the body from one place to another or to project the body upward, as in jumping and hopping. Walking, running, galloping, skipping, and sliding are other examples of locomotor skills.

Nonlocomotor skills are performed in place, without appreciable spatial movement. These skills are not as well defined as locomotor skills. Included in this category are bending and stretching, pushing and pulling, raising and lowering and twisting and turning.

Body management skills are an important component of movement competency. Efficient movement demands integration of a number of physical traits, including agility, balance, flexibility, and coordination. A basic understanding of movement concepts and mechanical principles used in skill performance is necessary for quality movement.

Manipulative skills (developed when a child handles an object), **rhythmic movement skills** (involve motion that possesses regularity and a predictable pattern), **gymnastics skills** (which help develop body management skills without the need for equipment or apparatus), **game skills** (which contribute to the child's total development by allowing children to experience success and accomplishment), and **sport skills** (learned in the context of application through an approach of skills, drills, and lead-up activities) are examples of **specialized motor skills**. In developing specialized skills, progression is attained through planned instruction and drills.

The *development of motor skills* follows an orderly sequence. During the stage known as early childhood (age 2 to approximately the end of the sixth year), a child develops the fundamental locomotor and nonlocomotor skills of running, jumping, leaping, hopping, skipping, sliding, dodging, stopping, swinging, twisting, bending, turning, and stretching. A child also begins to develop the basic manipulative skills of throwing, catching, and striking. Many of these fundamental motor skills are learned prior to kindergarten and, in most instances, through a process of exploration. During this time, teachers should help children tune up awareness of how various parts of the body move separately and together to create coordinated patterns. For example, Mrs. Adams does this through teaching her class "The Duck Song," in which children "flap their wings," put their toes in a make-believe pond to test the water, and "fluff their tail feathers." During the first two years of elementary school, the continuing development of these fundamental skills should be through a program that emphasizes exploration of movement rather than refinement of skills. This is primarily important when a child is learning the basic manipulative skills of throwing, catching, and striking. The latter skills can be effectively learned through informal and creative games programs.

As children move into middle childhood, they begin to refine fundamental motor skills and to develop more complex combinations of locomotor, nonlocomotor, and manipulative skill patterns. Increased physical size and strength, coupled with improved perceptual and cognitive development, contribute to a child's ability to perform more coordinated movement patterns with greater speed and accuracy.

During the late childhood stage, the more specific movement skills required of games, dance, and gymnastics begin to show some refinement. In game activities, the ability to move objects (e.g., balls) through a variety of complex game situations develops. Similarly, dance and gymnastics skills become more fluid and creative as the performer acquires greater skill and understanding of the finer aspects of an individual movement or sequence of movements. **Rhythm** is the ability to repeat an action or movement with regularity to a particular rhythmic pattern. It is an essential ingredient of all movement, whether throwing a ball, dodging a player, or dancing a waltz. Rhythmic activities play an essential role in individual development.

Consider the following practice question:

During a lesson for fourth graders on the fundamental movement skill of kicking, Mr. Iglesias organizes his students into groups of three for an activity. The groups are to determine the optimum place on the ball to impart force for kicking the ball into the air and which part of the foot to use. The groups are to experiment with different ideas and develop a solution to be compared with other group's solutions. At the end of the lesson, the solutions will be written down, read, and discussed. This activity is appropriate for developing learners' motor skills because it primarily focuses on:

A. refining the mechanics of the skill of kicking.
B. improving the accuracy of the skill.
C. retention through mental practice.
D. variable practice.

Choice *A* is the correct answer. This is a valuable method for teaching fundamental movement skills. Too often children are provided repeated opportunities for perfecting skills with little or no emphasis placed on the understanding of correct mechanics. By emphasizing understanding of correct mechanics, learners will be more likely to retain their skills and to be able to transfer their knowledge and ability to related activities.

Let's try another practice question:

Mrs. Huong has taught her class fundamental manipulative movement skills. Which of the following skills would be included in this instruction?

A. Throwing, kicking
B. Turning, twisting
C. Dancing
D. Jumping, sliding

While turning and twisting (*B*) and jumping and sliding (*D*) are fundamental skills, they are not classified as being fundamental *manipulative* movement skills. Neither is dancing (*C*).

The fundamental manipulative skills of throwing, catching, and striking are the foundation of all major individual and team sport activities. These skills involve controlling objects (such as a ball) with the hands or feet. The correct answer is *A*.

Growth and Development

Although the sequence of motor skill development is predictable, the *rate* at which these sequences appear may be quite variable. Each child is unique in that he or she has an individual timetable for developing. This phenomenon relates to a child's "readiness" to learn new skills, which refers to conditions that make a particular task appropriate to master. Heredity, gender, nutrition, family size, the home environment, and culture all modify the basic developmental sequence. In physical education, we need to develop a foundation of psychological and perceptual-motor readiness, while at the same time allowing the child to take full advantage of his or her present maturational level.

Three development patterns typify the growth of primary-grade children:

1. Generally, development proceeds from the head to the foot (**cephalo-caudal**). Coordination and management of body parts occur in the upper body before they are observed in the lower extremities. This is the reason most students can learn to throw before they learn to kick.
2. Development occurs from inside to outside (**proximodistal**). Children can control their arms before they can control their hands.
3. Development proceeds from general to specific. Children become competent in **gross motor skills** (large body movement) before they develop refined motor patterns (**fine motor skills**).

Without sound knowledge of the developmental aspects of motor behavior, one can only guess at the educational techniques and intervention procedures to use in skill development. The process of motor development should constantly remind us of the individuality of the learner. Each individual has his or own unique timetable for the acquisition and development of movement abilities. The EC-4 teacher should maintain his or her own records and provide activities that deal with changes in children's development (recording height and weight). Teachers should ensure that these activities do not somehow suggest that "taller is better," etc., but that children understand that their bodies grow and change at different rates.

Girls are often separated for their talk on menstruation in the fourth grade. This onset can be a development which can be very difficult psychologically if it should come early. As girls mature earlier and earlier, even primary teachers need to be ready for this event and the difficulties that can accompany it as a health issue. Teachers should answer questions forthrightly, though with consideration to age-appropriateness.

Consider the following practice question:

The students in Mrs. Matthews' third-grade class have shown important variations in terms of their overall physical development and their current skill levels. Which principle should Mrs. Matthews follow in developing a physical education program to meet the students' needs in this class?

A. Plan units with activities that focus on relatively simple and basic objectives that all learners will be able to achieve.

B. Intersperse units requiring only relatively low skill levels with those that require sub-
stantially higher skill levels.

C. Plan units with activities that give all children opportunities to improve their current
skill levels.

D. Minimize the total number of units planned in order to give all children ample time to
develop and refine their skills.

Children should be provided opportunities to enhance existing skills (*C*). Skilled students
who are not given the opportunity to continue skill development can become bored and
frustrated. The resultant behavior is often a lack of interest in activity or development of behavioral problems. This would be a likely result of Choice *A*. Choice *B* may cause frustration
in both the skilled participants who do not need exposure to basic activities, as well as the
unskilled participants who will not achieve the higher-level skills. Physical Education standards recommend that children be exposed to a variety of activities, with the goal of developing proficiency in many and competence in some. As a result, answer *D* is not in compliance with this standard. The correct answer is *C*.

Assessment and Evaluation

There are many kinds of assessment (both formal and informal) and evaluation,
but all should be done to improve instruction and increase learning and skills.
Ways to assess student learning and skills include the use of checklists, logs,
tests, and scoring rubrics. Informal assessments is often done on the spot when
a teacher observes and corrects or reinforces a student's performance.

Scoring rubrics are rating scales that list multiple criteria related to a task or
motor skill performance. The criteria are performance levels students are expected to achieve. To employ this method of assessment requires accurate
knowledge of different stages of acquiring skills so that a child's pattern of development can be observed and categorized.

Observation checklists are another means of gathering meaningful information about children. In this technique, criteria governing proper technique for
the movement pattern are listed, and the child's performance is checked against
these points. A teacher may want to keep a list of playground behaviors, recording such behaviors as (a) whether the child plays alone or in a group and for
how long and how often, (b) the physical level of play [active: vigorous, rough
and tumble, games with rules, etc.; or passive: talking, walking, sitting, waiting,
etc.], (c) play with the same or opposite gender, (d) location of the play, and (e)
if the play was adult directed or assisted (Daniels, Beaumont, & Doolin, 2002).

Skill checklists incorporate skills listed across the top of a roster in which class
progress is recorded. The value of using this assessment tool is that it allows the
instructor to be alerted to youngsters who are in need of special help. Checklists
are usually most effective when skills are listed in the sequence in which they
should be learned.

Standardized tests are useful in evaluating measurable outcomes. These types
of tests have been administered to large samples of youngsters, and the results
are useful for comparative purposes. These tests often require specialized equipment. The test results, or at least an interpreted summary, can be included in a
child's health record and can be part of a periodic progress report to parents.

It is important to remember just how this information will be interpreted
and used. Enough information must be collected to make a good judgment or
recommendation, and the information on development must be communi-

cated to parents and/or school health officials with proper concern for the child. If a teacher suspects that a child may have some physical developmental problems, it is wise to first consult with the school nurse and to collect information that would warrant further testing or medical attention, should it be needed.

Consider the following practice question:

How the curriculum is sequenced is important to the learner's sense of success. Which of the following statements best represents a developmentally appropriate sequence?

A. Relays should be introduced to develop skills.

B. Restriction of activities is best, so as to become competent in the one area before going on.

C. Lead-up games should be introduced to develop locomotor, nonlocomotor, and manipulative skills and to motivate children.

D. Cooperative behavior and skill development should be established before competitive situations are introduced.

Introducing competition (*A*) before skills are developed leads to frustration and often limits skill development. Although competition is a healthy strategy it should only be introduced *after* cooperative behavior has been established. Choice *A* can be eliminated, since introducing relays is not an effective skill development tool. Choice *B* is incorrect because the curriculum should be expansive rather than restrictive to allow children to explore *many* types of movement. Choice C could be appropriate for development of skills, but this queston asks about learners *sense of success*.

Positive Interactions and Personal Exploration in Physical Education

The TEKS in Physical Education state that students acquire the knowledge and skills for movement that provide the foundation for enjoyment, continued social development through physical activity, and access to a physically active lifestyle. In elementary school, children learn fundamental movement skills and begin to understand how the muscles, bones, heart, and lungs function in relation to physical activity. Learners begin to develop a vocabulary for movement and apply concepts dealing with space and body awareness. Learners are engaged in activities that develop basic levels of strength, endurance, and flexibility. In addition, children learn to work safely in groups, interdependently, and in individual movement settings. Team activities should reinforce working together to help all members achieve a goal and identify strengths that each member brings to a team. The best strategy for having children understand and obey rules is having them help establish desired guidelines. When children help make the rules, just as in classroom management, they feel more ownership and thus feel more compelled to comply. Occasionally, the teacher may ask children to play a standard well-known game with rules suspended (other than safety) to help them understand the rationale for following rules and maintaining fair play. As they progress through the elementary grades, learners can demonstrate mature form in fundamental locomotor and manipulative skills and can often maintain that form while participating in dynamic game situations.

Students should be taught key performance cues for basic movement patterns (such as throwing and catching) in the primary grades. They should learn game strategies, rules, and etiquette procedures for simple games and apply safety practices associated with physical activities. As learners mature, they combine locomotor and manipulative skills in dynamic situations with body control. The goal is for learners to demonstrate competence such as improved accuracy in manipulative skills in dynamic situations. Basic skills such as jumping rope, moving to a beat, and catching and throwing should be mastered and applied in gamelike situations.

? *Consider the following practice question:*

Angelina Elementary School sets goals at the beginning of each school year. Competent motor skill acquisition is one of these goals. Which of the following activities is *most* likely to be chosen to meet this goal for the early elementary grades?

   A. Team sports skills
   B. Locomotor skills and games
   C. Individual sports skills
   D. Aquatics program

The correct choice is *B*. Team sport skills (*A*) should be used to apply motor skills after competency has been developed. Practitioners often introduce team sport skills early in the instructional process. The result of this practice typically is the reinforcement of poor habits or frustration on the part of the student who has not yet mastered the skill. While individual sports skills (*C*) do provide an opportunity to teach competent motor skills, similar to team sport skills, they should be introduced *after* competent motor skills have been developed. Aquatics programs (*D*) provide the opportunity to develop components of health-related fitness but are not efficient means of developing competent motor skills. The answer is *B*.

All people want to be skilled and competent in the area of motor performance. The elementary school years are an excellent time to teach motor skills because children have the time and predisposition to learn. The types and range of skills presented in physical education should be as unlimited as possible. Because children vary in genetic endowment and interest, they should have the opportunity to learn about their personal abilities in a variety of skill types. The school years should be the years of opportunity to explore and experience many different types of physical activity. Thus the curriculum should be *expansive* rather than restrictive. It should allow learners to better understand their strengths and limitations and to learn what types of activities are available in the real world and what activities they prefer.

Designing and Implementing Activities

Developmentally based teaching in physical education has received emphasis in recent years. A developmentally based curriculum focuses on several important factors. First, every child passes through a series of developmental stages. For example, in the process of learning how to throw a ball, every child progresses through an initial and somewhat jerky stage, to a more focused second stage, to a final automatic step in which the movement is performed smoothly and effortlessly. A second important factor is that, although the majority of children follow similar sequences of motor development and arrive at developmental points at approximately the same age level, the rate of motor development varies; hence, the rate of development is not age-dependent. Children pass through each developmental stage according to their own levels of maturity and ability, rather than according to an exact chronological age or grade level. Although it is impossible for a classroom teacher to completely individualize a program for each child, it is possible to use new organizational techniques, new content areas, and new teaching strategies to allow children within any given learning experience in physical education to develop and learn according to their own levels of interest, ability, and previous experience. Having children set individual goals helps strengthen skills based on the current skills of learners. Social, emotional, cognitive, and psychomotor development must all be understood if developmentally appropriate programs are to be achieved.

Consider the following practice question:

When scheduling units and activities in physical education, it would be *most* important for a teacher to follow which of the following guidelines?

A. Activities of greater interest to learners should be alternated with those of lesser interest in order to maintain learners' motivation.

B. Class activities should coincide with the professional sports in season at that time.

C. Activities that are more familiar to learners should be alternated with those that are less familiar to ensure that learners regularly experience success.

D. Activities should build upon learners' previous experience and skills and should progress from simpler to more complex.

In presenting activities that build upon previous experience and skills (*D*), the teacher is more assured of the developmentally appropriate nature of the activity. By doing so, learners' motivation will be greater; therefore, alternating activities, according to interest as suggested in options *A* and *C*, is not necessary. Scheduling activities based upon seasonal considerations related to professional sports programs (*B*) is of little value in most cases. The best option is *D*.

What children learn can be applied in many settings. Learning is holistic; students use what they have learned in one area in many other areas. There is little doubt that learning to apply academic settings is an important process. Physical activity offers many opportunities for integrating subject matter and activity. For example, TEKS standards could be taught or reinforced by means of appropriate application of movement concepts. Examples of such academic integration include bringing together the fine arts and physical activity via posters, decorations, dancing, and costumes. Because the origins of physical education materials are diverse, geographical associations provide the classroom teacher with another source of learning experiences; games or dances of different cultures could be integrated into a lesson, for example. Studying geographical and climatic factors of various areas to see how they affect athletic performance is a natural integration of subject areas. Without using a great deal of imagination, it should be apparent how history, language arts, music, number concepts (mathematics), and so forth can serve in a symbiotic fashion along with physical activities.

Many children are kinesthetic learners who need movement in order to learn more quickly and better in all areas of learning. Providing for these learners can also increase movement while reaching the modality of these learners directly through movement activities, such as forming letters with the body, creative movement (becoming a seed, for example, and moving through the growing process), large floor games, pantomime and charades, and dance.

Physical education has recently undergone dramatic change. Not only has the emphasis shifted from the development of sport skills to a more holistic approach that emphasizes interdisciplinary concepts but the discipline has shifted its goals as well. Physical education plays a large role in enhancing the fitness and skill levels of learners so they have a background that allows them to develop an active lifestyle. People are commonly faced with many decisions that positively or negatively impact their level of wellness. The ability to make responsible decisions depends on a wide range of factors: (a) an understanding of one's feelings and clarification of personal values, (b) an ability to cope with stress and personal problems, (c) an ability to make decisions, and (d) an understanding of the impact of various lifestyles on health.

SUMMARY

This chapter has explored the role of health and fitness within the context of the Generalist exam. Health and fitness are rapidly evolving fields. Much has changed from the "PE" classes that many of us may have had as students. These new developments have helped to solidify the roles of these disciplines in the educational process.

Data provided by the U.S. Surgeon General delineate the fact that ours is a "nation at risk." Lack of exercise and obesity have been determined to be as serious as smoking. Unlike previous conclusions regarding the amount of exercise required in order to maintain a healthy lifestyle, the Surgeon General, in concert with the Centers for Disease Control, now maintains that a moderate amount of exercise will meet the demands of healthy, active living. Healthy students are more physically and mentally ready to learn. Although recess has an important role in unstructured play and developing socialization skills in children, please do not perceive physical activity time as simply an opportunity to provide students with outside time. Physical activity is an essential component of the learning process and should be treated accordingly.

REFERENCES

Bloom, B. S. (1956). *Taxonomy of educational objectives, Handbook I: The cognitive domain.* New York: David McKay Co. Inc.

Brewer, J. A. (2001). *Introduction to early childhood education: Preschool through primary grades* (4th ed.). Boston: Allyn and Bacon.

Cruickshank, D., Jenkins, D., & Metcalf, C. (2002). *The act of teaching* (3rd ed.). Boston: McGraw-Hill.

Daniels, D., Beaumont, L., & Doolin, C. (2002). *Understanding children: An interview and observation guide for educators.* Boston: McGraw-Hill.

Eggen, P., & Kauchak, D. (2001). *Education psychology: Windows on classrooms.* Upper Saddle River, NJ: Merrill Prentice-Hall.

Goleman, D. (1995). *Emotional intelligence.* New York: Bantam Books.

Kagan, S. (1992). *Cooperative learning.* San Juan Capistrano, CA: Resources for Teachers, Inc.

Luepker R. V., Perry, C., McKinlay, S. M., et al. (1996). Outcomes of a field trial to improve children's dietary patterns and physical activity. *Journal of the American Medical Association, 275,* 768–776.

Physical activity and health: A report of the Surgeon General (1996). Washington, DC: U.S. Department of Health and Human Services.

SUGGESTED READINGS

American Academy of Pediatrics. (1991). *Sports medicine: Health care for young athletes.* Elk Grove Village, IL: Author.

Inspaugh, D. J., & Ezell, G. (2001). *Teaching today's health.* Boston: Allyn and Bacon.

Gabbard, C., Leblanc, E., & Lowy, S. (1987). *Physical education for children.* Englewood Cliffs, NJ: Prentice-Hall.

Gallahue, D.L. (1987). *Developmental physical education for today's elementary school children.* New York: Macmillan.

Gill, E. (2007). A supersize problem. *Education Update, 49*(1). Retrieved on January 23, 2007 in www.ascd.org/portal/site/ascd/index.jsp/ and search for supersize.

Goals 2000: Educate America Act (1994). M.R. 1804.

Gordon, A., & Brown, K.W. (1996). *Guiding young children in a diverse society.* Boston: Allyn and Bacon.

Graham, G., Holt-Hale, S.A., & Parker, M. (1993). *Children moving.* Mountain View, CA: Mayfield.

Hellison, D. (2003). *Teaching responsibility through physical activity.* Champaign, Il: Human Kinetics.

Landy, J.M., & Burridge, K.R. (1999). *Fundamental motor skills and movement activities for young children.* West Nyack, NY: The Center for Applied Research in Education.

Mosston, M., & Ashworth, S. (1994). *Teaching physical education* (4th ed.). New York: Macmillan.

National Center for Chronic Disease Prevention and Health. (2000). The school health policies and program study (SHPPS). Retrieved on May 11, 2007, from www. cdc. gov/ healthyYouth/ shpps/ overview/ index. htm

Nichols, B. (1986). *Moving and learning—The elementary school physical education experience.* St. Louis: Times Mirror/Mosby.

Pangrazi, R.P. (2001a). *Dynamic physical education for elementary school children* (13th ed.). Boston: Allyn and Bacon.

Pangrazi, R.P. (2001b). *Lesson plans for dynamic physical education for elementary school students* (13th ed.). Boston: Allyn and Bacon.

Pangrazi, R.P., & Hastad, D.N. (1989). *Fitness in the elementary schools* (2nd ed.). Reston, VA: AAHPERD.

President's Council on Physical Fitness and Sports. (1991). *Get fit! A handbook for youth ages 6–17.* Washington, DC. President's Council on Physical Fitness and Sports.

Rink, J.E. (1993). *Teaching physical education for learning* (2nd ed.). St. Louis: Mosby.

Rothlein, L. Nutrition tips revisited: On a daily basis do we implement what we know? *Young Children, 44,* 30–36.

Schmidt, R.A. (1991). *Motor learning and performance: From principles to practice.* Champaign, IL: Human Kinetics.

U.S. Department of Health and Human Services. (1996). Physical activity and health: A report of the Surgeon General. Atlanta, GA: Author.

A HEALTH LESSON PLAN

The Human Heart

Grade Level: Pre-K/Kindergarten

Main Subject Area: Health

Integrated Subjects: Science, Music

Time Frame/Constraints: One period

Overall Goal(s): For children to understand where the heart is located in the body and that it works harder and healthier with exercise.

TEKS/TAKS OBJECTIVES:

§ 115.2. **Health Education** (b) Knowledge and skills; (1) Health behaviors. The student recognizes that personal health decisions and behaviors affect health throughout life. The student is expected to: (C) identify types of exercise and active play that are good for the body; (4) Health information. The student knows the basic structures and functions of the human body and how they relate to personal health. The student is expected to: (B) name major body parts and their functions;

§ 112.2. **Science** Scientific processes. The student develops abilities necessary to do scientific inquiry in the field and the classroom. The student is expected to: (C) gather information using simple equipment and tools to extend the senses; (D) construct reasonable explanations using information; and (E) communicate findings about simple investigations;

§ 117.3. **Music** (1) Perception. The student describes and analyzes musical sound and demonstrates musical artistry; (2) Creative expression/performance. The student performs a varied repertoire of music. The student is expected to: (A) sing or play . . . independently or in a group; and (4) Response/evaluation. The student responds to and evaluates music and musical performance. The student is expected to: (A) identify steady beat in musical performances; and (B) identify higher/lower, louder/softer, faster/slower, and same/different in musical performances.

Objectives:

• Students will complete a picture of what they believe a real human heart looks like.

• Students, in a center, will listen and describe their heartbeats at rest and after physical activity.

• Students, in a center, will construct a stethoscope.

• Students, in a center, will correctly place a magnetic heart on a body form.

• Students will sing "The Heartbeat Song."

• Students will each draw their own bodies with the heart in the correct area of the body.

Sponge Activity: Students draw a quick picture of what they think a real human heart looks like.

Environmental Concerns: This lesson is structured as mostly a center activity designed for small groups of two or three children to experience their own normal heartbeat/pulse during rest and during physical activity.

Center Set-up: The center should be set up on a table on the perimeter of the classroom. A free-standing, trifold poster board is used to display titles, images, instructions, and safety rules. Instructions supplemented by drawings or digital pictures should be displayed and labeled. The human figure drawing should be mounted where children can easily reach the heart area.

Focus or Set Induction: As a whole class, the teacher tells students, "Everyone clench your fist. This is about the size of your heart. Now clench your fist and unclench it until your hand feels tired. Let's keep doing that as long as you can. This is about what the heart does to pump blood through our bodies. How many times do you think it does that in a lifetime? About 3 billion times! Do you think it could get tired? That's why it has to stay a very fit muscle!" (If a large transparent container is available, the teacher can also fill it with water and show how clenching one's fist quickly in the water can push water out the top of the fist [or use two hands]).

Rationale(s): Teacher tells students, "Your heart is a muscle that works every minute of the day and night. Everyone make a 'strong man' muscle with your arm. Feel that muscle? Is it strong? What do people do to make their muscles strong? They go to the gym to lift weights or exercise. Because our heart is also a muscle, we can make it stronger with exercise so that it will be strong for a lifetime. How can you make it stronger, do you think? With exercise—that is correct! Today in the Heart Center you will discover how you know that your heart is getting exercised."

MAKING CONNECTIONS:

1. **Connections to Past or Future Learning:** Have you ever run or exercised so much that you can feel your heart beating very hard in your chest? Has a doctor or nurse ever taken your pulse? How did they do that?

2. **Connections to the Community:** Do people sometimes have trouble with their hearts? Where do they go if that happens? Talk about the local doctors, specialized doctors for hearts, and/or the hospital in the community.

3. **Connections to Culture:** Ask students if they know a time when we think of the heart in other ways (Valentine's Day). What is the symbol of Valentine's Day? Why do you think we use the heart as a symbol for love? (The heart can also beat faster with high emotions.)

4. **Connections to Student Interests & Experiences:** Have you ever been very scared? What happens to your heart then? Do we have sayings about the heart when it beats fast? (My heart skipped a beat! It made my heart race! My heart leaped to my throat! My heart is beating out of my chest!)

Pass around a tennis ball and have children squeeze it. Explain that this is about how hard your heart has to work to pump blood through the body.

Materials: (1) Inexpensive stethoscope [about $6 at Lakeshore Learning stores or others]; (2) stethoscope model consisting of two small funnels [from Home Depot or a dollar store] and about 25–30 inches of clear, 3/8 diameter plastic tubing [diameter depends on the funnel tube size]; (3) outline of a human figure [about the size of a small child] with a small magnet glued to the back side at the chest location of the heart with several Xs marked on the front side of the figure; (4) small laminated human heart image [downloaded from Web or copied from a book] with a small magnet glued to the back; (5) a variety of art supplies, including long sheets of paper; (6) illustrations of tasks; (7) diagram of body with heart shown in correct location; and (8) a kitchen timer.

Activities: Guided Practice: The teacher will model each of the following activities to be conducted independently by the children in the

Health Center: listening to a normal pulse with a stethoscope, listening to a pulse after physical activity, constructing a model stethoscope, and placing a heart image on a human outline.

Activity 1: Normal Pulse Instructions: Carefully place the stethoscope ear pieces in your ears. Place the small round end of the stethoscope on your neck just under your ear. Stand or sit quietly and listen. What do you hear? Describe the sound to your group. Repeat by placing the round end of the stethoscope on your wrist near the palm of your hand. What do you hear? Tell your group what you hear. (**Note:** Drawings or photographs about where to place the stethoscope are very useful to help students complete the tasks after modelling.)

Activity 2: Activity Pulse Instructions: Set your kitchen timer for two minutes. Walk in place for two minutes or sit down in a chair and get up 10 times in a row or until your timer goes off. Listen to your pulse again. What do you hear? Describe what you hear to your group. How is the pulse after standing and sitting (exercising) different from the normal pulse? Do the same by setting the timer for one minute and running in place.

Activity 3: Making a Stethoscope: Use the tube to connect the ends of the small funnels. Place the big, open end of one funnel over your ear. Place the other end on your wrist near your palm. What do you hear? How does this model work? (A diagram for this project should be available.)

Activity 4: "Where Is the Heart?" Use the small heart image and place it near the X on the human form drawing (where you believe the heart is). Each group member shows the others on their own body. (Students should check the body diagram that is placed in the center to be sure they are correct).

Independent Practice: Students will complete an art project using the materials of their choice to draw a heart on their body forms. The heart must be located in the correct general area.

Assessment: Participation in each activity (checklist). The heart on the student's drawing of his or her body must be located in the correct area.

What Will Students Do Who Finish Early?

Bookmark a Web site where a real heart can be heard. Have children listen. If a computer is not available, tape a real heart beat and have children listen.

Closure: Review major heart concepts: (1) the heart is a muscle; (2) the heart muscle squeezes to pump blood; (3) the heart pumping sound is the pulse; (4) activity increases the pulse rate; (5) the heart is in the human chest; and (6) exercise makes a stronger heart muscle. After all children have rotated through the Heart Center, children in a whole group will sing the "Heart Beat Song" (sung to the tune of "Frère Jacques").

Begin very slowly and speed up with each verse; put hand over heart and pat chest to the beat of the booms in the last verses; also have children do motions [like sleeping], then moving in place.

"The Heart Beat Song"

Hear my heart beat; hear my heart beat. Tick . . . tick . . . tick! Tick . . . tick . . . tick! (or can make ticking sound).

When I'm sleeping soundly, when I'm sleeping soundly, Tick . . . tick . . . tick! Tick . . . tick . . . tick! (or can make ticking sound).

(Sung a little faster).

Hear my heart beat; hear my heart beat. Tick, tick, tick! Tick, tick, tick! (or make ticking sound).

When I'm walking slowly, when I'm walking slowly. Tick, tick, tick! Tick, tick, tick! (or make ticking sound)

(Sung moderately fast)

Hear my heart beat, hear my heart beat. Boom, boom, boom! Boom, boom, boom!

When I'm skipping faster, when I'm skipping faster. Boom, boom, boom! Boom, boom, boom!

(Sung very fast)

Hear my heart beat, hear my heart beat. Boom, boom, boom! Boom, boom, boom!

When I'm when I'm running faster, when I'm running faster. Boom, boom, boom! Boom, boom, boom!

Ask children if this song has a steady beat. How is that like a heart beat? Did the song beat go slower and faster? How is that like a heart beat?

Ask students what the heart is (a muscle). Ask children to point to where their own hearts are in their bodies.

Modification for Students with Special Needs: Karla, in a wheelchair, will move her arms rapidly instead of running and standing/sitting.

Reflection: To be addressed after teaching the lesson.

DRAFT YOUR OWN HEALTH OR PHYSICAL EDUCATION LESSON PLAN

Title of Lesson: _____

Grade Level: _____

Main Subject Area: _____

Integrated Subjects: _____

Time Frame/Constraints: _____

Overall Goal(s): _____

TEKS/TAKS Objectives: _____

_____

_____

Objective(s): _____

_____

_____

Sponge Activity: _____

_____

_____

Environmental Concerns: _____

_____

_____

Rationale(s): _____

_____

_____

Focus or Set Induction: _____

_____

_____

Making Connections:

1. Connections to Past or Future Learning: _____

_____

2. Connections to the Community: _____

_____

3. Cultural Connections: _____

_____

4. Connections to Student Interests & Experiences: _____

_____

Materials: _____

_____

_____

Activities: Guided practice: _____

_____

_____

_____

_____

Independent practice: _____

_____

_____

_____

_____

Assessment: _____

_____

_____

What Will Students Do Who Finish Early? _____

_____

_____

Closure: _____

_____

_____

Modification for Students with Special Needs: _____

_____

_____

Reflection: _____

_____

_____

OBSERVING HEALTH AND/OR PHYSICAL EDUCATION EXPERIENCES/ACTIVITIES

During your visit to an early childhood classroom, use the following form to provide feedback as well as to reflectively analyze the room, the materials, and the teacher.

	Observed	Not Observed	Response
1. Movement is a daily part of the classroom.			If so, describe. If not, what types of movement could easily and logically be added?
2. Safety is discussed when movement is a part of the lesson.			If so, describe. If not, what was the result?
3. What could be discussed? If games are a part of the lesson, all children are included.			If so, describe. If not, how could each child be included?
4. All movements are developmentally appropriate.			If so, describe. If not, explain why not.
5. Alternative movements are provided for children with special needs (if applicable).			If so, describe. If not, what could be added?
6. Movement is integrated in other content areas.			If so, describe. If not, what could be added?
7. Movement is used as a way to invigorate a class after a long period of study.			If so, describe. If not, describe when and how movement could be useful.
8. Time is set aside for free play.			If so, what was the result? If not, could this element have been added? Explain why or why not.
9. A variety of equipment is available for children at different times.			If so, describe. If not, what equipment would be appropriate?
10. Ample space allows children and adults to move around freely.			If not, how could the area be rearranged?
11. Movement is appropriately assessed.			If so, describe. If not, what would be appropriate?
12. Health issues are mentioned during the day (e.g., cleaning hands, using a tissue, watching for too much sun).			If so, describe. If not, what could be added?
13. Healthy behaviors are noted by the teacher and rewarded in some manner.			If so, describe. If not, give ideas for what could be added.
14. There is a Health Center of some type in the classroom.			If so, describe. If not, give ideas for what could be added.
15. Health is integrated into other content areas.			If so, describe. If not, give ideas for what could be added.

	Observed	Not Observed	Response
16. The room is designed to help prevent transmission of illness (area for washing hands or hand wipes provided).			If so, describe. If not, give ideas for what could be changed or added.
17. The teacher ensures that the room and classroom equipment is sanitized often to prevent the transmission of illness.			If so, describe. If not, how can this be implemented.
18. When children are offered snacks or rewards in the classroom, healthy foods and drinks are used.			If so, describe. If not, what could be offered?
19. Children are encouraged to think at upper levels about health issues.			If observed, describe. If not, describe how this could be encouraged.
20. Health issues are discussed in a respectful way.			If so, describe. If not, suggest how this could change.
21. Health issues are discussed in a developmentally appropriate way.			If so, explain. If not, explain why not.
22. The teacher is a good model of healthy behaviors.			If so, describe. If not, how could this improve?
23. The issue of good mental health is addressed during the day (stress, emotions, peer pressure, etc.).			If so, describe. If not, describe instances where this could easily be addressed.
24. The teacher practices universal precautions with health issues (has gloves for incidents with bodily fluids, washes hands, etc.).			If so, describe. If not, how should this change?
25. Technology is used with health.			If so, describe. If not, what technological elements could be added?
26. Health is taught as a lesson that follows a structured lesson plan.			If so, describe. If not, how could this be accomplished?
27. Health learning is assessed in an appropriate way.			If so, describe. If not, how could this be accomplished?

TEST YOURSELF ON HEALTH AND PHYSICAL EDUCATION

1. As part of physical development, Mrs. Graham has her Pre-K students form a circle and asks one child to catch a medium-sized ball and then throw it to another child. When it is Kayla's turn to receive the ball, she closes her eyes, flinches, and turns her shoulder to the ball. Mrs. Graham should:
   A. skip Kayla's turn because it is obvious that Kayla is afraid in this game.
   B. call Kayla's parents to set up a conference about Kayla's development.
   C. recognize that this is an early stage of learning to catch.
   D. encourage Kayla to watch the ball and catch with her hands alone.

2. Mrs. Rutledge goes out to the track with her first graders at times because she is worried that her pants are becoming a little too tight. Her body fat (the percentage of fat to muscle) is greater than 26 percent—which does put her clearly in the "fat" category for women (it is 20 percent for men). She pants along with her first graders, but she also thinks that the coach expects too much of them. At the K–2nd grade level students should be expected to:
   A. run $\frac{1}{2}$–1 mile without walking.
   B. run $\frac{1}{8}$ of a mile without walking.
   C. run $\frac{1}{16}$ of a mile without walking.
   D. run about two blocks without walking.

3. Mr. McNeil was designing a mathematics lesson plan for his second graders with his student teacher, Sean. Mr. McNeil was in the process of adding a game where students were to bounce a ball a certain number of times, then pass it to someone opposite of them. The person who received the ball had to say how many times the child had bounced it before it was passed. If the answer was incorrect, the receiver had to pass it without bouncing. Sean looked puzzled at this activity and asked if it wasn't "a little young" for this group. "What's the purpose?" he asked. Mr. McNeil told him that the *best* reason to integrate this game in a mathematics lesson was:
   A. to improve spatial skills.
   B. to integrate kinetics with mathematics.

   C. to answer learning styles of diverse learners in this class.
   D. to add a manipulative element to the counting.

4. Although Mr. Herrera is not the coach, he sometimes works at recess with his students on the basic movement skills of catching, kicking, and moving objects with another object (a bat, a racquet, etc.). All three of these skills include beginning with:
   A. the arms slightly bent at the elbow.
   B. relaxing through the movement.
   C. eyes on the ball.
   D. the weight shift towards the object.

5. Mrs. Li has her children go through a short obstacle course that she designed in her classroom. One part of the course asks them to imagine that they are "walking over a tree branch that is over a stream." This part of the course is a simple line of duct tape on the floor. She is giving children an opportunity to improve their:
   A. agility.
   B. flexibility.
   C. balance.
   D. endurance

6. The best *complex* carbohydrate, or food that provides energy, is:
   A. sugar.
   B. fruits and vegetables.
   C. pasta, breads, and grains.
   D. dairy foods.

7. Mr. Getty has his children run a relay race in four teams. Children must run for a distance, go around a marker and return, touching a teammate's hand as they finish their part of the race. Students must run in place until their whole team has gone. This exercise is mostly related to:
   A. anaerobics.
   B. strength.
   C. aerobics.
   D. diastolic/systolic.

TEST YOURSELF ANSWERS AND RATIONALES FOR HEALTH AND PHYSICAL EDUCATION

Answer 1: Children develop physical skills at individual rates (*C*). Kayla is in the first stage of learning to catch, exhibited by her protective behavior when she is thrown a ball. In the next stage, Kayla will try to catch the ball using her whole body and will then progress to using her hands with her arms. Finally, she will catch with only her hands. Both choices *A* and *B* show that the teacher is unaware of these stages of development. Choice *D* would have her skip though the natural progression of development in this skill. The correct answer is *C*.

Answer 2: Choice *B* is correct. Fit children from K-2 should be able to run about 1/8 of a mile without walking. Children in third and fourth grade should be expected to run between 1/2 mile and 1 mile without walking. Mrs. Rutledge is also smart to understand the role of body fat in fitness. If she could get into the average category of 13 percent to 25 percent for women, she would be considered fit (8 percent to 20 percent for men). There are two important concepts to take from this question—information about body fat and information about expectations for children's exercise. The answer is *B*.

Answer 3: All of these answers are good reasons to integrate mathematics with movement. The *best* reason for this game, Mr. McNeil told Sean, was to help develop spatial skills. Children who are able to manipulate objects in physical activities such as throwing, catching, rolling, bouncing, or striking objects are more easily able to deal with mathematic problems that involve spatial skills. The answer is *A*.

Answer 4: The most important element each of these skills has in common is starting with one's eyes on the ball. The answer is *C*.

Answer 5: *Agility* (*A*) refers to being able to change one's position easily. *Flexibility* (*B*) refers to how much range of motion one has in his/her joints. *Endurance* (*D*) refers to how long one's muscles are able to work/contract. In this case, Mrs. Li is asking students to safely work on their equilibrium as they pretend they are *balancing* along the pretend line. The answer is *C*.

Answer 6: Although sugars can provide energy, they are called *simple* carbohydrates and are not the *best* source. It is pasta, breads, and grains that are the complex carbohydrates and the *best* choice for fuel food. The answer is *B*.

Answer 7: *Anaerobic exercise* (*A*) is related to weight training, or strengthening the body's muscles with slow movement. *Strength* (*B*) refers to how much force muscles are able to put forth. Choice *D, systolic* (contraction) and *diastolic* (relaxation) refers to measuring of one's blood pressure (as in "140 [systolic] over 90 [diastolic]"). *Aerobics* (*C*) involve the body in a total active workout to increase the intake of oxygen. The answer is *C*.

9 Preparing to Teach Theatre Arts in Texas

Kathryn L. Jenkins
University of Houston–Downtown

Janice L. Nath
University of Houston–Downtown

Joyce M. Dutcher
University of Houston–Downtown

The Generalist examination specifically asks teachers to be knowledgeable about the Fine Arts for music and art in Domain V. There is, however, an interesting discrepancy between the Generalist exam and the Texas curriculum prescribed by the Texas Essential Knowledge and Skills (the TEKS), which all teachers in Texas are required to provide for their students. The Fine Arts TEKS for students present requirements for each grade level in music, art, *and* the theatre arts, but there are no specific competencies for theatre arts on the Generalist examination for teachers. Nevertheless, the TExES competencies clearly state that teachers *must be aware of* the TEKS for *each* content area and grade level. Therefore, we have elected to include a chapter on theatre arts based upon this statement about the TEKS and because information in this chapter may also be embedded in both the competencies and questions on the Generalist in other content areas. We also decisively believe that the use of theatre arts for children creates positive and enriching learning experiences throughout the curriculum.

If you have already studied for the TExES PPR (Pedagogy and Professional Responsibilities), you undoubtably remember learning about dramatic play and its benefits for young children. This chapter will remind you of those benefits and inform you about other information for the theatre arts TEKS with the hope that you will see the value of providing quality opportunities for children—not only for dramatic play but also by engaging students often in informal and formalized theatre arts activities. This chapter will also show you how to integrate theatre arts into other content areas in ways that will make your classroom an exciting place for children to learn.

What Are Theatre Arts Experiences?

There are two main types of experiences that teachers provide within the realm of theatre arts for children—dramatic play and drama activities. **Dramatic play** refers to situations in which the child freely initiates role-play from either the real world or from pretend/make-believe. *Play* is the key word for this concept. As soon as young children develop the ability to pretend, they are ready to engage in dramatic play (Wortham, 2006). **Drama activities** refer to both **structured drama** that requires student participation in set, directed ways (scripted plays, skits, etc.) and other **creative drama experiences** where children are involved in *creative* activities related to drama. These include such activities as creating improvisational stories or situations, writing their own plays, or participating in the integrated arts (such as creating costumes, using puppets or masks, designing sets, and setting drama to music).

Dramatic Play

Teachers of younger children clearly understand how important the process of *dramatic play* is for child development. The process of engaging in play can involve children's negotiation of roles, the development of rules, the location or creation of props, and so forth. Teachers should provide time and a positive environment for children to engage in the process of dramatic play—both individually and cooperatively. Teachers may also encourage dramatic play for young children by providing specific props in a particular area or **center**. For example, a teacher may "set the stage" in a Home Improvement Center for encouraging children to role-play those tasks commonly found in and around their homes. Props such as tools in a tool box, pretend cleaning supplies, gardening equipment, and related dress-up clothes would encourage specific types of dramatic play and role-taking (yard work, cleaning, building, repairing, etc.). Many types of centers have specific purposes for development in particular content areas through dramatic play. For example, a Grocery Store Center would offer mathematical concepts, such as sorting, measuring, and counting as children role-play customers and sales persons. A Transportation Center with various land vehicles, airplanes, and boats would offer science and social studies concepts, such as classifying and community job roles, while a Pet Center would help children delve into various science concepts, such as living and nonliving things and social development in the areas of caring and responsibility. An enriched indoor (and outdoor) environment is essential for the young child to engage in many types of exploration of roles in play. Centers should also include a number of costumes and other types of props related to these types of centers. These need not be "complete" costumes or absolutely realistic props, especially if funds are short. Hats, vests, a lab coat, or other simple items can suggest a wealth of characters (McCaslin, 2006), can spark children to use their imaginations, and can expand children's exploration of various roles—especially those of adults.

Sustaining and extending activity is also important to dramatic play; thus, teachers may observe children's interest and follow up with materials that will appropriately prolong and enrich a play theme. For example, Mrs. Kelly notices that Hanna and Miguel, who are in the Home Center, are pretending that their baby brother is hurt. Mrs. Kelly chooses that time to introduce a medical kit with Band-Aids and other home medical props to the center. She also asks those children who are in the Clinic Center to join in helping with Hanna and Miguel's "baby brother". Later, Mrs. Kelly sees children in the Home Improvement Center pretending to plant flowers in their garden. To expand interest in both of these centers, she makes a note to bring some seeds and plants the following day "to sell" at the "store" so that children will purchase them and plant them in the outside play area.

Drama Activities

Teachers may also provide opportunities in theatre arts through structured or scripted dramas or other dramatic activities. These experiences come in many formats such as unison movements to poems or songs, skits, and plays. Miss Chen, for instance, teaches her Pre-K students a choral poem about "Five Little Pumpkins" with motions and voice inflections. Ms. Herrera asks children to use felt board characters to "retell" a story in her kindergarten class, as children use "character voices" in the retelling. Mrs. Fenten has her second graders use puppets to problem solve a "situation" in which two animals are arguing over the same toy. Mr. Irving assigned his third-grade class roles of the main characters in reenactments of stories to help reinforce children's abilities to develop sequencing skills in more exciting ways. Mrs. Mitchell's fourth-grade class puts on an entire play written for children by professionals (including both singing and dramatic speaking parts) for a PTO meeting. In many of these types of structured experiences, children must take on specific assigned characters, movements, or situations—with varying degrees of freedom on how much they are allowed to improvise or vary from a script. Children may also be involved in a number of other dramatic experiences. For instance, Ms. Claire tells children the *Legend of the Bluebonnet,* and afterward, children write their own short skits that follow the story line. Miss Arwen's class helps to build a puppet theatre, and Mrs. Mitchell's class also designs and constructs sets for their fourth-grade play.

Let's try a question:

As a recently hired first-grade teacher, Miss Loya, was asked by several teachers who had been teaching for some years why she integrates theatre arts activities into her lessons. Which statement *least* supports the incorporation of these activities into other lessons?

A. These activities address various modalities and multiple intelligences.
B. These activities help "less" exciting lessons become more motivating.
C. These activities promote creativity and critical thinking skills.
D. These integrated activities help in completing the required time set by the state for many of her content areas.

All of these choices are valid to some extent. There are several multiple intelligences and modalities integrated by including theatre arts activities—particularly linguistic, spatial, interpersonal, and bodily kinesthetic (*A*). Lessons certainly become more exciting for children (and, thus, more motivating) when theatre arts activities are used (*B*). Many of the theatre arts activities (particularly dramatic role-play) involve problem solving, creativity, and critical thinking (*C*). Even Choice *D* is somewhat true, but it is the *least* substantial reason for supporting the use of theatre arts in a general curriculum. There are *many* more substantial reasons for doing so. The correct answer is *D*.

What Are the TEKS in Theatre Arts for Students in EC-4 Classrooms?

For each grade level, the Theatre Arts TEKS (2006) include four strands:

1. Perception
2. Creative expression/performance
3. Historic and cultural heritage
4. Critical evaluation

Within each of these strands, the TEKS describe specific theatre arts knowledge and skills that teachers *must* provide in classrooms across the state. Each grade level includes and builds upon the knowledge and skills that were introduced in Pre-K and/or the previous grades so that a teacher should be familiar with *all* grade levels of the TEKS. After a brief description of each of the four theatre arts strands and what should be the focus in each grade level, this chapter will elaborate how they can be an integral part of the curriculum.

Perception

Sometimes, we do not think about *all* of the areas that are important in child development—only about our core "subjects" like reading and mathematics. However, *perception* is an important base for many of the tasks that we ask of children within these "core areas" as they grow (in addition to those in the other fine arts and in physical fitness). In helping students develop *perception* through the theatre arts, teachers can provide drama and theatre experiences that help young children make better sense of themselves, others, and their environment. Activities in the perception strand improve children's skills in *insight, awareness, sensitivity,* and *observation.* As these perception skills develop, students become more aware and more understanding of the world around them.

It is difficult for children to manage themselves without being able to fully understand and "read" themselves and others for understanding. This is an important part of perception. Therefore, beginning in Pre-K, students should be provided with numerous opportunities to engage in dramatic play activities to enhance their social and communication skills. For kindergartners, teachers should include activities that enhance students' self-perception and awareness of others and of their environment through dramatic play. Kindergarten experiences should also engage students in expressive movement, exploration of space, imitation of sounds, and use of props. These areas set the stage for the observation and spatial skills children need for many academic tasks.

In first grade, this strand requires building upon kindergarten experiences. Children should now be provided with activities that increase their confidence through dramatic play. They should also begin to participate in the imitation of actions and the imitation and creation of both animate and inanimate objects. For example, when teachers say, "Let's pretend to be elephants," they are checking children's perception and understanding of this animal, allowing for expressive movement and imitation of sounds, and developing spatial skills.

Second graders should be reacting to sensory experiences and be involved in increased spatial awareness through expressive and rhythmic movement. Also at this grade level, children should participate in: (1) dramatic play that uses actions, sounds, and dialogue; (2) role-play; (3) imitations; and (4) re-creation of dialogue.

In third grade, students react to sound, music, images, and the written word with voice and movement added. Children who are in the third grade should be responding to sensory and emotional experiences in theatre arts and should be creating play space as they continue to develop the use of expressive and rhythmic movements. Through classroom dramatizations, students should be able to reflect on their environment, portray characters, and demonstrate actions.

Finally, in fourth grade, activities for perception should include all of the above. In addition, teachers will expand experiences for children in: (1) further development of body awareness and spatial perceptions; (2) using interpretive movements, sounds, and dialogue; and (3) imitating and synthesizing life experiences in dramatic play.

Creative Expression/Performance

Creative expression and performance is the second theatre arts strand and is an important part of developing higher-level thinking, particularly synthesis. In this strand, Pre-K teachers involve children in spontaneous and expressive dramatics by having them create or re-create stories, moods, or experiences. For example, Elena was telling her teacher about going to her grandparents' house right across the border in Mexico. Her teacher, Ms. Cain, quickly pulled up two chairs to represent a car and asked Elena to "drive them both" to her grandparents' house. Elena was then asked to point out and tell what she "is seeing along the way." To recall their experiences, young children should have many opportunities to express and interpret their unique feelings through body movements and voice.

Pre-K and kindergarten students should be encouraged to participate regularly in dramatic play and should be taught how to appropriately use their voices, to move safely in dramatic situations, and to assume simple roles/interpret characters from real life and from stories. One way the kindergarten teacher facilitates students in theatre design, direction, and production is by providing centers, as described earlier, with appropriate props and manipulatives. Children should begin to create their own play spaces, costumes, and simple materials and to plan dramatic play both alone and in cooperation with others.

First-grade teachers should include experiences in dramatizing limited action stories, poems, and songs. They should assist children in becoming more sophisticated at adapting their play environment and selecting aspects of the environment for use in dramatic play.

In second grade, students are ready to perform pantomime and puppetry, as they dramatize poems, songs, or limited action stories. They are also ready for more advanced role-play from real life or imaginative situations.

In addition to the experiences above, third grade teachers ask their students to participate in the performance of a number of different roles in real or imagined situations. Children are also involved with narrative pantomime, dramatic play, and story dramatization. When older, they are able to dramatize literary selections using shadow play, puppetry, pantomime, and imitative dialogue. They are expected to identify and use technical theatre elements like simple lighting, sound, or stage props.

Fourth graders extend these skills to include the development, description, and performance of characters (including characters' relationships and surroundings) using personal experiences, heritage, literature, and history. Performances and creative expression should also include dramatization of literary selections and simple student-created stories. These presentations may be in unison, in pairs, or in groups, along with collaborative **improvisation**, or acting without a script as the drama flows along. The teacher must also include issues involved with more advanced use of props, costumes, and visual elements, as children begin to alter spaces to create suitable environments for play-making in safe ways.

Historic and Cultural Heritage

The *historic and cultural heritage* strand in theatre arts requires that children relate theatre to history, society, and culture to increase understanding and insight. Thus, kindergarten children should be involved in situations in which they re-enact real and imaginary scenes or situations from a variety of cultures and stories from their community.

Building on these skills and knowledge, first and second graders should imitate life experiences from historical events in their community. Additionally, they should integrate diverse cultural dimensions in re-enactments from various historical periods from Texas and America and be able to identify diverse cultural dimensions in dramatic play.

Older elementary children are more deeply involved with culture and history. As students move into third grade, dramatic activities begin to illustrate similarities and differences in life and reflect historical and diverse cultural influences. Fourth-grade students should be able to explain theatre as a reflection of life in particular times, places, and cultures. They must also identify the roles of live theatre, film, television, and electronic media in societies.

Critical Evaluation

The last strand for theatre arts is *critical evaluation,* another area that is important in the development of higher-level thinking. Following this strand, teachers must help children *respond to* and *evaluate* theatre and theatrical performances. Goals of this strand include promoting children's discriminating judgment and critical thinking and developing their appreciation for the theatre arts—as Texas is cognizant of the need for good evaluative consumers of live theatre, film, television, and other performance-related technologies. The TEKS also convey that students should respond to and critique performances through live theatre, film, television, and other technologies.

Beginning in kindergarten but continuing throughout all grade levels, observation of performances and appropriate audience behavior are highlighted. Young children in the first grade should also begin to demonstrate an awareness of the use of music, creative movement, and visual components in theatre.

By second and third grade, students respond more extensively to dramatic activities by employing creative movement, visual components, and music and using simple evaluative processes to do so. For example, Ms. Jamison borrows simple instruments from the music room (cymbals, drums, bells, etc.) and has groups compose a musical background to a recreation of *The Three Little Pigs*. After each group's performance, the teacher asks the audience to critique the use of sound in the performance. Children should also be introduced to amateur and professional performances, and they should be comparing many of the vocations found in theatre arts.

Fourth-grade activities should include definitions of visual, aural, oral, and kinesthetic aspects of informal play-making and formal theatre and discussions of these elements found in art, music, and dance. Activities should also include opportunities to compare and contrast the ways ideas and emotions are depicted (character study) and also of theatre artists and their contributions. Teacher questioning, both before and after performances, should be at the forefront of this strand. In one example, Mrs. Burke reads her children a story that they will re-enact. She then asks children what the main characters' voices should sound like and why, how each should walk, and what expressions should be on their faces. Then she asks a group of children to walk through an "ad lib" of the first part of the story. She follows by having "the audience" tell why the performance was believable or not. Afterwards, she selects another group of performers and repeats the process. Children also increasingly select movement, music, or visual elements to enhance their classroom dramatizations.

Remember that the TEKS are always building blocks, so each grade level builds upon the knowledge and skills of the previous grades. Lessons can focus on one or all of the four strands of the TEKS. Each of the four strands allows for creativity and variety on the part of the teacher.

It's time to look at another question:

Mrs. Bertram holds a group discussion and asks her children about their favorite way to listen to a story. She then talks to them about the Pueblo tribe's oral history and storytelling as a way to pass down their Native American traditions. Because this oral tradition was so honored, these Native Americans created two types of dolls for their young children. One was known as the "storyteller doll" (who was always formed with an open mouth), and the other was the "listener doll" (representing the children who were gaining knowledge and heritage from the elderly storyteller). Mrs. Bertram then has children create their own "storyteller" and "listener" dolls of clay and puts them in a center, where children go to tell, retell, and listen to stories.

In the activity described above, which of the Theatre Arts TEKS strands has Mrs. Bertram *not* integrated into her reading/art lesson?

- **A.** Perception and Creative Expression/Performance
- **B.** Creative Expression/Performance and Historic/Cultural Heritage
- **C.** Perception, Creative Expression, and Historic/Cultural Heritage
- **D.** Historic/Cultural Heritage and Critical Evaluation

This integrated reading/art lesson is full of activities that can address the Theatre Arts TEKS and other areas such as language arts and art. It is easy to see that the *main* strand in theatre arts is *Historic and Cultural Heritage,* because of the cultural nature of the activity involving Native American traditions. *Perception* is also appropriately addressed because students increase their awareness, insight of others, and their oral communications skills, by telling and retelling stories in the role of Native Americans to others in the center and/or to their "listening dolls." Children are also performing as they tell and retell stories, so the *Creative Expression/Performance* strand is also covered. The only one of these four strands not related to this activity is *Critical Evaluation*—children are not being asked to judge or critique. The correct answer is *C.*

(If you are interested in this activity, you can see an example of these dolls at http://www.penfieldgallery.com/storytellers/JToya.shtml.)

Why Include Theatre Arts in Daily Activities?

You have already seen in the strands discussed above some of the key reasons that theatre arts is an important part of learning. Let's continue to investigate other benefits to children in theatre arts activities.

Theatre arts experiences can help develop children's communication skills along with cognitive and social skills—all within one experience! Skilled teachers provide abundant opportunities during the day for children to use language to invent various themes and roles in dramatic play and to negotiate with each other. As children observe others in theatre arts activities and dramatic play, they learn by absorbing a wide-range of interactions in assorted situations. An increase in understanding in both present and past life experiences takes place as children watch and participate, and they are able to gain and use a wider range of human responses in communicating (both verbally and nonverbally) various situations in real life. They have a chance to act out their fantasies, fears, and other human emotions in a safe environment.

Theatre arts is one of the most empowering uses of play for children in the early years; it is during play that children begin to control their own destinies. Thus, theatre arts activities capitalize on a child's intrinsic motivation to have a sense of control of their world and to express their knowledge, their concerns, and their curiosities. As teachers become more competent in encouraging and integrating appropriate theatre arts activities, children become more comfortable and confident in developing their roles, their creativity, and their confidence as role-players. All teachers learn, for example, that puppetry has a unique value, as children "shed" their own personas to "become" others. This experience often allows children to overcome their apprehension or shyness and become more empowered in expressing themselves.

Play usually begins as an independent activity with very young children and becomes more cooperative and social in nature as they grow older. Teachers should be consciencious of children's experiences as they play alone, with a variety of children, and with a variety of skill levels and/or various children's backgrounds. An unlimited number of positive results come from a teacher's care in structuring cooperative groupings in theatre arts. Students sharpen their skills for socialization as they listen to opinions and ideas of others, lead a group, follow the lead of others, establish roles and rules, communicate, scaffold, and problem-solve.

Theatre arts can also be seen through the lenses of several other domains. For instance, for the *cognitive* domain, students recall, explore, collaborate, analyze, problem-solve, and think (and act) creatively. As mentioned, children also reach higher levels of thinking when they discuss and critique performances and compare and evaluate various literary genres. When children act and use their bodies to move during theatre arts, they increase their development of the *physical* domain. Theatre arts activities also contribute directly to children's speech, as they learn to imitate and use their voices to create characters. According to McCaslin (2006), even though written language is highlighted in schools, speech is our most important means of communication. Speaking before an audience (even if that audience is just the class) is advantageous in improving speech. In the *affective/ social/emotional domain*, children develop empathy and understanding of others and learn more about feelings, emotions, and alternative choices in communication. Through role-playing, scenery design, prop-making, setting development and/or puppetry, children can also participate in self-analysis, perspective-taking, interpretation of cultures, and character development. Within the *affective domain*, young children also learn about their values, preferences, aesthetics, talents, strengths, and areas of needed practice.

There are even more benefits to including theatre arts. Theatre arts offer chances to integrate multiple intelligences and modalities, depending upon the activity. For example, children can be kinesthetic, inter- and intrapersonal, musical, visual, spatial, and so forth in many theatre arts activities. Children also grasp the idea of symbols more readily, as they pretend that one object is another, both in play and in drama productions. Finally, children who are involved in exciting activities, such as theatre arts, are more motivated to be in school.

As one can readily see, there is a strong case for integrating theatre arts into the classroom on a daily basis. Let's continue to look at how skilled teachers go about integrating theatre arts in their classrooms.

Let us try another question:

Mr. Xu has children pretend that they are first walking on a sticky surface, sliding over ice, then tip-toeing over hot stones. He then has them pretend that the room is filled with smoke, then flowers, and, finally, the smells of a pizza cooking. Finally, he has them pretend the room is freezing cold, wet, and then blistering hot. What is the *least* applicable rationale for doing this activity?

A. To encourage students to increase their sensory recall for creative writing
B. To provide a warm-up for some type of theatre arts experience
C. To provide movement for students after an activity that requires them to be in their seats for a long time
D. To prepare students for dramatic play

First, remember that we are looking for the *least* applicable rationale for this activity. Part of the rationale for using theatre arts is to enhance integration with other activities. This particular activity works very well as a sensory recall for creative writing (*A*). This type of activity would also be suitable for children as a warm-up for a more formal theatre arts activity (*B*). A warm-up can be an important part of having children "get into the mood" of improvisation and/or formal acting. This is also a theatre arts activity that can break up a period of sitting too long with some movements (*C*). The rationale that *least* applies is preparing students for dramatic play (*D*) because dramatic play is spontaneous and should be initiated *by children themselves* (although dramatic play in certain directions can sometimes be encouraged by the teacher). The correct answer is *D*.

What Is the Teacher's Role in Theatre Arts in Early Childhood Education?

Instructional Roles

Teachers take on many roles in theatre arts instruction. The teacher is charged with instructing students on the **elements of theatre arts:** plot or story line, theme, mood, characters, language/dialogue, and spectacle. Instruction also includes the *technical components of theatre:* set, props, lighting, sound, costumes, and makeup. *Technical skills,* such as creating scenery, applying makeup, or props designing are also important to include. As children become older, they are taught about the *forms of theatre* (comedy, tragedy, farce, and melodrama). These elements are important for performance but are also critical in helping children with writing their own dramas and critiquing performances.

In addition to organizing opportunities for children to learn and build their skills with the elements listed above, teachers will take on many other roles. One of the most important of these for a teacher in theatre arts is that of a *facilitator* or *guide.* In this role, teachers set up activities and assist along the way—but also know when to step out of the way to allow students' creativity to emerge.

Planning for theatre arts activities through written lesson plans and creating units of study and integration of theatre arts will allow for multiple teacher roles to help children to be more active and engaged in learning. These other roles may include *modeler, motivator, strategist, questioner, creative developer, small group designer, mediator, safeguard,* and *assessor.*

As *modelers,* teachers set the tone for children's comfort level, confidence, and excitement about creative activities. Teachers of young children are constantly being observed by their students. Children are always listening, analyzing, and reacting to how their teachers introduce new concepts or experiences. If teachers take on an excited, active role in theatre arts as role-players, set designers, puppeteers and/or polite audience members, their students often follow that lead. Teachers can also model inclusion by planning ahead for all children to participate equally.

Motivating teachers integrate theatre arts into those areas of the curriculum in which students feel confident and interested; that is, teachers seek connections to children's personal interests by using the TEKS, the local community, and children's developmental levels and background experiences to create purposeful theatre arts activities throughout the year. Teachers utilize exciting literature, cultural and historical backgrounds, familial connections, and all of the content areas to ensure that students fully understand the role of theatre arts in daily life as well as to allow for real-life problem solving. During theatre arts, motivating teachers probe students to think, analyze, question, and defend their choices. A favorite probe of early childhood educators is "What if?" questions to encourage children to develop multiple ideas and solutions in dramatic play ("What if your truck runs out of gas [in the Transportation Center]?" "What if your baby doesn't like the food you are feeding him? [in the Home Center]" "What if your dog [stuffed animal] runs away, since you don't have him on a leash?"). All ages of children need the teacher to support their creativity by using questions or providing activities that focus on the *process* of learning rather than simply looking for one answer. It is also important for a teacher to maintain balance by avoiding *constant* intervention to turn an unstructured dramatic play episode into a "teaching situation." Children can become disinterested and disempowered when a teacher frequently intercedes in their play to manipulate a situation into an opportunity to teach something. Motivation also includes opportunities to make choices, make mistakes, and to derive meaningful context from their own decisions.

As *mediators,* teachers observe and listen to children to ensure that interactions are emotionally safe and appropriate in each situation. Teachers should constantly monitor the feedback that children are giving and receiving to be sure that it is acceptable, accurate, and helpful. Teachers should deliver constructive and supportive comments that encourage children to continue their theatre arts activity but should also be certain to immediately halt any harmful criticism that could discourage a child from participating. When mediating, teachers should use questioning, situational perspective-taking, and past experiences to allow children to make their own decisions and corrections as much as possible.

Teachers must also be *assessors.* The lesson planning process is always completed by assessing children—informally or formally. Any authentic assessment tool can be utilized in theatre arts. Teacher-made checklists, rubrics, anecdotal records, and rating scales can all be used effectively. Through the integration of technology, teachers can allow students to self-reflect by having them use digital photos, word processing, electronic journals, and video-taping critiques. As teachers design lessons and activities to address theatre arts, they must consider how they will assess children's participation, behaviors, and skills. Areas such as oral language and social development, spatial abilities, gross- and fine-motor skill development, application of prior learning, cooperation, attitudes, concentration/attention, types of play, and activities chosen by children, can be tracked over time (Nath & Cohen, 2003).

During actual performances, the teacher moves from guide or facilitator to *director.* This role will be discussed more fully later in the chapter. The teacher's roles in theatre arts are multidimensional and may include being a co-player/collaborative participant. If a teacher wishes to teach in a way that guarantees active, creative students, he or she will serve in many roles.

Noninstructional Roles

As an early childhood educator, another theatre arts role involves keeping administrators, teachers, and special interest groups (such as a parent support group or a curriculum advisory group) informed about research, any pertinent issues/policies, curriculum trends, and legislative updates. Because research supports the important role of theatre arts in developing the whole child (cognitively, socially/emotionally, and physically), these activities should be a part of every classroom. Although afterschool theatre arts programs can be popular for children who wish to delve more deeply into this area, theatre arts should not be considered by a teacher as an "add-on" to their existing curriculum (whenever time allows) but should be included as an integral part of every EC-4 instructional program. Therefore, it is the educator's job to keep those who make and/or influence curricular and instructional decisions aware of needed support. Although finding support can seem discouraging at times, there are many ways to do so.

One effective way to communicate the importance of theatre arts is through students and their work. This may be done by showcasing theatre arts activities as part of an integrated curriculum that promotes creative thinking and/or problem solving. It can also be achieved through focused student presentations or performances. Setting up fieldtrips for key community performances or asking the district to provide professional dramatic performances at the school shows teachers' concern for fulfilling the theatre arts TEKS. Sometimes support results from merely talking to and having repeated conversations with influential people (the building principal, lead or socially influential teachers, and/or parents) about supporting theatre arts. The most important thing to remember is that support for theatre arts cannot be taken for granted. Teachers should be strong advocates for supporting theatre arts.

Because theatre arts is rarely funded at the preferred level, it is suggested that teachers do the best job possible with the resources that are accessible or available at a reasonable cost. Teachers can look for costumes and materials in secondhand shops, dollar stores, and garage sales, and ask building supply stores to help with construction materials. They can involve individual parents and PTOs with supply drives and fundraisers. Teachers can integrate art and mathematics when they need to make props or construct set designs in their classrooms (at age appropriate levels) by having students create backdrops and/or simple props when appropriate. In other words, they should be creative! It is through determination that the message will be conveyed that theatre arts is essential for children.

When beginning a program, a strategic plan can be designed that includes a budget and a timeline for implementing a more comprehensive program. The plan, along with authentic student work, can be presented to the building administrator before the school's next budget cycle. Funding can come through thoughtful planning and implementation.

Let's try another question:

Mrs. Jewett makes an effort each day to go into each one of her centers, but Ms. Beck enjoys going into the Home Center and the Clinic Center and working with small groups. What does Mrs. Jewett understand that Ms. Beck does not?

    A. The teacher is a role model.
    B. The teacher is a motivator.
    C. The teacher is a constant instructor.
    D. The teacher is a facilitator.

At times, the teacher should fulfill all of these roles. However, Mrs. Jewett understands that she must be a role model in dramatic play activities. As a female teacher, she knows that if she does not go into all of the centers, then girls may see her modeling a "hidden curriculum" that "girls do not play with machines or blocks or other 'boy' things," and boys may believe that females do not (or should not) go there. The correct answer is *A*.

What Are the Main Aspects of Theatre Arts That Teachers Should Consider?

Considerations in creating experiences in theatre arts include age and developmental appropriateness (including cognitive, social/emotional, and physical), material selection, technology, resources, time, space, and safety.

The best environment for theatre arts activities is one that engages *all* students in *active* learning. Young children need an unlimited number of opportunities and materials with which to experiment, discover, make choices, collaborate, and connect their personal experiences with content. Children experience a great deal of empowerment when they are able to *choose their own* activities and are *in control* of dramatic play, so offering many choices for this type of play is ideal. There is an optimum balance. Offering too few props and materials does not support high-quality dramatic play experiences, while offering too many materials can create confusion, distraction, and disruption (Driscoll & Nagel, 2005).

Teachers in early childhood classrooms need to learn how to *manage time* and *instructional resources*. Fostering an appreciation for theatre arts means structuring time for students with various skills and interests to explore personal paths of self-discovery and self-expression. It also means *allowing time* for children to develop critical and creative thinking skills and for analysis and reflection of production-centered activities. Some researchers (Johnson, Christie, & Yawkey, 1999) suggest that with *less than* 30 minutes, children do not have time in sociodramatic play to establish a story line, recruit role-players, assign roles, negotiate rules, or choose pretend props or construct new ones. If this process is interrupted numerous times, children stop trying. Teachers also need to consider opportunities for start-up, transition, and clean-up time. Time can be effectively addressed by strategically developing dramatic activities as a routine part of content-area instruction rather than an activity left to mornings or recess.

One of the easiest tactics to *support creativity* has to do, as mentioned, with time allotment and environmental design of theatre arts. Students need more than just time to perform their tasks. Older children should also have the benefit of time to create a good performance. Standards state that theatre arts should be considered both *process-centered* (children work through a *process* of creative drama) and/or *production-centered* (children participate in prewritten scenes, plays, and musicals). During the *process* of creating, children need "think" time, planning time, exploration time, and analysis and reflection time. Students are more encouraged to express themselves creatively if they know the expectations and have time to go through all of these processes. They are more motivated, their ideas are more developed, and their motivation more inspired when given time for development.

Teachers can also control creativity through offering open-ended or closed materials. **Open-ended (or flexible) materials** are those that encourage a wide range of ways in which to engage in role-play (Johnson, Christie, & Wardle, 2005). For example, a center supplied with water can become a sea for boats, a swimming pool for dolls, or a sink/float or measuring experimental lab. **Closed materials** can only represent one thing. For example, an airplane can only be an airplane, a truck only a truck. Both types of materials can be valuable, but teachers must consider what goal they have for children and think carefully about providing the types of materials appropriate for reaching that goal—but ideally providing open-ended materials more often.

Within the environmental framework, teachers must also consider children's development levels and their culture. Children are not likely to engage in dramatic play with toys or props that are *too abstract* for their reasoning level or that *are unknown* to them. Very young children (2–3 years) need more realistic props, while older children can be creatively involved with "low realism" props (Johnson, Christie, & Yawkey, 1999). In addition, these researchers remind us that ". . . the activity centers and thematic play materials found in middle-class-oriented schools or childcare centers are less familiar to lower-class children than they are to middle-class children. If young children are not familiar with objects, they tend to explore them initially, only later using them in imaginative play" (pp. 140–141). Appropriate *physical development* must be another consideration. When children do not have the skills to manipulate certain props or move in certain ways, they will not be inspired to explore and play. On the other hand, "children who are more advanced will be motivated by the intricacies of more details in play" (Nath & Cohen, 2003, pp. 81–82). To set the stage for experiences, it is important that teachers establish a positive, risk-free, encouraging learning environment; thus dramatic activities should provide diverse and culturally sensitive learning props and experiences for children who are in various cognitive and physical developmental levels. The environment should also accommodate multiple learning styles, and it should create an atmosphere for questioning, creative problem solving, and collaboration.

Teachers are responsible for providing a *safe learning environment* for their students—physically and emotionally. Physically, teachers should be certain that theatre arts activities are in spaces that allow for movement, for appropriate volume in voices, for comfort, and for physical safety. Safety cannot be assumed; teachers must actively inspect their sites often for potential hazards. Most dramatic activities require movement and louder voices, thus requiring a specified area in order to be safe and beneficial. Selected areas need to be assessed for both potential risks and possible disruptions. Considerations such as the nature of the activity, the number of students involved, furniture, props, media, location with regard to others, equipment, electrical outlets, storage, and the overall room design should not be overlooked when planning and structuring dramatic activities—both those that are teacher directed and those initiated by students.

Costumes and props should always be clean, and teachers should be aware of hygiene and safety issues. A teacher must be particularly vigilant when there are outbreaks of various types of communicable illnesses or other issues that can be spread through sharing of headwear, clothing, and other props. The same will be true of other toys, center materials, and games used in dramatic play. All of these should be sanitized often and checked for wear and tear (that could cause tripping, fall on top of children, or could be unsafe electrically).

Safety issues also include the young child's voice. The teacher must engage children in exercises that allow them to project their voices and use their voices in many ways without straining their young vocal chords. Students should have opportunities to practice using different volumes, tones, and inflections. These experiences allow children to learn appropriate and safe use of their voices. Poems can be used for choral speaking that provide safe practice for oral skills and improvement of speech habits.

Rules should be made and enforced for certain types of theatre arts activities, particularly centers, and the teacher must be ready to intervene to redirect hurtful physical or emotional behaviors. The purpose of much of the dramatic play during early childhood is to promote friendship, empathy, and perspective-taking among classmates, and the teacher is key to insuring a psychologically safe classroom. Young children often use dramatic play involving power. One rule should always be in effect—if any type of dramatic activity or play is physically or emotionally harmful to another, it has to change or stop. Again, there is a balance—too much teacher interference can undermine the children's problem-solving ability, but teachers must constantly monitor for excessive behaviors and situations that require teacher intervention.

Depending on the developmental stages of children and the activities planned, space requirements will vary. Young children often explore dramatic activities through center play. Yet they also need large open, carpeted spaces to participate in creative dramatics that involve coordination and large motor skills. Space should be allotted for both. Young children do well with space reminders (such as colored tape on the floor, centers divided by trunks, screens, or other furniture that cannot be knocked over). In addition, there should be space for individual, pair, and small group interactions. Whereas centers provide young children opportunities for creative and dramatic play, their space requirements may vary depending on the curriculum, current interests, and the needs of the children. Spaces that are too small for a group of children can cause them to become more aggressive, but too large of a space does not encourage interaction (Johnson, Christie, & Yawkey, 1999). When a center is not working, the teacher should first check the layout of the room. There should also be sufficient materials and props so children feel invited to work alone or in small groups. Centers also require easy-access storage space for materials that students may "unpack and pack," discover, sort, reorganize, or use for cleaning up. Theatre arts activities for older students have additional space requirements. As students begin to collaborate, design, plan, organize, construct, and analyze activities together, they need space and technology that will support their efforts. Additionally, there needs to be space available for explorations, performances, and productions.

Many teachers volunteer (or may be required) to put on theatre performances during the year for other grade levels or for parents. Dramatic performances in front of large audiences *can be* unsettling for some children and are not recommended by some specialists for very young children; however, many children who participate in theatre arts are eager to perform. If a presentation is undertaken, teachers must always meet the emotional and the physical safety needs of all children, and every effort should be made to create enjoyable theatrical experiences. This can be achieved with forethought and preparation. Designing a safe floor plan, for example, can prevent staging that is dangerous with many children moving about at once. Stage areas must be clearly marked with tape (fluorescent, if stage areas are to be darkened at times). Sets, backdrops, and risers should be checked for placement and stability and for ease and safety of movement around them by performers. Any special lighting, sound equipment, or electrical cords should be secured and taped down if applicable. Choreography and movement should be simply designed to eliminate unnecessary risks, and exits should remain clear. Ample rehearsal time should be scheduled in the actual performance area for children to feel comfortable with their roles and their stage area. Sufficient adult supervision should be in place during rehearsals and during the performance to help manage "the cast" so that the teacher/director does not become so frustrated with children that he or she resorts to anger and yelling. The idea is improvement of children's self-concept through drama—rather than to tear it down. In a performance, all members of the group should be able to participate in some way. Teachers should always ask parental permission for any performance that is outside the child's classroom. Some parents may be concerned for religious, personal, or other pertinent reasons and their wishes must be respected.

Children should also be instructed in good audience behavior. When children are attending a performance, part of safety is to be a considerate audience when many people are seated close together (particularly in a darkened area). When a class is attending a school or a formal presentation, teachers are obliged to arrive in plenty of time to seat their classes before the lights dim and the actors begin. Teachers should be careful not to arrive so early that children become restless prior to the beginning of the performance.

Teachers should address the following with students: (1) when they can and cannot leave their seats during a performance; (2) when they should remain silent so that performers do not have to strain their voices and so that others can hear; (3) when and how children should show their appreciation; (4) when and how they should return if an intermission is given; (5) if food or other objects are allowed in the seating area; (6) what a curtain call means, and other performance manners.

Many formal theatre performances for children have packets with excellent activities that teachers can use to orient their children prior to the performance and/or to engage students in activities afterwards. If a packet is not automatically sent, teachers should inquire if one is available. These may include discussions, drawing ideas, dances or songs to learn, reenactments for different endings, and so forth. Because reaction to the fine arts is also a personal experience, teachers are cautioned to avoid giving children the feeling that there is "a right or wrong" answer for many of these activities (McCaslin, 2006). If there are no prepared materials or they are inappropriate for one's class, teachers should prepare children for the experience and create developmentally appropriate activities so that the performance is more meaningful.

Let's try the following practice question:

Mrs. Hutchinson was a new teacher in an area of Houston in which the student population was about $\frac{1}{3}$ White, $\frac{1}{3}$ African American, and $\frac{1}{3}$ Asian. In accordance with her EC-4 teacher preparation, she immediately set up a Kitchen Center with cooking implements, dishes, silverware, pots and pans, etc., for her Pre-K class to encourage sociodramatic play. She noticed that many of her White and African American children were using the center very well for role-play, but her Asian children did not seem to be interested. Her *best* course of action would be to:

A. set up a more rigid schedule and monitor children to make sure that each child spends a definite amount of time there.
B. add implements such as chop sticks, a wok, and other kitchen tools often found in Asian kitchens.
C. change the center because students are obviously not motivated by it.
D. go into the center herself and invite the Asian children to role-play with her.

Requiring young children to be in a particular center (*A*) does not necessarily interest them or encourage role-play. A Kitchen Center is, most often, one of the most popular centers to include because children have a wealth of experiences that they can bring to role-play (*C*). Because it is a place to link the two most important environments of children (school and home), this center should not be removed. Teachers *are* encouraged to go into centers and help initiate, encourage, and/or extend play (*D*), but the *best* course of action to involve her Asian children would be to equip the center with implements that are found in their homes (*B*). Children are much more likely to initiate role-play when they are using culturally familiar items. Also, when there are less familiar items for children to use, researchers (Johnson, Christie, & Yawkey, 1999) suggest that teachers of culturally different children be especially cognizant to give them plenty of time to become familiar with materials that may not be familiar to them and create partnerships with parents to set up culturally appropriate play centers. Before assessing young children who are engaging with new items, these researchers suggest that children be given "a second chance to shine" (p. 145) in performing expressive behaviors. Their findings show that children often show considerable improvement when faced with a more familiar or similar item or situation again. The correct answer is *B*.

Bringing It All Together: How Do Teachers Plan for Activities That Address the Four Strands of the Theatre Arts TEKS?

Teachers can actively engage children in many forms of dramatic expression. Through appropriate materials and well-planned experiences (such as centers, puppetry, art, movement, creative dramatics, music, dramatic play, and a number of other ways), children can develop cognition, language, and social-ization. Using the four stands of the theatre arts TEKS as a base, teachers can address the objectives and state requirements through a variety of teaching strategies. The following are a few examples:

Perception

Poetry, construction, story comprehension, creative writing, music, move-ment, finger plays, and role-playing

Creative Expression/Performance

Story-telling, creative dramatics and writing, set-making, prop-making, pup-petry, music, movement, technical theatre, technology games, role-playing, costume design

Historic and Cultural Heritage

Re-creating, puppetry, creative dramatics, audience members

Response/Evaluation

Audience members, choosing music, critiquing renditions, creative movement, visual effects, listening and evaluating, set design, creating scripts and roles

Planning for the four theatre arts strands with a variety of teaching methods will work towards a long-term objective of integrating these into many other content areas of the classroom. Using a wheel format (see Figure 9.1) helps to il-lustrate flexibility in designing lessons and experiences for young children that can expose them to many aspects of a particular strand, or even several strands, through various actions, tasks, and opportunities. As you can see in the wheel, there are multiple behaviors that can be integrated with the various TEKS from other content areas.

The wheel begins in the center with the four strands as the foundation of a lesson plan or an experience and then expands to show some observable and measurable behaviors (verbs) in the second circle that exemplify each strand. The developmentally appropriate (DAP) experiences and materials circle (third circle) supports the multidimensional characteristic of each of the strands and illustrates various ways that teachers can address a strand in a large group, in a small group, or in centers. The outer edge of the wheel is a *sampling* of TEKS. The outer three circles are a small sample of the ways in which theatre arts can be integrated into the early childhood classroom.

How Can Theatre Arts Be Integrated into Other Content Areas?

Theatre arts has far-reaching influences in other areas of the curriculum—language arts, social studies, music, art, science, and even mathematics. One most often thinks of theatre arts in connection with language arts, but theatre

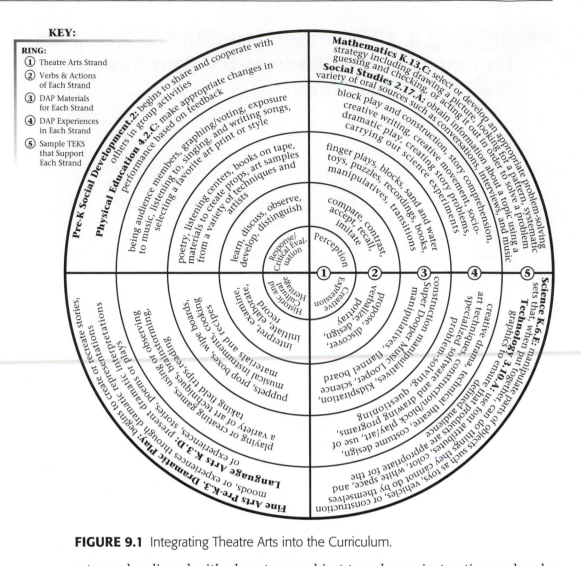

FIGURE 9.1 Integrating Theatre Arts into the Curriculum.

arts can be aligned with almost any subject to enhance instruction and make content more fun, more meaningful, and/or more concrete. Students engaging in movement, language, word problems, construction, and self-expression can simultaneously strengthen their skills in theatre arts and other content areas in exciting ways.

Through the use of a variety of settings (learning centers, small group lessons, and circle time), theatre arts can be comprehensively addressed in the curriculum. For example, while children are solving word problems in mathematics or engaged in scientific experiments, they may role-play and assign parts.

Furthermore, as young children listen to or create original poetry or stories or read literature they can use imagery, creative dramatics, and role-playing. Goldberg (2001) supports this issue by asking how a child's *acting out* of a story is different than simply reading it or listening to it. "When a child acts out a story she has read or heard, she has the opportunity to become the story—to internalize the characters, action, emotions. . . . I suggest that drama can be a fundamental tool that enables children to understand . . . by engaging with it" (p. 67).

Many theatre arts activities (such as choral reading) have considerable value in practicing oral language skills or second language learner skills in a "sheltered" manner and are suitable for any grade level (McCaslin, 2006). The natural tie of theatre arts to multicultural elements also helps bring children of many cultures together and helps them with the perspectives of others.

Through technology, children are also able to take on new characters in a game and direct the action. Using a variety of software, early childhood students can play with plot designs, character creating, and story telling and re-telling. For instance, children may use a simple PowerPoint with clip art characters to design a slide show of an original play. Students may also use Microsoft Publisher to create a mock newsletter for their original skit or characters. Children can video-tape their book reports as "newscasters," describing the plot of their books in "news terms," or they may role-play weather forecasters in a science class.

Other content-area experiences can rely heavily on theatre arts skills with role-play, imagery, plot and set design, use of props and visual elements, and story creating and telling. During social studies lessons, for example, children learn background knowledge and gain inspiration for their plots, props, and roles to play. Students can create and/or better understand the behaviors and symbols of certain heritages or cultures through portrayal of roles from different cultures or times. Children, given the knowledge for perspective-taking, realize their own connections to certain heritages or cultures or connect their own personal preferences for music, art, or literature with certain groups of people.

Most artistic experiences utilize some form of theatre arts. With music, for example, children can learn to use their creativity to visually express their rhythmical interpretations of certain pieces or match music to enhance a mood in dramatic readings or plays. As students artistically create dance movements, they use imagery, creativity, and evaluation. Students can also refine their artistic skills in prop-making, set-designing, and puppetry. In role-playing and creative dramatics, students can analyze and critique their skills, their likes and dislikes, and deepen their knowledge in many areas.

The Texas Professional Development and Appraisal System Alignment (PDAS) is the assessment document on which every teacher is evaluated. One will find a section for evaluation on teaching the fine arts for the required TAKS test (Texas Assessment of Knowledge and Skills). It can be found at www.cedfa.org/growing/PDAS_Elementary.pdf. This document is very helpful in showing alignment between other content areas and the theatre arts.

As teachers plan, there is a key approach to teaching theatre arts—that is to incorporate it naturally into other content areas in their lesson plans. Not only is it required, but it is good for children!

Let's look at another practice question:

Ms. Vasquez wants to introduce some words to her fourth-grade children in a vocabulary lesson. Which activity from the ones described below would be the *best*? She should:

A. write the words on the board and pronounce them, have children pronounce them with her, and then have students look them up in their classroom dictionaries and write down the definitions in their personal dictionaries.

B. use a puppet to "talk through" definitions.

C. explain the meanings and have students use the words in a short skit that they write and perform.

D. have children go to a center in which they can use a variety of materials to write the words.

The first activity (*A*) would be fairly boring to children. The teacher may want students to keep a personal dictionary, but Choice *A* would be an activity that should be used only *after* an introduction. Using a puppet as in Choice *B,* would not involve children being active learners. Although using a puppet may create some interest, it still uses a "telling voice," which would not increase the likelihood of children retaining the meaning. Choice *D* might be good for a spelling lesson, but it does not help with vocabulary development. Choice *C,* however, involves children in an activity that requires that they are actively constructing their own vocabulary meaning. This strategy is known as *Word Plays.* In this experience the teacher writes down a list of words (the number would depend on the grade level), pronounces them, and gives their meaning. Blachowicz and Fisher (2006) describe an example of this type of activity with first graders, after the teacher has told student teams to plan a drama using the words *quack, drip, mother,* and *hole.* Directions include having students describe a story, tell what kind of day it is, whom the story is about, what the problem is, and how it works out. Although each team came up with a different story to act out, one team presented the following drama:

Child 1: Once upon a time, there was a little duck who liked to play in the rain.

Child 2: He wanted to go outside on a rainy day, but his mother said, "You have to put on your boots."

Child 3: The little duck put on his boots and went outside to jump and play and quack all day. "Quack, quack, quack."

Child 4: The boots had a hole in them, but the little duck didn't know it.

Child 1: It was time to come in, because he heard his mother call, "Quack, quack, quack."

Child 2: The little duck came in with his boots. He didn't know that they had filled up with water, and they went drip, drip, drip all over the house.

Child 3: When his mother saw, she went, "Q-u-a-c-k! What is all that dripping all over my house. You are in trouble now!"

Child 4: Then she saw the hole, and the little duck helped her clean up all the drips. The mother hugged her little duck.

The correct answer is Choice C.

SUMMARY

Quite often, theatre arts activities are some of the most popular activities for children, parents, and teachers. Every principal knows that the way to entice parents to come to evening school meetings is for children to perform a musical or a play. Some people may not remember learning certain things in school, but most recall their performances in some type of dramatic activity during their school days. Linquist (1997) refers to these as "peak experiences that are remembered from a particular class activity or a performance and retold again and again" ("Remember when Ms. Guthery had the puppet theatre. . . ." or "When I was in school, we did this play in fourth grade and I was a . . ."). Perhaps this is one reason why Texas requires that teachers understand and implement the theatre arts TEKS throughout the early grades. Skilled teachers incorporate theatre arts in varied ways that contribute so much to children's growth and development. Many developmental areas, state objectives (TEKS), and life skills can be taught or enhanced through the use of theatre arts in the classroom.

GLOSSARY

Note: There are many terms in the theatre arts that, due to space constraints, could not be identified in the chapter. We have included some of these, however, to increase your terminology about theatre arts.

Aesthetic domain. The domain that focuses on the appreciation of the arts and sensory experiences.

Affective domain. The domain that focuses on valuing, self-awareness, self-esteem, and independence; this domain also covers appreciation, enjoyment, pleasure, etc., that are closely related to the arts; sometimes referred to as the "feelings" domain.

Centers. Areas for learning that contain open, closed, and child-centered materials offering choices to children (along with some structured activities) with regard to activity, materials, and/or approach.

Charades. Nonverbal acting; children in teams are asked to draw a card with a word or phrase; they can (1) indicate how many syllables the word has by a show of fingers, (2) show that the whole concept is being acted out by making a circle with hands, and/or (3) pull an ear to indicate that the word "sounds like" something else; one team member acts out the word or phrase while a timekeeper on the other side keeps time—the object being to have less overall guessing time than the other team.

Choral speaking. Children read or recite the same words together as one voice; can also be a call/echo as a "chorus" in answer to a single voice; provides a safe environment for shy children or children who do not speak English well.

Closed materials. Can only represent one thing during play (for example, an airplane can only be an airplane, a truck only a truck, etc.).

Cognitive domain. The domain that deals with different types of knowledge: logical-mathematical, social-conventional, scientific understanding, critical thinking skills, perception; often referred to as the "thinking" domain; related to Bloom's taxonomy (knowledge, comprehension, application, analysis, synthesis, and evaluation).

Collaborator/Co-player role. The teacher becomes an active "play partner" in sociodramatic play.

Construction. Curricular experiences that focus on creating meaningful representations of objects, events, or group of objects; students "construct" their own meanings rather than having the teacher "tell" them what the meaning is.

Creative drama experiences. Children are guided in improvisational stories or situations, writing their own plays, and integrated arts, such as creating costumes, puppets, masks, sets.

Creative dramatics. Spontaneous play that develops into assignment of roles and the design of a familiar plot to which children have been exposed through stories, poetry, and real life; allows for spontaneous interpretation and unique dialogue.

Creative expression. Children's verbal or nonverbal reaction or response to past experiences or imaginary experiences that can be observed through any variation of the arts, oral communication, or written communication.

Cultural heritage. Examining children within their community or home; or with family and in the neighborhood; or ethnicity with regard to their shared beliefs and traditions.

Developmentally appropriate. Material selection, lesson planning, activities, and interactions that align with children's developmental levels and focus on play, independence, and choices.

Drama-in-Education (DIE). Children are asked to become part of a dramatic moment (flight to the moon, a major archeological discovery, or other event in any content area) supported by resource materials, so they act and react accordingly in improvisation.

Dramatization. Presentation of a formally written play or skit with a memorized script; often includes props, backdrops, and costumes with assigned roles.

Dramatic play (also pretend play). Symbolic play for children in the age range of 2–7 years old; involves children using props, their imaginations, and role-playing to re-tell or represent real or make-believe scenarios; in schools, these are often encouraged by centers such as the water table with plastic manipulatives, Home Living Center, Pizzeria Center, Doctor's Clinic Center, and the Grocery Store Center, or in outside play areas, such as the sand box with construction vehicles. Unstructured play that expresses inner personal feelings and roles that depict imaginary or real-life experiences and personal stories.

Elements of theatre arts. Plot, theme, character, language, sound, and spectacle.

Improvisation. Students act "as they go along" without predetermined actions or a script.

Instructor role. The teacher provides information to children through words or activities designed towards a learning goal; the teacher directs sociodramatic play to teach content (for example the teacher might say, "Oh, no, Miss Baker! I see you only have one doughnut left, and there are two customers here. What can you do? Can you cut it in half? What is that called?") (This role must be done with care, as it *can* interrupt sociodramatic play, which teachers do not want to continuously do).

Language domain. The domain that focuses on listening skills, receptive language, expressive language, reading, writing, listening, and speaking.

Manipulatives. Concrete objects that allow children to problem solve or symbolize parts of a scenario.

Masks/Face Paint. Materials used in drama to enhance culture or symbolism; to allow an animal or thing to "come to life"; to classify an emotion or distinguish a particular character; and/or to "hide" the actor so he or she is more free and uninhibited when "becoming another."

Mock trial or meeting. A perspective-taking theatre arts activity in which children are assigned roles in terms of a court case (real or imaginary [for example, the trial of the wolf versus the three little pigs] or a meeting of some type (e.g., city council or school board).

Movement. Physical activities that help to develop fine- and gross-motor skills using locomotor skills, nonlocomotor skills, sensory awareness, eye-to-hand coordination, and a combination of any of those varied actions.

Open-ended (flexible) materials. Materials that offer a wide range of ways for children to engage with them during imaginative role-play (Johnson, Christie, & Wardle, 2005).

Pageant. Mini-skits that, when put together, show a series of events (e.g., the main events of the Texas Revolution, the Pilgrims leaving England and arriving in America, etc.).

Pantomime. Acting out ideas or characters with the body *only* (no words are spoken).

Perception. Opinions, viewpoints, or conceptions; the process by which people attach meaning to experiences.

Persona. A child is assigned an imaginary character, a real person, or a type of person (medieval knight, wagon train guide, etc.) who the child must research to become so familiar with

that the student can assume the *persona* of that person/character. Because there is no script, the child is required to ad-lib and answer questions as that person or character might do (or would have done), although children can also write their own script as the *persona* to perform.

Physical domain. The domain that deals with body awareness, fine-motor skills, gross-motor skills, health, safety, movement, and nutrition.

Play. A written work that has a script to be read or memorized and acted out; requires that actors follow the lines and directions written by the playwright.

Play leader. A co-player who tries to enrich and/or extend a sociodramatic play line.

Pretend play. Play that can include: make-believe; pretending with objects, art materials, construction materials, manipulatives, or props; thematic play, dramatic play, or sociodramatic play; story-telling, reenactment, or a story.

Process. Focusing on the way in which a child solves a problem or creates something instead of looking only at their final product or answer.

Prop boxes. A dramatic play kit in which materials and/or props are stored together. Most often these are on a theme of some type (children 3 years and under usually need more concrete or more realistic props; older children can more easily pretend with more abstract-looking props).

Puppetry/puppets. A teaching tool that can consist of a doll or other prop that has been created to represent a person, an animal, or an object and can be manipulated or transformed through the use of gestures, voices, or other actions.

Reaction story. Children listening to a story or event up to a certain point (not finishing it), then role-playing to show what they think should or did happen.

Readers Theatre. Children assume roles and read aloud the script of a certain story as they "act out" with their voices the parts of the story pertaining to their roles; interpretation is the aim rather than memorization.

Role-playing. A perspective-taking activity that allows children to analyze the thoughts, actions, behaviors, and dialogue of a character or player in a scenario or story; sophisticated role-play can involve the audience and role-takers in reenactments to question the soundness and/or preference of decisions and why, the feelings of all players, and possible improvements.

Scripted dramas. Structured events in which roles are assigned (historical or pretend); unison movements to poems or songs.

Shadow puppetry. A 2,000-year-old technique originating in the Far East and India in which a drama is presented using cut-out forms behind a screen with a backlight to cast shadows of the characters (most often mounted on and manipulated with sticks) and, sometimes including set design elements.

Simulations. A dramatic enactment of a particular situation in which students decide roles and make decisions (e.g., students may be divided into teams and tasked with simulating the building of the coast-to-coast railroad. They decide roles and decide how their teams will go about the task [i.e., should they build from each coast and meet, start in the middle and go out, etc.]. Then they are given popsicle sticks and reenact the building, with the team taking the least amount of time declared the winner).

Social domain. The domain that deals with social studies, social skills, and socialization.

Sociodramatic play. A type of dramatic play in which two or more children are involved and in which they communicate about the organization of their play, assign roles for play, and act out those created scenarios.

Story telling. Children create new endings, new characters, or completely new stories and share them either by dictating to a teacher (can be audio or video recorded or written down), drawing a picture, or recording them on paper.

Story re-telling. Children orally or dramatically share the sequence of events from a story or event.

Strands of Theatre Arts TEKS. (1) perception, (2) creative expression/performance, (3) historical and cultural heritage, and (4) critical evaluation experiences that teachers are required to provide in Texas classrooms.

Structured drama. Activities that require student participation in preset ways, usually with scripted dramas such as plays and skits in which roles are assigned or with unison movements to poems, songs, and chants.

Theatre in Education (TIE). A theatre genre that expects children to enter a situation where they are asked to "act out" decisions or solve problems in order to change attitudes or behaviors, stimulate intellectual curiosity, or motivate further interest in a topic or issue (McCaslin, 2006).

Thematic-fantasy play. After reading a book to children, they are questioned about the story, then props are used to construct a scene and children enact and re-enact the story.

REFERENCES

Blachowicz, C., & Fisher, P. (2006). *Using vocabulary in all classrooms* (3rd ed.). Upper Saddle River, NJ: Pearson.

Chapter 117, Texas Essential Knowledge and Skills for Fine Arts. Retrieved on February 20, 2006, from http://www. tea. state. tx. us/ teks/ 117toc. htm

Driscoll, A., & Nagel, N. (2005). *Early childhood education birth–8: The world of children, families, & educators.* Boston: Allyn & Bacon.

Goldberg, M. (2001). *Arts and learning* (2nd ed.). New York: Longman.

Johnson, J., Christie, J., & Wardle, F. (2005). *Play, development, and early education.* Boston: Pearson.

Johnson, J., Christie, J., & Yawkey, T. (1999). *Play and early childhood development.* New York: Longman.

Lallier, K., & Marino, N. (1997). *The persona book.* Englewood, CO: Teacher Ideas Press.

Laughlin, M., Black, P., & Loberg, M. (1991). *Social studies readers theatre for children.* Englewood, CO: Teacher Ideas Press.

Linquist, T. (1997). *Ways that work: Putting social studies standards into practice.* Portsmouth, NH: Heinemann.

McCaslin, N. (2006). *Creative drama in the classroom and beyond* (8th ed.). Boston: Pearson/Allyn & Bacon.

Nath, J.L., & Cohen, M.D. (Eds.) (2003). *Becoming an EC-4 teacher in Texas: A course of study for the Pedagogy and Professional Roles (PPR) TExES.* Belmont, CA: Thomson/Wadsworth.

PDAS: The Professional Development and Appraisal System and fine arts teachers. Revised 2002: Aligned with the Texas Assessment of Knowledge of Skills objectives. Retrieved on February 20, 2006, from http:// /www. cedfa. org/ growing/ PDAS_Elementary. pdf

Wisniewski , D., & Wisniewski , D. (1997). *Worlds of shadow: Teaching with shadow puppetry.* Englewood, CO: Teacher Ideas Press.

Wortham, S. (2006). *Early childhood curriculum: Developmental bases for learning and teaching* (4th ed.). Upper Saddle River, NJ: Pearson.

A THEATRE ARTS LESSON PLAN

Where the Wild Things Are

Grade Level: Kindergarten

Main Subject Area: Theatre Arts

Integrated Subjects: Language Arts, Music, and Art

Time Frame/Constraints: 2 or 3 days

Overall Goal(s): To guide children's understanding of reality versus fantasy; to assist children with recalling and summarizing the plot; to support children's understanding of emotions through the fine arts; to increase children's creativity in art and movement.

TEKS/TAKS OBJECTIVES:

§ 117.4. **Theatre Arts** (2) Creative expression/performance. The student interprets characters, using the voice and body expressively, and creates dramatizations. The student is expected to (D) participate in dramatic play;

§ 110.2. **Language Arts** (9) Reading/comprehension. The student uses a variety of strategies to comprehend selections read aloud. The student is expected to (C) retell or act out the order of the important events in stories; (11) Reading/text structures/literary concepts. The student recognizes characteristics of various types of texts. The student is expected to (C) distinguish fiction from nonfiction, including fact and fantasy;

§ 117.2. **Art** (2) Creative expression/performance. The student expresses ideas through original artworks, using a variety of media with appropriate skill. The student is expected to (D) develop manipulative skills when drawing, painting, printmaking, and constructing artworks, using a variety of materials;

§ 117.3. **Music** (4) Response/evaluation. The student responds to and evaluates music and musical performance. The student is expected to:

(B) identify higher/lower, louder/softer, faster/slower, and same/different in musical performances.

Objectives:

Individually: Each student will draw a picture of his or her bedroom.

Large group: The whole class will participate in a choral reading poem.

- The whole class, in a circle, will participate orally in an imagination process and make predictions about the book, *Where the Wild Things Are.*
- The whole class will listen to the teacher read *Where the Wild Things Are.*
- The whole class will participate in classifying real versus pretend/make believe/fantasy from the book and from real life on a chart.
- The whole class will participate in pretending to "put on emotions" and use sounds and their bodies to distinguish between emotions.

In Centers:

- Children will make "Wild Thing" puppets.
- Children will correctly select various musical background pieces to match various parts of the story.
- Children will select a correctly retold version of the story from three versions.
- Children will participate in a correct reenactment of the story in the Puppet Center.
- In cooperative groups, children will correctly draw an assigned part of the story. As a small group they will present their drawing to an audience and summarize the story.
- Students will participate as good audience members.

Sponge Activity: On a piece of paper, children will draw their own bedroom. Ask children to save it for later.

Environmental Concerns: Children need to be in a circle on the carpet. Make sure the area is clear and students are called to the floor as individuals or in small groups. Check each center after rotations to be sure materials/equipment are ready.

Rationale: Teacher: Sometimes we don't feel like ourselves. There are many emotions we experience. Knowing how emotions can affect us can help us to understand our true selves and others better. Sometimes make believe or fantasy can help us describe our feelings to others so they can understand us better. Have you ever felt like you were "grouchy as a crab or grumpy as an old bear" and wanted to "snap your claws" or "growl at someone" because you weren't feeling good? That is what we will talk about today.

Transition: As students are coming to the gathering area or carpet, the teacher can use the adapted focus song "Wolf Party" as a chant that introduces the lesson. It can be used as a transition to pretend play.

Focus or Set Induction: Have children think about the title of the poem and share what they think might happen at a party for wolves. Have children chant with the teacher as she reads the following poem. Afterwards, discuss how the wolves were feeling at the party. Ask how they expressed their feelings. Ask if children have ever felt like this at a party or another time when they wanted to participate with older children or adults. How did they express themselves?

Adapted from: **Wolf Party***

Original song and lyrics by Nancy Schimmel; music by Candy Forest.

Teacher: I wanna go to a party and howl at the moon

'Cause howlin' is really hip.

I wanna learn to howl like the big kids howl,

But all I can do is "yip."

ALL TOGETHER: I wanna go ah-oooo, ah-ooooo . . . !

Teacher: I hear my mommy and my daddy sing

And it sounds so long and cool.

I throw back my head and land flat on my back

And you know I feel like a fool.

ALL TOGETHER: I wanna go ah-oooo, ah-oooo . . . !

Teacher: Well, I went to a party with all of my friends

And we sang 'till the break of day.

I fell on my back, but everyone did

And that made me feel okay.

ALL TOGETHER: Now I can go ah-oooo, ah-oooo . . . !

Teacher: If you want to howl, just take a deep breath,

Close your eyes and throw your head back,

You don't need a moon, don't need to stay on tune.

You can howl like one of the pack.

ALL TOGETHER: Yeah, you can go ah-oooo, ah-oooo . . . !

* You can listen and download "Wolf Party" at www.songsforteaching.com

MAKING CONNECTIONS:

The following are questions the teacher can use to help students make connections.

1. **Connections to Past or Future Learning:** Remember when we talked about our last book and "retelling a story" so that if we wanted to describe a book we've read to someone else, they could clearly understand what it was about? We are going to use some of those same skills today. Remember that we talked about "how we wouldn't tell EVERY detail," but we would tell about the main actions that happened in order.

2. **Connections to Community:** Do you know anyone in Houston that "retells" stories as part of his or her job? (Show a short clip of news stories about kids from local channels and explain that they are retelling stories/ summarizing)

3. **Cultural Connections:** This story for today was written by a man from England (show on globe) who remembered how he felt when he was a child. Do you think that children all over the world have many of the same feelings? Do you think that you have the same kinds of feelings as other children in our school? In our class? What make you think so?

4. **Connections to Student Interests & Experiences:** (After the story is read use these prompts). This book was a make-believe view of how a little boy deals with his emotions. In real life, how do we feel when we want to be a little naughty? How do we feel in real life when we are disciplined? How do we feel when we still know that we are loved?

Materials:

Poem: "Wolf Party"

Book: *Where the Wild Things Are*

Short, taped newscast on a topic that is appropriate for young children

Globe

Clip art or drawings of people or animals that express feelings or are related to emotions ("ox suit" for "frustrated with a burden," "bull head" snorting with anger, "bouncing bunny" [excited], "timid mouse" "wasp" etc.)

Drawing paper

Brown paper bags and a variety of art materials (for "Wild Thing" puppets)

Pre-recorded music

Three taped versions of the story

Paper bag with pictures and labels of emotions

"Wild Thing" puppets

Activities: Guided Practice.

1. Ask children to close their eyes and imagine or pretend that they could go *any* place they wanted. Have them share where that might be (some may share real places and others make believe places). Ask children if their places are real or make believe. Share yours. Ask children to tell you what it means to imagine and pretend. Ask them from where they think their ideas for imagining and pretending come. Show them the cover of the book, *Where the Wild Things Are,* and ask what they think the book might be about and if they think it will be real or pretend and why. Ask children to close their eyes again and imagine what they think the wild things are going to be (*big/small, nice/scary*) and what kinds of noises they might make, if any. Have children listen as you read the book and have them silently compare how their own wild things matched those in the book.

2. On a white board, make a T-chart that has one side for "real" and one side for "pretend/make-believe." Ask children to classify parts of the story (for example, trees grew in Max's bedroom, Max got in a boat, Max was wearing a wolf suit, Max's mother was angry, Max's mother brought him dinner, etc.). Ask children to classify some real life experiences (cartoon shows, pretend games vs. real events, etc.).

3. Talk about reasons behind Max's actions. Ask: Why he might be behaving in this way? Why do you think the author said, "Max put his wolf suit on"? Do you have a suit you put on sometimes? What kind of suit do you put on when you are (a) frustrated, (b) mad, (c) silly, (d) excited, (e) sad, and (f) happy? Let's all pretend we are putting on our frustrated suits. My frustrated suit is an ox suit (show picture), and I feel like I'm pulling against a heavy load. Demonstrate facial expressions and sounds in an ox suit. Ask if any child would like to show "his or her" actions. Have everyone act out their frustration suits. Continue with their *mad, silly, excited, sad, irritated,* and *happy* suits and actions. Have some examples ready (silly monkey suit, irritated crab suit, etc.).

4. Centers

Center 1: <u>Art Center:</u> Supply brown lunch sacks and a variety of open-ended materials so that students can create their own "Wild Thing" puppets.

Center 2: <u>Music Center:</u> Pre-record several types of music and have numbered picture cards of the main parts of the story. Have children match each musical selection to parts of the story. Be sure to have a protected tape or CD with voice saying, "Selection 1, 2, etc." Have children tell why they matched each section using music description (soft/loud, fast/slow, high/low). For example, "He was going to his bed, so I thought the music should be soft there."

Center 3: <u>Listening Center:</u> Tape three versions of the story—(1) a version with too many details so the plot gets lost; (2) a version out of order; and (3) the real version. Have children listen and tell each other which was the best version and why.

Center 4: <u>Emotions Center:</u> Have each student pick out an emotion (with a picture) out of a box. Have each student draw himself or herself in an "emotions suit" (as teacher showed earlier).

Center 5: <u>Puppet Center:</u> Have students use puppets to re-enact the story.

Independent Practice: In groups of 4, have children number off (1–4). Child #1 will draw the scene he/she remembers from the beginning of the story. Child #2 will draw a scene that he or she remembers from the first part of the "travels" in the story. Child #3 will draw from the second part of the "travels," and Child #4 will draw a scene from the ending. Each group will then discuss how they want to show their pictures in order and what they should say. Remind each child about voice projection and being a good audience member. Each group will then present to the class. Ask each group to explain which pictures show something real that Max did and which show something make believe.

Assessment: Centers: (1) <u>Completion:</u> Did each child complete a puppet? (2) <u>Checklist for music:</u> Was each child able to recognize music that matched emotions from the story? Was he or she able to explain the match (fast/slow sounds, etc.)? (3) <u>Reading Comprehension Checklist:</u> Did each child select the correct version of the story and explain why? (4)

<u>Satisfactory/Unsatisfactory:</u> Did each child draw a reasonable emotion suit for the emotion that he or she drew out of the bag? (5) <u>Participation:</u> Did each child participate?

Independent Practice:

Group presentation: Was the story in order and the summary correct? Did each child speak clearly? Did each child participate as a good audience member?

Individual drawing: Did each child complete a drawing? Did the drawing show a good representation of the part of the story assigned?

What Will Students Do Who Finish Early?

Ask students to redraw their bedroom when on an "emotional journey" or put pictures that students drew in order so that you can post them on the wall.

Closure: Ask each child to recall their favorite part of the story. Ask children to explain the difference between their bedrooms and Max's bedroom.

Modification for Students with Special Needs:

Shon (with hearing difficulties) will need to be seated close to the teacher when the story is read and when groups are presenting. Charlene, who has difficulty holding a pencil, will use large markers or an assistance grip/roll.

Reflection: To be addressed after teaching the lesson.

DRAFT YOUR OWN THEATRE ARTS LESSON PLAN

Title of Lesson: _____

Grade Level: _____

Main Subject Area: _____

Integrated Subjects: _____

Time Frame/Constraints: _____

Overall Goal(s): _____

TEKS/TAKS Objectives: _____

_____

_____

Sponge Activity: _____

_____

_____

Environmental Concerns: _____

_____

_____

Rationale(s): _____

_____

_____

Focus or Set Induction: _____

_____

_____

Making Connections: _____

_____

_____

1. Connections to Past or Future Learning: _____

_____

2. Connections to Community: _____

_____

3. Cultural Connections: _____

_____

4. Connections to Student Interests & Experiences: _____

_____

Materials: _____

_____

_____

Activities: Guided practice: _____

_____

_____

_____

_____

_____

Independent practice: _____

_____

_____

_____

_____

Assessment: _____

_____

What Will Students Do Who Finish Early? _____

_____

Closure: _____

_____

Modification for Students with Special Needs: _____

_____

Reflection: _____

_____

OBSERVING THEATRE ARTS EXPERIENCES/ACTIVITIES

During your visit to an early childhood classroom, use the following form to provide feedback as well as to reflectively analyze the room, the materials, and the teacher.

Environment	Observed	Not Observed	Response
1. Ample space allows children and adults to move around freely.			If not, what could be changed?
2. Dramatic play and/or prop play area are accessible to children for a portion of the day.			If so, for how much time?
3. Free play occurs for a portion of the day.			Is the time sufficient? Explain why or why not.
4. Peer interaction is encouraged through a variety of centers and small group activities.			If so, how? If not, in what ways could the teacher encourage this?
5. Dramatic play materials and/or props are displayed and stored at the child's level in many places throughout the room.			If not, what could be changed?
6. Centers offer opportunities for dramatic or prop play in various content areas.			If so, describe. If not, what changes could be made?
7. Puppets and/or props are used to stimulate skills on different levels.			If so, what skills do you see being developed? If not, what could be changed?
8. When children initiate dramatic or sociodramatic play in any center, they are encouraged and supported on different levels.			If so, what are the teacher's actions or responses? If not, what opportunities were missed?
9. When children are onlookers, they are helped to become involved in specific activities with a specific role.			If so, by whom (their peers or the teacher)? If not, what could the teacher do?
10. Children can be seen utilizing role-playing, sociodramatic play, audience behavior and/or prop-making in several areas of the classroom throughout the day.			If so, give an example from another experience. If not, what would you change?
11. Children are allowed to be in control of their learning, their experiences, and their interactions.			If so, what is the effect? If not, how could this change?
12. Alternatives are provided for students who are not comfortable engaging in active participation of theatre arts.			If so, list the alternatives. If not, what could be added?
13. Theatre arts is integrated during whole group time in a developmentally appropriate way.			If so, describe. If not, give ideas for what could be added in a developmentally appropriate way.

	Observed	Not Observed	Response
14. Theatre arts is integrated during circle time in a developmentally appropriate way.			If so, describe. If not, give ideas for what could be added in a developmentally appropriate way.
15. Theatre arts is integrated during independent small group time in a developmentally appropriate way.			If so, describe. If not, give ideas for what could be added in a developmentally appropriate way.
16. Theatre arts is integrated during teacher-led small group time in a developmentally appropriate way.			If so, describe. If not, give ideas for what could be added in a developmentally appropriate way.
17. Children are comfortable creating roles and actions for play without prompting.			If so, when and how did you see them doing this? If not, why do you think that is?
18. Children are using imaginative play in a variety of times throughout their day.			If observed, describe some of these times. If not, describe how this could be added.
19. Children are using imaginative play in a variety of places in the room.			If observed, describe some examples of where. If not, suggest some areas.
20. he room has at least 4 or 5 different play centers set up to which children have access at some point.			If so, list them. If not, suggest some that could be developed.
21. Theatre arts is integrated in a variety of centers.			If so, describe one observation of this and include the center in which you saw it. If not, in which centers could integration take place and how?
22. Children are allowed age-appropriate independence in the centers to elicit creative expression.			If so, describe. If not, how could this change?
23. A wide variety of developmentally appropriate materials are accessible to children in several centers that would support theatre arts.			If so, list a few and include in which center they are located. If not, what materials could be added?
24. Many age-appropriate pretend play materials are accessible (e.g., props, blocks, manipula-tives, puppets, vehicles, character clothes, books, audio/visual materials) in many different centers.			If so, list what you observe. If not, list what could be added.
25. Teachers play an active role during center time, asking questions, facilitating play, and encouraging active participation and a variety of responses.			If so, list some of the questions you heard the teacher ask that qualify as higher-order thinking or creative thinking cues. If not, what opportunities were missed?
26. Students are comfortable and are responsive to the teacher's questions and cues throughout their play and group experiences.			What does the teacher do (or not do) to create a comfort level?

	Observed	Not Observed	Response
27. The schedule provides a balance of active and sedentary types of play.			If so, list what types of play you see. If not, how could this be changed?
28. A variety of theatre arts activities occur daily.			If so, list what activities you see. If not, list what could be added.
29. During a variety of times throughout the day the teacher engages as an active participant in play.			If so, discuss an example you observed. If not, what could the teacher have changed about his or her role?
30. Children's responses and interpretations are accepted.			If so, describe some of the responses from the teacher. If not, give the reactions of the children.

TEST YOURSELF ON THEATRE ARTS

1. Mrs. Lasner wants to integrate a lesson with mathematics, reading, and theatre arts. What activity from the following would allow her to do this in the most effective manner?
   A. Students dramatize a story they have read using shadow puppets they create from basic shapes.
   B. Students act out a story that Mrs. Lasner wrote and read to them about different shapes.
   C. Mrs. Lasner has students go on a walk to see what kinds of shapes they can find in the real world around them and then re-enact their walk.
   D. Mrs. Lasner has students rotate through three centers—one where students work with shapes, one where they read a story, and one where they participate in a short dramatic activity.

2. What activity below would offer Mrs. Glenn's fourth-grade class the *best* option for higher-level thinking about famous scientists?
   A. Researching on the Internet and writing a research paragraph about a famous scientist
   B. Creating a poster about a famous scientist to celebrate a week of "Famous Scientists"
   C. Participating as a character in a play about several famous scientists
   D. Participating in *persona taking* about several famous scientists

3. Ms. Quan conducts the following activity in her fourth-grade social studies class:

   Ms. Quan has children volunteer to take part in a reading. They read *Susanna of the Alamo: A True Story* aloud and write a script using the dialogue from the book (for example, they might start with Santa Anna's speech to the wives of those killed at the Alamo). The characters (*Santa Anna, Susanna,* and *Sam Houston* plus a *narrator*) read their scripts to the class, using their voices to convince the audience of their characters' pain, anger, sadness, and other emotions (Laughlin, Black, & Loberg, 1991).

   What type of activity does this describe?
   A. Role-play
   B. Readers Theatre
   C. Pantomime
   D. Reaction story

4. Mrs. Johnston asked her fourth-grade class during social studies time to get their "city council hats" on because she wanted their help in designing an evacuation plan that would work in case another strong hurricane threatened the Texas coast. Dramatizing a *mock meeting* has children working at what level of thinking?
   A. Analysis
   B. Evaluation
   C. Comprehension
   D. Application

5. Because of the varied theatrical activities Ms. Espinosa has been known to incorporate in her classroom, she has been put in charge of her school's theatre arts curriculum. She attributes her success to understanding and applying general skills she learned by reading the state's *EC-12 Theatre Standards.* In planning the school's curriculum, which of the following are the *most* important factors for Ms. Espinosa to consider?
   A. Age, developmental levels, prior experiences, and interests of students
   B. The lack of resources and expenses that would be incurred
   C. Students' ability to read and memorize their parts
   D. The availability of volunteers who can assist with the productions

6. Creating centers is one way of incorporating dramatic play activities into the curriculum. Which statement *best* illustrates an appropriate integration of theatre arts in an early childhood classroom during centers?
   A. Children receive rewards to go to centers for "free play" once their work has been completed.
   B. Children go to centers to work on assigned group projects.
   C. Individuals or small groups select their centers at structured times for dramatic play around themes, people, or situations.
   D. Individuals are given materials to make puppets that communicate their feelings at any given point in time.

7. Mrs. Ritika furnishes her interdisciplinary young childhood centers for dramatic play with materials that are termed "open-ended materials." Which of the following is *not* considered an open-ended type of material?
   A. Sand
   B. Water
   C. Clay
   D. Miniature airplanes

8. Mr. Carpenter's fourth-grade students have just completed reading an age-appropriate biography of Stephen F. Austin. Students are now given the option to either retell a favorite story from the biography as if they were the notable character in the story or to retell the story from the perspective of another character. Which of the following is *not* a true statement?
   A. Assuming the role of a notable character in order to retell a story in a biography encourages creative expression and reflection in a historical context.
   B. Listening and evaluating stories/events from multiple perspectives increase students' sensitivity to emotions and problems others have faced throughout the human experience.
   C. Role-playing activities are more appropriately integrated into the curriculum at lower grade levels.
   D. Retelling stories from another character's perspective elicits both critical and creative thinking.

9. At recess, Ms. Hart observes her preschoolers imitating animals they saw during a recent visit to the zoo. She decided to let them play a little longer. Which statement *best* supports her decision to let the play time continue a bit longer?
   A. The activity was helping students to express and develop their perceptions about other living creatures.
   B. The students were motivated and having fun remembering their experiences.
   C. The physical movement allowed them an emotional release of their feelings.
   D. She wanted to assess her students during group play.

10. Ms. Beal volunteers once a week in her son's first-grade classroom to read limited action stories to small groups of children. As she reads, the children are encouraged to act out parts of the story line. The *most* important aspect of this activity is that it:
    A. creates an awareness of individual learning styles.
    B. accommodates young children's short attention span.
    C. provides memory experience by imitating and creating actions and sounds.
    D. strengthens parent volunteerism in the school.

TEST YOURSELF ANSWERS AND RATIONALES FOR THEATRE ARTS

Answer 1: Choice *B* is appropriate—but perhaps not the *best.* The integration of all three topics is present, but children are not involved with much mathematics unless they help construct shapes for the play. Choice *C* is a good activity for mathematics, but the reading component is not there (only listening), and the drama component would not be very valuable. Choice *D* does not involve any *true* integration between the three content areas—they are all separated. Choice *A*, however, is a very thorough integration. First, children read a story. They then construct shadow puppets using basic shapes (for example, a duck can be constructed of two circles [the head and body], a square [the neck], two small rectangles [the legs], and three triangles [the tail and two feet]). They cut out the characters and tape a large flex straw to the form with a toilet tissue roll taped to the bottom of the straw as a handle. To help recall the characters and the sequence of the story, children then reenact the story using the shadow puppets behind a screen with a backlight. Children are actively involved in all three content areas. Shadow puppetry is a very popular activity with children because construction time can be short, there is a low cost for construction, there is less mess, fewer art skills are required, rehearsal is less tiring and time-consuming, there is a greater range of visual effects (and children are not as critical as they can be of 3-D effects because of their sophistication with special effects of movies and video games) (Wisniewski & Wisniewski, 1997). The correct answer is *A.*

Answer 2: Choice *A* does not really involve higher-level thinking—it is simply reorganizing and repeating what the child has read. Choice *B* is similar, although there is some small amount of synthesis-level creativity in the presentation and more integration of content areas. Choice *C* adds interest, but the student is basically only repeating lines that have already been written—rather than thinking and creating. Choice *D*, however, requires that the student research a famous person and be so familiar with his or her life, the times, actions, inventions, contributions, ideas, and personality, etc., that the student can act like and answer as that famous scientist. This requires a great deal of higher-level thought (Grimes & Marino, 1997). The answer is *D*.

Answer 3: Choice *A* involves having students take on a particular role and *ad-lib* rather than to read from a script. Choice *C*, *Pantomime*, uses actions and body movement only to indicate characters, types of characters, or events. No voice is used. Choice *D*, a *Reaction Story* or an unfinished story, has children listening to a story or event up to a certain point, then role-playing to show what they think should or did happen. Choice *B*, *Readers Theatre*, is described in this vignette. The answer is *B*.

Answer 4: Bloom's taxonomy progresses from the lower levels of thinking (knowledge, comprehension, and application) to the higher levels (analysis, synthesis, and evaluation) [a good way to help you remember the order is the silly saying, "Know children and always share everything"]. This activity reaches into the evaluative level of thinking (*B*). Children, playing the roles of members of a town council, would first analyze what did (and didn't) work for Houston and New Orleans during the mass evacuations, they would create new plans (*synthesis*), and finally would evaluate the new and old plans. The answer is *B*.

Answer 5: Ms. Espinosa's principal knows that theatre arts are a required part of the Texas curriculum (the TEKS); therefore, appointing a faculty member to be in charge of a theatre arts curriculum helps insure that they will be taught. Ms. Espinosa knows that, most likely, there will always be a shortage of officially funded resources for this area (*B*), so part of her job will be to ask teachers to be creative in obtaining resources for their children. She also knows that children will have different levels of reading and memorization abilities (*C*), so part of her position will be to ask teachers to find resources to address this so that all children in the school can be included. Volunteers are not automatically needed for each dramatic experience (*D*),

but it is definitely a plus for larger productions. Therefore, all of these choices are somewhat correct. However, the question asks for the *most* important factor. Choice *A* brings the most important factors to the forefront—children's ages, developmental levels, connections with prior experiences, and interests. These are the areas that *all* content areas need to consider *first and foremost* when developing any curriculum. The correct answer is *A*.

Answer 6: Choice *A* means that some children, more than likely, would seldom get to go to a center, as some rarely finish their work early. Assignment of a group project (*B*) takes away from the main rationale for dramatic play—that is, child empowerment—as *children* need to control the role taking. Choice *D* does not indicate an integration of activities—it only focuses on psychosocial development (with a concentration on emotions). By providing a structured time, the teacher ensures that all children will have opportunities to participate in a number of integrated themes (home, post office, restaurant, etc.) upon which a variety of content areas can be touched. In later elementary classrooms, a teacher may want to have children rotate through centers so that all students will participate in the activities at some point (in addition to having free choice); however, we are specifically looking at a young childhood class in this question. The correct answer is *C*.

Answer 7: Open-ended materials refer to those types of materials that offer a wide range of ways to engage in role-play with them (Johnson, Christie, & Wardle, 2005). For example, a center furnished with sand can become a dump ground for trucks, a mountain range, a bakery center for "mud pies," and so forth. Choices *A*, *B*, and *C* are all open materials, as is most Montessori equipment. Choice *D*, miniature airplanes, can only represent one thing—miniature airplanes and cannot be used to represent anything else. This is true of other toys such as trucks, spaceships, jigsaw puzzles (with only one final fit), and other similar materials. Teachers need to provide children with both types of materials—but with more opportunities for open-ended materials. Teachers should understand the different functions and values of both types of materials clearly. The answer is *D*.

Answer 8: Choices *A*, *B*, and *D* are all true statements for these activities. Remember that we are looking for a statement that is *false.* Choice *C* says that theatre arts is not really as effective for older elementary children, and that is certainly *not* true. Role-playing may be appropriately integrated throughout the EC-4 program. The correct answer is *C.*

Answer 9: One part of the curriculum for young children is to focus upon animals. This type of dramatic play always seems to be a motivating way for them to learn, so *B* is true—although not the *best* support for continuation of play. Choice *C* involves *emotional* release, which is not really a part of this activity (although, if the question would have spoken to the *physical release of energy,* it would have been true). Choice *D* could be an opportunity to gain assessment, as she watches for children's development in this area; however, again it is not the *best* choice. Choice *A, imitation,* allows children to refine what they have observed at the zoo and to develop a deeper knowledge and perception about animals. Allowing for more time encourages children to reflect more thoroughly and illustrate in more detail what it is that they understand about animals from their experiences at the zoo. This is the *best* choice for allowing students to continue. The correct answer is *A.*

Answer 10: Choice *A,* a focus on learning styles, is important. Children are getting an additional aspect to their *bodily-kinesthetic* awareness as they act and move. Choice *B* is also an important feature, because every teacher knows that she or he can hold young children's attention longer when listening is broken up by movement. Choice *D* is important as well, because bringing parents into the school community strengthens children's learning. However, the *most* important reason to have them act out parts is that this use of a dramatic activity can help children recall parts of the story by making it memorable through action. The correct answer is *C.*

10 Teaching English as a Second Language (ESL) in Texas

William J. Kortz, Jr.
University of Houston–Downtown

Janice L. Nath
University of Houston–Downtown

Many classrooms in Texas no longer look the way they did twenty years ago, when most children spoke English as their first language. Now, nearly *every* school in Texas has children for whom English is their *second* language, and they come to our Texas classrooms with the added burden of not only having to learn the vocabulary and sentence structure of a new language but also the content curriculum required by Texas (the TEKS [Texas Essential Knowledge and Skills]). To meet the needs of these children, many school districts throughout the state require that teachers have ESL (English as a Second Language) certification prior to being hired or to become certified in ESL as soon as possible after they begin their employment. This chapter discusses how to study for and obtain your ESL supplemental certification.

About Texas ESL Certification

Currently, there are two ways to obtain a Texas ESL certification by testing. One is by taking the lower grade level (EC-4) Generalist/ESL TExES test (#104) (which is a combination of content area and supplemental ESL test items). For those who have already completed their teaching certification in Texas, only the EC-12 ESL supplemental certification test (#154) is needed. The state can change its requirements, so be sure to check their Web site (www.sbec.state.tx.us) for the most current information.

ESL instruction is built upon state and national standards that entail knowledge and classroom applications considered to be best practices for teachers who have students for whom English is not their first language. For these classrooms, there is a growing body of knowledge that teachers should know and skills that they should possess. **Texas ESL standards** for teachers include *seven* areas to be learned and tested: (1) prerequisite understanding of English language concepts and acquisition of English, (2) methodologies, (3) oral communication, (4) literacy skills and assessment, (5) ESL foundations, (6) multicultural and multilingual perceptions, and (7) third-party awareness for a comprehensive overview of ESL instruction. As you study this chapter, you should complete a learning cycle of connecting the standards, domains, and competencies (what a teacher should know and be able to do) to the pedagogical vocabulary, strategies, methodologies, and various assessments that a teacher will apply in the ESL field. To gain a good grasp of these areas, you will hopefully read each standard, study the competency list that helps to define each one, and complete the practice questions located throughout this chapter and in the State Board for Educator Certification (SBEC) Preparation Manual #104 that can be downloaded from the Web at http://www.texes.ets.org/prepMaterials.

Teachers should understand that ESL instruction is good for all students, all ability levels, all ages, all grade levels, and all diverse backgrounds. In fact, since ESL instruction is so heavily grounded in the English language arts and developmental stages of first language acquisition, all teachers would do well to consider this supplemental certification as a means to improve their professional practice for *all* classrooms. There are many ways to continue to improve one's ESL teaching skills, and you are urged to seek these out in workshops, online courses, college courses, and similar professional development. To obtain ESL certification by simply testing, however, one must gain a full understanding of the importance of what follows in this chapter. Table 10.1 gives a conceptual overview of each of these components. The descriptors, or indicators, will follow in each subdivided section of this chapter.

Let us first look at a logical organization pattern of the information that we will study for this certification (Table 10.1). Note that the standards can be divided into three important key areas (or domains) that ESL teachers must consider: what should happen before the classroom (or preparation before teaching ESL), what should happen in the classroom (or during teaching ESL), and what should happen outside the classroom (or continuous professional development and community/resource outreach).

Table 10.1 divides the standards into three categories (or domains) discussed in this section and lists the competencies that belong with each. To see how these three domains are weighed on the exam, Table 10.2 divides and describes each domain and the approximate percentage of each in the ESL supplemental section to the EC-4 Generalist content-area exam.

Domain I is based on the assumption that an ESL teacher will have considerable knowledge of the learner and a clear understanding of how acquisition

TABLE 10.1   Standards, Domains, and Competencies in ESL Programs

Domain I	*STANDARD I* (concepts, structure, and conventions of English)
Before the Classroom	*Competency 001* The ESL teacher understands fundamental language concepts and knows the structure and conventions of the English language.
	STANDARD III (L1 & L2 language acquisition)
	Competency 002 The ESL teacher understands the processes of first language (L1) and second language (L2) acquisition and the interrelatedness of L1 and L2 development.
Domain II	*STANDARD IV* (ESL methods & instruction)
In the Classroom	*Competency 003* The ESL teacher understands ESL teaching methods and uses this knowledge to plan and implement effective, developmentally appropriate instruction.
	STANDARD III (L1 & L2 language acquisition)
	Competency 004 The ESL teacher understands how to promote students' communicative language development in English.
	STANDARD I (concepts, structure, and conventions of English)
	Competency 005 The ESL teacher understands how to promote students' literacy development in English.
	STANDARD V (ESL academic content, language, and culture)
	Competency 006 The ESL teacher understands how to promote students' content-area learning, academic-language development, and achievement across the curriculum.
	STANDARD VI (formal and informal assessment)
	Competency 007 The ESL teacher understands formal and informal assessment procedures and instruments used in ESL programs and uses assessment results to plan and adapt instruction.
Domain III	*STANDARD II* (foundations of ESL)
Outside the Classroom	*Competency 008* The ESL teacher understands the foundations of ESL education and types of ESL programs.
	STANDARD V (ESL academic content, language, and culture)
	Competency 009 The ESL teacher understands factors that affect ESL students' learning and implements strategies for creating an effective multicultural and multilingual learning environment.
	STANDARD VII (family and community involvement)
	Competency 010 The ESL teacher knows how to serve as an advocate for ESL students and facilitate family and community involvement in their education.

TABLE 10.2   ESL Domains* and Weights

Domain I	Language Concepts and Language Acquisition (25% of the test)
Domain II	ESL Instruction and Assessment (45% of the test)
Domain III	Foundations, Culture, Family, and Community (30% of the test)

of one's first language (as well as one's second) takes place. This is seen as *prerequisite knowledge* for the ESL teacher *before* he or she enters the classroom.

Domain II concentrates on planning, implementing, evaluating, and modifying ESL instruction—in other words, all that takes place *in the classroom*. Students' linguistic ability and conceptual understanding are considered during lesson planning to ensure that students are capable of acquiring new vocabulary and higher levels of *lexical* (or academic) *application*. Then, the teacher uses engaging instruction, applications of appropriate technology, and special methodologies and strategies. Finally, a combination of formal, informal, and authentic assessment is employed, interrelated in daily oral and content-area lessons to measure how much the student has achieved. Much of what is brought to the classroom by way of prerequisite knowledge from Domain I will be developed to a higher level in Domain II. This keeps the continuum of professional development constant as the ESL teacher reflects on classroom experiences to continuously improve requisite knowledge and skills.

Domain III includes those areas with which the ESL teacher is affiliated *outside of the classroom* to make instruction better in the classroom. Such topics include further understanding the foundations of ESL instruction, the importance of culture in any language, and involving families and community in the curriculum as a powerful impetus to instruction and support. As ESL teachers learn more about their students in the classroom, they should place equal emphasis on learning more about the language used in students' homes and culture by going outside the classroom to investigate and collaborate with families, communities, and other quality resources.

The ESL teacher can be expected to have a classroom with only a few ESL children, a classroom of all children who are **English Language Learners (ELLs)** who may speak only *one* language (such as Spanish), or a classroom of children who may speak a *variety* of languages other than English. ESL is not, however, a bilingual certification or program in which the teacher actually instructs partly in English and partly in the student's native language. An ESL teacher is not expected to speak another language—although it is certainly helpful. All ESL instruction takes place in English with the use of special knowledge and skills to help children gain English more quickly.

In concluding the overview to this certification, one can see that what a teacher has in terms of prerequisite knowledge will grow from year to year, due to what he/she does *inside* and *outside* the classroom. The teacher must always remember, however, that the expectations for each child are different, based upon past learning experiences and a multitude of other circumstances. Yet, Table 10.3 in the discussion of Domain I shows the state TEKS-based expectations concerning listening, speaking, reading, and writing for elementary students. If a student is unable to perform these required tasks and learning for his or her grade level due to the lack of English and, perhaps even deficiencies in his home language, he or she is still expected to achieve state benchmarks. Thus, what is ideal on paper may sometimes not be what is *real* in the classroom for children coming from a variety of experiences. Nonetheless, the teacher and the students are held accountable for their state test scores long before either is usually ready. The impact that an ESL teacher can make is, therefore, extremely important. Teachers who seek continuous learning will grow with the knowledge and experience that each new year's experience offers—as does the quality of collaboration with families, colleagues, and community that the teacher works to establish. These areas of *before*, *inside*, and *outside* the classroom guide the ESL teacher in professional development as he or she begins to work with ELLs at multiple learning levels.

DOMAIN I Language Concepts and Language Acquisition/ Preparation Before Teaching ESL or Before the Classroom

Standard I Concepts, Structure, and Conventions of English, and Standard III L1 and L2 Language Acquisition

Competency 001: The ESL teacher understands fundamental language concepts and knows the structure and conventions of the English language.

- Fundamental language concepts
- Language structure
- Conventions of language
- Phonology
- Morphology
- Syntax
- Lexical understanding
- Semantics
- Discourse
- Pragmatics
- Registers of language
- Social versus academic language
- Modifying instructional materials
- Delivery of instruction
- English language proficiency
- Interrelatedness of listening, speaking, reading, and writing
- Word formation
- Grammar
- Sentence structure

Facing the task of learning English requires the prerequisite understanding that **fundamental English language concepts** (basic English rules) are essential for an ELL to become fluent. The **structure** (*formal* systematic arrangements of a language) and **conventions of English** (*generally accepted usage*) are acquired in the beginning by oral interactions as an ELL concurrently builds higher levels of **lexical understanding** (terms used in *academic content,* such as mathematics, science, and social studies).

As an ESL teacher, one should become adept at being able to initiate an individual child's instruction at his or her *developmentally appropriate level* (Wertsch, 1985). To find that level, the teacher should informally assess the prior knowledge and skills of students through simple **oral discourse** (conversation). Moreover, literacy skills should be built through the **interrelatedness of listening, speaking, reading, and writing**. Teachers should document academic achievement in terms of increased understanding that will measure the value of *instructional delivery* in the ESL classroom. This delivery will depend entirely on where students are academically and on the dynamics of the class (i.e., differences in perception about learning, attention to detail, lack of concern for academics, etc.). **Social** versus **academic language** must be intertwined in the curriculum because true **English language proficiency** does not happen if the learner is not exposed to a rich environment of dialogue that he or she can comprehend, hands-on problem solving, and the chance to frequently reflect on previous verbal and cognitive processes.

When acquiring a second language, it is imperative to understand that language ability level has no set age or grade level. Children in the sixth grade may be starting at the same spot as those children who are two years old. The key difference is that the sixth grader has more fully learned his or her **first language (L1)** with all the rules of language and may have the ability to quickly **transfer language skills** from L1 to the **second language (L2)**. However, the problem in acquiring a new language for older learners is that making oral mistakes can be embarrassing, which can severely hamper new learning. On the other hand, most young children are rarely concerned with errors and continue to practice and forever ask "why."

Before a student ever steps into an ESL classroom, the teacher needs to understand the characteristics of human development, diversity in learning, the expected knowledge base for students according to the state of Texas (the TEKS), and how learning occurs in terms of acquisition, cognition, and metacognition. Hopefully, much of that information was learned for the Pedagogy and Professional Responsibilities (PPR) TExES exam required of all Texas teachers. If not, you are recommended to read *Becoming an EC-4 Teacher in Texas* (Nath & Cohen, 2002). From here, the teacher should be able to create an environment of equity for students and engage the class with effective instruction. In the course of regular classroom instruction, the teacher works on perfecting students' oral communication skills—being careful to avoid biases while children are learning second language words and phrases to aid in later instruction. At this point, implementing technology to present and represent information in innovative ways and assessing the effectiveness of instruction through student evaluation becomes important. When assessments help reveal a specific need, the teacher should focus on a student's weak areas and make efforts to immediately improve them (often in collaboration with colleagues who may have the same student for other content areas). What is learned about students' strengths and weaknesses should be shared with families in a manner that they can easily understand and do not find offensive. From working with families, teachers will continue to grow in multicultural awareness. In keeping up with these demands, teachers shall remain vigilant to improve and advocate for all ESL students, as there is an ethical duty to share one's expertise with educators at all levels.

A starting place for growth is to gain a clear conceptual overview of the **English Language Arts (ELA)** competencies. Table 10.3 shows a comprehensive look at each developmental stage in ELA. Each ESL teacher in Texas is expected to know and apply strategies for instruction for each of the following ELA competencies. It is also suggested that you study Chapter 2 in this book on teaching reading/language arts for a thorough review of many of these concepts and terms.

Try this question:

The following question tests knowledge of *English concepts*, *structure*, and *conventions*. See how you do with your knowledge and application of understanding!

Take note of the following sentence: *Jorge gave his grandmother a kiss.* In this sentence, the word *grandmother* is a/an:

- **A.** indirect object.
- **B.** direct object
- **C.** prepositional phrase.
- **D.** appositive clause.

First, determine what Jorge is giving (or what was *it* that he *directly* gave). The *direct* object (*B*) was a kiss. *To whom* was it given? He gave the *direct* object (the kiss) to his grandmother (who is the *indirect* object or the *receiver*). Choice *A* is the correct answer.

A prepositional phrase (*C*) begins with words such as *across, before, toward, to, from, at, in, up, with*, and so forth and is followed by a noun or a pronoun that creates some type of relationship or direction (*down* the stairs, *on* the counter, *within* her heart). An appositive clause (*D*) is a noun or pronoun that usually follows another noun or pronoun to describe or clearly identify the first one in some manner (for example, Ms. Kelly, *the teacher*, . . .).

For a teacher to be able to help ELLs, it is extremely important to understand English grammar and structure and the mistakes that ELLs can make. For example, an ESL teacher noticed that all her ELLs missed a mathematics word problem that read: *Jack put 3 cans on the shelf and then he put 3 cans on the floor. How many cans did he have altogether?* The ELLs had read the word *can* as a verb rather than a noun and could not decipher what the question was asking. A good ESL teacher could anticipate this problem and help ELLs understand English structure. Be sure to go back to Chapter 2 if you are uncertain about your English/language arts information. The correct answer is *A.*

In order to best create a positive environment for ELLs, the ESL teacher understands that expectations to learn English involve the eleven vital areas of learning listed in Table 10.3:

1. Oral language
2. Phonological and phonemic development
3. Understanding the alphabetic principle
4. Literacy development
5. Word analysis and decoding
6. Reading fluency
7. Reading comprehension
8. Research and comprehension skills in the content areas
9. Writing conventions
10. Development of written communication
11. Assessment of developing literacy

TABLE 10.3   EC-4 Generalist English Language Arts Competencies for ESL (ESL EC-4 Generalist)

Competency 011 (Oral Language) The teacher understands the importance of oral language, knows the developmental processes of oral language, and provides children with varied opportunities to develop listening and speaking skills.

Competency 012 (Phonological and Phonemic Awareness) The teacher understands phonological and phonemic awareness and employs a variety of approaches to help children develop phonological and phonemic awareness.

Competency 013 (Alphabetic Principle) The teacher understands the importance of the alphabetic principle for reading English and provides instruction that helps children understand the relationship between printed words and spoken language.

Competency 014 (Literacy Development) The teacher understands that literacy develops over time, progressing from emergent to proficient stages, and uses a variety of approaches to support the development of children's literacy.

Competency 015 (Word Analysis and Decoding) The teacher understands the importance of word analysis and decoding for reading and provides many opportunities for children to improve their word-analysis and decoding abilities.

Competency 016 (Reading Fluency) The teacher understands the importance of fluency for reading comprehension and provides many opportunities for children to improve their reading fluency.

Competency 017 (Reading Comprehension) The teacher understands the importance of reading for understanding, knows the components of comprehension, and teaches children strategies for improving their comprehension.

Competency 018 (Research and Comprehension Skills in the Content Areas) The teacher understands the importance of research and comprehension skills to children's academic success and provides children with instruction that promotes their acquisition and effective use of these skills in the content areas.

Competency 019 (Writing Conventions) The teacher understands the conventions of writing in English and provides instruction that helps children develop proficiency in using writing conventions.

Competency 020 (Development of Written Communication) The teacher understands that writing to communicate is a developmental process and provides instruction that promotes children's competence in written communication.

Competency 021 (Assessment of Developing Literacy) The teacher understands the basic principles of literacy assessment and uses a variety of assessments to guide literacy instruction.

These competencies begin with students' use of *oral language,* the first level of language development, and build upward. Do not forget that the ESL teacher is really responsible for two main sets of competencies—the English Language Arts (ELA) presented in Chapter 2 and those ESL competencies presented in this chapter (or more, if teaching content). Thus depending upon the circumstances, the teacher may also be self-contained in a classroom and be held responsible for other content area competencies such as the TEKS for mathematics, science, social studies, and so forth.

One of the most difficult obstacles for many new ESL teachers to overcome is the idea that language could or *could not* be grade-level or age-level specific. This means that a fourth-grade ESL teacher should become thoroughly aware of the ESL TEKS from the early childhood level (the Pre-Kindergarten Curriculum Guidelines) up through the upper grades. The English ability of a particular ESL fourth grader, for example, could be anywhere along the continuum of Pre-K–4 ESL. This also means that, for those who have not attended to the grammar rules for a long time, it is time to revisit them for the purpose of providing developmentally appropriate lessons for ESL students—no matter what their language levels. Knowing these TEKS, especially those for reading and language arts, at each grade level is the responsibility of an ESL teacher (Wertsch, 1985). Table 10.4 summarizes these ESL TEKS.

Try this question:

Mrs. Schultz greeted her new third-grade student from Italy who arrived on Monday morning. Mrs. Schultz quickly made time to talk with Elena, who spoke only a little English. Mrs. Schultz asked Elena if she had any pets at home, and Elena answered, "I gots two cat." Although Mrs. Schultz continues later with more assessment, this informal oral assessment gives her a good start on beginning Elena's instruction. At what level of the TEKS in ESL Language Arts and Reading should she begin?

A. Pre-K–K
B. K–1
C. 1–2
D. 3–4

This question asks us to closely examine Table 10.4. In Grade 2, one finds that children should learn to use singular and plural nouns and adjust verbs for agreement. This is clearly a skill that Elena is lacking. The correct answer is *C.*

Competency 002: The ESL teacher understands the processes of first language (L1) and second language (L2) acquisition and the interrelatedness of L1 and L2 development.

- L1 and L2 acquisition
- Theories
- Behaviorist theory
- Nativist theory
- Cognitive development theory
- Cognitive processes
- Memorization
- Categorization
- Generalization
- Metacognition
- Synthesizing
- Idiomatic expressions
- Syntax
- Phonology
- Morphology

TABLE 10.4   Summary of Pre-K–Grade 4 TEKS in ESL Language Arts & Reading

Pre-K

Communication and literacy begin. Interact with responsive adults and peers. Develop listening comprehension, phonological awareness, functions of print, motivation to read, appreciation for literary form, print awareness, and letter knowledge.

Kindergarten

Develop oral language. Begin to read and write. Extend vocabulary and conceptual knowledge. Follow directions. Discuss the meanings of words. Express complete thoughts. Listen to children's literature and informational material. Listen attentively, ask, and respond to questions and retell stories. Distinguish fiction from nonfiction. Identify and write the letters of the alphabet. Segment and identify the sounds in spoken words. Write the letters, name, and other words. Dictate for others to write.

Grade 1

Develop oral language. Become independent readers and writers. Listen attentively and connect experiences and ideas with information and ideas presented in print. Listen and respond to a wide variety of children's literature. Books heard introduce new vocabulary. Recognize features of texts. Develop print with spoken language. Decode words. Read (orally and silently) with fluency and understanding. Demonstrate comprehension. Become adept writers. Use subjects and verbs and write complete sentences. Become more proficient spellers.

Grade 2

Read and write independently. Use spoken language. Understand purposes for speaking and listening. Hold the attention of classmates. Recognize a large number of words and word identification strategies. Read regularly for understanding and fluency in a variety of genres. Read to acquire new information. Summarize what is read and represent ideas. Use references to build word meanings and pronunciation. Revise and edit writing to make ideas more clear and precise. Use appropriate capitalization and punctuation. Use singular and plural nouns and adjust verbs for agreement. Penmanship is legible. Compile notes into outlines.

Grade 3

Read and write more independently. Spend significant time engaged in reading and writing for assigned tasks and projects. Listen critically to spoken messages, contribute to discussions, and plan oral presentations. Read grade-level material fluently and with comprehension. Use root words, prefixes, suffixes, and derivational endings to recognize words. Demonstrate knowledge of synonyms, antonyms, and multi-meaning words Distinguish fact from opinion. Support ideas and inferences by citing portions of the text discussed. Read in a variety of genres. Write with more complex capitalization and punctuation. Write with contractions and homonyms. Write longer and more elaborate sentences and organize writing into larger units of text. Write several drafts to produce a final product. Master manuscript writing and use cursive writing.

Grade 4

Read and write for extended periods. Become critical listeners and analyze a speaker's intent. Adapt spoken language to the audience, purpose, and occasion. Read classic and contemporary selections. Read with a growing interest. Expand vocabulary across the curriculum. Read for meaning and paraphrase. Connect, compare, and contrast ideas. Identify and follow varied text structures. Produce summaries of texts and more sophisticated analysis of characters, plots, and settings. Use different forms of writing for specific purposes. Writing takes on style and voice. Write in complete sentences. Use adjectives, adverbs, prepositional phrases, and conjunctions. Become proficient spellers. Edit writing based on knowledge of grammar and usage, spelling, punctuation, and other conventions of written language. Produce a polished written composition. Use visual media and compare and contrast visual media to print.

There are several ideas about how human beings learn their **first language (L1)**. Some theorists tell us that language is a "human condition"; that is, we are born with an innate "ability" for it to happen. As soon as we are exposed to language, this ability "kicks in." This is called the **nativist theory**. Others say that language is learned in a **behaviorist** way, so when we are reinforced after making certain sounds by our caregivers and others, we repeat and/or correct what we hear. **Social cognitive** and **social cultural** theorists believe that we learn our first language through continuous social interaction and through modeling with adults and peers who are more knowledgeable, as those "models" adjust their language to fit the level of the young child or learner and make sure to increase the difficulty as children's language skills develop. This theory explains why many people use "baby talk" with very young children but do not use it as the child grows older.

Those who study language acquisition also believe that learning one's first language progresses through certain stages, beginning at birth. These stages include: (1) listening before being able to speak, progressing into (2) cooing and babbling. Other early stages that perhaps have more relevance to teaching a second language are the *use of one word* for communication (*Drink!*). Next comes using two words with *pivots* (a small group of words to which another is added to create a meaningful sentence of sorts . . . *byebye* car, *byebye* ball, *see* toy, *hi* plane, *all* broke) and *adding descriptive words* but without articles ("give big piece"; "throw red ball"). Language learners also progress through a stage where there is overgeneralization of the application of a rule for *all* cases (such as adding *–ed* to make the past tense as in "She *wented* to the store."). These stages are important to know because researchers tell us that second language acquisition parallels these (not including the *very* early stages). Thus it is important for the ESL teacher to take on various roles, such as the behaviorist reinforcer, and provide specific feedback that caregivers normally would give (sometimes referred to as *motherese*). For example, a child might say, "Sue good girl!" and mom gives appropriate feedback by saying, "Yes, (smiling) Sue is a very good girl today!" or "No, (frowning), Sue is a bad girl today."

In language acquisition, there are also five other important hypotheses concerning how newly arrived English Language Learners (ELLs) tackle the grueling task of comprehending and speaking a new language (Krashen, 1992). The following section describes each of these five hypotheses:

1. Acquisition-learning hypothesis
2. Natural approach
3. Affective filter hypothesis
4. Comprehensible input hypothesis
5. Monitor hypothesis

Most college graduates have had to learn another language at some point in their schooling, so it will be most helpful to remember what helped your learning (or *not*) and apply those experiences to the following language theories and strategies. It is also helpful to create an empathy needed for understanding the ELL by thinking back on one's own struggle to grasp another language. Remember, too, that an ELL is not only besieged with the language but with a new culture—*and* trying to study content—all at the same time. The ESL teacher must know and apply strategies based on these suppositions for the purpose of helping students attain communicative competence.

In order to best create a positive environment for language acquisition, the ESL teacher should understand that learning a new language takes place through multiple oral interactions in the target language (English). Therefore, it is important to have numerous examples of what the intended outcome should sound like modeled by native speakers. It is only after a student has heard and processed the correct word or phrase in several ways that it shows up in his or her conversation. For this reason, it is of paramount importance that the ESL teacher is a continuous active listener, participant, and reinforcer in normal conversation. Teachable moments in simple conversations with students lend many opportunities for ELLs to quickly relate meaning to structure, without damaging their pride. Stopping conversation to impose a language rule can often create confusion or embarrassment, and the teacher must be cognizant of being careful not to crush the self-esteem of the learner in these early exchanges. Keeping low-key, natural (rather than more stressful) conversations going—with plenty of examples of how English is to be used at the given moment—is the constant duty of the ESL teacher. Let us look more closely at each of these important hypotheses.

The Acquisition-Learning Hypothesis (Meaning to Structure with Two Theories Combined)

In the first hypothesis, Krashen (1992) states that there are two distinct types of learning used to understand and communicate in a second language: (1) *acquired knowledge* and (2) *learned knowledge*. Both are connected as the student progresses towards learning English. Language **acquisition** often occurs unconsciously and automatically in various types of interactions with another language and/or with native speakers to produce an output (either oral or written). For example, if traveling in a foreign country, one might subconsciously acquire the foreign term for *stop* because the word is posted on all stop signs on the roads, and the traveler recognizes the shape and placement of the sign. This same traveler might be able, should a young child run out into a dangerous situation, to say the word *stop* in the foreign language—not really understanding from where the word was acquired. A traveler might also pick up the foreign word for *thank you* after hearing it several times when a salesperson hands over a purchase. Acquired knowledge is also the basis for developing "an ear" for how to say things or why we can understand what someone has uttered without having *formally* studied another language.

For Krashen (1992), **learned knowledge** is purposefully gained knowledge about a language, its structure, and the way it functions. Thus, the sort of *formal classroom knowledge* obtained through grammatical graphing of sentences is different from the knowledge of grammar obtained (or *acquired*) through interpersonal communication. As a beginning foreign language learner, for example, one may be able to say a few phrases and conjugate some verbs correctly, but when faced with an actual conversation, the speaker may become lost. Therefore, knowledge about grammar must also be intentionally learned through some formal work—and consistently practiced in listening and in speech. The rules simply must be used in conversation to the point that speech actually sounds correct to the ELL student. This makes the modeling of correctly spoken English (with grammar rules entrenched) extremely important for language learners on a regular basis. When learning grammar rules, an ESL student can usually verbalize those rules and state why something is said for one reason or another. However, actually employing those rules while participating in the flow of English conversation is difficult, especially in the beginning, and multiple application situations are required. In comparison, structures and concepts of English acquired through communicative experiences become available more automatically. Meaningful and purposeful communicative experiences in cooperative situations provide some of the best opportunities for learners to link a language rule with its oral application in normal conversation.

Linking meaning is a primary process of language acquisition, but the study of hard and fast grammar rules involves the development of new, sometimes difficult concepts that may or may not exist as a parallel to the learner's primary language (as two examples, some languages use verb endings only in place of a pronoun and a verb—thus pronouns are not commonly used; some languages do not have contractions or high frequency irregular sight words). An ESL teacher must also remember that a student may not even speak or write his or her first language correctly or understand mechanics and conventions well. English concepts are, for them, not only difficult, but they need to learn more rules about general language structure they never needed before. The linking of grammatical terminology to completely new language concepts is part of what Krashen calls *learning*. Conscious efforts made by an ELL to use more advanced grammar at higher levels of *lexical* understanding (academic English) would also be a part of learned knowledge.

With the concepts of *acquisition* and *learning,* then, comes the mental linking of *meaning to structure* through conversation and from the study of grammar. Therefore, there is always a need for the ELL to read, write, speak, and listen regularly—even at the earliest stages of language development. Acquisition will take place during meaningful communication, but the study of grammar is important to continue language development and for understanding. Studying how sentences are put together in the new language will facilitate processing future understanding and allow easier meaning/structure connections that are the basis of deeper acquisition. The two are inevitably intertwined—but with Krashen (1992) emphasizing communication experiences first.

The Natural Order Hypothesis

According to the second hypothesis in language acquisition (Krashen & Terrell, 1996), convergent research suggests that language tends to be acquired in a *predictable, rarely variable order.* For example, students of English acquire the progressive form (for example, Janna *is talking*) before the present tense (Janna *talks*). The use of plurals is also acquired early, whereas possessives (such as *Juan's pencil*) are not. However, no research reports the exact order learning and applying the rules of language for each and every student. Moreover, the Natural Order Hypothesis assumes that the order of *acquisition* and the order of *learning* may be different. For example, students of English who study the rules of verb conjugation (learned early in grammar-translation methodology) may take several years before being able to use these correctly in formal and informal conversation. Thus, it appears that, although some grammar rules are learned early, mastery in the conversational use of other rules only happens after substantial periods of communication in the second language.

The Affective Filter Hypothesis

The third hypothesis states that language acquisition takes place in *low-anxiety, comfortable situations*. Students who are asked to stand up and speak to the entire class when they are feeling inadequate and pressured will surely not be able to get past their internal turmoil; hence, this emotional block prevents the disposition for language learning. While rote learning can take place under adverse conditions, language *acquisition* requires that students be able to attend to input and output in a more relaxed environment. This means that students with high-anxiety perceptions about making oral mistakes, poorly motivated students, and those with lower self-esteem often experience problems in acquisition activities. The best programs are those that attempt to remove stress and pressure. *Accelerated language programs,* for example, seek to override anxiety factors by having students play games, sing songs, and even take on the name and persona of someone else, so that it is not "the actual student" who might make a mistake—but "another." Programs of this nature often suggest an environment of playfulness in which students acquire much language in social situations, and *Suggestopedia* techniques enhance learning by including music, relaxation, and room decoration to heighten the senses and allow acquisition to "simply flow in." ESL teachers should make efforts to continuously use these types of strategies.

Also supported by research is allowing students to wait a short time to participate in English when they do not yet feel ready. This early "silent period" allows beginning ELLs to listen and gain confidence before forcing any output.

The ESL teacher is cognizant of the importance of students being interested in the activities in which they participate and in which they feel at ease with their peers. Classroom interactions need to be supportive rather than competitive in nature. If the student does not (or cannot) attend to the input, acquisition will not take place. Both a sincere interest in the success of students and a trusting ESL teacher/student relationship are essential.

The Input Hypothesis

The fourth hypothesis in Krashen's (1992) language acquisition hypotheses, the Input Hypothesis, attempts to explain that language acquisition can occur within the context of communication as the student attends to both spoken language and gestures that often accompany oral speech. Spoken language and gestures contain vocabulary, grammatical forms, inferred meaning, and other structures to be acquired. Comprehension takes place when the learner concentrates on the *meaning* expressed during the *total* communication process and is successful in connecting *meaning to structure;* that is, language acquisition occurs during the course of regular, natural conversation. There is a twist to this theory, however! Very similar to Vygotsky's zone of proximal development (Wertsch, 1985), the teacher determines a zone of conversation that slightly challenges the ELL in English—yet remains understandable for the learner—perhaps through the use of extra cues, such as pointing, gestures, pictures, and analogy to known vocabulary. This is sometimes called **i + 1**, meaning that the teacher considers the student's ability level to comprehend *input* (i) and adds one *level* (+1) above that.

The Input Hypothesis for the ESL teacher is one of the *most* important to use but is usually the least understood in ESL instruction. It tells us that what ELLs say is in direct relation to what they heard *and* understood. Thus, the Input Hypothesis should concern itself with the interchange of *understandable* ideas—focusing on the zone in which each child can comprehend. Acquisition, according to this theory, is entirely dependent on **comprehensive input** presented in all levels of discourse, ranging from informal conversation to high levels of lexical (academic) understanding. ESL students will first understand new words and grammar used in conversation; then the student will reproduce those words in other meaningful interactions. The reproduction of this spoken, comprehensible exchange is indispensable for development and continued success in the English language. No amount of explanation and drill can substitute for real communicative experiences; thus, the ESL teacher must continuously provide those experiences within the confines of the daily routine to ensure that she or he is using *comprehensive input* for each individual child's level and that the zone of exchange is slightly challenging.

 ## The Monitor Hypothesis

Finally, the Monitor Hypothesis blends *acquired knowledge* and *grammatical knowledge* in regular conversation—with a twist. Language learners use their formal knowledge about language and the way it functions as a "monitor" to guide correct output *before* the production of a sentence—a quick "think before you communicate" brain function. Monitoring speech with grammar rules is usually limited to situations in which there is time to think about it. Most students monitor relatively well when given ample time "to think about it" before answering. However, monitoring is very difficult for most second language learners during a normal conversation because the rapid pace does not lend itself well to giving ample time for this type of monitoring. As well, some students are very poor at monitoring in all situations. That is why it is imperative for the ESL teacher to become an active and participatory speaker and listener when students inaccurately monitor their output. For instance, with the help of the ESL teacher, most students can monitor their errors with little lost time or loss of self-confidence (i.e., a student says, "I haved it yesterday but today, no," and the ESL teacher uses **circumlocution** for the purpose of letting the student hear how the English should sound by saying, "You say you *had* it yesterday. Where were you when you *had* it last? You *had* it in your pocket, or you *had* it in another place?" The student replies, "I *had* it in my pocket." In this exaggerated repetition of the word *had,* the ESL teacher modeled the correct usage enough times that the student could easily self-monitor and continue talking about other matters.

Since monitoring with a formal knowledge of grammar learned through drill-and-practice is difficult in real-time contexts, it makes more sense to use acquisition-oriented activities in the ESL classroom. Grammar exercises are primarily to be done as written work or homework in order to give adequate time for reflection on and use of those rules. Finally, the Monitor Hypothesis reminds us that the ability to achieve on formal paper-and-pencil exams should never be compared with the ability to use such measures in natural, spontaneous conversation.

This question tests the ESL teacher's knowledge and application skills related to the competency of language acquisition. See how you do!

Which situation *best* encourages acquisition of language?

A. Researching a social studies issue on the Internet
B. Academic language proficiency
C. Interpersonal communication
D. Writing a term paper for science

Language acquisition is not really "taught." By providing language interaction in the classroom, language is *acquired.* It is only after students have perfected understanding through listening and speaking that they can also apply high levels of conceptual skills. For that reason, the ESL teacher knows that higher levels of cognitive application come when ESL students have had plenty of practice in interpersonal communication (or work with the context of speaking and listening in English) (C). The idea of *basic* interpersonal communication is what Cummins (1979) referred to as **BICS (Basic Interpersonal Communication Skills)** that students usually develop within *six months to two years.* Researching (A), academic language proficiency (B), and writing papers inundated with lexical terminology (D) are all skills referred to by Cummins as **CALPS (Cognitive Academic Language Proficiency Skills)**. These skills can take anywhere from *five to seven years* to learn; therefore, they are not part of a reasonable answer to this question. With that said, it is easy to understand how many students in ESL struggle so intensely to barely pass when the instruction they receive leaps past BICS and heads directly to trying to make sense of higher-order conceptual understanding in CALPS. When teachers move too quickly into teaching at the CALPS level, there may be ELLs who are still trying to acquire simple basic language (BICS) at the same time they are required to use high-level academic terms in English. Language is best acquired through common interaction with native speakers and the environment, including culture and experience. The correct answer is *C.*

DOMAIN II ESL Instruction and Assessment/In the Classroom/During Teaching

Standards I Concepts, Structure, & Conventions of English, III L1 & L2 Language Acquisition, IV ESL Methods and Instruction in the Classroom, and V ESL Academic Content, Language, and Culture, VI Formal and Informal Assessment

Competency 003: The ESL teacher understands ESL teaching methods and uses this knowledge to plan and implement effective, developmentally appropriate instruction.

- Planning instruction
- Developmentally appropriate instruction
- Texas Essential Knowledge and Skills (TEKS)
- English language arts and reading curriculum
- TEKS (listening, speaking, reading, writing, viewing/representing)
- Instructional goals
- Diverse characteristics and needs
- Content-based ESL instruction
- Active instruction
- Critical thinking
- Communicative competence
- Technology tools
- Classroom management
- Teaching strategies

Planning for effective instruction that is developmentally appropriate *and* particular to ESL will always begin with a firm understanding of student expectations (perhaps best found in the **Texas Essential Knowledge and Skills [TEKS]**). The TEKS, especially the English language arts and reading curriculum as it relates to ESL, are important to address daily, especially in areas such as listening, speaking, reading, writing, and viewing/representing. *Viewing and representing* is an extra domain that stresses the importance of using computers with ELLs, due to the ease of combining audio, visual, tactile, and graphical organization of content and conceptual overviews.

What is important for ESL teachers to remember is that even through the ESL TEKS may be written for the "ideal" level of student achievement, these aims may often need readjusting to the current student levels in English acquisition *and* cognitive academic language proficiency levels (CALPS). The ESL teacher must constantly assess students' individual academic levels and plan methodological strategies that will match students' current achievement and future goals in language mastery. The following explains the role of the TEKS in more detail:

- The TEKS are required knowledge for each grade level in all subject areas; therefore, each grade-level listing is prerequisite knowledge for the next grade level. Looking at the TEKS from the previous grade level will ensure that the ESL teacher knows what students *should* know and *should* be able to do upon entering their respective grade levels. Studying the TEKS for the grade level to which a teacher is assigned will help him or her understand what children should know when they exit that grade at the end of that academic year.
- The TEKS are not "*how* to teach content"; they are the listed content knowledge and skills required for all students at each grade level. The order and emphasis placed on teaching the TEKS is up to the ESL teacher. Methods should be matched to this list of knowledge and skills to provide the most appropriate approach in an effort to ensure student achievement.
- The ESL TEKS are divided into the domains of listening, speaking, reading, writing and viewing/representing, and each of these areas should be included on a daily basis.

ESL Methods

First, the ESL teacher must understand that methodologies are a body of practices, procedures, and rules that are especially effective for ELLs. The teacher should learn about those methods that work for learning English and those that work well with ESL learning in the content areas (such as with mathematics for ESL, science for ESL, etc.).

- *Linguistic instruction* should include initiating frequent interaction with English-speaking peers (cooperative groups) as well as materials for language acquisition and cognitive development.
- *Sheltered English* (or Specially Designed Academic Instruction in English/ SDATE) is an instructional approach used to make academic instruction in English understandable to ESL students. In the lesson plan, the teacher combines (1) cognitively challenging instruction in a content area, (2) English language, and (3) a focus on social/affective development. In the sheltered classroom, teachers use physical activities and visual aids in the content areas (such as science, social studies, and other subjects) in flexible group interactions.
- *Reciprocal teaching* refers to an instructional activity that takes place in the form of a dialogue between teachers and students using segments of text. The dialogue is structured by the use of four strategies: summarizing, question generating, clarifying, and predicting. The teacher and his or her students take turns assuming the role of teacher in this dialogue.

Other Methodologies Recommended for the ESL Classroom

- Audiolingual (new materials are presented in the form of a dialogue.)
- Brainstorming (asking students to give all they know on a topic; this gives the teacher a concrete view on what the class knows about a topic.)
- Buddy System Pairing (combining a beginning speaker with a more capable speaker.)
- Computer Assisted Instruction (CAL) (use of computers in education and training.)
- Computer-Assisted Language (CALL) (computer technology is used as an aid to the presentation, reinforcement, and assessment of material to be learned; usually includes a substantial interactive element.)
- Communicative Approach (or the functional approach; based on the theory that language is acquired through exposure to meaningful and understandable messages, rather than learned through the formal study of grammar and vocabulary.)
- Community Language Learning (especially for adult learners who might fear appearing foolish; so the teacher becomes a "Language Counselor.")
- Conferencing (one-on-one discussion with student to discuss assignments.)
- Cooperative Learning Groups (heterogeneous groups with varying levels of English provide support for each other.)
- Counseling Learning (CL) (facilitation of learning by closely monitoring and guiding student engagement as needed to enhance success.)
- Critical Pedagogy (teacher leads students to question ideologies and practices considered oppressive.)
- Critical Thinking (ELLs are as capable as other students of thinking at higher levels—they just may not have the English to explain; ESL teachers must apply instruction at the linguist level to include critical thinking tasks.)
- Debate (students gain oral skills through arguing meaningful issues with their peers.)
- Direct Method (a teaching technique in which the English language is used from the very beginning.)
- English for Special Purposes (English for science, technological, or other academic or occupational specializations.)
- Grammar Translation (vocabulary is taught in the form of isolated word lists.)
- Journal Writing and/or Drawing (students write or illustrate each day on a topic.)
- Language Experience Approach (LEA) (student dictates as the teacher writes down what was said.)
- Logs on Learning (having students write down each day what they understood about main concepts.)
- Model Reading (using big books and pointers to model the reading process and words.)
- Natural Approach (pioneered by Krashen, this approach combines acquisition and learning as a means of facilitating language development in adults.)
- Notetaking (teacher gives a note page or outline that is partially filled out or asks students to write down important facts as he/she specifically accentuates these points during a lesson.)

- Participatory Approach (a teaching strategy designed to promote productive and mutual learning among a group of students.)
- Role-play (students practice situations that are common in order to feel comfortable in the language.)
- Semantic Mapping (a visual strategy for organizing vocabulary around a theme to expand and extend thought.)
- Silent Way (a method to teach languages in which the teacher doesn't speak but uses manipulatives to explain.)
- Story Telling (teachers encourage students to "work up" a family or traditional tale to perform or tape for others.)
- Suggestopedia (teachers use visualization, games, play, taking on of a persona, relaxation techniques, music, etc.)
- Total Physical Response (TPR) (Asher, 2000) (teacher assesses understanding by the learner responding to teacher directions.)
- Using drama
- Using E-mail/the Internet
- Using literature
- Using photographs (students make inferences, draw conclusions, use expression, increase vocabulary from viewing or making photographs.)
- Using songs/music/rhyming chants (a memory technique and an opportunity to hear pronunciation.)
- Whole language/integrated or thematic instruction (lessons include content from several areas rather than being divided into specific content areas such as *only* social studies or *only* mathematics; see example lesson plan at end of chapter.)
- Writing Response Groups (gentle critiquing and improvement by students of each other's writing.)

Teacher Strategies for ESL Learners

- Read aloud to children often.
- Use slow, clear speech that is appropriately loud.
- Paraphrase often.
- Correct mistakes by restating the sentence with correct usage and meaning rather than the grammar rule(s).
- Repeat vocabulary in various contexts (especially from students' real world experiences).
- Use gestures/body language/pantomime to help with understanding.
- Limit slang and idioms.
- Use frequently used words in speaking, reading, and writing (classmates' names, pets, signs, school items, etc.).
- Provide use of hands-on manipulatives or concrete items and point to models, pictures, diagrams, props, maps, and other visuals; provide films or other technology as demonstrations.
- Check often for understanding.
- Label many parts of the classroom with English words (wall, window, door, desk, bookshelf, etc.).
- Scaffold and build from prior knowledge.
- Use graphic organizers.
- Provide multiple, meaningful, and motivating ways to engage in a concept.
- Provide age-appropriate materials for older students as well as younger students.

- Provide experiences for *all* to participate in social interaction.
- Provide a routine schedule and some permanent physical spaces so students feel safer by knowing exactly what to expect through a structured environment.
- Use repeated, simple questions that become routine throughout the day during reading and listening times (Who? What? What's that? Where? When?).
- Use prereading techniques to set exact expectations for the purpose of reading.
- Teach about context clues often.
- Contextualize activities, making them applicable to real-world situations (i.e., measuring items in class with a tape measure, using the computer to develop research skills, using a checklist and a digital camera for field-trip data collection, etc.).
- Teach children about various types of research skills and resources (dictionaries, Internet, etc.) so they can become more independent translators in and outside the classroom.

Technological Tools and Resources

Using and integrating technology can greatly enhance instruction. Here is a list of some technological tools and resources.

- Voice recognition and recording software
- Databases and word processors
- Working with multimedia presentations using graphics
- Teaching research skills on the Internet in the content areas
- Using taped read-alongs
- Using e-mail to pair students up with e-pals for the purpose of communication in written English
- Presenting electronic portfolios for the purpose of reflection on previous cognitive activities and directing future efforts accordingly (highly metacognitive)
- Using appropriate software for different ESL learning levels (beginning, intermediate, and advanced), which include necessary visual, graphical, and oral components
- Documenting family and community and their events
- Providing feedback to learners immediately
- Providing student evaluations, modifications, implementation of new curriculum, methodologies, and special needs

Management and Teaching Strategies

The best possible management and teaching strategies include purposeful, effective, and engaging lessons that require students to work in a *variety* of settings with others, particularly cooperative groups. However, there will be a need for management in the classroom. Rules should be few but inclusive, simple, and easy to understand (e.g., respect others' things, walk safely, listen until it is your turn, etc.). They should include student input and consistently be in place so that children feel there is a safe classroom structure. Consequences must be based on equity. Guiding new ELLs in helping them understand school rules and American norms for classroom behavior should be a priority for the ESL teacher, as students and parents from other parts of the world bring different expectations of classroom behaviors with them. Feeling able to navigate through the day with correct behavioral expectations does a great deal to lower anxiety for a new language learner.

Effective management of engaging instruction invokes establishing deadlines to finish class work, cooperative work, and individual projects. Placing a time limit on assignments automatically makes the lesson *metacognitive* in nature because the ESL student will have to internalize the quantity, quality, and time limitations to finish tasks. The ESL teacher never waits until the end of deadlines to monitor students' progress. Effective monitoring occurs during various stages of student work; therefore, ESL students who are meeting expectations should be effectively praised, while those that are struggling should be helped in an individual manner (both the student and teacher find ways to become successful according to the task criteria).

Understanding students' cultures is also important in management. For example, ESL teachers who demand that their Hispanic or Asian children "look them in the eye" will not have those children follow these directions. In these cultures, children do not look fully into an adult's eyes as a learned sign of respect. Guiding along with some cultural understanding are keys to good ESL management.

Let's try a couple of questions that depict a sample of the ESL teacher's knowledge and application skill relating to the competency of ESL methodologies:

Why would Mr. Guthrie, an ESL teacher, invoke the *"first three-before-me"* rule (ask three classmates before asking the teacher) whenever a student asks him about the meaning and pronunciation of a word?

- **A.** It helps engage the student in meaningful and independent problem solving that will lead to higher levels of confidence.
- **B.** It models what an adult would do in an inquiry-based approach.
- **C.** It makes the student think at very high levels of reasoning.
- **D.** It encourages the student to invoke a research-based approach for similar problem-solving situations.

In order to best create a positive environment, the ESL teacher understands that learning involves oral acquisition. This means that the ESL teacher should often insist upon authentic problem solving in cooperative learning contexts. The *"first three-and-then-me"* rule asks students to ask three members of their cooperative group for the answer before he or she asks the teacher. This creates the supportive view that others can be valued resources (*A*). In this scenario, modeling by the teacher (*B*) is important to begin with, but ultimately, it is the responsibility of the students to find answers and get busy with the task. Thinking at high levels of reasoning (*C*) is also important, but simply thinking of the meaning and the pronunciation of a word is not a higher-level thinking activity. As well, encouraging (or cheerleading) students to invoke a research-based approach (*D*) is often a good strategy—but it does not ensure either a product or a process from the student (i.e., that they are engaged in problem solving or actually coming up with an answer that feels right). The student expectation, according to state standards, requires the *student* to perform, not the teacher. For this reason, one can infer that the answer is *A* because engaging the student in the process of peer-based problem solving is half the battle to secure a product (achievement). The correct answer is Choice *A.*

Mrs. Mengistu teaches third-grade ESL. She is planning a unit on pets. Which of the following should she do *first*?

A. Have students go into a Pet Center.
B. Read a short book on pets to them.
C. Have cards with the names and pictures of various pets printed on them and have students use these for flashcards.
D. Have children tell what pets they have and match them with pictures.

Teachers should always begin with what children know and their own experiences (or the known to the unknown). Therefore, the answer is *D*.

Competency 004: The ESL teacher understands how to promote students' communicative language development in English.

• TEKS listening and speaking
• Linguistic environment
• Conversational support
• Rich, comprehensible language environment
• Communication experiences in English
• Interrelatedness of listening, speaking, reading, and writing for oral language proficiency transfer from L1 to L2
• Individual differences
• Developmental characteristics
• Cultural and language background
• Academic strengths
• Learning styles
• Appropriate feedback

Students Acquire Language in a Low-Anxiety Environment with Comprehensible Input: This Supports Listening and Speaking Skills

Even after becoming certified in ESL instruction, the ESL teacher will often wonder what to do with newly arrived ELL students. According to the Affective Filter Hypothesis, Krashen (1992) believes that students should not be pushed too hard and made to feel they *must* speak English "right this second." When anxiety levels are high, the affective filter is high; thus we can expect interference with the learning process. As a strong reminder in order to combat this, the ESL teacher understands that the affective filter should be as low as possible and must be accompanied by the teacher's use of **comprehensible input;** that is, where the language used is based on simple, already familiar terms (i.e., the level at which the child can comprehend or understand what is being said or offered to him or her in print). When students are at ease and using language *and* when they have conceptual familiarity within their L1, they will find it easier to generate English oral communication. There are a wide variety of techniques for keeping the affective filter level low and the input comprehensible for the child. Some examples are sticking to simple, nonidiomatic language, talking in small groups, using gestures, and avoiding harsh criticism on mistakes. The ESL teacher will be most successful when students are interacting in communicative activities that they enjoy about topics that concern them. Students must *always* feel that they can express their ideas in English without fear of direct, interruptive grammatical correction or reprimand. The goal is for them to express themselves and develop a positive attitude toward their new language then work on refining it.

Speaking Supports Language Acquisition

Much of an ESL teacher's job is to set up informal and formal experiences that encourage children to speak in their new language. Speaking supports language acquisition in several ways:

- It provides more opportunities for comprehensible input (via conversation).
- It gives students an avenue for participation in the L2 that contributes to identification with English language and culture. Language and culture are impossible to divide, and when one learns a second language, the culture of that language must also be considered part of the package.
- It prepares children for necessary communicative interactions with native speakers outside the classroom. An ultimate duty of the ESL teacher is to provide frequent opportunities for students to seek out native speakers, which, in turn, will provide them with more comprehensible input/output and contextual, hands-on practice in English.
- It helps to create a sense of community, as the ESL teacher and students share opinions, perceptions, and life experiences in small groups or whole-class discussions. Students should come together and support peers in problem solving and social communication, while at the same time build their confidence and pride as they become more successful in acquiring new skills.

Speech Emergence Is Distinguished by Grammatical Errors

When students begin speaking in whole sentences, they make many errors. This is to be expected and never underestimated, since this is an important part of the process in learning. It is those students who take the risks and make mistakes who learn. Those students who may appear to be well-behaved yet are not making mistakes (because they are not using the new language—even after allowing for a "silent period"), are often the ones who should cause the most concern. One simply cannot learn a language without making mistakes. Indeed, no intense self-monitoring of speech in the early stages of acquisition should be advised.

Early speech errors that arise during communication activities do not usually become permanent nor do they affect students' future language development. In fact, they lend themselves to opportunities for the ESL teacher to model correct usage, which gives students the ability to self-monitor without loss of time, thought, or self-respect. As in an example, Veronica overgeneralizes a plural rule by saying, "The childs went to the lunch" (when the correct word is *children*) by applying the plural rule of adding *-s* to the word. What she is doing is a natural progress in language learning, and the astute ESL teacher uses this active listening opportunity of circumlocution to exaggerate the correct oral use of the word. The teacher might say, "Oh, so the *children* already went to lunch, Veronica? When you saw the *children,* what time was it? Did the *children* have their money or sack lunches with them?" *Interference* from the structure of the home language can also occur often. For example, in many languages, the modifying adjective follows the noun (i.e., in French one says, "Le chat noir" or "the cat black"). During such communication activities, the ESL teacher should pay attention primarily to factual errors. If there are no factual errors, the teacher can expand and rephrase students' responses in grammatically correct sentences. This allows learners to hear a well-modeled example of communication in English and provides an opportunity to internalize and mimic the correctness of the situation.

The production of speech with few errors depends on a number of factors that cannot always be controlled by the teacher or students. Some forms and structures (e.g., idioms, prepositional phrases, and figurative meaning) require a large number of communicative experiences before acquisition is complete, and no amount of direct correction of speech errors can speed up the process. For this reason, the ESL teacher does not expect students to speak English without errors, especially early in the acquistional process; however, steady improvement in speaking English is expected through regular practice. It is not expected that students' errors fossilize, that is, become habits. Fossilization is not a problem in ESL classes; it appears to be more common among second-language learners who live and work in the environment of the new language and who never have the opportunity to interact in a sheltered environment like that of the ESL classroom. It usually takes several years of daily language use with repetitive mistakes for the mistakes to become so ingrained as to be truly fossilized.

Speech Emerges Step-by-Step

There are two very important reasons *not* to require *beginners* to speak English immediately—that is to give students a silent period: (1) students' anxiety levels (affective filters) will be lower if they are not pressured, and (2) students' understanding of spoken English will develop faster due to the use of comprehensible input. Students who are not pressured at once to produce English feel more comfortable with the language and pronounce it better when they begin to feel more at ease and start to speak in their own time. However, when a student does begin to speak, every opportunity to practice should be provided.

The Natural Approach (Krashen & Terrell, 1996) is based on the following tenets:

- Language acquisition (an unconscious process developed through using language meaningfully) is different from language learning (consciously learning or discovering rules about a language), and language acquisition is the only way competence in a second language occurs (acquisition/learning hypothesis).
- Conscious learning operates only as a monitor (or editor) that checks or repairs one's output (monitor hypothesis).
- Grammatical structures are acquired in a predictable order, and it does little good to try to learn them in another order (natural order hypothesis).
- People acquire language best from messages that are just slightly beyond their current competence (input hypothesis), but learners must be able to comprehend/understand at least the rest of what is being said to them or what is written.
- The learner's emotional state can act as a filter that impedes or blocks input necessary to acquisition (affective filter hypothesis).

Beginners who are in the Natural Approach are allowed to pass *naturally* through three stages:

Level 1: Comprehension
Level 2: Early Speech
Level 3: Speech Emergence

In Level 1, students need not respond in the target language. During this pre-speech stage, the ESL teacher asks questions that can be answered with "yes" or "no" or some other single words. This is the perfect opportunity to employ the **Total Physical Response (TPR)** a method, in which the ESL teacher is the "command giver" and the recently arrived student is the "order taker" (Asher, 2000). Student comprehension is assessed by the student physically performing the requested action/gestures ("Give me the pencil," and the student does so). Exaggerated body language and physical movement is often used to present and represent ideas and concepts. In Level 2, students respond with single words or short phrases, and, by Level 3, they are able to produce longer utterances. Keep in mind that students will continue to pass through these stages as they are introduced to new content areas in subsequent lessons. Words and structures presented may not be fully acquired until much later.

The Goal of the Natural Approach Is Communicative Competence

Communicative competence is reached when a student is able to ask a native speaker for directions on how to get from one location to another and can then understand the details given by the responding native speaker (Krashen & Terrell, 1996). For this to happen, the ESL student needs enough *receptive vocabulary* to adequately attend to what the native speaker says with the subject matter. **Receptive vocabulary** is the amount of spoken language one processes aurally (with regard to sound or the ear), and is usually up to four times greater than an individual's ability to speak. Asking for directions is good practice because of the limited output needed for a native speaker to provide a sufficient explanation when much more vocabulary than the original question is needed to answer. There are at least four components of proficiency in communicative competence:

1. Discourse competence
2. Sociolinguistic competence
3. Strategic competence
4. Linguistic competence

Discourse competence is the ability to interact with native speakers using various communication strategies, conversation, narration, inquiry for information, directing others, and so forth. **Sociolinguistic competence** is the ability to interact in different social registers using appropriate rules and politeness for that situation. There are five social registers in which people communicate (i.e., formal, consultative, informal, frozen, and intimate registers; Payne, 2005). **Strategic competence** is the ability to make use of limited linguistic resources to express ideas and to understand input (what is being said). For example, an American traveler in France went into a shop armed with a map. Not knowing the words for *I'm lost,* the traveler plunked down the map on the counter and asked the salesperson, "Où est ici?" ("Where is here?"), after which the shopkeeper pointed out their location on the map. This allows the traveler to communicate and operate strategically with limited language. **Linguistic competence** is the ability to use the *correct* grammatical form and structure to express a given meaning. Linguistic accuracy is important (but later on in the acquisition process) and does not weigh as heavily as a needed skill in *early* production of a second language. Linguistic accuracy continually improves as the learner matures in English. Even when linguistic proficiency is augmented with reading and writing skills, communicative competence develops from multiple communication experiences, not from just covering the material in a single lesson plan or unit!

Comprehension Comes Before Production

This principle follows the same path as the acquisition process. It is impossible to attach meaning to oral language if the learner has few opportunities to hear an expression often in context (for example, idioms such as "get over it"). In this example, the listener may think he or she has to jump or climb over something when the phrase is taken literally. Classroom activities should be designed to introduce most new vocabulary, idioms, high frequency irregular words, and grammatical forms and structures in communicative contexts *before* students are expected to produce these types of word phrases in their speech. Thus, most ESL instruction should start with input activities before moving on to ask for output (production) activities. In addition, it is important to precede these initial activities with a regular review of new vocabulary and phrases in which new words and grammatical forms and structures are introduced or reviewed for comprehension *before* students are expected to use them. This is especially important for content-area vocabulary that students will find later in subject areas like mathematics, science, and social studies.

Group Work Encourages Interaction and Creates Community

When students begin to be able to communicate orally in English, they should be encouraged to work in pairs and small groups on cognitive tasks that allow application of their growing language skills. By problem solving and interacting with peers in group work, students find more opportunities to speak in their new language, while giving the teacher the opportunity to monitor interactions. At this stage, group work often allows students to enjoy interacting with others on a personal basis, and this helps them to feel freer to express themselves in the context of social participation. From observation and listening during these interchanges, the teacher can then target more skills for individuals (such as answering questions and helping individuals with pronunciation, grammar, and concept development). The time students spend working in small groups should increase methodically so that the students themselves become the source of much of the communicative interaction.

See how you do with your knowledge and application of understanding of ESL methodologies.

While speaking with her ESL teacher, Monica remarks, "My mother think I get in trouble at school." In order to help the student understand her verbal mistake, the ESL teacher should:

A. tell her that the third-person present tense is exactly opposite from what it is in her language and, therefore, requires adding an "s" to the word *think*.

B. say, "Why does your mother think that?"

C. say, "Your mother really thinks that? If she thinks that, do you want me to tell her how well you are doing in school?"

D. understand that this is a developmental stage, and this will pass as Monica develops in English.

In order to create the best environment for language acquisition, the ESL teacher understands that a main purpose of ESL is motivating children to start saying things in English. It is important not to crush the self-esteem of students by interrupting conversations to point out grammatical errors, especially in the beginning which would happen in Choice A. This detracts from listening and speaking in normal conversation. ESL teachers should model correct speech through several oral versions of what the intended outcome should sound like from a native speaker (*circumlocution;* Choice C). When students have heard and processed the correctly modeled speech multiple times, the correct version will begin to appear in their own speech. For that reason, the importance of the ESL teacher being an active listener and participant in normal conversation is critical! Stopping conversation to impose a language rule (*A*) only creates confusion. Asking a question that requires even more language can confuse the ELL (*B*), but keeping the conversation going with plenty examples of how English is to be used is the duty of the ESL teacher—making the *best* answer Choice C. Teachers will understand that Choice *D* is a development stage, but simply understanding this does not help Monica with her verbal mistake. The correct answer is *C.*

Competency 005: The ESL teacher understands how to promote students' literacy development in English.

- Prior literary experiences
- TEKS related to the reading and writing strands
- Interrelatedness of listening, speaking, reading, and writing for developing literacy
- English is an alphabetic language
- Phonological knowledge and skills
- Phonemic awareness skills
- Letter-sound associations
- Phonograms
- Sight-word vocabularies
- Phonetically irregular words
- High-frequency words
- Reading comprehension
- Vocabulary
- Text structures
- Cultural references
- Facilitating reading comprehension
- Transfer literacy and skills from L1 to L2
- Developmental characteristics
- Cultural and language background
- Academic strengths
- Learning styles
- Instructional strategies
- Resources for literacy development
- Interrupted schooling
- Literacy status in the primary language

One way of promoting students' literacy development is by including the Texas Essential Knowledge and Skills (TEKS) in literacy development activities. The TEKS English Language Arts and Reading competencies at all grade levels are important to know because each student may be at a different development level on this continuum. The idea in literacy is that:

- the English Language Arts TEKS, which are ESL TEKS as well, are divided into listening, speaking, reading, writing and viewing/representing domains related to the reading and writing strands (http://www.tea.state.tx.us/rules/tac/chapter110/index. html).
- proficiency levels are *not* necessarily age or grade specific; students are divided into Beginner, Intermediate, and Advanced levels, and the ESL teacher must quickly be able to informally assess each student in order to individualize appropriate instruction.

- *beginning* ESL students, through carefully sequenced listening opportunities, expand their vocabularies to evaluate and analyze spoken English for a variety of situations and purposes.
- *intermediate* ESL students produce spoken English with increasing accuracy and fluency to convey appropriate meaning.
- *advanced* ESL students participate successfully in academic, social, and work contexts in English using the process of speaking to create, clarify, critique, and evaluate ideas and responses.

Interrelatedness

Because there is an interrelatedness of listening, speaking, reading, and writing, the ESL teacher should select and use the most effective strategies for developing students' literacy in English.

- The ESL student may exhibit *different* proficiency levels within the **four language components: listening, speaking, reading,** and **writing.** For instance, he or she may be a star at reading English but not in writing in English. Because the student is classified as ESL, each child has different skills, shortcomings and strengths, interests, and perceptions about English language learning.
- Listening, speaking, reading, writing, and viewing/representing are functions of language that should be taught concurrently, making the awareness of computer instruction and learning important for both the teacher and student.

English is an Alphabetic Language

An important part of helping ESL students starts with the ESL teacher understanding that English is an **alphabetic language** (symbols/letters reflect the pronunciation of a sound). The ESL teacher should apply effective strategies for developing ESL students' phonological knowledge and skills. Some of the most important issues are:

- **phonemic awareness skills** (e.g., skills needed to recognize that a spoken word consists of a sequence of individual sounds), and
- **sight-word vocabularies** (e.g., phonetically irregular, high-frequency words, for example, *thought, one, though, been, have*) which require other skills instead of decoding skills to read. Such words cannot be pronounced letter by letter nor do they follow English language rules. Each word has its own rule for pronunciation with no graphophonic clues. A teacher will want to measure both accuracy and fluency. Accuracy in reading can be measured by assessing students' oral reading mistakes in using word analysis knowledge for decoding those words they do not know. Most ESL students have primary languages that are *more* phonetic than English, making **word analysis skills** (sounding out/phonics) extremely important to teach regularly in the classroom. Determining if a problem is a decoding or a word-analysis issue is imperative in order to plan curriculum and choose the proper methodologies to address these separate English Language Arts (ELA) skills. Fluency is also important for a teacher to assess by determining if a student comprehends enough to be able to read with feeling and expression.

Reading Comprehension

The ESL teacher also knows factors that affect ESL students' reading comprehension such as vocabulary text structures, cultural references, and prior knowledge. A teacher can help by: (1) establishing a purpose for reading and listening, (2) retelling and acting out story events, and (3) helping children to make inferences.

Transfer of Literacy

Cognitive skills transfer from one language to another. Students who are knowledgeable about literacy and subject matter in their first language will be able apply this knowledge and these skills to their second language. An ESL teacher understands that learning a second language does not mean learning *many* of the rules of language, literacy, or content knowledge again; the idea is to identify language rules that students can possibly transfer from their L1 to their L2. ESL teachers can use these to help students leap into their new language. Of course this may take some inquiry into the child's home language and its structure on the part of the teacher, and it will also require that an ESL teacher thoroughly know the rules of English grammar.

Individual Differences and Personal Factors

Individual differences (e.g., developmental characteristics such as cultural/language background, academic strengths, and learning styles) affect ESL students' literacy development. Thus, the ESL teacher should get to know his or her ESL student as quickly as possible. Knowing each individual student can facilitate finding skills already acquired and applying those skills to new learning environments. Language deficits can exist in both the L1 and the L2. Tests in both languages can help to determine academic need. Also, individual students show an affinity for different learning styles and problem-solving tasks, depending on the academic task. When the ESL teacher is aware of learning styles or modalities (preferences for learning such as visual, auditory, tactile, or kinesthetic), he or she can bring these successes to new academic problems. Solving problems that require a metacognitive (*reflective*) process are similar across disciplines. Therefore, demonstrating how old success breeds new success makes an effective connection between students' prior knowledge and their new academic challenges.

Personal factors also affect ESL students' English literacy development, and the ESL teacher must consider effective strategies for addressing these factors. These might include issues in their native country or here such as interrupted schooling, literacy development (such as familiarity with the structure and uses of textbooks and other print, specialized language and vocabulary, etc.), the status of a student's ethnicity and/or his or her primary language, and/or students' prior learning experiences. In many instances, the ESL population is highly mobile, creating gaps in learning. Knowing about learning gaps can be of great help to the ESL teacher in terms of diagnosing (then filling) those gaps for increased student achievement.

Three critical areas have seen suggested by Peregoy and Boyle (2005) for the teacher to learn about new students: (1) determining the country of origin and the language spoken at home, how long the child has been in the U.S., and any unusual circumstances of immigration (trauma, etc.); (2) discovering as much as possible about prior schooling, including information on literacy in the home language, through any obtainable records or through interviews with caregivers; and (3) obtaining basic information on culture, religion, customs, food preferences/restrictions, and cultural role expectations of adults and children.

This question relates to literacy skills.
See how you do in this area!

Jorge, a fourth-grade ELL, is accustomed to a language that is more phonetic than English. What skill is needed in English (in addition to previous skills for his primary language) as he reads for fluency?

    A. Phonemic awareness
    B. Word analysis
    C. Alphabetic principle
    D. Decoding

When a language like English is entrenched with *nondecodable* words like *through, thorough, one,* and *have,* children need extra skills to read fluently. When coming across irregular sight words such as *have,* for example, the student cannot sound out each letter. *Have* would sound differently because the a would become a strong sound such as *hay + v +* the long *e* sound, as in Choice *A.* The skill needed to determine how irregular words are to be sounded out when reading for fluency might not even be in existence in a student's L1, adding difficulty to their reading process. Therefore, the skill of **word analysis** (*B*) is an extra ability needed for English fluency. When analyzing miscues in reading fluency, the ESL teacher should clearly distinguish mistakes between decodable words and high-frequency irregular sight words requiring "word analysis" skills. Literacy also involves *making connections* between the spoken sounds and symbols or letters in written language, or the **alphabetic principle** (*C*). However, choice *A* cannot be the answer because the question asks for *a skill* rather than a principal. The ESL teacher should also clearly know what *phonetic* means and why it is such an important stage of development for the ESL student. When a language is phonetic (spelled the way it sounds), it is easy to read out loud with fluency because **decoding** (*D*) is the only needed skill. Words like *cat, bat, sat* are sounded out by each letter. The correct answer is Choice *B.*

Competency 006: The ESL teacher understands how to promote students' content-area learning, academic-language development, and achievement across the curriculum.

- Content-area learning
- Academic-language development
- Achievement across the curriculum
- Effective practices, resources, and materials for content-based instruction
- Critical thinking
- Cognitive-academic language proficiency
- Preteaching key vocabulary
- Apply familiar concepts
- Cultural backgrounds
- Hands-on and other experiential learning strategies
- Using realia
- Media
- Visual supports to introduce and/or reinforce concepts
- Developmental characteristics
- Cultural and language background
- Academic strengths
- Learning styles/modalities
- Cognitive-academic language development
- Personal factors that affect content-area learning
- Prior learning experiences
- Familiarity with specialized language and vocabulary
- Familiarity with the structure and uses of textbooks and other print resources

Applies Knowledge of Effective Practices, Resources, and Materials

Effective practices that include how learning occurs in different stages of understanding (i.e., acquisition, cognition, and metacognition) are very important to an ESL teacher. When students are engaged in content-area reading versus simple narrative reading, the nonfictional, informational type of texts require a different approach. Science, history, mathematics, health, and other subjects all have specialized vocabulary and concepts. All new vocabulary must be *pretaught* for children to have any chance of understanding whatever follows in the lesson, and every opportunity should be made by an ESL teacher to provide visuals and models of the new language, vocabulary, and concepts. In the realm of content-area instruction, the ESL teacher knows that language arts is embedded in each of these subject areas. For this reason, the ESL teacher is aware that there are two types of simultaneous lessons taking place: (1) **linguistic** [the ability to comprehend new content terms when listening and to use them in speech] and (2) **conceptual** [academic application of abstract reasoning]. While taking advantage of effective practices, resources, and materials, the ESL teacher should be:

- engaging students in critical thinking (higher-order thinking as noted through Bloom's taxonomy);
- developing students' cognitive-academic language proficiency skills, better known as CALPS (Cummins, 1979);
- providing cooperative group work so that the teacher can monitor the level of linguistic challenge for the student in the new content-area vocabulary and conceptual understanding;
- listening critically to interpret and evaluate;
- using multiple types of strategies for learning and using the multiple intelligences information; and
- being aware that cognitive skills transfer from one language to another, and students who are literate in their first language will apply these skills (and other academic proficiencies) to the second language.

Instructional Delivery

The ESL teacher should always use **instructional delivery** practices or **strategies** that are effective in facilitating ESL students' comprehension in content-area classes by:

- preteaching key vocabulary;
- applying familiar concepts from students' cultural backgrounds;
- applying prior learning experiences to new learning;
- using hands-on (contextualized) and other experiential learning strategies;
- using **realia** (real-life examples), media, and other visual supports to introduce and/or reinforce concepts; and
- using technology to provided enriching experiences.

Let's try a question on the teacher's knowledge and application skill as it relates to the competency on content-area instruction:

During a social studies unit, a fourth-grade ESL teacher, Mr. Billingsly, introduces travel distance in terms of miles and kilometers. In order to understand the distance, students measure by walking around the school with the teacher and placing a red flag on the path for one kilometer walked and a blue flag for one mile walked. By the end of one mile, the time, number of feet, and the distance of a kilometer and a mile are logged by students and discussed. Distances are measured by the use of a pedometer, which measures feet, kilometers, and miles. Time is measured by a stop watch. The teacher's lesson is particularly effective for students' *academic language* (CALP) because it:

A. provides students with innovative approaches to learning.
B. supports content-area learning in a contextual, language-learning environment.
C. encourages students to make language experience connections to prior knowledge.
D. reinforces recognition of traveling distances.

In order to best create an environment for content-area achievement, the ESL teacher understands that academic language (CALP) in courses such as mathematics, science, and social studies will require both linguistic and conceptual skills. *Linguistic skills* are those used to read, write, speak, and listen to nonfictional or informational vocabulary found in content-area instruction. *Conceptual skills* include the ability to take linguistics skills to a higher level of abstract understanding and eventually to be able to learn without the need for concrete examples (in other words, *abstract reasoning*). For most students, this is begun through hands-on and participatory (*cooperative*) problem solving. In this lesson, actually walking the given distances helps ESL students build language experience with the vocabulary that they are challenged to learn and later apply. Therefore, the lesson implements the use of a contextual, lexical language-learning environment (*B*). Students develop both linguistic use of the language in the context of the lesson, while building conceptual understanding of measurement conversion. This approach not only encourages students to make language connections to concrete activities, it also provides language experience for later reflection of distance measurement. Hence, the best answer is what the author calls the "umbrella" answer (an answer under which the rest also fits); that is, Choice *B* because it supports achievement by tying language to the concept through active contextualized learning. Choices *A* and *C* may be true but are more about what the teacher is doing for the students rather than the students engaged in a hands-on (or in this case "feet on" experience). Choice *D*, even though it is good (the recognition of traveling distances) does not touch on students *vocalizing* their understanding for monitoring of understanding. The correct answer is Choice *B*.

Competency 007: The ESL teacher understands formal and informal assessment procedures and instruments used in ESL programs and uses assessment results to plan and adapt instruction.

- Formal assessment
- Informal assessment
- Authentic/alternative assessment
- Using assessment results to plan and adapt instruction (assessment loop)
- Test design, development, and interpretation
- Select, adapt, and develop assessments
- Diagnosis
- Program evaluation
- Standardized tests
- State-mandated LEP policies
- LPAC (Language Proficiency Assessment Committee)
- Identification, placement, and exit of ELLs
- State-mandated standards, instruction, and assessment
- Individual student needs
- Teacher-made tests
- Peer assessment
- Portfolio assessment
- Proficiency level
- Performance assessment

Test Design, Development, and Interpretation

This competency directs the ESL teacher to know basic concepts, issues, and practices in order to select, adapt, and develop assessments for varied purposes. Some of these purposes may include: program placements, diagnoses, ESL lesson and program design, implementation, evaluation, and modification. ESL teachers should plan for and be aware of on-going assessment opportunities—both those that are informal (oral questioning, observation, etc.) and those that are formal (usually in the form of standardized tests). For the purpose of assessing how well the teacher has taught, and even more importantly, how well the students have achieved, the following are critical areas to consider:

- **Diagnosis:** centers on finding solutions to a problem or roadblock that hinders a child's advancement in some way. Then, after a "treatment" has been introduced, it is incumbent upon a teacher to determine if this solution worked. An assessment loop includes: (1) observing a problem or roadblock in learning, (2) planning for a solution that may include a new curriculum, new strategy, etc., (3) evaluating the results to determine the amount of success, and (4) beginning the cycle again.
- **Program evaluation:** deciding which program best serves ELLs (i.e., bilingual, ESL, dual language, etc.) and being able to make recommendations accordingly; making judgments about particular programs.
- **Proficiency level:** desired for students (90 percent or better determines proficiency and no less should be accepted). Texas is a data-driven educational system and evaluation data of student performance determines effectiveness of teaching.

Evaluation measures should always be in place *prior* to instruction as part of the instructional planning process. In good planning for *all* instruction, teachers should begin with clear goals and solid objectives. This provides a benchmark to gauge differences in student achievement before and after instruction. Well-written objectives for individual learning levels help teachers to set measurable learning advancements for children. Pre- and post evaluations show how much growth took place; thus, the teacher can determine the effectiveness of his or her instruction and make a decision to reteach or continue instruction.

Formal, Informal, and Authentic Assessments

The ESL teacher applies knowledge of formal, informal, and authentic or alternative assessments in order to measure in terms of standardized state scores, developmental benchmarks, and actual real world skills for intended outcomes:

- **Formal assessment** evaluates student achievement for accountability and is measured *after* students have ample time to demonstrate mastery of intended objectives. These include standardized tests, TAKS tests, and benchmark testing.
- **Informal assessment** is often done orally or through observations as new material is being covered to readjust instruction as the teacher determines that a lesson is too advanced or too easy for students while monitoring the flow of learning. This type of assessment may also include mastery checklists, observations, informal inventories, data collected from others besides the ESL teacher, daily assignments, homework, projects, and so forth.

- **Authentic assessment** is usually understood to be real-life situations and/or **portfolio assessment.** Portfolios are designed to place students in the assessment "loop" to help them self-assess. By reflecting on previous learning and choosing artifacts that demonstrate intended learning outcomes and growth, they are given a sense of pride in their accomplishments, and, most importantly, directed toward improvement of learned skills the next time similar tasks are to be completed. An important aspect of *authentic assessment* is that skills such as actually making a multimedia presentation, "keeping a checkbook," delivering a speech in public, following directions for baking a cake, etc., may not be items tested on standardized tests, but they are indeed skills for which students apply their academics to real-world situations.

 ## Standardized Tests

The ESL teacher knows the types of standardized tests commonly used in ESL. Generally, there are two:

1. **Criterion-referenced tests** (such as the Texas Assessment of Knowledge and Skills [TAKS]) are standardized because the results can be *generalized.* This means the results of several demographic areas on the same test can be grouped together and assumptions can be made about all test-takers' performances, both overall and by individual items on the test. During this type of testing, those who administer the test must follow the same (or standard) rules of implementation and proctoring to ensure that the conditions for *all* test takers are as nearly the same as possible. This type of test is also called criterion-referenced because students are expected to know specific given material for each grade level and subject. For example, the TAKS examination tests specific knowledge and skills listed in the TEKS; the TExES ESL tests specific knowledge of the competencies found in this chapter. The student will receive a *percentage score* (i.e., 70 percent to pass, 90 percent to demonstrate mastery) for this type of test.

2. **Norm-referenced tests** such as ITBS, SAT, etc. are also standardized tests because they try to insure that test-taking conditions are the same for all students (*reliability*). However, students cannot possibly know all the material for each grade level and subject, so there is not a specific list of criteria *per se*. Scores are used to compare students against other demographic areas, and students are given *percentile scores* (i.e., scores are reported in terms of how well the student scored compared to similar test takers who have taken the same exam, as shown on a bell curve) instead of percentage scores. For instance, a student scoring in the 40th percentile on a norm-referenced English language arts test on their grade level would automatically be eligible to exit the bilingual/ESL program because this score would indicate that the student performed as well or better than 40 students of out 100 that took the same test. Of course, the same student would fall into the category of being monitored for success over the *next two years* due to the Language Proficiency Assessment Committee (LPAC) who maintains the responsibility for exiting ELL students.

   Mean, **median**, **mode** are used to determine information on tests about students. The *mean* is an average score (all scores are added and the sum is divided by the total number of scores); the *median* is the one score that falls right in the middle of all scores (in a group of tests in which the scores are 80, 90, and 100, the median is 90); and the *mode* is the score from a number of scores that occurs most often (in a group of test scores of 80, 90, 90, and 100, 90 is the mode).

Test bias often occurs for ELLs because tests can contain certain cultural references to which only English speakers and even, perhaps, only Americans (or even Americans from certain areas of the country) can relate. For example, *silos* (grain storage facilities) are a common site in the northern part of the United States but are rarely seen in the South. Thus a test item requiring knowledge of a silo to get the correct answer (for example, "A silo is a cone on top of a ____ ." [cylinder]) might find students from the North scoring higher, and many from the South lost. When ELLs cannot make a connection to this type of information, they get the item wrong—not because they are less smart but because the item is tied to a culture of which they are not a part. Test makers try to ensure *validity* (does a particular test *really* test what it is suppose to test) by item analysis to search for items like those just mentioned. The mathematics item in the example above would *not* be a valid one because a child may know what a cylinder is but not a silo. ESL teachers must be especially vigilant for test bias both on standardized tests given to ESL students and, especially, on their own teacher-made tests.

State-Mandated LEP Policies

The ESL teacher, more than likely, will be a regular member of the **Language Proficiency Assessment Committee (LPAC)**, which is responsible for the main purposes of recommending English Language Learners (ELLs) identification, placement, and exit in bilingual/ESL programs. The following guidelines are in place:

- State guidelines determine the makeup of the committee, functions of the committee, how often the committee meets (must meet at least once per year per student), other tasks of the committee, and administrative forms.
- If there are 20 or more ELLs at one grade level in a district, an ESL program is required.
- All students in an ESL or bilingual program are considered under federal as well as state guidelines (civil rights issue as a federally-funded program).
- Each student must have returned a home language survey, and those parents or students who mark that English is not their home language must take a language test within four weeks of their enrollment date.
- Any student who is found to have dominance in a language other than English should be offered a placement in an ESL program, but the *recommended* placement is decided by the LPAC.
- All students determined to be eligible for LPAC services must still have *parent permission* to be enrolled in a bilingual/ESL program. Those students not given parental permission are considered "waived" and will receive *no* special services. They are expected to meet annual testing requirements in English, regardless of the student's ability level in English. This can also make a school's TAKS test scores very low if children are unable to test well in English. The hope is for the ESL teacher to provide adequate reasoning for the parent to sign permission for student ESL services and then collaborate with families and the community for continued support.
- To exit an ESL program, a student must pass his or her Language Arts (Reading) TAKS test and, in addition, have his or her guardian's signature.
- After exiting, each student will be monitored by the LPAC for at least two years.

Let's try a policy question:

Mr. Long, a superintendent in a small district in northern Texas, was watching his enrollment of children who would be ELLs in the third grade. How many ELL children must there be before he must hire a third grade ESL (or bilingual) teacher?

A. 20
B. 15
C. 30
D. 10

If there are 20 or more ELL children in one grade level, an ESL program is required. The correct answer is *A*.

Instructional Relationships

In an effort to make connections to teacher and student standards, competencies, and expectations, the ESL teacher understands *assessment relationships* among:

- on-going, continuous assessment;
- state-mandated standards, which are the Texas Essential Knowledge and Skills (TEKS) or the requisite knowledge for grade levels and subjects;
- instruction of the TEKS, commonly known as the curriculum or student expected knowledge and skills;
- methodologies used in the classroom;
- assessment of instruction, which evaluates the planning implementation, evaluation of instruction, and reteaching or redirecting of instruction when needed; and
- the immediate need to address any professional development needs (based particularly on student performance on state measures).

The ESL teacher often needs to individualize instruction and assessment in order to address student needs and learning goals. Thinking in terms of measuring everything planned, implemented, evaluated, and redirected should be a continuous goal for ESL teachers. Where gaps in student achievement occur, particularly as revealed by annual state measurements (the TAKS) of students' progress, the teacher should plan to come together with fellow colleagues in an effort to plan professional learning activities that will provide both linguistic and conceptual improvement for the coming academic year.

See how you do with your knowledge and application of understanding on assessment!

Before beginning a mathematics lesson, Ms. Pruneda, an ESL teacher, has her fourth-grade students discuss their understanding of converting measurements from ounces to pounds and pounds to tons. The reason for this type of informal assessment is to:

A. encourage low-ability students to participate in the learning.
B. promote a sense of what will be covered as an advanced organizer or focus activity.

C. provide a sense of excitement about the content.

D. determine the appropriate developmental level of instruction at which to begin, according to the prior knowledge of the class.

Even though a good ESL teacher would like to (*A*) ensure that *all* students participate, that (*B*) he or she provides an advanced organizer or focus of the lesson to come and an enticement for students to become involved in the lesson is provided (*C*), in this case, it is *most* important for the teacher to start instruction at the correct developmental level. The answer, therefore, is Choice *D* and is based on the teacher discovering the prior knowledge of all students in the class. When educators talk about assessment, there must also be an observable, measurable product or process. As another hint, although participation by each student can be observed and measured informally, this question asked *why* the teacher should do this *before* the lesson. The correct answer is *D*.

DOMAIN III Foundations, Culture, Family, and Community/ Outside the Classroom/Continuous Professional Development and Community/Resource Outreach

STANDARDS II Foundations of ESL, V ESL Academic Content, Language, and Culture, and VII Family and Community Involvement

Competency 008: The ESL teacher understands the foundations of ESL education and types of ESL programs.

- Historical, theoretical, and policy
- Self-contained
- Pull-out
- Newcomer centers
- Dual language
- Immersion
- Apply research findings
- Instructional and management

Historical, Theoretical, and Policy Foundations

An ESL teacher should know the historical, theoretical, and policy foundations of ESL education and use this knowledge to plan, implement, and advocate for ESL programs that are truly effective. These areas include the following:

- *Historically,* immigrants have tried to maintain their home languages and cultures by providing instruction in their native languages, normally by speaking that language at home or by sending children to afterschool or Saturday L1 classes. With the influx of large numbers of immigrants, the Nationality Act of 1906 was passed to make sure that English would be learned but was later judged unconstitutional. In 1968, the Bilingual Education Act provided funds for bilingual/ESL programs. In addition, the **Lau vs. Nichols Act** of 1974 established rules to determine when districts must implement bilingual/ESL programs (typically, when a district has determined that there are 20 or more students across the district at the same grade level needing bilingual or ESL instruction, the district is bound to act and provide such services).

- *Theoretically,* **English as a Second Language (ESL)** is an educational approach in which **limited English proficient (LEP)**, or ELLs, are instructed in the use of the English language and in the various content areas in English.

Thus instruction is based on a special curriculum that typically involves little or no use of the native language and is usually taught during specific school periods; often students are "pulled out" of their regular classroom for language arts. For the rest of the school day, students are normally taught in a mainstream classroom, an immersion program, or a bilingual program (U.S. General Accounting Office, 2006).

- *State and national policy* tells all districts that they are required to conduct an ESL program and shall conduct *continuous* diagnosis and periodic assessment in the language of instruction to determine the program's impact and student outcomes in *all* subject areas. Annual reports of educational performance should reflect the academic progress in *either* language of the ELL students. Districts should also report the progress of their students annually. Each school year, the principal of each school campus (with the assistance of the campus level committee) must develop, review, and revise the *Campus Improvement Plan* for the purpose of improving student performance.

Types of ESL Programs

An ESL teacher should know the types of ESL programs (sometimes also termed **ELD** or English Language Development programs) along with their characteristics, goals, and research findings on effectiveness (Baker, 2001). Programs should include:

- **self-contained:** students have the same teacher for all subjects (except, perhaps, for special classes, such as music, art, or kinesiology [P.E.]);
- **pull-out:** students are taken out of regular classrooms for ESL instruction for a certain length of time, normally for language arts but return for most of the day;
- **Newcomer Center:** an entry program for supporting newly arrived immigrants that is short term (normally only up to a year), during which time the home language may be used at times for instruction but English and social adjustment is the focus;
- **immersion:** students are placed in a bilingual program in which the L1 home language is used only as needed, if at all, to clarify English instruction. Logically, students in bilingual lower grade classes will indeed use the L1 at a higher percentage to clarify English, whereas students that have greater English skills will incorporate much less help from the L1;
- **dual language:** (*two-way immersion*) native English speakers and students with another language are placed together; half of the day is taught in English and half in the home language of the other students—with the goal of both groups becoming bilingual. This type of program provides two main objectives, pride in L1 and a peer role model for L2. Research on this type of program is becoming quite promising; and
- **structured English immersion:** the student is taught in English using ESL techniques with the goal of English being foremost without concern for maintenance of the home language.

Make Appropriate Instructional and Management Decisions

ESL teachers must take into account all *external* forces that have a bearing on what it means to implement and maintain an ESL program (i.e., students' needs and achievement, rules governing such programs, and district and campus plans). Since ESL instruction is a federally regulated program and funded through federal money, it is imperative that specific records be kept, rules followed, and deadlines met. This is because students have a "property right"—meaning that they should expect a product for their efforts (such as a diploma upon graduation or, in this case, to speak English). Hence, many rules and regulations at the federal, state, and district levels are implemented to ensure that expectations are met. Districts not in compliance with state and federal standards can suffer adverse consequences. The No Child Left Behind Act of 2001 was a federal expectation that implemented measures to ensure that all states addressed accountability expectations. As a result, state and local education agencies became aligned with federal policy for the purpose of student achievement, namely reading on grade level by third grade and continuing to read on grade level for the remainder of a student's academic career. With such strict accountability measures in place with the component of second language instruction, many districts pay stipends to attract and retain quality ESL teachers.

Convergent Research Applied

It is the ethical and legal duty of the ESL teacher to keep abreast of important educational issues and findings about ESL and seize opportunities to collaborate with other professionals, families, and the community to improve instruction. Research is constantly being generated to help ESL teachers better understand what works and what may not work for ELLs. ESL teachers should always apply current knowledge of research findings related to ESL education (including research on instructional and management practices) to assist in planning and implementing effective programs (Baker, 2001). It behooves the ESL teacher to subscribe to professional journals and belong to professional organizations that advocate for ESL instruction.

Answer the following question relating to the competency on ESL foundations:

Which of the following programs, according to convergent research, *best* promotes pride in the primary language while still fostering academic language success in the target language?

    A. Transitional bilingual
    B. ESL
    C. Two-Way Dual Language
    D. Submersion

In this question, research firmly supports programs in which pride in the primary language (L1) is valued and maintained. The only program that maintains the L1 after English instruction is Choice C, two-way dual language. Transitional bilingual programs (A) in the state of Texas methodically replace Spanish with English as more English is acquired. This means that by the end of fifth grade, the student should be ready to enter into an environment of complete English instruction with no more L1 support. *ESL instruction* (B) is completely in English as well as *submersion* (D), where no program is offered (usually referred to as *immersion* or the "sink or swim" approach). However, in Choice C, two-way dual language, monolingual speakers of L1 and monolingual speakers of L2 come together in the same classroom (usually representing equal numbers of students for each language) to learn both languages. Two-way dual language can be called a "serpent model" because it involves switching instruction between the two languages—either by every other day delivery or half a day in the

L1 and half a day in English. When the two groups of monolingual speakers come together, they share the same anxiety and pride, depending on whether the current instruction is in the primary language or the target language. This builds pride in the primary language because it is valued and maintained and, at the same time, provides a model and mentor of language support by peers who speak the opposite language. The answer is *C.*

Competency 009: The ESL teacher understands factors that affect ESL students' learning and implements strategies for creating an effective multicultural and multilingual learning environment.

- Cultural and linguistic diversity
- Developmental characteristics
- Academic strengths and needs
- Preferred learning styles
- Personality
- Sociocultural factors
- Home environment
- Attitude
- Exceptionalities

- Affective, linguistic, and cognitive needs
- Cultural bias
- Stereotyping
- Prejudice
- Ethnocentrism
- Diverse cultural and socioeconomic backgrounds
- Awareness of and respect for linguistic and cultural diversity

---

Cultural and Linguistic Diversity

Cultural and linguistic diversity in the ESL classroom and other factors may affect students' learning of academic content, language, and culture. The following should be a focus of an ESL teacher as he or she prepares instruction:

- age (in terms of language acquisition, is neither related to age level nor grade-level specific);
- developmental characteristics (influenced by students' L1 and L2 experience and age [as one would consider if the child was not ESL]);
- academic strengths and needs (due to students' cultural/linguistic background and previous academic experience);
- preferred learning styles and modalities (thinking preferences and oral, visual, tactile, and kinesthetic modalities);
- personality (interpersonal, intrapersonal);
- sociocultural factors (religion, cultural rites of passage, expectations for genders, values, etc.);
- family unit (single, traditional, nontraditional, extended);
- home environment (low or high socioeconomic, abuse or neglect, family illiteracy, etc.);
- attitude (predisposition to learning may vary due to culture/language);
- exceptionalities, special education, gifted and talented, etc. (Section 504 is a civil rights law that prohibits discrimination against individuals with disabilities. Section 504 ensures that the child with a disability has equal access to an education. The child may receive accommodations and modifications.) Remember that an ELL could have any of the special needs that other children may have in addition to ESL needs. The ESL certification is supplemental because an ESL teacher must also be qualified to address children with special needs.
- **self-fulfilling prophecy**—a teacher's beliefs will create experiences for success when they feel that ESL children (1) can learn English quickly, (2) can compete with native English speakers, and (3) that bilingual children have advantages over monolingual children.

Diversity: Multicultural and Multilingual

Creation of an effective multicultural and multilingual learning environment should be a priority for the ESL teacher. It is also incumbent upon a teacher to ensure that he or she does not stereotype a culture (Bennett, 1998). For example, Puerto Ricans are generally considered Hispanic, but their culture is very different from that of Mexicans or Argentineans, just as the Japanese culture is very different from other Asian cultures such as Korean, Chinese, or Vietnamese. All cultures within an ESL class should be celebrated. Language and culture cannot be separated; therefore the ESL teacher would benefit from learning more about the particular cultures and languages represented in his/her classroom. For instance, if one is in an ESL class where the L1 is Spanish, one would expect to hear such terms as *mariachi* (Mexican musician), *aplácate* (calm down!), *tacos* (tortillas wrapped around a wide variety of meat and other ingredients), and so forth. However, those words may or *may not* mean the same thing or be understood by Hispanic societies that reside distantly from Mexico. As a parallel example, for a Texan the English word "boot" is footwear, but from the perspective of an English speaker from Britain, a "boot" is also recognized as the trunk of a car. The teacher who is not that fluent or speaks a particular dialect of another language must also attend to translations that he or she attempts in another language. The use of some verbs may be confusing and occasionally offensive (i.e., "discussion" in Spanish means *to argue*, while in English it means *to talk over,* so if a teacher asks children to have a discussion with this word in Spanish, he or she may be confused as to why children begin to argue).

Cultural Bias

There are a number of factors that contribute to cultural bias (Bennett, 1998). Because ESL children are from an increasing number of cultures, the ESL teacher should reflect upon these factors daily to be sure that there is a culturally responsive learning environment in place. **Bias** is defined as prejudice or to influence in a particular, typically unfair, direction. The unequal direction in most classrooms involves language used by a teacher that is not familiar or understandable to students. Bias occurs in teaching, testing, and other areas of education in which comprehensible or familiar ideas are *not* used, leaving many ELL students at an academic disadvantage. Cultural bias contains the following elements:

- **stereotyping** (false notions or conceptions of other races, etc.);
- **prejudice** (intolerance or hatred of other races, etc.);
- **ethnocentrism** (belief one's own group is superior to others); and
- **unfamiliar language used**, resulting in a disadvantage to those who do not understand and an advantage to those who do.

Sensitivity and Respect

The ESL teacher must always demonstrate sensitivity to students' diverse cultural and socioeconomic backgrounds and show respect for language differences. A teacher in an ESL classroom quite often represents all Americans to children and their parents, so this is not to be taken lightly. It should be a goal of the ESL teacher to learn all there is to know about his or her students (especially if there is a particular language or culture that is predominant in the area), and the teacher should try to learn some basics of the language of his or her students. Teachers have an opportunity to learn language and culture from their students—if they will take advantage of the situation.

The more the ESL teacher knows about his/her students, the better children respond to intended learning outcomes. Even learning a few words of the child's language is a step, but the teacher should definitely seek information on differences in social values (including differences in child rearing), personal space, cultural comfort level in touching, patterns of communication with body language, and in ways of listening and talking, especially with reference to the adult/child communication norms. One reminder, however, is that each child and family member is an individual and should not be automatically slotted into a stereotype of a particular culture simply because they are a recent arrival from a particular country. The Web is full of sites that give information about almost every country, and there are many suggestions in travel guides (or business travelers' guides) for interactions with the culture and descriptions of social norms of a particular country.

It is not required that teachers take on the beliefs and values of others, but understanding differences always helps in communication and gaining respect with families and their children. For example, in the Thai culture it is very distasteful to touch someone on the head, to point one's feet at someone else, or to shove an object at someone with one's feet. Direct eye contact is disrespectful towards elders in many Hispanic and Asian cultures, whereas in America, if children do not make eye contact, it is seen as being "guilty." In Spain and Brazil, and in many Middle Eastern countries, the sign Americans make to signal "OK" is considered offensive—even obscene. Cultural differences may also deal with attention to (or lack of attention to) time, dress, diet, grooming, and other body language. A savvy ESL teacher who does a bit of research can make children and their families feel more at ease as they are learning about America and its ways. Teachers can also avoid mistakes in judging children's knowledge and behavior versus their culturally different responses.

Strategies for Awareness

There are effective strategies for creating an awareness of and respect for linguistic and cultural diversity among students. Foremost, the teacher always models appropriate behavior. The ESL teacher must be careful to attend to such issues in the context of actual teaching and demonstrating what linguistic and cultural diversity looks like and how it should be supported by way of classroom examples. Each child should feel equally welcomed and equally served by the education received in a classroom. As an advocate for ESL students, the ESL teacher has limited control of the world outside the confines of the classroom, but he or she should be a constant example for students in appropriate dress, conversation, body language, politeness, and overall behavior.

The following question relates to the competency of multicultural and multilingual environments:

A new ESL teacher has been assigned to a classroom that includes students from several different ethnic, cultural, and language backgrounds. In order to *best* address the needs of the class, which supposition should be used to guide instruction?

A. Students should be paired with others who have similar backgrounds in order to ensure goals and objectives will be understood.

B. Students tend to learn best when they have choices in their own learning and assessments.

C. Students from any one of the various backgrounds can be expected to display a wide range of abilities, shortcomings, and interests.

D. Students from different backgrounds learn best when there is no mention of differences between them.

In order to best understand multicultural and multilingual issues in the classroom, the ESL teacher knows that language and culture *cannot* be separated. However, within Latin, Asian, and other cultures, there are many linguistic and cultural differences. First, the ESL teacher must be clear on the term *supposition*—it is a belief thought to be true based on *incomplete* evidence. What the ESL teacher should believe about different ethnic, cultural, and language backgrounds *should be* true or at least measurable in order to include supporting evidence. For this reason, we find that Choice *A* is not measurable because simply pairing students with similar backgrounds in no way supports that they will meet goals and objectives of learning. Choice *B,* giving students a choice in their own learning and assessment, is good motivational theory when children have choices at times. However, we will see that there is a better belief for a multicultural/multilinguist class. In Choice *D,* making no mention of the differences between students is not good for anyone. In fact, *celebrating* differences should be a focus of multicultural and multilingual awareness, although it is also very beneficial to examine what children have in common as well. This leaves Choice *C,* because it is held to be true. Students from many different backgrounds, cultures, or languages *can* be expected to display a wide variety of abilities, strengths, shortcomings, and interests. Each child will be an individual case. The correct answer is *C.*

Competency 010: The ESL teacher knows how to serve as an advocate for ESL students and facilitate family and community involvement in their education.

- Family and community involvement
- Advocating educational and social equity for ESL students
- Participating in LPAC (Language Proficiency Assessment Committee) and ARD (Admit, Review, and Dismiss) meetings
- Serving on SBDM (Site-Based Decision Making) committees
- Serving as a resource for other teachers
- Facilitating parent/guardian participation
- Communicating and collaborating effectively with parents/guardians
- Community members and resources positively affect student learning
- Accessing community resources

Teacher as an Advocate

ESL teachers must have considerable knowledge about laws and effective strategies to advocate for educational and social equity for ESL students. In this competency of family and community awareness, it becomes obvious that the ESL teacher must step *outside* the classroom to stand up for ESL children and their right to learn. This is accomplished by participating in:

- **the Language Proficiency Assessment Committee (LPAC),** which recommends identification, placement, and exit of English Language Learners (ELL) in bilingual/ESL programs.
- **the Admit, Review, and Dismiss (ARD) Committee,** which determines identification, placement, and exit of special education students and the appropriate **Individual Education Plan (IEP)** for such labeled students. An ELL may also be identified as having special needs.

- the **Site-Based Decision Making Committee (SBDM)** which is charged with planning for better student achievement each year at the *building level,* including ELL achievement.
- becoming a resource for other classroom teachers by serving as a mentor, sharing research and techniques, taking time to gain joint assessments of students they may have in common, and so forth.

Family Involvement

Every teacher hopefully knows the importance of family involvement for their children. However, in the education of ESL students, the teacher must go a step further in facilitating parent/guardian participation in their children's education and school activities. Although a language difference may make communication difficult, it is not necessary that the parents of ESL students speak English in order to have parental involvement. Many aspects of involvement are fruitful without speaking English. The ESL teacher must communicate with parents because:

- family support has a direct relationship to student achievement.
- families should be encouraged to help their children in academic topics using their *native language* when they are not fluent in English; having parents/guardians trying to help in nonfluent English for mathematics or science homework, for example, may confuse students on the academic concepts. Helping in the student's L1 also promotes pride in native culture and language.
- parents can provide support by making sure there is space in the house to do homework and research, establishing routines for doing school work, seeing that necessary school items are provided so students do not waste time in gathering supplies (i.e., paper, pencils, etc.), and visiting the school, seeking to collaborate, and attending students' events.

Family Collaboration

The ESL teacher applies skills for effectively communicating and collaborating with the parents/guardians of ESL students in a variety of educational contexts. This means that, whatever it takes, the ESL teacher finds the means to communicate the mission, goals, and routines of effective instruction with the parent. If there is no common language between the parent and the ESL teacher, every effort should be made to finding someone in the building or using other students who can translate. Some focus areas should be:

- collaborating. Asking for family information about the child, support, and advice can help teachers more quickly understand individual characteristics of students;
- making the school a welcoming place. For example, one ESL teacher sent a videotape to her ESL students' homes before the first day of school to help parents and children feel comfortable finding the classroom from the point of view of a visitor walking up the walkway to the school, signing in at the secretary's desk, walking to the child's classroom, "meeting" the ESL teacher at her door, and going through the classroom. Another school provides a parent room where caregivers can meet for socialization, receive free English lessons several mornings a week from English-speaking parents, help teachers prepare materials, if desired, and so forth;

- remembering that the entire family is new to this country and that they are often embarrassed, uneasy, or even fearful of communication with teachers; some families may even see the school as a state agency that might report on their immigration status—rather than as a helpful entity;
- having ESL children serve as translators can put them in a difficult spot at times, especially when problems exist, and they are caught between powerful people in their lives. A teacher candidate recently told about having her fourth-grade ESL teacher calling to report some "bad" behavior—which she promptly "translated" to "excellent" for her parents. Her advice is to never (if possible) have students translate information to their parents, in which the child has a stake.
- supplying parents with a developmental look at their child's progress in each area taught is crucial (i.e., beginning of the year work, middle of the year work, and mastery of intended learning outcomes);
- having teachers try their best to encourage parents to come into the schools (establishing social events at which children are performing and/or where there is food is often profitable; transportation and babysitting can also be problematic, so one school district runs its buses during Open House and provides some classrooms with volunteer babysitters for very young children—with excellent results);
- having teachers communicate by many means that parents understand (avoiding jargon, providing plenty of time for translations/understanding to occur);
- making sure that the medium used to communicate important information (e-mail, phone conversation, conferencing, etc.) can be easily used by each child's caregiver(s), and, if not, provide adequate alternative measures to insure the information is getting home (i.e., if a Web site is used to inform families and community of important school events and procedures, make sure that all intended parties have access and the language skills necessary) or provide an alternate and appropriate form of communication; when needed, teachers seek out and arrange translators who can help in *all* home languages of the students in the classroom; and
- sending take-home literacy or other projects in which parents are able to participate in their children's education.

Community Members and Resources

Community members and other human resources can positively affect student learning in the ESL program. The ESL teacher should access community resources to enhance the education of these students. This means that the ESL teacher must:

- actively seek successful community member models from the same ethnicity, culture, gender, and so forth. Jumping into abstract ways of conveying the same information will never have the same impact as having a real person who "looks like you" share his or her skills, perceptions, and/or advice on how to be successful. Language experience is built by making it easier to process conceptual ideas based on meaningful concrete experiences (i.e., instead of reading about what it takes to be an engineer, a doctor, etc., have someone come and talk with students who comes from the same socioeconomic and cultural situation as them). No matter what the discipline, a real person provides an opportunity to answer questions that are of interest to students as well as providing a model of success, leading children to think, "If that person can overcome his second language adversity and succeed, so can I!"

- seek community support in school activities (i.e., one-on-one literacy help from the retired community, financial support for equipment from local businesses, discounted rates on field trip activities and other educational supplies, etc.).
- be innovative and think "outside the box" when it comes to asking for outside support and expertise. When students have the opportunity to interact with successful people outside of education, they can begin to internalize the importance of the authentic connection of education to becoming a successful and productive citizen.

Let's try a question on family and community awareness for ELLs:

Ms. Zhang is a fourth-grade ESL teacher. She has children who have a variety of home languages but who are working on level with the fourth-grade TEKS. Ms. Zhang is trying to decide how to best provide information on the school Web site so that it can be easily understood by parents. She has thought about translating the information to all the languages represented in her diverse class. What strategy would *best* accomplish this?

- **A.** Send a flyer home in English (so that she will know which parents have the English skills to translate) to ask for those parents who are able to come to school and work with the teacher on this project.
- **B.** Call or e-mail students' families with a message translated into their own languages in order to solicit help in this matter.
- **C.** Have students from each language group translate the information from English to their native languages.
- **D.** Ask the LPAC specialist in the building to recommend people for this task.

Involving family in the learning environment helps student success, so we might be encouraged to select Choice A. Unfortunately, that would leave out particular languages in which family members do not have a good grasp of English. However, teachers do want to remember that there are many things caregivers can do to ensure they are active participants in their child's academic life *without* speaking English well. Each family will participate at their own comfort level—provided the teacher opens the doors for a variety of ways to do so. Choices B and D are also tempting because we know that family and community involvement in schools is part of these competencies. However, there is a better answer.

By having the students translate Web information into their primary language in an effort to better inform parents, the ESL teacher has captivated the resources of the class community, student's pride in their primary languages, and inferred to all who may see the Web site that this class celebrates all languages and cultures. For this reason, the *best* answer is *C*.

GLOSSARY

Academic language development. Involves student development in semantic and syntactic features, such as vocabulary items, sentence structure, transition markers, and cohesive ties, and/or specialized language functions and tasks that are part of a *content-area classroom* routine, such as defining terms, explaining historical significance, reading expository text, and preparing research reports (Wertsch, 1985).

Academic language. Lexical language or language needed to comprehend and communicate about content-area subjects, such as mathematics, science, and social studies.

Academic English. Includes vocabulary that is used beyond social conversations; the vocabulary needed to communicate effectively in content-area classes and to comprehend various texts in different content-area classes; "the ability to read, write, and engage in substantive conversations about math, science, history, and other school subjects" (*Research Points,* AERA, 2007); skills related to mastery of academic English include summarizing, analyzing, extracting and interpreting meaning, evaluating evidence, composing, and editing. It relies on a broad knowledge of words, concepts, language structures, and interpretation strategies.

Achievement across the curriculum. ESL teachers must not only help students achieve in learning English but also know and use ESL strategies to help students in the content areas, such as mathematics, science, social studies, art, music, and health/P.E.

Acquisition. The *subconscious* process of learning to comprehend and communicate in a language gained through meaningful interactions in the target language in natural communication (as opposed to book learning, study of grammar, and drill).

Advocating educational and social equity for ESL students. Participating in LPAC and ARD (Admission, Review, and Dismissal) meetings, serving on SBDM (Site-Based Decision Making) committees, serving as a resource for other teachers, etc., in order to ensure that each ELL has the same chance of success as those who are not ESL.

Alphabetic language. English is a written language in which symbols (the alphabet) reflect the pronunciation of the words; Greek, Russian, Thai, Arabic, and Hebrew are also alphabetic languages; it may or may not be the case that students' first language is alphabetic (but symbolic or ideographic), possibly making the transfer to English more difficult.

Alphabetic principle. Making connections with the fact that symbols stand for sounds in a written language.

Apply familiar concepts. Using prior knowledge from students' cultural backgrounds and prior experiences to connect new learning; using hands-on and other experiential learning strategies; using realia, media, and other visual supports to introduce and/or reinforce concepts.

Apply research findings. ESL teachers *must* stay current in the latest research on ESL learners.

Assessment to plan and adjust instruction. Continuously asking "how is this student progressing" through informal and formal means, then changing techniques to address both the needs of the class and of individuals.

Attitude. When working with young readers, struggling readers, or readers for whom English is not their primary language, it is important to emphasize activities that will promote students' positive mindset toward reading and the development of their reading skills.

Authentic assessment. A form of assessment in which students are asked to perform real-world tasks (or as near to real world as the classroom allows) rather than pen-and-paper drills.

Behaviorist theory. A belief that humans learn language through reinforcement.

BICS (Basic Interpersonal Communication Skills). Students can usually develop the basic ability to communicate *socially* in a new language within six months to two years.

Categorization. The basic cognitive process of arranging information into classes or categories (i.e., classification, sorting).

CALPS (Cognitive Academic Language Proficiency Skills). Proficiency in *academic* language development needed for content areas with specialized, lexical terminology; usually takes 5–7 years to develop.

Circumlocution. Correcting an ELL's statement by restating the student's mistake several times in correct English within a conversation rather than drawing direct attention to it or provide a rule.

Cognitive processes. Memorization, categorization, generalization, metacognition; involved in synthesizing and internalizing language rules for second-language acquisition.

Communicative competence. Having the skills to speak and comprehend when spoken to in order to communicate in a language.

Community resources. Positive community role models and resources can positively enhance student learning in the ESL program.

Comprehensive input. Teachers must be sure that the language they are using to address students (input) can be understood by ELLs, especially in academic subjects.

Concept. A general idea derived or inferred from specific instances or occurrences; something formed in the mind; a thought or notion. ELLs must often gain academic concepts at the same time they are grappling with learning English.

Content, language, and culture. Factors may affect students' learning of academic content, language, and culture (e.g., age, developmental characteristics, academic strengths and needs, preferred learning styles, personality, sociocultural factors, home environment, attitude, exceptionalities).

Content-area learning. Learning in mathematics, science, social studies, music, etc., that requires both *linguistic* and *conceptual* skills, particularly with the academic or lexical vocabulary.

Conventions of language. General agreement on or acceptance of certain practices or attitudes in the use of language, including grammar, spelling, punctuation, language usage, capitalization, legibility, sentence structure, and paragraphing; language practice or procedure widely observed in a group, especially to facilitate social interaction; a custom: for example, the usage of *y'all* for *you* in the South.

Critical thinking. The intellectual process of actively and skillfully conceptualizing, applying, analyzing, synthesizing, and/or evaluating information gathered from (or generated by) observation, experience, reflection, reasoning, or communication.

Culture. Socially transmitted behavior patterns, arts, beliefs, institutions, and all other products of human work and thought; these patterns, traits, and products are considered the expression of a particular period, class, community, or population.

Cultural and language background. Language and culture work together in language development and cannot be separated; furthermore, the importance of understanding individuals' cultures and language backgrounds is paramount for promoting language development.

Cultural and linguistic diversity. ESL teachers can expect to have students from many diverse backgrounds; teachers should gain knowledge in each individual's cultural and linguistic background rather than stereotype an "umbrella" culture (i.e., not all Hispanics come from the same country or culture; Hispanics come from Europe, the Caribbean, and Asia as well as North, Central, and South America with cultural and language differences that are not necessarily the same dialect or culture as that of Mexico).

Cultural bias. Stereotyping, prejudice, or ethnocentrism that causes one group to look down upon another group or to see their own group as superior; also, assessments that are unfair because they contain items based on cultural references unknown to those who are "outside" the culture and could not be answered correctly without that knowledge.

Delivery of instruction. Delivery of instruction can be found in several different areas: learner support and resources, instructional design and delivery, assessment and evaluation of student learning, use of technology, teacher use of student feedback, addressing learning styles, etc.

Developmental characteristics. Social, emotional, academic, and behavioral features that are interrelated parts of language development.

Developmentally appropriate instruction. Refers to Vygotsky and the "zone of proximal development" or "the distance between the actual development level as determined by independent problem solving and the level of potential development as determined through problem solving under adult guidance or in collaboration with more capable peers" (Wertsch, 1985). For ESL purposes, a teacher should slightly challenge the student with input.

Diagnosis. The critical analysis of language development for ESL students.

Discourse. Verbal expression in speech or in writing.

Discourse competence. The ability to interact with native speakers using various communication strategies, social registers, conversation, narration, inquiry for information, directing others, and so forth.

Dual language. A language approach emphasizing equality of educational opportunity for both English and non-English-speaking children through an educational process that validates and fully develops both languages and instills a mutual respect for both language learners; students are taught half the time in the L1 of half of the students and half of the time in the L1 of the other half.

ELLs (English Language Learners). Students who are placed in ESL or bilingual classrooms; formerly, the label was Limited English Proficient (LEP).

Engaging instruction. Motivating instruction that increases the involvement of students and seeks for them to take ownership of their learning and do meaningful and effective work.

English language arts and reading competencies (ELA). The basis of ESL instruction; all ESL teachers must also attend to these and the ESL competencies.

English language proficiency. Proficiency in English for ESL students is typically determined upon passing a standardized English language test. A score of 70 percent for criterion-referenced tests or fortieth percentile for norm-reference tests are adequate levels to be labeled *proficient*. Students are tested on their ability to comprehend English in order to be exited from an ESL program; students are monitored for the following two years after exiting to ensure academic success in the regular English classroom.

Enhanced learning. Provides improved, advanced, or sophisticated features to the learning process (computer software is one such medium that enhances instruction and learning with cutting-edge functionalities that include interactions, immediate feedback, guided practice, self-direction in learning, etc.).

ESL programs. Types of ESL programs include self-contained, pull-out, Newcomer Centers, dual language, and immersion.

ESL standards for Texas teachers. (1) Prerequisite understanding of English language concepts and acquisition of English; (2) methodologies; (3) oral communication; (4) literacy skills and assessment; (5) ESL foundations; (6) multicultural and multilingual perceptions; and (7)

third-party awareness for a comprehensive overview of ESL instruction.

ESL teaching strategies. Groups of activities specially designed to produce outcomes that create an effective multicultural and multilingual learning environment leading to positive ELL student achievement.

Ethnocentrism. A belief in the superiority of one's own ethnic group.

Facilitate learning. To increase the likelihood, strength, or effectiveness of learning.

Familiarity with the structure and uses of textbooks and other print resources. ESL teachers understand that children from other countries may not know how to address print resources, such as magazines, newspapers, and Web-based articles (for example, children may not understand the concept of reading by scanning left to right).

Formal assessment. A structured measure of learner achievement over a period of time, usually meaning the use of tests and exams (which are often standardized, such as the Texas Assessment of Knowledge and Skills [the TAKS test]).

Foundations of ESL education. The ESL teacher knows the historical, theoretical, and policy foundations of ESL.

Fundamental language rules. The fundamental rules of language at initial stages of language development.

Generalization. A language principle, statement, or idea having general application: *change y to i and add ed.*

Grammar. The branch of linguistics that deals with syntax, morphology, and semantics.

Hands-on and other experiential learning strategies. Using manipulatives and other concrete objects in the context of building conceptual understanding.

High-frequency words. Words that appear many more times than most other words in spoken or written language.

i + 1. The teacher assesses the learner's language level and adds one level to it to encourage challenging learning; as in Vygotsky's zone of proximal development.

Identification, placement, and exit. The major role of the Language Proficiency Assessment

Committee (LPAC) that is based on student achievement and standardized tests scores.

Idiomatic expressions. Expressions that are sentences or phrases that do not exactly or literally mean what they say, so that even if one knows the meaning of every word used, they can rarely be understood due to cultural and linguistic differences (for example, "Does the cat have your tongue?").

Immersion. Method in which the home language is rarely (if ever) used, and then only to clarify English.

Informal assessment. Ongoing appraisal by casual observation, discussion, or by other nonstandardized procedures.

Instructional and program management practices. All ESL program decisions should be data driven.

Instructional goals. Clear statements of what teachers want learners to accomplish.

Instructional strategies for ESL. Specific activities (what the teacher and students do) that should be based on accepted ESL methodologies or theory and designed to expand the thinking potential of students.

Integrate technology tools. Combining technology (i.e., hardware, software, peripherals, and use of the Internet, etc.) with content area and reading/language arts to enhance instruction.

Interpretation of results. Understanding formal, informal, and authentic assessment procedures and instruments (both in English proficiency and academic achievement); used in ESL programs to plan and adapt instruction as needed.

Interrelatedness of listening, speaking, reading, and writing. ESL teachers teach all of these areas in concert to increase mastery in English (because what students learn in one area will help in others).

Interrupted schooling. ELLs may have not had the opportunity to attend school regularly, which becomes a personal factor that can have an effect on ESL students' English literacy development.

Language. Involves communication of thoughts and feelings through a system of arbitrary signals, such as sounds, gestures, or written symbols. Such a system includes rules for combining the components and is used by a nation, people, or other distinct community.

Language Proficiency Assessment Committee (LPAC). Maintains responsibility for identification, placement, and exiting of ELLs from an ESL or bilingual program; monitors ELLs for success for two years after exiting.

Lau vs. Nichols. Established that a district must provide an ESL or bilingual program if there are 20 or more ELLs in a grade level.

Learned knowledge (versus acquistion). The conscious, intentional study of a language, its structure, and the way it functions through formal work.

Learning styles. Preferences for thinking and learning in specific ways that facilitate ESL students' communicative, literacy, and cognitive-academic development.

LEP (Limited English Proficiency). Has been commonly replaced by the Office of Civil Rights with ELL (English Language Learner), which is less negative in its connotation.

Letter-sound associations. The understanding that a written letter "stands" for a certain sound; *phonics.*

Lexical understanding. Vocabulary belonging to a particular subject (as in mathematics, science, or social studies) that one must understand in order to navigate through that particular content area.

Linguistic competence. The ability to use the correct grammatical form and structure to express a given meaning.

Linguistic environment. A supportive, positive oral/speaking environment with considerable conversational opportunities is important for ESL development.

Literacy development. Literacy development usually occurs in stages starting with oral language development and continuing to high levels of oral and written language applications. Therefore, the continuum of eleven ELA EC-4 competencies is written in this prescribed order.

Literacy status in the primary language. The level of a student in his or her native language will have an effect on the level to be achieved in L2; the better one knows his or her L1, the easier it is to learn L2.

Mean. Average of a number of scores.

Median. A score that falls in the middle of a range of scores.

Metacognition. Awareness and understanding of one's own thinking and cognitive processes; thinking about one's thinking.

Methods (of instruction). Methodologies that are identifiable techniques that can be widely used in ESL instruction, examples include "total physical response" (Asher, 2000), sheltered English, grammar translation, and computer-assisted instruction. More methods can be found in the third ESL competency.

Mode. The most frequent score in a number of scores.

Modifying instructional materials. The teacher uses assessment and appropriate data to determine what are the most appropriate materials for achieving instructional goals and changes them based on continuously gathered feedback.

Morphology. The study of the structure and form of words in language or a language, including inflection, derivation, and the formation of compounds. The smallest segment of sound that carries meaning, e.g., *un-true,* where *un* is a segment of sound and *true* is the smallest segment of sound that carries meaning. Words are the interface among phonology, syntax, and semantics.

Multicultural and multilingual learning environment. An effective, supportive, and respective environment (Bennett, 1998) that addresses the affective, linguistic, and cognitive needs of students from many countries (who may speak a variety of languages) and facilitates students' learning and language acquisition.

Nativist theory. Belief that humans are born with the innate ability for speaking language, and when exposed to language, this ability "kicks in"; an innate propensity for language acquisition.

Newcomer Centers. A bilingual or ESL program that makes use of facilities to separate first-year ELLs from the general population and takes advantage of ESL methodologies to better enhance academic success for this population of students. The Newcomer Centers serve these students through a program of intensive language development and academic and cultural orientation, for a limited period of time (usually from 6–18 months), before placing them in the regular school language support and academic programs.

Oral discourse. Conversation.

Overgeneralization. A language learner applies a rule to all circumstances (for example, adding *–ed* to the past as in "I *goed* to the store" or "He *stoled* my pencil").

Personal factors. Prior learning experiences, familiarity with specialized language and vocabulary, familiarity with the structure and uses of textbooks and other print resources, special needs, etc.

Phonemic awareness. Skills for the ability to hear, identify, and manipulate individual sounds (or *phonemes*) in spoken words; teachers should teach phonics skills as they are a good predictor of overall reading success, spelling, and comprehension; teaching the alphabetic principle (sound-to-symbol awareness) is effective in promoting phonemic awareness.

Phonetically irregular words. Words that are not pronounced like the rules that *should* govern them state.

Phonograms. Characters or symbols, as in a phonetic alphabet, that represent a word or phoneme (smallest unit of the sound system of a language) in speech.

Phonological knowledge and skills. Include phonemic awareness skills, knowledge of English letter–sound associations, and knowledge of common English phonograms.

Phonology. The study of speech sounds in language or a language with reference to their distribution and patterning and to tacit rules governing pronunciation.

Pragmatics. Language messages often consist of interpretation not based on the exact words (although not idioms). For example, if a boy asked a girl who was not interested in him on a date, she might reply in the *negative* by saying, "You've got to be kidding me, right?" or if someone asked, "Where is the rest of that homemade pie?" and the reply was, "Well, John was here . . ." that would mean John ate it (Payne, 2005).

Preferred learning styles. Learners have thinking and modality preferences (visual, auditory, tactile, or kinesthetic) that teachers should tap into to enhance individual success.

Prejudice. The act or state of holding unreasonable preconceived judgments or convictions about a particular group of people.

Preteaching key vocabulary. Before a content-area lesson begins, teaching the vocabulary necessary to understand the particular lesson helps in building linguistic and conceptual understanding with required informational, nonfictional vocabulary.

Prior literacy experience. Some ESL children may or may not have had formal or informal experiences with literacy due to interrupted schooling, poverty, etc.

Proficiency. The ESL teacher understands the difference between language proficiency and academic achievement (cognitive) and knows that ESL students who do not acquire the new language with the academic concepts will suffer academically.

Program evaluation. The systematic collection of information about the activities, characteristics, and outcomes of an ESL program to make judgments, improve effectiveness, and/or develop informed decisions about future development.

Pull-out. An ESL model in which students leave the regular classroom for a period of time during the school day in order to work with a special ESL teacher alone or in a small group.

Reading comprehension. Factors that affect ESL students' reading comprehension, including vocabulary, text structures, and cultural references.

Realia. Real things, such as photos, posters, books, souvenirs, and postcards; types of real material that the teacher can introduce to make instruction more concrete.

Receptive vocabulary. The amount of spoken language one can aurally process, which is usually up to four times greater than an individual's ability to speak.

Registers of language. (1) *Casual* [language used with family and friends that is not always "correct" English]; (2) *consultative* ["correctly" spoken English]; (3) *formal* [very "correct" English used in academic situations and business]; (4) *frozen* [words do not change and most people know them well, such as the "Pledge of Allegiance" and religious passages such as the Lord's Prayer]; and (5) *intimate* [language that is used between lovers or with wanted and unwanted sexual connotations] registers in English; ESL students can blunder by using conversation in the wrong register, so ESL teachers must also address this aspect (Payne, 2005).

Respect for language differences. The teacher demonstrates sensitivity to ELLs in showing students that they can achieve; simply because students currently do not have sufficient English skills, they are not necessarily below-average learners.

Rich, comprehensible language environment. The ESL teacher understands the role of a linguistic environment and conversational support in second-language development and uses multiple opportunities and activities for communication in English.

SBDM (Site-Based Decision Making) Committee. Schools in Texas each have a committee established to make decisions that will impact the achievement of children at their particular schools; ESL teachers should serve on this committee to advocate and ensure the rights of ELL children.

Sentence structure. The grammatical arrangement of words in sentences and the patterns and conventions of written and spoken English.

Self-contained. ELLs are taught with regular English-speaking students for the entire day, or students are placed in an ESL classroom with ESL students with similar needs in language arts and the remaining content-area subjects taught there as well.

Self-fulfilling prophecy. A teacher's *belief* in a student's (or students') success or failure will influence the end result.

Semantics. The study of meanings of words, expressions, and sentences.

Sight-word vocabularies. Phonetically irregular words, high-frequency words (*could, know*, etc.).

Social versus academic language. Vernacular or commonly spoken English (BICS) versus lexical or academic English (CALPS).

Social cognitive and social cultural theories. Belief that language is learned through social interactions and models (who adjust their levels for children).

Sociocultural factors. Includes religion, rites of passage, expectations for genders, values, and so forth.

Sociolinguistic competence. The ability to interact in different social registers using appropriates rules and politeness for that situation.

Standardized tests. Tests such as the Texas Assessment of Knowledge and Skills (TAKS test) that are uniformly developed, administered, and scored so that students are on an equal footing in terms of the conditions of testing and item biases.

State-mandated LEP (Limited English Proficient) policies. Includes the role of the LPAC (Language Proficiency Assessment Committee) and procedures for implementing LPAC recommendations for ELL identification, placement, and exit.

State-mandated standards, instruction, and assessment. The ESL teacher understands he or she must plan instruction according to Texas standards (the TEKS), implement instruction according to research-based methods and strategies, and assess student achievement (through the TAKS) in order to improve student achievement.

Stereotyping. Holding beliefs about a group of people that places them in categories that often lessen their chances of interaction and diminishes their potential; believing that individuals hold certain identified characteristics simply because they belong to a particular group.

Strategic competence. The ability to make use of limited linguistic resources to express one's ideas and comprehend input.

Structure. Formal systematic arrangements of a language.

Syntax. The grammatical arrangement of words in sentences.

Synthesizing. Integrating analyses of data to discover facts and/or develop knowledge concepts or interpretations.

TEKS (Texas Essential Knowledge and Skills). Teachers are required by the state of Texas to teach these for each grade level in content areas and in English Language Arts; ESL also has TEKS for each grade level.

TEKS in English Language Arts. Listening, speaking, reading, writing, and viewing/representing.

Test bias. Test construction which can skew the test scores toward or against a particular group(s) of test takers; this can often work for American children and against ELLs.

Text structures. Incorporating cause and effect, comparing and contrasting, sequencing, main idea, etc., to apply effective strategies for facilitating ESL students' reading comprehension in English.

Theories. Models based on currently accepted hypotheses; beliefs derived from many supporting studies.

Total Physical Response (TPR). A method used for assessing understanding; when the ESL teacher gives a command and the recently arrived student performs the command correctly or not (Asher, 2000).

Transfer from L1 to L2. Students can use concepts learned about their first language (L1) and can transfer these to help learn their second language (L2) more easily; language transfer theory supports that literacy skills and concepts learned in the first language will transfer to the second.

Visual supports. Video and graphics generated by computer projecting makes content-area concepts easier to understand because complex matters can be easily represented and presented by modern electronic media.

Word analysis skills. Students can "sound out" words that they cannot automatically recognize by sight through phonics strategies that relate to the alphabetic principle (a letter stands for a sound).

Word formation. The basic part of any word is the root; a prefix at the beginning of a root word and/or a suffix at the end can be added to change the meaning.

REFERENCES

American Educational Research Association (2007). *Research points.* Retrieved on January 1, 2007, from *http://www.aera.net/publications/?id=314/.*

Asher, J.J. (2000). *Learning a language through actions* (6th ed.). Los Gatos, CA: Sky Oaks Productions.

Baker, C. (2001). *Foundations of bilingual education and bilingualism* (3rd ed.). Bristol, PA: Multilingual Matters Ltd.

Bennett, C.I. (1998). *Comprehensive multicultural education: Theory and practice* (4th ed.). Boston: Allyn & Bacon.

Cummins, J. (1979). Cognitive/academic language proficiency, linguistic interdependence, the optimum age question and some other matters. *Working Papers on Bilingualism, 19,* 121–129.

Government Accounting Office of Records. (2006). *No child left behind act: Assistance from education could help states better measure progress of students with limited English proficiency.* Retrieved on January 5, 2007, from http://www.gpoaccess.gov/gaoreports/index. htm

Krashen, S.D. (1992). *Fundamentals of language education.* Torrance, CA: Laredo Press.

Krashen, S.D., & Terrell, T.D. (1996). *The natural approach: Language acquisition in the classroom* (revised ed.). Englewood Cliffs, NJ: Prentice Hall.

Nath, J.L., & Cohen, M.D. (Eds.) (2002). *Becoming an EC-4 teacher in Texas: A course of study for the Pedagogy and Professional Responsibilities (PPR) TExES*. Belmont, CA: Thomson/Wadsworth.

Payne, R.K. (2005). *A framework for understanding poverty* (4th ed.). Highlands, TX: aha! Process Inc.

Peregoy, S., & Boyle, O. (2005). *Reading, writing, and learning in ESL: A resource book for K–12 teachers* (4th ed.). Boston: Pearson/Allyn & Bacon.

Texas Education Agency. (1997). *Texas Essential Knowledge and Skills (TEKS)*. Retrieved on June 6, 2006, from http://www.tea.state.tx.us/teks/index.html. Austin, TX.

Texas Education Code. *Texas Essential Knowledge and Skills*. (1998). Retrieved on January 16, 2007, at http://wwwtea.state.tx.us/rules/tac/chapter110/index.html

State Board for Educator Certification (2007). *TExES preparation manuals*. Retrieved on January 5, 2007, from http://www.texes.ets.org/prepMaterials/.

Wertsch, J. V. (1985). *Vygotsky and the social formation of mind*. Cambridge, MA: Harvard University Press.

RESOURCES

Center for Applied Linguistics: www. cal. org

Center for Research on Education, Diversity & Excellence: www.crede.ucsc.edu

National Clearinghouse for English Language Acquisition: www.ncbe.gwu.edu

Bilingual Research Journal: http://brj.asu.edu/

IDRA Newsletter: http://www.idra.org/Newslttr/Newslttr.htm

National Association for Bilingual Education: http://www.uc.edu/njrp/

LEER MAS: http://www.tea.state.tx.us/curriculum/leermas/

Handbook for the Implementation of Bilingual/English as a Second Language Education Program: http://www.esc19.net/Handbook/Resources/Terminology.pdf

AN ESL LESSON PLAN

The following plan has been developed based on Texas Essential Knowledge and Skills (TEKS) for the Kindergarten through Grade 1 levels for acquisition, cognition, and metacognition in L2. What is important to remember is that second language acquisition and learning does not have grade level or age level specificity—rather a language level ability (i.e., beginning level, intermediate level, or advanced level). Some school districts distinguish levels as in pre-production, early production, speech emergent, intermediate fluent, and advanced fluent, or, levels 1–5 respectively. Therefore, the TEKS (Tevas Essential Knowledge and Skills) for the lower grade levels make great ESL lessons for early listening, speaking, reading, and writing development, depending on the developmentally appropriate level of the learner.

Title of Lesson: Pets

Grade Level: Second–Fifth

Main Subject Area: ESL

Subjects Integrated: Language Arts, Math, Science, Social Studies

Time Frame/Constraints: Depends on grade level

Overall Daily Goal: Constantly build on acquisition (listening and speaking), cognition (hands-on), and metacognition (reflection) of all instruction, linguistic and conceptual.

TEKS/TAKS OBJECTIVES:

§ K-3.15 **Reading/inquiry/research.** The student generates questions and conducts research about topics using information from a variety of sources, including selections read aloud.

Objectives: Students will view a multimedia or PowerPoint presentation on pets (viewing).

Students will listen to the teacher telling about his or her pet experience(s) (listening).

Students will participate orally in a KWL chart and tell about their own pet experiences (speaking).

Students, in groups, will research an assigned pet on the Web (reading).

Students, in groups, will complete a poster on an assigned pet (listening/speaking).

Students will write sentences on their favorite pets (number will be assigned on an individual basis, according to English level) (writing).

Environmental Concerns: Be sure to place students in heterogeneous groups with regard to English levels so that there is a stronger English speaker in each group. If a child has just lost a pet or had to leave a pet behind, it could be emotional for him or her.

Sponge Activity: Students review visual images on a looped multimedia or PowerPoint Slideshow of many types of pets (dogs, cats, fish, gerbils, turtles, snakes, birds, etc.) with names of the pets beneath each picture.

Focus: The teacher will tell about her experience with pets. Students complete the first two parts of a K-W-L chart (what they *know, want* to learn, and what they *learned*) about pets. (When students share their understanding and past experiences in a whole-class forum about such items, the ESL teacher is informed as to what level of understanding is pervasive.)

Connections to Past or Future Leaning: K-W-L chart.

Connections to Community: Ask students where they can obtain pets in their community and where they can get supplies to care for pets. What are the most popular pets in their community? Where in their community do they take a pet if it gets ill or is injured?

Cultural Connections: Are there pets that are more popular in some cultures than in others? Are pets more respected in some cultures (example, in ancient Egypt cats were seen as gods). In English culture, if you cross the path of a black cat, it is seen as good luck, but in American culture, it is seen as bad luck.

Connections with Student Interests and Experiences: Tell if you have a pet(s) at home. If not, what pet would you most like to have? Why? Do you care for the pet?

Rationale: Many families would like to keep pets, but they are not sure how much it will cost or how to care for them. Knowing this information in advance may help decide whether or not to obtain a certain type of animal for a pet.

Materials: PowerPoint presentation of pets; bookmarked Web sites for the level of English needed; list of pet foods and other needed supplies and their costs; poster boards; art paper for illustrations

Activities: Guided Practice: Students will view looped PowerPoint slideshow and review vocabulary words for each pet. The teacher will ask students to complete the "K" & "W" in a K-W-L chart on pets. The teacher will show other vocabulary with pictures related to pet supplies (bowl for fish/turtle, litter, leash, etc.). Groups will be assigned a pet and will look on specially bookmarked Web sites at the price of obtaining their assigned pet and to obtain information about their pet's care. Groups will examine a list of food prices from a local pet store to care for their pet and determine how much it might cost to keep their assigned pet per week. Groups will complete a poster on their assigned pet, giving basic information on their pet, its needs, and cost per week. They will have a choice of presenting it to the class or putting it up on the wall so others can see. In a whole class setting, students will complete the "L" of the K-W-L chart.

Independent Practice: Students will write complete sentences in English on what pet they would like the most and why.

What Will Students Do Who Finish Early?

Students will illustrate their own pets or their favorite type of pet.

Assessment: Each group will complete a poster showing three areas: their pet, its basic needs, and how much it costs to keep it each week. All students will have a walk-about to view the posters. Each child will receive an individual paper assignment to complete a specific number of sentences in English (according to individual levels), explaining why he or she would most like to have a specific pet. The teacher will assess on an individual basis, according to level.

Closure: The teacher will play "20 Questions" with students ("I'm thinking of a pet . . . "). Students have to ask the teacher questions to guess the pet about which the teacher is thinking.

Modifications: Number of sentences assigned will be according to level of individual student.

Reflection: Add after teaching.

DRAFT YOUR OWN ESL LESSON PLAN

Title of Lesson: ————————————————————————

Grade Level: ——————————————————————————

Main Subject Area: ————————————————————————

Integrated Subjects: ———————————————————————

Time Frame/Constraints: ——————————————————————

Overall Goal(s): ————————————————————————

TEKS/TAKS Objectives: ———————————————————————

————————————————————————————————————

————————————————————————————————————

Objective(s): ——————————————————————————

————————————————————————————————————

————————————————————————————————————

Sponge Activity: ————————————————————————

————————————————————————————————————

————————————————————————————————————

Environmental Concerns: ——————————————————————

————————————————————————————————————

————————————————————————————————————

Rationale(s): ——————————————————————————

————————————————————————————————————

————————————————————————————————————

Focus or Set Induction: ——————————————————————

————————————————————————————————————

————————————————————————————————————

Making Connections: ————————————————————————

————————————————————————————————————

————————————————————————————————————

1. Connections to Past or Future Learning: ——————————————

————————————————————————————————————

2. Connections to Community: ——————————————————————

————————————————————————————————————

3. Cultural Connections: ————————————————————————

————————————————————————————————————

4. Connections to Student Interest(s) & Experience(s): ————————

————————————————————————————————————

Materials: _____

_____

Activities: **Guided practice:** _____

_____

_____

_____

_____

Independent practice: _____

_____

_____

_____

_____

Assessment: _____

_____

What Will Students Do Who Finish Early? _____

_____

Closure: _____

_____

Modification for Students with Special Needs: _____

_____

Reflection: _____

_____

EVALUATION OF EC-4 ESL EXPERIENCES/ACTIVITIES

During your visit to an ESL classroom, use the following form to provide feedback as well as to reflectively analyze the room, the materials, the students, and the teacher.

	Observed	Not Observed	Response
1. Teacher adapts to children's language level on an individual basis.			If so, how? If not, what could be changed?
2. Teacher adapts content-area language to the appropriate level (comprehensible but slightly challenging input).			If so, how? If not, what could be changed?
3. Teacher links content to past learning.			If so, how? If not, how could this have been accomplished?
4. Teacher makes use of the growing capacity of computers for audio, visual, and tactile advantages in modern applications.			If so, how? If not, how could this have been accomplished?
5. Teacher makes connections to children's backgrounds.			If so, how? If not, how could this have been accomplished?
6. Teacher uses various multiple intelligences and modalities.			If so, how? If not, how could this have been accomplished?
7. Teacher makes use of body language and gestures to aid comprehension.			If so, how? If not, how could this have been accomplished?
8. Teacher makes use of concrete items (realia) to aid comprehension.			If so, how? If not, what could be added?
9. Teacher makes use of specific ESL strategies/and methodologies to aid comprehension.			If so, describe. If not, what could the teacher add?
10. Teacher models tasks to aid in comprehension.			If so, how? If not, what effect did this have on a completed project?
11. Teacher checks for understanding often to ensure comprehensible input.			If so, how? If not, how could this have been accomplished?
12. Teacher integrates other content areas and/or uses thematic units.			If so, describe. If not, what could be added?
13. Teacher provides an effective guided practice.			If so, describe. If not, what were the results?
14. Teacher provides an authentic (real-world) connection (rationale) and/or tasks for learning.			If so, how? If not, how could this have been accomplished?

	Observed	Not Observed	Response
15. Teacher uses authentic assessment for skills (i.e., multimedia presentations, speeches, building projects, writing "real" letters, etc.).			If so, how? If not, how could this have been accomplished?
16. Teacher facilitates (as well as teaches) the lessons.			If so, how? If not, describe other roles the teacher may have used? Tell if they were effective.
17. Teacher provides various seating configurations (whole group, cooperative groups, partners, and independent).			If so, describe. If not, what configurations would have been more appropriate?
18. Teacher uses various assessment instruments in written work.			If so, describe. If not, give ideas for what could have been added in a developmentally appropriate way.
19. Teacher uses various ongoing assessment instruments in oral work.			If so, describe. If not, give ideas for what could be added in a developmentally appropriate way.
20. Teacher provides materials that are developmentally as well as linguistically appropriate.			If so, describe. If not, give ideas for what could be added.
21. Teacher effectively preteaches all important content terminology before lessons begin (provides visuals, graphs, etc.).			If so, describe. If not, give ideas for what could be added.
22. Teacher clearly defines the stage of the lesson (i.e., acquisition [new learning], cognition [cooperative learning], and metacognition [reflective learning]).			If so, describe. If not, give ideas for what could be added.
23. Teacher makes the objective for the lesson very clear and provides students with expectations for the product, process, quantity, quality, and time limit of the intended learning.			If so, describe. If not, give ideas for what could be added.
24. Teacher demonstrates collaboration of family and community somehow in the teaching process.			If so, how? If not, how could this be accomplished?
25. Teacher introduces objectives that are clearly measurable and understood by students to direct their own learning.			If so, describe. If not, give ideas for what could be added.
26. Teacher clearly demonstrates expertise in ESL and in English, so as to serve as a good model.			If so, describe. If not, explain.
27. The environment is positive and relaxed for students.			If so, describe. If not, what could be improved and how?

	Observed	Not Observed	Response
28. Students make use of the interrelation of reading, writing, speaking, and listening as they are engaged in their own learning.			If so, describe. If not, what could be improved and how?
29. Students vocalize key terms often.			If so, describe. If not, when could this element be added?
30. Students are self-assessing and continually reflecting on the product, process, quantity, quality, and time limits involved in their learning.			If observed, describe some examples of where. If not, suggest some areas.
31. Students transition efficiently between whole class, cooperative groups, and individual lessons with minimal waste of valuable time.			If observed, describe some examples. If not, suggest some areas for improvement.
32. Students are involved with technology (i.e., word processors, databases, audio/video files, interactive computer programs, Internet investigations, computer reference materials, multimedia presentations, etc.).			If so, list those that are currently set up to which children have access. If not, describe how technology could improve this classroom.
33. If the program is a pull-out, students transition easily to their regular classroom.			If so, describe. If not, discuss what changes could be made to help.
34. Students understand clearly which type of learning will take place (i.e., acquisition [new learning], cognition [cooperative learning], and metacognition [reflective learning]).			If so, describe. If not, give ideas for what could be added to aid understanding.
35. Student uses content-area language orally with appropriate linguistic use of the lexical (academic) terms.			If so, how? If not, what could be changed?
36. All students participate orally.			If so, how? If not, how could this be accomplished?
37. The teacher projects a caring and respectful attitude with each child.			If so, how? If not, how could this be accomplished?
38. Students use strategies to solve problems.			If so, how? If not, what could be added?
39. Students use reference materials, both concrete and technological, to support learning.			If so, how? If not, how could this have been accomplished?
40. Students are engaged in contextual (hands-on) activities to enhance understanding of abstract concepts.			If so, how? If not, how could this have been accomplished?

	Observed	Not Observed	Response
41. Students work cooperatively and share leadership and support roles.			If so, how? If not, how could this have been accomplished?
42. Students understand the concept involved in the lesson.			If so, tell how you would know. If not, how could this have been accomplished?
43. Students make use of organizers, rubrics, timers, journals, and other support materials.			If so, how? If not, how what could be added?

TEST YOURSELF ON ESL

1. Mrs. Bradford's lesson for today focuses on <u>phonology.</u> On what will students work?
   A. Pragmatic language
   B. Graphemes
   C. Target sound
   D. Syntax

2. Helene said to her father, "Dad, I gotted this toy out of the closet." The language error committed by the child is common for children of her age. In which area of language development is she having trouble?
   A. Overextension
   B. Hyperbole
   C. Overgeneralization
   D. Assimilation

3. Trang, a mid-level ESL student, would have the most problems with which of the following statements?
   A. She got to school on time.
   B. She got against the wall to be safe.
   C. She got under the umbrella when it started to rain.
   D. She got over not making the cheerleading team.

4. What two language theories usually go together in order to promote *beginning* ESL students in speaking English?
   A. Affective filter-comprehensible input
   B. Self-monitor–affective filter
   C. Acquisition and learning theories
   D. Comprehensible input–self-monitor

5. Mr. Kuan pairs up Sunil, a new student from India, with Meera, also from India, who has been in the United States for more than two years. Which of the following is the *most* important reason for Mr. Kuan's actions?
   A. It insures that there will be someone who can translate important information to the new student when the need arises.
   B. It takes advantage of the affective filter theory and acclimates the new student to the class with little wasted time.
   C. It ensures that the ESL teacher will not have behavioral problems with a student who is bored when he cannot comprehend.
   D. Students paired together who are from the same language and culture base tend to learn more quickly.

6. Mrs. Sarenson, a beginning ESL teacher, is taking advantage of the district Web site to keep parents informed of class activities, homework assignments, school events, and so forth. What is the *most* important thing she should keep in mind using this type of medium?
   A. To use an attractive, colorful, and hyper-linked format so it is easy to find.
   B. To give written instructions that are simple and easy to understand.
   C. To supply the information to caregivers in other ways, in case they do not have access to the Internet.
   D. To send home flyers for parents that give explicit instructions on how to use computers in the school, public library, or other computers connected to the Internet so they will be able to access information in various locations.

7. Mr. Verde, the ESL teacher, regularly leads a class discussion in English with beginning level students about things he knows that students understand in their primary languages. He is sure this will help students acquire new English vocabulary because:
   A. students who do not perform well in English will have a model for dialoguing.
   B. this process encourages students to set a purpose in their interactions.
   C. students should make direct connections between their prior knowledge and the ability to translate terms mentally.
   D. activating prior knowledge, regardless of the language in which it was learned, will facilitate acquisition of new vocabulary and subsequent conceptual understanding.

8. When planning content-area curriculum, the ESL teacher should first:
   A. determine if students are too linguistically challenged by the unit's language goals and objectives.
   B. plan the assessment that will be used at the end of the unit.
   C. develop a rubric that will ensure that students follow the goals and objectives of the unit.
   D. use grading scales that will allow each level of learner to achieve at his or her own pace.

9. Ms. Zheng reads a passage to her third-grade intermediate-level students and comes across an expression the students do not understand. The phrase was, *out of the blue* (meaning *all of sudden* or *out of nowhere*). The teacher quickly realizes the need to teach language like this on a regular basis. These type of phrases are called:
    A. a nonstandard regionalism of English.
    B. idioms.
    C. dialectic phrases.
    D. lexical references.

10. Languages such as Spanish, German, Italian, Vietnamese, and French are alphabetic. Some students from these diverse backgrounds have varying levels of difficulty when reading English because:
    A. prior knowledge of the alphabet from a student's first language will not transfer to English.
    B. phonetic differences with English tend to create confusion with figurative meaning.
    C. phonemic awareness in the first language is unique to that language only.
    D. the phonetic irregularities of English can make understanding difficult especially when decoding or reading aloud.

11. What are the two most important areas an ESL teacher must consider when planning new lessons and curriculum in mathematics, science, and social studies?
    A. Language acquisition and learning theories in the instruction
    B. Linguistic and conceptual challenges of the instruction
    C. Authentic and formal assessment of the instruction
    D. Formative and summative evaluations of the instruction

12. ESL learning in the content areas begins with:
    A. encouraging students to make sure they identify areas that they did not understand well and ask for help in those areas.
    B. calling on the more advanced students, so lower-level students will benefit from the dialogue.
    C. speaking clearly and using language that is not biased in nature.
    D. previewing unfamiliar terminology, representing and presenting new concepts in a variety of ways, and providing multiple opportunities to reflect on cognitive learning.

13. In addition to formal assessment in the ESL classroom, Mr. Rosenthall also uses authentic assessment. The purpose of authentic assessment would be to:
    A. provide a measure that is more reliable than other measures.
    B. provide the benchmark by which all students will be compared for grading.
    C. provide a rubric for students in order to determine what is done and what remains to be done.
    D. provide for measuring actual skills "from the real world."

14. The Texas Assessment of Knowledge and Skills (TAKS) examinations are released to the public each year after all districts have completed testing. These exams can be located online for current and previous even-numbered year TAKS testing at the Texas Education Agency Web site (1997). Each item on the answer keys for TAKS includes the objective measured and Texas Essential Knowledge and Skills (TEKS) expectation for the student. The intent of showing both the objective and the student expectation for each item on the TAKS answer keys is to:
    A. make parents aware of school performance.
    B. help school personnel better analyze test results and plan professional development.
    C. justify the validity and reliability of formal state testing.
    D. single out schools and districts not performing at acceptable levels so the state can plan adequate interventions.

15. Which Supreme Court decision supported the contention that non-English-speaking students do not have equal access to education when instruction is delivered in English only?
    A. The Bilingual Education Act, Title VII of 1968
    B. The Nationality Act of 1906
    C. The Lau vs. Nichols Decision of 1974
    D. The National Defense and Education Act of 1958

16. According to the rules of the Language Proficiency Assessment Committee (LPAC), how often should this committee follow up on students who have exited the program? LPAC committees must monitor the progress of exited LEP students for:
    A. two academic years.
    B. one academic year.

C. every semester.

D. until the student graduates from high school.

17. An elementary third-grade ESL teacher, Mrs. Strahan, has been told by her grade-level team that they will be celebrating *Cinco de Mayo,* Mexico's Independence Day. However, after some research, she finds out that this information is "not exactly true," and the true Mexican Independence Day is in September. *Cinco de Mayo,* she finds, represents only an important battle that Mexico won against a European force. However, from what she understands, this is a very large event the school celebrates each year. She has already planned for students to bring in photos, food, clothes, and other relics related to *Cinco de Mayo.* What should she do *first* in light of her new cultural awareness?

A. Cancel class participation this year because the information is wrong.

B. Promote cultural awareness and respect by going along with it this year since she is new to the team.

C. Bring this issue to the grade-level team immediately and try to work toward consensus on a reasonable adjustment in light of the new information.

D. Tell her students about what she has learned and have them tell their parents in case any of them would be offended by this error.

18. During an informal conversation, a third-grade ESL student from the Caribbean tells his ESL teacher that he is embarrassed to invite his parents to the student award celebration because his parents did not go to school. He is afraid that his parents will not be accepted by others. The student's comment about his parents shows that:

A. he does not respect his parents.

B. he is experiencing culture shock.

C. he still needs more time to acculturate to the ways of this part of the United States.

D. he is experiencing cultural and social conflict.

19. Maria, a fourth-grade ESL student, tells her teacher, Ms. Newhauser, that she has to miss school again the following day. Concerned about the child missing school so often, the teacher asks if there is anything she should know or do for Maria. Upon further explanation, the student reports she is going with her parents to get the lights turned on for their new apartment and that Maria has to translate for them (just like when she translated for them to purchase some larger items like their washer/dryer and helped translate during their doctor's appointments). Worried that this may cause undue stress on the student and cause her to miss too much class time, the ESL teacher should:

A. inform the parents by phone call or personal visit that their daughter is expected to be in school, and if absent, the school does not receive funding from the state according to "average daily attendance."

B. explain to the mother that it is not appropriate for the parents to put such a burden on a fourth-grade student and that, in addition to the stress, it will cause the student to get behind and possibly fail.

C. arrange for the student to make up the work and send supplemental instructions for the work to the parents to ensure the student does not get too far behind.

D. obtain the parents' permission to call ahead to the light company to determine if there are people there who can translate for them and ask if they can make a reservation for these services.

20. Some parents of ESL students have made it clear they do not want to cause any problems with the school by interfering with what the teacher is doing in class. Many of them are under the assumption that the school is a state institution, and parent collaboration is not allowed or encouraged because they may have nothing to offer. What would be the *first* thing the teacher should do to change this assumption?

A. Communicate clearly that when parents are involved in the education of their children (whether they speak English or not), children tend to succeed academically.

B. Promise that all concerns will be dealt with according to parent wishes.

C. Explain that helping in school can only help improve English skills.

D. Plan various school events designed to help parents be more involved in the academic affairs of their children.

21. Mr. Gladstone greeted his new student, Bonhwa, when Ms. Carlton brought him into the teacher's regular fourth grade classroom in October. "I have a new fourth grader for you for this year, Todd," she said, "and he doesn't speak any English yet." "What!" said Mr. Gladstone, "Why aren't you taking him to Susan's ESL class?" Ms. Carlton replied:
    A. "Her room is full. There isn't any more space right now. We'll place him later."
    B. "His parents would not sign for special language services."
    C. "We have four weeks to get him tested, so he will be with you for those four weeks."
    D. "We don't have an ESL class in Korean, Todd."

22. Mrs. Vadelia was asking the rest of her LPAC if they had to meet for Roberto this year. "He passed his Language Arts/Reading test and his parents signed off when I had him last year in the third grade," she noted. Which response is correct:
    A. "No, we don't have to meet. He's 'good to go.'"
    B. "Yes, because you signed him off too early."
    C. "Yes, we have to meet about him through his fifth grade year."
    D. "Yes, we have to meet about him through his sixth grade year."

TEST YOURSELF ANSWERS AND RATIONALES FOR ESL

1. *Phonology* is target sound or patterning of speech sounds in a language (*C*). Choice *A*, *pragmatics*, represents the ability to understand meaning when the words do not translate exactly (for example, "Dude!" in some areas of the country means, "Hello, how are you?"). *Graphemes* (*B*) are simply letters of a language (which represent letter sounds as in *ph, th,* or *sh* that represent a phoneme). Syntax (*D*) represents the order or grammatical formation of sentences. The correct answer is *C*.

2. *Overgeneralization* (*C*) is the normal developmental process in learning English, ex-

tending the application of a rule of language to every case. Here, she adds –*ed* to an irregular verb to make the past tense. *Overextension* (*A*) is the overuse of a single word children in the early development of spoken language employ to denote meaning (i.e., a child learns what a cat is but makes the assumption that all four-legged animals are cats even when such subsequent animals may be horses or dogs). *Hyperbole* (*B*) is an intentional or obvious exaggeration. *Assimilation* (*D*), in second language theory, is when a student replaces his or her native language with English and may also give up one's home values and culture. The correct answer is *C*.

3. "Getting over" something is using English *figuratively,* not *literally*. Such idioms are very difficult for ESL students to understand. Choices *A, B,* and *C* are all *literal;* that is they mean exactly what they say. The correct answer is *D*.

4. A low affective filter (low level of nervousness) and comprehensible input (understanding speech) (*A*) are two things needed simultaneously in order for beginning English Language Learners to begin conversing in the target language. Self-monitoring (*B*) is only possible after early literacy speech is apparent and output of speech begins to follow a more grammatically correct format. Acquisition and learning theories (*C*) distinguish subconscious and conscious learning respectively. Comprehensible input–self-monitor theories (*D*) are two theories mentioned at very different stages of language development. The correct answer is *A*.

5. When beginning-level ESL students arrive at a new school and begin with a new teacher, it is most important to pair them up with someone who can speak their language (when possible), who knows the rules and routines. The student can more readily engage in classroom activities and lessons without concern. All of these answers have some merit, but we are looking for the *best* one. Choice *A* ensures that there will be someone who can translate important information to the new student when the need arises, but the continued

act of translating makes it unnecessary to attend to English as much. When students figure out the routine of the class, they should be separated from students who speak the same language if possible, to take advantage of attending to more English. Considering that a teacher may have behavioral problems with a student who is bored when he or she cannot comprehend can certainly be a factor, but it is not the *most* important issue for a newly arrived student (*C*). Quickly getting ESL students into a routine of engagement and purposeful learning is paramount. The belief that students paired together who are from the same language and culture base tend to learn more quickly (*D*) is a common misconception. In order to learn English, it is better (after the initial arrival) to pair students with others who do not share the same language in order to investigate and problem solve with the target language of English in common. The answer is *B*.

6. Even though using technology is the goal of many schools these days, the ESL teacher cannot forget that *many* parents, particularly those who may have just arrived, still require more traditional methods to disseminate important information (*C*). They simply may not have access to the Internet or know how to use it. To use an attractive, colorful, and hyperlinked format so it is easy to find (*A*) does not get the job done with parent and guardians. Presenting written instructions that are simple and easy to understand (*B*) may be desirable, but they are useless if they are not read because the parents don't use the Internet. Sending home flyers for parents that give explicit instructions on how to use computers in the school, public library, or other computers connected to the Internet so they will be able to access information in various locations (*D*) may be condescending and could cause alienation problems. It is also very possible that some parents could not get to these places. The correct answer is *C*.

7. Activating prior knowledge, both factual and conceptual, is helpful when ESL students understand content but not the English words. All students, in all languages, have many things in common that they understand (e.g.,

riding in a car, eating supper, going shopping, working, sleeping, and having animals). The only thing they lack is the vocabulary to talk about these things. The *best* answer is *D*.

8. All of these options have merit for ESL instruction. However, if students are linguistically challenged in their ability to speak content-area or lexical (academic) words in mathematics, science, and social studies (for example, *quadratic equation, scientific method, apartheid*), they will have difficulty understanding the concepts (when they are not understood in either the L1 or L2). First, an ESL teacher must determine linguistic abilities. The *best* answer is *A*.

9. Idioms (*B*) are one of the most difficult areas of English for ESL students to understand because they have no literal meaning, making them truly confusing when translated. Examples include, "starting from scratch", which is an equestrian term of lining up horses for a race at the point where a straight line had been scratched in the dirt (in the days before starting gates), or, "I would kill for a hamburger right now"—the speaker really does not intend to kill anyone but would *really* like to have this particular food. A *regionalism* of English (*A*) is a speech form, expression, custom, or other feature peculiar to, or characteristic of, a particular area. A *dialect* (*C*) is considered a language with a common root to another language (as in Hawaiian Pidgin English), but may not even be understood well by majority language speakers. *Lexicon* (*D*) refers to the vocabulary of a particular language, field, class, or subject—a language within a language. The correct answer is *B*.

10. Phonetic irregularities (*D*), exhibited by words such as *thought, have, mother, the,* and *been,* are words that are not *decodable* (or able to be read graphophonically), and they do not follow regular English rules. They also may not have representative sounds in other languages. This part of English acquisition and learning requires the ESL teacher to teach word analysis skills and physically model how to produce such sounds. Prior knowledge of the alphabet from a student's first language (*A*) *will* transfer to English. The fact that phonetic differ-

ences with English will tend to create confusion with figurative meaning cannot be substantiated (*B*). It is not an easily measurable variable for such advanced understanding of English. Phonemic awareness in the first language being unique to that language only (*C*) is not completely true. Since all the languages mentioned are alphabetic, many of the target sounds are the same. The correct answer is *D*.

11. Content-area instruction has two major components, *linguistic* (language) skills and *conceptual* (cognitive) skills. The ESL teacher knows that in order to master mathematics, science, social studies, etc., the ELL must acquire new content vocabulary, use that vocabulary in cognitive activities with peers while speaking and problem solving, and frequently reflect on what has been learned and what can be improved in future attempts to learn similar vocabulary and concepts. Language acquisition and learning theories (*A*) are rather global and are not measurable. Authentic and formal assessments of the instruction (*C*) are done *after* linguistics and conceptual understanding take place. Formative and summative evaluations of instruction (*D*) are steps the ESL teacher takes during and after lessons, although the teacher should plan for measuring how much children learn during the planning process. The *best* answer is *B*.

12. Content-area understanding starts with previewing unfamiliar terminology and making sure that, when the new lexical language shows up in reading, the ESL student will not be confused on pronunciation or the concept (*D*). In addition, teachers should represent and present new concepts in a variety of ways including maps, charts, graphic organizers, pictures, and images (all of which can be done in conjunction with technology). Finally, teachers should provide multiple opportunities to reflect on cognitive learning. Too often, ESL students, even adults, are too shy or timid to ask for help (*B*). Calling on the more advanced students so lower-level students will benefit from the dialogue is not inclusive and also singles out those that are not advanced (*B*). This can be demoralizing for the less advanced students.

Even if you raise the level of your voice and speak clearly, this won't help (*C*). You simply must preteach all vocabulary and use visuals when possible. The correct answer is *D*.

13. Authentic measures of intended learning normally refers to assessing by "other than paper and pencil." For example, in order to assess public speaking ability, the student should give a speech, or in order to effectively use multimedia, the student should manipulate a computer and the required software. These types of skills are authentic to real-world applications and are necessary to accompany purely cognitive skills. The correct answer is *D*.

14. Instruction must be informed by data obtained through assessment. This assessment may be informal, formal, or authentic. Released TAKS tests are a good way to obtain more formal data on students at the beginning of the school year, which will inform both the student and teacher of achievement on state-expected knowledge and skills. The data can also be used to inform professional development needs in instruction. Answer *B* is cause for future action and improvement; the others are not. The *best* answer is *B*.

15. In the famous Lau vs. Nichols Decision of 1974 (*C*), it was found that one of the major purposes of bilingual education was to keep the student on grade level by providing content instruction in the L1 while acquiring English. Simply providing instruction in English is not equal access to education if the student does not know English and loses out on content instruction. Choice *A*, the Bilingual Education Act, Title VII of 1968, gave money to bilingual education but not much direction as to how to plan and implement good programs. Choice *B*, the Nationality Act of 1906, found to be unconstitutional, gave immigrants a certain amount of time to learn English or else. Choice *D*, the National Defense and Education Act of 1958, was the first federal legislation that promoted foreign language curriculum. The correct answer is *C*.

16. Students who have exited ESL programs and who have passed the proper standardized tests (indicating that they can effectively

operate in a regular English-speaking program) must still continue to be monitored by the LPAC for continued success for a period of two years. The correct answer is *A*.

17. Any curricular concerns in a grade level or department must be brought to the team and a proper solution must be found. In the event that all team members do not agree on the best solution, competent professionals should work towards "consensus" in the best interest of students. This particular issue would *not* be hard to correct with the proper understanding while avoiding the cancellation of an important tradition (*A*). The fact that it has become mislabeled does not negate the fact that it is an important celebration in many parts of Texas. The answer is *C*.

18. Some students in ESL classes *can* lean towards English as being superior to their home language for many reasons and can also begin to see their families in a negative light. Cultural and social conflict can occur if there's a perception that their first language is not important or they should be ashamed of it or their home culture in some way. The ESL teacher should realize that it is important to foster pride in the L1 and find many opportunities to celebrate the differences in language and cultural backgrounds. The correct answer is *D*.

19. A family's needs often come before their concern for school policies (*A*). Choice *B* is true, but it is very harsh when translations are truly needed for important matters. It is in the best interest of the student to be in school without interruptions and without having to make up work. The ESL teacher knows there are many avenues to get help in a number of languages other than English. Collaborating can frequently keep both parents and teachers informed about the needs of students and the family. Being so direct (*A*) may cause the ESL teacher more problems than remedies in further communication with this family, and the same is true with Choices *B* and *C*. The correct answer is *D*.

20. Whether parents do or do not know English or are reluctant to participate in school affairs, they can be instrumental in the academic success of their children if they simply become involved in the efforts of their children in regards to academics. There are many ways to be supportive without much contact with the school itself. However, they should always be encouraged to attend and participate in school events, and teachers should work towards events that invite parents into school (Literacy Night, Math Night, etc.). Promising that all concerns will be dealt with according to parent wishes (*B*) is simply not feasible or reasonable. Explaining that helping in school can only help improve English skills (*C*) can be condescending and threatening. Many parents are already overwhelmed by the idea of commanding English (*D*). Planning various school events designed to help parents be more proficient in the academic affairs of their children (*D*) is a very good idea; however, one does not have to come to school in order to support their children. Parents can provide a home environment and routines that support the academic efforts of the school. Parents coming to school are an added bonus, but many parents will never take advantage of this avenue. The *best* answer is *A*.

21. The principal tells Mr. Gladstone that the student will be with him for the *rest of the year*. Therefore, we can eliminate Choices *A* and *C* (even though *C* would be true [a school does have four weeks from time of enrollment to test a child]). An ESL class is never conducted in another language (only bilingual classes), so Choice *D* would be a misleading statement (and incorrect). However, if parents do not sign for their children for special ESL or bilingual service, the child cannot receive them automatically from the school, and he or she will be placed in a regular classroom. Bon-hwa will be expected to meet all the district and state objectives in English. The correct answer is *B*.

22. The LPAC (Language Proficiency Assessment Committee) must meet at least once a year for the two years following a child's exit from an ESL or bilingual program to ensure that the child is still successful in a regular classroom; therefore, Choice *A* is incorrect. Choice *D* would indicate three years of meetings. The teacher cannot simply "sign him off," so Choice *B* is incorrect. The correct answer, two years, is *C*.

Name Index

Adams, M.J., 34
Adams, W., 57
Alleman, J., 218
Allen, R., 224
Armstrong, D., 164
Asher, J.J., 490, 496
Ashlock, R., 101
Baghban, M., 62
Baker, C., 510
Bandura, A., 274
Barber, B., 236
Barton, K., 168
Baruth, L., 158
Beal, C., 228
Beaumont, L., 422
Bennett, C.I., 512
Blachowicz, C., 456
Blevins, W., 41
Bloom, B.S., 163, 168, 313, 314, 398
Bolick, C., 214
Boyer, E.L., 320
Brewer, J.A., 403
Brody, R., 236
Brooks, J.G., 89
Brooks, M.G., 89
Brophy, J., 218
Calfee, R.C., 70
Carlton, R.A., 105
Carmen, R., 57
Chapin, J., 153, 163, 168, 224
Christie, J., 449, 451, 452
Clay, M.M., 70
Cobb, P., 99
Cohen, M.D., 447, 450, 478
Cornett, C.E., 320
Cramer, R.L., 34
Cummins, J., 487, 502
Daniels, D., 422
Davis, K., 213
Davis, R.B., 89
De la Roche, E., 312
Dobbs, S.M., 320, 321
Dooley, N., 162
Doolin, C., 422
Driscoll, A., 120, 449
Duthie, C., 63
Duvall, L., 223
Eggen, P., 405
Elkonin, D.B., 31
Ellis, A., 162, 167
Epstein, A.S., 308
Farris, P., 161, 163
Feldman, E. B., 314
Fisher, P., 456

Fitzgerald, A., 105
French, L., 71
Fullan, M., 319
Gardner, H., 300, 301, 316, 320
Gay, G., 225
Goldberg, M., 454
Goleman, D., 406
Grant, S., 162, 164, 167
Guzzetti, B., 161
Halliday, M., 54
Hasan, R., 54
Hepler, S., 161
Hickman, J., 161
Howden, H., 105
Huck, C., 161
Johnson, A., 163
Johnson, J., 449, 451, 452
Johnson, M., 308, 313
Kauchak, D., 405
Kindler, 300
Krashen, S.D., 482, 483, 484, 485, 493, 495, 496
Kutiper, K., 39
Lampert, M., 99
Levstik, L., 168
Lichtenberg, B.K., 99
Linderman, M.G., 306, 321
Linquist, T., 456
Lundsteen, S.W., 51
Lynch-Brown, C., 225
McCaslin, N., 439, 445, 454
McCormick, S., 69
McGee, L., 40
McGowan, T., 161
Maher, C.A., 89
Malaguzzi, L., 300
Manning, M., 158
Manzo, A.V., 54
Martorella, P., 228
Massialas, B., 224
Maxim, G., 160, 161, 170, 171, 236, 237
Meyer, B., 54
Miller, S.A., 306
Mittler, G.A., 303
Morris, A., 162
Morrow, L.M., 50
Nagel, N., 120, 449
Nath, J.L., 447, 450
National Center for Chronic Disease Prevention and Health Promotion, 417
National Center for History in the Schools (NCHS), 167, 168, 169

National Council for the Social Studies, 160
National Council of Teachers of Mathematics (NCTM), 89, 102, 105, 110, 112, 113, 117, 119
Noddings, N., 89
Ogle, D.M., 50
Parker, W., 153
Payne, R.K., 496
Perfumo, P., 70
Perkins, D., 163
Piaget, Jean, 23, 96, 274
Pitri, E., 316
Richgels, D., 40
Savage, T., 164
Seefeldt, C., 171, 213, 215
Spandel, V., 67
Spring, C., 71
Stanford, B., 225
Stauffer, R.G., 50
Stearns, P., 167
Sternberg, R., 163
Stiggins, R., 67
Swartz, R., 163
Szekely, G., 306
Szyba, C.M., 305
Terrell, T.D., 495, 496
Terry, C.A., 39
Texas Education Agency (TEA), 153
Texas Education Code, 236
Tomlinson, C., 225
Tompkins, G.E., 33
Troutman, A.P., 99
U.S. General Accounting Office, 509
Vacca, J.A., 55, 56
Vacca, R., 55, 56
Van de Walle, J., 108
Vansledright, B., 162, 164, 167
Vygotsky, L., 274
Walker, B.J., 54
Wardle, F., 449
Wertsch, J.V., 477, 480
Wilkinson, A., 51
Wilson, B., 317, 320
Wineberg, S., 168
Wortham, S., 438
Wright, S., 300, 301, 316
Yawkey, T., 449, 451, 452
Yopp, H.K., 32
Ziegler, A., 62

Subject Index

Admit, Review, and Dismiss (ARD) Committee, 379, 514
Aesthetics, 318, 319–320
Affective domain, 398
Algebra, 103–108
Alphabetic principle, 32–35, 42, 501
Alternative certification program (ACP), 4
American Association for the Advancement of Science, 260
Art, 299–322
    age-appropriate, 306
    analysis, interpretation, and evaluation of, 312–315
    appreciation of art histories and diverse cultures, 307–312
    cognitive and artistic development, 316
    creative expression in, 304–307
    culture and, 307–312
    elements of, 302–303
    language and, 320–321
    mathematics and, 321
    perception in, 301–304
    principles of design, 303
    roles of, 307
    science and, 321
    social studies and, 215, 321
    studio, 318
    TEKS-related correlations, 300–301
    Western history of, 309–311
Art criticism, 318, 319
Art history, 307–312, 318, 319
Artistic development, 316
Art-making media, 305–306, 319
Assessment
    authentic, 164, 504–505
    of developing literacy, 69–73
    in ESL programs, 487–488, 504–505
    formal and informal, 422, 447, 504–505
    formative and summative, 163, 275–276
    in mathematics, 95–102
    in music, 380–383
    in physical education, 422
    portfolio, 70–71
    in science, 275–276
    in social studies, 163–164
    in theatre arts, 447
Assessment and instruction of developing literacy, 69–73
Authentic assessment, 164, 504–505
Bar graph, 170, 264
Basal reader, 40–41
Bias, 512
BICS (Basic Interpersonal Communication Skills), 487
Bidialectism, 23
Bilingual education, 23
Blending, 30, 34
Bloom's taxonomy, 98, 163, 168, 313, 314, 398
Books, 39–40, 161
Business, 240–241, 242–243

cycles of, 242–243
    government regulation of, 242
Calculators, 119, 120
CALPS (Cognitive Academic Language Proficiency Skills), 487
Cardinal directions, 213–214
Cardiovascular fitness, 415–416
Certification programs, 4
Charts, 170, 264–265
Checklists, 31
Child developmental levels, 157
Choral reading, 26
Citizenship, 154, 155, 226–228
Civilizations, early, 173
Classification, 92
Climate, 217
Cognitive development, Piaget's theory of, 96, 274
Communicative competence, 496
Competencies, 2–3
Competency statement, 2
Comprehension
    ESL and, 500–501
    evaluative, 49
    ineffective, 47
    inferential, 49
    literal, 49
Compromise, 181
Computer-administered test (CAT), 4
Computers, 120, 158–159
Concept books, 39
Consumer Price Index (CPI), 243
Content areas, integrating, 160–162
Context clues, 43
Contextual setting, 22
Contradictory issues, 164
Convergent question, 53
Conversation, 25
Cooperative groups, 157
Coordinated approach to Child Health program (CATCH), 401
Corporations, 241
Creative expression, through theatre arts, 441–442
Criterion-referenced tests, 70, 505
Cultural bias, 512
Cultural diffusion, 218
Cultural diversity, 22
    challenge of, 223–226
    designing learning opportunities for all students, 162–163
    in ESL programs, 512, 513
    in music, 370
Cultural geography, 218
Culture, 223–226
    art and, 307–312
    geography and, 154, 212, 213
    science and, 155
Data collection, 92
DEAR (Drop Everything and Read), 47
Decision making, personal and social, 278
Decoding, 22, 41–44

Democracy, concept of, 228, 229
Democratic classrooms, 228
Diagnostic tests, 275
Directed Reading-Thinking Activity (DRTA), 49
Discipline-Based Art Education (DBAE), 316,
    317–322
Divergent question, 53
Diversity, multicultural. *See* Cultural diversity
Domains, 2–3
    music in, 367–368, 369–374
Drama, 26, 157, 438–439
Due process, 229
Earth science, 285–287
Economic indicators, 243
Economics, 154, 155, 226–228, 238–245
    business and, 242–243
    consumer influence and, 239—240
    government expenditures, 241–242
    international, 243–244
    structures of business, 240–, 241
    of Texas, 244–245
    types of economic systems, 238–239
Elkonin box, 31
Emergent literacy, 36–37
English, as an alphabetic language, 499
English as a second language (ESL)
    acquisition-learning hypothesis, 483–484
    affective filter hypothesis, 484
    assessment in, 487–488, 504–505
    basics of, 487–488
    certification, 474–476
    comprehension before production, 497
    conventions of English and, 477–483
    cultural and linguistic diversity, 511–512
    effective practices, resources, and materials,
        502–503
    effect of community members on, 516–517
    family involvement and collaboration, 515–516
    foundations of, 508–513
    goal of communicative competence, 496
    individual differences and, 500–501
    input hypothesis, 485–486
    instructional relationships, 507–508
    management and teaching strategies, 491–494,
        509–511
    methods recommended, 488–491
    monitor hypothesis, 486
    natural approach in, 496
    natural order hypothesis, 484
    pre-K to Grade 4 TEKS in, 481
    programs, 23, 473–517
    reading comprehension, 500–501
    speech emergence and, 494–499
    speech errors in, 494–495
    standardized tests in, 505–506
    standards, domains, and competencies in, 475
    state-mandated LEP policies, 506
    teacher as advocate, 514–515
    technological tools and resources for, 491
    test design and development, 504–505
    types of, 509
English Language Arts (ELA) competencies, 478,
    480, 499
English language concepts, 477–483

English Language Development Program (ELD),
    509
English language learners (ELLs), 23, 476, 483, 506,
    508, 514–515
English language proficiency, 477–483
Environment, 220–221
Environmental Protection Agency (EPA), 221
Estimation skills, 105
Evaluations, 163–164
    of art, 312–315
    in music, 381–383
    physical education and, 422
    theatre arts and, 442–443
Evaluative comprehension, 49
Experts, as resources, 159
Explorations, 175–177
Fantasy, 39, 225
Feldman Model of Art Criticism, 314
Fine Arts. *See* Art
Fitness, 415–416
Folktales, 39, 224
Foreign policy, 190–194
Formative assessment, 163, 275–276
Fundamental skills, 419
Gender discrimination, 225–226
Generalist (TExES) exam
    item formats, 3–4
    preparing for, 1–17
    standards, domains, and competencies, 2–3
Geography, 155, 213–223
    climate, 219–220
    content of, 215–223
    culture and, 154, 212, 213, 218
    natural resources/environment, 220–221
    of Texas, 221–223
Geometry, 109–117
Gifted students, 163
Global education, 224
Goals 2000: Educate America Act, 408
Government, 154, 155, 173, 174, 177–183, 185,
    226–236
    content of, 228–236
    foundations of, 229–230
Government revenues and expenditures, 241–242
Grapheme-phoneme relationship, 42
Graphemes, 33, 42
Graphic information, interpreting, 57
Graphic organizers, 52
Graphophonemic knowledge, 33
Graphs, 169, 170, 264–265
Gross Domestic Product (GDP), 243
Gross National Product (GNP), 243
Guide-O-Rama, 56
Health, 397
    basic, 400–402
    healthy relationships, 403–404, 406
    illness and disease, 404–405
    mental and physical, levels of, 398
    nutrition and, 402–403
    refusal skills, 407
    safety and, 411–413
    school facilities, 402
    standards and competencies, 399–400
    stress, 409–410

substance abuse, 405–406
technology and, 410–411
Health and physical education, 397–426
Healthy People 2000, 398
History, 154, 155, 167–211
  methods of historians, 171
  Texas, 203–210
    earliest inhabitants, 203–205
    early European exploration and development, 205–207
    revolution, republic, and statehood, 207–210
  United States, 172–211
    exploration and settlement, 178–179
    foreign policy, 189–194
    international relations between superpowers, 194–197
    national unity, 179–183
    the present, 197–200
    reform movements, 187–189
    regional differences, 183–186
  world, 172–175
  see also Social studies
Holidays, 200–203
Human activities, basic, 218
Hypothesis, 272
Identification requirements, 5, 14
Immersion, 509
Inclusion, 163
Income tax, 241–242
Individual education plan (IEP), 377, 514
Industrial Revolution, 183, 186–187
Inferential comprehension, 49
Informal Reading Inventory (IRI), 71
Information, locating skills, 56
Instructional delivery, 502–503
Interlocking study guide, 56
International affairs, 189–197
International System of Units, 267
Invented spelling, 30, 62
Inventions, 210–211
K-W-L (Knowledge, Want to Know, Learned), 50, 274
Language
  art and, 320–321
  four components of, 499
Language acquisition, 477–483, 485, 494–499
Language arts and reading, 18–73
  alphabetic principle, 32–35
  assessment, 69–73
  literacy development and practice, 36–40, 69–73
  oral language, 20–28
  phonemic awareness, 28–32
  phonological awareness, 28–32
  Pre-K to Grade 4, 19
  reading comprehension, 48–60
  reading fluency, 44–48
  word analysis and decoding, 41–44
  writing, development of, 61–65
  writing conventions, 65–69
Language experience approach (LEA), 22–23
Language Proficiency Assessment Committee (LPAC), 506, 514
Learning cycle, 274
Learning disabilities, 163

Learning theories, 21–22, 274
Legends, 224
Letter naming, 33, 34
Life science, 282–285
Limited English proficiency (LEP), 23, 506, 508
Line graph, 169, 264, 265
Listening, 24, 51
Listening-thinking strategy, 54
Literacy
  development, 36–40
  emergent, 36–37
  transfer of, 500
Literal comprehension, 49
Literary elements, 40
Literature, 39, 224–225
Management skills, 6–7
Manipulative variable (MV), 266, 272
Maps, 170–171, 214, 216
Material Safety Data Sheet (MSDS), 261
Mathematical perspectives, 117–121
Mathematical processes, 117–121
Mathematics, 88–121
  algebra, 103–108
  art and, 321
  classification and data collection, 92
  common difficulties for children, 114
  geometry, 91, 109–117
  in learning centers, 100
  mathematical perspectives, 117–121
  mathematical processes, 117–121
  measurement, 91–92, 109–117
  number and operations, 90–91
  number concepts, 95–102, 103–108
  overview of, 89–90
  patterns, 91, 103–108
  pre-kindergarten guidelines, 90–92
  probability, 109–117
  problem solving, 102
  relating to other content areas, 110
  sample questions, 94
  science and, 110
  spatial sense, 91
  standards and competencies for, 90–94
  statistics, 109–117
  technology and, 117, 120
Mathematics manipulatives, 92–93, 97–98
Measurement
  mathematics applications, 91–92, 109–117
  nonstandard, 113, 115
  in science, 267
Metric system, 267
Miscues, 43, 70
Mock trials and meetings, 157
Morphemes, 42
Motor skills, 419–421
Movement
  music and, 365
  physical education and, 418–420
Multiple-choice exams, 9–11
Music, 334–384
  age-appropriate, 368–369
  American, 353–354, 357–361
  assessment, 380–383
  careers in, 361–362

Music (*continued*)
   copyright laws and, 384
   creating, 371
   dancing and, 358, 359
   and diversity, 370
   in the domains, 367–368
   duration of sound and, 335–337
   dynamics, 346–347, 352
   evaluating musical performances, 362
   form, 344–346, 358
   health and safety in, 377
   history of, 353–357
   home, community, and, 376–377
   importance of teaching, 362, 369
   instrument families, 348
   movement to, 365
   notation, 341–344, 352–353
   pitch and melody, 340–344, 346
   planning music lessons, 365–366
   resources for, 375–376
   rhythm and, 337–340
   singing and playing, 351–352, 362–363
   special needs children and, 377–380
   speech and, 372
   teachers' professional responsibilities, 383
   teaching children, 362–363
   technology and, 374–375
   tempo, 347
   of Texas, 353, 354–357
   timbre and tone color, 348–351
   visual and aural knowledge of, 335
Myths, 224
National Center for History in the Schools (NCHS), 167
National Council for the Social Studies, 152–153, 160, 165
National Council of Teachers of Mathematics (NCTM), 2, 89
   Standards for Mathematics, 89
National Research Council, 260
National Science Educational Standards, 260
Natural resources, 220–221, 240
Noninterlocking guide, 56
Nonstandard dialects, 23
Nonstandard measurement, 113
Norm-referenced tests, 505
Note taking, 8, 24, 52
Number and operations, 90–91
Number concepts, 95–108
Nutrition, 402–403
Obesity, 403
Occupational Health and Safety Act (OSHA), 261
Oracy, 51
Oral expression, 25
Oral language, 2, 20–28
   development of, 37
   types of delivery, 30
Patterns, 91, 103–108
Pedagogy and Professional Responsibilities. *See* PPR (Pedagogy and Professional Responsibilities)
Perception, through theatre arts, 440–441
Performance-based assessment, 164
Performance tasks, 100
Phonemes, 30, 33, 42

Phonemic awareness, 29–31, 499, 501
Phonics instruction, 42
Phonological awareness, 29–31
Phonology, 22
Photographs, 171
Physical education, 397, 414–417
   assessment and evaluation, 422–423
   designing activities, 424–426
   growth and development, 421
   positive interactions in, 423–424
Physical science, 279–282
   key ideas of, 280–281
Picture books, 25, 39
Pie chart, 170, 264–265
Play, 157
Poetry, 39–40
Political science, 229
Pollution, 221
Portfolios, 70–71
   sample, 66
PPR (Pedagogy and Professional Responsibilities), 3, 5, 10–11, 13, 368, 478
Prediction, 116
Print association, 36
Probability, 109–117
Problem-solving software, 159
Process standards, 102
Professional Development and Appraisal System Alignment (PDAS), 455
Professional growth, 164
Professional organizations, 164
Professional Roles and Responsibilities. *See* PRR (Professional Roles and Responsibilities)
Prohibited items, 14
PRR (Professional Roles and Responsibilities), 19, 478
Psychomotor domain, 418
Public Law 94–192, 377, 379
Pull-out programs, 509
Question-Answer Relationships (QARs), 47, 53
Questioning, 52–54
Questions, convergent and divergent, 53–54
Readers' theater, 26
Reading
   fluency, 46
   functional part of, 24
   oral, 25–26, 50
   word-by-word, 46
   see also Language arts and reading
Reading comprehension, 48–50. *See also* Comprehension
Reading fluency, 44–48
   components of, 46–47
Reading Miscue Inventory, 70
Reciprocal Questioning (REQUEST), 54
Reciprocal teaching, 488
Reflective teaching, 164–165
Reform movements, 187–189
Registration, 5, 13
Religions, early, 173, 174
Renewable and nonrenewable resources, 221
Repeated story reading, 50
Rereading stories, 26
Responding variable (RV), 266, 272

Retelling stories, 26
Retest, 16
Rhyming, 29–30
Rhythm, 303, 337–340, 420
Rubrics, 31
Running record, 70
Safety, 411–413, 450
Scaffolding, 37
School health facilities, 402
Schwa sound, 43
Science, 259–290
  art and, 321
  assessment, 275–276
  basic process skills, 271, 272
  data collection, 264
  earth and space, 285–287
  history and nature of, 276–278
  instruction, 260–262, 273–275
  life, 282–285
  mathematics and, 110
  personal and social decision making, 278–279
  physical, 279–282
  political, 229
  reform efforts, 260
  technologies and, 262–268
  TExES science lesson, 289–290
  tools, materials, and equipment, 262–268
  unifying themes, 288–289
Scientific inquiry, 269–272
Scientific method, 272
SCORER, 57
Segmentation, 22, 30
Self-fulfilling prophecy, 511
Semantic map, 24
Sheltered English, 488
Singing, 362–363
Social science instruction, 156
Social Security, 242
Social skills, 157
Social studies, 152–245
  art and, 215, 321
  assessment and evaluation, 163–164
  building thinking skills, 163
  citizenship and, 236–237
  classroom materials for, 214–215
  competencies defined, 154–155
  culture and, 154, 223–226
  economics and, 226–228, 238–245
  elementary level, 155–156
  engaging all students in, 162–163
  geography and, 154, 215–226
  government and, 226–236
  interdisciplinary issues, 160–162
  intradisciplinary areas, 160–162
  knowledge and skills for teachers and students, 154
  reflective teaching, 164–165
  science and, 165–166
  scope and sequence of, 155–156
  social science instruction, 156
  teaching history, 154, 165–211
  technology use in, 158–159, 165–166
Social studies skills, 155
Society, 165–166

Software, 158–159
Sounds
  awareness of, 31
  duration of, in music, 335–337
Sources, primary and secondary, 169
Space exploration, 198
Space science, 285–287
Speaking activities, 26
Special needs children, music and, 377–380
Speech emergence, 494–495
Spelling
  invented, 62
  stages of development, 69
SQ3R (survey, question, read, recite, and review), 54–60
SSR (Sustained Silent Reading), 47
Statistics, 109–117, 169
Stereotyping, 512
Story retelling, 50
Study skills, 1, 6–9
Subject areas. *See* Content areas
Substance abuse, 405–406
Summarizing, 50–51
Summative assessment, 163, 275–276
Supply and demand, 239–240, 241
Syllable, 43
Syntactic patterns, 24
Tables, 170
Tall tales, 224
Technology
  health and, 410–411
  in mathematics, 117, 120
  music and, 374–375
  science and, 262–268
  social studies and, 158–159, 165–166
Test anxiety, 12–17
Test bias, 506
Test-taking skills, 1, 9–17, 57
Texas
  earliest inhabitants, 203–205
  early European explorations and development in, 205–207
  economics of, 244–245
  geography of, 221–223
  music of, 353, 354–257
  revolution, Republic, and statehood of, 207–210
Texas Administrative Code, 153
Texas Art Education Association (TAEA)
Texas Assessment of Knowledge and Skills (TAKS), 57, 89, 260
Texas Education Agency (Tea), 93–94
Texas Education Code, 153, 236
Texas Essential Knowledge and Skills (TEKS), 2, 89, 103, 153, 260, 398, 437
  for Pre-K to Grade 4, 93–94
Texas Examinations of Educators Standards (TExES) test framework, 153
Texas Hazardous Communication Act (HazCom), 261
Texas Primary Reading Inventory (TPRI), 31–32
  components of, 33
TExES *Competencies*, 2
TExES *Standard*, 2
Textbooks, 168, 1612

Theatre arts, 437–456
activities for, 453
in EC-4 classrooms, 440–443
Theatre arts (*continued*)
historic and cultural heritage in, 442
important aspects of, 448–452
and other content areas, 453–455
reason for including, 444–445
teacher's role in, 446–448
types of experiences, 438
Thematic units, 25, 160
Thinking skills, 163, 237, 314–315
historical, 168
Timelines, 170
Trade, balance of, 243
Trade books, 25, 214
United States history, 175–211
U.S. Constitution, 181–182, 229, 230
writing of, 230–231

Vocabulary
expanding, 24–25
receptive, 496
sight, 43
sight-word, 499
Word analysis and decoding, 41–44
Word analysis skills, 24, 41–42, 43, 499, 501
Word processing, 158
Word recognition skills, 42, 47
World history, main events in, 172–175
Writing conventions, 65–69, 72
Writing process
developing stage, 62
emergent stage, 62
mechanics, 62
phases in, 63–64
Writing selections, content for, 64
Writing workshop, 63
Yopp-Singer Test of Phonemic Segmentation, 32
Zone of proximal development, 44, 274